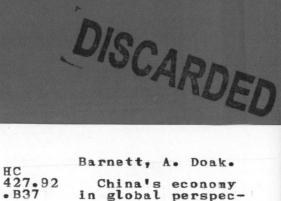
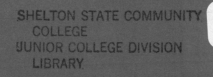

China's Economy
in Global Perspective

BY A. DOAK BARNETT

Communist Economic Strategy: The Rise of Mainland China
(1959)

Communist China and Asia: Challenge to American Policy
(1960)

Communist China in Perspective
(1962)

Communist Strategies in Asia: A Comparative Analysis
of Governments and Parties
(editor, 1963)

China on the Eve of Communist Takeover
(1963)

Communist China: The Early Years, 1949–1955
(1964)

The United States and China in World Affairs
(editor of manuscript by Robert Blum; published posthumously, 1966)

China after Mao
(1967)

Cadres, Bureaucracy, and Political Power in Communist China
(with a contribution by Ezra Vogel, 1967)

Chinese Communist Politics in Action
(editor, 1969)

The United States and China: The Next Decade
(editor, with Edwin O. Reischauer, 1970)

A New U.S. Policy toward China
(Brookings, 1971)

Uncertain Passage: China's Transition to the Post-Mao Era
(Brookings, 1974)

The United States, China, and Arms Control
(with Ralph N. Clough, Morton H. Halperin, and Jerome H. Kahan;
Brookings, 1975)

China Policy: Old Problems and New Challenges
(Brookings, 1977)

China and the Major Powers in East Asia
(Brookings, 1977)

China's Economy in Global Perspective
(Brookings, 198)

A. DOAK BARNETT

China's Economy
in Global Perspective

Copyright © 1981 by
THE BROOKINGS INSTITUTION
1775 Massachusetts Avenue, N.W., Washington, D.C. 20036

Library of Congress Cataloging in Publication data:

Barnett, A. Doak.
  China's economy in global perspective.
  Includes bibliographical references and index.
    1. China—Economic conditions—1976– .
  2. China—Economic policy—1976– . I. Title.
HC427.92.B37   330.951'057   81-1193
ISBN 0-8157-0826-2   AACR2
ISBN 0-8157-0825-4 (pbk.)

1 2 3 4 5 6 7 8 9

To my brothers and sister

ROBERT W. BARNETT

EUGENIA BARNETT SCHULTHEIS

H. DEWITT BARNETT

Foreword

SINCE the death of Mao Tse-tung (Mao Zedong) in late 1976, Chinese policies have undergone profound changes. Mao and China's leading "radicals" had for years insisted upon "uninterrupted revolution," giving priority to ideological and social transformations aimed at achieving an egalitarian society. During the Cultural Revolution of the late 1960s and early 1970s, they created turmoil throughout the society. Since 1977, China's post-Mao leaders, with Vice Premier Teng Hsiao-ping (Deng Xiaoping) taking the lead, have shifted priorities and reoriented policies in far-reaching ways, stressing the need to establish political stability and to accelerate economic growth. They have been remarkably pragmatic, eclectic, and experimental in searching for new solutions to China's problems. In economic affairs, they have moved toward a new strategy of development at home and have begun to involve China in the world economy to an unprecedented degree.

In 1980, Teng called the current period "another turning point in Chinese history" and stated that Peking's modernization program "is in a real sense a new revolution." An essential component of this new revolution, he indicated, is a dramatic turning outward. "China," he declared, "has now adopted a policy of opening our doors to the world."

The shifts now occurring in China's domestic economic policies call for basic structural and systemic changes that would move the country toward a Chinese version of "market socialism." The changes in China's foreign economic relations call for a rapid increase in trade, growing imports of capital goods and technology, greatly expanded international scientific and technological exchanges, the encouragement of foreign investment in China, and a new willingness to borrow abroad.

In earlier years, when China's leadership stressed self-reliance and the

ix

country's economy was relatively isolated, little attention was paid to either the actual or the potential importance of China in the world economy. Now, it is clear that China's developmental experiments and growing role in the world economy are potentially of major international importance.

Despite its low per capita income, China today has the sixth largest gross national product in the world. It is becoming a significant market for capital goods and technology, and its expanding exports of raw materials and low-cost manufactured goods are having an increasing impact on world markets.

In two specific fields, its importance is especially great. As one of the three largest agricultural producers in the world, China feeds more than a fifth of the world's population. Since the 1960s, it has also been the largest grain importer among the developing nations, and its grain imports are still rising. China is the third largest producer and consumer of energy in the world, and since the early 1970s it has been an exporter of modest quantities of oil and coal. In the immediate future, trends in energy output and consumption in China are likely to create a tight energy supply situation, domestically, which probably will limit and might even reduce its energy exports. If Chinese offshore oil is vigorously developed during the next few years, however, China conceivably could become a significant energy exporter in the second half of the 1980s, at a time when the world's energy problems are likely to be even more difficult than at present. Because of these facts and possibilities, any serious analysis of global food and energy problems in the future must take China into account.

In carrying out its new policies, China will face formidable obstacles and problems both at home and abroad, and it remains to be seen how successful and lasting the policies will be. These policies also will pose a variety of new problems and issues—as well as new opportunities—for leaders in the United States, other major nations, and international organizations dealing with global problems.

In this study, A. Doak Barnett analyzes the recent changes in China's economic policies at home and abroad, the opportunities and problems they create, and their prospects for success. The study deals broadly with China's trade, technology imports, and foreign borrowing. It also discusses China's present and future roles in world food and energy balances. In discussing the new policy issues that face other nations as a result of China's emergence on the international scene, the study devotes special attention to the problems and prospects of U.S.-China economic relations and discusses policy issues now facing policymakers in Washington.

While focusing on recent trends, the author has analyzed them against the background of the past three decades of Communist rule in China. He projects likely trends for the rest of the 1980s on the basis of statistical and other data available as of mid-1980.

Barnett has studied China and U.S.-China relations continuously since the 1940s, and in recent years he has been personally involved in many new relationships that have developed between the United States and China, serving as a member of the U.S.-China Joint Commission on Scientific and Technological Cooperation, Consultant to the National Security Council and Department of State, member of the Academic Advisory Board of the National Council for U.S.-China Trade, Vice-Chairman of the Committee on Scholarly Communication with the People's Republic of China, and Board member (and former Chairman) of the National Committee on U.S.-China Relations.

Barnett wishes to thank a number of persons who read and commented on early drafts of this study, especially Robert Michael Field, Dwight H. Perkins, and Michel Oksenberg, who made valuable suggestions concerning the entire manuscript, but also those who commented on particular parts, including: Martin Abel, Mary B. Bullock, Joel Darmstadter, Robert F. Dernberger, Richard Gilmore, James P. Grant, Herbert E. Horowitz, James A. Kilpatrick, Charles Liu, Nicholas H. Ludlow, Martin M. McLaughlin, John Mellor, Leo A. Orleans, J. Ray Pace, Robert B. Oxnam, Fred Sanderson, Lyle Schertz, Benedict Stavis, John D. Steinbruner, Anthony M. Tang, Thomas B. Wiens, and Joseph A. Yager. None of these, of course, bears responsibility for the final product.

He also acknowledges his indebtedness to James B. Stepanek and Neal B. Hoptman who, in the early stages of the study, assisted him in his search for materials, to Monica Yin, who managed his research files and typed many versions of the manuscript, and to Joan Spade and Robert L. Londis, who at different times assisted in manuscript typing and preparation. Finally, he expresses his appreciation to Andrea De La Garza and her associates at Editorial Experts, Inc., who copy-edited the manuscript, and to Florence Robinson who prepared the index.

The Institution is grateful to the Ford Foundation and the Rockefeller Brothers Fund for generous financial support of the study.

The views expressed in this book are the author's own and should not be ascribed to the Ford Foundation or the Rockefeller Brothers Fund, or to the trustees, officers, or other staff members of the Brookings Institution.

BRUCE K. MACLAURY
President

November 1980
Washington, D.C.

Contents

xiii

Appendix Tables

A Note to Readers

THIS is a large book on a big subject. To readers who may be intimidated by its length, I make the following suggestions.

Although all five parts of the book are closely interrelated, each also stands on its own. Any reader who has a special interest in a particular subject—China's new domestic economic policies, its trade and foreign economic relationships, its roles in the world food and energy systems, or U.S.-China economic relations—can turn directly to the part that deals with it. The table of contents is a guide to topics covered in each part.

The book contains a great deal of statistical information. Since much of the subject matter is unfamiliar to all but a few China specialists, and since the figures on China's economy are controversial even among them, it seemed necessary to include many data. Any reader not interested in detailed figures can focus attention on my broad discussion of and generalizations about trends, problems, and policies and skim sections filled with statistics.

A. D. B.

A Note on Statistics

FOR almost two decades, until recently, there was an extreme paucity of reliable, official Chinese statistics. During the 1950s Peking (Beijing) released fairly extensive figures on the Chinese economy. Some were summarized in State Statistical Bureau, *Ten Great Years* (Peking: Foreign Languages Press, 1960). Others were collected and published in Nai-Ruenn Chen, editor, *Chinese Economic Statistics: A Handbook for Mainland China* (Aldine, 1967). However, in the 1960s and early 1970s virtually no overall national statistics were released, and foreign government specialists and scholars working on China were compelled to make independent estimates, based on laborious collection and analysis of fragmentary data. The Central Intelligence Agency (CIA), with a large staff of economic specialists dealing with China, has published more extensive statistical estimates on the period from 1949 to the present than any other body outside China; its estimates probably have been more widely used by the scholarly community than those from any other source.

In the mid-1970s, Peking again began to publish a few national statistics. Then, in mid-1979, the State Statistical Bureau and certain other central government agencies released, for the first time in two decades, overall national statistics on key aspects of the economy; the amount of official information released has slowly increased since then. The official Chinese figures are still limited, however, and interpretation of them presents problems because of differences between Chinese and Western statistical practices and uncertainties about the effectiveness and reliability of the Chinese statistical system in many areas and sectors. Nevertheless, the recently published official Chinese statistics provide important new data on the Chinese economy that are now the best available, though they should be used cautiously and with some qualifications. Unfortunately, however, these statistics cover mainly the years starting with 1977; the statistical vacuum of the previous two decades persists (although some Chinese officials have indicated that eventually statistics on earlier years will be released).

In this book I have made full use of the recently published official Chinese figures, but since the study deals not only with recent events but also with long-term trends, I have had to rely heavily for the earlier years on non-Chinese estimates made by U.S. government agencies, international organizations, business organizations, and private scholars. Not surprisingly, these estimates vary, and the choice of which to accept presents difficult problems since there is still debate over some of them. Because of this, I have fully documented in my notes, tables, and appendix the sources for all the figures I have used.

At various points in the book, especially in the notes, I discuss in detail the problems relating to the figures used for particular economic sectors; however, a few general comments on the statistical sources I have mainly used, especially for the years before 1977, are appropriate at the start.

For estimates on China's industrial output, agricultural production, and gross national product (GNP), I have relied heavily on CIA publications. Most of the CIA's production estimates have been remarkably accurate; when Peking published official statistics for 1977 and 1978, in only a few areas (some of which will be mentioned later) did the CIA's estimates prove to be far off the mark. Since mid-1979 the CIA, taking into account the new official Chinese data, has adjusted some of its figures for earlier years; I have used these revised figures when possible. The CIA's estimates of China's GNP are still open to debate (see part I, note 288); nevertheless, I believe they are still the best available series on China's GNP covering the entire period since 1949. The reader should not forget, however, that they are estimates and probably will have to be revised eventually as more data become available.

The statistics on China's foreign trade are among the most reliable and complete of any figures on the Chinese economy, since they were constructed in large part from data published by countries that deal with China. Both the CIA and the U.S. Department of Commerce have published extensive series of figures on China's foreign trade. The figures differ to some degree because of variations in the statistical methodologies used (for example, Chinese imports are sometimes given cost, insurance, and freight [c.i.f.], sometimes free on board [f.o.b.] or free alongside ship [f.a.s.]). But the differences are not great. I have used both series since the different ways of breaking down and analyzing the data have been useful for different purposes. In making international trade comparisons, I have mainly used CIA figures plus International Monetary Fund statistics on the trade of other nations and total world trade.

Except for the years for which official Chinese figures are available, my principal sources for agricultural statistics on China have been the CIA and the U.S. Department of Agriculture (USDA). Here, as in the case of the trade figures, there are differences in the calculations made by different U.S. government agencies, but generally they are not great. For world agricultural trends, I have relied mainly on USDA statistics, supplemented by figures from the CIA and the United Nations Food and Agricultural Organization. For China's population, apart from the official Chinese figures available, I have relied to a considerable extent on estimates made by the Foreign Demographic Analysis Division of the Department of Commerce. For world population trends, I have used figures from a variety of sources, including U.S. government agencies, UN bodies, and private organizations dealing with population issues.

On energy, especially oil, I have relied heavily (except for the years for which official Chinese figures are available) on CIA estimates, but I have also made use of estimates in several independent scholarly studies. However, in analyzing long-term world energy trends and projections of future trends, I have relied mainly on UN statistics, supplemented (for recent years) by data from the CIA, U.S. oil industry sources, the Organization for Economic Cooperation and Development, and several private studies.

On all of these subjects, I have used current press reports for some very recent figures and estimates.

The complexity of the subjects dealt with and the variety of the sources used have inevitably created problems of interpretation. It is virtually impossible to achieve total statistical consistency; the reader will have to judge how adequately I have dealt with these problems.

In writing this study, I confronted special problems because of the rapid pace of change, both in China and worldwide, and because many of the organizations making the statistical estimates have periodically revised their figures for past years. Each year, the CIA has updated its entire series on China's GNP to give figures in the dollar values of a new base year (usually, the year before the estimates are published). Further-more, not only the CIA but also the USDA, the Department of Com-merce, and UN agencies often revise figures on agricultural and indus-trial output in past years on the basis of new data.

It is no simple task to keep completely up to date, either on actual developments or on the latest statistical data and estimates. Unavoidably, the figures in the book include some that already could be updated if time were available to do so. However, in general, I have used the latest figures or estimates available as of mid-1980.

However, the numbers used in this volume or, for that matter, any economic statistics on China should not be regarded as precise. At best, they provide only approximations of—or good clues to—reality. I be-lieve, nevertheless, that the data used in this study are adequate to provide a sound basis for judging broad economic trends and problems, and for examining their implications for other countries and analyzing the policy issues these pose for decision makers in Washington and elsewhere.

A. D. B.

A Note on Romanization

No SYSTEM of transliterating Chinese into English is wholly satisfactory. Many romanization systems have been devised, each of which has good and bad points. For several decades, the Wade-Giles system was the most widely used in English-language writings on China. Even when this system was generally accepted, however, there was no complete consistency in usage. Well-known place names were generally romanized on the basis of a different system used by the Chinese postal authorities; the names of certain well-known leaders were often based on other, often idiosyncratic, transliterations, sometimes based on southern (Cantonese) rather than northern (Mandarin) pronunciation. Moreover, even when using the Wade-Giles system, most authors writing for a general audience modified it by eliminating umlauts, which are used for certain *u* sounds, and apostrophes, which are used to differentiate aspirated from nonaspirated sounds (for example, Wade-Giles uses *p'* for *p* and *p* for *b*).

Some years ago, the Chinese devised a new system, called pinyin (or hanyu pinyin). Like the Wade-Giles system, it is based on the standard northern dialect (Mandarin, kuo-yu, or pu-tung hua). Unlike Wade-Giles, however, it uses a different alphabetical symbol for each different Chinese sound and abandons the use of the apostrophe to differentiate aspirated and nonaspirated sounds. Peking's State Council finally decided that, from January 1, 1979, on, pinyin would be used in all English-language materials published by agencies of the People's Republic of China. (Even when deciding this, the Chinese authorities again allowed for exceptions for certain well-known historical places and persons, for which traditionally used forms of romanization could still be employed.)

Subsequently, the U.S. government, the United Nations, most American news organizations, and many if not most American scholars switched from Wade-Giles to pinyin.

The change has been confusing for the majority of ordinary English-language readers who are not specialists on Chinese affairs. For them, although the Wade-Giles system created some difficulties, the pinyin system created even more. Linguistically, pinyin is in many respects clearer and less confusing than Wade-Giles for those who know the system. However, some of the letters used to represent particular sounds make a large number of Chinese words unintelligible, or at least unpronounceable, for average English-speaking readers who have not learned the system. For example, the use of *x* for the sound *hs* (or, roughly speaking, *sh*), *q* for *ch*, and *zh* for the sound *j* is extremely confusing to nonspecialists. Perhaps, in time, average readers in the West may become familiar with the new system. However, during this transitional period, many still find the Wade-Giles romanization easier to understand than the pinyin system.

Because this book is aimed at a broad readership, not just at China specialists, I have adopted the following policies regarding romanization in this volume.

In the text, I use traditional postal system spellings for well-known Chinese place names and a modified Wade-Giles system (without apostrophes or umlauts) for all other Chinese words, including personal names, lesser-known place names, and other Chinese terms. In Chinese names, surnames come first, following Chinese usage (but in Japanese and Korean names the order is reversed and surnames are given last, since this is now the usual practice in Western publications). The first time that any Chinese name or term appears in each part of the text, I indicate, in parentheses, what the new pinyin spelling is, even when it is identical with the Wade-Giles form.

In the notes, although I use modified Wade-Giles or traditional postal spellings for any comments I make, titles of publications and names of authors are given in the romanization used in the publication cited; however, apostrophes and umlauts have been deleted from all Wade-Giles romanizations. (As a result, over time, the citations for certain publications appear with different romanizations; for example, what was the *Peking Review* before 1979 has been the *Beijing Review* since January 1979.) The first time that any Chinese name or term appears in each part of the notes, whether it is romanized according to Wade-Giles or pinyin spelling, I give the alternative in parentheses (or in brackets if it is within a title or quotation).

Like all compromises, this one is less than wholly satisfactory and creates some anomalies, but I believe that the result is suitable for this volume. Appendix table 3 lists the modified Wade-Giles, full Wade-Giles, and pinyin forms of the Chinese names and terms appearing in the book.

A. D. B.

Introduction

OF ALL the major powers, China until recently has been the least involved in the web of global interdependencies that has developed during recent decades. Attitudes rooted in history, as well as recent international politics, partially explain this fact. Traditionally, the Chinese viewed their country as a civilization unto itself and felt little need for contact with the outside world. Because of this, the forcible "opening" of China by the Western colonial powers in the 1840s was traumatic. The Chinese viewed these powers as culturally inferior even though they were more advanced scientifically, technologically, and militarily. The Western impact contributed to the disintegration of the traditional Chinese political and social system, which began a long period of revolutionary change.[1] For the first time, the Chinese had to confront the reality of the modern multistate international system.[2] Since then, for a century and a half, they have been trying to answer some basic questions. To what extent should China involve itself in the world economy and modern international community? And precisely what international roles should it try to play?

There has been continuing debate in China over the desirability, and possibility, of borrowing useful ideas and techniques from more technologically advanced modern nations while at the same time preserving the essence of China's traditional culture.[3] Repeatedly, some relatively cosmopolitan leaders have argued for more active Chinese participation in the international community and extensive borrowing of ideas and values as well as technology from the West, accepting that this would result in far-reaching cultural change within China. Others, essentially nativist or isolationist in orientation, have advocated minimal interaction with the outside world and placed highest priority on the need to preserve China's cultural distinctiveness. Between these extremes, many have favored selective borrowing from the West through carefully regulated contacts. Most in this last category have recognized the need to obtain scientific and technical knowledge as well as material goods from economically advanced nations, but they have argued that while doing so China should, and could, preserve its distinctive values and institutions.

In the nineteenth century, many influential leaders maintained that China could catch up with the rest of the world in material terms by learning and applying Western "techniques" while still preserving the "essence" of Chinese culture. Their slogan was, use Chinese learning for "ti" (ti) (essence or substance) and Western learning for "yung" (yong) (function or utility).[4] This view has resonated in Chinese policy debates since that time. During the three decades since the start of Communist rule, many of the issues that were at the center of earlier debates have continued to divide Chinese leaders. The fundamental question of whether—or at least to what extent—China should "join the world" has yet to be finally and definitely answered. Moreover, in recent years the old issues have been complicated by new kinds of ideological, political, and economic dilemmas.

When the People's Republic of China was first established in 1949, its leaders initially decided to move rapidly to join the world or, to be more precise, that part of it ruled by other Communist regimes. For a combination of ideological, military-security, and economic motives, they concluded that China should not only ally itself militarily with the Soviet Union but also emulate its institutions and basic policies. Peking (Beijing) stated explicitly that it viewed a foreign nation as the model for China, something few Chinese leaders had ever done before.[5]

In the 1950s China's relationships with the Soviet Union and other "socialist camp" members were unlike any foreign relationships in China's past. Chinese leaders called for borrowing virtually everything that could be borrowed from the Soviet Union, including basic values and institutions as well as science and technology, and they developed extensive educational and intellectual as well as military and economic links of a kind unprecedented in Chinese history. Instead of asserting that China was a model civilization, sufficient unto itself, Peking's leaders now proclaimed that their country was an integral part of the Communist bloc led by Moscow. Although Peking never opted for total economic integration into the bloc—they chose, for example, not to join the Council for Mutual Economic Assistance (COMECON), through which the economies of the Soviet Union and Eastern Europe were linked—nevertheless, China became closely tied to and dependent on the Soviet Union.

During the 1950s Chinese relationships with the rest of the world remained limited. Although they developed political and economic ties with the non-Communist Third World and some links with Japan and Western Europe, these remained restricted. This was not entirely a matter of choice.[6] The Korean War and resulting confrontational relations between Washington and Peking helped to impose isolation upon China. Nevertheless, Peking's own policies, stressing its alignment with Communist bloc nations, all of which in that period limited their contacts with the non-Communist world, ensured that China would be fairly isolated from the mainstream of developments in the international community and relatively uninvolved in the global economy.

China's identification with the "socialist camp" did not last for long, however. During the late 1950s and early 1960s Sino-Soviet ties quickly unraveled. The causes of the Peking-Moscow split were complex; they have been thoroughly analyzed elsewhere and need not be detailed here. In brief, differences between leaders in the two countries led, step by step, from ideological debates to political and territorial disputes, and ultimately to military confrontation.[7] In the process, Peking's leaders openly rejected the Soviet model, disengaged China's interests almost completely from those of the Soviet Union, and ended China's dependence on Moscow. The alliance that had looked both monolithic and permanent in the 1950s proved in fact to be very fragile. It can be argued that, from a historical viewpoint, the close Sino-Soviet ties of the 1950s were an aberration, and that, in light of China's history, an eventual reaction against dependence on a foreign power and reassertion of China's sense of uniqueness, independence, and self-sufficiency were probably inevitable. (However, relatively few people—whether historians, political scientists, or others—predicted the split, and those who did failed to foresee that it would come so soon.)

Although the Sino-Soviet split was precipitated by causes that had relatively little to do with China's old cultural attitudes and dilemmas, the way in which the Chinese reacted to Moscow as their conflict evolved revealed that the question of how—and how much—China should involve itself with the international community beyond its borders remained unresolved. It became clear that many Chinese leaders were strongly influenced by assumptions, attitudes, and goals very similar in some respects to those of many nineteenth century Chinese leaders. From the late 1950s on, Mao Tse-tung (Mao Zedong) and his closest supporters demonstrated that, although they were determined to modernize and strengthen China, they believed it was necessary to restrict China's external relationships severely, fending off foreign influences that might subvert China's "essence" and obtaining only what was absolutely necessary from other nations.[8] The "essence" that Peking's leaders now tried to protect was very different, of course, from the cultural values that nineteenth century Chinese leaders idealized. In the late 1950s Mao reasserted the values embodied in his own version of Marxism-Leninism, not those of traditional Confucianism.[9] Nevertheless, once again Peking's leaders stressed what was uniquely Chinese, at the same time reasserting, as earlier leaders had, the universal validity of the values China stood for.

In the late 1950s China turned inward, and from 1960 on one of its prime slogans was "self-reliance."[10] Adopting a do-it-yourself, bootstrap approach to development, Peking cut back its foreign economic and cultural ties. While in this period the Chinese carried on essential trade, and expanded diplomatic and political activities in the Third World, for both ideological and political reasons they were essentially inward looking. Peking's leaders tried to reduce all foreign influence on China, especially from the other major powers, whether Communist or non-Communist.

Their stress on self-reliance reached a peak during the Cultural Revolution, in the late 1960s, when diplomatic and political ties with other nations were reduced to a low level. Within China, there were outbursts of xenophobia reminiscent of the Boxer Rebellion at the turn of the century as well as outbursts in earlier centuries. In the early 1960s some Chinese leaders tried to reverse the nativist trends in Peking's economic policy, and reportedly at least a few argued for a more pragmatic and outward-looking general foreign policy, but they failed.[11]

By the early 1970s, however, change had begun, including a significant rise in China's foreign trade. But the ideal of self-reliance remained predominant until the death of Mao in 1976. In a fundamental sense, it represented a revival, in modern form, of the traditional idea that China should be an entity unto itself, restricting its dealings with the outside world in order to limit the corrupting effects of foreign influence.

The most militant supporters of self-reliance during and immediately after the Cultural Revolution were the top "radicals" in China's Politburo, but the policy bore Mao's imprimatur. It may have acquired considerable mass support by appealing to primordial cultural attitudes, latent xenophobia, and strong nationalist feelings shared by many ordinary Chinese. In the early 1970s, however, other leaders, including Premier Chou En-lai (Zhou Enlai), responding to economic necessities, argued for greater pragmatism in both domestic and foreign economic policy, and Chinese policy gradually acquired a more outward-looking orientation.[12] Foreign trade, and the importation of technology from abroad, increased fairly rapidly. This trend provoked strong opposition from the radicals, and during 1974–76 there was a climactic debate over "self-reliance" between those who emphasized the need for ideological purity and those who believed that economic imperatives required broader relationships with the rest of the world.[13] This was part of a broad struggle over revolutionary and developmental issues, over the general direction in which the revolution should move, the strategy of development China should pursue, and the relative priority of revolutionary goals and values and developmental aims and economic growth.[14] The fundamental question was what type of society China should develop in the future. Arguments over domestic and foreign economic policies were inevitably linked. China's radicals espoused a developmental strategy stressing egalitarian social goals that was premised on the ideal of self-reliance; they argued that China's involvement in the world economy had to be minimized to preserve China's ideological and revolutionary values. China's leading "pragmatists" maintained that China had to broaden its foreign economic and other relationships in order to solve its most pressing domestic problems and accelerate modernization and economic growth.

The debates remained unresolved as long as Mao lived. However, almost immediately after his death in September 1976, and after the purge of China's top radicals (the "Gang of Four") in October, dramatic policy shifts began to occur. Since then, far-reaching changes have occurred in virtually every field of policy in China. Peking's dominant post-Mao leaders have proclaimed a philosophy that is frankly pragmatic, and the new policies they have adopted add up to a form of de facto de-Maoization. To date, they have preserved Mao as a national symbol of historical importance, but they have downgraded his importance and have either reversed or substantially modified most of the policies associated with his name during the last decade and a half of his rule. Peking's leaders now assert that Chinese must "seek truth from facts," "emancipate" their "minds," and avoid being trapped by any (including Maoist) dogmas. They also emphasize that China must learn whatever it can from any foreign country whose experience provides lessons that can be adapted to help China achieve its goals.[15]

China's new leaders have proclaimed that "modernization" and accelerated economic development are the country's priority aims. In adjusting priorities, they have shifted emphasis from equity to efficiency and from egalitarianism to growth. In late 1978 they announced that the Chinese revolution had entered a new period, in which the primary focus of all efforts would be on economic objectives and technological revolution rather than on egalitarian ideological values and political revolution.[16] Their stated goal is to make China a fully developed nation by the end of the century through rapid modernization of its agriculture, industry, military establishment, and science and technology, encompassed by the slogan "four modernizations." Achievement of the four modernizations, Peking now emphasizes, will require cultural, social, and institutional as well as economic change; in Marxist terms, the "superstructure" of society and "the relations of production" must be altered to develop China's "productive forces."[17]

This extraordinary shift in philosophy, priorities, and policies has begun to have far-reaching effects not only on China itself but also on its relationships with the outside world. It is not easy to predict confidently what the ultimate consequences will be. Policies are still being evolved, and many are still experimental. Implementing them will be extremely difficult. Moreover, while solving some problems, these policies will create new ones and have undesired side effects. Although the new policies appear to enjoy fairly broad support, they face some internal opposition. Possibly, at some point they could provoke a political backlash, resulting in another swing of the policy pendulum, or at least a slowing down in the pace and extent of change. Even assuming that current policies continue essentially unchanged for the indefinite future, it is difficult to estimate what degree of success they will have, or what the unintended as well as the planned consequences will be.

The immediate impact on China's attitudes toward, and relationships with, the outside world has been fairly dramatic, however, especially in the economic field. Although self-reliance continues to be an officially approved slogan, for all practical purposes it has been abandoned as an immediate imperative, even though it continues to be a long-term goal. China's leaders now stress that the success of the nation's modernization policies depends fundamentally on learning as much as possible, as fast as possible, from many different kinds of countries: the economically advanced industrial nations (especially non-Communist nations such as Japan, the Western European countries, and the United States), some

Eastern European countries (especially Yugoslavia, Hungary, and Rumania), and even certain relatively successful developing areas (including South Korea, Taiwan, Hong Kong, and Singapore).[18]

Peking now calls for rapid expansion of foreign trade; the importation of large quantities of machinery, equipment, and complete plants from abroad; and a much more active policy of acquiring advanced scientific knowledge and technological know-how from foreign countries through increased two-way contacts, training, and exchanges. Chinese leaders also emphasize the need to learn foreign techniques of organization and management. And they have begun to open the door to some cultural influences from "bourgeois" societies.

Despite the far-reaching changes in China's foreign economic policy, which have paralleled major shifts in China's domestic development goals, strategies, and policies, Peking's security policy has not been fundamentally altered. In fact, there has been remarkable continuity in certain aspects of China's political and strategic approach to the outside world.

Since 1949 a complex mixture of influences and motivations has shaped China's overall foreign policy. One has been a strong, nationalistic desire to assert China's rights internationally and obtain recognition of China as a major power. Another has been an ideologically motivated impulse to encourage revolutionary change beyond China's borders, through support (mainly moral but some material) of political movements within foreign countries and advocacy of structural changes in the international system. By far the most important determinant of China's overall foreign policy, however, has been the determination of Peking's leaders to enhance China's national security in the face of perceived threats from other major powers—Japan in the 1930s and 1940s, the United States in the 1950s and 1960s, and most recently the Soviet Union.[19]

Recognizing their position of military weakness relative to other major powers, China's leaders have tried to enhance their country's security by pursuing, with a fairly high degree of consistency, a distinctive balance-of-power strategy, conceived of in "united front" terms and aimed at encouraging as many countries as possible to oppose the power or powers believed to pose the greatest threat to China at any particular time.

In the late 1960s Mao and other Chinese leaders concluded that the Soviet Union had become their principal enemy, and they embarked on a policy aimed at encouraging more active opposition to it by all other nations, especially the major non-Communist industrial powers.[20] Since Mao's death, China's leaders have continued this effort, and so far there has been little change in either their political or economic relations with the Soviet Union (although, as will be discussed later, at some point Peking could modify its policy toward Moscow for economic as well as for tactical political reasons).

Although "grand strategy" has had a significant influence on Chinese thinking, not all Chinese foreign policy decisions can be explained in terms of its national security calculations or even its nationalistic and revolutionary motivations. Some of Peking's actions have been reactions to the policies of other nations or to events beyond their control. Others have represented pragmatic, ad hoc efforts to achieve limited objectives or to promote specific interests—including economic interests. In general, however, during the past three decades military-security considerations, politics, and ideology have taken precedence over economics in determining overall foreign policy.

During the period since Mao's death, however, economic factors have become much more important in shaping China's general approach to the outside world. One reason is that for the first time since the 1950s economic growth and modernization have been given priority over Maoist ideological aims in domestic policy. In many respects the expansion of China's economic ties with the non-Communist industrial countries reinforces its primary foreign policy goal of mobilizing international support in opposition to the Soviet Union. But today economic interests are less subordinate to ideological and political aims than in the past.[21] New foreign economic ties have already begun to affect the basic pattern of China's foreign relations. If this trend continues, in time it could alter China's general relationships with the outside world in fundamental ways, creating new networks of interlocking interests, relationships, and interdependencies.

To date, the most visible effects of China's new economic policies have been on its relationships with the advanced industrial nations of the non-Communist world, but its growing foreign economic ties are also subtly affecting its relationships with the Third World, and it is at least possible that a pragmatic Chinese leadership may in time reassess its policy toward Moscow as well.

Until recently, China's involvement in most international organizations has been severely limited, but this too is changing.[22] To date, insufficient attention has been paid to its actual and potential importance in relation to many global issues, such as those concerning world trade, technology transfers, energy, natural resources, the environment, population, the oceans, the international financial system, and general relationships between developed and developing nations (North-South relations). Because of the relatively small size of China's trade in the past, as well as its general unwillingness to participate actively in cooperative international approaches to solving global issues, the Chinese role has not seemed sufficiently important to most observers to deserve much attention. Even though, following the seating of the People's Republic in the United Nations in 1972, the Chinese became increasingly vocal in articulating their views on some international problems, especially in UN conferences, and their positions had a certain influence on Third World attitudes and North-South debates, the prevailing view in the West was that China could be virtually ignored in analyses of most basic international economic problems and did not have to be included in efforts to devise solutions for them.

This view was always shortsighted. Because of its sheer size, China has played an important role in the world economy, no matter what the extent and character of its foreign economic relationships at any time. With between one-fifth and one-fourth of the world's population, it is the largest single concentration of humanity anywhere.[23] Despite its relative poverty, measured in per capita GNP, and the fact that it produces only about 4.6 percent of the world's gross product, China today nevertheless is the world's sixth largest producer of goods and services.[24] Its defense budget is the third largest in the world.[25] It is the third largest producer and consumer of "primary energy," the third largest producer of coal, and one of the top dozen producers of oil.[26] Its untapped natural resources are huge; for example, it is estimated that its proven and probable reserves are at least the third (and maybe second) largest in the world in coal and are probably about tenth in oil and fifteenth in gas.[27] It also has large resources of many nonferrous minerals.[28] Even in rankings of mining and industrial production, China's position is near the top of the list in gross output of many basic commodities and products. By the mid-1970s, for example, it had become first in the world in production of tungsten; third in synthetic ammonia; fourth in pig iron, primary tin, chemical fertilizers, and cement; fifth in rolled steel and metallurgical coke; and eighth in primary aluminum.[29] In certain manufactured goods, China's production also ranks near the top of the list. In cotton fabric, its output is first in the world (slightly above India's); it ranks second (surprisingly) in radio receivers, fourth in freight cars, sixth in mainline diesel locomotives and tractors (excluding garden tractors), and ninth in trucks and buses.[30]

In sum, despite its low standard of living, China, because of its size, is one of the world's major producers and consumers. Any country that has such a huge population and accounts for a significant portion of the world's production and consumption of goods and services occupies an important place in the global economy, whatever its direct economic interaction with the rest of the world. From a global perspective, one cannot ignore what a country with more than one-fifth of the world's population produces and consumes; what resources it possesses, develops, and uses; and what the resulting environmental, social, and political effects are. No matter whether China is inward looking or outward looking, its economic policies and performance will have significant effects on mankind's future.

In a few areas of world trade, moreover, China already has become an important factor internationally.[31] For example, it has been the world's largest importer of chemical fertilizer since the early 1970s. In recent years it has been the seventh ranking importer of minerals. It has also been one of the largest importers of steel. However, because its general level of foreign trade has been relatively low, it has received little attention in most analyses of international issues. Even though it has the world's largest population and the sixth largest GNP, China has not ranked higher than between twentieth and twenty-fifth in world trade in recent years; in 1977 it ranked thirty-seventh.[32] In 1977 its imports accounted for only 0.7 percent of total world imports; its share of total world exports was roughly one-half of 1 percent.[33] However, China's turning outward since 1977 indicates that it could play a larger and more significant international economic role in the future. If so, its relevance to and involvement in major global issues will certainly grow.

The purpose of this study is to analyze the changes now taking place in China's foreign economic relations, their possible implications for both China and the broader international community, and the policy issues—as well as economic opportunities—they are likely to pose for other nations, particularly the United States. The starting point is an analysis of the domestic Chinese economy and the changes that are occurring in Chinese policies. This requires an examination of the basic shift that has taken place in China's development strategy, and the effects that the changes in its domestic policies are having on its foreign economic relations. The study then analyzes in detail China's prospects for increasing its foreign trade and acquiring advanced technology from abroad. This requires an examination of the factors that will affect the size, composition, and direction of China's trade and, specifically, its capabilities for acquiring foreign capital goods and technology. Judging Peking's future prospects also requires an assessment of the problems it faces in absorbing new technology from abroad and possible methods for paying for it. On this basis, tentative conclusions can be reached about China's general prospects for expanding its foreign economic relations, the problems that it is likely to encounter, and the policy issues that other nations will face as their economic relationships with China grow.

Following this general discussion of China's expanding economic relationships with foreign nations, the study analyzes in detail China's present and future international roles on two key issues in the global community: world food and world energy. On both issues, China's international roles are already more significant than many people realize; they are certain to become increasingly important in the years ahead. The study attempts, in the context of global food and oil trends, to examine current developments affecting China's domestic supply and demand and its trade, and to assess the actual and potential importance of this trade, both to China itself and to the world economy. The linkages between Chinese interests and those of the global community relating to food and energy are clearly growing. This opens new possibilities for greater Chinese involvement in cooperative international programs in these fields. It also raises new policy issues for the United States and other nations.

I

China's Modernization Program

TO UNDERSTAND China's new foreign economic policies, it is essential to examine the changes that have occurred since late 1976 in Peking's (Beijing's) domestic economic development strategy, since the policy shifts at home and abroad have been closely interconnected; to understand the *reasons* for these shifts, it is necessary to examine China's record of economic performance in the 1950s and 1960s and the problems that Peking's leaders faced when Mao Tse-tung (Mao Zedong) died. Although in many respects China's development over the past three decades has been remarkable, the performance of the economy has been erratic, and periods of rapid growth have been interrupted by serious setbacks.[1] Over time, many of Peking's leaders concluded that certain fundamental problems remained unresolved.

There has been almost continuous debate in China, especially since the late 1950s, over developmental priorities and the best strategies to solve the country's most pressing economic difficulties.[2] The pendulum has swung several times between policies emphasizing mass mobilization techniques aimed primarily at achieving Maoist egalitarian goals and more flexible, pragmatic policies designed mainly to accelerate growth. Mao himself (and, during the final years of Mao's life, radical leaders acting in his name) dominated economic decision making in the late 1950s and again in the late 1960s, during the Great Leap Forward, the communization program, and the Cultural Revolution. Each of these upsurges of revolutionary mobilization resulted in setbacks to the economy. After each, other leaders, such as Liu Shao-chi (Liu Shaoqi), Chou

En-lai (Zhou Enlai), and Teng Hsiao-ping (Deng Xiaoping), supported by others in China's bureaucracies, moved policy in more pragmatic directions, emphasizing economic recovery and renewed growth. The roots of many current policies can be found in actions initiated by China's leading pragmatists during the early 1960s to cope with the severe economic depression that followed the Great Leap, and during the early 1970s to repair the damage done by the Cultural Revolution.[3]

The likelihood of a shift away from ideological dogmatism after Mao's death was predictable long before his demise.[4] There is reason to believe that for many years a majority of the top leaders in China's Party, state, and military bureaucracies, especially its economic planners and administrators, favored a shift toward more flexible, growth-oriented policies. Mao's views on economic policy probably had only minority support from the early 1960s on, but they prevailed because of his charismatic power and unique role as Party chairman. Even Premier Chou En-lai, the only individual at the top among China's post-1949 leaders whose relationship with Mao was never ruptured (although in certain periods it was strained), clearly favored a development program based on more practical policies. In tracing the origins of their current program, China's present leaders stress that Chou first proposed a program of "four modernizations" in 1964, then repeated his proposal in 1975, long before the concept was officially proclaimed to be the center-piece of Chinese policy in early 1978.

In his Report on the Work of the Government, made to the Third National People's Congress (NPC) in December 1964, Chou, discussing the third Five Year Plan (scheduled to start in 1966), asserted that the Communist Party must "strive to build China into a powerful socialist state with a modern agriculture, modern industry, modern national defense and modern science and technology."[5] But soon thereafter political conflicts shattered the unity of the Chinese leadership, making it impossible to translate these slogans into concrete plans. The turmoil of the Cultural Revolution forced postponement of any new modernization program for more than a decade.

Then, in January 1975, at the Fourth National People's Congress—the first session since 1964–65—Chou again called for initiation of an essentially pragmatic new modernization program. Reminding his audience that he had proposed this earlier in 1964, he urged adoption of a two-stage program:

On Chairman Mao's instructions, it was suggested [by Chou himself] in the

Report on the Work of the Government to the Third National People's Congress that we might envisage the development of our national economy in two stages beginning from the Third Five Year Plan: The first stage is to build an independent and relatively comprehensive industrial and economic system in 15 years, that is before 1980; the second stage is to accomplish the comprehensive modernization of agriculture, industry, national defense, and science and technology before the end of the century, so that our national economy will be advancing in the front ranks of the world.[6]

Chou gave few details about the course he was proposing, but behind-the-scenes work began on a new Five Year Plan, and Teng Hsiao-ping, China's quintessential pragmatist, was groomed to be his successor. As Party General Secretary, Teng had been a key organizational leader in Peking from the mid-1950s to the mid-1960s. Subsequently he had been purged during the Cultural Revolution, and only recently had been rehabilitated with Chou's backing and apparently Mao's as well.[7] Teng set to work defining a set of very new economic policies. Three documents, drafted under his aegis in 1975, called for a major shift away from Maoist ideological priorities toward increased pragmatism.[8] Although drafts were circulated within the Party, they were not published, and they soon became the target of violent political attacks by China's radicals, who succeeded in obstructing their implementation.[9] However, they foreshadowed policy changes that were to take place soon after Mao's death.

When Mao died and China's leading radicals were purged, the main immediate obstacles to policy change were removed. A number of Peking's leaders immediately pushed for adoption of new policies, some similar to ones introduced experimentally in the early 1960s, others virtually identical to many proposed in 1975. Chou En-lai's 1975 speech, the planning work done during 1974–75, and the proposals drafted under Teng's direction during 1975 provided the starting point for defining the new modernization program. However, to help legitimize the move toward more pragmatic policies, the new leadership also revived, in late 1976, a broad programmatic statement Mao had made twenty years earlier (which had never been openly published in China) in a period when he had been much more flexible and moderate in his approach to economic policy than he was in the following two decades.[10] But the real patron saint of the post-Mao policies was Chou En-lai, and the real prime mover pushing for their rapid implementation was Teng, who, after his second purge by Mao and the radicals in early 1976, was rehabilitated a second time in 1977 and again assumed a key position in the leadership.[11]

As changes in China's economic policies began rapidly to occur, Peking's leaders appeared to feel a sense of great urgency about the need to stimulate very rapid growth as well as to adopt a new approach to economic development.[12] Trends in the mid-1970s just before Mao's death helped to create this feeling. During 1975–76 the Chinese economy had performed very poorly.[13] Agricultural production, including grain output, stagnated in both years (and in the following year as well).[14] Although total gross national product (GNP) continued to increase in 1975, there was apparently no real growth in 1976. Stagnation in agriculture, a major cause of the general economic slowdown, was due in part to bad weather, but the political instability caused by the conflict between China's radicals and pragmatists during Mao's declining years, which intensified as Mao's death approached, also had an extremely adverse effect on the economy. Conflict at the top levels of the leadership was accompanied by political strife at the factory level, which resulted in industrial slowdowns and even some factory closures.[15] (Political strife had also been a major reason for the decline in GNP in 1967 and the lack of growth in 1968, at the height of the Cultural Revolution.[16]) No-growth and agricultural stagnation were profoundly disturbing to China's leaders, since the country's population continued to grow by roughly 15 million a year.

There doubtless were different views within the leadership (as there were among foreign observers), however, about the extent to which economic stagnation in 1976 was due to temporary, short-term factors or to more fundamental structural problems. Some Western analysts argued that the primary causes of the poor economic performance were unusually bad weather (a temporary factor), the Tangshan (Tangshan) earthquake of 1976 (a one-time disaster), and political disruptions, uncertainties, and lack of consensus with the leadership during the succession struggle (which in theory could be remedied to a large extent by reestablishing political discipline and order), rather than basic weaknesses in the economy or the regime's economic policies per se.[17] Probably some Chinese had similar views. The overall performance of China's economy during the first seven years of the 1970s did not provide the basis for any prima facie case that China's economy was in such deep trouble that its leaders had to opt for major policy changes. Despite stagnation in 1976, during the seven years from 1970 through 1977[18] China's total GNP apparently increased at an average annual rate of over 6 percent, and the rate of growth in industrial output was close to 9 percent.[19]

However, the economic concerns of China's pragmatists in 1977 focused not only on the immediate situation but, to an even greater extent, on the country's inability to solve certain basic, long-term, structural economic problems which, if not resolved, would almost certainly produce slower growth—and conceivably major economic crises—in the future. The view held by Teng Hsiao-ping, who emerged openly in mid-1977 as the main architect of new policies, was that China's economic difficulties were rooted in fundamental problems that demanded far-reaching changes in economic development strategy, not merely cosmetic policy changes. By 1977–78 this view prevailed.

Even though during 1977–78 many press discussions of China's economic problems were highly propagandistic and placed most of the blame for the country's difficulties on "sabotage" by the so-called radical Gang of Four, by 1978 the leadership had begun to articulate with remarkable frankness the view that ever since the late 1950s certain basic problems had obstructed China's economic development, and that therefore new policies were essential to sustain and accelerate soundly based, long-term modernization and growth.[20]

To understand the policy shifts that have occurred since 1977, it is necessary to understand these basic problems. To obtain a balanced view of China's record over the past three decades, however, it is also necessary to recognize the regime's economic accomplishments.

Economic Record: Major Accomplishments

Despite its ups and downs, China's economy has grown tremendously since 1949, and the Chinese have built a substantial industrial foundation, on the basis of which the country's leaders hope to achieve even greater growth in the future. The country has achieved respectable long-term rates of overall growth, and it has distributed output in a relatively equitable fashion. It has avoided excessive foreign debt, and it has minimized the effects of problems such as unemployment, uncontrolled urbanization, neglect of rural society, and inflation that have been endemic in many other developing countries. Peking's success in promoting both growth and equity convinced some people that China's Maoist developmental policies provided a good model for other developing nations to emulate[21] (although China's recent economic difficulties and policy shifts have confused many of those who once viewed the "Maoist model" with an almost totally uncritical eye).

Judged on the basis of its rate of overall growth, China's economic record since the 1950s has been fairly impressive in comparison with the record of many other large developing countries. As table 1-1 shows, during the quarter century from 1952 (the year before China's first developmental plan got under way) through 1977, the nation's GNP rose from roughly $92 billion (in 1977 U.S. dollars) to about $370 billion, quadrupling in twenty-five years.[22] During that quarter century, China's average annual rate of growth was a little over 5.7 percent. During the twenty years from 1957 through 1977 (which may provide a better benchmark for evaluating China's long-term growth rates), it was about 5.5 percent. In per capita terms, the average during 1957–77 was close to 3.4 percent.

These long-term rates are misleading in some respects, however, because great variations occurred over time. The rate of growth was very rapid in the 1950s (averaging over 8.8 percent in the six years from 1952 through 1958). Then, during 1960–61, there was actually a negative rate of growth, and China's GNP declined from $145 billion in 1959 to $112 billion in 1961. (These and the following GNP figures are in 1977 dollars.) This was followed by another period of rapid growth during the five-year period from 1961 through 1966, when China's GNP increased at an average rate of almost 12 percent. GNP just reached $157 billion in 1964, however, which was only slightly above the 1958 level, and in 1966, at $196 billion, GNP was only 28 percent above the 1958 level; the high rate achieved during 1962–66 obviously was due in large part to "catch-up" gains rather than to new growth. In 1967 GNP again declined, due to the effects of the Cultural Revolution, and thereafter it did not surpass the 1966 level again until 1969, when it reached $210 billion. Subsequently, rapid growth resumed in the early 1970s; the average rate during the six-year period from 1969 through 1975 was almost 8.5 percent. Although 1976 was another year of no growth, in 1977 the economy began moving forward again, and it has continued growing ever since.

Despite long-term growth, the erratic pattern of ups and downs[23] disturbed many Chinese leaders who felt, and still feel, that China cannot

TABLE 1-1. *China: Estimated GNP (U.S. Government Estimates, December 1978)*

Year	GNP (billions of 1977 dollars)	Population (midyear, millions)	GNP per capita (1977 dollars)
1949	54	538	100
1950	67	547	122
1951	78	558	140
1952	92	570	161
1953	98	583	168
1954	102	596	171
1955	112	610	184
1956	121	625	194
1957	128	639	200
1958	153	654	234
1959	145	667	217
1960	141	680	207
1961	112	692	162
1962	124	705	176
1963	139	720	193
1964	157	734	214
1965	172	749	230
1966	196	765	256
1967	188	781	241
1968	189	798	237
1969	210	816	257
1970	244	834	293
1971	261	852	306
1972	273	869	314
1973	308	885	348
1974	320	900	356
1975	342	914	374
1976	342	930	368
1977	370	946	391
1978	407	964	422

Sources: GNP figures are CIA estimates from (1) National Foreign Assessment Center, Central Intelligence Agency, *China: Economic Indicators*, Reference Aid ER 78-10750, December 1978, p. 1; and (2) Arthur G. Ashbrook, Jr., "China: Shift of Economic Gears in Mid-1970's," in Joint Economic Committee, *Chinese Economy Post-Mao*, 95 Cong. 2 sess. (Government Printing Office, November 1978), p. 208. In a few cases where there are minor differences, source 1 estimates are used. Population estimates are from the source cited in table 3-1. Figures are rounded. Per capita GNP figures are my calculations. For later CIA estimates giving GNP figures through 1978 (in 1978 dollars), see appendix table 1.

afford to experience slowdowns and setbacks such as those of the early 1960s, late 1960s, and mid-1970s. Yet, unquestionably, China's long-term rate of growth has been respectable. While it has been considerably lower than that achieved by some of China's rapidly developing Asian neighbors (including Korea and Taiwan, as well as Japan), it has been much higher than any growth rate achieved in pre-1949 China; it has also been above the rates achieved during most of the last three decades in other large, heavily populated Asian countries such as India and Indonesia.[24]

One important explanation for China's growth rate has been its high level of investment. Before 1949, the rate of capital formation in China— that is, its gross investment as a percentage of its gross output—was probably only about 5 percent.[25] By 1957 this rate had risen to about 20 percent, and since then it has been at least 25 percent and in some years well over 30 percent, a very high level for a densely populated country with low per capita income.[26] It was close to twice the level achieved in India, for example.[27] (However, the Soviet Union's level of investment has been comparable.[28])

By far the largest share of China's investment since the 1950s has gone into industry. Not surprisingly, the growth rate of China's industrial sector has been most rapid.[29] With 1957 as a base of 100, the index figure for China's industrial production in 1977 was 572, compared with 48 in 1952 (table 1-2). (In 1979 the Central Intelligence Agency [CIA] estimate for 1978 put the figure at 651.) The growth rate in industrial output during the twenty years from 1957 through 1977 was 9.1 percent (or 6.8 percent per capita), and for the quarter century starting from 1952 the rate was 10.2 percent. Consequently between 1952 and 1977, the increase in China's industrial output was eleven- to twelve-fold; between 1957 and 1977 it was almost six-fold. (A 9 percent rate results in a doubling every eight years.) In achieving this rate of industrial growth, the Chinese have not only expanded output in the few industrial centers they inherited in 1949; they have also built up many entirely new ones, scattered over the country,[30] and have developed medium- and small-scale rural plants in towns and communes throughout China.[31]

The fastest growth has been in producer goods industries. According to U.S. government estimates (see table 1-2), with 1957 as a base (100), the production index for these industries was 602 in 1975, compared with 39 in 1952.[32]

The growth in machine building was the most rapid. With 1957

TABLE 1-2. *China: Selected Economic Indicators (U.S. Government Estimates, December 1978)*

Indicator	1952	1957	1965	1970	1971	1972	1973	1974	1975	1976	1977	1978
Agricultural production index (1957 = 100)	84	100	101	126	130	126	142	146	148	148	146	151
Total grain (million metric tons)	161	191	194	243	246	240	266	275	284	285	286	295
Cotton (million metric tons)	1.3	1.6	1.6	2.0	2.2	2.1	2.6	2.5	2.4	2.3	2.0	2.2
Hogs (million head)	90	115	168	226	251	261	...	287	...	...	290	...
Industrial production index (1957 = 100)	48	100	199	316	349	385	436	455	502	502	572	646
Producer goods index (1957 = 100)	39	100	211	350	407	452	513	536	602	...	...	...
Machinery index (1957 = 100)	33	100	257	586	711	795	930	992	1,156	...	...	...
Electric generators (million kilowatts)	*	0.3	0.8	2.3	2.9	3.6	4.3	5.1	6.0	6.6	...	...
Machine tools (thousand units)	13.7	28.3	45.0	70.0	75.0	75.0	80.0	85.0	90.0	85.0	...	...
Tractors (thousand 15-horsepower units)	0	0	23.9	79.0	114.6	136.0	166.0	150.0	180.0	190.9	221.8	271.0
Trucks (thousand units)	0	7.5	30.0	70.0	86.0	100.0	110.0	121.0	133.0	135.0	150.0	181.0
Locomotives (units)	20	167	50	435	455	475	495	505	530	530	555	...
Freight cars (thousand units)	5.8	7.3	6.6	12.0	14.0	15.0	16.0	16.8	18.5	19.0	21.0	...
Merchant ships (thousand metric tons)	6.1	46.4	50.6	121.5	148.0	164.6	209.4	288.4	313.6	318.8	...	...
Other producer goods index (1957 = 100)	41	100	200	294	336	371	415	429	472	...	...	...
Electric power (billion kilowatt-hours)	7.3	19.3	42.0	72.0	86.0	93.0	101.0	108.0	121.0	128.0	141.0	162

Coal (million metric tons)	66.5	130.7	232.2	327.4	353.6	376.5	398.1	410.6	479.6	488.0	546.6	605
Crude oil (million metric tons)	0.4	1.5	11.0	28.2	36.7	43.1	54.8	65.8	74.3	83.6	90.3	100.3
Crude steel (million metric tons)	1.3	5.4	12.2	17.8	21.0	23.0	25.0	21.0	24.0	21.0	24.0	31.7
Chemical fertilizer (million metric tons)	0.2	0.8	7.6	14.0	16.8	19.8	24.8	24.9	28.8	24.3	38.0	48
Cement (million metric tons)	2.9	6.9	16.3	26.6	31.0	38.1	41.0	37.3	47.1	49.3	56.2	67.8
Timber (million cubic meters)	11.2	27.9	27.2	29.9	30.7	33.2	34.2	35.2	36.2	36.7	37.2	39.2
Paper (million metric tons)	0.6	1.2	3.6	5.0	5.1	5.6	6.0	6.5	6.9	7.0	7.1	...
Consumer goods index (1957 = 100)	60	100	183	272	272	295	334	347	368	...	...	...
Cotton cloth (billion linear meters)	3.8	5.0	5.7	8.5	...	...	...	...	9.6	8.9	10.0	11.1
Wool cloth (million linear meters)	4.2	18.2	...	...	...	...	...	65.2	...	...	...	...
Processed sugar (million metric tons)	0.5	0.9	1.5	1.8	1.9	1.9	2.2	2.2	2.3	...	...	...
Bicycles (million units)	0.1	0.8	1.8	3.6	4.0	4.3	4.9	5.2	5.5	...	...	...

Source: Adapted from NFAC, CIA, *China: Economic Indicators*, December 1978, p. 1. At the time of this writing, this source was the most up-to-date, comprehensive set of indicators published by the CIA. For later CIA revisions (as of July 1979) of some of these indicators, see appendix table 2, in which most figures for 1976–78 have been modified somewhat, and a few (for example, those for electricity and timber) have been greatly changed.

*Negligible.

as a base, the index for machinery production, which was 33 in 1952, reached 1,156 in 1975; today it is substantially above the 1975 figure.[33]

In contrast, consumer goods production grew much more slowly. With 1957 as a base, the index for all consumer goods rose from 60 in 1952 to 368 in 1975. Thus, during the twenty-three years from 1952 through 1975, when the output of producer goods was increasing more than fifteen-fold and that of machinery thirty-five-fold, consumer goods increased only a little over six-fold. Output of cotton cloth—in many respects the most important manufactured consumer product in China— increased only two- to three-fold, from 3.8 billion linear meters in 1952 to just over 10 billion meters in 1977.[34]

The growth in agriculture has been less rapid. (Agriculture will be discussed in detail in part III, but a few figures indicating the general pattern of growth will be given here.) Although since the 1950s agriculture has grown much more rapidly than in the pre-Communist period, not only has the rate been much slower than in industry, as one would expect; it has consistently lagged behind the regime's hopes and needs. According to U.S. government estimates, China's total production of "grain" (including soybeans and tubers) rose from 161 million tons in 1952 to close to 283 million tons in 1977, an increase totaling 122 million tons, or just under 76 percent, in twenty-five years.[35] While this was a creditable performance, when translated into per capita terms, the rate of growth was much less impressive and varied considerably over time. Over the quarter century, while the average rate of increase of *total* grain output was 2.3 percent, since population growth during the same period averaged more than 2 percent a year, in per capita terms the rate of growth was very low—at most, not more than a quarter of a percent or so per year, and perhaps not that much. For the twenty years from 1957 through 1977, the average rate of increase in total grain output was around 2 percent. Then, from the mid-1960s on, the rate rose and from 1965 through 1977 averaged about 3.2 percent a year (despite stagnation during 1975–77). In the early 1970s, however, the rate was very erratic, with large ups and downs. (China's rate of growth of *overall* agricultural output, that is, including cash crops and other non-grain agricultural production, was comparable to that of grain. With 1957 as a base, the index figures for 1952 and 1977 were 84 and 146, respectively, indicating an average annual rate of growth of about 2.2 percent from 1952 through 1977 and 1.9 percent from 1957 through 1977.[36])

It has been an achievement to sustain an agricultural growth rate above that of population growth, and many observers would include this in any list of Chinese successes. However, in light of the regime's steadily increasing needs for agricultural products—for industrial use and export as well as consumption in China—the performance of agriculture has created serious problems and been a cause for deep concern for China's leaders. Actually, the rate of increase in China's agriculture has been somewhat below the average for all developing nations,[37] and it has kept ahead of China's population growth by only a razor-thin margin.

What has made the "Chinese model" attractive to some observers in other developing nations has been Peking's apparent success in coping with many of the social consequences of development that have plagued most developing nations.[38] The Chinese have distributed the fruits of development in a more egalitarian fashion than have most developing countries. (A few areas, such as Taiwan, have also achieved success in this regard, by very different methods, but they are the exception rather than the rule.[39]) During the past three decades China has been able to eradicate most of the worst poverty, and at least since the end of the post-Leap depression it has maintained a floor under the country's standard of living, guaranteeing at least minimal consumption for the majority of the population and raising the level of nutrition among the poorest groups in society.[40] It also has substantially raised the national standard of health.[41]

In reality, China has not been as egalitarian as some outside observers have assumed.[42] Although income differentials have been reduced, they are still substantial. For example, although in factories the highest wages have generally been three to four times as large as the lowest regular wages (not counting those of apprentices), in urban areas some of the highest incomes have been close to twenty times those of persons at the bottom of the socioeconomic ladder. Party and government officials have enjoyed many perquisites not included in their regular salaries. Moreover, a large gap has continued to exist between urban and rural incomes, and in the countryside there have been sizable variations in incomes among communes, brigades, and teams as well as between individuals. Nevertheless, by raising the income level of those at the bottom levels of society, ensuring the availability of basic essentials to most of the population, eliminating most "conspicuous consumption," and controlling corruption, the regime has prevented the kind of polarization of the wealthy elite and the poverty-stricken masses that has been characteristic of a large number of developing nations.

In contrast to many other poor countries, China also has made progress in improving the quality of life in rural areas, working mainly through the collective organizations called communes. Although the commune system as originally introduced in the late 1950s did not work, and the regime soon was compelled to retreat to a pattern of rural organization similar to that of its pre-1958 collectives (even though the name commune was retained), for the past decade and a half China's system of agricultural collectivization has been viable and relatively stable, although not optimally efficient.[43] The system has had many advantages from the regime's point of view, and some important pluses— as well as minuses—from the perspective of China's peasants. It has made possible effective mobilization of rural labor and capital for productive purposes, ensured at least subsistence income to commune members, and facilitated agricultural planning and the rapid popularization of new agricultural methods and techniques. Since the early 1960s, when Peking's leaders decided to give higher priority to agricultural develop-ment[44] and began to increase modern "inputs" into farming, the communes have played an important role in helping to disseminate the knowledge and materials required to accelerate agricultural modernization.

Although the urban-rural gap in China continues to be large, from the 1950s on the regime took steps to try to narrow it. Most notably, it steadily raised the prices of agricultural goods and reduced the prices of manufactured goods needed by the rural population, thereby im-proving the peasants' terms of trade in their relations with urban areas.[45] During the 1960s and early 1970s the regime's policies in the fields of health and education had a definite pro-rural bias. Simple, low-level education was greatly expanded in the countryside, and cooperative rural health services, relying heavily on a newly developed corps of paramedics (the so-called barefoot doctors), were developed.[46]

Observers from less well-organized developing nations have been im-pressed by the Chinese Communists' demonstrated capacity to mobilize huge amounts of labor for projects of many kinds, in both rural and urban areas. From the early 1960s on Chinese leaders placed increasing emphasis on the importance of labor-intensive projects. Even though a large percentage of Peking's centrally allocated investment funds still were allocated to large-scale industries—both civilian and military— China in recent years has developed medium-sized and small enterprises on a scale unparalleled in most other developing nations. Many of the regime's initial experiments with such industries in the 1950s—including the "backyard steel furnaces" set up during the Great Leap—were failures, but subsequent efforts have been more rational. In many fields a significant percentage of national output in recent years has come from small plants and mines. U.S. government analysts estimated that in 1977, for example, small enterprises accounted for 33 percent of coal output, 60 percent of chemical fertilizer output, and 64 percent of cement output.[47] Recent Chinese figures indicate that, at least in coal, the output of small mines was even higher than U.S. estimates suggested, accounting for 45 percent of total coal output in 1978.[48] Even in pig iron and crude steel, medium and small plants produced roughly 28 percent and 15 percent, respectively, of total national output in 1977. However, small-scale enterprises, while solving some problems, have created new ones. Many have been inefficient, involved high production costs, and been unable to turn a profit. Consequently, Chinese planners are now thinking of consolidating or closing many of them.

Another Chinese accomplishment that has impressed outside observers has been Peking's seeming ability, until recently, to check excessive urbanization and large-scale urban unemployment, which have plagued most developing countries. They accomplished this not simply by encouraging labor-intensive projects, mobilizing workers and peasants for public works on a massive scale, and assigning virtually everyone some sort of work; but equally important, they maintained strict control over all internal migration, preventing what in the 1950s they called the "blind flow" of peasants from the countryside to the cities.[49] In the 1960s and early 1970s China actually reversed the flow by sending between 10 million and 20 million young people (mostly graduates of junior or senior middle schools) out of the major cities to rural or frontier areas; until recently about 10 million of these reportedly have remained in remote areas.[50] As a result, even though many medium and small cities in China grew substantially from the 1960s on, the population in most of China's largest cities increased only slowly, in comparison with those in other developing countries; in some cases it even declined.[51] By all of these means, the Chinese Communist regime alleviated many of the social problems usually associated with rapid modernization, and it reduced the "social overhead" costs that large-scale urbanization normally involves. (During the past few years, however, there has been a sizable illegal flow back to the cities of urban youth previously "rusticated," creating a serious new problem.)

The ways in which China's leaders attempted, throughout the 1960s and early 1970s, to inspire the country's workforce through nonmaterial incentives—that is, by using ideological and nationalistic appeals and providing rewards other than monetary incentives—also impressed many foreign observers, especially from Third World countries. The Maoists' goal was to inculcate the entire population with a new revolutionary ethic, based on a greater sense of social responsibility, and to stimulate the population to work hard for the collective good—to "serve the people"—rather than to work for private gain.[52] In parallel with this effort, the regime attempted, especially in the late 1960s, to increase worker and peasant participation in the management of both industrial enterprises and communes and to encourage a mixture of old, middle-aged, and young cadres in all bodies responsible for supervising management. From the late 1950s on, China's leadership also attempted to stimulate "local initiative," decentralizing certain decision-making and managerial functions to the provinces, counties, and lower levels.[53] Although the central authorities never relinquished key decision-making powers regarding national planning and maintained overall control of national allocation of resources, they did provide some leeway for the adaptation of policies to local conditions.

Another Chinese Communist achievement was its success in controlling—or at least limiting—inflation. Once the lid had been placed on inflation in the 1950s, China's leaders were able to restrain price rises and to avoid almost entirely—until very recently—the kind of destructive inflation that many other rapidly developing societies have experienced. They accomplished this by subjecting most commodities to strict controls, rationing basic necessities, and pursuing generally conservative fiscal policies. As a result, prices in state-operated stores were held in check, although since the mid-1960s "free market prices" have been rising gradually. Then, during early 1979, signs of inflationary pressures began to reappear, even in prices charged in state-operated stores.[54]

In recent years, also, the Chinese have implemented one of the most vigorous population control programs anywhere in the world.[55] Population policy was a highly controversial issue in China during the 1950s and was the focus of intense policy debate; the regime's actual population policies vacillated. However, once Mao fully endorsed a serious program of birth control, the regime mobilized its impressive organizational talents to mount a major effort to slow population growth (although Chinese leaders still insisted on calling it population planning rather than birth control). By encouraging late marriages, use of contraceptives, and "planned child-bearing"—using education and propaganda, organized social pressures, and varied sanctions and penalties to back up its efforts at persuasion—the regime began to achieve results by the early 1970s, especially in urban areas. (The coercive element in the country's population-control policies has recently increased significantly.) The evidence points to a significant drop in the annual rate of population growth, from well over 2 percent in the late 1960s to considerably under 2 percent in the mid-1970s[56] (although the decline occurred more in urban than in rural areas). Peking now claims that the population growth rate is dropping rapidly; the State Statistical Bureau's figures show the rate to have been 1.2 percent in 1978 and slightly under that in 1979.

Finally, more than any other large developing nation, from the 1960s until recently China relied essentially on its own resources and was able to minimize its foreign indebtedness.[57] Even though, as will be discussed later, China has not been debt-free, despite its claims, it has been more "self-reliant" than most other developing countries. After paying off the Soviet debt it acquired during the 1950s, Peking proclaimed that it would not accept any long-term foreign loans. (Its indebtedness during the 1960s and early 1970s consisted of short- and medium-term credits.) And it became a donor of substantial foreign aid to other developing countries.

Unresolved Problems: Motives for Change

In light of these accomplishments, China's economic record since the 1950s can be regarded as a success story in important respects. Yet identifying achievements gives only part of the story. Despite successes, the Chinese failed to solve certain fundamental economic problems, and Peking's concern about these problems has steadily mounted over time. China's new leaders obviously believe that unless more progress can be made in solving these problems, the country will face an uncertain economic future. Their basic rationale for carrying out far-reaching changes in China's approach to development since 1977 has been that more flexible and pragmatic policies are essential to deal with China's most serious underlying economic problems, and that their solution is imperative to speed up overall growth and modernization.

The most fundamental of China's unresolved problems has been the lag in the nation's agricultural output in relation to its growing needs.[58] In the seven years from 1970 through 1977, the average annual rate of increase in grain output and total agricultural production was lower than the long-term average since the mid-1960s. Poor weather during the three years 1975–77 was one of the major explanations for this, and output rose as soon as the weather improved. Nevertheless, the leadership has been deeply disturbed by the fact that, *in per capita terms*, China has made little real progress since the 1950s, despite the priority given to agriculture and the steady increase in modern inputs to farming ever since the early 1960s. In 1978 a leading Chinese official, Hu Chiao-mu (Hu Qiaomu), head of China's new Academy of Social Sciences, stated frankly, "The average per capita grain distribution in 1977 only matched that of 1955."[59] And in mid-1979 a Hong Kong newspaper, *Ming Pao* (*Ming Bao*), reported that Vice Premier Li Hsien-nien (Li Xiannian) had admitted in a major speech to a Party meeting that 100 million Chinese were not getting enough to eat.[60] Moreover, China's need for industrial as well as food crops has continued to rise inexorably. The Chinese will face many difficulties as they try to speed up agricultural growth in the period ahead; these will be discussed in detail in part III. Suffice it to say here that the country's entire economic future will depend, in a fundamental sense, on how well its agricultural sector performs; China's new leaders clearly recognize this fact.

Another almost equally disturbing problem has been China's failure, ever since the late 1950s, to achieve any significant increase in the productivity of industrial labor. Hu Chiao-mu stated in 1978 that although labor productivity had increased during the first Five Year Plan period (1953–57) at an average annual rate of 8.7 percent (and wages rose at an annual rate of 7.4 percent in the same period), "after 1958, wages did not increase in due time and growth of labor productivity was not normal"; the result, he said, was that for twenty years "industrial growth depended entirely or for the most part on increasing the number of workers" (to which he should have added "and capital equipment").[61] If labor productivity had continued to grow at the same rate as during 1953–57, he noted, by 1977 it would have been three times what it was. Conceivably, this official statement exaggerated the problem. It is difficult to believe that with all of the buildup of industry there has been *no* increase in labor productivity. Nevertheless, the estimate is probably not far off the mark, because of the inefficient use of industrial labor in China.

Moreover, in rural China the productivity of the peasants is much lower, not surprisingly, than that of the country's urban workers. The progress the Chinese have made in recent years has been in raising per acre yields, not per peasant output. In a speech made in March 1978 to a National Science Conference, Vice Premier Teng Hsiao-ping, after acknowledging that labor productivity in China's iron and steel industry was "only a small percentage of advanced levels abroad," added that "average annual output of grain per farm worker is about 1,000 kilograms in China, whereas in the United States it is over 50,000 kilograms, a disparity of several dozen times."[62]

China's new leaders recognize that it will be difficult, if not impossible, to continue indefinitely trying to achieve large production increases mainly by adding labor and capital. Raising efficiency and labor productivity has been set, therefore, as a top-priority national goal. It is doubtful if the Chinese themselves fully understand the reasons for the stagnation in labor productivity in China over such a long period—which, if it was as bad as Peking says it was, was really extraordinary. They do recognize, however, that basic weaknesses in China's incentive systems and management practices have been major causes and that the remedies must include significant changes in the country's economic *system* as well as in its policies.

In light of the low level of labor productivity in China, the maintenance of "full employment" (or something close to it) has been less impressive than many observers believed. While China was able to avoid most overt unemployment from the 1950s until recently, the economy has been characterized by tremendous underemployment.[63] Because of very inefficient use of labor and widespread labor redundancy, China, despite its huge labor force, has actually encountered labor shortages at times, in both agriculture and industry. The overstaffing in most Chinese economic enterprises has been readily apparent to foreign observers visiting the country; it is now evident, from what Chinese officials themselves are saying, that the situation has been even worse than it appeared on the surface. Many reports now also indicate that overt unemployment is on the rise. The *Ming Pao* report on the speech by Li Hsien-nien cited above reported that Li stated that in mid-1979 China had 20 million people unemployed.[64] The determination to cope with new unemployment problems, as well as to raise the efficiency and productivity of labor, underlies many of the regime's new economic policies.

One reason for low labor productivity was the ineffectiveness, in practice, of the Maoist approach to incentive policy, which viewed any pursuit of personal material gain as corrupting. Until late 1977, there had been no major wage raises in China since the 1950s (although a few people received minor increases, mainly by being promoted to higher grades, in the 1960s). Material incentives were reduced during the Cultural Revolution, and the elimination of bonuses resulted in a lowering of real incomes for many workers (in some cases by perhaps as much as 10 percent).[65] Recent statements by Chinese leaders show that they believe the lack of adequate material incentives has been one of the major causes of China's low labor productivity ever since the 1950s.[66] The Maoist hope that a "new socialist man" could be created obviously has not been realized. Although Chinese culture for centuries has promoted a strong work ethic, and many visitors to China have been impressed by the fact that its workers and peasants seem to work harder than those in many developing nations, the evidence suggests that the work ethic has been seriously weakened during the past two decades in China. In comparison with earlier years, and with other areas in East Asia that are populated by Chinese or strongly influenced by traditional Chinese culture, the efficiency of the labor force in the People's Republic is now low.

Popular dissatisfaction with China's low average standard of living has been rising ever since the 1960s, and this presents major political as well as economic problems for the country's leadership. Since the early 1970s evidence filtering out of the country has indicated that many ordinary Chinese have become increasingly impatient with the lack of improvement in the country's basic living standards.[67] As China's overall economy has developed, expectations—or at least hopes—have risen more rapidly than has the supply of consumer goods or the incomes necessary to purchase them. The need to respond to these rising expectations also underlies many of the regime's new policies.

Low labor productivity has not been the only index of the inefficiencies that have been built into the Chinese economic system in the years since the 1950s. The use of capital, in many different kinds of industry, has also been relatively inefficient, and in some instances capital–output ratios have been high.[68] In operating some of the large industrial enterprises constructed in China during the 1950s with Soviet assistance, for example, the Chinese have not yet fully mastered the production methods necessary to achieve full-capacity, standardized, serial production.[69] Perhaps in part because of the size of such enterprises, there has been relatively little innovative change in production methods since the 1950s—far less, for example, than in some smaller enterprises, especially in Shanghai (Shanghai), which had entrepreneurial experience predating 1949.[70] In many industries, including ones producing consumer as well as producer goods, output often has been below capacity. Even in many small-scale industries the use of capital often has been high.[71] In numerous Chinese plants, varied types and levels of technology—some relatively capital-intensive and others very labor-intensive—have been used in different operations in the production process in a single enterprise. In theory, such a mixture at times may make sense in light of China's factor endowments; because of China's scarcity of capital and abundance of labor, the use of men rather than machines and of unmechanized or semimechanized methods in some parts of the production line (together with highly mechanized or even automated methods at other stages) can sometimes be rational. In practice, however, the mixture has often caused slowdowns and inefficiencies in the total production process, resulting in less than fully effective use of high-cost capital items.[72]

China's new leaders recognize the need and potential for more efficient use of the country's existing capital stock as well as its labor force. They now frankly state that during the next few years, while new, more technologically advanced plants are being built, a large share of the production increases projected in China's development plans must come from more efficient operation of existing enterprises. Party Chairman Hua Kuo-feng (Hua Guofeng) made this clear in early 1978 when he outlined Peking's plans for the period through 1985. "In the next eight years," he said, "and especially in the next three years, our existing enterprises must be the foundation for the growth of production."[73] (Hua claimed that because of the radicals' "interference and sabotage between 1974 and 1976," China "lost about 100 billion yuan in total value of industrial output, 28 million tons of steel, and 40 billion yuan in state revenues."[74])

Although political disruptions have been a major reason for below-capacity production in industrial plants during certain periods, especially during the late 1960s and early 1970s, there have been more fundamental causes, traceable to inefficiencies in planning and management. Planning mistakes by authorities at all levels (compounded at certain times, for example, in 1976, by a virtual breakdown of central planning and a de facto decentralization going far beyond anything China's central planners desired) have resulted in frequent imbalances of a serious sort, which have created crippling shortages and bottlenecks. At times these have forced some enterprises to curtail or even halt operations.[75] Pricing policies have often been unrealistic, diverging greatly from real market values (as the present leadership puts it, prices have ignored the "law of value"),[76] resulting in costly misallocations of resources. Generally, in its planning and management the regime has placed primary emphasis on the need for enterprises to meet physical output targets rather than norms relating to quality, costs, or profits, and this emphasis has frequently resulted in serious waste.[77] Repeated changes in management procedures and relationships within enterprises have created confusion. In the late 1960s and early 1970s the regime gave increased power to political functionaries, or representatives of the masses, or both, and reduced the authority of professional managers and technical experts, which had adverse effects on efficiency and created uncertainties that disrupted operations.[78] Today Peking's planners emphasize the past weaknesses in China's planning and management practices, and they stress the need to make major changes in the way the entire Chinese economic system is organized and functions in order to raise its level of efficiency.

Finally, Peking's leaders now acknowledge, more explicitly than ever in the past, that technologically China lags far behind the developed world and in some respects has fallen further behind during the past two decades, especially since the start of the Cultural Revolution. Hua Kuo-feng, in February 1978, declared, "The gap between our own and the advanced world scientific and technological level which had been narrowing [before the "interference and sabotage" of the Gang of Four] has widened again in recent years."[79] Shortly thereafter, Fang Yi (Fang Yi), the new head of China's scientific establishment, when outlining plans for developing science and technology during the period 1978–85, asserted, "Compared with advanced world levels in science and technology, our country is now lagging 15 to 20 years behind in many branches and more still in some others."[80] In the judgment of qualified foreign observers and analysts, China's technological lag behind advanced world standards may be only five to ten years in some fields, but the gap is thirty to forty years in others.[81]

Since the 1950s China's scientific and technical development (both civilian and military) essentially has relied on the knowledge obtained during the massive transfer of technology to China at that time from the Soviet Union. Although subsequent acquisition of new technology from the major non-Communist industrial nations, especially since the early 1970s, has helped to upgrade China's technological levels in certain fields, the process of catching up with recent worldwide developments has just begun. Despite China's accomplishments in some fields of high technology (including those relating to nuclear weapons and missiles) and its efforts to encourage mass innovation, it is now recognized that the radicals' policies toward education, research, and intellectual development between the mid-1960s and mid-1970s had disastrous effects. China lost a generation of trained scientific and technological manpower, and its research establishment was unable to keep up with the accelerating worldwide pace of technological change. In most fields it has yet to achieve an independent capacity for innovation.[82]

Recognition of basic problems such as these convinced China's post-Mao leadership that to speed up economic growth, major changes in policy and in the structure of the country's economic system were essential. Whether or not they exaggerated the seriousness of some of the problems they inherited is arguable. Certain problems were unavoidable in such a huge developing economy, especially an economy operating under a planned, socialist "command system." Other problems probably should be blamed more on the lack of consensus and on conflict within the leadership than on flawed policies. From the late 1950s on, the periodic economic and social disruptions resulting from political struggles were a primary cause of many of China's economic difficulties. Whether or not the new policies adopted by Peking will really solve these problems, and what new difficulties and dilemmas they will create, remains uncertain. Nevertheless, China's present leaders have shown a greater willingness than at any time during the past three decades to acknowledge, openly and frankly, the weaknesses of China's economy and the shortcomings of past economic policies, to recognize the seriousness of the difficulties they face, and to begin experimenting with remarkable flexibility and pragmatism to find new approaches to unsolved problems. As Teng Hsiao-ping said in a speech to a National Science Conference in March 1978, "Backwardness must be perceived before it can be changed."[83] Peking's post-Mao leaders now recognize China's backwardness and proclaim their determination to change it.

New Economic Goals and Policies

Immediately after Mao's death and the purge of China's top radical leaders, it became clear that an era had ended in China and a new stage in the country's development had begun. The direction in which policy would shift became clear within a few weeks after Mao's passing, and a little more than a year after the succession Peking spelled out in detail an extraordinarily ambitious program of modernization. The "ten year" plan announced by the Chinese in early 1978 outlined one of the most ambitious programs of rapid development ever proposed by a developing nation. Policy changes occurred at a breakneck pace throughout 1978 as the regime tried to start implementing its new programs as rapidly as possible.

The initial production targets set by China's leaders were so high, and the projected pace of change so rapid, that in many respects the new program looked like another Great Leap Forward, based this time, however, on a philosophy fundamentally different from that which motivated the Leap of the 1950s. Most of the priorities and approaches symbolized by Mao, and pushed by China's top radicals during the final years of Mao's life, were modified or reversed.

The Chinese press started to signal this shift immediately after the purge of the radicals. For a period, many old slogans used in past policy debates were reiterated, but they were turned on their heads, and the Gang of Four was accused of the same errors and crimes they had accused China's leading pragmatists of committing.[84] Within three months of Mao's death, a reinterpretation of his legacy had begun. In December 1976 Peking's leaders published for the first time Mao's April 1956 essay "On the Ten Major Relationships," which contained many views quite different from those he advocated in his later years.[85] In April 1977 the leadership released the fifth volume of Mao's Selected Works, covering 1949 through 1957, the period before Mao began pushing the policies emphasizing revolutionary egalitarianism and mass mobilization that had led first to the Great Leap Forward and later to the Cultural Revolution.[86]

At first, it appeared that in many respects China's post-Mao leaders were simply returning to policies similar to those of the 1950s. Some leaders doubtless intended this. However, before long, especially after Teng Hsiao-ping's second political rehabilitation in July 1977, it became evident that the new programs unfolding in China represented a great deal more than simply a return to the past. By late 1977 and early 1978, the policy statements made by top leaders indicated that Peking was moving to adopt a developmental strategy far more flexible than anything the Chinese Communists had attempted.

Officially, Teng Hsiao-ping, after his rehabilitation, was merely a Vice Premier; Hua Kuo-feng occupied the positions of Party Chairman and Premier. From the start, however, it was evident that Teng was the prime mover behind the major policy changes being introduced, and by the latter part of 1978 there could be no doubt that he was the most powerful individual in the leadership. On several occasions during 1978, when both Hua and Teng delivered speeches, there were indications of differences in philosophy and over policy between the two men. Teng called more openly for far-reaching and essentially pragmatic policy changes, while Hua (whose legitimacy as Chairman rested on the claim that Mao had chosen him as his successor) continued to place more emphasis on Maoist concepts of egalitarianism and mass mobilization.[87] Whatever differences existed, however, they were contained during 1978, and a kind of modus vivendi appeared to evolve between them; Teng functioned as the main architect of China's policies even though Hua occupied the top symbolic leadership posts. Their relationship probably continued to involve tensions, but they seemed able to cope with them through compromise (with Teng's views carrying more weight on economic issues but Hua's still having some influence on political and ideological issues).[88]

Despite continuing differences within the leadership, a strong consensus emerged during 1977–78 in support of the general direction of economic policy being urged by Teng, and the content of the regime's new policies began to be revealed in a series of speeches and reports emanating from important Party and government meetings and conferences. The first indications of the forthcoming changes surfaced in late 1976 and early 1977, but statements at that time were still not very specific, and many reflected some "traditional" Maoist values. This was true, for example, of Hua's speech in December 1976 to the Second National Conference on Learning from Tachai in Agriculture, and to a lesser extent of the speeches made by Hua, Vice Premier Yu Chiu-li (Yu Qiuli), head of China's State Planning Commission, and others in May 1977 at a National Conference on Learning from Taching (Daqing) in Industry.[89] Nevertheless, these statements began to provide some details about the policy shift under way.

Then, from mid-1977 on, the nature and scope of the shift were elaborated in much clearer terms. In August, the Party's Eleventh Congress (the first since 1973) officially approved both China's new Party leadership headed by Hua and the new policies symbolized by Teng.[90] Hua's political report to the Congress dealt more with ideological and political issues than with economic policies, however, and he still put more stress on the importance of Mao's legacy than Teng did; nevertheless, Hua's report helped to lay the theoretical basis for increasingly pragmatic and growth-oriented policies. He emphasized the need for faster development of China's "productive forces" and also for "revolution in the realm of the superstructure," including accelerated technological change and major changes in educational policy.[91]

The Party Congress did not produce any detailed outline of the regime's economic plans, but in the months that followed a series of more specific programmatic statements appeared, and the shape of China's new development policies became increasingly clear. In October, at a meeting of the Standing Committee of the Fourth National People's Congress, Vice Premier Yu Chiu-li, speaking on behalf of the State Council, presented a frank and realistic analysis of the country's economic situation and began to define the tasks that lay ahead.[92] In December Vice Premier Fang Yi, slated to become head of the revived State Scientific and Technological Commission, discussed in some detail new policy directions for the fields of science and education.[93]

Finally, in February 1978 Hua Kuo-feng, as Premier, addressed China's National People's Congress (the top "legislative" body in the Peking government), presenting a major "Report on the Work of the Government," which outlined in some detail China's basic economic plans, policies, and targets, not only for its current Five Year Plan period (1976–80) but also for the years through 1985—and even in very general terms for the rest of this century.[94] (By this time China's leaders had merged their plans for 1976–80 and 1981–85 into a single "ten year" plan, even though two years had already passed.) This report was the most important and in many respects the most specific statement on long-term economic goals and policies that any Chinese leader had made in public since the 1950s. It attempted to define a framework for the development of China's economy for many years ahead and a guide for policy during the entire period between 1978 and 2000. Probably Teng, together with the top economic planners and technocrats in Peking, played a larger role in drafting these plans than Hua did (it was frankly acknowledged that the plans were based on initial work done under Chou En-lai's supervision in 1974–75, when Teng served as Chou's main deputy on economic matters),[95] but in delivering the report Hua identified himself with the plan and assumed responsibility for it.

In the months following the National People's Congress, policies in many economic and related fields were further defined, with increasing detail, in a series of important meetings and conferences. In March, Fang Yi submitted a draft "Outline National Plan for the Development of Science and Technology" to a large National Science Conference,[96] and in April Teng and others spelled out new educational policies at a National Conference on Educational Work.[97] There were many other national conferences of this sort, including a National Finance and Trade Conference in June and July;[98] in July the Central Committee announced a new (draft) "Thirty-Point Decision on Industry" (which was not, however, immediately published).[99] Throughout this period, the Chinese press was full of articles explaining the policy changes.

Gradually, the official statements and supporting press articles made it clear that the changes proposed would not only alter past policies in almost every important field relating to economic development, but would also, if fully implemented, involve significant changes in the structure of the economy. One of the most important early statements indicating the new leadership's willingness to modify—or at least to experiment extensively with—their basic economic system was an article by Hu Chiao-mu, the head of the newly established Chinese Academy of Social Sciences. Reportedly first delivered as a speech to the State Council in July 1978, then published in October, this important statement, entitled "Act in Accordance with Economic Laws, Step up the Four Modernizations," called for extensive systemic changes in the economy designed to expand its productive capacity and raise its level of efficiency and productivity.[100] What Hu proposed, essentially, was that China should move in the direction of some kind of "market socialism"—although he did not use that term in his article—drawing upon the experience of many other nations and adapting it to China's situation.

The shift in China's basic economic policies also began to be apparent during 1978 in the actions and behavior of Chinese government bodies and officials. Foreign governments and businessmen dealing with the Chinese saw evidence of new flexibility in China's foreign economic transactions.[101] Although the changes occurring within the country's internal economy were less visible, nevertheless foreign visitors also saw that trends toward increasing pragmatism were beginning to reshape Peking's approach to dealing with most economic problems at home as well as abroad. The internal and external policy changes were intimately linked; consequently, although the primary purpose of this study is to analyze how China's relationships with the world economy are changing, it is necessary first to examine and evaluate the nature and scope of China's overall economic plans and the policy changes that are now occurring within China.

Initial Targets for 1978–85

When Hua Kuo-feng first announced China's basic quantitative production targets for 1985, some did not seem unreasonable, but many were so high that they were almost certainly unattainable. It appeared that the leadership, in its rush to "get the economy moving," let optimism run roughshod over realism. (Less than a year later, however, they faced realities and undertook a major "readjustment," which will be discussed below.)[102]

The initial "ten year" plan outlined by Hua called for total "capital construction" investments (under the state budget) during the eight years 1978–85 "equivalent to the total for the past twenty-eight years."[103] In regard to specific sectors, the plan called for an average rate of increase in the value of total agricultural output of 4 to 5 percent a year and an average annual rate of increase in industrial output of "over" 10 percent.[104] The average rate of increase in total GNP implied by these figures was probably between 8 and 9 percent a year.[105] For reasons that will be discussed later, there was virtually no possibility that China could achieve all of the targets set for the period 1978–85. In particular, the projected growth rate in agriculture appeared too optimistic; if this was the case, obviously there was little prospect of achieving the overall increase in GNP projected in the plan. Although many of the specific measures proposed in the plan made good sense, the timetables for achieving some of them appeared unrealistic.

Hua's speech specified various measures to achieve rapid modernization of agriculture, mainly through raising per acre yields but also by trying to expand acreage (it was originally indicated by more than 13 million hectares).[106] Large-scale projects were called for to harness major rivers; one ambitious project proposed to divert Yangtze (Yangzi) River water to areas north of the Yellow River. The regime asserted that its hope was that by 1980 all grain-deficient areas in China would become self-sufficient and that by 1985 there would be one mou (one-sixth of an acre) of "guaranteed stable high yields" land for each member of the Chinese rural population.[107] The grain output target set for 1985 was 400 million tons, which would require an increase of 41 percent over 1977, implying an average annual rate of increase of 4.4 percent during the eight years from 1977 through 1985.[108] The plan also called for an increase in the amount of "marketable grain" in China by two- to threefold in eight years, much if not most of which was slated to come from twelve "large commodity grain bases" and expanded state farms.[109] The plan reemphasized the need for land improvement, better water control, increased use of chemical fertilizers and pesticides, the introduction of new seeds, and improved methods of cultivation. It also placed high priority on accelerated agricultural mechanization and electrification; the target was to achieve 85 percent mechanization of "all major processes of farmwork" by 1985.[110] According to the plan, China's agriculture should move toward greater specialization, and it was proposed that a "number of bases" be developed for specialized production of cash crops such as cotton, edible oils, and sugar.[111]

Even though the plan gave high priority to agricultural development, the largest share of state investment during 1978–85 seemed slated for the industrial sector to expand basic industries and develop the country's transportation infrastructure. Hua asserted that in eight years the regime planned to build 120 "large-scale projects," some requiring construction of new plants, mines, or transport facilities, and others involving expansion of existing ones; primary emphasis would be on major heavy industries—metallurgy (ferrous and nonferrous), fuels, electric power, other raw and semimanufactured materials, and transportation equipment and facilities—all of which have created bottlenecks in China's development.[112] Top priority was given to steel, which Chinese planners over the years have usually labeled the "key link" in industry, just as they have generally called grain the key link in agriculture. The specific projects called for included construction of ten large iron and steel complexes (at least three of which would be new, while the rest would probably involve expansion of existing facilities). The target for steel production in 1985 was set at 60 million tons, more than double the 1977 output of less than 24 million tons.

Apart from steel plants, Hua indicated that of the 120 large-scale projects 9 would involve construction of nonferrous metal complexes (probably including both aluminum and copper plants), 48 would relate to fuels and power (including eight major coal mines, ten oil and gas fields, and thirty power stations), and 11 would be in the field of transportation (including six new "trunk" railways and five "key" harbors). The remaining forty-odd unspecified major projects in the plan probably included plants in the fields of machine building, chemicals, petrochemicals, electronics, computers, and communication equipment.[113] Hua asserted that with completion of all of these projects, the country would have "14 fairly strong and fairly rationally located industrial bases," under the supervision of "6 major regions," integrated into a "comprehensive" national "system."[114]

Hua also called for "vigorous development" of light industries producing textiles, sugar, paper, and other consumer products. This clearly was an important part of the overall plan, necessary to fulfill the promises made to try to raise living standards for both workers and peasants.[115] Peking's planners recognized that light industrial plants could be constructed fairly cheaply and rapidly and that profits from their output would be a major source of new investment funds.[116] Hua declared that all provinces in China should "achieve self-sufficiency in ordinary light industrial products as early as possible."[117] Although neither he nor other leaders discussed at that time specific targets for light industry, Hua's report made it clear that the regime intended to accelerate the rate of development of light industry substantially. (Some foreign analysts inferred from Chinese statements that the rate of increase in the output of light industry would be higher than that of heavy industry, but it is debatable whether this rate was built into the original plan.[118] However, in his 1979 report calling for major modifications of China's development program, Hua asked specifically for a faster rate of growth in light industry than in heavy industry, and China achieved this.[119]) The Chinese said little in 1978, however, about plans to increase investment in light industry, although they did indicate that they hoped to speed up development of petrochemical industries and expand other oil-based industries such as synthetic fibers and plastics.[120] Some of their statements suggested that investments in light industry would be quite limited, at least compared with those made in large heavy industries. Initially, they stressed that production increases should come mainly from more efficient use of existing plants.

Finally, the plan called for a dramatic lowering of China's population growth rate. In his report Hua declared that the regime's goal was to lower the annual rate of population growth in China to less than 1 percent within three years.[121]

Evaluation of Initial Targets

Once the ten-year plan was unveiled, the achievement of the "four modernizations" became China's highest priority domestic goal. With an air of euphoria and seemingly unlimited confidence, the regime's propaganda apparatus went into high gear to explain the new program to the Chinese people and to promote its rapid implementation.[122]

Almost as soon as the program started, however, some leaders within China and many analysts abroad questioned the feasibility of achieving certain of the announced objectives. While Peking's new pragmatism and flexibility augured well for China's future development, its inclination to try to go "too far too fast" did not. It was evident that China's leaders had still not carefully sorted out their priorities. In effect, they set maximal goals in virtually every field without adequate analysis of the resources and skills necessary to achieve them on anything like the schedule they had set for themselves. They had not, in sum, made many of the hard choices that ultimately they would have to face.

Realistic assessments of rates of increase in investment, production, and overall growth that are plausible are not easy to make. A variety of factors will influence the country's actual economic performance during the next few years; these variables are so numerous, and the problems so complex, that any predictions could be far off the mark. Nevertheless, it is possible to form some general judgment about what is plausible—or implausible—by examining China's past economic performance and by identifying some of the most important stimuli and constraints that will influence economic performance in the period immediately ahead. If one compared the targets initially set in early 1978 with China's actual performance during the past twenty to thirty years, certain new targets did not seem totally unreasonable, but some clearly were overambitious.

The implied investment target for 1978–85 was extremely ambitious, yet it was not totally implausible, based on certain assumptions about future growth rates.[123] If, for example, China's GNP were to grow at an average annual rate of 8 percent from 1977 through 1985 (slightly less than the planned rate of growth implied by the sectoral output growth targets announced by Hua), its total GNP would rise from $370 billion in 1977 to $689 billion in 1985 (in 1977 dollars; it obviously would be considerably higher in 1985 dollars), and its cumulative GNP during all eight years would amount to about $4.266 trillion. If China were able to maintain an investment rate of 25 percent—a rate well below that of the recent past—its annual investment would rise from $93 billion in 1977 to $173 billion in 1985, and its total investment during the eight years would total $1.069 trillion (in 1977 dollars). This doubtless would be close to the probable total investment made during the previous twenty-nine years. The cumulative total of China's GNP during 1949–77 conceivably may have been around $5.2 trillion (in 1977 dollars), and, if one were to assume that at least 20 percent of gross output during the entire period went into investment—which probably is too low—total investment during 1949–77 might have been just over $1 trillion.[124] (In early 1980 Teng stated that China's "capital construction" had totaled 600 billion yuan.[125])

If one were to assume that during 1978–85 China's economy grows at an average rate of 7 percent a year, its GNP would rise (in constant 1977 dollars) from $370 billion in 1977 to $654 billion in 1985, and cumulative GNP over the period would total $4.176 trillion. At a 25 percent rate of investment, annual investment would rise from $93 billion to $159 billion, and the cumulative total would be $1.009 trillion. If one assumes that China's average rate of growth is "only" 6 percent, its GNP would rise from $370 billion in 1977 to $612 billion in 1985, and the cumulative total for the eight-year period would be $3.882 trillion. At a 25 percent rate, investment would be $93 billion in 1977 and $148 billion in 1985, and the cumulative total would amount to $971 billion.

All of the above calculations are crude. Nevertheless, this kind of rough calculation indicates that the regime's stated objective of investing as much during the 1978–85 period as it did during the entire previous twenty-nine years was not as implausible as it might have appeared at first glance. A specific $600 billion figure for probable total investment during 1978–85 reportedly was mentioned by one high-ranking Chinese official in 1978.[126] Even though the report did not specify what "investment" meant, that figure, although unquestionably very ambitious, could not be said to be out of the realm of the plausible, although for several reasons that will be discussed later it may prove to be too optimistic, and by early 1979 Chinese officials themselves were describing it as being somewhat too high.[127] The above calculations show, however, that even if China's GNP grows at "only" 6 percent a year, and if the investment rate averages "only" 25 percent a year, China in theory might be able during 1978–85 to invest a total of around $800 billion (assuming the U.S. government estimate of $370 billion for China's GNP in 1977 is not wildly off the mark).

It is possible that the average rate of growth of China's GNP will be below 6 percent during 1978–85—as some analysts argue that it probably will—or that the rate of investment might drop more than is now expected, in part because of increasing pressures for greater consumption. Nevertheless, on balance, the regime's initial investment target, although vague, was not totally beyond the bounds of plausibility.

The same cannot be said, however, about the plan's (implied) projection of an average annual rate of GNP growth of 8 to 9 percent during 1978–85. China seems unlikely to achieve the planned growth rate for agriculture set by Hua, and while the projected rate of increase in industrial output, though very ambitious, is more reasonable, it too could prove to be too high.

The target that Hua set for industrial growth—more than 10 percent a year—is only slightly above the average annual rate of 9.1 percent achieved during 1957–77. In light of the tremendous effort that the regime now plans to make to increase output, the prospect for sizable investments in at least some industries, and the possible impact of the regime's new policies aimed at increasing economic efficiency, a modest rise in the rate of industrial growth is possible if its new policies work.

Not long ago, some recent studies by foreign analysts predicted, however, that the rate of growth in China's industrial output might decline slightly in the period ahead. One analyst, for example, forecast that the average rate during 1975–90 might be 7 percent.[128] He argued that several trends would tend to lower the rate: a reduced overall rate of national investment (due to an increase in consumption), a smaller share of total investment allocated to industry (due to the increased need for investment in agriculture and other sectors), and a lower rate of increase in output from any given amount of investment (due to a shift toward more capital-intensive industries with higher capital–output ratios). Another analyst predicted that because of the economic setbacks and inefficiencies of recent years, Chinese industrial output might grow rapidly for a short period, as China makes "catch-up" gains, but that thereafter it probably would not be able to sustain a rate of growth as high as 9 percent.[129] He gave a number of reasons for this judgment: China's lack of foreign exchange to pay for needed plant imports; its lack of the skills needed to coordinate its economic plans and absorb new plants and technology rapidly and efficiently; its increasing need to devote industrial output to agriculture and other sectors; its shortage of skilled personnel; and, most important, "the inflexibility and the lack of dynamism of a socialist command society in dealing with the complexities of modern technocratic society."

The problems mentioned by these analysts highlight some of the difficulties China will certainly face in trying to raise its rate of industrial growth. However, both analysts made their estimates before the announcement of some of the most important recent policy changes designed to stimulate greater efficiency throughout the Chinese economy. While it is too early to judge what effects the new policies will have—and it is possible that China's target for industrial growth may prove to be too optimistic—if Peking implements its new policies effectively it could come close to achieving the target.

The most serious questions raised from the start about the broad targets contained in Hua's report concerned agriculture. In calling for an average annual rate of agricultural growth of 4 to 5 percent (4.3 percent for grain specifically) during 1978–85, China's leaders seemed unrealistically optimistic.[130] They were right in recognizing the critical importance of accelerating agricultural growth, but neither China's past performance nor its immediate future agricultural prospects would appear to justify such an ambitious target. Since China's agricultural problems and prospects will be discussed in detail in part III, suffice it to say here that a rate of 4 to 5 percent would require a huge jump not only over the 2 percent rate achieved during the quarter century 1952–77 but also over the 3 percent rate attained in the period from the mid-1960s through the mid-1970s. As the later discussion will show, even if effective policies are pursued, raising the rate of agricultural growth in China may become harder rather than easier in the period ahead, and instead of being between 4 and 5 percent, the rate could well be closer to 2 or 3 (or, at most, 3-plus) percent during 1978–85.

If these judgments are correct, the overall rate of GNP growth certainly will be lower than that implied in Hua's report. Instead of being between 8 and 9 percent, it seems more likely to be between 6 and 7 percent, assuming, optimistically, that industry grows at a rate of about 9 percent and agriculture at a rate of 2 to 3 percent or slightly higher.[131]

Achieving even these rates would constitute a fairly impressive accomplishment and will not occur automatically. Some analysts have predicted that instead of rising above past long-term rates (under 6 percent during the quarter century 1952–77 and about 5.5 percent during the two decades 1957–77), the rate of growth in China's GNP might drop in the period ahead to around 5 percent. (One analyst forecast a rate of 5 percent during 1975–90;[132] another estimated that in the 1980s it would "drift downward to below 5.5 percent."[133]) Raising the average rate to 6–7 percent will require a major effort, therefore. Whether or not the regime can succeed in doing so will depend not only on its investment policies but also on how successful China's leaders are in implementing their new policies designed to raise efficiency throughout their economy.

Finally, the goal of reducing China's rate of population growth to less than 1 percent in three years (that is, by 1981) also sounded extremely optimistic, despite official claims that by 1979 it had dropped to under about 1.2 percent.[134] Some Western analysts make more pessimistic projections, for various reasons (which will be discussed further in part III). If China's economic plans are based on assumptions about demographic trends that are too optimistic, unanticipated population growth will obviously require significant adjustments in many other aspects of the plan, which could contribute to a lower overall growth rate.

Far-reaching Economic Policy Changes

While crude macroeconomic calculations such as those above suggest that some of the growth targets the Chinese initially set for themselves were too optimistic, Peking's present emphasis on accelerated growth, and its sizable long-term investment plans, should result in a significant expansion of China's productive capacities *if* its new policies can be effectively implemented. However, the "if" is crucial; China's performance will depend fundamentally on the ability of its leaders to manage their economy much more effectively than in the past.

Peking's leaders now give clear evidence that they are prepared to alter the country's policies in very significant ways to try to make their economic system more efficient and productive, and the new policies adopted or proposed since 1977 are more important in many respects than the specific targets announced.[135]

One of the most urgent objectives of Peking's post-Mao leaders has been to restore order and discipline in the economy—and in the polity and society as a whole. They recognize that they must prevent any recurrence of the factional infighting, political conflict, and social instability that crippled China's economy during Mao's final days if their modernization plans are to succeed. Soon after Mao's death they adopted "stability and unity" as one of their key slogans[136] and immediately placed prime stress on the need to restore discipline and stimulate hard work at the working level of the economy, in industrial enterprises and communes. Numerous steps were also taken to reemphasize the importance of "rules and regulations," which the radicals—in the name of Mao and under the slogan "it is right to rebel"—had strongly attacked.

After a decade of social disorder, it was not easy to restore order at a grassroots level, and during 1977–78 widespread purges and demotions of persons associated with the Gang of Four during the Cultural Revolution created some new tensions. Nevertheless, the regime gradually succeeded in achieving a higher degree of social order than China had enjoyed for many years.[137]

From the start, the new leadership relied on the carrot (increased incentives) as well as the stick (purges and a clampdown on radical factionalism) in restoring discipline among China's workforce. Proclaiming a new incentive policy, the leadership openly rejected the extreme egalitarianism and austerity previously demanded by China's leadership and frankly appealed to popular desires for personal material gain and improved living standards.[138] The issue of "material incentives" had been one of the most hotly debated questions in the long conflict between the radicals and pragmatists in the years preceding Mao's death. To the radicals, restricting what they called "bourgeois rights" was essential if China was to make progress toward achieving the ultimate goal of an egalitarian communist society.[139] In practice, although they bitterly attacked every proposal for increasing material incentives and opposed bonuses, piece-rate wage payments, and promotions, they were not able to alter the basic incentive system as much as they would have liked. Even in the mid-1970s, when "bourgeois rights" were under heavy attack, workers in Chinese industrial enterprises were still paid according to the eight-grade wage system introduced in the 1950s, and peasants' income in most of China was still based on a work point system that had changed relatively little since the reorganization of the communes in the early 1960s. Nevertheless, the radicals had been able to hold in check the mounting pressures for increased material incentives.

In contrast, China's new leaders, convinced that the low productivity of labor and the decline of the work ethic were due in large part to the lack of material incentives, proclaimed that all labor must be paid according to "the socialist principle of 'to each according to his work.' " While continuing to pay most workers on a time basis (according to the long-established eight-grade wage system), they reintroduced some piecework pay to supplement the time-rate system and restored the practice of paying bonuses for good performance.[140] In the fall of 1977 they raised the wages of more than half of China's urban working force by about 10 percent (10 to 15 percent for the lowest paid workers, who were the main beneficiaries) and promised to try to raise wages periodically in the future, within the limits of China's capabilities.[141]

They also promised to increase the availability of consumer goods, raise living standards gradually, and give the greatest rewards to the most productive workers.[142] Initially, the steps taken were not very far-reaching. The wage raises were relatively small. (Moreover, the initial raises did not significantly increase differentials; in some cases they actually narrowed the gap between high and low wage earners, since a large share of the benefits went to China's lowest paid workers.) However, though the size of the initial wage increases was not spectacular, even small raises were psychologically important in a country where wages had been virtually frozen for almost two decades. The leadership assured the population, moreover, that the steps taken were just the beginning. Many Chinese statements emphasized that Peking planned to raise wages further—and suggested that in the future wage differentials would grow. Leaders declared that everyone must "oppose egalitarianism," a slogan that was a far cry from the radicals' assertion that China must "restrict bourgeois rights." To support the new policy they quoted statements by Mao that under socialism "there can be no absolute equality," and "absolute equality is wrong."[143]

It is not likely, however, that China now will—or can—totally abandon egalitarian ideals, which were at the heart of the Maoist vision. China's new leaders will probably continue trying to maintain a minimal floor under consumption, to guarantee basic subsistence to all, and to oppose excessive conspicuous consumption. Nevertheless, they clearly are determined to use material incentives as a major means to try to spur harder work and increased productivity, and they appear quite willing to tolerate the almost inevitable widening of income differentials that this eventually will produce.

Increased use of material incentives should have favorable effects on labor productivity, but exactly how much they will help to raise productivity remains to be seen. The policy involves some risks and dangers. Although extreme Maoist egalitarian policies tended to weaken labor enthusiasm, they also encouraged a kind of Puritan austerity that supported the regime's policy of maximizing investment and restricting consumption. It is difficult at present to judge how much the regime can afford to expend in implementing its new incentives policy. In practice, there probably will be severe limits on the amount of resources the regime can allocate to increase workers' wages and peasants' incomes.

Yet the new policy has raised hopes, released long-repressed pressures for improved living standards, and stimulated increasing consumer demand. For almost thirty years China's leaders strongly discouraged the "revolution of rising expectation";[144] now they seem to be deliberately encouraging it. It is very likely, however, that in China, as in many other developing countries, rising expectations will outpace the regime's capacity to meet growing consumer demands. If the output of consumer goods lags behind rises in consumer income, inflationary pressures will increase and black markets will grow. China's leaders are aware of this danger and appear determined to increase consumer goods production fast enough to balance rising incomes and demand, but this may be difficult to do. It is almost certain, therefore, that once again—really for the first time since the 1950s—the problem of inflationary pressures will be added to Peking's list of significant economic problems.[145] Official Chinese figures issued in early 1980 revealed that in 1979 there had been an overall increase nationally of 5.8 percent in retail prices.[146] Many sensible steps to solve some of China's fundamental problems—including the effort to provide more adequate incentives and stimulate labor productivity—will create new problems.

Achieving an equitable balance between urban and rural consumers in China has long been difficult and may now become increasingly complex. The Chinese are trying to use increased material incentives to motivate both farmers and urban workers. They have declared that the principle of "to each according to his work" must be fully implemented in communes as well as factories, and they stress the need to also base rewards for peasants essentially on labor productivity (rather than on ideological and political criteria).[147] Great emphasis has been placed on the need to give more authority to small production teams, which ultimately distribute income among peasants, as well as to encourage "private" plots, rural "free markets," and "sideline" occupations through which enterprising peasants can earn extra income.[148] There has even been some discussion—as there was in the early 1960s—of increasing the role of individual peasant households in the rural system (which, if done, would be a step away from collectivization).[149]

China's new leaders have promised to raise rural incomes and standards of living and to continue trying to narrow the urban-rural gap. The most practical way to do this is by raising the prices of agricultural products and lowering the prices of industrial products, thereby narrowing the so-called scissors price differential. During 1949-78 the differential was narrowed significantly when the purchase prices for agricultural products doubled while the retail prices of industrial products rose only 28 percent. However, since 1978 they have promised to make greater adjustments of prices to narrow the differential further.[150] In late 1978 the Central Committee announced plans for a 20 percent increase in the purchase prices for agricultural products.[151] By the end of 1979 this had been carried out, and purchase prices of many other products had also been substantially raised.[152]

What the net effect of raising both urban wages and agricultural prices will be over time is difficult to judge, however. The government continues to subsidize certain rationed food necessities in the cities to try to keep the prices paid by urban workers for essentials relatively low, but in 1979 many other prices rose, and it is clear that raising the prices paid for agricultural commodities, like increasing urban wages, will contribute to growing inflationary pressures. (Conceivably, higher urban wages and increased agricultural prices could cancel out many of the benefits for workers or peasants or both.) The effort to raise both urban and rural living standards, maintain a reasonable balance between workers' and peasants' interests, narrow the urban-rural gap, increase supplies of consumer goods fast enough to meet rising incomes and expectations, and at the same time contain inflationary pressures will not be easy. China's present leaders believe that the risks inherent in their incentives policies are worth taking, however, in order to raise productivity and infuse a new element of dynamism into the Chinese economy.

The new incentives policy has been only one part of a wide-ranging "series of economic reorganizations and reforms"[153] initiated or proposed since 1977–78 and aimed at raising productivity and efficiency through major improvements in national planning, economic organization, enterprise and commune management, and the development of the country's human resources. Some of the most radical proposals are still being debated in Peking. The implementation of others is proceeding cautiously and experimentally. If all the changes proposed were to be fully and effectively implemented, they would significantly change the way the Chinese economy functions and over time could have important social and political effects.

To end the confusion in the country's economy, steps were taken to strengthen national planning and improve overall management of the economy. Greater real authority was given to many national planners and certain national institutions in ways that increased centralized control in important respects.[154] Many older leaders who had played key roles in economic planning and management in earlier years, such as Chen Yun and Li Hsien-nien, assumed influential positions in the top leadership, and an increasing number of technocratic administrators and scientific planners—men such as Yao Yi-lin (Yao Yilin), Yu Chiu-li, Po Yi-po (Bo Yibo), Chang Ching-fu (Zhang Jingfu), Li Chiang (Li Qiang), Ku Mu (Gu Mu), Kang Shih-en (Kang Shien), Wang Jenchung (Wang Renzhong), and Fang Yi—acquired a greater voice in decision making.[155] The top-level bodies in the government dealing with economic matters were reorganized and strengthened; several that had existed earlier but had gone out of existence—including the State Scientific and Technological Commission—were re-created.[156] The importance of economic ministries was again stressed, and their authority was increased in certain respects. The creation (or restoration) of six major regions to supervise economic affairs in the provinces was proposed; this could help to improve economic administration. Although it is not yet clear exactly what functions the regions will have, they should strengthen central planning.[157] (However, they might also create, as similar regional organizations have in the past, a potential danger of localism.)

Peking's public release of data on its economic plans and statistics on performance seemed to show the growth of a broader consensus on and greater confidence in economic policy, at least within the leadership, than had existed for many years. It also indicated an improved capacity to plan at the national level. Competent economists, possessing skills in extremely short supply in China, were again in good standing;

some, such as Sun Yeh-fang (Sun Yefang), who had been denounced for their "revisionism" and "Libermanism" in the 1960s were rehabilitated, and the new Chinese Academy of Social Sciences, created in 1978, from the start gave high priority to economic training and research.[158] China's top planners even asked a few foreigners—including Saburo Okita, one of Japan's top economic planners—to visit China and serve as consultants, something that would have been unthinkable in the 1960s.[159]

However, while strengthening Peking's overall control over national economic planning and management in important respects, China's leaders nevertheless appeared prepared to move further toward decentralization than ever before, mainly by increasing the decision-making authority granted to basic productive units—industrial enterprises and rural communes and their subunits—and by allowing market forces to influence economic decisions much more than in the past.

Balancing the interests of central and local authorities is a fundamental, continuing, and in some respects insoluble problem in a country as large as China, and over the years numerous shifts have occurred between centralization and decentralization. Ever since the late 1950s, however, when there was a major shift toward decentralization, virtually all Chinese leaders have stressed the need to allow some scope for "local initiative" under overall central planning.[160] The question has been, how much? Since 1978 the trend has been toward granting more authority to local units in new ways.

Peking's leaders have asserted that to achieve "proportionate development in a planned way," it is necessary "to transform the semi-planned status to a fully planned status" with "comprehensive balancing" that "does not leave any loophole,"[161] stressing that, although Peking should give "full play to local initiative," nevertheless "local initiative must yield to the State's overall interests." However, at the same time they have emphasized that the main responsibility of central planners is to determine broad policy, decide on overall allocations of resources, and "coordinate" the economy, *not* to make "administrative decisions" concerning the details of day-to-day operations.

One of the most dramatically new and potentially significant features of China's new economic approach since 1977–78 has been the stress placed on the need to take market forces more fully into account than before and to give greater authority to the managers of enterprises, rather than relying on "administrative" decision making by higher-level government bureaucrats.[162] "While State power can help the economy develop faster," it is now acknowledged, "it can also work the other way, and political power may cause great damage to economic development." Today, a leading China Party intellectual is able to admit with remarkable candor that "inappropriate centralization or decentralization often results in damaging the development of economic construction."[163]

All economic policies and decisions, Hu Chiao-mu declared in 1978, must be based on "objective economic laws," especially "the law of value"; in short, prices must be based on realistic calculations of costs.[164] He proposed general implementation of a "contract system" under which all or most economic transactions would be based on specific contracts signed between enterprises (or communes), between the state and enterprises or collectives, and even between different levels of state authorities.[165] Many official statements have called for substantially increased scope for decision making at the enterprise level. "Economic administration cannot primarily depend on purely administrative methods," Hu stated; "the maximum volume of economic work should be switched from the governmental administrative scope to that of enterprise management. . . . The enterprises themselves should also reduce the scope of management by pure administrative measures to the minimum and expand the scope of management by relying on economic measures," and they must "adapt to the structure of product supply and marketing and to the objective needs of other economic activities."[166]

While increasing incentives for both workers and peasants, and stimulating local initiative by giving greater authority to local enterprises, Peking also has attempted to regularize economic activity by strengthening nationwide "rules and regulations." In 1978, as noted earlier, the regime issued its so-called Thirty-Point Regulations for Industry (its complete title was a "Resolution [Draft] on Some Problems of Accelerating Industrial Development"), an elaboration of the so-called Twenty Points drafted in 1975 that had been based on the regime's so-called Seventy Points formulated in 1961.[167] Although the targets and norms that all Chinese enterprises must try to fulfill (the "five fixes" and "eight economic and technical norms") have not basically changed, the relative importance of various norms definitely has.[168] Previously, enterprises were judged primarily on the basis of whether or not they fulfilled their gross, quantitative output targets. Since 1977–78 increasing stress has been placed upon costs, quality, and profits.[169] The new emphasis on profits is particularly significant. The regime also insists that enterprises improve their accounting, raise the quality of their products, and avoid waste in manpower, materials, and financial resources. Chinese planners have promised that enterprises, as well as individuals, will be rewarded for good performance and penalized for shortcomings and mistakes,[170] and they have attempted to introduce a higher degree of accountability into the economy as a whole in ways that will affect both managers and workers. Successful enterprises will be allowed to keep a part of their profits, either to expand production or to improve workers' welfare.[171] With a shift of greater authority to the enterprises, efforts have been made to reduce the staffs of bureaucratic organizations and cut red tape.

There has been a major shift in the regime's position on the importance, and roles, of professional managers, technicians, and "experts" in enterprise management. The Revolutionary Committees established in enterprises during the 1960s were soon abolished, and since 1978 the regime has stressed that professional managers, using the expertise of all their technical specialists, should make the key decisions relating to production. While managers still are to be subject to overall direction by local Party committees, the leadership urges that the functions of professionals and Party apparatus be differentiated more clearly. Not only has the authority of the former in making production decisions been increased; some official statements have emphasized that the primary responsibilities of Party organization men should be essentially ideological and political, and the Party has urged its organization men to learn more about economic issues and managerial problems. The Party has asserted that one of its major responsibilities is to give adequate support to professional managers and technical personnel so that the latter can do their jobs more effectively.[172]

At national and regional levels, the Chinese have begun organizing a number of large "specialized companies," similar to the thirteen so-called trusts set up in the 1960s, especially during 1964–65, by Liu Shao-chi and Teng Hsiao-ping. (They lasted only briefly and were a target of attack by radicals for many years thereafter.)[173] These "corporate-type" bodies are designed to achieve a new level of efficiency and productivity in key fields. It is claimed that they will be able to operate more flexibly, base their decisions mainly on economic criteria, and improve coordination within the broad fields in which they operate. It is hoped that substantial benefits will flow from new economies of scale and from a combination of increased specialization and improved coordination of related activities. It is intended that these specialized companies will be freer from local political interference than most enterprises in the past and will have greater operational autonomy, but that they will operate under policy supervision exercised by national ministries and overall planning bodies. Whether in practice these actions will tend more to decentralize decision making or to increase central control of basic policy remains to be seen. There is little doubt, however, that while corporations could develop great power, they probably will contribute to increased efficiency and better coordination in many fields.

Initial moves toward establishing large-scale specialized companies occurred in 1977–78 in the petroleum and agricultural machinery industries. By the end of 1978 corporations were also established or planned for coal, steel, textile fibers, railways, and other fields.[174] In certain respects the new "specialized companies" appear to have been modeled on large-scale corporations in the West. "The experience of developed capitalist countries," the head of China's Academy of Social Sciences has stated, "tells us that to organize specialization and cooperation according to different trades and localities and organize scattered enterprises into specialized companies (including national companies, regional companies, incorporation of enterprises of the same trade, and incorporation of enterprises of related trades) is not only an inevitable trend in modern industrial development but also an objective demand in developing industry at high speed with high standards."[175]

The establishment of these specialized companies has reflected a new emphasis on the need for greater specialization throughout the economy in order to raise technical levels and operational efficiency. Decrying the past tendency in China to establish "make-everything-you-need enterprises," the regime has called for a rational division of labor between enterprises and localities.[176] In both industry and agriculture, the regime states that what is now needed is a new combination of "specialization and coordination."

China's new policies also have placed tremendous stress on the necessity to develop new forms of "scientific management."[177] The Chinese today are frankly eclectic, and they are actively borrowing from the experience of a wide variety of countries. Although they have shown special interest in the Yugoslavian and other East European countries' experiences, they also have stated explicitly that they intend to learn all they can from scientific management in the non-Communist industrial nations. Endorsing Lenin's statement that Communists must "learn from the bourgeoisie," the Chinese now maintain that "capitalist countries' economic management methods have merits worthy of our learning." They are interested not only in obtaining advanced technology from Japan, Europe, and the United States but also in learning from and adapting for use in China production and management systems developed in these countries.[178]

The new emphasis on improved management has also been applied to the communes, especially their lowest subunits. Policy statements have stressed the desirability of giving production teams more autonomy and authority so that they can "run their own affairs"—and run them "democratically." They also have advocated increased specialization in agriculture and wider use of the "contract system," even in transactions between communes and their subordinate units and between commune units and their members.

Two other important trends have been the regime's emphasis on the need to improve financial control over, and direction of, the economy and its call for more comprehensive and effective economic laws and judicial organs to handle economic transactions and disputes. "Many economic management functions of the state can be performed by the bank [that is, the People's Bank of China] more flexibly and efficiently than [by] administrative organs," Hu asserted in 1978.[179] From now on, the state banking system is expected both to "promote and supervise" the activities of economic enterprises through their credit and loan policies and to monitor their performance, instead of simply doling out wage and capital construction funds as requested.

Chinese leaders have acknowledged, and clearly recognize, that these changes will create new problems. As Hu put it, "while implementing the contract system, developing specialized companies, strengthening the bank's role, and promoting other measures ... we expect various complicated disputes to arise"; therefore the regime must "strengthen economic legislation and economic judicial work."[180] The new policies will require much greater attention to laws and legal procedures than in the past, and since 1977–78 the Chinese have been formulating (and codifying) many new laws.[181] (A similar trend started in the mid-1950s but was aborted when Mao reemphasized the need for radical revolutionary change.)

The many changes proposed and implemented experimentally since

1978 represent a remarkable attempt to modify the Chinese economic *system*. China's economy doubtless will remain a socialist, state-dominated system, and in many respects it will still be a "command" economy. However, to the extent that the new policies are effectively implemented, they should increase the link between economic decision making and market forces; result in more realistic pricing; create new incentives for managers, workers, and peasants; and introduce new elements of economic competition into the system. They also should broaden financial instead of bureaucratic controls; relate economic transactions to legally based contracts; increase the importance of cost accounting, quality control, and profit making; generally strengthen the role of law in economic affairs; promote increased specialization; and encourage more "scientific" management. All of this clearly would change the system significantly—in the direction of "market socialism." Under no foreseeable conditions will the economic system be totally changed; Teng and his colleagues are not "restoring capitalism," as the radicals charged. If China does move gradually toward "market socialism," the end result will be distinctively Chinese, not a copy of the system in Yugoslavia or elsewhere. Nevertheless, the changes could be profound.

If the new policies succeed, they should, as Peking's leaders hope, contribute to greater efficiency and increased productivity. However, the transition from old to new methods of operation could create considerable confusion—and have some disruptive effects—in the short run. China's leaders doubtless have taken this as well as other risks into account, but most seem convinced that the potential economic gains outweigh the possible risks.

Education, Science, and Technology

Two other areas, closely related to economic development, in which major policy changes have occurred since 1977–78 are those relating to education and to science and technology. China has suffered an acute shortage of skilled manpower in many fields, in part because training and research in many scientific and technological fields lagged so badly in the late 1960s and early 1970s. The policy shifts in these areas have been extremely important, therefore. The context for these changes has been a basic shift in the regime's policy toward intellectuals and a dramatic swing of the pendulum in the long Chinese debate over the importance of "redness" (ideological purity) or "expertness" (professional skills and knowledge); this has reflected an even more fundamental ideological change.[182]

Underlying all the recent changes in China has been a profound ideological shift, a major reordering of the priority given to competing values inherent in China's brand of Marxism-Leninism. In place of the Maoist stress on class struggle, continuous revolution, and egalitarian social goals, the men dominating the present leadership—above all Teng Hsiao-ping—have elevated pragmatism and economic growth to the status of primary guiding principles or goals.[183] Whereas Mao in his later years was preoccupied with "contradictions" (and the conflicts they cause), Peking's leaders now stress the crucial importance of "practice" (and the need for pragmatic compromises resulting from concrete experience).[184] This emphasis is summed up in the slogan all Chinese are now exhorted to follow: "Seek truth from facts."[185] To Chinese who fully accepted the Maoist vision, this doubtless represents extreme "revisionism" and a move toward the "capitalist road." Some would call the recent trend an abandonment of ideology. It clearly represents at least a major adaptation and modification of Maoist ideology. In the judgment of many, it has amounted to what can be called de facto de-Maoization. (Conceivably, this trend could lead eventually to a more overt, extensive reinterpretation of—or even a rejection of—Maoist thought, although many factors will tend to inhibit China's leaders from going that far.) However, to Teng Hsiao-ping and those who share his views, it is simply a necessary adaptation of Marxism-Leninism to cope with China's problems, under changing circumstances, in a practical and realistic fashion.

This ideological shift has undergirded the new policies adopted in the fields of education, science, and technology and Peking's changed attitudes toward intellectuals in general. Since 1977–78 the political and social status of all intellectuals, especially of scientists and technicians, has risen dramatically.[186] Political and ideological controls over them have been relaxed, and their working conditions have been improved significantly. The leadership's motive has been to mobilize all the expertise and professional talent available to China, with relatively little regard for ideology, to support the regime's development program. (This was true also when similar policies toward intellectuals were carried out, briefly, in 1956.) One result of the loosening of political controls on intellectuals has been a cultural "thaw" that, although limited, is important and genuine.

Major changes in educational policies were revealed in a series of meetings held during 1977–78, culminating in a National Education Work Conference convened in April 1978.[187] The policies enunciated at these meetings focused above all on raising the quality of training, especially in higher education, to produce effective experts and professionals, particularly in science and technology, who can help meet the manpower requirements and provide the skills needed for the country's modernization programs.[188] This has involved a basic reversal of the educational policies introduced during the Cultural Revolution, which had been promoted by China's radicals right up until they were purged.

During the late 1960s and early 1970s Chinese educational policy stressed egalitarian values and glorified "redness," denigrating expertise and professionalism.[189] Priority was given to primary and secondary rather than to higher education and to rural rather than to urban schools. Commune-level schools in the countryside were greatly expanded, while institutions of higher education were severely attacked; for many years all major universities were closed. Educational administration was decentralized, curricula were simplified, and the length of training was reduced at all levels. (In primary schools, courses were generally cut from six to five years; in secondary schools, from six to four or five years; and in higher education, from five or six to three or four years.) Ideological and political controls over education were increased through Revolutionary Committees and "Mao Tse-tung Thought Propaganda Teams," and the political and ideological content of courses was increased. Great stress was put on combining education and work, and large amounts of time were allocated to physical labor. Pedagogical methods were changed; in the process, the traditional authority of teachers was greatly weakened. Entrance examinations were abolished (access to education was based in large part on political recommendations), and all elitist special schools were abolished.

In respect to every one of the above policies, the trend has been reversed.[190] The main stress today is on quality and talent. Primary attention is focused on higher education. Centralized administration has been restored; so too have "key schools" at all levels for students who show special talent. The length of courses has been gradually extended. Students are now tested for admission and at every stage of their schoolwork. Revolutionary Committees and propaganda teams have been disbanded. Ideological and political content has been cut back, and the time devoted to physical labor has been reduced. Teachers' authority has been restored, and educational leaders have attempted to reestablish discipline over students. Curricula are being revised. In addition, graduate programs have been reestablished, though still only on a small scale, and there is a new stress on learning from abroad. Foreign language training (especially in English) is being given great emphasis.

The number of students in higher education is still very small in relation to China's population and in light of the country's urgent need for skilled manpower. By late 1979 there were just over one million students in 633 regular institutions of higher learning, and only about 19,000 graduate students.[191] These numbers will unquestionably rise substantially in the next few years, but a shortage of qualified teachers will make it difficult to expand higher education very rapidly without adversely affecting quality, on which the leadership currently puts such great stress. There is much less need for expansion of lower-level educational institutions; in 1979 China had nearly 147 million students in primary schools and just under 60 million students in regular middle schools.[192] But to upgrade the overall system of education, quality will have to be improved at lower levels, too. The "key schools," which are now receiving such great emphasis, are designed to be centers of excellence. They are assigned the ablest students and are given special financial support.[193] The Chinese will also continue to work to achieve universal literacy (which now probably stands at about 70 percent).[194] Their stated aim is to achieve universal ten-year primary and secondary education in urban areas and universal eight-year education in rural areas by 1985.

After a decade during which Chinese universities were in chaos and the quality of higher education was debased, the quality of education in higher institutions is on the upgrade. Assuming that present policies continue, the Chinese should be able to reconstruct an educational system that can supply much if not most of the trained manpower that it needs. But this will take considerable time. China will continue to encounter serious shortages of skills as its modernization program proceeds.

Recognition of this problem led Peking's leaders in 1978 to make one of the most audacious choices they have made in recent years: to send large numbers of students abroad to study science and technology in the industrialized capitalist countries—including the United States,

Japan, several Western European countries, Canada, and Australia.[195] Some estimates of the total number that Peking plans to send abroad eventually are in the tens of thousands. (A leading Chinese diplomat told me in early 1979 that in his opinion perhaps 10,000 would be sent abroad in the next few years.[196]) However, the Chinese will have great difficulty finding enough qualified students to meet such targets, and the numbers probably will be smaller than those some predict. Nevertheless, the total will be in the thousands.[197] (Most of the first contingent sent to the United States and Europe in 1978–79 were mid-career scholars or "students" in their thirties and forties who had received their basic education before the Cultural Revolution; they were sent abroad for retraining to upgrade their skills.)[198]

The educational changes now taking place will be essential to help China meet its skilled manpower needs for its development program. But it is questionable whether even the rapid expansion of quality education at home and the crash training of students abroad will produce results rapidly enough to fulfill all of China's needs. The new policies, moreover, will raise new problems. Within China, they will tend to create a new intellectual elite, and many Chinese who fail to "make it" in the competitive system will be frustrated and resentful. Those who go abroad may, on their return, regard themselves as a special elite within China's elite—as some past generations of "returned students" tended to do. It is difficult to predict what effects education in capitalist societies—in fact, several quite different capitalist societies—will have on those trained abroad, how well the regime will be able to absorb them back into a socialist system, and what the long-run impact will be on Chinese society. Both the elitist trends in education and the exposure to capitalist societies will involve risks, adding to the complexities of social change in China in the period ahead. But they will enhance China's prospects for achieving its economic goals. As in the case of other policy changes described earlier, Peking's present leaders undoubtedly understand the dangers and costs but believe that the potential benefits are enormous. They seem to accept the calculated risks.

Another striking aspect of the change in Chinese policy since 1977–78 has been the leadership's glorification of science and scientists. Fang Yi, China's top scientific planner, proclaimed in 1978: "The modernization of science and technology is the key to the four modernizations, and scientific research must go ahead of economic construction."[199] China's top political leaders, including both Hua and Teng, made similar statements. In February 1978, for example, Hua declared: "Modern science and technology, which are characterized mainly by the use of atomic energy and the development of electronic computers and space science, are experiencing a great revolution. . . . To catch up quickly with the dramatic changes in modern science and technology and rapidly transform our backwardness in these fields are important and indispensable steps for the speedy development of our economy and the strengthening of our national defense. This is a matter to which our whole Party, army, and nation must give close attention."[200] Teng, at about the same time, asserted: "The crux of the four modernizations is the mastery of modern science and technology. . . . Modern science and technology are undergoing a great revolution. . . . How [worldwide] have the social productive forces made such tremendous advances and how has labor productivity increased by such a big margin? Mainly through the power of science, the power of technology."[201] Teng also, in the same speech, basically redefined the class status of China's intellectuals. "The overwhelming majority of them are part of the proletariat," he said, adding, "Those who labor, whether by hand or by brain, are all working people in a socialist society."[202] An ideological reformulation of this kind has far-reaching implications in a socialist society.

Many discussions in Chinese publications since 1977 have glorified science and technology to an extent unprecedented during the past thirty years.[203] In some respects they recall the atmosphere in China half a century earlier, in 1919, when some of China's leading intellectuals proclaimed that "Mr. Science" and "Mr. Democracy" would be China's saviors.[204] Now, some Chinese again seemed to be moved by an almost blind faith in science and technology as the panacea for China's problems, suggesting the emergence of a new kind of "scientism," an almost religious approach to science. But this is not true of all Chinese. Many simply show a sober, realistic recognition that in the contemporary world science and technology are crucially important to economic development and have faced up to China's relative backwardness in these fields in a hardheaded fashion. Peking's planners have recognized that accelerated economic development requires rapid advances in science and technology.

Starting in mid-1977 Peking convened a series of conferences on science and technology. Building upon planning work done in 1975 (and even earlier in 1972) under the aegis of Chou En-lai and Teng Hsiao-ping, these meetings worked out new policies and goals.[205] Finally, at a major National Science Conference in 1978, Fang Yi unveiled an "Outline National Plan" covering the years 1978–85.[206] This plan called for greatly increased investment in, and rapid enlargement of, China's research and training facilities in science and technology. It called for a rapid increase in the number of "professional scientific researchers" in China to a total of 800,000 by 1985. It spelled out plans for the establishment of many new research institutions, the reopening of those closed during the Cultural Revolution, and creation of a "unified system," with effective "coordination" of all efforts.

Prime emphasis was placed on the need for full and effective use of China's available scientific talent. Scientists were promised much better treatment, professionally and individually, with at least five-sixths of their time reserved for professional work and ideological and political intrusions on their time minimized. Those subjected to political attacks in the past were promised rehabilitation, and many who previously had been assigned jobs inappropriate for persons with their training and skills were reassigned. Peking also announced that awards and titles for achievement would be restored.

Once again, research in basic theory was recognized to be of fundamental long-term importance, and the new plan called for strong support of both basic and applied research. Fang Yi and others stressed the importance of individual achievement as well as collective effort. Rapidly, steps were taken to revive scientific and technological societies, journals, and conferences. In addition, Peking strongly endorsed the need to expand international contacts and exchanges. (China's leaders also decided to give stronger support than ever before to the development of the social sciences, through a newly established Chinese Academy of Social Sciences.)[207]

The national plan for scientific and technological development, as revealed in 1978, gave priority to research in eight general areas: agriculture, energy resources, materials, electronic computers, lasers, space sciences, high-energy physics, and genetic engineering.[208] It also outlined research tasks in twenty-seven "spheres," which included, in addition to the "two major departments of basic and technical sciences," such broad fields as national resources, agriculture, industry, national defense, transport and communication, oceanography, environmental protection, medicine, finance and trade, and culture and education. These research priorities obviously related directly to immediate economic development problems. One striking feature of the plans, however, was that they also called for major work in basic theory and in high-technology fields on the frontiers of modern development, including nuclear energy, electronic computers, semiconductors, lasers, and space technology.[209]

China's new stress on scientific and technological development unquestionably should contribute significantly to the regime's efforts to accelerate economic growth; faster progress in scientific and technological research and training probably is a prerequisite for more rapid modernization. In this, as in other aspects of the regime's programs, however, Chinese leaders may have set some unrealistic goals and started off trying to do some things too fast.

Even though the basic sciences and advanced fields of high technology, which were badly neglected in the past, clearly are important for the country's long-term development, there is a danger that the swing of the pendulum in China's policies toward science and technology is too great. With only limited resources, if Peking were to invest huge sums in costly projects in basic science and high technology, progress in less exotic fields that are important to China at its present stage of development might be slowed. The targets for the next few years may prove to be overly ambitious because of the country's acute shortage of skilled personnel. Large domestic training programs and efforts to learn as much as possible as fast as possible from other nations (not only by training Chinese abroad and expanding international exchanges but also by inviting more foreign experts and teachers to China)[210] will help, but probably not rapidly enough to enable China to achieve all the targets set for the next few years. In this field, as in others, the Chinese still face hard choices regarding priorities.

Political Context

From the time China started on its new course in 1977–78, one key question has been whether or not the new policies will last. The answer, clearly, will depend on political developments as much as on economic performance in the period immediately ahead. To come close to achieving the objectives its leaders have set, China must maintain greater political stability than it has in recent years. If there is no continuity of policy, and China again experiences violent zigzags such as those characteristic of the past two decades, it will almost certainly fall far short of its modernization goals. So far, political trends since Mao's death have generally been encouraging in this respect.

Today China enjoys a greater degree of political stability than it has for years. Compared with the 1960s and early 1970s, when serious conflicts fractured the top leadership and basic policy differences resulted in many disruptive policy shifts, the period since 1977 has so far been characterized by relative stability and unity. The initial phase of the succession, after the Gang of Four had been ousted, was smoother than many had expected. The quick purge of the top radicals made possible the formation of a leadership in which, while there still was by no means unanimity, there was a strong majority that seemed to agree on the general direction in which China should move. The past polarization between incompatible, irreconcilable radical and pragmatic viewpoints appeared to end when the Gang was purged. Whether or not the radicals in fact had plotted to seize power through a coup, as was alleged, for many years they had exerted an extremely divisive influence.[211] Their continuation in positions of power would have guaranteed continuing factional strife in Peking's highest decision-making bodies. While a collective leadership including them might have been possible—many observers believed this was likely following Mao's death—such a leadership probably would have had great difficulty formulating and implementing clear-cut policies. The likely prospect would have been for continued factionalism and further power struggles. Instead, immediately after Mao's death the new leadership acted with vigor and decisiveness, made visible progress in strengthening Party discipline and restoring order in society, and showed real boldness in initiating new policies.

Nevertheless, it was clear that power relationships were far from static. One cause of tension was the persistence of resentments and suspicions between those victimized by the Cultural Revolution and those who benefited from that upheaval.[212] This cleavage existed not only at the top but at all levels of the society. In addition, policy debates over political and ideological issues—as well as over specific economic policies—continued.

In 1979 it was still too early to judge whether the first stage of the post-Mao succession was over or whether the leadership changes that had occurred were only the first acts in a drama that would continue for some time. What was clear was that leadership stability would depend on a small number of top leaders—above all on Hua Kuo-feng and Teng Hsiao-ping, and perhaps also Party elder Yeh Chien-ying (Ye Jianying), who played a stabilizing, restraining, and compromising role during the early succession period.

It was impossible for outsiders to know the real relationship between Hua and Teng. Some analysts argued that a situation in which one man, Hua, held the most prestigious positions in a regime (Party Chairman and Premier), while another, Teng, ostensibly his subordinate, exercised greater real power, was inherently unstable. Yet it appeared in 1978–79 that a relationship evolved that was at least tolerable to both. Teng's political base for power was unquestionably stronger than Hua's from the start; as a result, Hua may have recognized that he was simply unable to challenge Teng's real power. Being much younger (at fifty-nine) than Teng (who was seventy-three in 1977), Hua may have decided to bide his time, gradually building up his base of power and hoping ultimately to acquire enough power to match his status after Teng's demise. Teng doubtless was tempted at times to use his power to occupy the posts that carry the greatest prestige in China.[213] Yet he seemed to recognize that to try to change the top leadership through another power struggle might endanger the success of the entire modernization program to which he was so strongly committed.

Although on the surface China's top leadership was comparatively stable from late 1976 on, there were tensions under the surface and gradual changes in power relationships within the Politburo and the Central Committee, and at provincial and lower levels as well.[214] The main trend, however, was a steady strengthening of the political base of Teng's power. During his days as Party Secretary-General in the 1950s and 1960s, Teng developed a wide network of supporters in all of China's bureaucracies (including the military establishment); he now used past ties effectively to bolster his position.

During 1977–78, with Teng's backing, most of the surviving leaders who had been purged for opposing Mao in earlier years were rehabilitated. (Some were exonerated posthumously.)[215] Step by step, Teng was able to place close associates and supporters in key positions in the central Party organizations and in the most important government ministries and commissions. The post of Party Secretary-General was revived and filled by Hu Yao-pang (Hu Yaobang), clearly a "Teng man."[216] Many changes also occurred in provincial-level posts; most of the new appointees were men linked to Teng. In the Party, a nationwide campaign against all those who had been closely associated with the Gang of Four resulted in purges, demotions, and criticism affecting large numbers of middle- and low-ranking cadres, many of whom were at least potential opponents of Teng and his policies. Some evidence suggests that Teng periodically urged going even further in "purifying" the entire Party to suppress all potential opposition and discredit the radicals' views, but that certain leaders—probably including Yeh as well as Hua—argued successfully for restraint.

Finally, in December 1978 the Central Committee's Third Plenum decided "to close the large-scale nationwide mass movement to expose and criticize Lin Piao [Lin Biao] and the Gang of Four and to shift the emphasis of our Party's work and the attention of the whole people of our country to socialist modernization."[217] Steps to tighten Party discipline continued, however, under a new Central Commission for Inspection of Discipline, headed by Chen Yun (Chen Yun); like Teng, he had long been noted for his pragmatism.[218] Chen was elected to the Politburo and became a Vice Chairman of the Party. In sum, from the time of his second comeback in early 1977, through his official rehabilitation in July 1977, the Party's Eleventh Congress in August, the Fifth NPC in March 1978, and then the Central Committee's Third Plenum at the end of the year, Teng was able to steadily strengthen his political power and build solid support for his policies.

However, there remained in the Politburo several leaders who had risen to power during the Cultural Revolution and who were potential opponents. These included leaders such as Wang Tung-hsing (Wang Dongxing), Chen Hsi-lien (Chen Xilian), Wu Teh (Wu De), and Chi Teng-kuei (Ji Dengkui), and possibly Hua too.[219] They constituted a relatively weak minority, but their continued presence in the Politburo was clearly galling to Teng. Periodically, including at the time of the Central Committee's Third Plenum in late 1978, there were reports that these men might be purged, but in each case these proved to be false. Conceivably, Teng considered ousting them but was restrained by others. Nevertheless, Teng's star steadily rose while those of his potential opponents declined. It appeared, on the surface, at least, that the philosophical and policy differences between Teng and Hua gradually narrowed, mainly as a result of Hua's moving closer to Teng's positions.

However, during 1978–79 debate continued on a number of ideological and political as well as economic issues,[220] including how far to go in purging persons who had been associated with the Gang of Four, the extent to which Mao's general ideological line and the Cultural Revolution should be openly repudiated, and the way in which the legacy of

Mao as a leader should be handled. There were also debates on the extent to which formerly purged leaders should be rehabilitated or exonerated and the degree to which there should be steps toward political relaxation allowing for freer expression of public opinion. Some differences continued, also, on many of the new policies, including the priority given to economics over politics, the downgrading of ideological reform, the glorification of pragmatism, the stress on material incentives, the elevation of "expertness" over "redness," and the return to more elitist educational policies. In a broad sense, Teng's views prevailed on most key issues, but he did not have his way on everything. There was no question, moreover, that many of those at various levels who had been purged or demoted, or whose interests had been damaged by the policy changes, harbored resentments against Teng personally as well as against the new Party line.

The political changes during 1978–79 were not confined to the Party; the new leadership worked to restore discipline and morale within all the regime's bureaucracies and tried to create a new political atmosphere throughout the country, taking varied steps described by foreigners as political "liberalization" or "relaxation."[221] While putting new stress on the need for greater "democracy" within the Party itself, Peking also loosened general political controls significantly, under the old slogan of "Letting a Hundred Flowers Blossom."[222] The most dramatic result of this political relaxation was the eruption in late 1978 of new wall poster campaigns (at "Democracy Wall" in Peking and similar places elsewhere), open street corner debates, and some public demonstrations by small dissident groups of students, workers, and peasants (especially former "Red Guard" members who earlier had been sent to rural areas). The beginnings of an "underground" or unofficial press also appeared.[223] Although much of the public criticism expressed through these outlets focused on past Maoist policies, some was directed at Mao himself; there were criticisms of current conditions and policies as well, including a few impassioned pleas for Western-style democracy in China.[224] The leadership was divided on how far to let such trends go, but by early 1979 it began to pull back and impose limits.[225]

Another important element in the leadership's move toward "liberalization" was the adoption of a new policy toward victims of past purges and political campaigns. Peking publicly "cleared" large categories of Chinese who had been the targets of class struggle and discrimination for three decades. Thousands who had been jailed as "Rightists" in 1957 were released.[226] In early 1979 the Central Committee decided to remove old pejorative class labels (such as "landlord" and "rich peasant") from millions of Chinese who had worn these "hats" ever since the 1950s and who as members of the so-called five elements had been subjected to serious discrimination and periodic political attacks for years.[227] More than at any time since 1949, the regime now stressed the importance of "socialist legality"[228] and promised to draft adequate laws not only concerning economic matters but also dealing with criminal justice. Steps toward codification of laws, interrupted in the 1950s, were resumed, and legal training and research were revived.

The trend toward political relaxation was accompanied by a real cultural thaw, which not only had an invigorating effect on China's artists, writers, and intellectuals but probably had a wider immediate impact on ordinary Chinese, through popular entertainment, than many of the regime's other political moves.[229] The restrictions on traditional and foreign cultural influences previously enforced by the radicals, especially by Mao's wife, Chiang Ching (Jiang Qing), were greatly relaxed. Artists and writers were granted considerably more freedom for individual expression than they had enjoyed in the past. Suddenly, China's theaters began showing previously banned traditional operas, old Chinese movies, new plays, and even foreign motion pictures, many dealing with themes that had been considered subversive before 1977. The publishing industry became more active, and more daring, than it had been for many years. Accompanying these changes was a significant relaxation of the puritanical revolutionary code of personal behavior that the Maoists had emphasized so strongly; the effects on social mores were immediately visible, especially in major cities.[230] Women began to try new hairstyles, use cosmetics, and wear more colorful clothes. Western-style dancing was permitted in some places. Romance was no longer denounced as unrevolutionary. In general, the leadership suddenly legitimized much greater freedom to express personal feelings and individual aspirations. It was no longer mandatory to say that one's only goal was "to serve the people"; people now could speak of their own hopes and ambitions, and many did.

As these political and social trends developed, ideology (at least as articulated during the Maoist period) was steadily deemphasized. All old ideological issues were reexamined, and step by step Mao was cut down to human size.[231] Starting in late 1978, occasional direct criticism of Mao and what he stood for began to appear, first in wall posters, then (in implicitly critical forms) in official publications. Debate continued within the leadership over how far to go in "demythologizing" Mao, and at one point Peking seemed on the verge of adopting a policy of open de-Maoization.

Early in 1979, Lu Ting-yi (Lu Dingyi), once deputy head of the Party's Propaganda Department under Mao, wrote an article in the *People's Daily* that, while effusively praising Chou En-lai, unambiguously indicated that Mao had been wrong at the historic Lushan (Lushan) Central Committee Plenum in 1959. What Lu specifically said was that Peng Teh-huai (Peng Dehuai), who criticized Mao at that time, was "correct" and that "the opposition to him" (meaning Mao) "was wrong"; this "erroneous 'left' tendency," he added, "later developed into a line, and was only corrected after the Gang of Four was smashed in October 1976."[232] The implication—apparent to all Chinese readers—was that in many respects Mao had been fundamentally in error ever since the late 1950s. Even though the Chinese press soon thereafter asserted that the Party was not carrying out any de-Maoization (or "de-Maoification") program but was simply "restoring Mao Tse-tung Thought to its original form,"[233] in fact the media began to treat Mao as a flawed leader who, although right in his views up to 1959, had been wrong during the last two decades of his life.

In contrast, Chou En-lai's reputation steadily rose; he was generally portrayed as an unblemished leader. Lu stated that Chou "was correct for 41 years after the 1935 Tsunyi [Cunyi] meeting."[234] Mao's mausoleum was closed for a period in the winter of 1978–79, and there were rumors that some kind of monument to Chou would be built. By late spring in 1979, however, Mao's mausoleum had been opened, and those who had been openly critical of him were at least temporarily reined in.

Even though it seemed unlikely that China's leaders would decide to denounce Mao openly, as Khrushchev had attacked Stalin in 1956, it was hardly necessary for them to do so. By 1979 what Mao had stood for in his later years had been discredited, and virtually all his old foes had been rehabilitated. No matter how the leadership decided to handle Mao's legacy, the myth of infallibility that had girded his reputation was greatly weakened, and many of the core values of Mao's Thought were no longer accepted as the foundation for Chinese policy.

Most ideological and political, as well as economic, trends in China during 1977–78 appeared to enjoy fairly wide popular support.[235] After years of exposure to intense ideological indoctrination, political "struggles," and manipulated social tension, large numbers of Chinese seemed to yearn for increased stability, law, and order and to favor some political and ideological relaxation and fewer restrictions on cultural activity and social behavior. (A few ardently argued for much greater freedom for political expression—even for democracy in the Western sense.)

However, there was little basis for concluding that China's leaders had suddenly been able to eliminate all the profound differences and divisions that had developed in China during the last two decades of Mao's rule. While the opponents of change were doubtless in a minority, there unquestionably were significant groups in the society that disapproved of much that was taking place, some because of ideological convictions, others because their personal interests were adversely affected.

One can only make informed guesses about the probable lineup of supporters and opponents as the regime changed course during 1977–79. Probably most economic planners, senior Party administrators, and technocrats were basically supporters. In fact, a large percentage of older Party leaders of all sorts, many of whom had at one time or other been hurt by Mao's vindictiveness, doubtless were generally supportive of Teng and his pragmatic approach to policy. The overwhelming majority of scientists, artists, professionals, and intellectuals almost certainly were among the most enthusiastic backers of the new policies; many obviously were exhilarated by the changes under way. Some Chinese youths, who saw new opportunities opening up for them in education as well as in the economy, probably had similar feelings. Many, if not most, urban workers may have felt relief and new hope because of the wage increases, the new attention to material incentives, and the prospect that their lives might be less politicized and more stable. Many peasants have reacted similarly, and for comparable reasons. In fact, large numbers of ordinary Chinese seemed relieved by the deemphasis of ideology and "return to normalcy," of a kind, which buoyed hopes for greater stability, reduced tension, a somewhat freer life, and perhaps an improved standard of living.

But developments during 1977–79 probably were viewed with alarm, distaste, or at least uncertainty by some groups in China. Committed Maoist ideologues must have viewed most of the new policies as a betrayal of what they had believed in and fought for. Party members and bureaucrats who had been purged or demoted because of their association with the radicals—there were many—were unquestionably bitter. Most who had joined the Party during the Cultural Revolution probably felt uneasy, at best, about their future. Some older Party members who came from lower-class backgrounds and had fought for the revolution in the 1930s and 1940s must have resented the new glorification of professionals and intellectuals, many of whom were not even Party members; the new policies threatened to have adverse effects on their political status. And among important groups of youth there were increasing signs of cynicism. Many frustrated young people were increasingly audacious in expressing their dissidence. Many of the millions who had been sent to the countryside in the late 1960s and early 1970s now returned to the cities and showed their unhappiness openly. Some illegally organized demonstrations; others engaged in crime and other antisocial activities.[236] This "lost generation" (the young Red Guards who had rebelled in the late 1960s because they were both idealistic and frustrated and because Mao told them it was "right to rebel") now provided raw material for a small but active "democratic" movement.

As always, the feelings and attitudes of China's huge mass of peasants were the most difficult to judge. Many probably felt new hope because of the leadership's promise to raise rural living standards. Others, however—particularly younger ones—may have feared that the new policies affecting education, health, and the economy generally might in the long run benefit urban areas more than rural villages, reversing the trend of the previous two decades.[237]

The reactions of China's military leaders and rank and file were also impossible to assess accurately. Many doubtless endorsed the leadership's emphasis on the need for military modernization. However, some may soon have been disillusioned because, in reality, the military establishment was not given very high priority in the leadership's allocation of resources (despite an increase in the defense budget in 1979).[238]

The political and social changes of 1977–79 were paralleled by fast-moving economic developments. China's modernization program really got under way in 1978. However, it did not take long for some leaders to recognize that they faced huge problems in trying to accelerate the country's development. By late 1978 Party leaders decided to modify their original plans; as will be discussed in detail below, in mid-1979 they announced that the entire modernization program would be significantly modified and slowed down and that China would undergo a period of "readjustment."

The political trends of the previous three years did not slow down, however. Within the leadership one climax occurred in early 1980, the result of which was that Teng Hsiao-ping won a clear political victory over a majority of potential opponents at the summit of power in China. By February 1980 he and his closest supporters had created a more unified, stronger top leadership than China had enjoyed at least since the 1950s. It was a leadership strongly committed to continue moving in the general direction defined during 1977–79 to carry forward the general policies that Teng had so strongly promoted—and symbolized. Even within the framework of the consensus that had emerged, Peking's leaders still struggled with many unresolved problems and debated specific policies. Nevertheless, the consolidation of a "Tengist" leadership at the start of a new decade enhanced the prospects for stability in China's top elite and continuity in policy in the period immediately ahead.

On January 16, 1980, Teng delivered a long and important "Report on the Current Situation and Tasks" to a cadre conference in Peking attended by 10,000 people. In this report, he spelled out his vision of China's future, outlining his views on China's problems and the Party's priorities for the 1980s.[239]

Teng discussed "three major tasks" for the decade. First on his list was the need to protect China's security and cope with the Soviet threat ("to oppose hegemonism and safeguard world peace in international affairs"). Second was "to bring about the return of Taiwan to the motherland." Although the need "to step up economic construction, that is, to step up the building of the four modernizations" was listed third, he made it clear that "modernization is the core of the three major tasks," on which success in achieving the other two goals would depend. "National defense construction cannot be carried out without a certain economic foundation," he said; "the main aim of science and technology is to serve economic construction." Although he noted that internationally the 1980s had started off badly (with "incidents" in Afghanistan as well as in Iran, Vietnam, and the Middle East), there was no militant posturing in his speech, and he stressed the need for peace. "Our strategy in foreign affairs," he said, "is to seek a peaceful environment for carrying out the four modernizations. This is not a lie, it is the truth." He also stated that although the 1980s would probably be "a decade of extremely great turmoil and filled with danger . . . we have confidence in being able to put off the outbreak of war." "If a large-scale war breaks out," he stressed, "we will have to fight and halt implementation" of the current "general line."

Teng's discussion of Taiwan was also devoid of militant rhetoric or threats. Unification "will remain an important task on our agenda," he said, and China should "strive to attain this target in the 1980s," but he indicated, implicitly but fairly clearly, that this should be accomplished peacefully. In fact, he suggested that it would only be possible when China had caught up with or surpassed Taiwan economically. "We must achieve a certain degree of superiority over Taiwan in economic development," he said, adding that "we cannot succeed without this." Throughout his report, he made it clear that economic modernization must be given top priority and that both China's security and the goal of national reunification would depend on its success.

Teng admitted that some people in China "doubt the socialist system," others are "confused," and still others are "dissatisfied" because "progress is too slow" or because they believe "that there is not much chance of carrying out" current policies; despite this fact, Teng asserted, the Chinese should have "confidence as we enter the 1980s."

He discussed frankly many of China's past economic shortcomings and failures, as well as its early achievements. He stressed, however, that virtually since the start of the Communist regime (at one point he said for twenty years, but at another point he said for thirty years), China had never really made economic development the main "focus" of its work. Moreover, it had experienced grave setbacks during the Cultural Revolution. Over time, as a result, "many problems accumulated." However, now, Teng said, China should "concentrate on looking ahead. . . . We are currently seeking a road suitable to the actual conditions in China," and "perhaps we can now seriously explore a relatively good road"—a "socialist" not a "capitalist" road, but nevertheless a new one. He stressed that "we should be neither impetuous nor tardy" but should "promote the economy a bit faster and a bit more economically." He also talked about the need for numerous changes in the economic system: "expanding enterprise self-management rights," "democratic management," "developing specialization and coordination," "combining planning regulation with market regulation," "combining advanced and medium technology," and "making rational use of foreign investment and technology."

In defining basic economic goals, he showed notable realism. His speech contained no talk about rapidly catching up with the major industrial nations, which leaders had proclaimed to be China's goal in the 1950s; in fact, he discussed why this was not possible, at least in terms of per capita output, because of China's huge population. Instead, he said that China would do well to achieve a per capita national output of about $1,000—close to Taiwan's today—by the end of the century. While admitting that this amount still would be less than average per capita output in Singapore or Hong Kong today, he nevertheless maintained that it would make China a "comfortably well-off society," at least by comparison with its own past and present.[240]

In discussing the regime's recent policies and accomplishments, he noted its success in creating new jobs in 1979, increases in the output of light industry (accompanied by cutbacks in capital construction), and current experiments in enterprise self-management. But he emphasized that China faces many difficult problems and tasks in the period ahead. He stressed that the country needs better planning, correction of existing economic imbalances, and improved education. While promising that the regime would continue to implement a system of payment according to work, he criticized indiscriminate, excessive, and wasteful use of bonuses in 1979 (and announced that there would be no spring festival bonuses in 1980).

Teng's comments on foreign policy were quite short. After stating that it would be necessary to continue opposing Soviet "hegemonism" (without really harping on this theme), he briefly reviewed recent foreign policy accomplishments, including improved relations with Japan, the United States, and other Western countries and increased cooperation with the Third World. He maintained that China's Vietnam incursion in early 1979 had had the effect of "stabilizing the Southeast Asia situation and will continue to do so in the future," and did not threaten a repetition of the use of force. In general, he emphasized how much China's international contacts had expanded, asserting that this had "set a new pattern in our country's diplomacy."

One striking aspect of Teng's report, however, was that even though he began by emphasizing that China's modernization program is the "core" of the country's tasks in the period ahead, what seemed uppermost in his mind was the need to maintain sufficient political and social order to ensure the success of the modernization program. The greater part of his speech discussed "four problems": ensuring the continuity of China's current basic "political line" (which, he said, Yeh Chien-ying's major speech on October 1, 1979,[241] had "summarized in a relatively complete way" for the first time); ensuring political "stability and unity"; recapturing a "pioneering spirit"; and developing a better "force of cadres" in China.

Teng argued that the regime had achieved many political successes since the purge of the Gang of Four. He pointed out that 2.9 million people had been "rehabilitated" (including a large number of purged top leaders, ten of whom he listed by name), that most of the incorrect verdicts made during the Anti-Rightist campaign of the 1950s had been rectified, and that the discriminatory labels previously placed on intellectuals, and most of those placed on landlords, rich peasants, and capitalists, had been removed. He discussed the changes that had already occurred in leadership and ideology, the regime's efforts to enhance "democratic life" in the society, and the new reliance on law; he also argued that policy was now "on the right track" in education, science, cultural work, and many other fields. China had "restored Mao Tse-tung Thought to its original state," he asserted. He implied that in the future the regime would avoid the kind of "movements," or campaigns, that were so disruptive in the 1950s and 1960s. All of this, he maintained, had already "transformed" the Party and state and had created a political situation of "stability and unity and liveliness and vigor."

But what most concerned Teng, obviously, was the need for further steps to restore the leadership role of the Party and its political cadres in Chinese society (he noted that China had 38 million Party members and 18 million cadres), to revitalize the Party as an institution, to improve its ability to carry out China's modernization, and to maximize the probability that his approach to development would be followed after he was gone. He insisted that there must be better party discipline and that the policies of the central leadership—especially the Central Committee—be faithfully followed. He also called for the development of new, better-qualified Party members and cadres, who would be "specialists" as well as "socialists," and discussed at great length the shortage of such people in many fields (law and education, specifically). He strongly urged faster generational change in China's leadership at all levels and stated that people in their forties and fifties—especially competent persons around age forty—should now be promoted, while older comrades should be retired. Calling for restoration of a "pioneering spirit of plain living and hard work," he strongly criticized those who seemed interested mainly in privileges. What he proposed was essential, he argued, to carry out the four modernizations effectively and also to "uphold the four basic principles—socialism, the dictatorship of the proletariat, Marxism-Leninism–Mao Tse-tung Thought, and Party leadership."

Teng placed special stress on the imperative of maintaining "social order" in China and made it very clear that although China's leaders remained committed to raise the "material *and spiritual* [emphasis added] living standard" of the Chinese people, encourage freer expression of opinions, promote more "democratic life" in Chinese institutions, encourage greater creativity among artists and writers, and develop a meaningful legal system, they were equally determined to set limits on political freedoms in order to prevent activities that could "lead to chaos."[242] While in 1978 Teng had been one of the key leaders encouraging "liberalization," he now obviously was more concerned about how to maintain social stability during a period of enormous social change in China. "Turmoil," he said, "can only lead to retrogression."

He discussed various "factors of instability," including "remnants" of the radicals' organizations and ideology, "factional elements," and some "counterrevolutionaries" with foreign links. But he devoted special attention to the "so-called 'democrats' and 'dissidents'" who had conducted large poster campaigns during 1978–79 (and then had been reined in by the Chinese leaders), persons who showed "extreme individualism" and tendencies toward "anarchism," and those who opposed the socialist system and Party leadership, thereby threatening to "sabotage social order." He asserted that while such people should be handled by legal means, they should be treated "severely" (he defended the regime's jailing of the well-known dissident, Wei Ching-sheng [Wei Jingsheng] in 1979). He also proposed elimination from the state constitution of the article that had guaranteed the right to the so-called four greats (including writing "big character posters" and holding "great debates").[243] None of this constituted a "retraction," Teng maintained; the leadership never had "relaxed," he argued, to the point of allowing totally free expression that could create social disorder.

To summarize, Teng emphasized that while major changes will occur in the Chinese economy and society as China modernizes, there will be a need for more skilled, effective Party leadership and discipline; and that while greater freedom of expression, creativeness, and legality will be necessary, there will have to be—in his view—clear limits on such freedoms to prevent the development of open dissident movements and to maintain social order. To most Westerners, such a position contains basic contradictions. It is possible, and perhaps probable, however, that most of China's leaders as well as many ordinary Chinese agree with Teng. However, to tread the delicate path he has tried to define—encouraging increased creativity, legality, and expression of opinion but at the same time preventing "destabilizing" or subversive political activities and views—will not be easy.

In the weeks following Teng's report, the text was widely distributed and discussed in Party and non-Party meetings all over the country as the leadership prepared for a new Central Committee Plenum (although the report was not actually published until after the Plenum). At about the same time, Teng published an article in the *Bangkok Post* (an odd choice) which articulated some of his views to a wider audience in the outside world.[244] In it he proclaimed, "We are standing at another turning point in Chinese history"; and "For us in China this is in a real sense a new revolution."

China's radicals, he said, had "put false choices before the Chinese people." "We do not want capitalism," he declared. "We do want a socialist society with a prosperous economy." He made clear that this required a new kind of relationship with the rest of the world. For years, he said, China was "cut off from the rest of the world," at first because isolation was "imposed on us" but then because "we isolated ourselves!" He maintained that starting in the late 1960s "conditions in the world changed," and now "we have learned to use this favorable international climate to accelerate our advance towards the four modernizations."

Acknowledging that skeptics both abroad and within China doubted whether "we can attain the goals we have set for ourselves," he argued that there are "four reasons for thinking we can." First, China is "rich in natural resources." Second, over the last thirty years, despite the fact that "we did some stupid things," "we were nevertheless able to lay the groundwork" for modernization in agriculture, industry, and technical development. (He stated that China's investment in capital construction over thirty years had totaled 600 billion yuan.) Third, "the Chinese people are not a stupid people." The "problem is how to bring their inventive genius into full play." That, he asserted, is "why we are calling for the emancipation of people's minds" and letting "a hundred flowers bloom." Here, as in his Party report, however, he said there would be limits on free expression of opinion, and he defended the clampdown on "democracy wall" in Peking to prevent "anarchy." Fourth, he said, "China has now adopted a policy of opening our doors to the world, in a spirit of international cooperation"—which will encourage "mutual stimuli" and "cross fertilization" on which all countries that have modernized, he stressed, have depended.

The problems China faces in its modernizing course are indeed "complex," Teng admitted; the country needs a "restructuring of the national economy," a reduction of personnel in agencies that are "overstaffed," and new jobs for redundant employees. "A whole generation of youth ... was inadequately educated" (some show remnants of the "poisonous influence" of the radicals); and the country must solve basic shortages of scientific and technical talent. It must also find the right mix of "automation, mechanization, and manual operations."

Nevertheless, he maintained, "we have ample grounds for optimism." China plans "to put to good use" the "managerial skills of the capitalist countries" (which are "part of mankind's common heritage"). It also would "like to expand the role of the market economy." This will not, however, mean that China will move toward capitalism; although there will be capitalist elements in the economy, from investment by foreigners and Overseas Chinese, "public ownership will predominate." "Under the socialist system," Teng maintained, "a market economy can exist side by side with a planned production economy [which he labeled a "two-sector" system]—and they can be coordinated."

Teng stressed that much in China's modernization program is still experimental. "As we move into the 1980s," he said "it is hard to envisage the outcome of improvements two or three years hence. They will take time. It will take a little longer to see the outlines of our achievements, as they take shape." But he expressed optimism about the prospects for China's economic success and stressed its international significance, declaring that "we can certainly expect the world economy to undergo a fundamental change when China modernizes"; because it has a population of about a billion, "the modernization of China will be an important factor in the whole world's prosperity."

Finally, Teng declared, men of his age must be "concerned about arranging for what comes after" and "find good and reliable successors, so that once a succession takes place, new turmoil will not break out again." China planned to "introduce a retirement system for our officials," he announced, and he pledged that "by 1985 I shall become only an adviser or consultant." (In mid-March, some top Party leaders privately reported that in an unpublished speech, Hu Yao-pang said that Teng would resign as Vice Premier before the end of 1980.)[245]

Teng's comments about laying the basis for continuity of leadership and policy in the future revealed what was then occurring in China, although the outside world did not learn the details until some weeks later. The process Teng had started during 1977–79, by which in a step-by-step fashion he had placed "his" men, or at least men generally supportive of his views on modernization, in key posts throughout China, was speeded up in late 1979 and early 1980. Half a dozen of China's key regional military commanders were replaced by somewhat younger men, and Teng turned over one of his posts, that of People's Liberation Army (PLA) chief of staff, to a protege.

Finally, the Central Committee met in Peking in late February 1980 (in the Fifth Plenum of the Eleventh Central Committee). When it issued its Communiqué on February 29,[246] the world learned that Teng had been able, in effect, to complete the first stage of the post-Mao succession by restructuring Peking's top leadership in such a way that the predominance of his influence—and basic views—was clear for all to see.

The Fifth Plenum "decided to approve the resignations"—that is, it purged by legal Party means—of all the most important holdovers on the Politburo from the Cultural Revolution: Wang Tung-hsing, Chi Teng-kuei, Wu Teh, and Chen Hsi-lien, and deprived them of all Party and state posts. Two new members, both in their early sixties, were elected to the all-powerful Standing Committee of the Politburo: Hu Yao-pang and Chao Tzu-yang (Zhao Ziyang). Hu was Teng's close protege, whom Teng earlier had made Party Secretary-General, and he now emerged as the key organization man within the Party apparatus. There was immediate speculation that he might eventually rise to the Party chairmanship. Chao was the dynamic and innovative Party leader in Szechwan (Sichuan), the province that throughout 1979 had been in the forefront of economic experimentation. Observers speculated that he would later be appointed Premier (replacing Hua Kuo-feng in that post) and become the key Party leader in the state apparatus. This became very plausible when Teng, in April, told foreign visitors that Chao was in charge of "the day-to-day work" of the government.[247] Adding them to the Standing Committee—which already included Yeh Chien-ying, Li Hsien-nien, and Chen Yun, as well as Hua and Teng—appeared to make China's top policy-making body (with one possible exception, Hua) united on the need for a basically pragmatic approach to China's modernization, although not all shared identical views by any means on specific issues, such as how far to go in decentralization or in moving toward market socialism. Since all the others, except for Hua, were in their seventies or eighties, both Hu and Chao emerged as possible successors to Teng in real power terms. Moreover, as a result of the removal of four potential opponents of the Party's new policies, the Politburo as a whole now appeared to be united by a firmer consensus than at any time in two decades. This not only increased the real prospects for continuity in basic policy in the period ahead, but it also lessened the uncertainty about a possible reversal of policy that must have persisted among lower-level leaders and cadres as long as holdovers from the Cultural Revolution had remained on the Politburo.

The Plenum also established a new Central Party Secretariat, making it a powerful permanent office under Politburo leadership. Hu Yao-pang's title was changed from Secretary-General to General Secretary (the latter indicating a more powerful position), just as Teng's had been more than a quarter century earlier when his first rise to the top occurred. (Teng had become Secretary-General in 1954, then General Secretary in 1956.)[248] Ten others were elected to the Secretariat: Wan Li (Wan Li), Wang Jen-chung, Fang Yi, Ku Mu, Sung Jen-chiung (Song Renqiong), Yu Chiu-li, Yang Teh-chih (Yang Dezhi), Hu Chiao-mu, Yao Yi-lin, and Peng Chung (Peng Chong).[249] Half were on the Politburo; the others were Central Committee members. This group in some respects was unprecedented for two reasons. First, its membership was more heavily weighted in favor of economic administrators, planners, technocrats, and Party intellectuals than any comparable top body in the Party's history. Most, of course, had held numerous jobs that involved essentially Party work or political administration, and many had had military experience as commissars if not commanders (as most old Chinese Communist leaders had); however, the majority now carried economics-related responsibilities in their current jobs. (Of course, all top Party jobs are also political.) Only one was an active military man. This clearly was a body geared to manage China's new economic modernization policies. Second, it was a group that consisted almost entirely —with the exception of two in their early seventies—of men in their sixties; more than half were sixty-five or younger. By the standards of some countries, they would not be considered young, but compared to China's recent leaders they certainly were. It seemed probable that most would be capable of operating effectively as leaders for at least five to ten years. Their appointments therefore reflected a significant (even though still limited) "generational" change.

All of these changes left Hua Kuo-feng in limbo. Possibly he would remain as a figurehead. Possibly he might be eased out—with either Teng himself or Hu or Chao becoming Party Chairman. The chance that he could assert real power now seemed slim. Surprisingly, three months after the Plenum, Hua seemingly challenged current policy for the first time in two years by criticizing material incentives, but most observers interpreted this as a defensive action by an increasingly isolated man rather than a real challenge to the current line.[250]

Perhaps the most important symbolic act of the Plenum was the formal, complete, official rehabilitation of Liu Shao-chi, who had once been Chairman of State and Mao's chosen successor and the most important single target of political attack (with whom Teng had been closely linked) during the Cultural Revolution. He was the last of the major leaders purged by Mao in the 1950s and 1960s to be rehabilitated, and his exoneration in effect closed a long chapter in China's history.[251]

The Communiqué did not discuss policy issues at any great length. Apart from generally endorsing the leadership's program of "four modernizations" and the "policy of readjustment, restructuring, consolidation, and improvement of the national economy," adopted in mid-1979, it mainly discussed steps to "uphold and improve Party leadership," reviewed the draft of a revised Party constitution (which among other things would abolish "the existing system of lifetime jobs for cadres"), adopted "Some Criteria About the Political Life Within the Party" (which had been approved in principle by the Politburo the previous February),[252] and endorsed the view that article 45, guaranteeing citizens the right to "speak out freely, air their views fully, hold great debates, and write big character posters," should be deleted from the state constitution. It also called for convocation of the Twelfth Party Congress ahead of schedule.

The Communiqué stated that "the session did not specifically discuss economic work" (the national economic plan for 1980 had already been formulated during the previous November-December, it said), and some difficult economic issues remained to be thrashed out before, during, and after the new Party Congress. What the Plenum accomplished was the consolidation of a leadership with increased capability and commitment to implement China's modernization program along the general lines already adopted.

Consolidation of leadership at the top could not, however, answer many basic questions about the long-term effects of the political and social changes initiated during 1977–79. Although these changes cannot be estimated with accuracy, over time they could have a significant impact on the nature of the society and the political as well as the economic system. There is little possibility that the trends toward political relaxation will lead rapidly toward "democracy" in the Western sense, at least in the foreseeable future. With its huge population, authoritarian tradition, and immense population, China always has lacked the cultural, social, and political basis for pluralistic democracy. The imposition in 1949 of a Communist system, ruled by a Leninist Party, further limited the possibilities. Yet, if the policies initiated since 1977 persist, the political system could gradually change in several ways.

There could be an increased tendency, for example, for certain types of interest groups to coalesce and work more openly to promote their own political, cultural, or economic objectives. Even if the political relaxation that occurs is limited and the Party places greater stress on discipline, there may be more open expression of dissatisfaction by dissident groups. There probably will be increased bureaucratism, as Mao always feared, even though the new leaders will try to combat it; at the same time the tendency of many groups to challenge this trend may increase. There is little doubt that elitism will grow and that Maoist egalitarian goals will be increasingly compromised. This will probably create new tensions and resentments, though these are likely to be more like those widespread in other rapidly developing countries than like the semi-religious conflicts between Maoists and non-Maoists that fractured and at times paralyzed China in recent years.

Although the old ideological issues that made conflicts between radicals and pragmatists so bitter in the 1960s and early 1970s will not disappear, Chinese politics will probably not soon be polarized into "two lines" to the extent that occurred in the last years of Mao's life. In society as a whole, there is likely to be a weakening of revolutionary commitment and idealism. This will contribute to the growth of social problems familiar in most other developing societies, especially in cities, if urban unemployment grows.

The central issues in politics in the period ahead will be different from those of the past. Some Chinese may continue to argue about egalitarianism versus pragmatism or "true Marxism-Leninism–Mao Tse-tung Thought" versus "revisionism." But increasingly the most important debates probably will be over allocation of resources, that is, about who gets what and what works and what does not.

Chinese society, in short, has entered a very new period. Both the new economic development policies and the political and social changes create inevitable uncertainties. There will be new tensions and possibly considerable social and political confusion as China attempts to implement its policies. It seems unlikely, however, that these could create the kind of disintegrative forces that some other rapidly developing countries, such as Iran, have confronted. China is not starting its modernization programs from scratch; the processes of change now being accelerated have been under way for several decades. Moreover, it is an extraordinarily well-organized society. Although the process of institutionalizing the Chinese political and social system is far from complete, the Communist Party controls an organizational apparatus that has impressive capabilities for mobilizing, controlling, and instructing the population. Moreover, even though rapid economic and social change will have unsettling effects, there will be strong integrative forces at work. Despite the weakening of ideology (at least in its Maoist form), Marxism-Leninism in some form probably will continue to be a strong influence in society. And Chinese nationalism, superimposed upon cultural foundations that are as strong as in any other modern nation, will continue to be a powerful unifying force. Even though the changes now occurring will create new problems, they should improve the regime's prospects for accelerating economic development and general modernization. If things work out as Peking's leaders hope, the new policies could inject a new dynamism into the economy and stimulate new creativity in the society.

Three Years of Economic Readjustment (1979–81)

China's modernization program started off with excessive optimism. After Hua Kuo-feng's February 1978 outline of the plan, the fanfare surrounding it created a euphoric atmosphere, raising unrealistic expectations both within China and abroad; 1978 was a year of frenetic effort at home and unprecedented trade activity abroad.[253]

Within months, however, multiplying problems and continued debate became evident, and by year-end the Party had decided to modify its initial program in major ways. At a watershed meeting of the Central Committee in December, China's leaders in effect temporarily shelved the original plan to concentrate first on immediate problems. Subsequent public and private statements by Chinese leaders in early 1979 revealed that a major "reassessment" was in process.[254] Not only did Peking scale down many short-run goals, but in the spring some major projects were halted and negotiations for many large-scale imports of plants and machinery were temporarily suspended.

The Party's Third Plenum in December 1978, while announcing a major "shift [in] the emphasis of our Party's work . . . to socialist modernization," called for important "revisions" in the original plan and major reform in "the structure of economic management."[255] In contrast to the original plan, which focused attention on huge new "capital construction" projects, especially in heavy industry, the Plenum's Communiqué asserted that "the whole Party should concentrate its main energy and efforts on advancing agriculture as fast as possible because agriculture, the foundation of the national economy, has been seriously damaged in recent years and remains very weak on the whole."

Following the Plenum, the official press began to discuss the need for a cutback in capital construction and a general adjustment that inevitably would result in a somewhat slower pace of overall growth than originally projected. In February 1979 an editorial in the *People's Daily* (*Renmin Ribao*) entitled "Emancipate the Mind for an Overall Balance in Economic Development"[256] stressed that China must avoid "impetuosity or rashness" as well as "right conservatism."[257] "Judging from our experience in the past 30 years," it said, "China suffered more from rashness than from conservatism." Analyzing the country's 1978 plans, the editorial asserted, "The scale of some capital construction projects was too large and beyond the reach of material and financial resources," adding that "setting some plan figures too high" was an example of the current "phobia" involving "fear of being conservative." The editorial strongly criticized the original plan's overemphasis on "steel as the key link." What China must achieve, it declared, is "the best proportionate relationship for developing the national economy—in which minimum investment can yield maximum results and in which existing economic conditions are fully used to satisfy society's needs to the greatest extent." In its readjustment of priorities, Peking reemphasized that China must give first priority to agriculture, second to light industry, and third to heavy industry. "Agriculture and light industry require smaller investment, but they produce quicker results and this meets the needs of the people," said the February *People's Daily* editorial.

Although these statements signaled a cutback of certain heavy industry targets, there were at first few details on which industries would be affected and how. However, certain shifts of priorities soon became clear. "Steel investments should be proportionately reduced," the *People's Daily* declared, and priority within the heavy industrial sector should be given to China's "weak links in industrial production," including "coal, electric power, transportation, and building materials." In the immediate future, it asserted, plans should stress projects that "accumulate funds, introduce advanced technology, and quicken the pace of construction"; they should give priority to developing "professions and trades that will produce quick results, earn more profits and foreign exchange, and compete on the international market." This clearly implied that increased attention would be given to light consumer goods industries producing for both the domestic and foreign markets.

Word gradually filtered out of China, through various sources, about some of the probable changes in targets. Most notably, Chinese officials privately indicated that the cutback in the goal for steel output would be sizable, probably reducing the target for 1985 from 60 million tons to somewhere between 40 million and 50 million—perhaps around 45 million tons.[258] There was also evidence, despite the increased priority being given to agriculture, that agricultural mechanization would be slowed, and the regime's approach to mechanization modified.[259] High-level Chinese officials privately indicated that a rapid introduction of tractors and other large-scale machinery might be a mistake. Mechanization of agriculture would continue, they said, but at a slower pace, and it would not be viewed as a panacea for agricultural modernization but simply as one part of a complex mix of policies. They also indicated that while capital investment in steel and heavy industry generally would be cut, the development of certain heavy industries would continue to receive high priority; these included fuels (coal, oil, natural gas, and others), electrical power, and modern transportation, all of which have created continuing economic bottlenecks in China, as well as a variety of minerals and other raw materials that China itself needs and also can export.[260] Giving continued priority to these fields was essential to overcome past shortages that had prevented full utilization even of China's existing industrial plants, to strengthen the country's basic infrastructure and build the foundation for future industrial development, and to develop exportable raw materials to earn more foreign exchange to help finance China's ambitious import plans.

In the spring of 1979, the Party and the government convened a series of major conferences to discuss changes in economic plans and priorities. Few official statements emanated from these meetings, but their debates and decisions were reflected in the press as well as in visitors' reports and other sources. A particularly important, though unpublicized, Party Central work conference was convened in April in Peking. In June a reputable non-Communist Hong Kong newspaper, the *Ming Pao*, reported that Vice Premier Li Hsien-nien had stated at the conference[261] that China is facing an "economic crisis." The shortage of foodgrain was such, he reportedly said, that 100 million people in the country were not getting enough food, the monthly grain ration was simply not sufficient for workers engaged in heavy work, and nonstaple foods were also insufficient. (The paper said Li indicated the average monthly grain ration in China was 29 catties, or about 32 pounds.) According to the report, Li also stated that China had a current budget deficit of 10 billion yuan due to excessive investments in large new projects as well as to the increases in wages and bonuses granted in 1978. He also said that China's unemployment had risen greatly in recent years and now stood at 20 million.[262] It was not specified whether this figure referred only to urban areas, but Peking's statements on unemployment usually do; if this was the case, Li's statement implied that urban employment had risen to perhaps 10 percent of the total urban population, and close to 20 percent of the urban workforce. Whether or not this was accurate, clearly unemployment had again become a very serious—and openly acknowledged— problem for the first time since the 1950s. By the spring of 1979, Chinese officials started to talk about it, even to foreigners.

Policy Adjustments

Following the decisions made in Party conferences during late 1978 and the first half of 1979 to alter economic priorities, top government bodies then translated the decisions into specifics. The results were unveiled at the second session of the Fifth National People's Congress held in June 1979.

As Premier, Hua Kuo-feng made the keynote address, as he had in February 1978. Two other top economic leaders also delivered important reports, and the State Statistical Bureau (SSB) released a major collection of statistical data, the first of its kind since the 1950s. Together, Hua's "Report on the Work of the Government," Vice Premier Yu Chiu-li's "Report on the Draft of the 1979 National Economic Plan," Finance Minister Chang Ching-fu's "Report on the Final Accounts of 1978 and the Draft Budget for 1979," and the SSB's "Communiqué on Fulfilment of China's 1978 National Economic Plan" gave a more detailed picture of the state of the Chinese economy, its recent performance, and plans for the immediate future than any available since the late 1950s. Chinese leaders did not immediately try to fill the statistical vacuum that had existed for two decades, but they published a fairly wide range of statistics for the years 1977–78 (the period since Mao's death and the radicals' purge) and announced major targets for 1979.

The reports showed that China had experienced a successful recovery and period of rapid (too rapid) growth in the two years since Mao's death. They also reinforced the basically pragmatic thrust of the country's modernization policies that had evolved during 1977–78. However, they discussed frankly the serious economic difficulties facing China— some of them problems inherited from the past, others created by the regime's efforts to introduce a new approach to modernization too rapidly. China's leaders now publicly admitted that aspects of their initial modernization plans and some of the targets announced in early 1978 were unrealistic. No revised targets for 1985 were immediately announced, but it was evident that many had been, or were being, re-examined and in many cases reduced.

When the targets set for 1979 were revealed, they showed that in the immediate future the modernization program would be slowed, at least in comparison with the rate projected in the original plan, for at least three years and possibly for more, to enable the Chinese to put their economic house in order in preparation for a sustainable, sound program of rapid economic growth thereafter. In general, the statements made at the 1979 NPC were notable for their realism. Peking's leaders appeared to have overcome the euphoria of 1978, corrected many previous errors, and adjusted their course in ways that would increase their chances of long-run success.

In his report, as in previous reports on government work (delivered by Chou En-lai in the 1950s and 1960s), Hua began with an analysis of ideological and political issues. There were almost no traces of Maoist concepts of mass mobilization and revolutionary egalitarianism in what he said, as there had been in some of his earlier statements. He almost seemed more "Tengist" than Teng. How much the report reflected Hua's personal views was not clear (all such reports must have the Politburo's endorsement). It clearly did represent the Party's new line, however.

Since the "historic turning point" (at the Third Plenum in December 1978), when the Party Central Committee "shifted the focus of the work of the whole nation to socialist modernization," Hua declared, the nation has been dedicated to "emancipating the mind" and "seeking truth from facts" (slogans associated with Teng) which were "laid down" as "principles" by the Plenum.[263] "The nationwide discussion on the criterion of truth," he asserted, "has helped to emancipate the minds of cadres and masses alike," breaking the "mental chains" forged by "Lin Piao and the Gang" and making it possible to approach problems by "proceeding from reality and integrating theory with practice." While he spoke favorably of Mao, the "mental chains" he was referring to obviously were those associated with Mao and the radicals in the 1960s and 1970s. By stressing Mao's call for "integrating theory with practice," he in effect argued for pragmatic values identified with Mao in his earlier years. Hua downgraded Maoist concepts of "contradiction" and class struggle. As Teng (and Liu Shao-chi[264] before him) had, he called for a virtual ending of class struggle. Analyzing "the class situation and class struggle in China" as of 1979, he said, "Of course, there are still counterrevolutionaries" and others in China who still "seriously disrupt socialist public order," and "we recognize" that "class struggle has not yet come to an end," but "class struggle is no longer the principal contradiction in our society." There is "no longer any need," he stated, "for large-scale and turbulent class struggle waged by the masses, and therefore we should not try to wage such a struggle in the future." Landlords and rich peasants have "ceased to exist" as "classes," "capitalists" are now "a part of the people," and there is "no conflict of fundamental interests" among workers, peasants, intellectuals, and other patriots who support socialism. He reported that the work of "removing the Rightist label" from those so designated in the past had been completed and that progress had been made in "changing the status" of landlords and peasants.[265] The "supreme *political* task" (emphasis added) now, he declared, is "the realization of the four modernizations."

Hua asserted that to "bring the superiority of the socialist system into full play," it is necessary to "promote socialist democracy and strengthen the socialist legal system," as well as to raise the people's level of political consciousness and understanding of Marxism-Leninism–Mao Tse-tung Thought. "Only with full democracy," he said, "will they [the people] generate the drive to study and solve the various problems of the national economy, to put forward every kind of practical and imaginative proposal . . . and to make important innovations, inventions, and discoveries," adding that "the more socialist democracy develops, the better modernization can be achieved." Decrying "autocracy, bureaucracy, love of privilege, the patriarchal style of work, and anarchism," he called for "freedom and discipline," talked about the need for "freedom of the person and legitimate economic rights," and said "every ordinary worker has his inviolable rights." "A citizen should be protected by the government," Hua stated, "against any restraint in enjoying and exercising the rights to freedom of the person, of speech, correspondence, publication, assembly, association, and religious belief, as long as he does not violate the Constitution or the provisions of specific laws based on it."

While these statements did not herald the start of Western-style democracy in China, they did reveal a new concern about citizens' political rights. As had been the case in the mid-1950s, when a comparable trend occurred, the need for political "relaxation" was directly linked to the demands of economic development.[266] Hua reported that the regime had speeded up the process of drafting many national laws and noted that government departments and local authorities also were drafting many new rules and regulations. He called for experimentation with a "system of workers' congresses" based on elections of leaders (or, where elections are inadvisable, local opinion polls) in grassroots enterprises and establishments.[267] He stressed also that greater attention should be given to letters and visits to Party and government institutions from the "masses." In general, he proposed there should be greater flexibility in transferring or replacing ineffective or undesirable leadership personnel. He called for abandoning the idea of an "iron rice bowl" (that is, virtually permanent job assignments without respect to performance) and advocated learning from foreign practices of personnel management. "We should make an extensive study of domestic *and foreign* [emphasis added] experience," he said, "and establish and improve systems concerning the examination, assessment, supervision, reward and punishment, removal, rotation, and retirement of cadres."

Hua's articulation of many ideological, political, and economic ideas that had been associated mainly with Teng indicated that by mid-1979 Teng's pragmatic philosophy had triumphed. As a result, the top leadership appeared more genuinely "collective" than before. Although on the surface it appeared that Hua's star had risen, at least to some degree, Teng was obviously *the* leader, since his ideas and drive had been instrumental in setting China on its new course.

While Teng unquestionably played a major part in the policy reassessment during the first half of 1979, several others among China's top administrators and technocrats apparently were key actors in the process of readjusting economic policies and goals. Some reports suggested that Chen Yun was the key individual advising a readjustment of economic policy and cutback of targets. The seventy-nine-year-old Chen had been a top economic administrator in the 1950s, but was pushed aside by Mao after his opposition to the Great Leap Forward in the late 1950s. He resurfaced briefly in the early 1960s, but fell again during the Cultural Revolution, and was not fully rehabilitated until late 1978. He is said to have strongly urged cutting short-run targets to levels more realistic than those initially announced in 1978. Chen emerged as head of a new State Financial and Economic Commission, which was theoretically responsible for overall economic coordination in China.[268]

By mid-1979 the consensus among the dominant leadership appeared to be strong in regard to the basic directions of policy in spite of intense continuing debate on specific issues such as how much to decentralize or to allow market forces free play. Although the reassessment of 1979 required the leadership to admit serious mistakes publicly, no political heads rolled immediately. The remaining members of the Politburo associated most closely with Maoist ideas and the Cultural Revolution were largely excluded from the exercise of any real decision-making power, however, and eight months later were ousted. In articulating the leadership's policies and plans, Hua expressed the consensus of those making up the dominant Politburo majority, who looked mainly to Teng for leadership.

The economic sections of Hua's report began with an analysis of "the solid achievements in economic recovery and growth during the past two years and more," giving statistics indicating that during 1977–78 these achievements had, in fact, been impressive. He then declared that since the Third Central Committee Plenum's call for "revisions" in China's economic plans, the State Council had undertaken an "overall analysis of our economic construction" and had concluded that "the country should devote the three years beginning from 1979 to readjusting, restructuring, consolidating, and improving the national economy in order to bring it, step by step, onto the path of sustained, proportionate, and high-speed development." He discussed at length the reasons why such a readjustment was required.

"To this day," Hua declared, "the superiority of socialism has not been consistently and effectively brought into play, and we have achieved far less than we should have." In the initial formulation of the ten-year plan, he admitted, "we did not take . . . into full account" the problems resulting from the disruptions of recent years; as a result "some of the measures we adopted were not sufficiently prudent."

Hua stated bluntly, "The main problem now facing us is that our agricultural expansion cannot as yet keep up with the needs of industrial development, and at times cannot even keep up with the demands of a growing population." He summarized a variety of other major problems as follows:

Many important products of the light and textile industries are insufficient in quantity, poor in quality, and limited in variety, so there are not enough marketable goods. Although the coal, petroleum, and power industries, and the transport and communications services, have grown at a relatively swift pace, they still lag behind what is required by our expanding economy. Coordination within and between industrial departments is lacking in many respects. In capital construction, far too many projects are being undertaken at the same time, and many will not contribute to our production capacity for years. There are obvious shortcomings in the structure of our economic and enterprise management which seriously dampen the enthusiasm of their workers and staff, and of the enterprises, localities, and central departments as a whole. These shortcomings all hinder us from making better use of our manpower, equipment, and circulating funds.

To illustrate the effects of existing shortcomings, Hua stated that 24 percent of China's industrial enterprises were run at varying degrees of loss, 43 percent of major industrial products from key enterprises were qualitatively inferior to the best produced in the past, and 55 percent of enterprises used more raw and semifinished materials than during their best past periods.

A readjustment of plans and targets was therefore "crucial," Hua asserted, "to rectify the serious disproportions in our economy" and improve the "coordination" of various sectors. The State Council, he reported, had set five general objectives for the next three years, 1979–81:

(1) To achieve a relative correspondence between the growth of grain production and other farm and sideline production on the one hand and that of population and of industry on the other.

(2) To achieve a growth rate for the light and textile industries equal to or slightly greater than that of the heavy industry....

(3) To alleviate the current tense situation in the fuel and power industries and the transport and communications services by increasing production and practicing economy....

(4) To resolutely narrow the scope of capital construction, concentrate

our forces on major projects, improve their quality, reduce cost and shorten construction periods.

(5) To bring about, on the basis of rising production, a further increase in the average income of all peasants from the collectives, and in the average wage of all non-agricultural workers and staff.

And in adjusting the economy, Hua stated, the regime must also implement "overall reform of the structure of economic management, carried out firmly and step by step," so that economic practice conforms with "objective economic laws," especially the "law of value," as well as the principle of "to each according to his work." "The egalitarian tendency . . . must be resolutely checked." In addition, he stated, "local authorities must be given greater powers in planning, capital construction, finance, materials, and foreign trade," and "specialized companies and complexes of an entrepreneurial nature must be formed." Thus, he made official policy many of the proposals put forward by Hu Chiao-mu a year earlier.

After discussing general objectives, Hua listed ten specific tasks or policies that the State Council had set for the period immediately ahead, which for the most part simply elaborated upon and outlined the five general objectives.

First, . . . concentrate effort on raising agricultural production. . . .

Second, . . . speed up the growth of light and textile industries. . . .

Third, . . . overcome the weak links in our economy: the coal, petroleum and power industries, transport and communications services, and building materials industry. . . .

Fourth, . . . curtail capital construction and try to get the best results from investment. . . .

Fifth, vigorously develop science, education, and culture and speed up the training of personnel for construction. . . .

Sixth, continue to do a good job in importing technology, make use of funds from abroad and strive to expand exports. . . .

Seventh, . . . take active and steady steps to reform the structure of economic management. . . .

Eighth, preserve basic price stability; readjust those prices that are irrational, while strengthening price control. . . .

Ninth, raise the living standards of the people step by step as production rises. . . .

Tenth, continue to do a good job of family planning and effectively control population growth. . . .

While this list codified many new policies that had been spelled out gradually throughout 1977–78, they also highlighted the important changes in short-term policy resulting from the regime's 1979 reassessment of plans: a cutback, at least temporarily, in overall investment; an increased stress on investment with relatively quick payoff; a shift of priorities away from investment in heavy industry and toward agriculture and light industry; concentration within the field of heavy industry on eliminating key bottlenecks and solving basic infrastructure problems; greater attention to price policy; and increased emphasis on improving living standards and incentives, reforming methods of planning and management, and further developing scientific and technical training and research.

Hua's report went beyond these generalities and discussed many specific policies and problems related to each of the major tasks outlined. Yu and Chang also dealt with many of these, even though they concentrated attention on quantitative data rather than on broad policy.[269] The details in all three reports deserve careful attention, because they were intended to define a framework for China's entire modernization program at least through 1981.

In discussing agriculture, Hua underlined the necessity to increase output not only of grain but also of meat and other nonstaple foods, cash crops, and raw materials. Yu stressed the need to overcome the lag in output of aquatic products as well. Hua emphasized the importance of recent Central Committee decisions on "Some Questions Concerning Acceleration of Agricultural Development (Draft)" and "Regulations Concerning the Work in the Rural People's Communes (Preliminary Draft)," the latter of which, he said, would be submitted, after trial implementation, to the NPC in 1980 for approval.

Highlighting the importance of China's small production teams operating under the communes, Hua said that their role as the "basic accounting unit" should be "protected," and he emphasized that "private" plots and rural free markets should be preserved for a "long period." He noted, and Yu discussed at some length, the regime's plans to increase the prices of agricultural and sideline products and to remit or reduce the agricultural tax and commune enterprise tax when conditions justified doing so. All three reports discussed Peking's plans for raising peasant incomes. Hua promised greater support for agro-scientific research and extension work and continued promotion of mechanization (though with less priority than in 1978) and emphasized the need for improved agricultural leadership and management, calling on county leaders to do a better job in "guiding" the communes. He promised further efforts at reclamation and farmland capital construction and an increase of acreage with "high and stable" yields.

In discussing industry, Hua said that for now "we must mainly rely on tapping the potential of large numbers of existing enterprises, renovating and transforming them and enabling them to reach or approach modern standards." He called for a speedup in the growth of light industry, again stressing that these industries "require relatively small investment and bring quick returns" and "satisfy the daily needs of the people and of foreign trade and accumulate funds [through profits and taxes] for modernization." He called for more effective measures to modernize light industries. Building new "key" plants in the light industrial sector should be accelerated, he said, but equally important, "greater efforts must be made to renovate and transform existing enterprises." He promised that successful light industries would be "guaranteed" the fuel, power, and raw materials that they need. He exhorted them to "turn out large numbers of top-quality, brand-name products to meet market needs at home and abroad."

Hua's discussion of heavy industry focused on overcoming existing "weak links." He admitted that there was "tension or even imbalance" in the coal industry between excavation and tunneling; new mines should be built, he said, and existing ones should undergo "technical transformation." He emphasized the need for increased geological surveying to discover new oil and other resources, and for a "rational balance between extraction and reserves" (that is, a slowing of the depletion rate). He also called for faster construction of both thermal and hydropower stations. (He did not mention nuclear power stations as he did in 1978.) There was particular urgency in Hua's call for energy conservation, which, he asserted, "will be for some years the most important and surest means of removing the pressure on fuel and power supplies." Roughly estimated, Chinese enterprises and transport and communications services now waste 20 billion to 30 billion kilowatt-hours of electricity a year (roughly 8 to 12 percent of 1978 output) and "tens of millions" of tons of coal, Hua said, and he called for all regions and departments to try to save 2 to 3 percent in their use of coal and electricity and 5 to 10 percent in their use of gasoline. He reported that China planned to pass an energy act "as soon as possible" and would enact "unified regulations concerning the allocation and supply of electricity."

Yu elaborated on many of these themes. He stated that power plants using oil would be converted back to coal as soon as possible, and all new enterprises would have to document the fact that on completion they would have an assured source of fuel and power. He also asserted that the unified distribution of electricity would be through power grids within and between provinces that would be controlled by the Ministry of Power Industry, which would ensure that power is available for the "best enterprises." Hua made a parallel statement: planning commissions at all levels, he declared, should "firmly halt the operations of those enterprises which, producing low-quality, overcostly, or unwanted goods, have long remained in the red," while supplies of fuel, power, and raw and semifinished materials should go to those that "produce urgently-needed, good-quality, low-cost products and yield large profits," so that they can "operate at full capacity."

The metallurgical industry, Hua stressed, should in general focus on qualitative upgrading rather than quantitative expansion in the immediate future. The steel industry in particular should aim at "improving quality and increasing variety and specifications" in order to produce more high-grade and alloy steels. Increases in output should be pushed mainly in the cases of nonferrous metals and steel products that are rare or in short supply. The machine-building industry "should do its utmost to produce more high-grade machinery," and the electronics industry should be "vigorously developed."

All the reports made to the NPC emphasized that in the immediate future the line should be held on investment, and, in fact, that "capital construction" should be cut to some degree. Hua specifically stated that "all localities and departments should . . . halt projects not urgently needed at present," and "priority should be given to the construction of key projects" in the weak sectors. "Concerted efforts" should be made, he said, "to shorten building times, reduce construction costs, and assure that all projects are completely up to required standards." It is necessary, he said, to "raise the proportion of increase in fixed assets to overall investment." (In passing, he stated that environmental problems must be taken "into account.")

Yu underlined these points. "We have far too many projects under construction, with unsatisfactory results," he said. "They have consumed a great deal of the country's financial and material resources without providing it with new production capacity in time. In order to concentrate our forces and raise the efficiency of our investment, we must make determined efforts to cut down the number of capital construction projects." Those already scheduled should be reexamined, and "construction must be terminated or put off in those projects which are not urgently needed by the state or where favorable construction conditions do not exist." Chang stressed the same theme. "Capital construction is too large in scale and spread over too many projects for the country's financial and material resources at present," he said, and there are "serious disproportions" and imbalances among sectors; "returns from investments are very unsatisfactory," and "the proportion of accumulation in the State revenues exceeds reasonable limits." He also declared, "In management, there is shocking confusion and waste in some production units and in some organizations."

While calling for a cutback in capital construction investment, all three men emphasized the need for expanded and better education and scientific and technical research and training, more effective use of pricing and incentives policy, and expanded trade and foreign economic relations; and they all gave some specifics on particular plans and policies in these areas.

Promising increased spending on science, education, culture, and health, they put special stress on the critical importance of "key" scientific research institutes and universities (and "key" lower-level schools as well). However, Hua also called for new efforts to eliminate illiteracy and universalize primary school education, which he said had been "on the point of completion" in the 1960s but had been "set . . . back many years" by the radicals' policies. He placed considerable emphasis on the need to expand secondary-level vocational schools, both to create new skills and to "help solve the unemployment problem for large numbers of middle school graduates."

Discussing structural and managerial change in the economy, Hua reported that "the departments concerned under the State Council" had already produced initial drafts or measures dealing with several "urgent" questions relating to the "restructuring of economic management," including trial regulations concerning "rewards and penalties for workers and staff," trial measures for the "enlargement of the power of decision of enterprises," measures for the gradual "replacement of investment by bank credits in capital construction," a preliminary program for "reform of the financial system," and regulations on foreign trade and foreign currency. After trial implementation and revisions, he said, these would be published by the State Council. Chang was specific in regard to one of the reforms. In November 1978, he said, the State Council had decided to initiate experimentally an "enterprise fund system," under which successful enterprises could keep a portion of their profits and use them for workers' welfare or other purposes. But, Chang admitted, "judging from experience during trial implementation, certain stipulations are not entirely suitable and need to be improved after further study."

After reiterating the Chinese leadership's desire to keep prices stable, Hua discussed the regime's intention to use price policy to increase incentives and promised continued efforts to raise both rural and urban living standards gradually, with priority to rural areas. Both he and Yu showed understandable concern, however, about some of the dilemmas the new policies would involve. Hua said that in early 1979 the State Council, implementing an earlier Central Committee decision, decided to raise the state purchase price of the main farm and sideline products. Yu revealed the details, stating that the decision was to raise the grain price by 20 percent for regular state purchase quotas and an additional 50 percent for above-quota grain. The average price increases for eighteen major farm and sideline products would be 24.8 percent, he said. Hua acknowledged that this would have some inflationary effects in the cities but argued that while some urban families would "unavoidably be slightly affected," those hurt would just be a "few," and "the actual living standards of the great majority of workers and staff and other urban inhabitants will not suffer."[270] The government, he said, has done "its utmost to allocate funds for improving the livelihood of workers and staff and the urban population in general," but resources allocated for this "cannot be very large," and "we hope our workers and staff and other urban inhabitants will understand." Yu promised that in 1979 urban wages would again be raised for "a part of the urban workers and staff." Commenting on the restored bonus system, Hua emphasized that bonuses should be based on merit, not offered to all workers at year-end. The SSB had revealed that "most" units gave year-end bonuses in 1978.

Hua showed concern about growing urban unemployment. The government is "very much concerned" about "the people waiting for work," he said, and would push a job-creating program. We "will try to multiply the opportunities for employment by efforts to develop handicrafts, repair and renovation services, commerce, service trades, fish breeding and poultry farming, restaurants, tourism, urban public utilities, parks, and public gardening and other undertakings. . . ." There was also a note of urgency in Hua's comments on population. The SSB claimed that by 1978 the rate of annual population growth had dropped to 1.2 percent (twelve per thousand), but it revealed that by year-end mainland China's total population was about 958 million (the total figure officially given was 975.23 million, including Taiwan). Hua, warning that the numbers of persons of marriageable age would be higher in the 1980s and 1990s, said that penalties as well as rewards would be used to reinforce family planning. The birth rate target he set for 1985 was 0.5 percent (five per thousand). Not long thereafter a Chinese official said the birth rate target for the year 2000 was zero.[271] (Although most of Hua's report concerned domestic problems and policies, he gave much more attention than in his 1978 report to trade and other foreign economic relations, which will be discussed in part II.)

Budget and Investment Shifts: Outlines of China's New Course

The reports delivered at the NPC provided a skeletal picture of China's economic situation and new policies; the flood of statistics released put flesh on the bones. In particular, the SSB's Communiqué on performance in 1978,[272] Yu's report on China's 1979 economic plan, and Chang's report on China's 1978 and 1979 budgets[273] gave quantitative content to the Chinese leaders' general statements.* (For details, see tables 1-3 and 1-4.)

The state budget provides a good starting point for examining recent trends in China's economy and Peking's priorities and policies. The published data show that in 1978 there was an enormous jump in both state revenues and state expenditures. This was possible because of the remarkable recovery during 1977–78 and reflected the regime's ten-

---

*The figures used in this discussion are drawn from the NPC reports and SSB Communiqué unless otherwise noted. Figures for 1978 and targets for 1979 were given by the Chinese in concrete terms; many of those for 1977 are inferred from statements about percentage increases over 1977. The figures are given in Chinese yuan rather than dollar equivalents because of the difficulty of determining valid dollar equivalents. For a discussion of this problem, see note 288. The yuan figures are extremely useful for analyzing trends and relative values within the Chinese economy, even though they do not provide a basis for international comparisons.

TABLE 1-3. *China: Official Data on Output, Budgets, and Investment (Value), 1977–79*

Item	1977[a] (actual)	1978 (actual)	1979[a] (plan)	1979 (actual)
National income; state finance				
National income (percentage increase)	8.0	12.0	...	7.0
National income (billion yuan)	...	315.0	...	337.0
Gross value of industrial and agricultural output (billion yuan)	(506.7)	569.0	(608.7)	617.5
Gross additions to fixed assets (billion yuan)	(26.0)	35.6	...	41.8
Investment in capital construction (billion yuan)[b]	(36.5)	47.9	(50.0)	50.0
Funded by state budget	(29.5)	39.5	40.0[c]	39.5
Funded by local sources	(7.0)	8.4	(10.0)	10.5
Distribution of state investment in capital construction (percent)				
Share of agriculture	...	10.7	14.0	...
Share of light industry	...	5.4	5.8	...
Share of heavy industry	...	54.7	46.8	...
State revenue (billion yuan)	(87.5)	112.1	112.0	...
State expenditure (billion yuan)	(84.4)	111.1	112.0	...
Industry				
Gross value of industrial output (billion yuan)	(372.8)	423.1	(457.0)	459.1
Heavy industry (percentage increase)	...	...	7.6	7.7
Light industry (percentage increase)	...	...	8.3	9.6
Agriculture				
Gross value of agricultural output (billion yuan)	(134.0)	145.9	(151.7)	158.4
Domestic trade				
Commodities purchased by commercial departments (billion yuan)	(156.6)	174.0	...	199.2
Manufactured goods	(115.3)	128.0	...	140.6
Farm produce and sideline products	(41.3)	46.0	...	58.7
Total retail sales (billion yuan)	(141.0)	152.8	175.0	175.3
Retail sales of major consumer goods (percentage increase)				
Pork	...	15.0	...	25.0
Sugar	...	19.0	...	9.3
Cotton cloth	...	4.3	...	3.6
Synthetic cloth	...	13.9	...	52.7
Machine-made paper	...	20.5	...	...
Coal	...	4.5	...	...
Foreign trade				
Total trade (billion yuan)	(27.2)	35.5	44.0	45.5
Exports (billion yuan)	(14.0)	16.8	19.2	21.2
Imports (billion yuan)	(13.3)	18.7	24.8	24.3

dency to set overly ambitious goals when it initiated its modernization program. In 1978 total state revenues (these figures cover only the central or national budget, not those of local governments) were 112.111 billion yuan (of which 45.100 billion yuan was from industrial and commercial revenue and 44.000 billion yuan was from state-owned industrial enterprises). Total state expenditures were 111.093 billion yuan. The increase over 1977 was huge—almost 28 percent.[274] Most came from income from state-owned industrial enterprises, which rose 35 percent; the rise in industrial and commercial revenue was 12.6 percent. Both increases reflected the rapid growth of China's industrial output in 1978.

The increase in state expenditures in 1978 was even larger. Central budget expenditures during the year rose a whopping 31.7 percent over 1977. (As a result, even though there was still a budget surplus of 1.018 billion yuan in 1978, it was smaller than the 1977 figure of about 3.158 billion yuan.) In short, China began its "four modernizations" program with an unrestrained spending spree.

While the 1978 figures reflected the economic surge that actually occurred that year, the planned budget for 1979 provided a good measure of the slowdown resulting from the reassessment of early 1979. The 1979 budget called for rigidly holding the line on expenditures. Both revenues and expenditures were scheduled to total 112.000 billion yuan—a level almost exactly the same as that of 1978.[275] In general, the figures showed that the 1979 budget for most major categories of state expenditures would be a tight one—at least by comparison with 1978.

The shifts in priorities and investment strategy resulting from Peking's readjustment policies are clear from the budget for expenditures in 1979. After the investment splurge of 1978, Peking decided to limit, perhaps even to cut, investment, though its figures were confusing.

Sources: State Statistical Bureau Communiqué, in Foreign Broadcast Information Service, *Daily Report—People's Republic of China*, June 27, 1979, pp. L11–L20; Yu Chiu-li, "Report on the Draft of the 1979 National Economic Plan," in FBIS, *Daily Report—PRC*, July 2, 1979, pp. L13–L18; and Chang Ching-fu, "Report on the Final State Accounts of 1978 and the Draft State Budget for 1979," in FBIS, *Daily Report—PRC*, July 3, 1979, pp. L6–L19; and SSB Communiqué, in FBIS, *Daily Report—PRC*, April 30, 1980, pp. L1–L10. Figures are rounded; therefore some totals differ from the sum of components and from figures in the text that are not rounded.

a. Figures in parentheses are derived from Chinese statements on percentage changes.

b. These investment figures are from Yu Chiu-li's report and the SSB Communiqué in 1980; see above and pp. 103, 113.

c. Including foreign loans used for capital construction.

TABLE 1-4. *China: Official Data on Industrial and Agricultural Output, 1977-79*

Item	1977 (actual)	1978 (actual)	1979[a] (plan)	1979 (actual)
Production				
Coal (million tons)	550.0	618.0	620.0	635.0
Crude oil (million tons)	93.6	104.1	106.0	106.2
Electric power (billion kilowatt-hours)	223.4	256.6	275.0	282.0
Rolled steel (million tons)	16.3	22.1	...	25.0
Pig iron (million tons)	25.1	34.8	...	36.7
Crude steel (million tons)	23.7	31.8	32.0	34.5
Timber (million cubic meters)	49.7	51.6	...	54.4
Cement (million tons)	55.7	65.2	...	74.0
Sulphuric acid (million tons)	5.4	6.6	...	7.0
Soda ash (million tons)	1.1	1.3	...	1.5
Caustic soda (million tons)	1.4	1.6	...	1.8
Chemical fertilizer (million tons of nutrient)	7.2	8.7	9.6	10.7
Insecticides (thousand tons)	457.0	533.0	...	537.0
Ethylene (thousand tons)	302.7	380.3	...	435.0
Plastics (thousand tons)	524.0	679.0	...	793.0
Chemical medicine (thousand tons)	35.2	40.7	...	41.7
Power generating equipment (million kilowatts)	3.2	4.8	...	6.2
Machine tools (thousand units)	199.0	183.0	...	140.0
Motor vehicles (thousand units)	125.4	149.1	...	186.0
Tractors (thousand units)	99.3	113.5	...	126.0
Hand tractors (thousand units)	320.5	324.2	...	318.0
Internal combustion engines (million horsepower)	27.4	28.2	...	29.1
Locomotives (units)	293.0	521.0	...	573.0
Freight wagons (units)	6,396.0	16,950.0	...	16,042.0
Steel ships (thousand tons)	634.3	865.9	...	809.0
Chemical fibers (thousand tons)	189.8	284.6	(300.0)	326.0
Cotton yarn (million bales)	12.3	13.3	...	14.7
Cotton yarn (million tons)	...	2.4	...	2.6
Cotton cloth (million meters)	10,151.0	11,029.0	...	12,150.0
Cotton cloth (million square meters)	...	10,286.0	...	11,430.0
Machine-made paper and paperboards (million tons)	3.8	4.4	...	4.9
Sugar (million tons)	1.8	2.3	...	2.5
Salt (million tons)	17.1	19.5	...	14.8

TABLE 1-4 (*continued*)

Item	1977 (actual)	1978 (actual)	1979[a] (plan)	1979 (actual)
Detergents (thousand tons)	257.0	324.0	(350.0)	397.0
Bicycles (million units)	7.4	8.5	(9.5)	10.1
Sewing machines (million units)	4.2	4.9	(5.3)	5.9
Wristwatches (million units)	11.0	13.5	(15.2)	17.1
Grain (million tons)	282.8	304.8	312.5	332.1
Cotton (million tons)	2.0	2.2	2.4	2.2
Oil-bearing crops (million tons)	4.0	5.2	...	6.4
Sugar cane (million tons)	17.8	21.1	...	21.5
Sugar beet (million tons)	2.5	2.7	...	3.1
Jute, ambary, hemp (thousand tons)	861.0	1,088.0	...	1,089.0
Silk cocoons (thousand tons)	216.0	228.0	...	271.0
Aquatic products (million tons)	4.7	4.7	...	4.3
Livestock (year-end number)				
Hogs (million head)	291.8	301.3	...	319.7
Sheep and goats (million head)	161.4	169.9	...	183.1
Large animals (million head)	93.8	93.9	...	94.6

Sources: SSB Communiqué, in FBIS, *Daily Report—PRC*, June 27, 1979, pp. L11–L20; Yu Chiu-li, "Report on the Draft of the 1979 National Economic Plan," in FBIS, *Daily Report—PRC*, July 2, 1979, pp. L13–L28; Chang Ching-fu, "Report on the Final State Accounts of 1978 and the Draft State Budget for 1979," in FBIS, *Daily Report—PRC*, July 3, 1979, pp. L6–L19; and SSB Communiqué, in FBIS, *Daily Report—PRC*, April 30, 1980, pp. L1–L10. Figures are rounded.
a. Figures in parentheses are derived from Chinese statements on percentage changes.

The Finance Minister, discussing the 1978 budget, said that total expenditures for capital construction (including local and reserve funds) amounted to 45.192 billion yuan, a huge 50.2 percent increase over 1977. Of this, he stated, 39.500 billion yuan came from the central state budget, while the rest—5.692 billion yuan—came from "regular reserve funds," local budgets' "standby financial resources earmarked for capital construction," and "other reserve funds put aside for capital construction."[276] In 1979, he said, "appropriations for capital construction" would total 39.000 billion yuan, of which 36.000 billion yuan would be "capital construction investments" (presumably this referred to central budget expenditures comparable to the 39.500 billion yuan figure in 1978) and 3.000 billion yuan from "reserve funds for capital construction." Whereas in 1978 the proportion of capital construction to total budget expenditures was 40.7 percent, in 1979 it would be reduced to 34.8 percent.[277]

Yu Chiu-li presented slightly different figures.[278] He stated that in 1978 central and local budgeted expenditures on capital construction totaled 47.900 billion yuan, of which 82 percent, or 39.500 billion yuan, was in the central budget (which he said was 34 percent above 1977), while 18 percent, or 8.400 billion yuan, was in local budgets (20 percent above 1977). Yu, like Chang, said that in 1979 capital construction investments from the central budget would drop to 36.00 billion yuan, but in addition there would be 4.000 billion yuan from "foreign exchange loans," so that the total central investment would be 40.000 billion yuan. Construction outlays by "localities and departments" would amount to an additional sum of "nearly" 10.000 billion yuan, he said, which seemed to imply that total central and local investment might be near 50.000 billion yuan. (His figures appeared to indicate that of planned investment in 1979, 72 percent would come from the state budget, 8 percent from foreign loans, and 20 percent from local budgets. The proportionate rise in the percentage from local budgets from 18 to 20 percent and the reliance on foreign loans were significant changes.) Yu stated correctly that "despite *reduction* [emphasis added], the scale of capital construction outlays is still fairly large." The figures did show that in 1979 there would be a cut in planned central budget allocations for investment, and a drop in their percentage of total state expenditures. However, it appeared that if investments financed by foreign loans were added, and if some increase occurred in local investments, as Yu's figures suggested was possible, the total of all investments from central and local budgets and foreign funds might be slightly higher than in 1978. What was clear, however, was that the regime decided in early 1979 to prevent any large rise in state investment comparable to that in 1978.

Equally important, China's leaders decided to modify investment priorities, raising the priority of agriculture and light industry and reducing that of heavy industry. The figures on budget allocations clarified the dimensions of this shift, which was significant, even though in 1979, as in previous years, capital-intensive heavy industry would continue to account for the bulk of total government investments.

Compared with 1978, the percentage of total state capital construction investment allocated to heavy industry was scheduled to drop in 1979 from 54.7 percent to 46.8 percent, while allocations to agriculture would rise from 10.7 percent to 14.0 percent and those to light industry from 5.4 percent to 5.8 percent. If the two years' capital construction investment totals to which these percentages should be applied are the 40 billion yuan figure for 1979 (including foreign loans) and the 39.5 billion yuan figure for 1978, which seems probable, but not certain, the figures indicated that in 1979 central state investments in heavy industry would drop by 2.887 billion yuan, or 13 percent, from 21.607 billion yuan in 1978 to 18.720 billion yuan. At the same time, central investments in agriculture would rise by 1.373 billion yuan, or 32 percent, from 4.227 billion yuan to 5.600 billion yuan (although Chang said *total* agricultural capital construction investments would be 7.800 billion yuan), and those in light industry would rise by 247 million yuan, or 12 percent, from 2.133 billion yuan to 2.380 billion yuan.[279]

The increases in investment in both agriculture and light industry, while not huge in absolute terms, were important. It is not easy to shift investment allocations rapidly. The jump in agricultural investment was particularly impressive. Nevertheless, the figures showed that despite the "deemphasis" of heavy industry, it would still account for close to one-half (46.80 percent) of total state (that is, central) investments in 1979 and would be 3.34 times as large as those in agriculture and 7.87 times as large as those in light industry.[280] (Because of the capital-intensive nature of heavy industry it probably will continue to absorb a high proportion of China's limited investment resources.)

Apart from investment, statistics on other major budget items relating to agriculture and industry throw further light on trends in China's economy and economic policy.

In 1978 16.778 billion yuan—or 15.103 percent of total state budget expenditures—were spent on the following, related to the operation of enterprises (mainly industrial): funds for "tapping the potential of enterprises and for their renovation," circulating funds, funds for geological surveys, and other "undertakings in industry, communications, and commerce." Although the Finance Minister gave no breakdown of how much went to each, probably a large part was for circulating (that is, operating) funds (which in earlier years generally came from sources other than the budget). He stated that by 1979 a "striking problem" emerged because in the previous year industrial enterprises obtained about 25 percent more circulating funds than they were entitled to, so that "huge sums in circulating funds are lying idle." The 1979 budget called for a cut in such funds to 4.300 billion yuan, but listed the three other allocations relating to the operation of enterprises: 600 million yuan for bank credits, 2.900 billion yuan for "tapping the potential of enterprises" and "transforming" them, and (what seemed to be a new budget line item) 2.700 billion yuan for "subsidizing the trial manufacture of new products." The four items totaled 10.500 billion yuan; if, as seems likely, this figure was comparable (despite a different classification) to the 16.778 billion yuan relating to enterprises in 1978, the 1979 budget called for a huge cut, probably mainly due to a reduction in enterprise circulating funds, despite new allocations to stimulate innovation.

The 1979 budget also called for a cut in funds for operating expenses allocated to agriculture, including the communes, from 7.695 billion yuan in 1978 to 7.050 billion yuan in 1979, but Chang went to great lengths to explain that "the total sum going to agriculture" would be larger than ever. He pointed out that if one adds to the 7.050 billion yuan figure for operating expenses the circulating funds for rural enterprises and social relief, 7.800 billion yuan for rural capital construction, and 2.550 billion yuan for agricultural loans, the funds going to agriculture in 1979 would total 17.400 billion yuan. With 7.000 billion yuan more, which increased state purchase prices for farm and sideline products plus tax reductions or remissions would add to rural incomes, he said, the total would be more than 24.000 billion yuan. "Never since the founding of the People's Republic has the state allocated such a big sum for agricultural expansion," he declared. The increase in funds going to agriculture was one of the most notable features of Peking's financial plan for 1979.

The rise in the defense budget was also striking, however, and raised a question as to whether military expenditures would escalate in the future, with adverse effects on China's long-term development program. Hua in his NPC report did not mention any increase in military spending (though he included modernization of national defense among the four modernizations). In fact, he stated that "after producing military supplies of the required quality and quantity, the defense industries should also strive to turn out more products for civilian use, especially consumer durables,"[281] which seemed to imply a deemphasis of military spending consistent with the priority given to "civilian" development in China's modernization program evident during 1977–78. However, the Finance Minister's budget report made clear that, in fact, following China's military incursion into Vietnam in early 1979, Peking had to increase its defense budget substantially.

In 1977, Chang indicated, China's defense budget amounted to 14.906 billion yuan, or 17.67 percent of total state expenditures. In 1978, it rose by 12.60 percent to 16.784 billion yuan. This increase was very modest in light of the 28.2 percent rise in total state expenditures in 1978, and as a percentage of the total budget, defense dropped to 15.11 percent. But, in 1979, Chang reported, the defense budget would increase by 3.446 billion yuan, or 20.53 percent, to 20.230 billion yuan, and rise to 18.06 percent of state expenditures. This was particularly striking because overall state expenditures were to be held at roughly the same level as in 1978, and centrally allocated investment was slated for cuts. The announced increase in the military budget was much larger than the increase in budgetary funds allocated for capital construction in light industry and agriculture. (These budget figures do not reveal total defense spending, much of which is excluded or hidden in other categories of expenditures, including that for capital construction. U.S. government analysts estimate that China's total military spending in many years has been close to 10 percent of GNP.)[282]

Chang did not give any breakdown of the military budget and provided little explanation for the reasons behind the large increase, but he did link it directly to the Vietnam incursion. "Last February and March," he said, "when our country was compelled to launch a limited counter-attack in self-defense against the aggression by Vietnam, there was some increase in military spending. In addition, our border defense needs to be strengthened. It is therefore reasonable that the proportion of our spending on national defense and preparations against war should increase, to some extent, its proportion in the total budget." The rise in the military budget therefore probably reflected a temporary jump in operating costs, not a trend toward an increase in overall military spending.

The question of how much China will feel compelled to spend on its military establishment will be a critical one in the period ahead. Although the distinction between military and civilian investment is not always clear-cut, it is an important one. To date, China's overall modernization program has clearly given highest priority to development of the civilian economy, and, despite the regime's commitment to military modernization, there had been little evidence of any significant rise in military procurement (although, after the cutback that had occurred in 1972, after the purge of Lin Piao, military procurement rose some). Since the start of the four modernizations, it appears to have had fourth priority.[283]

Peking's civilian-dominated top leadership has argued that to improve defense capabilities in the long run, it is essential first to build up the country's basic economy. While recognizing that some steps to modernize defenses immediately are vitally important, they indicate that far-reaching military modernization will be possible only when the country's economy is much stronger. (Although Chinese military representatives did a lot of window shopping for military equipment in Europe during 1978 and early 1979, they bought little.)[284] On the surface, the country's top military leaders appear to have accepted this argument (although doubtless they would like to have more, and debate on the issue has continued).[285] In some respects this is surprising, in light of the key role military men have played in Chinese society, their importance during the succession period, and China's need to improve its defenses against possible threats from the Soviet Union. Yet there is no question that because of China's limited resources, any big increase in military spending would tend to have adverse overall economic effects, probably slowing the pace of general economic development. The need to increase military spending in 1979 may help to explain the cutback in investment in heavy industry.

While it is not yet clear whether the increase was attributable primarily to the results of the Vietnam incursion, in which case the rise might be a temporary one, or whether it presaged a major shift in priorities, likely to continue for some time, probably it was the former. There had been no dramatic developments in bilateral Sino-Soviet relations in 1978–79 to intensify Chinese perceptions of any immediate Soviet threat sufficiently to justify a major urgent shift of resources to the military. Yet the possibility cannot be excluded that Chinese military leaders, who are acutely aware of China's military weakness relative to the Soviet Union, were able to capitalize on the Vietnam conflict (which highlighted some of the shortcomings of China's forces) to argue for greater budget allocations over an extended period. If the shift was mainly Vietnam-related and short term, which seems most likely at this point, the impact on China's ten-year plan as a whole may not be great. If, however, it signaled the start of a long-term change in priorities, the effects on China's economic development program could be serious.

Some other budget figures provided valuable indicators of the scale of various programs related to China's modernization. In 1978 expenditures on culture, education, health, and science (all lumped together in Chang's figures) rose by 24.9 percent to 11.266 billion yuan, or 10.14 percent of state expenditures. The budget for 1979 called for a further increase of 7.2 percent to 12.080 billion yuan, or 10.79 percent of state expenditures. This was a significant rise. These figures, moreover, covered only operating funds, not total relevant expenditures. Chang stated, for example, that in the field of science, if one adds to the budget figure (which covers only the operating expenses of the Academy of Sciences, the State Scientific and Technological Commission, and their affiliates) the capital construction funds allocated to these bodies and investments and operating expenses related to science made by other departments, the total would be 5.870 billion yuan, which he said was about 10 percent above the figure for 1978. (These figures, he said, did not include expenditures on scientific research in "grassroots units," because of a lack of statistics on such expenditures.)

The remaining expenditure figures presented by Chang were relatively minor in the total budget. In 1979 1.000 billion yuan was allocated to foreign aid, and 1.600 billion yuan for "regular reserve funds." He gave no figure for "administrative expenses," but the 1979 figure probably was about the same as in 1978, when it was 4.332 billion yuan, or 5.14 percent of total expenditures.

Economic Performance during 1977–78

During 1977–78 the Chinese economy recovered rapidly from the setbacks of 1975–76. The restoration of relative stability helped. This alone was responsible for many of the immediate gains. The shift from Maoist to pragmatic policies also began to have some immediate effects. Probably the most important stimulus, however, was the enormous 50 percent increase in capital construction expenditures in 1978. As a result of all these factors, the economy grew at a rate far above the long-term rate since the 1950s.[286]

According to official figures, China's "national income" grew by 8 percent in 1977 and 12 percent in 1978, and in 1978 totaled 315 billion yuan.[287] (Even though it is difficult to convert these national income figures accurately into dollar equivalents, there are reasons for concluding that they probably imply that China's GNP in dollars was close to the U.S. government estimates used throughout the study.)[288] In 1978 gross industrial and agricultural output (in value) increased by 12.3 percent to 569 billion yuan (national income is lower because it is calculated "net"). Gross industrial output grew 13.5 percent to 423 billion yuan, and gross agricultural output by 8.9 percent to 146 billion yuan. All these increases were far above long-term rates.

The detailed State Statistical Bureau figures released in 1979 provided the first official quantitative portrait of the Chinese economy since the 1950s. The data on Chinese industry showed big jumps in the output of key industries after 1976.[289] Major increases occurred in most heavy industries. Steel output soared by 33.9 percent, rising to 31.78 million tons in 1978, largely because of improved use of existing capacity. Coal output jumped by 12.4 percent, and in 1978 was 618 million tons; this increase was well above the long-term coal growth rate (but a good deal of the total may have been low-quality coal from small mines). Crude oil production increased by 11.1 percent to 104.05 million tons; this rise was below the long-term rate but comparable to that of the previous two to three years. Electricity output jumped by 14.8 percent, faster than the rate for all industry; in 1978 it was 256.55 billion kilowatt-hours. Cement rose 17.2 percent, well above the long-term rate, to 65.24 million tons. Increases in many other industries were also impressive (see table 1-4). There were exceptions, however. The output of machine tools dropped 8.0 percent to 183,000 units, and production of hand tractors rose only 1.2 percent, to 324,200, and internal combustion machines by only 2.8 percent, to 28,180. There were probably special reasons for these cases, however; the drop in machine tool output may have been due to reduced production of smaller and relatively ineffective tools, and the slow growth of hand tractors may have been attributable to a greater emphasis placed on larger units, the output of which rose 22 percent, to 113,500 units.

A large percentage of the 1978 production increases in heavy industries came from more effective use of existing plants and factories, but there were some additions to capacity. Altogether, 99 new large- and medium-size capital construction projects and 297 additional individual projects in such plants were completed and put into operation during the year; probably most were in heavy industry. Capacity added during the year included steel, 1.12 million tons; coal, 11.51 million tons; crude oil, 10.00 million tons; power-generating equipment, 5.05 million kilowatts; cement, 1.89 million tons; railway lines, 806 kilometers; and highways, about 35,000 kilometers. Extensive prospecting identified important new reserves, including 8.8 billion tons of coal and 2.2 billion tons of iron ore. More than 15 million meters of drilling was done, but no figure was given for new oil reserves discovered.

Major production increases also occurred in light industries. Output of cotton cloth increased 8.6 percent, to 11.029 billion meters; cotton yarn 8.1 percent, to 13.28 million bales (or 2.38 million tons); machine-made paper and paperboard 16.4 percent, to 4.39 million tons; and sugar 24.8 percent, to 2.267 million tons. The rise in production of certain consumer goods was even faster. The output of bicycles rose by 14.9 percent, to 8.54 million; sewing machines by 14.7 percent, to 4.865 million; and wristwatches by 22.4 percent, to 13.51 million. These increases, reflecting greater stress on incentives and living standards, were just the beginning of a sharp upward climb.

While the figures published revealed considerable progress in 1978, they also highlighted how far China has to go to modernize and raise living standards. To illustrate, China's per capita output of electricity in 1978 was less than 270 kilowatt-hours, compared with more than 10,000 kilowatt-hours in the United States. Its railways mileage, totaling just over 50,000 kilometers, equaled less than 1 kilometer for every 200 square kilometers of territory. And the annual output of bicycles amounted to one for every 112 persons, even though the bicycle is the principal form of mechanical transport for the average Chinese.[290]

The jump in agricultural output was even more impressive, compared with long-term growth rates. The 8.9 percent increase in the overall value of agricultural output was extremely high by past standards. It was due in large part to an impressive 7.79 percent increase in grain output to 304.75 million tons in 1978, a record level. Although this was not the largest annual increase since 1949 in percentage terms (for example, grain output is estimated to have increased 10.8 percent in 1966, 13.0 percent in 1970, and 10.8 percent in 1973) or, for that matter, in absolute terms (estimated output increased 28 million tons in 1970 and 26 million tons in 1973), it clearly was one of China's best years.[291] Some other crops—though not all—did even better than grain. The output of sugar cane increased by 18.9 percent, to 21.7 million tons; oil-bearing crops by 30.0 percent, to 5.218 million tons; and cotton by 5.8 percent, to 2.167 million tons (table 1-4). Only animal husbandry and the output of aquatic products lagged badly; the stock of hogs at year-end had increased by only 3.3 percent, to 301.29 million, and that of large animals by 0.1 percent, to 93.89 million. The output of aquatic products actually dropped by 0.9 percent, to 4.66 million tons.

Part of the increase in farm output in 1978 was due to steadily increasing use of modern inputs. The average amount of chemical fertilizer applied per hectare of farmland in China rose 39 percent, to 89 kilograms, and on the 4.3 million hectares of farmland sown with new hybrid rice, average output reportedly increased by more than 700 kilograms per hectare. (The increase in China's fertilizer output was 1.455 million tons, in nutrient, rising to 8.693 million tons; this alone probably accounted for a large percentage of the increase in grain output. New seeds accounted for a good deal of the rest; the claimed increase of yields on land sown with new hybrid rice alone amounted to more than 3 million tons.)

Official data revealed other accomplishments, and shortcomings, during 1978. Carrying out its new incentive policy, the regime raised the average annual wage of workers and staff in state enterprises by close to 7 percent, to 644 yuan in 1978. The overall increase in the wage bill for urban areas rose 10.49 percent, to 56.9 billion yuan. (The percentage increase in the total wage bill in urban collective enterprises was 12.36 percent, higher than in state enterprises; in such collectives total wages rose to 10.0 billion yuan, while in state enterprises the rise was 10.09 percent, to 46.9 billion yuan.) However, the increase of employment lagged seriously. The workforce in all enterprises rose only 4.25 percent, to 94.99 million, an increase of only 3.87 million jobs, in a year when population increased by almost 10 million. The regime claimed, though, that the productivity of workers in state industrial enterprises rose significantly, by 12.3 percent. This was the beginning of an encouraging trend.

Overall domestic trade increased at roughly the same rate as national income. In 1978 commodities purchased by state commercial departments increased by 11.10 percent, to 174 billion yuan; purchases of manufactured goods increased by 11 percent, to about 128 billion yuan; and purchases of farm and sideline products rose by 11.30 percent, to 46 billion yuan. Retail sales lagged behind national income, however, rising only 8.3 percent, to 152.75 billion yuan. (These figures revealed that in 1978 roughly 30 percent, by value, of industrial and agricultural and sideline products was distributed through the state commercial network.) Sales of some basic consumer goods increased more rapidly. Machine-made paper sold rose by 20.5 percent, synthetic cloth by 13.9

percent, pork by 15 percent, and sugar by 19 percent; consumer durables such as bicycles, wristwatches, sewing machines, radios, and television sets reportedly grew "even more rapidly." But some lagged: cotton cloth sales increased by only 4.3 percent and coal by 4.5 percent. The first signs of inflationary pressures also appeared in 1978. While the state's retail prices for most basics, including grain, edible oil, cotton cloth, and coal, reportedly were "stable," it was reported that the prices of some items such as vegetables and fruit "rose slightly."

Important advances were made in science and education. The number of institutions of higher learning increased from roughly 400 to almost 600. New enrollments in such institutions jumped by almost one-half to 400,000, raising the total number of students in institutions of higher learning from 620,000 to 850,000; those graduating in 1978 totaled 165,000. Despite showing progress, the figures on students at various levels highlighted the enormous task China faces in developing adequate high-level skills. In 1978, although China had 146.24 million primary school students and 65.48 million students in regular middle schools (plus another 880,000 in secondary technical schools), it had only 850,000 in institutions of higher learning (plus 550,000 in factory-run colleges and universities). In short, while most young children were enrolled in primary schools, fewer than one-half of their graduates could find places in middle schools, and only 1 to 2 percent of middle school graduates could be accepted into regular institutions of higher learning. While China, with close to a billion people, had less than 1 million students in regular institutions of higher learning in 1978, the United States, with roughly one-quarter of China's population, had approximately 12 million students in institutions of higher learning.[292]

1979 Slowdown and Future Prospects

China's rapid growth during 1977–78 was impressive but simply not sustainable. By late 1978 the economy was overheated and plagued by shortages and imbalances. Some slowdown was inevitable, whether planned or unplanned. The decisions made by Party leaders between December 1978 and mid-1979 to slacken the pace of growth deliberately, check the rise of investment, and alter priorities during a three-year "readjustment" were designed to make the slowdown orderly. The growth and production targets for 1979 unveiled by the State Planning

Commission in June revealed what Peking intended the readjustment to mean, quantitatively;[293] when the SSB published another communiqué at the end of April 1980,[294] the figures showed what had actually occurred. Overall, growth had slowed but was still fairly rapid. Clearly, the economy had considerable momentum. Performance in particular sectors did not exactly match the regime's targets, however; some goals were not fulfilled; others were exceeded. Many bottlenecks, which had been evident earlier, were highlighted. However, the figures showed that at least some of Peking's new policies—for example, those stressing the need for greater attention to consumer demands—were being seriously implemented. Although not a spectacular year economically, 1979 was not a bad year either. It appeared that in the face of great difficulties, the readjustment was under way, even though many questions about the future remained unanswered—and unanswerable.

According to the SSB's figures, national income rose 7 percent in 1979, to 337 billion yuan. The rate was well below 1978 and slightly below 1977 but was good nevertheless. The surge did not immediately turn into a crawl. Gross industrial and agricultural output rose 8.5 percent, to over 617 billion yuan. Gross industrial output grew by the same rate, 8.5 percent, to over 459 billion yuan. This was a large drop from the 13.5 percent achieved in 1978 but was somewhat above the plan for the year and close to China's long-term industrial growth rate. Gross agricultural output again increased unusually rapidly, by 8.6 percent, rising to over 158 billion yuan; this was not much below the 1978 rate and exceeded the original plan for the year.

These detailed figures on different sectors illuminated both the positive effects of China's new policies and the great problems they face. Moving Chinese society with its huge population and its swollen bureaucracies onto a new course will not be easy. The statistics showed, however, that the regime's shift of priorities in 1979 had produced results, though not all that were hoped for.

Despite Peking's calls for reining in state investment, "capital construction" expenditures totaled 50 billion yuan, which was what Yu Chiu-li had indicated it would be; according to the SSB, it was 4.4 percent above the comparable figure for 1978. "Fixed assets" provided to capital construction units, nationwide, totaled 41.800 billion yuan, a 17.4 percent increase. The number of large- and medium-size construction projects completed and put into operation also rose, totaling 128 major projects and 340 units within other large projects. By early

1980, leading Chinese officials and economists were publicly complaining about the difficulty of actually cutting back capital construction and urged a further reduction of national investment, at least as a proportion of national income.

The breakdown of the investment figures nevertheless revealed significant changes. While investment from the central budget was 39.500 billion yuan, the same as in 1978, capital construction by "departments, localities, and enterprises" rose 25 percent, to 10.500 billion yuan, a reflection of the regime's efforts to decentralize some economic decision making.

The shift of investment, to give larger shares to agriculture and light industry and less to heavy industry, was clearly reflected in the output figures for the year. According to the SSB's final figures, grain output rose by an impressive 9.0 percent, to 332.115 million tons (far above the plan for the year, which had called for a 2.54 percent increase). This claimed rate of increase was even above that in 1978, which had been an excellent year. There was some question about whether or not part of this rise was statistical rather than real—that is, whether or not it was due in part to better or more comprehensive statistical coverage (a month before the SSB report, a vice chairman of the State Planning Commission had said that 1979 grain output was 324.900 million tons).[295] Even if this was so, a significant rise doubtless occurred. The reasons were several. The effect on peasant incentives of a 22.1 percent overall increase in state purchase prices for farm products and the decentralizing of decision making to communes and work teams were important, as was good weather. But increased investments in (or related to) agriculture were unquestionably a significant factor in the grain output increase and the even more impressive 23.3 percent rise in output of oil-bearing crops, which totaled 6.435 million tons. The average amount of chemical fertilizer per cultivated hectare rose again, by 20 kilograms, or 22.5 percent, to 109 kilograms. Electricity consumed in rural areas increased 11.7 percent, to more than 22 million kilowatt-hours. The country's stock of large- and medium-size tractors rose by 20 percent, to 667,000; hand tractors by 18 percent, to 1.671 million; and power-driven irrigation and drainage machines by close to 9 percent, to more than 71 million horsepower.

Not all crops did as well as grain and oil-bearing seeds, however. Cotton output rose only 1.8 percent, to 2.207 million tons (even though China's state farms did better, increasing their cotton output by 8.9

percent). As a result, China was forced to increase its raw cotton imports and accelerate domestic production of chemical fibers. Sugar cane production rose only 1.9 percent, to 21.508 million tons (although sugar beet output, a secondary source for sugar in China, jumped 15 percent, to more than 3 million tons). Aquatic products actually dropped again by 7.5 percent, to 4.305 million tons.

The regime's determination to take immediate steps to stimulate incentives and respond to consumer desires in rural as well as urban areas was clear. The big increase in state purchase prices for farm products was the most notable indicator of this, but trends in the animal husbandry industry and meat production were another. China's stock of hogs rose 6.1 percent in 1979, to almost 320 million (roughly one hog for every three persons); and meat output (pork, beef, and mutton) rose a remarkable 24.1 percent, to 10.624 million tons. (Even with this rapid increase, however, per capita meat production was still only 11 kilograms, or 24 pounds, per person per year!)

The stress on both improving incentives and meeting consumer needs was strong in industry, too. Reversing policies pursued during the past three decades that had ensured that heavy industry would grow more rapidly than light industry, plans for 1979 had called for increases of 8.3 percent in light industry and 7.6 percent in heavy industry. Final statistics for the year showed that while heavy industry grew at roughly the rate called for, light industry grew even faster than planned. The actual growth rate in heavy industry was 7.7 percent (output rose to 261 billion yuan, which was 57 percent of the value of gross industrial output), while the rate for light industry was 9.6 percent (with output rising to 198 billion yuan, or 43 percent of gross industrial output).

The rates of increase in the most important consumer goods industries (and related heavy industries) were very impressive; in all but a few cases they were above 1978 as well as long-term rates, and most were above the original targets set for the year. Output of chemical fibers rose 14.4 percent, to 326 thousand tons; cotton yarn 10.5 percent, to 2.630 million tons; cotton cloth 10.2 percent, to 12.150 billion meters; machine-made paper 12.3 percent, to 4.93 million tons; and sugar 10.1 percent, to 2.5 million tons.

Consumer durable industries grew even faster. They were, in fact, the most rapidly growing sector of Chinese industry in 1979, as the following rates of increase in output indicate: bicycles, 18.1 percent; radio sets, 18.2 percent; sewing machines, 20.8 percent; wristwatches,

26.4 percent; cameras, 30.0 percent; and television sets, 157.1 percent. Their starting point was so low, however, that output of most remained tiny in relation to China's population. The 10.09 million bicycles, 13.81 million radio sets, and 17.07 million wristwatches produced amounted to roughly one of each of those items for fifty to one hundred Chinese. The output of 5.87 million sewing machines was enough, very roughly, for one per thirty to forty households. And the television sets and cameras produced, 1.329 million and 238,000, were about one per 730 persons and one per 4,000 persons, respectively. China certainly did not become a "consumer society" overnight. Nevertheless, the trend was significant.

There were other signs of the increasing stress on incentives and living standards. Total retail sales (by value) increased 14.7 percent in current prices (and 12.4 percent in constant prices). Retail sales of pork rose 25 percent; leather shoes, 26 percent; synthetic cloth, almost 53 percent; bicycles, sewing machines, radios, and watches, between 18 and 40 percent; television sets, 200 percent; and cassettes, 300 percent.

Heavy industry, starting with an enormously larger base, continued to grow, but at slower rates. The most notable slowdowns were in fuels and energy. Crude oil output grew at only 2.0 percent; coal, 2.8 percent; and natural gas, 5.7 percent (to 106.15 million tons, 635.00 million tons, and 14.51 billion cubic meters, respectively). The electric power industry did better, increasing output by 9.9 percent (to 282 billion kilowatt-hours), which was above the growth rate of all industry, but not by much. These relatively low rates were not unexpected; in fact, they were slightly above the original targets for the year. In 1979 Peking's planners stressed the short-run need in these fields to improve quality (for example, by producing more high-quality coal from large mines), intensify exploration, and create new capacity for future production increases. They also stressed conservation, and at year-end reported that fuel use per unit of output (by value) in the economy as a whole was cut 5.1 percent. Nevertheless, the energy situation remained tight.

Iron, steel, and cement output grew somewhat faster than energy sources did; pig iron grew by 5.6 percent, to 36.73 million tons; crude steel by 8.5 percent, to 34.48 million tons; rolled steel by 13.1 percent, to 24.97 million tons; and cement by 13.3 percent, to 73.90 million tons. In some cases the growth rate was faster than specified in the original plans, which called for little increase in output but improvement in the quality of products in these industries during the readjustment period.

(For example, the planners had called for steel production in 1979 almost exactly equal to 1978.)

The performance of other industries varied greatly. (For details, see table 1-4.) Important chemicals, plastics, and chemical fertilizers grew at relatively rapid rates—mostly between 10 and 20 percent. The production figures for some machinery and equipment rose at comparable rates, and a few items increased even more rapidly, but the output of others actually dropped. (For example, the production of large and medium-size tractors rose by 10.5 percent, and output of power-generating equipment by 28.4 percent, but machine-tool production dropped 23.5 percent.)

The planners' focus on creating new capacity in 1979 had some immediate payoff and was likely to have more in the future. For example, the capacity added during the year included almost 40 million tons of coal, 8 million tons of oil, 4.65 million kilowatts of power-generating capacity, and more than 2 million tons of steel.

What these figures showed was that despite the intended deemphasis of heavy industry, there was a considerable, almost built-in, momentum in the growth of some heavy industrial goods.

One of the fundamental dilemmas the Chinese already face, which will become increasingly difficult in the period ahead, is that they wish to—and need to—increase output in agriculture, light industry, and heavy industry simultaneously. Agriculture still provides the underpinnings for their entire economy, and increased output of consumer goods is essential to the success of their new incentives policy; yet expansion of heavy industries—especially those essential to the economy's basic industrial infrastructure—is also a prerequisite for the kind of overall modernization they envisage. With limited resources, the choices they face are not likely to become easier during the next few years.

The SSB figures and other statistics on 1979 also highlighted two problems that became very visible in 1978 and are likely to grow more serious in the period ahead: unemployment and inflation. The 7 million new urban jobs created[296] were roughly what had been planned, but fell far short of what was needed to cope with China's unemployed and underemployed; the new jobs amounted to just a little over half of the 12.83 million increase in population during the year. And the fact that SSB, for the first time, published an official figure on the average nationwide rise in retail prices—5.8 percent—was a sign of increasing official concern about inflation (which may actually have been higher than the SSB indicated, although it said its figure covered rural markets as well as all state prices and "negotiated" prices).

The SSB's statistics included another figure of importance: during 1979 worker productivity (per person output of workers and staff members) in state industrial enterprises again rose, by 6.4 percent, to 11,790 yuan. If correct, this figure was an encouraging sign that the regime's new policies aimed at raising efficiency were beginning to take hold. In Peking's overall modernization program, efforts to "restructure" and "improve" as well as to "readjust" and "consolidate" the economy are crucial. However, it was still too early to judge the likely long-term effects of their reform experiments. Approximately 3,000 key enterprises were designated "experimental enterprises" in 1979. The experience of these enterprises will have a major impact on future development policies, but so far outsiders know relatively little about them.[297] In March 1980 Chao Tzu-yang, who recently had taken charge of the "day-to-day work" of the government (according to Teng), discussed several of the concrete problems of successfully implementing these experiments and reforming the economy.[298] He placed special stress on the need for more realistic price policies (otherwise, he noted, giving more autonomy to enterprises to stimulate their initiative may have little effect, since profits and losses may simply reflect artificial prices, not actual performance). He also indicated that at least two more years of experimentation would be necessary before large-scale reform on the basis of current experiments would be desirable.

A number of other statements made by high Chinese leaders from the fall of 1979 through the spring of 1980 indicated that the "readjustment" period would almost certainly last more than three years, that long-term plans were still under debate, and that in the immediate future growth was likely to be somewhat slower than in 1979.

In September 1979 Teng told a group of Overseas Chinese that the readjustment period might be extended; this was the first authoritative indication of this possibility.[299] The Communiqué of the Party's Fifth Plenum in February 1980 revealed that the regime was still "working out a long-term program for development of the national economy, an economic system, educational plans, and an educational system suited to the needs of this development."[300] In January an article in the *People's Daily* had complained that in "the year since we started readjusting the national economy, the government has not formulated any interim or long-term program for economic development but only put forward the principal quotas to be achieved by 1985."[301] In April Li Jen-chun (Li Renjun), a Vice Minister of the State Planning Commission, stated that in 1980 China's gross industrial and agricultural output might grow by only 5.5 percent, with gross industrial output rising 6 percent and gross agricultural output 3.8 percent, all substantially below 1979 rates.[302] At about the same time, Hsu Ti-hsin (Xu Dixin), head of Peking's Economic Research Institute, asserted that because the readjustment had gotten a late start in 1979, it would continue at least through 1982 and possibly into 1983.[303] Chinese planners were still working on a ten-year plan covering 1980–89, he said, and were dividing it into two periods: 1980–82 and 1983–89. He also indicated that some of the regime's original targets for 1985—including the 400 million ton goal for grain production and the 60-odd million ton steel output target—might now be moved back to 1989 or 1990. During 1980 continued signs of bureaucratic confusion, policy debates, and new evidence that energy and grain supplies might become increasingly tight in the future suggested that China's rate of growth during the year might be even slower than Peking's planners had anticipated.

As of mid-1980, therefore, there were new uncertainties about just how much China could achieve, and how fast, in the first stages of its modernization program. Trends during 1978–80 underlined the difficulty of making predictions. Almost everyone, Chinese and foreigners alike, had been too optimistic in early 1978. By 1980 the mood was more sober, and the tendency both at home and abroad was not only more realistic, but in some cases pessimistic. However, it would almost certainly be a mistake to judge China's prospects solely on the basis of the immediate situation in 1980. The Chinese will continue to face serious problems and difficulties throughout the 1980s, and "readjustment" may in practice have to be an almost continuous process, as China wrestles with the multiple tasks of setting realistic priorities, evolving sound policies, and accommodating conflicting interests; and as the leadership, trying to overcome deep-rooted inertia and some inevitable opposition, attempts to inject a new dynamism into an economic system that has many built-in rigidities and suffers from serious shortages of capital and skills as well as of planning and managerial experience. There will be continued debate on basic questions: how much to allocate to investment and how much to consumption; how to divide investments and skills between agriculture and industry, and in industry between producer and consumer goods; how to divide economic resources between civilian and military needs; the degree and type of decentralization that should be implemented; and how far to go in mixing "market economy" elements and state planning.

Despite the problems and uncertainties, however, it seems clear that China's shift to a new, more flexible and pragmatic approach to national economic development is historic, and over time should enhance its prospects for sound, sustainable development. The readjustment should give the country a breathing period, providing an opportunity to lay more solid foundations for accelerated growth in the future. Many of the policies adopted during 1977–79 will almost certainly be implemented gradually in the period ahead. Whether or not they will guide China's development for the rest of this century remains to be seen; much will depend on actual results over the next few years.

To retain political support for present policies, Peking does not necessarily have to show dramatic results immediately. However, in time it clearly must achieve real economic progress that produces tangible benefits affecting the lives of average Chinese. The critical period may be the middle years of the 1980s. For the next two or three years, as Peking tries to build the foundations for more rapid growth, the payoff conceivably may be limited. But present policies probably will have to show significant results by the mid-1980s. Ultimately, both the policies and China's present leaders could stand or fall on the country's economic performance during this period. Whether or not the policies succeed will therefore have political as well as economic consequences.

Several key factors are likely to determine the degree of China's success. Its investment policy will be one, though by no means the only critical one. Another will be its ability to focus primarily on civilian rather than military goals. Equally important will be its ability to develop fairly rapidly the required human resources by training large numbers of competent personnel, some abroad, but mainly at home. Perhaps most important, the regime's success or failure in implementing reforms in planning, organization, and managerial practices to increase efficiency and productivity will be critical. There is no doubt that to encourage innovation and achieve self-sustaining growth, systemic changes in China's economy are necessary.

In light of all that is now known, what rate of overall economic growth is it reasonable to expect China to achieve during the period ahead? The rate doubtless will be well below the 8 to 9 percent rate initially defined as Peking's goal. However, it is plausible that with reasonable luck, following its current readjustment, China may be able to achieve average rates of growth averaging 2 to 3 percent or more in agriculture, 8 to 10 percent in industry, and 6 to 7 percent in overall GNP. Some analysts predict rates that are higher. Other analysts, less optimistic, predict a GNP rate averaging 5 to 6 percent.[304] Some would consider even this figure to be too optimistic. But it would be a mistake to underestimate the potential effect of the forces that the present Chinese leadership is now trying to release.

Saburo Okita, one of Japan's leading economic statesmen and planners, recently wrote, "China's economic programs over the next 20 years should be one of the great constructive developments in East Asian and, indeed, in world history.[305] For the first time, a Chinese leadership strongly committed to rapid modernization, and possessing an organizational apparatus capable of mobilizing the country's huge population and resources, is approaching development problems in an essentially experimental, pragmatic way.

What China achieves economically during the 1980s will depend fundamentally on domestic factors. However, more than at any time during the past two decades, its achievement will also be determined by the new foreign economic relationships that China is now developing. When Teng said in early 1980 that "China has now adopted a policy of opening our doors to the world" and "modernization would be impeded if we rejected international cooperation," he was doubtless right.[306] One of the most remarkable changes since Mao's death has been Peking's turning outward economically. Although this has been influenced by recent general trends in the international community, fundamentally it has been rooted in the changes that have occurred within China, which produced a new outlook and strategy of economic development. Peking's present leaders recognize that the success of their new economic policies at home will depend greatly, and probably in many respects directly, on the effectiveness of their new foreign economic policies. In the readjustment since 1979, this outward orientation has not been changed; in fact, it has been reaffirmed.

China's turning outward obviously has major implications for China's future; it also has important potential implications for the rest of the world. These implications will be examined in the rest of this volume. This will require an analysis in some detail of the changing character of China's overall trade and other foreign economic relationships, the opportunities and problems that these create for other nations, and the possible consequences not only for the Chinese but for the global community as a whole.

II

Trade and Technology Imports

DURING 1977–78 the shift in Chinese attitudes toward economic relations with the outside world was remarkable. Peking's (Beijing's) leaders initiated what some observers called a "great leap outward," adopting economic policies more internationally oriented than at any time since 1949. They decided to "join the world" economically because they recognized that rapid modernization of the kind they envisaged would require expanded trade and increased imports of plants, machinery, equipment, management know-how, and scientific and technical knowledge, especially from the advanced capitalist nations. This orientation contrasted sharply with that of the 1960s and early 1970s, when "self-reliance" had been stressed as one of the regime's fundamental principles. During 1974–75, just before the death of Mao Tse-tung (Mao Zedong), "self-reliance" had become one of the hottest subjects of debate between China's radicals and pragmatists.

Debate over "Self-Reliance"

Despite the fact that self-reliance was one of the fundamental principles underlying China's policy, and had been ever since 1960, Chou En-lai (Zhou Enlai) and other leaders who shared his view that increased trade was a necessity began to take steps in the early 1970s to expand the country's foreign economic relations,[1] but their moves were opposed by China's top radicals.[2] Then, in early 1974, after his comeback as Chou's principal deputy, Teng Hsiao-ping (Deng Xiaoping) started to hint of policy changes. In a speech to the United Nations General Assembly in April, while reiterating old slogans, he asserted: "self-reliance in no way means 'self-seclusion' and rejection of foreign aid."[3] In July, Li Chiang (Li Qiang), Minister of Foreign Trade, declared that "it is necessary for China's foreign trade to develop in steady steps." (He still, however, opposed the idea of accepting foreign loans or developing joint ventures.)[4]

The radicals were not long in responding to signs of change in foreign economic policy. In August 1974, "Down with Underestimation of Oneself," an article published in the radicals' Shanghai (Shanghai) journal, *Study and Criticism*, strongly denounced plots "to worship things foreign and sell out the country."[5] "To view foreigners as a hundred percent perfect and ourselves as totally incompetent," the article said, "is a spiritual shackle." The authors, writing under a pseudonym, declared that "we have firm faith in the strength of the masses of the people, and we are convinced that by maintaining independence, keeping the initiative in our own hands and relying on our own efforts, we shall be able to rapidly develop our science and technology and change China's outlook."

Despite the opposition, Teng began in 1975 to formulate concrete changes in foreign as well as domestic economic policies. A document outlining ways to speed up China's industrial development (one of the three major policy statements drafted under Teng's supervision and circulated at that time within the Party) stated, "In catching up with industrially advanced countries, the industrially backward countries invariably rely on adoption of the most advanced technology"; the statement stressed that China must "learn with open-mindedness all advanced and good things from foreign countries," and "usher in advanced techniques from abroad in a planned and selective manner."[6] To do this, it said, China must "export as much as possible." The document called for the industrial sector to "aggressively increase production of items that can be exported," and it endorsed contracts with foreign companies to help develop China's coal and petroleum—contracts under which China would "pay back [for equipment imported] with the coal and petroleum produced." A plan for the development of science and technology, drawn up in the fall of 1975, also argued strongly for "learning the good points of foreign countries" and advocated greater study of experience abroad, increased gathering of scientific and technical information, more foreign language study, and expanded contact with the international scientific community.[7]

The radicals counterattacked with a salvo of polemical blasts. An article in August 1975, titled "Self-Reliance Is a Question of Line,"[8] stated:

For more than the last two decades, the struggle centering on adhering to or opposing the line of independence and self-reliance has been very sharp. Out of their sinister efforts to subvert the dictatorship of the proletariat and restore capitalism, Liu Shao-chi [Liu Shaoqi] and Lin Piao [Lin Biao] frenziedly hated and stubbornly opposed this line. They vainly tried to sell out state sovereignty and once again bring "wolves" into our country, frantically advocating servility to things foreign and the doctrine of trailing behind at a snail's pace. ... To achieve real success by following the spirit of independence and self-reliance, it is necessary to continuously deepen the criticism of servility to things foreign and the doctrine of trailing behind at a snail's pace, both of which have their deep social and historical roots in China and still poison the minds of a section of the people today. ... We should ... give full prominence to the spirit of independence and self-reliance. ... Learning from foreign countries must be combined with a spirit of independent creation. It is wrong to imagine that foreign technology is flawless.

The same month, "Liang Hsiao (Liang Xiao)" (a pseudonym used by the radicals), in an article, "Comment on Lin Piao's Philosophy of National Betrayal,"[9] called for a long struggle against the "revisionist line of capitulation, national betrayal and fawning upon foreign powers and admiring foreign things." "Liang" argued, "Should we admire and cherish blind faith in foreign things and, believing that 'the moon abroad is rounder than China's,' rely on others in doing everything, we would lose our political and economic independence and again become a colony or semi-colony." In October a long article titled "The Yang Wu [Yangwu] Movement and the Slavish Comprador Philosophy," by the same group, again using the name "Liang Hsiao," put the debate in historical perspective, linking it to the nineteenth century movement to learn foreign technology while protecting the essence of Chinese culture.[10] The proponents of that movement were actually "the first group of slavish compradors" to hold power in modern China, and they "sold out the national interests and compromised with and capitulated to foreigners," the article asserted; "they could only copy from other countries and rely on foreigners in every way possible." Subsequently, it said, others advocated a similar line. It accused Hu Shih (Hu Shi), for example, of advocating "wholesale Westernization," in order to undermine "the national consciousness of the Chinese people." Liu Shao-chi and Lin Piao were no better, the article stated. Liu, it charged, had said that "our door is open to all" and "if in [the] future imperialism should come to China to open mines and factories, share the profits with us on an equal basis and work to our mutual advantage, it may be permitted to do so."

By April 1976, after the radicals had engineered Teng's second purge, they zeroed in on him by name as the major focus of their attacks. In an article titled "Thoroughly Criticize the Slavish Comprador Philosophy Publicized by Teng Hsiao-ping,"[11] the authors of the 1974 article "Down with Underestimation of Oneself" strongly attacked Teng ("the biggest unrepentant capitalist-roader"), saying that he "fundamentally denied that we could rely on our own strength to realize the four modernizations" and "again and again advocated relying on exports to secure imports for the development of industry, and made an exaggerated description of the technology and equipment introduced from other countries." This kind of policy, the authors said, "will only lead to the sinking of China once again into the status of an economic satellite of imperialism." In August an article attacked Teng for putting forward the "so-called 'major policy' under which China would sign 'long-term contracts' with foreign countries, with the foreign capitalists supplying the 'most up-to-date and the best equipment' to be 'paid for' by China with its mineral products. This 'major policy,' " it said, "was purely a policy of out-and-out capitulation and national betrayal."[12]

There were numerous other articles elaborating on these themes. At the time many observers thought that the radicals' charges were extravagant, but soon after the purge of the Gang of Four China's new leaders rapidly shifted away from self-reliance, precisely in the ways that the radicals had attacked Teng for advocating, and a flood of articles appeared denouncing the radicals' views. When the 1956 article by Mao Tse-tung, "On the Ten Major Relationships," was published for the first time, commentaries on it pointed out that he had asserted that "our policy is to learn from the strong points of all nations and all countries." (Mao also had said, however, that "we mustn't copy everything indiscriminately.")[13] In January 1977 an article strongly denounced the recently purged Gang of Four for their "organized, planned and premeditated wild attack against foreign trade over the issue of our country's oil exports."[14] It gave details on how the radicals had obstructed China's foreign economic relations and declared, "We are using exports to obtain needed materials in return and to import needed equipment and technology in an effort to implement the principles of 'making foreign things serve China' and combining learning with creation," to enhance China's "ability to build socialism with independence, initiative, and self-reliance and accelerate the socialist construction." The radicals had acted "against the tide of history," it said, by preaching an "isolationist policy." In February, another major article, titled "Foreign Trade: Why the 'Gang of Four' Created Confusion," gave additional details on the radicals' obstructionism and further argued the case for expanded trade.[15]

Similar articles were published throughout 1977, and increasingly they stressed the need for China to adopt an ambitious, flexible technology acquisition policy and to learn foreign management techniques as well as to expand trade. An article in July, "Self-Reliance and Making Foreign Things Serve China—Notes on Studying Chairman Mao's 'On the Ten Major Relationships,' "[16] asserted: "Every nation and country as it develops is bound to absorb and make use of, to a greater or lesser degree, scientific and technological achievements of other nations and countries. . . . Presumptuous conceit and blind rejection of all things foreign are anti-Marxist and unscientific. . . . We dare to put forward the slogan of learning from foreign countries precisely because we have full confidence in our own country."

In October an article by the Mass Criticism Group of the State Planning Commission titled "Why Did the 'Gang of Four' Attack 'The Twenty Points'?" argued strongly not only for increased imports of "advanced techniques" and "complete sets of equipment" but also for "the usual practice of deferred payment or payment by installments," and by increased exports of commodities such as coal and oil.[17] A radio "talk" in the same month, titled "Do We Need to Import Advanced Technology?"[18] asserted:

Rather than negating the principle of self-reliance, learning from foreign countries' fine experience and emulating other people's good points and importing the needed technology and equipment from abroad will strengthen our capability to develop our economy through self-reliance. . . . With regard to foreign countries' scientific and technological achievements that the Chinese people do not have at present, we should use them as much as possible. . . . We must seize the present good opportunity and race against time to develop and strengthen our country by adopting various methods, including learning from the strong points of all countries.

Another radio "talk" in November quoted Teng as saying, "We should consider the modern advanced world level as a starting point and honestly and humbly study all advanced sciences and technology and create new things in the study."[19]

From early 1978 on, official statements endorsing the new policy of turning outward were made by many of China's top leaders. After Hua Kuo-feng (Hua Guofeng), in his February 1978 report to the Fifth National People's Congress (NPC), had declared that "there should be a big increase in foreign trade" (China, he said, "should build a number of 'bases,' for supplying industrial and mineral products and agricultural and sideline products for export"),[20] others soon made longer, more specific, and stronger statements and began to spell out some of the details of the regime's new policies.

At China's National Science Conference in March, Teng declared:[21]

A person must learn from the advanced before he can catch up and surpass them. Of course, to raise China's scientific and technological level we must rely on our own efforts, develop our own inventions, and adhere to the policy of independence and self-reliance. But independence does not mean shutting the door on the world, nor does self-reliance mean blind opposition to everything foreign. Science and technology are a kind of wealth created in common by all mankind. . . . It is not just today, when we are scientifically and technically backward, that we need to learn from other countries; after we catch up with the advanced world levels in science and technology, we will still have to learn from the strong points of others. . . . We must actively develop international academic exchanges and step up our friendly contacts with scientific circles of other countries.

Fang Yi (Fang Yi), the Poliburo's specialist on science, called for a plan to send many Chinese technical personnel abroad for study and work, the strengthening of cooperation with other countries to learn about their scientific and technical research *and* their "experience in organization and management," and the inviting of foreign experts and advisers to teach and work in China.[22] In June 1978 at a National Finance and Trade Conference, Vice Premier Li Hsien-nien (Li Xiannian), criticizing those who favored "some kind of self-contained or semi-self-contained economy," asserted that "we are going to use up-to-date science and technology to transform step by step all the sectors of the national economy"; this, he said, requires greater specialization and division of labor and a widening of the area of exchange at home as well as "exporting more for more imports of advanced technology and equipment."[23] In October Hu Chiao-mu (Hu Qiaomu) went further in his advocacy of learning planning and management techniques from capitalist countries, beyond simply importing equipment and technical know-how from them.[24] "The planned management and other management systems within capitalist factories in the early years have now been developed into a modern, highly efficient planned management and other management systems of the big companies," he said; they act "according to objective laws of economy" and have "rich experience in using these laws skillfully." Hu cited Lenin to support the view that Communists must "learn from the bourgeoisie" and from "first-rate capitalist experts."

Lenin's name was also invoked to support joint ventures and borrowing abroad. An article titled "How Did Lenin View the Introduction of Advanced Technology and the Admission of Foreign Capital?" said that Lenin "held that the best of the workable methods [to develop the Soviet Union's economy] at that time was to admit foreign capital and use it to stimulate domestic industry,"[25] and "Lenin and Stalin adopted a series of important measures to quickly develop the socialist economy, to effectively use external factors, and to acquire foreign capital and advanced technology." These measures, it said, included acquiring foreign capital through loans, importing large quantities of machines and equipment, concluding contracts for foreign technical assistance, hiring foreign technicians and experts to work in the Soviet Union, and sending people abroad for study and inspection tours. These measures also included organization of "joint companies" with "foreign capitalists" (the Soviet Union holding at least 51 percent of the shares) and granting "leases" and "concessions" to foreign capitalists willing to develop mines, forests, and oil fields in the Soviet Union. "Lenin's ideas on acquiring advanced technology and foreign capital did not fully materialize," the article stated, but "judging by those which did materialize, his ideas played a great role in socialist construction in the Soviet Union." Publication of this article was the first indication that China's leaders were considering conventional borrowing abroad.

In the same month an article titled "What Is the Difference Between a Name and Reality?"[26] asserted that "advanced capitalist enterprises run their businesses well and with high efficiency, although they employ few men." It continued:

This shows they adopt scientific management methods. If we learn to apply them systematically, they will be conducive to improving our work. However, scientific management was once given the very unpleasant name "bourgeois control, restriction, and repression." If you learned from foreign technology, you would be accused of "restoring capitalism." It is obvious that learning from foreign technology does not harm state sovereignty but is beneficial to socialist construction. But the fear of such accusations as "national betrayal" and "capitulationism" compelled us to follow the path of the "gentleman of ancient time.". . . All we ask about these things is whether they are advanced and whether they are useful to the proletariat. We don't care what the Gang labelled them. Practice has already proved that the results of introducing things foreign are good and that we have not become "foreign slaves" because of them. This being the case, we should not be afraid of being this or that. . . . Practice is the only way to decide whether a name is supported by facts.

(What the Gang of Four really favored, the article said, was "socialism of poverty.")

In December an article titled "Importing Technology Must Not Follow 'A Single Pattern' " analyzed in a fairly sophisticated way the country's need for greater flexibility in considering all the available means to import technology.[27] China should continue importing "complete sets of equipment," as in the 1950s, it said, but by no means should it rely on this method alone, because it is very expensive and "is not likely to help raise the levels of domestic research and production" and because it does not necessarily transfer knowledge of "the technological processes essential to manufacture" (including "basic designs and vital aspects of production technology").

The article pointed out that some countries have "practically discontinued" complete plant imports and Yugoslavia, Rumania, and Japan have "focused on acquiring technology and other more advantageous approaches," such as "securing franchises for manufacturing certain lines of equipment or collaborating in designing and producing them," thereby raising their level of "scientific research, designing, and manufacturing facilities." These countries, it said, have speeded their development "by combining acquisition of technology with facilities for production, supply and marketing, importing with exporting, and new enterprises with old enterprises after they have been renovated." It stressed that in technology acquisition there are many different "options in contracting, processing, and assembling operations for joint production, in jointly financed operations, compensatory trading, and so on" and in "cooperative arrangements whereby the interested parties may conduct research and produce designs together or form engineering or designing firms on a partnership basis." There are also, the article pointed out, various other "channels" through which technology is transferred, including "sending experts and qualified people abroad for training, participating in academic conferences and technological study groups, holding forums and exchanging papers and technical information, and so on," and "there are different forms of payment." The author was impressed in particular by the experience of Japan which, he said, had spent $5.8 billion from 1950 to 1975 importing more than 26,000 "technological items," as a result of which Japan "overtook and surpassed developed capitalist countries in Europe and America."

As these official statements and articles showed, during 1977–78 China's leadership basically reversed the trend of the previous decade and a half, rejected the old self-reliance doctrine (without, however, abandoning it as a long-term goal), and called for flexible foreign economic policies aimed at significantly broadening China's links with the world economy.

In mid-1979 the report delivered by Hua Kuo-feng to the National People's Congress made clear that even if latent opposition continued, as it doubtless did, the new "open door" policy was viewed by Peking as essential to China's modernization and would continue despite the "readjustment" of overall economic plans. Although Hua's report to the 1978 NPC session had said relatively little in detail about trade and other foreign economic relations, his 1979 NPC report placed great stress on them.[28] "Economic exchanges between countries and the import of technology are *indispensable major* [emphasis added] means by which countries develop their economy and technology," he said; "we must work hard to learn all that is worthwhile learning from foreign countries, selectively import advanced technology of which we are urgently in need, and not wall our country off from international exchanges." Hua indicated that Peking's reassessment had resulted in less change in foreign economic policy than in domestic policy and that efforts to expand trade rapidly would continue. "Both in the 3-year period of economic readjustment and in *subsequent years* [emphasis added]," Hua stated, "we shall be taking energetic steps to develop foreign trade, expand economic cooperation and technical exchange with foreign countries, and employ various appropriate means, current in international practice, to absorb funds [that is, borrow] from abroad."

Hua asserted that the "planned import of advanced foreign technology and the use of funds from abroad do not stand in contradiction to our country's policy of readjustment"; instead, they are essential "to strengthen the weak links in our economy and transform and improve our existing enterprises." In particular, he said, "if conducted in a rational way, our cooperation with foreign countries in production technology, compensatory trade, and joint investment enterprises will promote the restructuring, consolidation, and improvement of our enterprises"; this will require, however, "organizing vast numbers of technicians and workers to study, assimilate, and master advanced foreign technology." He stressed that "while it is important to import the essential complete sets of equipment [plants], it is even more important to bring in advanced manufacturing technology and skills." To be able to afford this, he stated, "we must raise our ability to pay," and the "major and most reliable approach is a vigorous expansion of exports." "Each and every department," he stated, should "draw up short-term and long-term export plans." China also should make a major effort to expand tourism and other exchange-earning activities.

Yu Chiu-li (Yu Qiuli) also dealt at length with foreign economic relations in his report to the 1979 NPC, reinforcing many of the points Hua had made but paying more attention to the problems involved.[29] He indicated that although a big push would be made to expand both exports and imports, there would have to be some adjustments in import policy. "The import of new technology and of complete sets of equipment must be preceded by proper investigation and study" and "in an orderly way," he said, emphasizing that the "purchase of manufacturing technology should be stressed and that of complete sets of equipment minimized." "Priority should be given," he stated, "to those projects which require less investment, produce quicker results, and earn more foreign currency, and this work must be combined as far as possible with the transformation of existing enterprises."

While the plan called for a large increase in imports of capital goods and technology (and an "appropriate increase in the import of general and consumer items"), Yu said that "nothing should be imported that can be made and supplied at home," and all departments and localities applying "for import of new technology and equipment" must "present plans for repayment of the sums of foreign currency involved and must make sure that they can manufacture necessary accessories in China." "We must increase foreign currency earnings by *every possible means* [emphasis added]," he declared, and, like Hua, he stressed the responsibility of all "departments and localities" in this respect and urged more efforts to earn exchange from "non-trade channels."

To increase exports, he called for more "flexible forms" of trade; a policy giving priority for fuel, power, and materials to plants producing for export; and greater efforts to improve the quality and variety of export products tailored to sell in "the international market." China should also "develop tourism in a big way" to increase foreign exchange earnings, he said. He added that China "should do more processing and assembly," as well as compensatory trade and cooperative production, and "should initiate joint ventures with Chinese and foreign investment." (To facilitate trade expansion and increased imports of technology, the NPC adopted a new law on foreign investment formally authorizing the formation of joint enterprises; the law was fairly general, but the Chinese said that the State Council was working on detailed regulations and measures.)[30]

Great Leap Outward during 1977–79

Peking's decision to turn outward produced results almost immediately. By 1978 the Chinese were expanding their overall trade and technology imports rapidly and experimenting with numerous approaches and methods that had been taboo before 1977. It was evident that they were, in a sense, "throwing away the book," abandoning old inhibitions and adopting—or at least experimenting with—a wide variety of means to obtain and pay for the plants, equipment, technology, and other imports that China needed.

During 1977 the Chinese had begun sending large numbers of technical missions and trade representatives to virtually all the major industrial nations to investigate possible imports and potential suppliers. In addition, unprecedented numbers of foreign businessmen were invited to China to brief the Chinese on their products and services.[31] As it turned out, however, 1977 was a year of preparation rather than dramatic action. Peking's trade experts were laying the groundwork for an import program of unprecedented scope, but they were not yet ready to start buying on a large scale. American estimates show that China's foreign trade rose from about $13 billion (in 1976) to roughly $15 billion (in 1977), an increase of between 13 and 14 percent; but this rise was merely a prelude to the spectacular jump soon to come.[32]

During 1978 Chinese activity on the world market suddenly exploded. According to U.S. estimates, overall trade increased by close to 40 percent (in current prices), from about $15 billion (in 1977) to roughly $21 billion, with imports (cost, insurance, freight [c.i.f.]) increasing by 56 percent, from $7.1 billion to $11.1 billion, and exports (free on board [f.o.b.]) rising 26 percent, from just under $8 billion to $10 billion.[33] China entered into serious negotiations with thousands of foreign corporations and businessmen and indicated a strong interest in importing literally tens of billions of dollars worth of capital goods and technology. During the year the Chinese also signed some important general trade agreements with major capitalist nations, each of which established a framework for trade. Month after month, particularly during the second half of 1978, dozens of huge "deals" were reported by the Western press; some involved enormous potential sales (in billions of dollars) of machinery, equipment, technology, and services.

Many of the reports were misleading, however. Often those writing them failed to distinguish between firm purchase orders (embodied in concrete contracts) and letters of intent, general agreements, protocols, initialed agreements, negotiations, or simply expressions of possible interest by the Chinese. Others focused less on the size of immediate commitments (which were often for preliminary start-up work and therefore relatively small) than on huge deals that might result but were by no means certain. Often little information was given on the time period involved, and it was difficult to judge how large the year-to-year purchases and deliveries might be. Estimates of the value of the complete plants China actually purchased during 1978 therefore varied considerably.

A U.S. government study estimated in early 1979 that during 1978 Chinese negotiators had probably actually signed contracts for close to $7 billion of complete plants and had indicated an active interest in purchases of plants, equipment, and related technology that conceivably could total (if they were eventually consummated) about $40 billion.[34] A large percentage were in the fields of metallurgical and petrochemical plants. Contracts for petrochemical plants totaled more than $3 billion, and those relating to iron and steel amounted to close to $3 billion. (The schedules for deliveries were not clear, however, and, as will be noted below, in the spring of 1979 some deals, including the largest one in the field of steel, were temporarily suspended, to be renegotiated.) The study stated that plant purchases under "discussion" were allocated roughly as follows: steel, $22 billion; coal and electric power, $6 billion; transportation equipment, $4 billion; nonferrous metals, $1.5 billion; agricultural machinery and chemical plants, $600 million; and equipment and services relating to petroleum and gas, several billions of dollars. (The Chinese also negotiated for possible large-scale purchases relating to communications, electronics, and instruments, but the study provided no dollar estimates for these fields. Machine-building equipment and facilities being discussed were said to total only about $70 million, a low figure, doubtless because of China's substantial domestic capabilities in this field.)

Some estimates were even higher (but these clearly overstated the total of firm contracts). A National Council for U.S.-China Trade

(NCUSCT) study, which attempted to aggregate all reports of contracts known to have been signed or under negotiation by the Chinese during 1978, estimated that China's signed contracts for foreign purchases of plants, machinery, equipment, steel, and grain totaled close to $17.5 billion and that the Chinese had discussed deals that could eventually total $43 billion or more.[35] Another calculation made by the same organization in the spring of 1979 indicated that purchases of plants, machinery, and technology under contracts actually signed by China in 1978 (for delivery over several years) totaled $11.4 billion (not counting the $2.6 billion temporarily suspended in the spring) and that other deals, perhaps totaling $52 billion to $59 billion, were still "under negotiation."[36]

NCUSCT's breakdown of its $11.4 billion figure by broad categories indicated that Chinese purchases of plants, machinery, and technology during the year were allocated roughly as follows: iron and steel, $0.1 billion (with, however, roughly $2.6 billion more signed in late 1978 but temporarily suspended in early 1979); coal, $4.0 billion; other mining and processing equipment, $2.4 billion; port development, $2.1 billion; petrochemical plants and equipment, $0.5 billion; hotels, $0.5 billion; shipping, $0.5 billion; petroleum-related items, $0.4 billion; electronics, $0.3 billion; agriculture-related plants and equipment, $0.1 billion; power development, $0.2 billion; and construction plants and equipment, $0.2 billion. In the breakdown of the estimated $52 billion to $59 billion under "negotiation," by far the largest categories were planned investments related to steel, estimated at $19 billion (this was before Peking's economic "readjustment" of 1979), and transportation, $11 billion to $16 billion, although the estimates for at least four other fields totaled $3 billion or more each: mining (coal and other), $6 billion; petroleum, $3 billion to $5 billion; power development, $3 billion; and Western-built hotels (to encourage tourism), $3 billion. Subsequent developments showed that many of these estimates were much too high.

One important development during 1978 was the signing by the Chinese of several broad "framework" agreements with Japan and the European Economic Community (EEC) and with several governments within the EEC. In February China concluded a long-term agreement with Japan covering the years 1978–85.[37] It called for $20 billion in two-way trade, $10 billion each way. China's imports during this period (mainly during 1978–82) were to consist of perhaps $7 billion to $8 billion of plants and technology and $2 billion to $3 billion of machinery and construction materials. China's repayments were to be made largely with oil (the hoped-for amount being 47 million tons) and coal (8 million to 9.5 million tons). In March 1979 the accord was extended to cover the years through 1990, and the amount of two-way trade called for was substantially raised, reportedly to $40 billion to $60 billion.[38] A Japanese source estimated that during 1978 China actually signed contracts for $6.043 billion in plant purchases from Japan and another $1.303 billion in 1979 (and by early 1980, $3.863 billion were "in effect").[39] One optimistic Japanese source predicted that by 1990 the agreement might have stimulated a total of $100 billion in two-way trade.[40] Although the euphoria of the period produced some unrealistic hopes, nevertheless, the Sino-Japanese agreement did set a framework for substantially increasing trade.

The Chinese also signed a fairly general five-year agreement with the EEC, initialed in February 1978 and concluded in April. The key clauses in the agreement granted China most favored nation treatment, called for the establishment of a joint EEC-China economic commission, and proposed active steps to promote two-way trade.[41] In December of that year the Chinese signed an intergovernmental agreement with France calling for about $13.6 billion in trade over seven years, through 1985.[42] The agreement specified eleven fields that would receive special attention, including oil, steel, aluminum, aeronautics, electronics, and nuclear power. The Chinese expressed a desire to purchase, and the French a willingness to sell, two 900-megawatt nuclear power plants that, according to different reports, could cost at least $2 billion and possibly as much as $4.5 billion.[43] (The Framatome nuclear plants that were discussed contain U.S.-licensed technology, thus requiring U.S. approval or acquiescence of any sales, but it appeared that the U.S. government would not block such sales.) Although the Sino-French agreement, like the Sino-Japanese accord, merely set a "framework" for future trade—that is, particular deals would require contract negotiations later—it was expected to boost trade. (The French also agreed to arrange financing amounting to over $6.8 billion.)

In March 1979 the Chinese signed an agreement with the British, who hoped it would boost total Sino-British trade to at least $8 billion to $10 billion (and possibly $14.2 billion) during 1978–85.[44] Within its framework, there reportedly were agreements for Chinese purchases of about $2 million for such items as coal equipment and power and steel plants, and there were continuing negotiations regarding sales of other machinery, plants, and transportation equipment. In September 1978 it had been reported that the Chinese signed an "agreement" with the Germans, mainly to develop coal mines and facilities, which reportedly could eventually cost $4 billion,[45] but this was neither very concrete nor firm, although in 1979 the Germans offered sizable credits and began signing some contracts for sales. In December China signed an agreement with the Canadians covering the years 1978–85, which reportedly called for purchases of up to $10 billion of equipment, technology, and commodities (including grain).[46] There were other less important accords.

Many of the specific "deals" that the Western press reported under negotiation during 1978 involved extremely large projects; most were in fields one would expect, in light of China's original development plans—basic power, fuel, metallurgical industries, and transportation. Nippon Steel Corporation signed an agreement to help China build a large steel plant at Paoshan (Baoshan), near Shanghai (modeled on the ultramodern Kimitsu plant in Japan); the deal amounted to about $2 billion.[47] German, British, and French, as well as Japanese, companies bid for contracts for an even larger project: a huge steel plant that the Chinese reportedly hoped to build in north China. It was estimated that the first stage of this project, if it were to materialize, could cost about $9 billion, and that final costs of a plant of the size contemplated might cost $14 billion. The U.S. Steel Corporation reportedly signed an agreement to develop an iron mine and build an iron ore pelletization plant; estimates of possible eventual costs were said to be more than $1 billion. Bethlehem Steel signed a comparable agreement to develop a mine and build an ore processing plant, which reportedly would eventually cost more than $100 million. Various German companies gradually negotiated a wide range of large projects. The biggest said to have been discussed was the already mentioned $4 billion coal mining development project. In addition, the Germans reportedly agreed to build twenty-two nonferrous plants costing hundreds of millions (and possibly several billions) of dollars and five chemical plants said to be worth about $750 million. China also signed numerous agreements or contracts for the construction of petrochemical and synthetic fiber plants; the Japanese and the Germans were the main suppliers.

In the total value of contracts signed, the Japanese were far ahead of any other nation. According to an early U.S. estimate,[48] they obtained well over half of all contracts signed in 1978. According to a later calculation,[49] of the $40 billion or so of possible purchases of plants and equipment of all types being discussed in 1978 (for purchase during the period through 1985), Japan probably accounted for 25 percent, West Germany for 14 percent, the rest of Western Europe for 6 percent, and the United States for 3 percent; for the rest, there were still no clear front-runners.

In the field of nonferrous metals, the Chinese discussed a variety of contracts, including one with an American company, the Fluor Corporation, for construction of a copper plant that might ultimately cost $800 million.[50] Most important of all, during 1978, numerous oil companies—American, Japanese, and European—began discussions with the Chinese on exploration and development of offshore oil. According to most estimates, such oil projects might ultimately require investments of several tens of billions of dollars.[51] Peking also continued buying sizable amounts of oil machinery and equipment, as it had been doing for several years.

The Chinese discussed a variety of transportation and communications projects.[52] One involved a deal with Dutch companies for development of port facilities that might eventually cost $2 billion to $3 billion. The Chinese also discussed with the Japan National Railways ways to modernize the country's railway system (possibly including converting three trunk lines into high-speed corridors); this project, too, could ultimately cost several billion dollars (and might involve others besides the Japanese). With U.S. companies, the Chinese discussed the purchase of a satellite communications system; if, as some expected, the system eventually included a large number of earth stations, it could involve costs totaling between $150 million and $500 million. Several major automobile manufacturers—including Toyota, Mercedes-Benz, and General Motors—competed for contracts to modernize China's truck production facilities. In this case, too, the estimates of ultimate costs made by knowledgeable experts totaled several billion dollars.[53] China purchased a sizable number of ships, pieces of automotive equipment, and other transport items in 1978; it also bought three Boeing 747s for $150 million.

In 1978 the Chinese also discussed large projects to help develop tourism.[54] For example, they negotiated a $500 million general agreement with Intercontinental Hotels, a Pan Am subsidiary, to build and operate for a period of time a chain of new hotels in China and negotiated large-scale projects with other hotel companies, including Hyatt. (By 1979, however, it was apparent that Peking would not follow through on many of these; clearly they would continue to expand hotel facilities but would do so in less costly ways.) During the year they signed an agreement with the Coca-Cola Company authorizing bottling operations in China as well as Coca-Cola sales to China, mostly, it was believed, for tourist consumption. There was also serious discussion about building, with foreign assistance, a skyscraper trade center in Peking that, according to some estimates, might cost as much as $500 million.

Virtually all of China's purchases abroad during 1978 were civilian in nature, but the Chinese also shopped actively in Europe for certain types of military equipment.[55] They negotiated with the French, for example, for the purchase of the Milan, HOT, and Crotale anti-aircraft and anti-tank missiles; estimates of the possible costs ranged from $350 million to $700 million. The British indicated their willingness to sell the Harrier fighter (CV-STOL) planes to the Chinese, and according to some reports, the Chinese hoped eventually to purchase ninety of them at a cost of more than $700 million. It remained unclear, however, whether Peking would purchase any of this military equipment, at least on any significant scale.

Aggregating all of these reports made it evident that during 1978 the Chinese embarked on an unprecedented national "shopping spree." Almost all of its shopping (except for its ongoing purchase of needed commodities) was for plants and equipment needed for its original development plan for 1978–85. Peking's aim seemed to be to make arrangements as rapidly as possible for a large percentage of the imports that would be needed for their entire "ten year" development plan; and most of the deals discussed were ones requiring several years to carry out.

During the second half of 1978 there apparently were strong pressures from China's top leaders on those responsible for trade to act with dispatch to conclude initial agreements. In late 1978, however, China's leaders realized that they were going too fast, and when the regime undertook its "reassessment," they had to pause to sort out priorities in trade as well as in other fields, mainly to assess their ability to pay for and to absorb what they were considering buying. In February 1979 Peking suddenly called for a suspension of about $2.5 billion in agreements or contracts with Japanese manufacturers (including the agreements concerning the Paoshan steel plant).[56] They also halted or slowed many other negotiations that had been initiated during the previous months.

By mid-1979, however, when revision of the plan was announced, the Chinese had renegotiated (on better terms) the Paoshan steel agreements as well as other major contracts and had reactivated virtually all the Sino-Japanese agreements earlier suspended. They also signed important new agreements with American and other oil companies to begin seismic exploration off the Chinese coast and resumed active shopping for foreign technology. But in general they deliberately slowed negotiations with many foreign corporations.

By this time it was clear that Peking's purchases of plants, machinery, and equipment would be more cautious and more tightly controlled than during 1978. The Chinese modified some of their import plans and dropped or delayed a number of deals they had started negotiating in 1978. (Some of their huge steel projects were canceled.) Peking's attention shifted, as Yu indicated in his NPC report, to purchasing less expensive and less capital-intensive plants. Some grandiose projects were scaled down, and others were abandoned. The Chinese began to calculate more carefully their ability to pay for capital goods imports and gave higher priority to projects that could pay their own way through export of commodities or goods produced.

Nevertheless, the foreign trade target set for 1979 indicated that Peking hoped to import sizable amounts of capital goods and technology, including a few big and costly plants, but was debating what it could prudently borrow to help pay for them. There was no basic change in Peking's policy of pushing hard to increase trade to support its modernization program.

Peking's great leap outward during 1977–79 involved more than an increase in trade and a rise in the number of signed contracts for imports of plants and equipment. China changed its entire approach to foreign economic relations, and those responsible for trade showed remarkable flexibility and eclecticism in adopting new methods.

The first signs of increased flexibility had appeared in 1977 when the Chinese rapidly improved their staffing to handle trade problems both at home and abroad and showed increasing willingness to accommodate the requirements of foreign markets and the desires of foreign businesses.[57] Ideological polemics, which in the past had regularly intruded into business talks, disappeared. For a while, the Chinese continued to handle most of their trade through well-established and relatively inflexible mechanisms such as their semiannual Canton Fair; there was still little contact between foreign businesses and the ministries and enterprises that were the real end-users (and suppliers) in China. However, China's foreign trade corporations (under the Ministry of Foreign Trade), which provided some links between ultimate end-users and suppliers, assumed more important roles.

Then, during 1978–79, the Chinese started to develop entirely new kinds of relationships with foreign businesses.[58] Instead of restricting most contacts to the Canton Fair, the Chinese began to bring many other Chinese organizations into the process and to allow foreign businessmen to deal with varied institutions, in Peking and elsewhere. There were increased direct contacts between businesses and many ministries other than the Ministry of Foreign Trade and its subsidiaries, with many new national bodies set up to promote and regulate foreign trade and investment, and with new agencies and corporations established at the local level in key areas to deal with trade. Peking decided to permit foreign companies to establish offices in China and indicated that China's trading corporations planned to set up offices abroad.

The Chinese also began to discuss many forms of cooperative arrangements with foreign companies.[59] They designated certain areas and enterprises to produce mainly for export. And they started signing new types of agreements with foreign businessmen under which Chinese factories contracted to process or assemble goods for foreign companies, with foreign companies providing designs, expertise, and managerial advice and, in many cases, production equipment, parts, accessories, and packaging expertise. The Chinese explored a wide variety of joint operations and coproduction schemes, including commissioned processing and licensing of production technology. By late 1978 it was evident that the Chinese were especially interested in compensation, payback, and production-sharing agreements under which a foreign business would be repaid for its contribution (equipment, technology, advice, and so on) from the product of the enterprises involved. They also investigated the possibilities for barter agreements in which a foreign company would accept payment in goods other than those produced by an enterprise receiving foreign assistance.

Within a year, a sizable number of factories were operating under cooperative arrangements with foreign businesses. By early 1979 the number of factories in Kwangtung (Guangtong), the province adjacent to Hong Kong, with processing or assembling agreements with foreign companies exceeded 300.[60] In Peking there were factories producing, processing, or finishing more than forty kinds of products including cassettes, radios, digital clocks, and refrigerators.[61]

The new Chinese flexibility first affected small export-oriented operations, but by 1979 it was evident that it would apply to many of their largest development projects. With an awareness of China's need not only for imports of capital equipment but also for technology acquisition in a much broader sense, Peking indicated willingness—in fact eagerness—to have foreign companies send advisory, technical, and managerial personnel to work in China, as well as a desire to send larger numbers of technicians and workers to be trained abroad. Chinese leaders made it clear that they were interested in establishing closer, longer-lasting foreign economic relationships than any since the Sino-Soviet alliance days.

In late 1978 the Chinese revealed—first in private discussion with foreign corporations and later publicly—that they were prepared to negotiate "joint ventures" and to accept foreign equity investment in China. Somewhat earlier they had shown a desire to attract investment funds from Overseas Chinese and, in fact, had agreed on some joint ventures, both in Hong Kong and in China itself, involving equity holdings by persons of Chinese origin living abroad. Now they announced that they were interested in agreements involving direct investment by major foreign companies, including some of the world's largest capitalist multinational corporations.

In a press conference held in Hong Kong in December 1978 (itself an unprecedented event), Minister of Foreign Trade Li Chiang declared that "China welcomes joint investments with foreign firms whose equity shares in such ventures may run up to a maximum of anywhere near 49 percent with the length of such ownership up to negotiation."[62] In the same month, Vice Premier Li Hsien-nien stated in an interview, "We will support ourselves by our own efforts. But we will also support ourselves through countries prepared to cooperate with us, such as Japan, the United States, Canada, and the European Community. We are purchasing equipment, and their bankers are providing us with credits. They are constructing factories here, and we are paying for them with minerals produced. They are providing investment, and we are forming joint companies, but not in such a way as to harm our sovereignty."[63]

In discussions with foreign businessmen, Chinese officials indicated that Vice Premier Teng had approved the idea of foreign equity investment at least as early as October 1978 and that they were interested in discussing arrangements similar to some that the Yugoslavs had with foreign companies, in which the Chinese would own certain assets (including the land and buildings) while the cooperating foreign corporation would own other assets (machinery and equipment, for example).[64] In such arrangements, foreigners might participate in management, they indicated, and there would be clear agreements on the length of time for investments, repatriation of capital, a reasonable rate of return on investment, and the pricing policies necessary to achieve a reasonable profit.

Finally, in mid-1979, not only did the NPC approve a draft law on the formation of joint ventures, but it was revealed that the China Council for the Promotion of International Trade was preparing detailed drafts on company law and investment law, presumably on behalf of the State Council.[65] The joint venture law[66] authorized foreign businesses to incorporate in China and form joint "companies, enterprises, or other entities." The law stated that such joint ventures will be limited liability companies and that foreign partners will have to contribute at least 25 percent of the registered capital. (No upper limit was set, which implied that conceivably it could be 100 percent.) Industrial property rights, as well as capital goods and cash, will count as part of the investment capital, and contributed technology and equipment will have to be "advanced and appropriate" (with foreign companies liable for compensation to the Chinese if "outdated" technology is "intentionally" provided). Foreigners can serve on the boards of such joint ventures, but the Chinese will appoint the chairman and retain ultimate control (although foreign participants can appoint one or two vice chairmen). Decisions will be by "consultation," and disputes will be subject to conciliation or arbitration by an agreed-upon body. Boards will be empowered to act on all important matters, including staff appointments, pay scales, and hiring and firing, as stipulated by the agreement. Profits, after income taxes (that is, corporate taxes on gross profit), and allocations to reserve, bonus and welfare, and expansion funds will be divided according to shares of capital; in some cases a two- to three-year income tax exemption will be granted and, when funds are reinvested, there may be a partial restitution of taxes paid. Net profits can be repatriated in foreign exchange; the same will be true of salaries of foreigners employed, after payment of personal income taxes.

Following the publication of this law, the Chinese established a Foreign Investment Control Commission and Import-Export Control Commission (the former with responsibility for giving final approval to joint venture proposals), both headed by Vice Premier Ku Mu (Gu Mu), and a China International Trust and Investment Corporation (to help promote joint ventures), headed by a former Shanghai industrialist, Jung Yi-jen (Rong Yiren).[67] These men and others made statements indicating that China would be willing to guarantee a profit for foreign companies investing in joint ventures; that agreements could be for twenty, thirty, or more years; that (in theory at least) there would be no upper limit on the percentage of foreign contribution to capital investment; and that in addition to company and investment laws, new regulations or laws would soon be drawn up on corporate and individual taxes, patents, and customs.[68] Some statements suggested that the corporate profit tax might be 30 to 40 percent.[69] The level of profits allowed (or guaranteed), Jung said, "will not be less than those in other foreign countries." Ku declared that "China will insure more rights, give more convenience, and be more generous" to joint ventures than other countries are.[70]

However, even though by the fall of 1979 about thirty joint venture proposals were under consideration, most potential foreign investors were still cautious and inclined to wait until the legal framework was further clarified.[71] This hesitation was notably true of the Japanese. In fact, a special ad hoc committee appointed by the Japan External Trade Organization (JETRO) prepared an analysis that raised numerous questions and proposed that some changes in the joint venture law be considered by the Chinese.[72] Nevertheless, it seemed likely that in time, significant foreign investments would occur, although in 1980 progress in this direction was still slow.

A major explanation for these Chinese moves toward new forms of cooperation, and in particular for the great stress placed by the Chinese on compensation agreements and foreign investment, was Peking's increased awareness by 1979 that China will face a more serious payments problem than ever before. The adoption of new forms of cooperation was part of their answer to the problem. In addition, during 1978-79 the Chinese shopped worldwide for credits and loans.

During the previous decade and a half, Chinese leaders, as a matter of principle, had tried to come as close as possible to balancing their commodity trade each year, paying most of the costs of their imports by exports. In practice, however, they had been compelled even then to stretch out their payments, through so-called "progress payments," and to obtain substantial amounts of short-term commercial credit (usually for terms of six to eighteen months and mostly for imports of basic commodities such as grain, fertilizers, and steel); however, they had claimed that such credits did not constitute debt. In addition, they had obtained some medium-term commercial credits on a limited scale to finance the purchase of plants, machinery, and equipment, but the mechanism used, so-called "deferred payments," made it possible for them to claim that these credits (which were essentially supplier credits), also did not constitute debt. (Interest and capital repayment charges were built into one overall schedule of Chinese payments over a period of time, usually five years.) From the mid-1960s on, Peking claimed that it had no foreign debts, and it was extremely proud of this fact; moreover, in reality China's indebtedness was relatively small. In the early 1970s, when China's trade began to rise, the avoidance of obvious large-scale foreign indebtedness appeared to be the essence of the principle of self-reliance.

During 1977–79 this, like many past Chinese policies, appeared to be abandoned, and Peking indicated that it had a strong interest in foreign credits and loans. China started to obtain commercial loans by soliciting deposits by foreign banks in the Bank of China.[73] By early 1978, however, the Chinese were negotiating for large-scale syndicated loans from Western and Japanese banking groups. By the end of the year, they laid aside most inhibitions, and Li Chiang, in his December press conference in Hong Kong, explicitly stated that China would accept foreign government loans. The Chinese began negotiating for loans from several official export-import bank institutions (or loans guaranteed by them). They also showed increasing interest in concessionary loans from official aid institutions and applied to one United Nations agency for a loan and obtained it.

Because of the liquidity of many of the world's money markets, bankers from the economically advanced countries flocked to China, eager to extend credit to Peking. There was some hard bargaining, however, and the Chinese pressed for the lowest possible interest rates and the longest possible periods of maturity; in some cases they argued for loans designated in dollars (whose value was declining) rather than in harder currencies. Although the Organization for Economic Cooperation and Development (OECD) guidelines restricted institutions in member countries from giving many types of loans to developing countries at interest rates below 7.25 percent (for loans up to five years) or 7.50 percent (for longer-term loans), the Japanese and some others devised various ways to justify granting loans to China at lower rates.

The Chinese completed arrangements for a few foreign loans during 1978, but their most important financial agreements required fairly long negotiations, which continued into 1979. By late 1979, however, numerous major agreements had been consummated.[74] These gave China access to between $20 billion and $30 billion of foreign credits for the period through 1985. The largest and most important were general "framework" agreements in which governments, or consortia of foreign banks backed by governmental export-import banking institutions in the lending banks' countries, promised China large—in some cases, huge—lines of credit, mostly tied to purchases in their countries. The Chinese also obtained major loan commitments of a purely commercial sort.

According to data published by JETRO, in a seven-month period from December 1978 through June 1979 the Bank of China signed agreements for what JETRO labeled "governmental" credits (including government loan offers and commercial credit lines backed by national export-import banks) totaling $17.695 billion and "private sector" credits (from individual banks or banking consortia) totaling $3.448 billion, mostly for use through 1985.[75] JETRO listed the following "governmental" credit lines offered by China during this period: approximately $7 billion (F30 billion) from a consortium of eighteen French banks, guaranteed by the Compagnie d'Assurance pour Commerce Extérieur in December 1978; $5 billion guaranteed by the British Export Credit Guarantee Department and about $2 billion (420 billion yen) financed by the Export-Import Bank of Japan for Chinese resource development in March 1979; $1 billion from a consortium of four Italian financial institutions guaranteed by Mediocredito Centrale and $45 million from Australia's Export Finance Insurance Corporation (EFIC) in April; and about $2.3 billion from Canada's Export Development Corporation and $350 million from Sweden's Svensk Exportkredit AB in May. JETRO's listing of private credits extended to China included $5 million from the Bank of Montreal in January; $500 million from the Arab France Union Bank in March; five British loans from leading individual banks or consortia totaling $575 million in March and another $100 million in April; $100 million from the Canadian Imperial Bank of Commerce, $50 million from West Germany's Hessische Landesbank, and $10 million from the Bank of Chile in April; $2 billion from a Japanese consortium of twenty-two banks including the Bank of Tokyo in May; and $8 million from the First National Bank of Chicago and $100 million from Germany's Bayerische Vereinsbank in June.[76]

JETRO did not include on this list a Japanese line of credit for syndicated short-term credits totaling another $6 billion, so that the actual total for Japan alone was $10 billion—$2 billion long term, $2 billion medium term, and $6 billion short term.[77]

During the second half of 1979, the Chinese obtained further loan offers. German banks reportedly negotiated during 1978–79 for loans that might total several billion dollars. In the fall of 1978 the Chinese had signed a protocol with the Eastern Committee of German Industry looking forward to possible credit of about $4 billion (DM8 billion), mainly to finance coal mining development, and according to one source, the Dresdner Bank considered a loan of possibly as much as $14.7 billion[78] to finance a huge steel mill in North China (the reliability of this particular report was questionable, however, and in any case the Chinese ultimately postponed this project indefinitely). In October 1979 the West German government indicated that it was prepared to extend export credits "beyond the present level of about $1 billion (DM2 billion)." In November it was reported that German banks were making $869 million of credits available to China and that the government had promised to underwrite another credit of about the same amount.[79] In addition, China obtained other lines of credit during this period: $2 billion in August 1979 from Canada's Export Development Corporation and $100 million in January 1980 from A/S Eksportfinans, a Norwegian export credit institution.[80]

The interest rates on virtually all of these lines of credit were relatively low, in fact almost "semiconcessional."[81] Most of the government-backed loans were at the minimum interest rates allowed by the OECD's "gentleman's agreement" regarding loans to developing countries— 7.25 percent for five years and 7.50 percent for over five years (although interest on the largest French credit offers were 7.25 percent for seven years and 7.50 percent for over seven years). The interest on the Japanese Export-Import Bank's $2 billion loans was only 6.25 percent for ten years. The syndicated bank loans were mostly at 0.5 percent above the London Inter-Bank Rate (LIBOR), generally for five years, although at least one was 0.625 percent above LIBOR.

In mid-1979 the Chinese also began searching for very low interest concessional loans from foreign governments, and in October they obtained their first such loan of importance; while visiting Peking, Prime Minister Masayoshi Ohira offered China a $200 million credit (50 billion yen) at an interest rate of 3.0 percent for six port, railway, and hydropower development projects; reportedly, the Japanese government was committed to provide China with a total of $1.5 billion at this low rate.[82]

Until the fall of 1979 the United States was not really "in the game" in international financing offered to China for its development; only one small U.S. bank credit was extended to the Chinese. However, in August Vice President Walter Mondale promised that $2 billion of U.S. Export-Import Bank credit would be made available to China.[83]

The Chinese also turned for assistance to United Nations agencies. In January 1979 they obtained a small loan of $15 million from the UN Development Program; some reports suggested that they might eventually seek as much as $100 million from it.[84] In November China was granted $20 million from the United Nations to assist its program for refugees from Vietnam during 1979–80, and in early 1980 the UN Fund for Population Activities committed itself to spend $50 million over four years to assist China in its new census and general population control program.[85] These were harbingers of efforts to borrow larger amounts from UN agencies. In late 1978 and early 1979 Chinese officials indicated for the first time that they were seriously considering joining the International Monetary Fund (IMF) and the World Bank. The acting manager of the Bank of China told U.S. Senator John Glenn in the fall of 1978 that he had recommended to his government that it "rejoin" the IMF, and Vice Premier Teng told the president of Japan's Kyodo News Service in February 1979 that "there would be no hitch on China's part in joining IMF, if the Taiwan issue is settled."[86]

Despite the fact that they had been offered huge amounts of relatively cheap credit during 1979, as of mid-1980 the Chinese had drawn very little of it. It appeared that debate continued on the extent to which China should engage in such borrowing, and Peking showed greater prudence and conservatism about acquiring debt than most developing countries. They gave priority to efforts to maximize foreign exchange earnings from exports. In addition, they launched new drives to earn as much foreign exchange as possible from other sources, including Overseas Chinese remittances, tourism, and shipping. They also stressed the need, whenever possible, to arrange production-sharing, compensation, and processing contracts, which would have built-in provisions for repayment. They also began actively soliciting equity investment by large foreign corporations as well as by Overseas Chinese. They appeared to regard the huge lines of credit they obtained as a means of last resort to pay for essential imports, and although they already had the option of borrowing as much as $20 billion to $30 billion at relatively low rates, they seemed inclined to go slow in using this credit while they explored the possibilities of obtaining even more desirable financing or aid from the IMF, the World Bank, and UN agencies as well as concessional credits from foreign governments.

Developments occurred so rapidly during 1978–79 that it was difficult to keep track of the agreements China was making and even more difficult to calculate exactly what the likely scale of its purchases of capital goods and technology, or its borrowing, would be during the next few years. The Chinese themselves had difficulty keeping track of developments, which was one reason they decided to slow down and take a hard look at their financial situation as well as their production and trade during the "readjustment" of 1979.

Despite the uncertainties, however, a number of foreign experts and institutions attempted to estimate the possible scale of China's capital goods imports and foreign borrowing during 1978–85. One early study, made by the U.S. Department of Commerce in January 1979, predicted that during the seven-year period China might import $70 billion to $85 billion of "capital equipment" of all kinds, of which perhaps $50 billion would be "complete plants."[87] This was judged by many to be too optimistic, however, and a month later the Central Intelligence Agency (CIA) estimated that China probably could afford (on the basis of its own earnings plus loans) to import $30 billion to $40 billion of "industrial plants" by 1985.[88]

Estimates of China's likely borrowing also varied substantially, but many analysts believed that to obtain what it needs from abroad China might have to borrow between $10 billion and $30 billion during 1978–85. Some Japanese sources predicted that China might need to borrow $50 billion or more during that period.[89] The CIA calculated that to import $40 billion of plants by 1985, the Chinese might need to draw upon $15 billion to $20 billion of foreign credits.[90]

At this stage, no one, including the Chinese themselves, can be certain what they actually will need during the next few years. But it is possible to analyze key factors that will influence their performance. To obtain more than a superficial understanding of both the potentialities and opportunities and the problems and constraints that will determine the actual scale of China's foreign economic relations in the period ahead, it is essential to look at China's past experience in economic relations with the rest of the world, especially during the three decades since 1949. The following section will examine in detail the development of China's trade in recent years and its acquisition of foreign capital goods and technology to the present. This examination will provide a basis for assessing the factors that will determine what China may be able to do in the period ahead and for estimating its actual prospects.

China's Foreign Trade

Peking's current drive to expand its trade and imports of technology is especially striking because China has never been a major trading nation; during the 1960s, when proclaiming its self-reliance, China stressed that it had no desire to become one.[91] Even though in recent decades the Chinese have developed one of the world's largest economies (if measured in terms of gross output), their trade has been less than that of countries such as the Netherlands, Belgium, Denmark, South Korea, and even their claimed province of Taiwan. China's world rank in trade, already low, declined following the Sino-Soviet split; while in the late 1950s it had ranked eleventh or twelfth in world trade, by the 1960s its ranking had dropped to twenty-second or twenty-third.[92]

Calculated as a percentage of gross national product (GNP), China's total trade turnover (imports plus exports) has been among the lowest of any of the major nations, including other continental-size nations, but recently has been rising. Estimates must be crude, and they are subject to considerable possible error because it is difficult to know what exchange rates are valid to use in comparing dollar figures for China's trade with dollar estimates of its GNP. However, some Western specialists have estimated that in real terms China's total trade turnover generally has amounted to no more than 4 to 8 percent of GNP and generally has averaged not more than 6 percent.[93] Trade turnover may have been about 4 percent of GNP in 1977, 5 percent in 1978, and 6 percent in 1979.[94]

By any standard, these are small figures. The foreign trade of most large countries with big internal markets tends to be relatively low, it is true, as a percentage of GNP. In recent years, for example, the figures for India, the United States, and Japan generally have been under 10 percent, 10 to 15 percent, and about 20 percent, respectively, compared with more than 80 percent for the Netherlands and almost 100 percent for Taiwan.[95] (In the case of the United States, however, the percentage has been rising and in 1978 was over 15 percent.)[96] Compared even with these large countries, China's ratio has been low. Only the Soviet Union, whose foreign trade has generally amounted to 5 or 6 percent of GNP in recent years, has been comparable.[97] In per capita terms, China's trade almost certainly has been the smallest of any major nation. In 1976 (based on an estimate of 930 million for China's population that year) its foreign trade amounted to roughly $14 per person. By 1979 trade (in current dollars) had more than doubled, but per capita it was still only $29.

Trade and Growth

While small by these measures, foreign trade unquestionably has been important to China's economic growth. The long-term rate of increase of China's trade has been comparable to (although perhaps slightly lower than) the long-term rate of growth of its GNP.[98] In the twenty-five years from 1952 through 1977, as China's GNP (calculated in constant 1977 dollars) grew at an estimated rate of 5.7 percent, its trade (calculated in current dollars) increased at a rate of 8.7 percent, from $1.9 billion to $15.1 billion.[99] A comparison of GNP growth in *constant* dollars with trade growth in *current* dollars does not distort reality badly for the 1950s and 1960s, although it does for the 1970s because of the effect of worldwide inflation on the trade figures. A U.S. government study showed, for example, that in 1975 the "current dollar" value of China's trade with non-Communist countries (which accounted for almost 84 percent of its total trade that year) was 97 percent above its "real value" calculated in constant 1970 dollars.[100] If both trade and GNP are calculated in constant dollars, some studies show, the long-term rates of growth appear to be remarkably similar. One estimate of the real growth of China's trade from 1952 through 1977 indicated that, in constant dollars, the rate was 5.7 percent, about that of China's GNP during those years.[101]

China's trade growth, like the growth of its GNP, has been erratic, however. Trade fluctuations have reflected the ups and downs in overall GNP, and changes in trade also have influenced GNP growth rates, although not always immediately. In the period right after the Communist takeover, China's trade was extremely small; the $1.210 billion turnover in 1950 was well below the pre-Communist peak (table 2-1).[102] Thereafter, it rose steadily but in real terms probably did not surpass the 1928–29 level until the mid-1950s.[103] Then, during China's first Five Year Plan period, the rate of increase was impressive; total turnover increased 62 percent (in current dollars), at an average annual rate of more than 10 percent.[104] The increase was even more rapid in the late 1950s; in 1958 foreign trade rose by 23 percent and in 1959 by 14 percent. For the period from 1952 through 1959 the average rate of growth was 12.4 percent. World trade in that period is estimated to have increased at a rate of about 5 percent; the rate for all developing countries was just above 2 percent, and for all Asian countries other than Japan and China it was about 1 percent.[105] Judged by the rate of increase in its trade, therefore, China was in the vanguard, internationally, during the 1950s. In 1959 its trade reached $4.290 billion, a figure that was not surpassed until more than a decade later, in 1970.

In the early 1960s China's trade, like its GNP, plummeted to a low of $2.670 billion in 1962, below that of any year since 1954. During the decade as a whole, trade stagnated. Although from 1963 on there was a gradual rise, by 1969 trade still was below the peak of a decade earlier. From 1962 through 1969 the average rate of increase was 5.5 percent. For the ten-year period from 1959 through 1969 as a whole, there was no growth.

In the 1970s, trade began to increase again at a rapid rate, even though the debates in China over economic policy were still unresolved and China's radicals tried hard to obstruct the trend. In current prices the rise was spectacular. In eight years trade rose by 287 percent (in current dollars), from $3.895 billion in 1969 to $15.055 billion in 1977, an average annual rate of over 18 percent. In 1978, the first year of the post-Mao trade drive, it increased (in dollars) by about 40 percent, to more than $21 billion. (In yuan the rise was less—just over 30 percent.) The total rise, in current prices, from 1969 through 1978 was 442 percent, and the average annual rate of increase was almost 21 percent. In 1979 trade continued to rise rapidly. Calculated in current dollars (which depreciated further against the yuan during the year), it rose by about 40 percent to $28.245 billion.[106] (Calculated in yuan, it increased 28 percent to 45.500 billion yuan.[107])

However, because the figures in current dollars were inflated by rapidly rising world prices, they distorted the true picture, and in "real" quantitative terms the rise was less. Nevertheless, even taking account of inflation, the rate was impressive. The U.S. government study already cited indicated that in constant 1970 prices China's trade with non-

TABLE 2-1. *China's Balance of Trade, 1950–78*[a]
Millions of U.S. dollars

Year	Total trade				Communist countries				Non-Communist countries			
	Total	Exports	Imports	Balance	Total	Exports	Imports	Balance	Total	Exports	Imports	Balance
1950	1,210	620	590	30	350	210	140	70	860	410	450	−40
1951	1,900	780	1,120	−340	975	465	515	−50	920	315	605	−290
1952	1,890	875	1,015	−140	1,315	605	710	−105	575	270	305	−35
1953	2,295	1,040	1,255	−215	1,555	670	885	−215	740	370	370	0
1954	2,350	1,060	1,290	−230	1,735	765	970	−205	615	295	320	−25
1955	3,035	1,375	1,660	−285	2,250	950	1,300	−350	785	425	360	65
1956	3,120	1,635	1,485	150	2,055	1,045	1,010	35	1,065	590	475	115
1957	3,055	1,615	1,440	175	1,965	1,085	880	205	1,090	530	560	−30
1958	3,765	1,940	1,825	115	2,380	1,280	1,100	180	1,385	660	725	−65
1959	4,290	2,230	2,060	170	2,980	1,615	1,365	250	1,310	615	695	−80
1960	3,990	1,960	2,030	−70	2,620	1,335	1,285	50	1,370	625	745	−120
1961	3,015	1,525	1,490	35	1,685	965	715	250	1,335	560	775	−215
1962	2,670	1,520	1,150	370	1,410	915	490	425	1,265	605	660	−55
1963	2,775	1,575	1,200	375	1,250	820	430	390	1,525	755	770	−15
1964	3,220	1,750	1,470	280	1,100	710	390	320	2,120	1,040	1,080	−40

Year												
1965	3,880	2,035	1,845	190	1,165	650	515	135	2,715	1,385	1,330	55
1966	4,245	2,210	2,035	175	1,090	585	505	80	3,155	1,625	1,530	95
1967	3,915	1,960	1,955	5	830	485	345	140	3,085	1,475	1,610	−135
1968	3,785	1,960	1,825	135	840	500	340	160	2,945	1,460	1,485	−25
1969	3,895	2,060	1,835	225	785	490	295	195	3,110	1,570	1,540	30
1970	4,340	2,095	2,245	−150	860	480	380	100	3,480	1,615	1,865	−250
1971	4,810	2,500	2,310	190	1,085	585	500	85	3,725	1,915	1,810	105
1972	6,000	3,150	2,850	300	1,275	740	535	205	4,725	2,410	2,315	95
1973	10,300	5,075	5,225	−150	1,710	1,000	710	290	8,590	4,075	4,515	−440
1974	14,080	6,660	7,420	−760	2,435	1,430	1,010	420	11,645	5,230	6,415	−1,185
1975	14,575	7,180	7,395	−215	2,390	1,380	1,010	370	12,185	5,800	6,385	−585
1976	13,275	7,265	6,010	1,255	2,345	1,240	1,105	135	10,930	6,025	4,905	1,120
1977	15,055	7,955	7,100	855	2,520	1,370	1,150	225	12,530	6,580	5,950	630
1978	21,100	10,000	11,100	−1,100	3,200	1,600	1,600	0	17,900	8,400	9,500	−1,100
	(20,295)	(10,004)	(10,291)	(−289)	(3,088)	(1,562)	(1,526)	(36)	(17,207)	(8,442)	(8,765)	(−323)

Sources:: For 1950 through 1977, National Foreign Assessment Center, Central Intelligence Agency, *China: Economic Indicators*, Reference Aid ER 78-10750, December 1978, p. 39; for 1978, NFAC, CIA, *China: A Statistical Compendium*, Reference Aid ER 79-10374, July 1979, p. 13, which gives exports f.o.b. and imports c.i.f. The 1978 figures in parentheses are CIA statistics giving both exports and imports f.o.b., from NFAC, CIA, *China: International Trade Quarterly Review, Third Quarter 1979*, Reference Aid ER CIT 80-002, February 1980, pp. 3–8.
a. Data (except for 1978) are rounded to the nearest $5 million. Because of rounding, components may not add to totals shown.

Communist countries increased during 1970–75 at an average annual rate of close to 12 percent;[108] imports rose at a rate of 12.4 percent, and exports at 11.5 percent. After 1975 there continued to be price distortions but they were less than in the early 1970s, and the real growth rate in China's trade in the 1970s has again been well above the world average.

Although there has been a significant parallelism in China's GNP growth rates and the rates of growth in its foreign trade, it is no simple matter to identify cause and effect. Clearly, the fluctuations in trade have reflected, and in some respects been caused by, changes in the country's overall growth rate. Whenever Peking has initiated large investment programs designed to accelerate growth, its needs for imported capital goods have risen, and it has expanded exports to pay for increased imports. It also is true that increased purchases of foreign plants and machinery have tended to stimulate higher GNP growth rates. It is difficult to determine precisely how much rising rates of GNP growth have stimulated foreign trade or how much increased trade has pushed overall growth, but the linkage between the two has been important.

The relationship between trade and growth has differed markedly in different periods, however.[109] In the 1950s, especially from 1952 through 1959, China experienced growth that was at least to a degree trade-led (although no really large nation can rely on trade-led growth to the extent that smaller nations can). The rate of increase in trade, 12.4 percent in that period, was almost double the growth rate of China's GNP, which was 6.7 percent. In the 1960s the reverse was true; from 1959 through 1969, while trade stagnated, GNP grew by a total of 45 percent. Although the average rate of GNP growth was very low—only 3.8 percent—compared with either the 1950s or the 1970s, nevertheless there was some growth but no overall increase in trade over the ten-year period. In the 1970s China's growth was again trade-led. From 1969 through 1977, while GNP increased by about 76 percent (in constant 1977 dollars), at an average rate of about 7.3 percent, trade rose more than 275 percent in current prices (287 percent if Western estimates are used, 277 with the latest Chinese data for 1977),[110] at a rate of roughly 18.4 percent a year; in constant prices the average rate may have been close to 15 percent. As in the 1950s, trade has been growing at about double the rate of GNP.

Basic Approach to Trade

Despite the linkage between trade and growth, until recently the Chinese rarely indicated that they viewed exports as a major means to promote growth.[111] Unlike smaller nations that have deliberately pursued policies of export-led growth, China has tended to view exports primarily as a necessity, to pay for imports they felt to be essential, including complete plants, machinery and equipment, various semi-manufactured goods needed by Chinese industry, and basic commodities like food. Generally, in the past it appears that they first estimated their essential import needs in any particular year and then drew up an export plan to earn enough to pay for all or most of their import bill.[112] Now, however, some Chinese seem inclined to view an expansion of exports as desirable, in itself, as a means to exploit comparative advantage and spur growth.

China's policy has generally been one of import substitution; that is, to the extent possible the Chinese have used their limited foreign exchange to obtain imports to develop their domestic production capacities in order to reduce or eliminate future need to purchase the items imported. During the mid-1960s and early 1970s Peking's planners focused attention on the importation of "turnkey" plants to serve as prototypes that could be copied in China instead of viewing imports as a means to make large-scale additions to China's productive capacity in priority fields. Recently, this approach, too, appeared to be changing. The first sign was in the early 1970s, when Peking decided to import thirteen large chemical fertilizer complexes to expand very rapidly China's production capacity in a high-priority field (instead of simply purchasing only one or two plants to copy). Since 1977 this practice has occurred in a variety of fields.[113] However, China's planners probably still think essentially in import substitution terms, and they decided in 1979 to slow down imports of complete plants except in a few fields where making large-scale and rapid additions to capacity through imports seems imperative.

Throughout most of the past three decades, China's planners probably would have liked to focus their import policy mainly on the goal of obtaining needed capital goods and technology, and in certain periods, capital goods have dominated China's imports. However, necessity has forced them to purchase large quantities of certain basic commodities, including food, and various semimanufactured goods essential to both agriculture and industry, such as chemical fertilizers and steel. They probably have viewed the importation of such items as a stopgap measure, hoping that eventually they could expand their own production capacities to the point where domestic output would obviate the need for imports. But as China's development has progressed, its need to import certain commodities and semimanufactured goods has increased. Even though domestic output of food and fertilizers has risen substantially, demand has increased even more rapidly. And in the case of steel, although the Chinese have become increasingly able to meet their needs for low-quality steel, their requirements for high-quality steel products has steadily grown, resulting in an increase of imports despite the large rise in China's domestic steel production.

Simply stated, the raison d'être of trade, in Chinese planners' eyes, has been the necessity to import certain modern capital goods and technology, plus some basic commodities and industrial raw materials in short supply, and to try to export enough to pay for these imports. In the past, they never really aimed at trade maximization. In fact, like planners in most centrally planned economies, they have had a fairly strong bias against extensive involvement in the world market, for several reasons. Because of the impossibility of controlling and difficulty of predicting economic trends worldwide, increased dependency on external sources of supply and on foreign markets creates planning problems in a "command economy."[114] Extensive involvement in world trade creates new relationships of interdependence, if not dependence, which expose planners to uncontrollable and unpredictable external forces. All trade, while bringing benefits, creates vulnerabilities. Trade inevitably exposes a country to the effects of inflation and recession in other countries. In the early 1970s even China, despite its relative isolation from international market forces, was significantly affected by worldwide inflation, which greatly raised the prices that it had to pay for grain and fertilizer imports, and by recession in the non-Communist industrial nations, which adversely affected the markets and prices of many of its exports. Until recently, therefore, the strong predisposition of Peking's leaders has been to try to insulate and protect China's economy as much as possible from the vagaries of the world market.

The organization of foreign trade in China has also worked against maximization of trade opportunities.[115] As in most socialist nations, Chinese enterprises generally have not been oriented toward sales or profits, to say nothing of foreign trade. Meeting gross output targets has been their main preoccupation. Most producers have had few if any direct links to foreign trade; contacts with buyers and sellers abroad have been handled by specialized trading companies controlled by the Ministry of Foreign Trade. In the past most enterprises knew little about foreign markets, had virtually no links with foreign buyers or sellers, and lacked motivation to promote sales abroad. Even when their products have been marketed internationally, it has been difficult to be responsive to the requirements of foreign buyers.

Economic Imperatives

Despite the biases and impediments that have tended to limit China's trade, Peking's leaders, even while proclaiming their self-reliance, have never advocated complete autarchy. They have been compelled to rely on trade to meet many essential needs.

Two key economic determinants of the ups and downs of China's foreign trade during the past three decades have been (1) industry's unavoidable need for imports of certain capital goods and semimanufactured items and (2) the fluctuations in China's agricultural output, which have determined both China's need to import food (and inputs into agriculture) and its capacity to export agricultural products and agriculture-based manufactured goods. Although ideological and political shifts have had a significant impact on trade, as will be noted later, these economic factors have been of fundamental importance.

Each time China's leaders have decided to give priority to policies designed to speed up economic growth, especially industrial growth, they have been compelled to increase imports of capital goods and technology, and these imports clearly have stimulated growth. China's imports of plants, machinery, and equipment—to be discussed in detail later—rose rapidly during its first Five Year Plan period (1953–57), reached a peak during 1958–60,[116] dropped precipitously in 1961, and were at a low level during 1962–64. Thereafter, these imports rose rapidly for a brief period, from 1965 through 1967, then dropped again during 1968. Since 1969, they have again risen rapidly.

Each period of rapidly rising capital goods imports has been a period of increasing total trade, and each surge of imports of capital goods has helped to accelerate growth. Such imports did not guarantee uninterrupted rises in the country's overall rate of growth, however. At times, years of large imports of capital goods have been followed immediately by years of low growth. Other factors, especially China's agricultural performance, have been even more important as primary determinants of GNP growth rates. In the early 1960s China's crisis in agriculture was the prime cause of the country's worst depression of the post-1949 years, and much of China's expanded industrial capacity (to which the capital goods imported in the late 1950s had made a major contribution) was underutilized for several years. One effect of setbacks in both agriculture and industry was trade stagnation.

Because agriculture plays such a large role in China's economy, it is probably still the most important single economic determinant of trade. Even though agriculture's share of the gross domestic product has declined (according to one estimate, it was 47 percent in 1952 but only 26 percent in 1970)[117] while industry's has steadily grown (from an estimated 17 percent in 1952 to 42 percent in 1970), nevertheless agriculture's role in the economy continues to be crucial. Agriculture not only produces esesential food and provides a large proportion of the raw materials for Chinese industry (about three-quarters of the raw materials for consumer goods industries), it also accounts for a huge share of the country's exports. Until fairly recently, agricultural raw and processed materials totally dominated China's exports, and today they constitute well over one-half of the total, even though exports of minerals and other raw materials and manufactured goods made from them have steadily grown.[118] The fluctuations of China's agricultural output have also greatly influenced the character of its imports; the inability of the Chinese economy to meet the country's total needs for food, industrial products for agriculture (especially fertilizers), and agricultural raw materials for industry (especially textile fibers) has necessitated large imports of these items, especially following poor agricultural years.

Politics and Economics

Economic imperatives have been the primary determinants of China's trade but not the only determinants. Ideology and politics have had a significant impact on policy shifts that have greatly affected both the direction of China's trade and the regime's decisions on whether to increase or decrease imports of capital goods and technology, to expand trade or stress import minimization and substitution to an extreme degree, and to borrow abroad or not. All of the past swings of the pendulum in China's overall economic development strategy have been paralleled by shifts between relatively outward-looking and relatively inward-looking policies. During the 1950s, when China modeled its development on Soviet experience, it looked outward (toward the Communist bloc) and attempted to maximize its imports of capital goods; both trade and GNP grew rapidly. During most of the 1960s, following the Sino-Soviet split, when China experienced a serious depression, then glorified self-reliance and stressed egalitarian aims, trade stagnated, imports consisted mainly of basic commodities such as grain, and the rate of overall economic growth was low. The recent shift to a pragmatic growth-oriented strategy has led to the most outward-looking orientation—and the most active trade promotion efforts—in China's history; emphasis again is being placed on the desirability of maximizing imports of capital goods and technology. These major policy changes, which have generally resulted from ideological and political shifts between "right" and "left" lines, have not totally overridden economic imperatives, but they have resulted in trade patterns very different from what they would have been if decisions had consistently been made on the basis of economic considerations alone.

The strong bias against acquiring foreign debt from 1960 on, which was a major constraint on trade, was in part the result of the Sino-Soviet split. The Chinese felt that they had been "burned" by becoming too dependent upon the Soviet Union in the 1950s, which helps explain why they proclaimed self-reliance with such passion. It can be argued that Chinese leaders had no possibility of obtaining substantial financial assistance anywhere immediately after their break with Moscow and therefore were simply making a virtue of necessity. However, their commitment to self-reliance in the 1960s was more than that; for Mao and China's radicals it became an article of faith.

During the period of closest relations with Moscow, China had deficits in its overall trade balance each year from 1951 through 1955 (varying roughly between $150 million and $350 million annually), financed largely by Soviet loans and credits, which, although not very large, were extremely important to China's balance of payments.[119] Then, from 1956 through 1972, the Chinese maintained export surpluses in all but two years (1960 and 1970). Despite difficult economic circumstances within the country, the Chinese insisted on paying off their debts to Moscow as rapidly as possible, and they completed doing so in 1965. Throughout the 1960s Peking continued to pursue extremely conservative financial policies; from 1965 on it claimed that it had no foreign indebtedness and, in fact, it avoided all long-term debt. Its export surpluses generally were between $150 million and $200 million in the late 1950s, rose to near $400 million in the early 1960s, and were often close to $200 million from 1965 through 1972. In short, the Chinese operated on a pay-as-you-go basis from the late 1950s through 1972 (even though, as will be discussed later, they financed some commodity trade with short-term credits and briefly, in the mid-1950s, imported a few plants on medium-term credits disguised as "extended payments"). Peking's strong bias against long-term foreign debt was a major reason why, throughout the 1960s, its trade failed to reach even the level of 1959.

This inhibition began to change in the early 1970s, and during 1973, 1974, and 1975 China had sizable trade deficits. In fact, the $760 million deficit in 1974 was the largest in Chinese history up to that time; Peking soon slowed the growth of imports and strongly pushed exports. This effort turned the situation around, and in 1976 and 1977 China had the largest trade surpluses in its history ($1.255 billion in 1976 and $855 million in 1977). But by 1978 Peking's priority had again shifted to imports, and again China had a trade deficit, amounting to about $1.100 billion.[120] This time, instead of calling again for cutbacks in imports, Peking set a very high target for further trade expansion in 1979, and while pushing increased exports and other measures to earn more foreign exchange, it seemed determined to continue expanding imports despite the prospect of continuing deficits; it appeared prepared to finance deficits in part by borrowing. Such a policy would have been unthinkable prior to the ideological and political shift following Mao's death.

Politics also has had an enormous influence on the direction of China's trade. Politics has not generally determined particular trade deals; the Chinese generally have been shrewd judges of quality and price and have tried to take advantage of favorable price trends in specific import and export decisions. But broad shifts between trade partners have been strongly influenced by—and in some instances determined primarily by—the overall state of China's political relationships with the countries involved.

Although before 1949 China's trade was predominantly with the non-Communist industrial nations, immediately after the Communists' takeover, China began to shift trade toward the Soviet Union and East European nations. This shift was the result of a deliberate decision, made on political and ideological grounds, to reorient China's economy toward the Communist bloc. The economic agreements China made with other Communist nations, starting in early 1950, and the loans and technical assistance it obtained from them, supported this shift. From mid-1950 on, economic necessity also reinforced the trend. After the outbreak of the Korean War, the embargo imposed on China trade by the major non-Communist industrial powers severely limited Peking's trading options and probably made China go further in shifting trade toward the bloc than it otherwise would have.[121] (It was not until the late 1950s that some non-Communist industrial nations began reducing restrictions on trade with China; the United States did not start to do so until the early 1970s.) Nevertheless, the major reorientation of China's trade in the 1950s away from its traditional trading partners was in a basic sense Peking's own choice, dictated more by politics and ideology than by economics.

During the first half of the 1950s the proportion of China's total trade conducted with other Communist nations skyrocketed from 29 percent in 1950, to 51 percent in 1951, to 70 percent in 1952, and to 74 percent in 1955.[122] By the mid-1950s more than half of total Chinese trade was with the Soviet Union alone. During 1956–58 trade with bloc nations remained fairly stable, in value terms, but then it rose to peaks of $2.980 billion and $2.620 billion in 1959 and 1960, respectively. However, because Chinese economic links with non-Communist countries also significantly increased from 1956 on, trade with Communist countries gradually dropped as a share of China's total trade; during 1956–60 it varied between 63 and 69 percent.

Then in 1960, following the Sino-Soviet split, the Chinese again made a deliberate, major shift in the direction of their foreign trade, essentially for political reasons. As in 1950, the choice was not wholly Peking's, since Moscow withdrew all Soviet technicians from China and tried to use economic pressure to change Chinese policies. But clearly Peking, on its part, decided to disentangle its interests from Moscow's, and in the 1960s it rebuffed all Soviet attempts to restore old ties. As a result, trade with the Communist nations dropped rapidly. It declined to 56 percent of total trade in 1961, 34 percent in 1964, then in 1969 reached its nadir, $785 million, which was only 20 percent of total trade. By then, most of the trade was with Eastern Europe, not the Soviet Union; in 1969 trade with the Soviet Union was $55 million, a mere 1.4 percent of China's total trade.

As trade with bloc countries declined, China's non-Communist trade rose rapidly, from $1.370 billion, or 34 percent of the trade, in 1960 to $3.110 billion, or 80 percent, in 1969. In the 1970s trade with the Communist nations again rose in absolute terms, but it continued to decline as a percentage of total trade, accounting for only 17 percent in 1977. (By 1979 trade with the Soviet Union, totaling $355 million, was only 1.3 percent of China's total trade.)[123]

The Chinese paid a price for these major, rapid shifts in trading partners, both in the early 1950s and the early 1960s, since from a purely economic point of view they could have benefited from increased trade with both non-Communist and Communist nations. In the 1960s they experienced serious immediate problems as a result of the initial cutoff of Soviet capital goods and technical assistance, and shortages of replacement parts became a continuing problem. Moreover, they were unable to take advantage of the natural market existing for many Chinese export goods in the Soviet Far East. However, Peking was prepared to pay the costs in order to cut the Chinese umbilical cord to Moscow and reassert greater economic independence.

Political factors have also influenced the direction of China's foreign trade in less dramatic ways. On many occasions the Chinese have indicated that in their view the development of trade relations is an important means to pave the way for the establishment of diplomatic relations and to cement existing relations; some minor shifts in the direction of trade have been made with these purposes in mind. Political as well as economic motives led the Chinese to stress the importance of expanding trade with Third World countries. These motives also influenced certain decisions affecting trade with developed countries.[124] For example, before Austrialia formally recognized Peking, the Chinese often showed an obvious preference for Canada in its grain purchases; and before U.S. recognition, the Chinese generally treated the United States as a residual source of grain supply, although when tight world supplies in 1973–74 compelled them to look to the Americans as a major source, they did so with no compunction. In both instances, Peking hinted repeatedly that improved political relations would lead to larger Chinese purchases, which in fact proved to be the case.

In a few cases—though only a very few—the Chinese have used trade policy as an instrument of crude political pressure. The most notable instance occurred in 1958 when Peking temporarily halted trade with Japan to exert political pressure on the Japanese government.[125] Since then, there has been no comparable example of blatant Chinese manipulation of trade for political purposes. In general, small shifts for political purposes have had only marginal effects on Peking's overall trade pattern, and the most important factors determining the majority of *specific* Chinese trade decisions have been economic, not ideological or political.

Since the early 1960s the Chinese have talked a great deal about expanding trade with less-developed countries (LDCs), stressing the ideological and political significance of such trade. They have also had practical reasons for promoting trade with these countries, since as a group they buy more from China than they sell to it, and China earns substantial amounts of foreign exchange from them that it can use in trade with other nations. However, although China's trade with the LDCs has risen over the years, its economic relations with the non-Communist developed nations (DCs) have expanded even faster and are now far more important to it, above all because these countries possess the modern capital goods and technology that China needs.[126]

In the years from 1961 through 1970 China's trade with the LDCs (not counting Hong Kong and Macao, which constitute special cases) increased impressively by over 100 percent, from $397 million to $790 million. However, in the same period, trade with the non-Communist developed countries increased by 171 percent, from $824 million to $2.230 billion. From 1970 through 1977, the *rate* of increase in China trade with the LDCs was faster than the rate of increase in trade with the DCs; as a result, in 1977 trade with the LDCs was 4.11 times (in current dollars) the 1970 figure, while trade with the DCs was only 3.34 times the 1970 figure. But this trend did not last. Since China started its new modernization program, trade with non-Communist DCs has grown much faster than trade with the LDCs. From 1977 through 1979 trade with the former rose (in current dollars) 121 percent to $15.716 billion, while trade with the latter increased 65 percent to $5.568 billion. Trade with the LDCs will continue to be important but primarily for economic rather than political reasons, and above all to earn foreign exchange to finance imports from the developed countries.

Trade Partners: Recent Trends

Today the basic pattern of China's foreign trade is one in which it imports the items it needs most—plants, machinery, equipment, food, fertilizer, steel, and other semimanufactured goods—from the developed nations and helps to pay for these imports with net foreign exchange earned elsewhere, especially from trade with other developing nations and Hong Kong.

Until recently, China has generally aimed at achieving a rough balance in total trade, but it has never insisted on balancing bilateral trade exactly with individual non-Communist nations, and a triangular trade relationship has developed among China, the DCs, and the LDCs. In 1977, of China's total imports, 64 percent came from the DCs, 20 percent from the LDCs, and 16 percent from Communist nations. Of its total exports, 37 percent went to the DCs, 23 percent to the LDCs, 23 percent to Hong Kong, and 17 percent to Communist nations.[127] In 1979, 69 percent of imports came from the DCs, 18 percent from the LDCs, and 13 percent from Communist nations, while 42 percent of exports went to the DCs, 24 percent to the LDCs, 22 percent to Hong Kong, and 12 percent to Communist nations.

For many years China's deficit with the non-Communist industrial nations has been large, and it is still growing. In 1961 it totaled $380 million. By 1977 it had grown to $1.600 billion (table 2-2). Recently, China has energetically promoted exports to the DCs to narrow the gap between imports and exports. Its deficit as a percentage of its imports from DCs dropped from 63 percent in 1961 to 35 percent in 1977, but its absolute size has steadily grown. It more than quadrupled (in current dollar terms) between 1961 and 1977. Then, from 1977 through 1979 this deficit increased more than two times and (with both exports and imports calculated f.o.b.) reached $4.484 billion and rose to 43 percent of China's imports from the DCs.

During this same period, China's surplus in trade with the non-Communist LDCs has steadily grown and become increasingly important because it has helped China to finance other trade. In 1961, in its trade with the LDCs (not counting Hong Kong), China had a surplus of $49 million, equal to 13 percent of its trade deficit with the DCs. By 1977 this had risen $480 million, roughly 30 percent of its deficit with the DCs. By 1979 (with imports as well as exports calculated f.o.b.) the surplus reached $869 million; however, this was only 19 percent of China's deficit with the DCs.

Southeast Asia—especially Singapore and Indonesia—has been particularly important in China's favorable trade balance with Third World countries. In 1977 China had a total export surplus of $305 million in total trade with that region, including surpluses of $200 million in trade with Singapore and $146 million in trade with Indonesia (partially offset by deficits with the Philippines and Thailand). In 1977 it also earned surpluses of $230 million in the Middle East (mainly with Kuwait and Iraq), $215 million in sub-Saharan Africa (mainly with Nigeria), and smaller amounts in "South Asia" and North Africa. However, China had a large deficit, amounting to almost $410 million, in trade with Latin America (mainly with Brazil and Argentina). In the Third World, China has strongly pushed sales of low-cost manufactured items; to date most have been consumer goods, but sales of inexpensive producer goods have been rising. In Southeast Asia, however, a sizable proportion of China's exports has consisted of "traditional" Chinese products, mainly agricultural, sold to Overseas Chinese.

Although the surpluses it earns in Third World trade are important to China, Hong Kong is more important in this respect than all Third World countries combined. It is hard to overstate the crucial role Hong Kong now plays in China's overall trade. This small British colony, which Peking claims as Chinese territory but has no desire to take over at present, plays a special function in helping China pay for its trade with the developed nations. Although its population is only a little over 4 million, by 1977 China's two-way trade with Hong Kong amounted to $1.840 billion, which made it China's second largest trading partner, next to Japan.[128] (Actually, China's exports to Hong Kong in 1977, totaling $1.795 billion, were greater than those to Japan; they almost equaled its exports to all Third World countries.)

The most important fact about China-Hong Kong trade is that it is almost entirely one way. In 1977 China imported only $45 million from Hong Kong; consequently, China had a huge surplus of $1.750 billion, or 3.6 times the surplus it earned in trade with all Third World countries. This surplus was larger than China's total trade deficit with all non-Communist developed nations. By 1979 China-Hong Kong trade totaled $2.985 billion, and China's surplus had risen to $2.607 billion; however, this was now "only" 58 percent of its deficit with the DCs, which had soared since 1977. China's surpluses in trade with Hong Kong may not again cover its entire deficit with the DCs; nevertheless, the more these deficits grow, the more important Hong Kong will become to China as its main source of net foreign exchange earnings.

Some of China's exports to Hong Kong are re-exported (in 1977 30 percent of the total),[129] but most consist of food and manufactured

TABLE 2-2. *China's Trade by Area and Country, 1976–77*[a]
Millions of U.S. dollars

Area and country	1976				1977			
	Total	Exports	Imports	Balance	Total	Exports	Imports	Balance
Total (all countries)	13,275	7,265	6,010	1,255	15,055	7,955	7,100	855
Non-Communist countries	10,930	6,025	4,905	1,120	12,530	6,580	5,950	630
Developed countries	6,805	2,695	4,110	−1,415	7,450	2,925	4,525	−1,600
East Asia and Pacific	3,470	1,420	2,050	−630	4,205	1,620	2,585	−965
Australia	380	102	278	−176	631	124	507	−383
Japan	3,052	1,306	1,746	−440	3,509	1,473	2,036	−562
Western Europe[b]	2,675	985	1,690	−705	2,395	1,025	1,370	−345
Belgium–Luxembourg	93	46	47	−1	90	35	55	−20
France	571	169	402	−233	278	169	110	59
Italy	278	135	143	−8	240	140	100	−40
Netherlands	124	78	46	32	143	82	60	22
Norway	28	7	21	−14	121	10	111	−101
Sweden	79	44	35	9	103	51	52	−1
Switzerland	92	32	60	−28	99	34	65	−31
United Kingdom	277	136	141	−5	284	159	125	34
West Germany	952	236	716	−480	826	250	576	−325
North America	660	290	370	−80	850	280	570	−290
United States	351	202	149	53	391	203	188	14
Canada	309	90	219	−129	459	77	381	−304
Less developed countries	2,465	1,700	765	935	3,250	1,865	1,385	480

Southeast Asia	860	660	200	460	1,135	720	415	305
Indonesia	126	126	*	126	146	146	*	146
Malaysia	147	97	50	47	260	134	126	8
Philippines	94	54	40	14	194	79	115	-36
Singapore	295	254	41	213	324	262	62	200
Thailand	132	67	65	2	171	64	107	-43
South Asia	280	180	100	80	325	210	115	95
Iran	95	89	6	83	95	75	20	55
Pakistan	79	61	18	43	88	70	18	52
Sri Lanka	66	6	60	-54	78	29	49	-20
Middle East	440	285	155	130	520	375	145	230
Iraq	101	51	50	1	65	45	20	25
Kuwait	82	72	10	62	100	75	25	50
Syria	79	31	48	-17	106	43	63	-20
North Africa	175	110	65	45	225	130	90	40
Egypt	98	39	59	-20	90	45	45	0
Morocco	21	18	3	15	42	23	19	4
Sub-Saharan Africa	515	415	100	315	555	385	170	215
Nigeria	129	128	1	127	135	130	5	125
Sudan	53	26	27	-1	89	27	62	-35
Tanzania	53	38	15	23	36	17	18	-1
Latin America	200	60	140	-80	495	45	450	-410
Argentina	3	*	3	-3	117	1	117	-116
Brazil	10	*	10	-10	179	*	179	-179
Chile	66	16	50	-34	60	5	20	-20
Peru	70	15	55	-40	62	17	45	-28
Hong Kong and Macao[c]	1,660	1,630	30	1,600	1,840	1,795	45	1,750

TABLE 2-2 (*continued*)

Area and country	1976				1977			
	Total	Exports	Imports	Balance	Total	Exports	Imports	Balance
Communist countries	2,345	1,240	1,105	135	2,520	1,370	1,150	225
Soviet Union	417	179	238	−59	338	177	161	16
Eastern Europe	985	435	550	−115	1,220	600	625	−25
Czechoslovakia	126	56	70	−14	138	66	72	−6
East Germany	200	96	104	−8	225	110	115	−5
Hungary	71	31	40	−9	73	41	32	9
Poland	106	40	66	−26	116	56	60	−4
Rumania	451	202	249	−47	600	300	300	0
Far East[d]	620	460	160	300	630	420	210	210
Other[e]	320	165	155	10	330	175	155	25

Source: NFAC, CIA, *China: International Trade, 1977–78*, Research Paper ER 78-10721, December 1978, pp. 12–13. Exports f.o.b, imports c.i.f.
*Negligible.
a. Data for individual countries are rounded to the nearest $1 million. All other data are rounded to the nearest $5 million. Because of rounding, components may not add to the totals shown.
b. Including Spain, Portugal, Greece, and Malta.
c. Including entrepot trade with third countries; Hong Kong re-exports to third countries of $493 million in 1976 and $534 million in 1977; re-exports to China of $25 million in 1976 and $38 million in 1977.
d. Including North Korea, Mongolia, Vietnam, Cambodia, and Laos.
e. Including Yugoslavia, Cuba, and Albania.

goods consumed by the local, predominantly Chinese, population. The situation is unique and, therefore, permits Peking to earn a sizable part of the foreign exchange it requires by supplying the needs of one small group of Chinese (less than half of 1 percent of China's total population) in an area that Peking claims but does not control. If the Chinese were to take over Hong Kong, this would no longer be the case.

China's imports now come mainly from the non-Communist DCs, and today these are crucial to China's development; they will become even more important in the years immediately ahead. While in 1977 the $4.525 billion (c.i.f.) that China purchased from the DCs accounted for 64 percent of its total imports, by 1979 imports (f.o.b.) from the DCs rose to $10.100 billion, or 69 percent of total imports.

In recent years, Japan has been the most important source of these imports, followed by Western Europe, the United States, Canada, and Australia. In 1977 two-way trade with Japan was $3.509 billion, between 23 and 24 percent of China's overall trade, and of this its imports (c.i.f.) were $2.036 billion, almost 29 percent of China's imports.[130] By 1979 two-way trade with Japan was close to $6.5 billion (according to U.S. sources); Chinese imports (f.o.b.) were $3.680 billion, and exports totaled $2.791 billion. Japan accounted for almost 23 percent of China's total trade and 25 percent of its imports.[131] Japan is now by far the most important single source for China's imports of complete plants and other capital goods as well as for many basic commodities such as steel and fertilizers. Proximity and historical cultural ties, as well as the quality and price of Japanese products, help to explain this.

China's two-way trade with all West European countries in 1977 totaled $2.395 billion, which accounted for 16 percent of its total trade; imports (c.i.f.) from these countries amounted to $1.370 billion, or 19 percent of China's total imports. By 1979, trade with these countries had risen to $5.279 billion, or 19 percent of total trade, and imports totaled $3.391 billion, 23 percent of total imports. Western Europe clearly is now China's second most important source of industrial products, especially capital goods. Today, West Germany is the leader; next in importance are the United Kingdom, France, and Italy. In 1979 China's trade with West Germany totaled $1.894 billion; the United Kingdom, $746 million; France, $624 million; and Italy, $572 million. West Germany played the key role in China's imports; in 1979 the Chinese purchased $1.430 billion (f.o.b.) from West Germany, more than three times its imports from the United Kingdom, which was second. (China's trade with Australia and Canada in 1979 totaled $900 million and $647 million, respectively, with imports accounting for $734 million and $505 million of the totals; in both cases, grain constituted the bulk of China's purchases.)

In 1977 Chinese trade with the United States was only $391 million, or 2.6 percent of China's overall trade. Of this, Chinese imports accounted for $188 million; agricultural products were the largest items, but machinery and equipment and other manufactured goods had begun to be significant.[132] Then in 1978, as normalization of relations approached, trade with the United States began to rise rapidly. Peking resumed large-scale grain purchases from the United States (which had been cut off since 1974) and began buying more American manufactured goods as well. By 1979 the United States passed Germany and became China's third largest trade partner; it was second only to Japan as a supplier of China's imports. U.S.-China trade will be discussed in part V. Suffice it to say here that by 1979 it reached $2.318 billion, and Chinese imports from the United States totaled $1.724 billion.

China's trade with Communist bloc countries remains smaller than trade with either the non-Communist industrial nations or the Third World countries; nevertheless, imports from several of these countries are still important to the Chinese.[133] In 1977, when two-way trade with other Communist countries totaled $2.520 billion, China purchased $1.150 billion from them—$300 million from Rumania, $161 million from the Soviet Union, $115 million from East Germany, $210 million from Asian bloc nations, and lesser amounts from other Communist countries. In 1979, two-way trade with other Communist countries rose to $3.599 billion, with imports rising to $1.914 billion, including $544 million from Rumania, $190 million from the Soviet Union, and $264 million from East Germany. China's imports from Communist bloc countries include sizable amounts of valuable manufactured producer goods, and the Chinese have been able to obtain them on a pay-as-you-go basis. For more than two decades, from 1956 through 1978, their exports to these countries were greater than imports from them. In 1979, however, China had a deficit of more than $200 million in this trade. It is probable that if the political atmosphere affecting China's relations with bloc countries were to improve, the scale of trade with European Communist countries might rise substantially. China's trade with other Asian Communist nations, however, may decline both for economic reasons and because of the political deterioration of Chinese relations with Vietnam and some of the other nations involved.

If China continues to expand its overall trade and imports of capital goods and technology substantially, recent trends seem likely to be accentuated. Imports from Japan, Western Europe, and the United States will increase, certainly in absolute terms and possibly in proportionate terms as well. However, the Chinese will have to continue trying to expand exports to Hong Kong and the Third World as much as possible to help pay for growing imports. Although they will also try hard to increase sales in the industrial nations, they face stiff competition and protectionist resistance in almost all these nations. Sales to Hong Kong may increase, but it will not be easy to expand them indefinitely since the colony is small, buys mainly for its own use, and already obtains a high percentage of its imports from China. The Chinese will probably be compelled, therefore, to mount a major export drive to develop larger markets in the Third World countries, where China's potential for increasing sales is still large. In doing so, however, it will have to compete against many countries that are now well ahead of it in developing effective international marketing techniques. Its competitors will include not only some of the world's trading giants, especially Japan, but also other developing Asian economies, such as South Korea, Taiwan, Hong Kong, and Singapore (which some call "little Japans"), as well as India and Indonesia.

Composition of Trade: Changes over Time

The changes in the composition of China's trade over the past three decades have not been as dramatic as the shifts in direction; nevertheless, they have been significant, and knowledge of them is necessary to judge likely developments in the period ahead. Ideology and politics have had little to do, directly, with what China has imported and exported (although they have had an indirect influence through their impact on overall development strategy). Basically, the important shifts in the composition of China's trade have been the result of changes in the country's economic capabilities and needs, as the structure of its economy has evolved in the process of development.

In the mid-1930s China's total foreign trade turnover was generally between $800 million and $1 billion a year (in U.S. dollars of that period), or roughly $2 per capita, and its exports were overwhelmingly dominated by agricultural goods.[134] A wide variety of farm products, including textile fibers, animal products, vegetable oil, and tea made up at least two-thirds (some estimates put the figure as high as five-sixths) of China's exports. China sold some metals, ores, and manufactured goods abroad but not in large quantities. Its imports included substantial amounts of petroleum products, food, fibers, and manufactured products. Chinese imports of capital goods gradually grew in the 1930s, and by 1936 machinery and equipment constituted over 6 percent of total imports, and transportation equipment (vessels and vehicles) accounted for another 5 to 6 percent; total capital goods imports, therefore, probably accounted for 11 to 12 percent of all imports.[135] However, a large proportion of China's imports at that time consisted of consumer goods.

In the decade following the Communist takeover the character of China's exports did not change greatly. Exports continued to be dominated by agricultural products, although sales of textiles (which, of course, were agriculture based) and industrial materials increased. By 1959, of China's total exports, which amounted to $2.2 billion, 50 percent were agricultural products, 28 percent were textiles, 16 percent were industrial materials, and 5 percent were miscellaneous manufactured goods.[136]

On the import side of China's trade, however, the change was more striking. Manufactured consumer goods imports virtually ended, and imports of capital goods rose rapidly. In 1959, of China's $2.1 billion imports, machinery and equipment accounted for 48 percent, industrial materials for 36 percent, and chemical fertilizers for roughly 3 percent. Less than 1 percent were agricultural products.

Then, during the post-Leap economic crisis in China in the early 1960s, the composition of China's trade changed again. By 1962, of China's total imports of $1.150 billion, 50 percent ($575 million) consisted of agricultural products. Food alone (mainly grain) accounted for $460 million, 40 percent of total imports. Imports of industrial materials dropped but nevertheless continued to account for 27 percent of the total. While chemical fertilizer imports declined in absolute terms, they remained about 3 percent of total imports. The most dramatic change was the decline in imports of machinery and equipment, which by 1962 dropped to only 10 percent of total imports.

The composition of exports also changed, though not quite so dramatically. Despite their serious domestic agricultural crisis, the Chinese continued to export foodstuffs; in 1962 food sales abroad earned 16 percent of China's total export earnings of $1.525 billion. However, agricultural exports as a whole declined greatly, to 28 percent of total exports. As a proportion of all exports, sales of industrial raw materials rose, and by 1962 made up 20 percent of the total (even though in absolute terms their value declined slightly). The most significant change was the increase in the proportion of China's total exports made up of manufactured goods. Sales of textiles abroad rose to 35 percent of total exports in 1962 (even though their dollar value dropped slightly). Exports of other manufactured items also rose, in value as well as proportionately, and by 1962 amounted to 17 percent of total exports. Together, textile and other manufactured goods constituted more than half of all exports. However, because the bulk of these manufactured goods used agricultural raw materials, more than half of all exports continued to be agriculture based.

The situation in 1962 was abnormal because of the economic crisis in China following the Great Leap Forward; once recovery began, the composition of trade changed again. Some of the consequences of the crisis had lasting effects, however, and the pattern did not return to that of the 1950s. Despite a gradual recovery of China's agriculture from 1962 on, the Chinese were compelled to continue importing large amounts of food and other agricultural products. In 1965 foodstuffs still were the largest single category of imports, constituting 28 percent of the total; 22 percent consisted of grain alone. Imports of chemical fertilizer accounted for another 8 percent.[137] Together, food and fertilizers made up 36 percent of total Chinese imports.

Imports of machinery and equipment constituted only 18 percent of total imports in 1965, two-fifths of the percentage of such imports in 1959. Purchases of "crude materials," mainly for industrial use (textile fibers and rubber were the largest), accounted for 20 percent of all imports, and other semimanufactured materials accounted for over 17 percent. In the latter category, iron and steel accounted for about 8 percent, nonferrous metals for just under 3 percent, and textile yarn and fabrics for 2 percent. Chemicals other than fertilizers made up close to 5 percent. In 1965, therefore, imports of all raw and semimanufactured materials accounted for roughly 37 percent of China's total imports, about the same proportion as at the end of the 1950s. The biggest change since the 1950s had been the precipitous drop in capital goods imports.

There was no basic change in the pattern of China's exports in this period, although by 1965 its sales of foodstuffs had risen, both in absolute terms and as a proportion of total exports. Sales of crude materials and manufactured goods were not strikingly different as a proportion of total exports from what they had been in 1962, though both had risen in value.

Textiles continued to dominate China's manufactured goods exports. And well over half of the country's total sales abroad still were either agricultural commodities or agriculture-based products.

To be specific, by 1965 foodstuffs made up 26 percent of China's total exports; the main categories were grain, which accounted for 6 percent; animals and animal food products, 10 percent; and fruits and vegetables, 5 percent. Crude materials, mainly agricultural in origin, totaled 20 percent; of these, the most important were oilseeds, textile fibers, and crude animal materials, each accounting for close to 4 percent of total exports. Manufactured goods exports totaled 45 percent of all Chinese sales abroad in 1965, and of these, textiles alone made up 24 percent. Exports of metals, both ferrous and nonferrous, accounted for about 6 percent.

Thereafter, even though China's overall trade grew slowly during the second half of the 1960s, then rapidly in the early 1970s,[138] by 1977 its composition had not undergone fundamental changes; most of the trends that had emerged by the mid-1950s continued. Nevertheless, the beginnings of some shifts of significance were discernible, and the inauguration in 1978 of China's new modernization program pointed toward further changes.

Between 1965 and 1977 China's imports of foodstuffs rose greatly in absolute terms; in 1977 it spent $1.115 billion for such imports, $745 million for grain, and $320 million for sugar (table 2-3, part 1).[139] However, foodstuffs dropped as a percentage of total imports. During the years 1974–76, they averaged 14 percent of China's total imports (grain imports alone were 10 percent), and in 1977 the figure was 16 percent (with grain accounting for slightly over 10 percent), compared with a 1965 figure of 28 percent (22 percent for grain).[140] But since then, grain imports have continued to rise, and they could increase further in the years ahead (see part III, pages 355, 359).

Whether food imports rise or fall in the period ahead will be one of the key variables that will help to determine how much of its export earnings China will be able to use to import capital goods and technology. Moreover, trends in world grain prices will obviously have a large impact on China. Although future prospects will be discussed in detail later, it is worth noting here that if by 1985 China's grain imports have risen to a level of 15 million to 20 million tons a year, the annual cost would be $1.5 billion to $2.0 billion if the average price is $100 a ton, $2.25 billion to $3.0 billion if it is $150 a ton, and $3.0 billion to $4.0 billion if it is $200 a ton. There is little doubt that food will continue to be a major item in China's import bill.

Another key variable will be how much China must spend on imports of raw and semimanufactured materials for use in industry and agriculture. In recent years, imports in this category have been rising; the Chinese now use a very large proportion of their foreign exchange earnings to pay for them. Particularly striking has been China's growing need for imported steel. In 1977 Chinese purchases abroad of iron and finished steel totaled 5.8 million tons, and cost $1.570 billion, or 22 percent of all imports, compared with $145 million, or 8 percent, in 1965.[141] In volume China's imports of chemical fertilizers rose to 3.9 million tons in standard units, or 1.52 million tons in nutrient value, despite the development of China's own fertilizer industry; however, because of price trends, the per unit cost declined, and as a percentage of total imports fertilizers were roughly 5 percent in 1977 compared with about 8 percent in 1965 (even though their cost had risen from $145 million to $345 million). The same was true of textile fibers and rubber. In 1977 imports of both were higher than in 1965, but both had declined slightly as a percentage of all imports. In 1977 China's $500 million of textile fiber imports ($350 million of natural fibers, including 150,000 tons of cotton, and $150 million of synthetic fibers) were 7 percent of total imports, whereas in 1965 fiber imports had constituted 10 percent of all imports. To purchase 259,000 tons of rubber abroad, China spent $225 million in 1977, which was about 3 percent of total imports, compared with a little under 4 percent in 1965.

China's dependence on large-scale steel imports could create an even more troublesome payment problem than grain imports. The fact that iron and steel have constituted China's largest single category of imports in recent years may have been one reason why Peking's leaders initially set such a high target for increases in domestic steel production during the 1978–85 period. Yet, they were doubtless correct when they concluded, in 1979, that their original target was unattainable. Even though cutting the target was realistic, it probably means that for some years China will have to continue importing large quantities of iron and steel, especially specialized, high-quality steel; if so, such imports could use up a significant share of its foreign exchange earnings. If iron and steel imports were to grow at 10 percent a year, by 1985 they would cost well over $3 billion (even assuming no price rise) compared with $1.57 billion in 1977. If steel prices increase, the amount will be larger. To conserve as much foreign exchange as possible for capital goods imports, China will have to work hard to keep its imports of industrial supplies such as steel within bounds.

TABLE 2-3 (Part 1). *China: Commodity Composition of Imports, by Area, 1976–77*[a]
Millions of U.S. dollars

Commodity	1976					1977				
	Total	Developed	Less developed	Hong Kong[b] and Macao	Communist	Total	Developed	Less developed	Hong Kong[b] and Macao	Communist
Total	6,010	4,110	765	30	1,105	7,100	4,525	1,385	45	1,150
Foodstuffs	560	350	115	...	90	1,115	695	350	...	70
Grains	325	290	35	...	...	745	630	110	...	...
Fruits and vegetables	5	...	5	...	...	10	...	10	...	...
Sugar	200	60	55	...	85	320	60	205	...	55
Crude materials	895	245	435	15	200	1,445	415	810	20	200
Oil seeds	5	...	5	...	...	115	15	100	...	...
Crude rubber, natural	150	...	135	...	15	215	...	200	...	15
Crude rubber, synthetic	5	5	...	...	...	10	10	...	...	...
Wood pulp	60	60	...	...	...	55	55	...	...	...
Textile fibers, natural	190	15	175	...	...	350	50	300	...	...
Textile fibers, synthetic	115	115	...	...	...	150	150	...	...	...
Crude fertilizers, minerals	40	...	30	...	5	60	10	40	...	10
Metalliferous ores and scrap	125	25	15	...	85	110	20	35	...	55
Crude animal and vegetable materials	20	...	5	10	5	40	...	10	15	15
Petroleum and products	45	...	45	...	...	30	...	30	...	...
Animal fats and oil	15	15	...	...	...	35	35	...	...	...
Fixed vegetable oils	10	5	5	...	...	105	50	55	...	...

Chemicals	600	455	35	...	110	885	710	60	5	110
Elements and compounds	210	210	...	...	5	295	290	...	...	5
Dyeing materials	20	15	...	...	...	45	40	5	...	...
Fertilizers, manufactured[c]	230	100	30	...	95	345	215	55	...	75
Plastic materials	90	85	...	...	...	100	100	...	...	...
Manufacturers	3,900	3,045	165	15	670	3,555	2,670	145	15	725
Paper and paperboard	45	40	...	...	...	60	60	...	...	...
Textile yarn and fabric	125	115	5	...	...	175	155	5	5	10
Nonmetallic mineral products	15	10	...	5	...	15	5	...	...	10
Iron and steel	1,445	1,335	5	...	100	1,570	1,470	10	...	90
Nonferrous metals	260	110	130	...	20	265	120	105	...	40
Metal products, industrial	90	80	...	...	10	55	55	...	...	...
Nonelectric machinery	1,090	905	...	...	185	455	280	15	15	160
Electric machinery	210	185	...	...	25	105	65	...	...	40
Transport equipment	170	190	15	5	265	640	365	...	...	275
Precision instruments	60	40	...	...	15	25	10	...	...	15
Watches and clocks	15	15	...	...	...	10	10	...	...	...
Other	55	10	10	...	35	100	35	20	...	45

Source: NFAC, CIA, *China: International Trade, 1977–78*, pp. 14–15.

a. Data are rounded to the nearest $5 million. Because of rounding, components may not add to the totals shown. Ellipsis marks indicate that imports, if any, amounted to less than U.S. $2.5 million. Estimates are based on data reported by trading partners. Where data are incomplete, as for the less developed and Communist countries, estimates are based on fragmentary information from trade agreements and press reports and on commodity breakdowns for earlier years.

b. Including Hong Kong re-exports of third country goods to China.

c. Excluding phosphate rock, ammonium chloride, sodium nitrate, and potassium nitrate.

In 1977 imports in three broad import categories[142]—manufactures (other than machinery and equipment including transport equipment), chemicals (of which fertilizers were the largest), and crude materials (of which textile fibers and rubber were most important)—totaled $4.655 billion ($2.355 billion for manufactured goods other than machinery and equipment, $855 million for chemicals, and $1.445 billion for crude materials), which accounted for 66 percent of total imports. In 1965 the comparable total had been $970 million ($365 million for manufactures other than machinery and equipment, $230 million for chemicals, and $375 million for crude materials), which was 53 percent of total imports that year. These figures highlight that as China's economy has developed, its need for imported raw and semimanufactured materials to supply Chinese industry and agriculture has steadily grown, both absolutely and as a proportion of total imports, despite the increase of China's own production in most of these categories. Obviously, purchase of these commodities uses scarce foreign exchange that might otherwise be available to buy capital goods and technology abroad.

These trends have imposed major constraints in recent years on Peking's ability to increase its imports of capital goods. In 1977 the Chinese were able to allocate only $1.2 billion, or 17 percent of total imports that year, to purchase machinery and equipment abroad (which was less than it had to use for iron and steel imports alone); more than half of the $1.2 billion was for transportation equipment. In percentage terms, this was roughly the same as in 1965, when the Chinese had spent $330 million, amounting to roughly 18 percent of total imports, on machinery and equipment. The percentage was much lower in 1977 than in the 1950s, when it had been close to 50 percent. Even though China is now determined to increase its machinery and equipment imports greatly, both in absolute terms and as a percentage of total imports (and will need to do so to achieve its broad economic goals), its ability to do this in the years ahead will be determined in part by the demands placed on its limited foreign exchange resources by the necessity to import large quantities of food and raw and semimanufactured goods. Eventually, China's efforts at import substitution should reduce the need to import some semimanufactured goods, but this will take time. In the immediate future, as in the recent past, even if the Chinese are able to expand their own production capabilities, they will probably need to continue importing sizable quantities of such goods, especially higher-quality types.

Comparing the commodity composition of China's exports in the mid-1970s with the mid-1960s, there were no dramatic changes and some striking continuities. Sales abroad of foodstuffs in 1977 made up 25 percent ($2.025 billion) of all Chinese exports, and grain alone accounted for 6 percent ($455 million) (see table 2-3, part 2); as percentages of total trade, these figures were almost exactly the same as in 1965, when food accounted for 26 percent of total exports and grain alone for 6 percent. Exports of manufactured goods accounted for 43 percent ($3.415 billion) of total exports in 1977, compared with 45 percent in 1965; textiles alone (including yarn, fabrics, and clothing, almost all agriculture based) accounted for 23 percent ($1.860 billion) in 1977, which was roughly equal to the 24 percent made up by textiles in 1965. When the figure for exports of agricultural crude materials is added to those for foodstuffs and textiles, in 1977 well over half of all Chinese exports (perhaps close to two-thirds) were still either agricultural commodities or agriculture-based products, as was the case in the 1960s.

However, one new trend foreshadowed greater possible change in the future. In the early 1970s the first signs occurred of a determination to earn substantially more amounts of foreign exchange in the future from exports of the mineral products of extractive industries. The most important single new development in China's export trade in recent years has been the addition of oil to the list of major Chinese export commodities. When they began in 1973, exports of petroleum and petroleum products constituted only 2 percent ($80 million) of China's total exports. Immediately thereafter they rose to 8 percent ($525 million) in 1974 and to 13 percent ($910 million) in 1975.[143] During the next two years they remained at roughly the same level, 12 percent ($840 million) in 1976 and 13 percent ($1.015 billion) in 1977. Subsequently, however, the Chinese made it clear that they now hope to expand exports of products from all of their extractive industries, including oil, coal, and various other minerals. The degree of success they achieve in this respect will be another key variable that will help to determine how much they will be able to increase their total trade and their capital goods imports.

In the long run the size of China's oil exports may prove to be one of the most critical factors affecting its overall trade. General prospects in the field of energy in China are analyzed in part IV, but it is worth noting here that if by 1982 it could export 20 million tons of oil (which its present plans, including a commitment to raise oil exports to Japan to the level of 15 million tons by 1982,[144] indicate it would like to do), it

TABLE 2-3 (Part 2). *China: Commodity Composition of Exports, by Area, 1976–77*[a]
Millions of U.S. dollars

Commodity	1976					1977				
	Total	Developed	Less developed	Hong Kong[b] and Macao	Communist	Total	Developed	Less developed	Hong Kong[b] and Macao	Communist
Total	7,265	2,695	1,700	1,630	1,240	7,955	2,925	1,865	1,795	1,370
Foodstuffs	1,945	485	450	715	300	2,025	475	470	760	320
Live animals	230	180	...	230	...	250	...	...	250	...
Meat and fish	430	180	60	50	20	400	140	60	170	30
Eggs and dairy products	65	10	10	85	...	60	5	5	50	...
Grains	450	25	160	115	180	455	20	190	80	165
Fruits and vegetables	385	170	65	15	35	490	195	80	140	75
Teas and spices	140	45	65	5	10	150	55	60	20	20
Tobacco	35	15	15	...	...	30	...	20	5	5
Crude materials	1,805	1,135	145	215	310	2,045	1,280	170	245	350
Hides and skins, undressed	30	30	...	...	...	30	30	...	...	...
Oil seeds	85	65	5	10	5	90	55	10	10	15
Textile fibers	285	195	...	50	30	290	255	10	15	10
Crude minerals	65	45	5	10	10	75	50	15	10	15
Metalliferous ores	45	40	...	...	5	45	35	10	...	10
Crude animal materials	260	150	25	65	20	330	170	35	90	35
Coal	95	10	5	...	80	95	30	5	...	60

Crude oil	665	540	60	...	60	785	625	75	...	85
Petroleum products	175	15	25	65	75	230	10	25	110	85
Fixed vegetable oils	40	15	5	15	5	25	10	5	10	...
Chemicals	330	150	80	60	40	380	160	85	70	65
Medicinal products	40	10	15	20	...	50	10	10	25	5
Essential oils and soap	45	25	10	5	5	60	25	15	10	10
Manufactures	3,060	890	1,015	675	535	3,415	1,000	1,135	705	575
Leather and dressed skins	65	50	...	10	...	65	50	25	15	15
Paper	65	5	20	30	5	60	5	25	25	5
Textile yarn and fabrics	1,155	340	325	265	225	1,300	400	380	280	240
Nonmetallic mineral products	150	30	60	60	...	170	35	55	65	15
Iron and steel	105	10	55	15	25	110	5	75	15	15
Nonferrous metals	90	40	70	5	35	65	25	5	5	30
Metal products	105	10	55	25	5	180	15	100	25	40
Nonelectric machinery	140	10	40	25	50	140	70	70	20	45
Electric machinery	75	5	50	20	10	75	40	40	20	10
Transport equipment	70	5	50	...	15	55	5	35	...	20
Clothing	420	170	105	70	80	560	210	150	105	95
Footwear	65	20	20	10	15	65	25	25	15	...
Handicrafts and manufactures	320	155	80	55	25	370	170	115	65	20
Other	110	30	10	10	55	95	15	5	15	60

Source: Same as table 2-3, part 1.

a. Data are rounded to the nearest $5 million. Because of rounding, components may not add to the totals shown. Ellipsis marks indicate that exports, if any, amounted to less than U.S. $2.5 million. Estimates are based on data reported by trading partners. Where data are incomplete, as for the less developed and Communist countries, estimates are based on fragmentary information from trade agreements and press reports and on commodity breakdowns for earlier years.

b. Including Hong Kong re-exports of PRC-origin goods to third countries.

would then earn about $4.4 billion a year, assuming a price of about $30 a barrel, or about $220 a ton. If by 1985 it could export 50 million tons (which not long ago seemed to be Peking's target) and the price was $35 a barrel (about $256 a ton), it would be earning between $12 billion and $13 billion a year from oil exports. If oil prices were to rise to $40 a barrel (about $292 a ton), and China could export 50 million to 100 million tons a year, its oil exports could earn between $14 billion and $29 billion annually. It doubtless will not be able to achieve levels this high during the first half of the 1980s; for reasons that will be discussed later, oil exports are likely to be more important to China after 1985 than in the next few years. Recently, some Chinese have indicated to the Japanese that they may not be able to fulfill their near-term targets. Nevertheless, oil exports could be increasingly important to the Chinese from the mid-1980s on. How much Peking believes it will be able to prudently borrow during the next few years to finance immediate capital goods imports will probably be significantly influenced by its leaders' judgment on oil export prospects during the second half of the 1980s.

A second recent trend of great potential importance has been toward diversification of China's manufactured goods exports. Even though in 1977 exports of manufactured goods accounted for roughly the same share of total exports as in 1965, and textiles remained dominant among them (handicrafts were next), there have been many indications that the Chinese now recognize that they must try rapidly to broaden their manufactured goods exports. Starting some years ago, they began to develop markets for Chinese-made machinery and equipment as well as more varied consumer goods. By 1977 China's machinery and equipment exports totaled $270 million ($140 million nonelectric machinery, $75 million electric machinery, and $55 million transport equipment). This was only 3 to 4 percent of China's total exports, but Peking will try to expand such exports, and they are likely to increase gradually. The main opportunities they now see, however, lie in the field of consumer goods, and since 1977 it has become clear that the Chinese are determined to achieve a large increase in exports in this category.[145]

The task that China faces in expanding its textiles and other manufactured goods exports, in both new and old markets, is a challenging one. If, for example, the Chinese attempt to increase total exports at an average annual rate of 12 percent (in constant dollars) during the period 1980–85, they will have to rise from $13.5 billion in 1979 to almost $24 billion in 1985; and if they simply were to keep their exports of all manufactured goods, and of textiles specifically, at the same levels (as percentages of total exports) as in 1977 (43 percent and 23 percent, respectively), by 1985 China would have to find markets for more than $10 billion of manufactured goods of all types, including more than $5 billion of textiles. (If, during this period, prices rise and the ratio of manufactured goods to total exports increases, the overall figure will be higher; however, since the Chinese will try to diversify their manufactured goods exports, the figure for textiles might be lower.) These hypothetical projections are not predictions. Nevertheless, they give an idea of the size of the markets that China may feel compelled to try to develop in the period immediately ahead. It will face many difficulties in the process.

The character of China's exports could change more in the next decade than it has in the last. Because of the lag in China's agriculture (at least in relation to its needs), its huge labor force, and the size of its resources of oil, coal, and other basic raw materials, its comparative advantage in the period ahead will lie in increasing exports of oil, other raw materials, and labor-intensive manufactured goods (textiles and many others) as much as possible, while trying to reduce, at least proportionately, its exports of agricultural products.[146] It will also be in China's interest to shift, to the extent possible, from manufactured products using agricultural raw materials to those using mineral products (for example, from cotton textiles to textiles using synthetic fibers). Although no dramatic shift will be immediately feasible, Peking's leaders give evidence that they are thinking along these lines. And if the Chinese are able to increase their exports of low-cost manufactured goods, as well as oil, coal, and other minerals, China's international position as an exporter will undergo important changes as its position as an importer also changes.

Different Trade Patterns: With Developed, Developing, and Communist Nations

The differences in the character of Chinese economic relationships with the industrialized nations, developing countries, and Communist bloc states become clearer if one examines the direction of trade for particular categories of commodities. In 1977 the Chinese spent $1.2 billion for purchases of foreign machinery and equipment, its highest priority imports.[147] Of this, $710 million, or almost 60 percent, was spent in the non-Communist DCs. Almost all of the rest ($475 million, or 40 percent of the total) was bought from Communist bloc countries. Virtually none came from the LDCs. A similar pattern prevailed in China's trade in the intermediate industrial materials. In 1977, 94 percent of China's iron and steel imports ($1.470 billion of a total of $1.570 billion) came from the DCs, a small amount from other Communist nations ($90 million), and only a negligible amount ($10 million) from the LDCs. China also depends on the DCs for most of its imports of textile yarn and fabrics ($155 million of a total of $175 million in 1977). Only in the category of non-ferrous metals did the LDCs supply a significant share of sales to China ($105 million, or about 40 percent of China's total imports of such metals); even in this category, the DCs provided more ($120 million, or 45 percent) and the Communist countries a significant amount ($40 million, or 15 percent). Altogether, in 1977 three-quarters of China's imports of manufactured goods of all types ($2.670 billion of a total of $3.555 billion) came from the DCs, 20 percent from Communist countries, and less than 5 percent from LDCs. In 1977 China also obtained 80 percent of its imports of chemicals (including chemical fertilizers) from the DCs ($710 million out of $885 million total imports in 1977).

China is now dependent on the DCs, moreover, for most of its important food imports. In 1977, 85 percent of China's grain imports ($630 million of a total of $745 million) came from these countries, and only 15 percent from the LDCs (mainly Argentina). Of China's total imports of all foodstuffs, the LDCs provided a sizable amount (31 percent, or $350 million of a total of $1.115 billion), but the DCs provided much more (62 percent, or $695 million); 6 percent ($70 million) came from the Communist nations. Only in the case of sugar is China dependent primarily on the LDCs for a major food item; in 1977 it obtained from them almost two-thirds of its imports of this commodity ($205 million of a total of $320 million).

The one important major category in which China imports considerably more from the LDCs than from the DCs is "crude materials"; in 1977, 56 percent of its imports of such materials came from the LDCs. The LDCs provided the bulk of China's imports of natural textile fibers (86 percent, or $300 million, of a total of $350 million), crude natural rubber (93 percent, or $200 million, of a total of $215 million), and oil-seeds (87 percent, or $100 million, of a total of $115 million). Even in this category, however, the LDCs' dominance has subsequently been eroded as China has bought more cotton from the United States and increased its imports as well as domestic production of synthetic fibers (in 1977 it imported $150 million of such fibers, all from the DCs). In the future, it might rely more on synthetic rubber to the detriment of natural rubber imports. There appears to be little prospect, therefore, that the LDCs' exports to China could rise as a percentage of total Chinese imports in the period ahead; they are more likely to decline.

Although Chinese exports are more evenly distributed among various groups of nations, in 1977 the DCs accounted for the largest share ($2.925 billion, or 37 percent of China's total exports of $7.955 billion). However, other nations were not so far behind. The LDCs accounted for 23 percent ($1.865 billion), Hong Kong (and Macao) for 23 percent ($1.795 billion), and the Communist countries for 17 percent ($1.370 billion). An examination of the pattern of exports to each group provides clues to where China may try to expand sales in the period ahead.

China's markets for textiles, its largest single category of exports, are widely distributed. In 1977, of its total textile exports, which amounted to $1.860 billion ($1.300 billion of textile yarn and fabrics and $560 million of clothing), 33 percent ($610 million) went to the DCs, 28 percent ($530 million) to the LDCs, 21 percent ($385 million) to Hong Kong, and 18 percent ($335 million) to Communist countries.

However, the LDCs were China's largest export market for all manufactured goods. Of total exports in this category in 1977 ($3.415 billion), 33 percent ($1.135 billion) went to the LDCs, 29 percent ($1.000 billion) to the DCs, 21 percent ($705 million) to Hong Kong, and 17 percent ($575 million) to Communist bloc countries. In certain categories LDC markets are now particularly important to China. In 1977, 54 percent ($145 million of a total of $270 million) of China's exports of machinery and equipment went to the LDCs, compared with 28 percent ($75 million) to the Communist nations, 15 percent ($40 million) to Hong Kong, and 4 percent ($10 million) to the DCs. In 1977 China also sold to the LDCs plus Hong Kong a large percentage of certain other products, including 71 percent of its nonmetallic mineral exports ($120 million of a total of $170 million) and 82 percent of its iron and steel exports ($90 million of $110 million total). China's sales of handicraft goods were almost equally divided between the LDCs plus Hong Kong and the DCs; of a total of $370 million, $180 million went to the former and $170 million to the latter. The main export markets for China's nonferrous metals, however, were in the Communist nations, which in 1977 accounted for 46 percent ($30 million of a total of $65 million) of Chinese sales, compared with 38 percent ($25 million) for the DCs and only 15 percent ($10 million) for the LDCs plus Hong Kong.

The largest market for China's exports of foodstuffs is Hong Kong, which in 1977 accounted for 38 percent ($760 million of a total of $2.025 billion) of all food sales; 23 percent ($475 million) went to the DCs, 23 percent ($470 million) to the LDCs, and 16 percent ($320 million) to Communist bloc nations. Hong Kong bought two-thirds of China's exports of live animals, meat, fish, eggs, and dairy products ($470 million of a total of $710 million). However, China's grain exports ($455 million, most of it rice) went mainly to the LDCs ($190 million) and Communist bloc nations ($165 million). The only category of foodstuffs in which the DCs now provide China's largest markets is fruits and vegetables; in 1977 $195 million (of a total of $490 million) went to the DCs and $140 million went to Hong Kong.

The pattern is different, however, for crude materials, which accounted for 26 percent of all China's exports in 1977 ($2.045 billion, of $7.955 billion). The DCs now provide China with its major markets for exports in this category. In 1977, 63 percent ($1.280 billion) went to them, 17 percent ($350 million) to Communist countries, 12 percent ($245 million) to Hong Kong, and 8 percent ($170 million) to the LDCs. The DCs (mainly Japan) purchased 63 percent ($635 million of a total of $1.015 billion) of China's largest crude material export, petroleum and petroleum products, and 88 percent ($255 million of a total of $290 million) of its next largest, textile fibers. In the case of petroleum the Communists ranked second (taking $170 million, or 17 percent), Hong Kong third (taking $110 million, or 11 percent), and the LDCs fourth (taking $100 million, or 10 percent). The pattern of China's export of chemicals was similar; the DCs took more than two-fifths of China's total exports of $380 million, while the LDCs, Hong Kong, and Communist bloc nations each took close to one-fifth.

In light of China's existing trade patterns, certain trends and problems seem highly probable in the period ahead. As China tries to increase its purchases of plants, machinery, and equipment, the percentage of its import trade conducted with the non-Communist DCs, already very high, could increase further. China's imports of food and intermediate industrial goods probably will also continue to rise, and since most of these, too, will have to be obtained from the DCs, this will reinforce the trend toward reliance on the DCs for an increasing share of China's imports.

Even if China finances some of its imports with credit, it will have to expand its exports fairly rapidly to pay for its growing imports. How, and where, will it be able to do this? How much China can continue to expand its exports to Hong Kong is debatable, since Hong Kong is small and its imports of many Chinese commodities may be approaching a saturation point. Although exports of some commodities to the colony, including oil, coal, and many manufactured goods, probably can be increased further (and the foreign exchange earned from this trade will continue to be of vital importance to China), it is unlikely that China's net foreign exchange earnings from Hong Kong trade will grow as rapidly as its deficits with the DCs. The Chinese will have to try harder, therefore, to expand their export markets elsewhere, on a much larger scale than in the past.

China will certainly try to expand exports of all kinds to the major non-Communist industrial nations from which it obtains its most important imports. Chinese exports to them of crude materials, especially oil, coal, and other raw materials, will probably grow substantially during the next few years. Apart from such raw materials, labor-intensive manufactured goods, especially consumer goods, offer the Chinese the greatest opportunities for expanding exports fairly rapidly in the period ahead. They will doubtless mount a major export drive, therefore, to sell increasing quantities of such goods to both the DCs and the LDCs and perhaps to Communist bloc countries as well. Success will not come easily, however, in part because of growing import restrictions, especially in the DCs; nevertheless, exports of low-cost manufactured goods probably can be increased significantly, especially in the LDCs. Even though some other developing countries are more experienced in such trade, if the Chinese successfully implement their new policies, which call for much greater flexibility in trading methods, they probably will learn how to develop markets more effectively than in the past. Their labor costs are clearly lower even than those of most other developing countries already engaged in trade on a large scale, and this could give China an important advantage. Conceivably, therefore, the Chinese may gradually capture an increasing share of some of the world's major markets for low-quality, low-cost goods. If so, this will probably reinforce the tendency of South Korea, Taiwan, and others to focus on goods of higher quality, requiring relatively advanced technological methods of production.[148] Even though the Chinese will try to expand markets for their manufactured goods in both the DCs and LDCs, the potential in the LDCs may prove to be larger.

In sum, as China's trade expands, the percentage of its imports obtained from developed countries is likely to continue rising and become even more critical than at present. Yet exports to the LDCs will also become increasingly important to China because of its need to earn foreign exchange. Future trends probably will reinforce the triangular trade pattern that has already evolved, in which China obtains its most important imports from the non-Communist industrial nations but helps to pay for them with earnings from its trade with the Third World and Hong Kong. China's trade with Communist bloc nations probably will not grow greatly unless and until political relationships improve, although the potential for substantial increase exists and may become increasingly tempting over time.

Imports of Machinery and Equipment

Even though China's foreign trade remains small in relation to its GNP, it is much more important to the Chinese economy than this small percentage might suggest. Certain imports are essential to maintain economic and political stability. Grain, fertilizers, textile fibers, iron and steel, and nonferrous metals that the Chinese purchase abroad are necessary to keep their economy operating effectively, using their existing capacity. Imports of complete plants, machinery, equipment, and other forms of advanced technology are vital to the success of Peking's present modernization plans and China's long-term prospects for growth.

Technological change is recognized to be one of the most important variables affecting economic growth, and imports of machinery and equipment are one of the most important means to promote technological change.[149] In the words of a leading Western analyst of the Chinese economy, imports have been "crucial" to China's development because they have been a "highway for the importation of advanced technology and capital goods" and, therefore, "vital in the process of industrialization."[150]

The scale of China's imports of machinery and equipment and their importance in China's total import trade have varied greatly in the years since 1949, however. In periods when Peking has placed greatest stress on rapid growth, these imports have risen; in periods when it has emphasized social goals or experienced serious economic difficulties, these imports have dropped, sometimes precipitously. In 1952, on the eve of China's first Five Year Plan period, imports were small, totaling just under $200 million.[151] Then, during China's first Five Year Plan period, they rose very rapidly, reaching a peak of more than $900 million in 1959 (table 2-4). During 1952–60 they totaled close to $5 billion, averaging more than one-half billion dollars a year for the entire period. From 1958 through 1960 the average was considerably higher, more than $800 million a year. China's purchases of capital goods in the 1950s, all from the Communist bloc, were far above any it had made previously. One analyst maintains that they constituted "the most comprehensive technology transfer in modern industrial history."[152] Whether or not this is the case, they certainly constituted the largest rapid transfer of technology to China up to that time.

Following the Sino-Soviet split, China's imports of machinery and equipment were much smaller in the 1960s. During the post-Leap depression they dropped precipitously, to a low of $100 million in 1963. Thereafter they rose again, to more than $400 million in 1966, but in the late 1960s they slumped to about $200 million. For the entire 1961–69 period, they totaled only a little more than $2 billion, averaging under $250 million a year for the entire period, less than half the level of the previous nine years.

Starting in the early 1970s China's imports of machinery and equipment have again risen rapidly. Even before Peking initiated its new modernization program, they had reached a level above that of the 1950s. Between 1970 and 1974 they quadrupled, from about $400 million to $1.6 billion; then they soared to well over $2 billion in 1975. During 1976 they remained high, at $1.8 billion. Then in 1977 they were temporarily cut back because of China's large trade deficit in 1975, dropping to $1.2 billion in 1977. Nevertheless, during 1970–77, they totaled almost $9 billion, which was more (in current dollars) than the cumulative total from 1949 to 1970. The annual average was more than $1 billion for the entire eight-year period, and during 1974–77 the average was close to $1.7 billion a year. These current dollar figures overstate the actual rise, but even after adjustments are made for inflation, China's imports of machinery and equipment in 1975 were almost three times those of 1970 in real terms and may well have exceeded those in 1959, the peak year for such imports from the Communist bloc.[153]

The drop in 1976–77 was simply a temporary slowdown, and immediately thereafter China resumed its purchasing of machinery and equipment on a large scale. By the end of 1978 the Chinese had contracted for at least $7 billion, and possibly more, of machinery and equipment imports, and they were seriously discussing purchases of several tens of

TABLE 2-4. *China: Imports of Machinery and Equipment*[a]

	Imports (current U.S. dollars)			Exports (millions of U.S. dollars)		
Year	Total	Commu-nist	Non-Communist	Total	Commu-nist	Non-Communist
1952	193	181	12	2	2	*
1953	276	255	21	2	2	*
1954	381	368	13	47	47	*
1955	411	396	15	58	57	1
1956	545	503	42	52	50	2
1957	566	500	66	33	30	3
1958	715	645	70	40	33	7
1959	933	873	60	59	50	9
1960	840	790	50	39	33	6
1961	272	246	26	71	67	4
1962	102	86	16	70	65	5
1963	100	76	24	70	59	11
1964	162	101	61	62	52	10
1965	302	147	155	62	45	17
1966[b]	443	205	238	71	49	22
1967	335	133	202	92	72	20
1968	235	129	106	97	74	23
1969	214	115	99	88	63	25
1970	398	149	249	91	48	43
1971	481	222	259	119	55	64
1972	524	278	246	124	63	61
1973	797	296	501	172	97	75
1974	1,605	370	1,240	255	150	100
1975	2,160	440	1,710	335	240	100
1976	1,770	475	1,295	285	210	75
1977	1,200	475	725	270	75	195

Sources: Figures for 1952–73: CIA, *Foreign Trade in Machinery and Equipment Since 1952*, Reference Aid A ER 75-60, January 1975, p. 1. Both imports and exports are f.o.b. country of origin. Figures for 1974–77: CIA, *People's Republic of China: International Trade Handbook*, Research Aid ER 76-10610, October 1976, pp. 16–17; and NFAC, CIA, *China: International Trade, 1977–78*, pp. 14–15. Non-Communist trade statistics for these years give Chinese exports f.o.b. and imports c.i.f. Figures are rounded to nearest 5 million, so totals may vary from the added components.

* Negligible.

a. The terms machinery and equipment refer to those commodities included in section 7 (Machinery and Transport Equipment) of the Standard International Trade Classification (SITC). Section 7 of the SITC differs slightly from the Soviet classification of machinery, equipment, and transportation facilities; hence the data on non-Communist trade are not precisely comparable with the data on trade with the Soviet Union and other Communist countries.

b. In the original table, the total for 1966 was $433 million, an obvious error, which I have changed to $443 million. (Earlier CIA estimates for 1966 were $455 million.)

billions of dollars more. Actual imports of "technology and complete sets of equipment," according to Chinese figures, totaled about $880 million in 1978, and Peking's plans called for a 220 percent increase to about $3.0 billion in 1979.[154] Actual imports in 1979 fell short of the target but, nevertheless, according to the Chinese, increased to more than $2.75 billion, a new peak.[155]

The pattern as well as the scale of China's purchases of foreign machinery and equipment has changed over the years.[156] During 1952–61 China purchased almost all (well over nine-tenths) of its imports in this category from Communist bloc countries. Then, following the Sino-Soviet split, the bloc's share declined fairly rapidly, to roughly 50 percent in the mid-1960s. Thereafter, however, even though China's overall trade with Communist countries continued to drop and by 1970 accounted for less than 20 percent of total Chinese trade, Peking's imports of machinery and equipment from the bloc stabilized. During the eight-year period 1965–72 these countries provided almost half (47 percent) of China's imports of machinery and equipment, even though they accounted for only 23 percent of China's total foreign trade in the period.

However, since 1973 the Chinese have obtained an increasing share of their machinery and equipment imports from the non-Communist industrial nations. In 1976, 73 percent ($1.295 billion) of their total machinery and equipment imports ($1.770 billion) came from these nations and in 1977 the figures were 60 percent, or $725 million of a total of $1.2 billion.[157] This percentage has continued to rise as a result of China's surge of buying from Japan and the West.

However, continuation of this trend will depend on whether or not China can pay for what it wishes to obtain from Japan and the West. At some point the Chinese may be tempted to increase their imports of machinery and equipment from Communist nations. It is worth noting that Chinese imports of capital goods from the bloc (mainly, at present, from East European nations) continue to be important; in recent years capital goods imports from the bloc actually have fluctuated less than imports of such goods from the non-Communist nations. For example, in 1977, when China temporarily cut back its overall imports of machinery and equipment (mainly because of shortages of foreign exchange), the cuts were entirely in imports of these items from the non-Communist DCs, which dropped to $725 million (60 percent of the total). Machinery and equipment imports from Communist bloc countries remained at the same level as in 1976, $475 million (and they rose from 27 to 40 percent

of total Chinese imports of this kind). In both 1976 and 1977 machinery
and equipment dominated China's imports from the Communist countries, making up more than two-fifths of the total (43 percent in 1976,
41 percent in 1977).[158]

With large-scale Western credits available to it, China is less likely to
cut back its capital goods imports from the non-Communist nations suddenly or drastically, and even if they fluctuate from year to year, they
should increase substantially in the period ahead. However, the Chinese
may continue to look to the Communist bloc as a major source for certain types of capital goods, especially transportation equipment, if past
experience provides any clues to the future. It is at least possible that imports of other machinery and equipment from the bloc countries could
also rise, especially if there is any improvement in political relations
between Peking and Moscow.

The capital goods China has imported during the past three decades
have included items for virtually every modern industry in China and
many kinds of agricultural machinery and transportation equipment.[159]
In the 1950s and early 1960s imports of complete plants and machinery
for major industries predominated. However, since the early 1960s the
quantity of transportation equipment imported has grown significantly.
In 1976 transportation equipment accounted for 27 percent ($470 mil-
lion) and in 1977 for 53 percent ($640 million) of China's total imports
of machinery and equipment.[160] Sales of transportation equipment to
China by Communist nations totaled $265 million in 1976 and $275 million in 1977 and accounted for about half (56 percent in 1976 and 43 percent in 1977) of total Chinese imports of transportation equipment and
for more than half (56 percent and 58 percent) of all Communist sales
of machinery and equipment to China in 1976 and 1977.

Generally, when China has increased its imports of capital goods substantially, it has given high priority to the importation of complete
plants. In certain periods it has clearly viewed plants as *the* principal
means to acquire new, advanced technology. The first and, until recently, most important surge in Chinese purchases of complete plants
was in the 1950s. At that time they dominated China's capital goods imports. Soviet statistics indicate that in the decade 1952–61 imports of
complete plants accounted for 62 percent of China's total imports of
machinery and equipment from the Soviet Union.[161] Most of these
plants were bought under the provisions of 291 Sino-Soviet agreements
signed in the 1950s. In addition, the Chinese signed 100 agreements with

East European countries, many of which also involved the importation of complete plants.[162] According to one study, in China's worldwide trade during that same period imports of complete plants accounted for 37 percent of all its imports of machinery and equipment ($2 billion out of a total of $5.4 billion).[163]

In the early 1960s, during China's post-Leap depression, the importation of complete plants was halted entirely. During 1963–66 importation was resumed briefly on a relatively small scale; altogether, during those years the Chinese purchased fifty or more new plants from Japan and Western Europe. Few, however, were very large, and it is estimated that together they were worth about $200 million.[164] After 1966 the Cultural Revolution resulted in another total cutoff of complete plant imports that lasted into the early 1970s. Then, in late 1972 Peking decided to give high priority to the purchase of complete plants, this time entirely from the non-Communist industrial nations, with Japan the leading source, followed by the West European nations. As a result, plant purchases soared.

It is difficult to calculate precisely how much of China's machinery imports in recent years has consisted of complete plants, but the figures on the value of contracts signed for plant purchases provide one measure of the importance placed on such imports.[165] According to U.S. government estimates, contracts for whole plants and technology suddenly jumped in 1973 (from a small figure in 1972) to $1.259 billion. In 1974 the figure was lower, but still high; $831 million in such contracts were signed during that year. Thereafter, there was a lull for three years—the figures dropped to $364 million in 1975, $185 million in 1976, and $59 million in 1977—but in 1978 they skyrocketed to an unprecedented level, totaling $6.787 billion (and possibly more), making the 1973–78 total $9.485 billion. (Japanese estimates are not very different.[166]) The American data indicate that during the five years 1973–77 the Chinese contracted for the purchase of seventy or more complete plants and that in 1978 alone the number was close to the total of the previous five years.[167]

Then, in 1979 Yu Chiu-li and others cautioned against hasty purchasing and excessive emphasis on complete plant imports, and during 1979 contract signings dropped sharply, to $1.706 billion, according to a U.S. government estimate. Undoubtedly, the Chinese will continue plant purchases but possibly at a pace comparable to that in 1979 rather than that in 1978. Deliveries on most contracts will extend for several years. Annual imports of plants—that is, actual deliveries—should rise, however, and according to some optimistic projections, could range between $3 billion and $7 billion a year during the first half of the 1980s.[168] Because of the economic slowdown resulting from Peking's "readjustment" in mid-1979, these estimates are probably too high for the period immediately ahead but plausible for the period following the readjustment.

Imports of machinery and equipment probably will increase as a percentage of total imports, but it remains to be seen whether they reach the level of the 1950s. In the 1950s such purchases rose spectacularly as a percentage of total imports, from about 19 percent in 1952 to a peak of roughly 45 percent in 1959.[169] For the five-year period 1956–60 they averaged 40 percent. During the 1960s, when China's growth slowed, its need for food imports rose, its export capability declined, and its purchases of machinery and equipment dropped; at one point they reached a low of 8 percent of total imports (in 1963). Briefly, during 1965–67, the percentage rose to about 18, but thereafter it fell again, to 12 percent in 1969.

Since the start of the 1970s, it has risen significantly. During 1970–77 imports of machinery and equipment averaged 21 percent of total imports, and briefly, during 1976–77, they were 29 percent. The figure may eventually rise in the decade ahead. But if it rises dramatically, China's problems of finding enough foreign exchange to pay for the imports of grain, fertilizer, steel, and other commodities will multiply. China's actual imports of machinery and equipment during 1971–77 totaled $8.5 billion to $8.6 billion, averaging more than $1.2 billion a year; during the same period, its imports of iron, steel, and nonferrous metals totaled $9.8 billion, averaging $1.4 billion a year, and its imports of grain totaled $4.3 billion, averaging more than $600 million a year.[170] In the period ahead competing demands for foreign exchange to be used for capital goods imports clearly will create problems.

Even if China's imports of machinery and equipment increase sharply, they are not likely to constitute more than a small percentage of the country's total requirements for capital goods. In this respect, the situation has changed greatly in comparison to the 1950s. In the 1950s China had to rely heavily on imports to meet such needs, but since then China's own machine-building industry has grown extremely rapidly, at an average annual rate of almost 17 percent during the years 1952–75,[171] far higher than the growth rate for industry as a whole. As a result, the proportion of machinery imports to the total net annual additions to China's stock of machinery and equipment has declined steeply. According to several studies, during the 1950s imports of equipment probably contributed about 40 percent of the equipment component of investment in China, but by the early 1970s these imports contributed only about 10 percent (and possibly less).[172] Stated differently, by the early 1970s China's self-sufficiency in machinery had risen to more than 90 percent. According to another estimate, in the 1950s as much as a half of all machinery and equipment installed in China came from abroad, but by 1973 imports probably represented only about 6 to 8 percent of China's own machinery and equipment production.[173] As a proportion of China's total capital formation, imports of machinery and equipment are estimated by one analyst to have been close to 10 percent in the 1950s, but thereafter they dropped to perhaps as low as 3 percent by the early 1970s.[174] (If this estimate is correct, China's situation now is comparable with that of the Soviet Union. In recent years, Soviet imports of machinery from the West, which have accounted for close to 40 percent of its total imports from the West, are estimated to have provided about 4 percent of the Soviet Union's domestic equipment investment.[175] Moscow reportedly has bought more machines from East Germany than from the West, however, and if these were included, the percentage would be higher.)

While it is evident that over time imported machinery and equipment have provided a declining percentage of China's total needs, purely quantitative measures are misleading. They do not measure the qualitative impact of such imports. There is no doubt that ever since the 1950s imports of advanced types of machinery and equipment have played a crucial role in raising the technological level of Chinese industry, thereby contributing notably to China's growth. According to one estimate, during China's first Five Year Plan period imports of machinery and equipment were probably responsible for at least 20 percent and possibly as much as 50 percent of China's total growth.[176] No comparable estimate is available for recent years, but it is clear that the contribution of these imports to development and growth has continued to be much larger than one might conclude simply from statistics on their quantitative contribution to China's total capital stock. (In the Soviet case, even though imports have probably not accounted for more than 4 percent of domestic inventory in recent years, one estimate indicates that without them Soviet industrial growth during 1968–73 might have been 15 percent lower than it was.)[177]

Today Peking's leaders hope that the qualitative effects of imports of machinery and equipment will help rapidly to raise the technological level, efficiency, and productivity of China's entire economy. Whether or not this occurs will be determined by how much China imports and, more important, by how rapidly and effectively the Chinese are able to absorb the new technology and adapt it for use throughout their economy.

Technology Absorption

The frankness with which Peking's current leaders acknowledge the present shortcomings of the Chinese economic system and their need to acquire new knowledge as well as machinery from abroad augurs well for China's development in the period ahead. They now appear genuinely to recognize that it will not be sufficient just to buy plants and that to modernize they must rapidly improve their research capabilities, expand their training of skilled personnel, and acquire knowledge of foreign managerial and production methods as well as new scientific and technological information. They also acknowledge that while restructuring their economic system, they must establish new kinds of intellectual as well as economic relationships with the world community.

Despite these encouraging changes in official attitudes, however, the Chinese undoubtedly will encounter problems in trying to acquire, adapt, and absorb new technology at the pace that China's leaders seem to want, and they will have to overcome numerous and formidable impediments to change.

Rapid technology absorption is not a simple process.[178] Old cultural and political attitudes, shortages of skilled manpower, intractable social habits, institutional rigidities, and the manifest shortcomings of the existing planning and managerial systems in China will all pose major obstacles to effective use of much of the technology they import. The weaknesses in China's existing economic infrastructure will pose other obstacles. The intrinsic problems of trying to integrate advanced technology into an economic system in which the general technological level lags far behind that of the advanced nations will be enormous. Many of the organizational and institutional characteristics of Communist "command economies" tend to work against rapid technological change and innovation, as past experience in the Soviet Union and elsewhere, as well as in China, has demonstrated.[179] The incentive systems affecting managers, workers, and others have given inadequate rewards for the risks involved in experimentation, and decision making has tended to be conservative. Pricing policies have usually failed to give sufficient encouragement to the development of new or improved products. The inadequacy of the existing links between research and production, and between foreign trade and domestic economic activity, also has worked to impede change. Moreover, in China, the policies pursued when the radicals were in the ascendant so severely damaged the country's system of higher education, its research establishment, and its enterprise management structure that many of the effects may be long lasting; China's leaders are still trying to overcome them.

Nevertheless, the changes in Chinese attitudes are extremely important. They provide a much stronger ideological and intellectual basis than in the past for attempting to cope with the problems of rapid technological modernization. Now Chinese leaders at least recognize the huge dimensions of the tasks and problems they face. The author of the 1978 article on "Why China Imports Technology and Equipment" stated, "Technological progress was formerly timed by centuries, whereas major scientific and technological breakthroughs are now made every ten years or even every year."[180] Echoing Teng, this author emphasized that Chinese must first of all "acknowledge our backwardness so as to swiftly change our backwardness."

China's leaders are right when they stress the rapidity of technological change in the world today, underline China's relative backwardness, and emphasize the necessity of broadening scientific and technological as well as economic ties with the international community if China is to modernize more rapidly. Even under optimal conditions, it will not be easy to "catch up." According to one study, the "indicators" of modern scientific development worldwide have recently been doubling about every fifteen years.[181] Even countries at the forefront of scientific progress take many years to convert new knowledge into usable technology. Much technology uses discoveries that are twenty-five to thirty years old.[182] Frequently it takes ten years or more in the West to convert an innovative technical idea or invention into large-scale production and use.[183] Since China lags anywhere from ten to thirty years behind world levels in various fields of science and technology,[184] its only hope of "catching up" is to learn rapidly from more advanced nations.

China is not unique in this respect. Virtually all developing countries trying to speed up their modernization are compelled to obtain both knowledge and equipment on a sizable scale from foreign sources. In recent years, the developing nations as a group have increasingly recognized this and stressed the need for more efficient and speedy (and equitable) transfers of technology. Through organizations such as the United Nations Conference on Trade and Development (UNCTAD), they have tried to pressure the industrial nations to facilitate such transfers in new ways and forms that can help to accelerate their development without compromising their sovereignty.[185] China, which faces many problems similar to those of other developing nations, has strongly endorsed the proposals put forward by UNCTAD. But clearly Peking's leaders do not plan to wait for such collective efforts to produce results.

Although the Soviet Union and East European countries in many respects must be regarded as developed rather than developing nations, since the 1960s they too have given much higher priority than in the past to the acquisition of production technology from the West. In recent years, many of these countries have confronted what some have called a "crisis of efficiency," which has compelled them to recognize that in contrast to earlier years when they were able to promote fairly rapid growth primarily by additions of labor and capital, their future growth will depend increasingly on their ability to raise productivity and efficiency through technological and organizational change.[186] In their quest for new technology, many of these countries have broadened their economic ties with the West very significantly through a variety of new cooperative arrangements.

In a sense, China's policies now are based on a similar recognition by its leaders that they too face a "crisis of efficiency," and many of the cooperative arrangements they hope to work out with non-Communist corporations and governments are similar to ones pioneered by East European nations in their relations with the West. In some respects, however, the Chinese now seem to be even more flexible and eclectic, and less constrained by ideology and politics, than the Soviet Union and many East European countries.

The need to acquire technology from abroad is by no means confined to the LDCs and Communist nations in today's world. Even the most advanced industrial countries must depend to a significant degree on technology imports to keep up with the rapid processes of change now occurring worldwide; the most extensive technology transfers occur among these nations. According to one estimate, even the United States, in many respects the most technologically advanced nation in the world, obtained more than half of the knowledge affecting its growth in the 1950s from foreign sources.[187] According to another estimate, imports of machinery and equipment have recently accounted for as much as 11 percent of U.S. companies' total investment in these two areas.[188]

In light of these facts, although China's new attitudes toward technology acquisition appear extraordinary and audacious compared with attitudes in the 1960s, in a global context they are less remarkable. In fact, they indicate that China's leaders are now simply recognizing, in a way that leaders in most countries did years ago, the scientific and technological as well as economic realities of the contemporary world. In recognizing existing realities and committing themselves to an ambitious program of technology acquisition, they have taken a step of enormous importance, but it is only a first step. They still must learn how to acquire and absorb new technology most effectively, and this will doubtless require a great deal of trial and error.

Technology is transferred between nations in many ways.[189] One is the purchase of foreign individual machines and equipment that embody new technology and use of the imported items as prototypes to be copied. The Chinese have tried this method in several periods in the past. In many respects, however, this is a slow and ineffective method. It is difficult to "reverse engineer" complex machines, to learn the precise specifications of their materials and parts, and to understand the many considerations that influenced their design.[190] Often, attempts at reverse engineering take so long that the copies of imported machines are obsolete before they can be manufactured on a large scale. Reverse engineering, moreover, reveals little about the production and management systems that make efficient production possible.

Factors such as these argue in favor of purchases of complete plants, preferably together with extensive foreign managerial and production services as well as technical advice. This is a faster and more efficient way to acquire and absorb new technology. Recognition of this led to the large-scale buying, culminating in the shopping spree of 1978, and abandonment of a do-it-yourself approach. However, purchases of complete plants are expensive. Moreover, the effectiveness of even this method depends on many factors, including the availability of skills locally and the adequacy of the training and advisory services that come with the plants. If such services are restricted to the minimum required to get an imported plant into initial operation, the knowledge and skills acquired may be limited, the periods required to achieve full utilization may be long, and plant operations may be inefficient. Adequate assistance requires close cooperative arrangements with the suppliers, including, in many cases, the use of foreign experts for more than brief periods.

Cooperative arrangements made regarding a single plant may be insufficient to ensure effective utilization of the total technology imported. Often, the operation of one plant depends on many others, and successful planning must take full account of the institutional and social setting, the interrelations of numerous enterprises in large industrial complexes, and the general economic infrastructure, especially the availability of adequate energy and transportation. China's readjustment of plans in mid-1979 showed that many of its leaders and technocrats are aware of the problems, and since then their policies appear to have taken such complexities into account to a greater extent than in the past. Increasingly they have stressed the need for new kinds of cooperative arrangements with foreign corporations that will help the Chinese acquire the essential scientific, technical, production, and management expertise required for effective use of imported plants and machinery.

Recognizing the need to develop China's skilled manpower as rapidly as possible, the Chinese adopted a multifaceted approach to solving the problem.[191] In addition to attempting to raise the quality of China's own educational programs and sending advanced scholars and students abroad for study, they have expanded training in foreign languages to equip large numbers of people to use foreign materials and to work with foreign technicians, and they are sending some lower-level technicians and workers abroad for training in connection with specific purchases of foreign plants or equipment. China's success in absorbing new technology will depend on all these efforts.

Gradually, the number of foreign technicians and advisers invited to China is increasing, and they are staying for longer periods. Most are employees of foreign companies who go to China in connection with particular plant or equipment sales. Some, however, are now being hired directly by the Chinese, as teachers or advisers in Chinese institutions. From 1972 through 1977 about 3,000 foreign experts worked in China for varying periods of time; since then the number has been rising. If and when joint ventures develop on a larger scale, there could be a significant number of foreigners holding managerial positions in China. The Chinese do not seem likely to invite many foreigners to act as senior advisers to government agencies; their experience with the Russians in the 1950s still rankles deeply, and Peking almost certainly does not wish to repeat it. Nevertheless, they have begun to call on a limited number of foreigners for ad hoc advice to government agencies, and this practice could increase.

The Chinese have also stepped up their efforts to acquire technology through written sources and people-to-people contacts of all sorts. Although for many years they purchased a great deal of scientific and technical literature abroad, during the Cultural Revolution this declined. Now, however, it is being done more systematically and on a larger scale than ever, and new mechanisms are being devised to distribute the literature more effectively throughout China. Starting several years ago, Peking began to encourage foreign companies to hold exhibitions and conduct technical seminars in China; these have steadily increased over time. The Chinese have shrewdly used all such opportunities to try to upgrade their level of technological knowledge. The increased emphasis on scientific and technical research within China has been accompanied by a much more active policy of developing international exchanges. After a long period in the late 1960s and early 1970s, during which China's foreign contacts virtually dried up, Peking now sends large numbers of scientific and technical delegations abroad and is inviting an increasing number of foreign experts and specialists to visit China. The Chinese have also begun to participate much more actively than in the past in international scientific and technical conferences and organizations.

All of these steps should enhance the chances of success of China's new approach to technology acquisition, but there is no guarantee of success, and in attempting to absorb billions of dollars worth of advanced technology in a brief period, the Chinese will doubtless experience many failures, or at least partial failures.

No matter how effective their new education and training programs are, the Chinese will encounter serious skilled manpower problems for years, in almost all fields and at all levels. Training takes time; basic education requires many years. Although the Chinese being educated abroad should make a major contribution to raising the level of China's scientific and technological knowledge in the long run, how much impact they will have in the near future remains to be seen. Moreover, it remains to be seen how well China will be able to reabsorb "returned students" educated abroad in different kinds of educational systems. In some fields the Chinese may be unable to find enough qualified persons, from any source, to achieve their targets.

There will be serious problems resulting from the forced pace of development. Some new plants will suffer from lack of needed materials and parts; others may produce more than China's markets can absorb. The weaknesses in China's infrastructure in fields relating to power, fuels, materials, and transport will take years to remedy. And China's technological "dualism" (or technological "multiplicity")—its use of varied levels of technology in different plants or even within a single plant—will continue to create complex problems.[192] It will be difficult to achieve balance, integration, and complementarity because of differential rates of change and varying levels of technology in different fields and sectors of the economy. While importing advanced technology should make it possible to "leapfrog" ahead in some fields, bottlenecks and imbalances will emerge as a result of faster development in some fields than in others.

Some imported plants, while introducing new technology, may prove to be "inappropriate" in relation to the factor proportions of the Chinese economy and the basic characteristics of Chinese society. In the 1950s the Chinese imported a large number of big, capital-intensive Soviet plants that contributed little to solving China's employment problems. In 1978 it appeared that Peking's leaders might be following that same path. This issue was debated in China in early 1979, however, and as a result of the mid-year readjustment, Chinese planners are trying to avoid squandering resources on plants that are too capital-intensive and to stress the need to increase employment through continued efforts to develop small- as well as large-scale enterprises. Nevertheless, many of the imported plants could create new problems while solving old ones. They will help to advance the country's knowledge of new technology, but it remains to be seen whether they also help to maximize its ability to use its limited resources most efficiently.

While Peking's leaders now recognize that the efficiency with which they are able to use imported plants will depend on how rapidly the country can improve its industrial production and management systems, the Chinese have yet to fully master and apply advanced mass production techniques involving standardization and serialization; their past experience is not wholly reassuring.[193] Some large plants imported in the 1950s still have not developed efficient mass production. The Chinese have had greater difficulty in learning the management techniques necessary for efficient mass production than in acquiring basic production technology itself.

The proposed changes in the structure of China's economic system, designed to (1) improve planning, (2) relate production decisions to real costs, prices, and other market factors, (3) give professionals at the enterprise level more decision-making authority, and (4) strengthen incentive systems, could greatly enhance the chances of success. However, it remains to be seen how effectively the proposed changes can be implemented. Because of inertia and resistance from lower-level bureaucrats, the system cannot be changed overnight.

In the long run to absorb and fully utilize advanced technology the Chinese will have to disseminate it widely throughout the economy. Since the 1950s they have evolved some creative approaches to the problems of popularizing certain types of relatively simple technology, through national and regional conferences and the creation of organizational linkages between large and small enterprises, as well as through publications. For example, small- and medium-size plants producing certain types of motor vehicles have been developed in most provinces with help from larger factories in major industrial cities, and small-scale plants producing fertilizers and some other products have been developed widely at the county level and below on the basis of designs and equipment produced in major centers.[194] However, many of these small plants have been very inefficient.[195] Disseminating the advanced technology associated with new imported plants will involve different, and in many respects more complicated and difficult, problems. Some imported high technology will have only limited transferability to other plants until the technological level of the entire economy is raised.

Some of the most advanced large-scale plants now being imported may not fully realize their potentialities unless they can be substantially adapted and modified to fit the country's economic and cultural setting. Ultimately, the Chinese will have to develop an improved capability for independent innovative adaption; because the relationships among technology, production, and the use of end-products are dynamic rather than static, efficient utilization of plants will require an ability to change with changing conditions.[196]

For many years Peking has attempted to inculcate the Chinese people with new attitudes favorable to innovation. However, during the 1960s and early 1970s they emphasized the roles of ordinary workers and peasants.[197] They have just begun to create a structure of incentives and skills designed to maximize the potential for innovativeness on the part of China's planners, managers, scientists, and technicians, who unquestionably can contribute most to raising technological and economic levels throughout the economy. The contrast between the propensity to innovate in medium-size Shanghai enterprises with pre-1949 roots and the bureaucratic inertia in many large-scale plants imported from the Soviet Union in the 1950s points up the importance of experience, which takes time to acquire.[198] It may take many years for the Chinese to maximize the potential of plants they are now importing.

In the long run, to create a basis for scientific and technological self-reliance and sustainable economic growth, the Chinese will have to acquire improved independent design capabilities as well as better production and management skills. They should be able to do so gradually, and the experience derived from absorbing new plants as well as the training of large numbers of Chinese now under way will help. But they have only made a start toward acquiring all the knowledge they will require.

Finally, even if one assumes there will be no major ideological and political backlash in China leading to a reversal of current policies, the social problems resulting from rapid change will complicate the process of effectively absorbing the new technology. Forced draft modernization inevitably has some destabilizing effects, in part because of its differential impact on different groups in a society. No one can be certain what all the social and political consequences of the new policies in China will be. One can say that the process of change is not likely to be completely smooth; new social problems, requiring new responses, will arise.

These problems will not prevent China's leaders from importing large amounts of foreign capital goods and technology during the next few years. However, they will affect the speed and efficiency with which the country is able to absorb and use the technology, which will be a primary determinant of the overall success of their modernization program—and of the level of future technology imports. The problems are not hypothetical; they can be illustrated not only from the experience of other countries but from China's own record in the recent past.

The number two truck plant in Wuhan exemplifies the difficulties China will encounter in absorbing imported technology.[199] Begun in 1964 with large imports of Western equipment and technology, it was designed to produce 100,000 six-ton trucks a year. However, it did not produce its first truck until 1977, and although by 1978 it employed 160,000 employees in twenty-six factories, it was still operating at a fraction of its capacity—perhaps no more than one-seventh. Ineffective management appears to have been at the root of the problem.

The problems resulting from skilled manpower shortages can be illustrated by China's experience in producing aircraft and missiles. In the 1960s, to speed production of missiles (using Soviet technology of the 1950s), the Chinese were compelled to transfer technical personnel from work on air-breathing engines to work on missiles, with the result that aircraft development slowed down.[200] Shortages of skilled manpower were also partially responsible for delays in putting into full production some of the large fertilizer complexes (using very advanced technology) imported by the Chinese in the early 1970s.

The Chinese also encountered difficulties in getting into production the Rolls-Royce Spey aircraft engine, licensed from the British for production in China. One problem in this case was China's lack of certain kinds of high-quality alloy steel necessary to make essential parts (including turbine blades).[201] Chinese planners apparently did not realize this lack at the start and subsequently had to make special arrangements to import such steel.

China's steel industry provides one of the most notable examples of the effects of weaknesses in China's basic economic infrastructure. Some of China's largest steel facilities have been greatly underutilized in recent years, partly because of power shortages. Power shortages (and variations in electric voltage) have adversely affected many other industries as well.[202] (Variations in voltage can have particularly serious consequences, resulting in damage to sophisticated equipment.) Recently, American oil company representatives visiting China have reported that some imported equipment has been ineffectively used. In 1978, for example, one representative reported that blowout equipment on oil rigs in the Pohai (Bohai) Gulf area were inoperative, creating risks that could have costly results.[203]

There is no way to quantify the effects that problems such as these may have on Chinese development programs. However, it is probable that in many instances it will take considerably longer than Peking's leaders hope to put imported technology to work effectively in China. Whether or not they can efficiently use what they buy, even in the long run, is a question still to be answered; it will depend on how well they are able to implement their new policies calling for major changes in Chinese attitudes, values, institutions, and social and economic processes.

What China Can Afford

Despite all the problems and uncertainties they face, China's present leaders are determined to purchase billions of dollars worth of capital goods and technology in the 1980s. How much they actually will be able to afford will be determined in large part by what they are able to earn from exports, plus other earnings, but it will also depend on how much they decide to borrow.

Many of the cooperative arrangements the Chinese are now trying to work out with foreign businesses should help them develop larger export markets. In compensation and payback schemes, imported machinery and equipment will be paid for with products, and the Chinese also hope that foreign partners in joint ventures will help to open up markets abroad for Chinese-made goods. But there is little prospect that in the near future China will earn enough from exports to pay the total bill for all the capital goods that its planners now wish to buy. They recognize this and consequently are trying to expand nontrade earnings in every way they can, while debating whether or not to borrow on a large scale.

Nevertheless, any realistic estimate of what the Chinese may be able to buy abroad must start with an analysis of its trade potential. Prediction is difficult because so many variables are involved. Future trade growth will depend on how successful Peking's leaders are in implementing their new domestic economic policies, in carrying out the proposed reforms in their economic system, and in achieving a respectable rate of overall growth. It will also depend on the success they have in developing cooperation with foreign businesses and governments, adapting to the requirements of world markets, and expanding exports of raw materials and low-cost manufactured goods while holding down increases in imports of food, steel, and other commodities. There are uncertainties about all of these matters. Nevertheless, enough is known about China's past record, present situation, and future plans to make plausible estimates of what the Chinese may be able to accomplish during the next few years.

Trade Growth: Future Trends and Possibilities

Because China's economic policies are more trade oriented than ever in the past, there is little doubt that its foreign trade will grow in the period ahead, probably fairly rapidly. Ever since the end of the 1960s the rate of annual increase in Chinese trade has been impressive (averaging 18 percent a year in current dollars during 1969–77), and during 1978–79 it was spectacular (averaging about 40 percent in dollars and close to 30 percent in yuan).[204] However, imports have increased more rapidly than exports. According to official Chinese statistics, in 1978, while total trade increased 30.3 percent to 35.500 billion yuan, imports rose 41.1 percent to 18.740 billion yuan, but exports increased only 20 percent to 16.760 billion yuan, resulting in a deficit of 1.980 billion yuan, more than 10 percent of total imports.[205] According to the latest U.S. government estimates (calculating both exports and imports f.o.b.), in 1978, while total trade increased 37.8 percent to $20.231 billion, imports increased 55.4 percent to $10.264 billion, but exports increased at only half that rate, by 23.4 percent to $9.967 billion.[206]

In 1979, trends were comparable, and they produced the largest trade deficit in Chinese history. According to official Chinese statistics, total trade increased 28 percent to 45.500 billion yuan, imports rose 29.6 percent to 24.300 billion yuan, and exports increased 26.3 percent to 21.300 billion yuan, producing a deficit of 3.100 billion yuan, 12.8 percent of imports.[207] According to U.S. government estimates, total trade increased by 39.6 percent to $28.245 billion; imports rose by 43.6 percent to $14.741 billion; and exports increased by 35.5 percent to $13.504 billion, producing a deficit of $1.238 billion.[208] (If the Chinese figure for the deficit, in yuan, is converted into dollars at the average exchange rate for the year, $1.00 = 1.552 yuan, the figure for the deficit in 1979 would be $2 billion.)

Whether the Chinese will continue to allow imports to grow more rapidly than exports, covering the deficits with foreign loans and other earnings, or will slow imports in order to limit the deficits, remains to be seen. Their choice between these options will have a significant influence on the future rate of growth of total trade. Despite uncertainty on this score, however, past performance indicates that China should be able to continue expanding trade at a fairly rapid rate.

It is not likely to be able to sustain the 30 to 40 percent rates of 1978–79, even though some of its smaller Asian neighbors have done this; China faces too many constraints both at home and abroad. It certainly is plausible, however, that China can do as well as or better than it did in the 1950s, when trade grew at an average rate of over 12 percent from 1952 through 1959, or the first half of the 1970s, when the rate, in constant dollars, was also 12 percent. It is at least possible that during the next five to ten years the rate could average 10 to 15 percent in constant dollars and perhaps 15 to 20 percent in current dollars.

What would such rates mean? With $15 billion (the figure for 1977) as a base, a rate of growth of 10, 15, or 20 percent would result in two-way trade in 1985 of roughly $32 billion, $46 billion, or $65 billion, respectively. With $21 billion (1978) as a base, these rates would mean that 1985 trade would total $41 billion, $56 billion, or $75 billion. A reasonable estimate is that by 1985 China's two-way trade may have risen to somewhere between $40 billion and $60 billion.

If the rate of increase is in this range, trade as a percentage of GNP will rise significantly. Assuming that China's GNP in 1978 was close to $407 billion, and that GNP grows at 5, 6, or 7 percent a year (the likely range), the country's GNP in 1985 would be roughly $573 billion, $612 billion, or $654 billion, respectively.[209] Two-way trade of $50 billion would thus amount to between 6 and 8 percent of GNP. While this would be above what it has been in the recent past, it does not appear implausibly high.

If trade grows at approximately the rate indicated, the size of China's trade deficits will have to increase, even assuming that Peking will try hard to keep the gap between imports and exports from becoming dangerously wide.

If one hypothesizes that China's total trade might grow from $28.245 billion in 1979 to about $60 billion in 1985 (which would require an average rate of increase of somewhat over 13 percent) and that imports increase at an average rate of 14 percent and exports at 12 percent, by 1985 China's imports would be more than $32 billion, its exports just under $27 billion, and its deficit close to $6 billion. If China's imports grow at an average rate of 14 percent from 1979 through 1985, total imports during 1980–85 will be more than $140 billion. How much of this might plausibly consist of complete plants, machinery, equipment, and other forms of advanced technology? The Chinese probably cannot increase capital goods as a percentage of total imports to the level of the 1950s when it averaged 40 percent (during 1956–60). They may try, however, to achieve a percentage close to the recent level (29 percent during 1976–77). If during 1980–85 China's imports of machinery and equipment account for 30 percent of total imports, such imports (including complete plants) would total more than $40 billion, averaging about $7 billion a year during the period.

If China purchases foreign capital goods on this scale, such imports will rise significantly as a percentage of GNP and total investment in machinery and equipment. With the U.S. government's estimate of China's 1978 GNP ($407 billion) as a base and GNP growth calculated at a rate of 5, 6, or 7 percent for the years 1979–85, China's GNP in 1985 (in constant dollars) would be $572 billion, $612 billion, or $654 billion, respectively; its cumulative GNP for the period 1978–85 would total $3.885 trillion, $4.028 trillion, or $4.176 trillion.[210] In early 1980 the director of Peking's Economic Research Institute stated that China's rate of capital accumulation was 36.6 percent in 1978 and above 30 percent in 1979, and he urged that it be reduced to about 25 percent a year in the future.[211] If 25 percent of the above estimates of possible cumulative GNP is invested, cumulative gross investment during 1978–85 could be around $1 trillion.

In the 1950s investment in machinery and equipment accounted for close to 20 percent of China's gross investment in fixed capital during China's first Five Year Plan period, but by the early 1970s it was close to 30 percent.[212] If one calculates that China's investment during 1978–85 totals somewhere between $500 billion and $1 trillion and that 20 to 30 percent of that is for machinery and equipment, investment in machinery and equipment during the eight years could total anywhere between $100 billion and $300 billion; and if China imports $40 billion of this, the import component could be somewhere between 13 and 40 percent. Even the lower figure would be above that of recent years (which has been under 10 percent). The higher figure would be about that of the 1950s. However, something in this range is not implausible in light of the tremendous stress Peking now places on imports of advanced technology.

Despite the slowdown in plant purchases in 1979, complete plants still may account for a significant percentage of the machinery and equipment China imports in the period ahead. One U.S. government analysis, made in early 1979, estimated that if China were to import $48 billion of machinery and equipment during 1978–85, perhaps as much as $40 billion, or 80 percent, could consist of "major capital goods and technology" (presumably mostly complete plants).[213] This no longer seems plausible; it would be higher than the proportion of plants in China's total machinery and equipment imports from the Soviet Union during 1952–61 (which was 70 percent), and in light of recent Chinese statements warning against excessive emphasis on complete plant imports, the percentage almost certainly is too high. Nevertheless, imports of complete plants will doubtless increase considerably over the level of the 1960s. If they were to account for one-half to three-quarters of all machinery and equipment imports, they could total $20 billion to $30 billion. However, in light of the slowdown in plant purchases in 1980, they may be less than that.

Balance of Payments: Past Characteristics

The above calculations are crude. At best they suggest a range of possibilities. To get a clearer view of the realistic prospects, it is necessary to analyze China's entire balance of payments, its possible trade deficits, and its likely earnings from nontrade sources that could help pay for imports.[214]

According to Peking's official statistics, in 1978 China had a trade deficit of 1.980 billion yuan ($1.177 billion at the official exchange rate), equal to 10.57 percent of total imports; however, its net income from "nontrade" sources (that is, "invisible items") totaled 2.100 billion yuan ($1.249 billion), so that its overall balance of payments was actually favorable, showing a surplus of more than 120 million yuan ($71.347 million).[215] In planning for 1979, however, Chinese leaders expected an increased trade deficit, which could not be totally covered by earnings from traditional sources of "invisible" income. Yu Chiu-li stated that China planned to draw 4 billion yuan in foreign loans during the year (equal to $2.38 billion at the average 1978 exchange rate but $2.56 billion at the average exchange rate in 1979).[216] In 1979 the actual trade deficit, according to Chinese statistics, was 3.100 billion yuan, considerably above 1978. (Because of appreciation of the yuan, the deficit rose somewhat less in dollar terms, to roughly $2 billion.)[217] The trade deficit amounted to almost 13 percent of total imports, compared with less than 11 percent in 1978. (No data had been published by mid-1980 indicating how much of this was covered by nontrade earnings.)

During the next few years China's trade deficit could well continue rising. According to one American study in 1979, the deficit might reach a peak during 1981–83, mainly as a result of stepped-up purchases of capital goods and technology during 1979–81, and then drop thereafter, as deliveries on these purchases taper off. The study estimated that during 1981–83 China's trade deficits could reach peaks of $4 billion to $6 billion a year and that its current account deficits (even including invisibles) might range between a little more than $2 billion and close to $4.5 billion.[218] Another study made at about the same time estimated that during 1981–83, China's annual current account deficits could range between just under $3 billion and almost $8 billion.[219] Japanese studies at that time differed only slightly. One, for example, estimated that China might have trade deficits of $4.20 billion in 1980, $4.89 billion in 1981, and $5.65 billion in 1982 and that its overall current account deficits could total between $1.5 billion and $2.0 billion during those years.[220] These estimates, made before the full implications of the mid-1979 readjustment were clear, may overestimate China's purchases—and deficits—in the immediate future, but they may not be far off the mark for the period following the readjustment.

To understand what China can try to do to cover future deficits of this size, it is useful to analyze trends in China's overall balance of payments including nontrade transactions in its current account and possible borrowing, as well as its earnings from exports. In recent years both nontrade items and credits have become increasingly important to China, and this trend is likely to continue in the period ahead. China's past record as well as its current policies are relevant to an assessment of the role nontrade items may play in their balance of payments in the future.

One U.S. government study covering the years 1950–64 highlights several important facts about China's balance during the regime's first decade and a half.[221] In that period (which included the years when China received a variety of loans and credits from the Soviet Union), merchandise trade (that is, imports and exports) was overwhelmingly dominant in China's balance of payments. Invisible items in its current account were of minor significance. However, capital movements, even though relatively small, were of considerable importance. According to the study, during the first half of the period (1950–57) merchandise trade accounted for 77.8 percent of the total of credit items in China's overall balance (and 91.0 percent of current account items) and 83.2 percent of the total of debit items (95.5 percent of current account items). During the entire period from 1949 through 1964, trade accounted for 82.9 percent and 79.0 percent, respectively, of total credits and debits, and 93.7 percent and 95.0 percent, respectively, of current account credits and debits.[222]

"Invisibles," including Overseas Chinese remittances,[223] nonmonetary gold, freight and insurance payments and receipts, and interest payments on loans, together accounted for between 7 and 8 percent of the credits and under 4 percent of debits during 1950–57 in China's total balance, and during 1950–64 for under 6 percent of credits and just over 4 percent of debits.[224] Capital movements and changes in China's holdings of monetary gold accounted for over 14 percent of credits and almost 13 percent of debits in its overall balance of payments during 1950–57 and for over 11 percent of the credits and almost 17 percent of the debits during 1950–64.

The largest single invisible item, by far, on the credit side of China's balance consisted of Overseas Chinese remittances; on the debit side, payments for freight and insurance were the largest. According to the study, during 1950–64, China received a total of $1.235 billion from Overseas Chinese remittances (averaging roughly $82 million a year), and it paid out $810 million for freight and insurance (roughly $54 million a year on average). (Another study estimated that during the eighteen-year period 1950–67, Overseas Chinese remittances totaled $1.043 billion, averaging close to $58 million a year, and that in the same period China's payments for freight and insurance totaled $1.622 billion, averaging about $90 million a year.)[225] During the entire period through 1964, China's current account balance showed a credit of $215 million from additions to China's nonmonetary gold (with annual additions varying from $25 million to $45 million) and a debit of $195 million for interest payments (averaging about $13 million a year), plus an estimated $60 million (net) for other unspecified outpayments. In China's current account for invisible items alone, there was a surplus of $385 million during the fifteen-year period (with credits totaling $1.450 billion and debits $1.065 billion), or an average of over more than $25 million a year; remittances from Overseas Chinese more than covered China's current account deficits in other categories of invisibles.

Soviet loans, though limited in relation to Peking's needs, were important to China, particularly during the first half of the 1950s. They enabled the Chinese to maintain regular deficits in trade with the Soviet Union during 1951–55 (totaling about $1 billion), when Peking started to industrialize and to import Soviet capital goods on a large scale.[226] However, later repayments placed a fairly heavy burden on the Chinese, and it was particularly onerous during the early 1960s when, although China was suffering from a major economic crisis, for political reasons Peking decided to pay off its debt as rapidly as possible.

Estimates of the total Soviet loans and credits provided to China in the 1950s vary. There were only two publicly announced long-term developmental loans. The first, in 1950, was a five-year loan of $300 million (or $60 million a year), carrying a low annual interest rate of 1 percent; the second, in 1954, was for about $130 million (520 million rubles). However, the Russians also extended other credits of varying sizes to the Chinese. One U.S. government study estimated that total Soviet credits and loans drawn upon by China during 1950–57 were $1.405 billion.[227] This amount included miscellaneous credits totaling $645 million (mainly Korean war credits of close to $500 million) and $330 million for repurchase of Soviet shares in joint stock companies. In addition, in 1961 the Russians extended two short-term, interest-free credits: one of $320 million, apparently to roll over China's debt (which was necessary because of its economic difficulties at that time), repayable by the end of 1965; and the second, amounting to about $46 million, for sugar imports from the Soviet Union, which was to be repaid by 1967. Adding these amounts to the total raises the figure to more than $1.770 billion.

A later study estimated that total Soviet credits and loans to China actually amounted to more than $2 billion,[228] of which only the 1950 and 1954 development loans were specifically earmarked to finance imports of Soviet machinery and equipment. Apart from the two long-term development loans, the author of this study lists the following Soviet credits and loans to China: a loan of about $918 million, mainly to pay for military equipment received during and immediately after the Korean War (although a part may have been for other purposes); a credit of about $313 million in 1954, to be repaid in "several years," to help China pay for recovery of the Soviet shares in four Sino-Soviet joint stock companies; and a loan of about $570 million in 1955 to help China pay for the Soviet military materiel that was transferred to the Chinese when the Russians withdrew from the joint naval base at

Lushun (Port Arthur). This study did not include the 1961 loan of $320 million (which the author regarded simply as a moratorium on previous debt, without interest) or the 1961 credit of more than $46 million for sugar imports (which also carried no interest). If these amounts are added, the total would come to roughly $2.6 billion.

Still another study concluded that total Soviet credits can be calculated to have been as high as $2.240 billion, or as low as $1.370 billion, depending on the rates of exchange used for yuan-ruble conversions as well as on whether the 1961 loan is regarded as a moratorium or as a new credit.[229]

Whichever figures one accepts, all of the studies highlight certain facts about Sino-Soviet financial relations during that period. One is that Moscow gave no free grants to the Chinese. Another is that the bulk of Moscow's loans and credits were not long-term development loans; most were to help China pay for Soviet military equipment or the transfer to Chinese ownership of Soviet shares in joint enterprises (assets that were already in China) and to help finance short-term trade deficits or delayed repayment of past loans. The real financial assistance was quite limited, therefore. Soviet technical assistance and sales of machinery and equipment were crucial to China's development in the 1950s, but China had to pay its own way. (It is worth noting that the industrial machines and equipment removed from Manchuria by Soviet forces right after World War II, without payment, were worth an estimated $895 million, which exceeded Moscow's later development loans to China, all of which the Chinese had to repay.[230])

China began repaying the Soviet loans in 1954 and therefore was compelled to maintain a trade surplus in trade with the Russians from 1956 on. Chinese repayments (principal plus interest) were small before 1955 but rose to about $200 million a year from 1955 through 1960; they were about $150 million a year in 1961–62 and then rose to peaks of about $270 million in 1963 and $360 million in 1964.[231] By the time all loans and credits had been repaid in 1965, total Chinese repayments, it is estimated, amounted (with interest) to $2.294 billion.

During the 1950s and early 1960s several other nontrade items were important in the Chinese balance of payments. In the early 1950s China expropriated sizable amounts of convertible foreign currency held within China. One study estimates the total to have been $250 million, which helped China considerably in the new regime's early years.[232] However, this was a one-time operation. In the early 1960s, during the post-Leap economic crisis, China began to obtain short-term credits from non-Communist countries to help finance importation of grain, fertilizer, and some steel. Most of these were commercial credits, for periods varying from six to eighteen months. It is estimated that during 1961–64, total drawings of such credits amounted to $910 million and Chinese repayments to $700 million (eventually, the Chinese made full repayment, with interest).[233] This short-term credit facilitated an uninterrupted flow of key commodity imports during an extremely difficult economic period.

Finally, most surprisingly China became a significant aid donor itself in the 1950s and, in fact, from 1956 on was a net capital exporter.[234] According to one study, during 1950–64 China's deliveries on the credits and grants extended during those years totaled $1.205 billion.[235] Most went to other Communist nations (especially North Korea and North Vietnam, which, it is estimated, together received $1.065 billion), but starting in 1956 the Chinese also began giving aid to non-Communist developing nations. "Extensions" of aid by China to non-Communist developing nations, that is, aid commitments, totaled at least $723 million during 1956–64.[236] Aid deliveries were relatively small at the start, however, probably totaling only about $140 million during 1956–64. (The amount of repayments made to China on these loans was negligible, totaling only about $40 million by the end of 1964, $25 million from Communist recipients and $15 million from non-Communist ones.)

To summarize, during the Peking regime's first decade and a half, the Chinese obtained most of their international earnings from commodity exports. However, credits from the Soviet Union in the 1950s supplied limited but essential capital that helped finance imports of machinery and equipment, and in the early 1960s Western short-term commercial credits helped finance imports of essential commodities, especially grain. Overseas Chinese remittances more than covered China's current account deficits with non-Communist countries. Other invisibles were not very important in that period.

On balance, China did reasonably well in managing its payments problems until the late 1950s. Even though it consistently had sizable deficits in invisibles (especially freight and insurance) and itself extended considerable foreign aid, in the mid-1950s, it was able to increase its holdings of foreign exchange reserves steadily, to about $645 million in 1957 (which included an estimated $610 million in foreign exchange and $35 million in gold).[237] These were counterbalanced by clearing account balances owed to other Communist countries (perhaps $360 million), but even when this is taken into account, China's "net international financial resources" in 1957 probably amounted to about $285 million, equal to one-fifth of its total imports that year, and its foreign currency holdings of $610 million equaled 44 percent of its imports from non-Communist countries during the year.

During the late 1950s and early 1960s the balance of payments situation deteriorated. During the late 1950s China's imports soared briefly. Then, following the Great Leap, both exports and imports dropped, and an increasing portion of foreign exchange earnings had to be used to pay for imports of grain, purchased with short-term credits. In 1961–62 China had to sell a sizable amount of silver to help meet its obligations. Although its gold reserves increased, its foreign currency holdings dropped to $155 million, and its total reserves (including both currency and gold) by 1962 had declined to $320 million, not much more than half the amount in 1957.[238]

From 1963 on, however, China's position began to improve, and it was able to pay its international obligations without cutting imports or further reducing its reserves. As trade began to rise again, so too did its reserves; by 1964 they had risen to $400 million ($185 million in foreign currency balances and $215 million in gold).

By 1967 receipts in China's balance of payments totaled an estimated $1.955 billion, payments were $2.026 billion, and its deficit was $71 million.[239] The breakdown of estimated receipts for the year was merchandise exports (f.o.b.), $1.863 billion; freight and insurance, $7 million; Overseas Chinese remittances, $30 million; net drawing of Western credits, $50 million; and repayment of Chinese credits, $5 million. The breakdown of estimated payments was merchandise imports (f.o.b.), $1.774 billion; freight and insurance, $163 million; interest on Western credits, $10 million; and Chinese foreign aid, $79 million. (As these figures show, net outpayments on current account for freight and insurance totaled $156 million, close to 8 percent of total outpayments and almost 9 percent of the cost of imports.) China had a net capital outflow during the year; if it had not been a donor of foreign aid, it would have had a small surplus in its balance.

China's balance of payments during the next decade cannot be described in detail on the basis of available published studies. However, U.S. government analyses throw some light on trends during the early 1970s. In 1970, according to one estimate, in its financial balance with all non-Communist countries China had a trade deficit of $90 million (based on f.o.b. calculations of both imports and exports; if imports are calculated c.i.f., the deficit is $250 million) and a deficit in invisibles (including both services and "transfers," mainly receipts from transport costs and Overseas Chinese remittances, down payments for plants, and deliveries of China's foreign aid) amounting to $30 million, producing an overall current account deficit of $120 million.[240] China's drawings of supplier credits in 1970 totaled an estimated $275 million, and its debt service payments were $355 million. Its overall financial balance, therefore, showed a deficit of $200 million ($120 million on current account and $80 million on capital account).

Comparable estimates for 1977 showed significant changes.[241] In its dealings with non-Communist nations, China had a trade surplus of $1.140 billion (if imports are calculated c.i.f., the figure is $630 million) and a surplus from net services and transfers of $400 million, producing a current account surplus of $1.540 billion. It drew supplier credits amounting to $530 million and made debt service payments of $535 million. Consequently, although it had a slight capital account deficit, China had an overall financial balance surplus of $1.535 billion. This study indicated that while China's net deficits in services and transfers (including transport costs, Overseas Chinese remittances, down payments for plants, and foreign aid) varied greatly during 1970–76, over time they declined. Totaling $30 million in 1970, $15 million in 1971, $40 million in 1972, $240 million in 1978, and $370 million in 1974, they were "negligible" in 1975 and 1976. Then in 1977, instead of a deficit, China had a large surplus, about $400 million. A Japanese study estimated that by 1977 China's surplus in invisibles was even higher, about $532 million.[242]

These figures highlight two striking changes that had occurred in the nontrade transactions in China's balance of payments: instead of having a deficit in such transactions as it generally had in the past, by 1977 China enjoyed a sizable favorable balance; and instead of being a relatively small borrower of short-term credits, by 1977, even before the start of its new modernization program, it had become a fairly large borrower of medium-term, as well as short-term, credits.

Balance of Payments: The Future

Both of these trends should continue and become increasingly important in the period ahead. Official Chinese statistics show that in 1978 China's net "nontrading income" totaled 2.100 billion yuan (about

$1.250 billion), which more than covered the year's trade deficit of 1.980 billion yuan (close to $1.180 billion).[243] There are no official data on the breakdown of the $1.250 billion. U.S. estimates of Chinese net earnings from invisibles in its current account in 1978 were lower. One estimate, for example, calculated that its net tourist revenue during the year was $300 million; net transport revenue, $240 million; receipts from Overseas Chinese remittances, $400 million; and net payments on its own foreign aid commitments, $220 million; added together, these indicated net earnings on current account in all these categories totaling $720 million.[244] The reason for the discrepancy between this estimate and the official Chinese figure is not wholly clear, but possibly the U.S. estimate of China's foreign aid was too low. Peking did not release any figure on its aid in 1978, but its budget for 1979 called for aid of 1 billion yuan ($595 million at the average 1978 exchange rate, $641 million at the 1979 rate).[245]

Although it is not possible to make accurate predictions about likely Chinese net earnings from various nontrade transactions during the next few years, it is possible to identify some significant current trends and make rough estimates.

In recent years the Chinese have greatly expanded their merchant marine and earnings from shipping.[246] Between 1961 and 1975, according to one estimate, the number of merchant ships grew from 150 to 507 (370 under China's own flag and 137 under foreign flags). In 1961 their 150 ships totaled only 760,000 deadweight tons; in 1975 the 370 under China's own flag totaled 3.996 million deadweight tons, a 426 percent increase, and the 137 under foreign flags totaled another 1.7 million deadweight tons, raising its total merchant marine tonnage to 5.7 million. Of China's 370 flag vessels in 1975, 210 were engaged in foreign trade, and it is estimated that they carried about one-third of all China's total foreign trade. During 1976–78, according to statistics from Lloyd's (the London insurance firm), China purchased 228 foreign ships with a deadweight tonnage of 3.8 million, and a 1979 Lloyd's survey estimated that by then China had either under "its own registry or its direct control" a total of more than 10 million deadweight tons (not including coastal tonnage).[247] Since 1975 the amount of China's trade carried in its own vessels has risen rapidly; one authority estimates that in 1978 Chinese-owned ships carried about 70 percent of China's foreign trade.[248] The buildup of China's merchant marine will probably continue. One expert has predicted that by the early 1980s China's total fleet (including ships under foreign flags) may approach 12 million deadweight tons, and that by the mid-1980s it conceivably could reach 17 million deadweight tons.[249] Some time ago the Chinese indicated that, in their view, at least 50 percent of freight (and insurance, in both import and export trade) would constitute a "fair share" of cargo to be carried in their own ships; they appear already to have surpassed this, and now they clearly are striving to earn as much as possible from maritime activities (although doing so will not be without problems since many of their trading partners have a similar goal).[250] One study estimates that their net transport revenue could rise to $720 million in 1985.[251]

Chinese earnings from tourism already are substantial and should grow fairly rapidly in the next few years as a result of Peking's strong commitment to expand tourism and its current drive to build new hotels and facilities.[252] According to different Chinese statements, in 1978, at least 400,000 and perhaps as many as 700,000 persons (it is unclear whether this includes Overseas Chinese and perhaps visitors from Hong Kong) visited China.[253] Then in 1979, according to the State Statistical Bureau, 4.2 million "foreigners, Overseas Chinese, and Chinese compatriots from Hong Kong and Macao" visited China and spent 696 million yuan (about $446 million); the Bureau stated that this was 54 percent above the previous year, implying that in 1978 earnings from visitors had totaled 441 billion yuan (about $262 million at current exchange rates).[254]

In the period ahead Chinese earnings from tourism may begin to catch up with those of other Asian nations and grow along with them. In 1978, according to Asian Development Bank figures, Asian nations earned about $5 billion from 15 million visitors, and some travel industry analysts predict that by the end of the 1980s they may be able to earn $20 billion to $30 billion.[255] In 1978, Singapore reportedly earned $1.2 billion from more than 2 million visitors, Hong Kong $1 billion from 2 million visitors, Taiwan nearly $600 million from 1.3 million visitors, Japan $430 million from more than 1 million visitors, South Korea $430 million from 1 million visitors, and Thailand about $300 million from 1.5 million visitors. The Chinese are now determined to capture a reasonable share of this tourist trade, and there is good reason to believe that they will be able to do so. According to one U.S. estimate, Chinese earnings from tourism could rise to $1.260 billion in 1985.[256] A Japanese study estimates such earnings could total $809 million by 1982.[257]

Overseas Chinese remittances have also been increasing. To attract such remittances, Peking has again, as it did in some earlier periods, adopted policies giving relatives of Overseas Chinese special treatment, and it has adopted new procedures and established new enterprises to attract investments as well as contributions to relatives from Chinese abroad.[258] Estimates of the current flow of Overseas Chinese remittances vary, but all indicate a big increase compared with the 1950s and 1960s. One study estimated that in 1978 they totaled $400 million.[259] Another estimated that they amounted to $421 million.[260] Some Hong Kong sources estimate that remittances plus earnings from Chinese capital investments in Hong Kong now total $1 billion to $1.5 billion a year,[261] but these figures may be too high. However, it does seem at least possible that remittances could rise to $1 billion by 1985.[262]

While working hard to increase their current account earnings from shipping, tourism, and remittances, the Chinese appear to be reducing certain outpayments. Most notably, they appear to have decided to reduce China's foreign aid commitments in the period immediately ahead. According to estimates made by foreign analysts, starting in 1956, when China began giving aid to non-Communist developing nations, through 1978, China's pledges of economic aid (that is, aid "extended") totaled $4.756 billion.[263] The annual average of its aid commitments over twenty-three years therefore was more than $200 million a year, reaching a peak in the early 1970s. Commitments in the fourteen-year period 1956–69 totaled only $1.103 million, but then in the four years 1970–73 they were $2.43 million. The maximum in one year was in 1970, when almost $750 million was pledged; the annual average during the four years was more than $600 million. Since 1974 new commitments have steadily declined. They averaged just under $300 million a year during 1974–75, were about $100 million a year during 1976–77, and then rose slightly to $182 million in 1977 and $185 million in 1978.

Actual aid deliveries to the LDCs have been considerably lower than the above figures, however. During the entire 1956–77 period, deliveries to Third World countries totaled $2.26 billion, averaging just over $100 million a year for the twenty-two years.[264] In recent years, deliveries have risen. Although during 1956–67 they totaled only $445 million, averaging less than $40 million a year, during 1968–70 they averaged $70 million. Then, during 1971–76 they totaled $1.405 billion, averaging more than $230 million a year. After reaching a peak of around $300 million in 1976, however, aid deliveries to the LDCs dropped to $185 million in 1977 and $215 million in 1978. Foreign analysts have predicted that in the next few years Chinese aid deliveries would be kept relatively low, perhaps at a level of $200 million, or a little more, a year. It is hard to know, however, whether this will be possible. As of the end of 1978 the Chinese still had well over $2 billion in aid commitments to LDCs outstanding.[265] It may therefore be difficult to reduce deliveries substantially without unwanted political repercussions. The surprisingly large amount budgeted for foreign aid in 1979 (1 billion yuan, or roughly $640 million converted at the 1979 exchange rate) made this evident.[266] Nevertheless, the Chinese may try to cut their aid gradually, and they are likely to make fewer commitments in the near future.[267]

While the above trends should have favorable effects on China's balance of payments, in certain areas expenditures abroad will rise. For example, China will have to spend much more than in recent years, probably more than in the 1950s, to pay the costs of Chinese students and trainees abroad as well as the salaries of foreign experts in China. During 1951–62, according to one estimate, the costs of training Chinese students and others in the Soviet Union may have totaled about $60 million, or roughly $5 million a year,[268] and the foreign exchange costs for Soviet experts who worked in China during 1950–59 may have totaled around $100 million, or about $10 million a year.[269] If China sends students and trainees to non-Communist nations on the scale it apparently now plans and hires an increasing number of foreign experts, the costs could be considerably higher. If one hypothetically calculates that during the period 1979–85, 10,000 Chinese study abroad for an average of one year each (or 5,000 for two years each) and total annual costs for each are $10,000, the overall bill would be $100 million, or an average of close to $15 million a year. This may be more than China can afford, so, in fact, costs may be less. It is difficult to estimate the cost for foreign experts, but if significant numbers are involved, it too could be high.

Despite new expenditures of this sort, however, on balance China will probably earn substantial, and increasing, net surpluses from invisible items in its current account during the next few years. According to one estimate, these could rise to between $2 billion and $2.5 billion a year in the mid-1980s.[270] According to another estimate, Chinese net earnings from all services and transfers in 1985 might be about $2.760 billion.[271] Any estimate must be based essentially on informed guesswork; nevertheless, these figures are plausible, and they suggest that earnings from invisibles will be increasingly important to China in the period ahead. In fact, during the entire 1978–85 period they conceivably could amount to close to 10 percent of export earnings and cover one-half to two-thirds of China's annual trade deficits.[272] Thus, even though nontrade items will not account for a huge percentage of China's total international transactions, they could be of great importance.

International Borrowing: Potential and Limits

Even a substantial increase in Chinese earnings from both exports and nontrade transactions cannot completely solve their payments problems. They may have to consider borrowing abroad on a large scale. How much are they likely to need and be able to borrow without reaching a level of indebtedness that could be dangerous for both China and its international creditors?

Peking has not publicly revealed any definite targets for either capital goods imports or foreign borrowing for the next few years, but from what is known it is possible to estimate what Chinese leaders may hope to purchase and what they might have to borrow to help pay for it.

Right after Peking launched its modernization program, it appeared that in the period 1978–85 China's total imports of complete plants, machinery, and equipment might total $40 billion to $50 billion; to help pay for these imports, it might have to borrow at least $10 billion to $20 billion, and it probably could do this without taking unwarranted financial risks. At first, the Chinese seemed eager to sign many contracts for major capital goods and technology purchases for the entire period 1978–85 during a relatively short period of time, to ensure that as many as possible would go on-line and start operating before 1985 (construction in many cases would take three to four years or more). The offers of foreign credit that the Chinese obtained from the Japanese and Europeans left little doubt that they could borrow at least $10 billion to $20 billion, or more, if they wished.

Since mid-1979, the slowdown in plant purchases suggests that they will be more cautious than it first appeared in their purchasing policy during the next two to three years. They have been very conservative about borrowing, drawing little of the credit offered to them. One reason is that they are trying to determine how much concessionary credit they may be able to obtain from countries such as Japan and eventually from international institutions such as the IMF and the World Bank and its "soft" loan lending body, the International Development Association (IDA). However, although still very prudent, China could at some point decide to use more of the credits now available to it. It is possible that China will purchase several tens of billions of dollars worth of capital goods in the period ahead, but the buying period may well be stretched out over a longer time than originally anticipated.

Before discussing some of the analyses made by foreigners of what China could now prudently borrow, a further comment on its past borrowing record is relevant. Its financial relations with the Soviet Union already have been discussed, but a word should be added about its debt-service ratio (the ratio between annual debt repayments and annual export earnings) during the second half of the 1950s and first half of the 1960s. If this ratio is calculated by comparing China's estimated annual repayments on debts to the Soviet Union with its export earnings each year in trade with all Communist bloc countries, the ratio was almost 20 percent during 1955–58, averaged 15 percent during 1959–62 (increasing from 13 to 17 percent in that period), then rose to highs of 33 percent in 1963 and 50 percent in 1964 before dropping to below 8 percent in 1965, the year in which Peking paid off its last obligations to Moscow.[273] Calculated as a percentage of Sino-Soviet trade, the percentages were higher, reaching a peak of 114 percent in 1964! If the ratio is calculated by comparing debt repayments to the Soviet Union with total Chinese export earnings worldwide, the ratios are lower; the average was about 13 percent during 1955–58 and roughly 10 percent during 1959–62, then rose to 17 percent in 1963 and 20 percent in 1964 before dropping to 2 percent in 1965. Probably the most valid measure of China's debt-service load at that time is the one comparing its debt repayments with exports to the Communist bloc as a whole. This ratio, which reached a peak of 50 percent, was high—extremely high during 1963–64. International bankers become concerned when a country's debt-service ratio exceeds 25 percent.

One striking fact about Peking's record in that period, however, is that despite the rapid deterioration of Sino-Soviet relations from 1960 on, the Chinese not only paid off their debts to Moscow in full, but they did so ahead of schedule. In doing so, they gave high priority to fulfilling their financial obligations, even when they faced enormous domestic problems and their political relations with their creditors were bad.

In their borrowing from non-Communist nations, the Chinese have been equally scrupulous about repaying debts on schedule, even though their political relationships with most of these countries until recently have been far from close. Their record as a debtor to non-Communist nations since the start of the 1970s is particularly relevant to questions about the future. During 1970–77 China's total borrowing (virtually all from non-Communist nations) was substantial, even though its leaders continued (through 1976) to claim that China had no debt. Altogether, the Chinese obtained (that is, actually drew) about $4.860 billion in foreign credits and loans during this eight-year period.[274] Their annual drawings averaged about $250 million during 1970–72, were more than $500 million in 1973, and averaged $1.0 billion to $1.5 billion during 1974–75 and more than $500 million during 1976–77 (tables 2-5 and 2-6). However, most of the credits that they drew during this period—$3.740 billion, or roughly 77 percent of the total—consisted of short-term commercial loans, generally for periods ranging from six to eighteen

TABLE 2-5. *China: Foreign Debt Position, 1970–77*[a]
Millions of U.S. dollars

	1970	1971	1972	1973	1974	1975	1976	1977
Short-term credits[b]								
Drawn	275	240	240	530	840	920	225	470
Repaid	325	305	175	230	655	830	935	230
Net	−50	−65	65	300	185	90	−710	240
Interest[c]	30	30	15	20	50	65	95	25
Outstanding	325	260	325	625	810	900	190	430
Medium-term credits[d]								
Drawn	0	0	0	0	215	560	285	60
Repaid	0	0	0	0	0	0	20	215
Net	0	0	0	0	215	560	265	−155
Interest	0	0	0	0	0	0	5	65
Outstanding	0	0	0	0	215	775	1,040	885
Totals								
Drawn	275	240	240	530	1,055	1,480	510	530
Repaid	325	305	175	230	655	830	955	445
Net	−50	−65	65	300	400	650	−445	85
Interest	30	30	15	20	50	65	100	90
Outstanding	325	260	325	625	1,025	1,675	1,230	1,315

Source: NFAC, CIA, *China: International Trade, 1977–78*, p. 22.

a. All data are estimates based on contract terms, delivery schedules, and trade statistics and are rounded to the nearest $5 million.

b. Six- to eighteen-month credits for grain, for Japanese fertilizer in 1970, and for Japanese steel in 1975.

c. Estimated at 8 percent per year for 1970–74, 10 percent for 1975–76.

d. Five-year credits for complete plant purchases.

TABLE 2-6. *China: Financial Balance with Non-Communist Countries, 1970–77*
Millions of U.S. dollars

	1970	1971	1972	1973	1974	1975	1976	1977
Trade balance (f.o.b.)	−90	250	310	40	−555	−65	1,705	1,140
Net services and transfers[a]	−30	−15	−40	−240	−370	*	*	400
Current account balance	−120	235	270	−200	−925	−65	1,705	1,540
Debt service[b]	−355	−335	−190	−250	−705	−895	−1,055	−535
Supplier credit drawings[c]	275	240	240	530	1,055	1,480	510	530
Financial balance gap	−200	140	320	80	−575	520	1,160	1,535

Source: NFAC, CIA, *China: International Trade, 1977–78*, p. 23.
* Negligible.
a. Net total of estimated transport costs, overseas remittances, down payments for plants, and foreign aid.
b. Principal and interest.
c. Includes short-term and medium-term supplier credits.

months and carrying interest charges of about 8 percent during 1970–74 and 10 percent thereafter. Short-term borrowing of this sort averaged about $250 million a year during 1970–72, then rose rapidly to a peak of more than $900 million in 1975, dropping thereafter to roughly $500 million in 1977. These short-term credits were very important to China because they facilitated the flow of imports of key commodities, but they involved substantial costs. Interest payments varied between $15 million (in 1972) and $95 million (in 1976) and averaged close to $50 million a year. They totaled $330 million during the eight years. Some analysts deemphasize the significance of these short-term credits in assessing China's indebtedness because the Chinese repaid them rapidly; however, this borrowing did create a continuing debt; at the end of 1977 short-term credits still outstanding totaled more than $400 million.

From roughly the mid-1960s to the mid-1970s the Chinese avoided all long-term or even medium-term indebtedness, but in 1974 they again purchased some major capital goods with medium-term financing (generally loans for five years) under arrangements called deferred payments. In these, repayment of the loans, including interest, was usually melded into a general schedule of payments (so that interest charges were not identified as such). China's total borrowing of this kind during 1974–77 amounted to $1.120 billion; annual drawings amounted to $215 million in 1974, $560 million in 1975, $285 million in 1976, and $60 million in 1977. By the end of 1977 the Chinese had repaid $235 million, together with $70 million interest, but $885 million of medium-term debt was still outstanding. At the end of 1977 China's total outstanding debt, including both short- and medium-term credits, therefore, totaled about $1.315 billion. (Its peak level during the first seven years of the 1970s had been $1.675 billion, in 1975.)

As these figures indicate, China's borrowing rose to significant levels during the early 1970s, even before its decision in 1978 to consider borrowing in new ways and on a larger scale. Its year-end outstanding debt is estimated to have been $1.025 billion in 1974, $1.675 billion in 1975, $1.230 billion in 1976, and $1.315 billion in 1977 (see table 2-5). However, because its hard currency exports rose, its debt-service ratio remained well under the 25 percent "danger point."

When the ratio is calculated by comparing China's annual debt-service payments (principal plus interest on its short-term and medium-term debts) with its annual earnings from exports to non-Communist countries, it averaged 13.28 percent during 1970–77 but varied significantly from year to year, ranging from lows of 6.13 percent in 1973, 7.88 percent in 1972, and 8.13 percent in 1977 to highs of 21.98 percent in 1970, 17.49 percent in 1971, and 17.51 percent in 1976. During four of the eight years (1971 and 1974–76) it ranged between 13 and 18 percent.[275] (If the ratios are calculated using only the figures on repayments on medium-term debts, they are much lower. For 1977, for example, the ratio is only 4.26 percent instead of 8.13 percent. However, since short-term credits create real debts, even though they are "turned over" from year to year, and require repayment with interest, they should be included.)

China's total reserves (including both foreign currency and gold), which were at a low level at the start of the 1970s, are estimated to have risen to about $4 billion by late 1977.[276] (In mid-1978 Vice Premier Li Hsien-nien stated that the dollar value of China's reserves of foreign currencies alone totaled "well over 2 billion.")[277] By 1978 most estimates ranged between $3 billion and $5 billion.[278] This is not a huge amount for a country of China's size, but it appears to have been adequate in relation to the size of China's trade and debt. Reserves of this size are roughly equivalent to between one-fifth and one-third of the cost of China's imports in 1979.

China clearly has been reasonably prudent in its foreign financial dealings to date. Its debt-service ratio has not approached dangerous levels in recent years, and it has an excellent record of repaying debts on schedule. Many other countries have had higher debt-service ratios. World Bank figures show, for example, that while in some LDCs the ratio has been below 10 percent (and in a few even below 5 percent), in many it has been much higher. In 1975 the ratio was between 15 percent and 20 percent in countries such as Brazil, Zaire, Burma, and Bangladesh; between 20 and 25 percent in countries such as Sri Lanka, Sudan, Argentina, and Peru; between 25 and 30 percent in countries such as Egypt, Mexico, and Chile; and over 45 percent in Uruguay.[279] In 1978 the Soviet Union's debt-service ratio was 19 percent.[280]

Sometimes another measure is used to judge a country's foreign debt burden: the size of its debt as a percentage of GNP. By this standard, too, China's debt has been comparatively low. One analyst has calculated that in 1976 the Soviet Union's net foreign debt totaled $16.2 billion and amounted to 1.8 percent of GNP, the debt of East European countries (excluding Yugoslavia) totaled $25.6 billion and amounted to 8.1 percent of GNP, and the overall debt of all the COMECON Communist bloc countries (including Cuba but not Yugoslavia or the Asian Communist nations) was $43.1 billion and amounted to 3.5 percent of GNP.[281] By comparison, China's outstanding foreign debt in 1977 ($1.315 billion, including $885 million of medium-term debt and $430 million of short-term debt) was close to one-third of 1 percent.

During 1978–79, when China began actively shopping for foreign credits, it appeared initially to some that Peking might be throwing prudence to the wind. Chinese leaders responded to the concern expressed by certain foreigners by assuring them repeatedly that they did not intend to buy or borrow beyond China's real capacity to pay. These assurances are credible. Judging by their past behavior, they themselves would be disturbed if their debt-service ratio rose much above 20 percent for any prolonged period. Their predisposition probably will be to keep the ratio from rising beyond 15 to 20 percent.

Several studies indicate that Peking should be able to borrow $10 billion to $20 billion without excessive financial strain. One U.S. government analysis made in 1978 concluded that if one assumes that "Peking purchases $3 billion worth of plants each year for [sic] 1978–82 [that is, a total of $15 billion during five years] and that exports to the non-Communist countries increase at an average rate of 10 percent per annum," then "with a 7-percent interest rate and continued use of 5-year credits China's debt-service to export ratio would remain within safe limits, rising from 6 percent in 1981 to a peak of 18 percent in 1985."[282] It further calculated that, "Even if downpayment expenditures were included, the debt service ratio would hit only 20 percent. If Peking were to accept a [sic] 10-year credits the debt service ratio would range from 4 to 11 percent from 1981 to 1985, and including downpayments would peak at only 15 percent."

A CIA analysis in 1978 constructed two models covering the years from 1977 through 1986.[283] One model indicated that if China's average rate of increase in export earnings from trade with non-Communist nations were to be slightly over 15 percent a year during the nine years 1978–86 (25 percent in 1978–80, 15 percent in 1981–83, and 10 percent in 1984–86), during those years the Chinese might be able to import about $50 billion of capital goods, to borrow more than $13 billion, and still keep their debt-service ratio low—very low in the years 1978–84 but rising toward the end of the period to 10 percent in 1986. The second model suggested that if China's exports were to increase at a rate of 10 percent during 1979–86, the Chinese might be able to import

$37 billion of capital goods, to borrow almost $20 billion, and to have a debt-service ratio that remains low during 1978–83 but rises thereafter to 6 percent in 1984, 13 percent in 1985, and 21 percent in 1986. The calculation of debt-service ratios in these models does not include short-term credits, which in the years ahead could range between $500 million and $1 billion a year; if these were included, the debt-service ratios would be higher.

Still another study, published in mid-1979 by the National Council for U.S.-China Trade, concluded that China might import about $50 billion of capital goods and technology during 1978–85, or about 34 percent of the study's projection of China's total cumulative imports during the period.[284] The authors calculated that China's overall two-way trade during these years could increase at an average annual rate of 17.6 percent (in current dollars), reaching $63 billion in 1985. They predicted that imports would rise somewhat faster than exports (18 percent compared to 17 percent) during the period, and their patterns of growth would be different. Imports, they concluded, would increase at an extremely rapid rate at the start, then at a relatively low rate, and then start to pick up again at the end of the period, whereas the growth rate of exports, also starting high, then dropping, then rising again, would be considerably below the export growth rate at the start and considerably above it at the end.

For the entire 1978–85 period, according to this study's projections, China's cumulative trade deficits might total close to $18 billion. Almost $12 billion of this, it was estimated, might be covered by net surpluses from nontrade items (tourism, transportation, and remittances), which the authors expected to rise from $720 million in 1978 to $2.760 billion in 1985. The study suggested, however, that China would borrow on a significant scale, drawing close to $15 billion in loans during 1978–85 (of which almost $10 billion would be repaid by the end of 1985), with annual drawings varying between $2 billion and $3 billion in most years but tapering off at the end of the period. The study calculated that, depending on the types of loans and their precise terms, China's debt-service ratio might be in the range of 10 to 15 percent.[285]

All such estimates are based on informed guesswork. Neither the overall growth of China's trade nor the scale of China's imports of capital goods and technology is predictable in any precise way. The overall growth of trade will depend on many factors: the degree of political stability and continuity of policy in China, the performance of the Chinese economy as a whole, and the flexibility and skill with which the Chinese operate internationally. How much, and what, China can import will depend on what it can earn from exports of low-cost manufactured goods, nonagricultural raw materials, and varied nontrade transactions, and on how much steel, grain, and other commodities it will have to buy, as well as on how much it borrows from abroad and how rapidly and effectively it can absorb the capital goods and technology it does purchase.

There is uncertainty about all of these variables. However, despite the impossibility of making accurate predictions, certain developments are probable. During the years immediately ahead, China's overall trade is likely to grow fairly rapidly, perhaps at an average annual rate of 10 to 15 percent (in constant dollars). To support their modernization program, the Chinese will try to maximize imports of capital goods and technology; conceivably these could total between $40 billion and $50 billion by the middle or—more likely—the late 1980s. If they buy on this scale, they will have to finance their imports at least partially with foreign loans, and it is plausible that they might decide to borrow $10 billion to $20 billion for this purpose.

China and the International Community

Peking's new policies are involving the Chinese in the world economy and international community to a much greater extent than in the past, but it is not yet clear how far this trend will go, how long it will last, and what effects it might have on Peking's broad relations with the international community.

It is impossible to forget that in the 1860s, 1890s, 1920s, 1930s, and 1950s China started programs calling for expanded political, economic, and cultural relations with foreign nations, but in each case the trend was aborted as a result of ideological and political struggles at home, conflicts with foreign nations, or both. Ultimately, each time, nativist impulses reasserted themselves. One cannot exclude the possibility that China's new experiment might, like previous ones, prove to be no more than a temporary swing of the pendulum.

Yet, there are reasons to believe that China's current policies could have more significant and lasting effects. China today is stronger and, despite internal debates, more unified than in the past. Its present leaders appear firmly committed, on pragmatic grounds, to both rapid modernization and increased economic intercourse with the outside world. Moreover, most other nations are more genuinely prepared than in the past to accept China as an active participant in the global community.

Today China's foreign contacts are increasing rapidly, both quantitatively, through increased trade, technology transfers, and financial dealings, and qualitatively, through expanded institutional and personal contacts, exchanges of scientific and technical knowledge, and greater intellectual interaction in the field of ideas and culture. The impact of the qualitative changes, both within China and on its relations with foreign nations, could have far-reaching effects since new ideas are often catalysts for ideological, political, and social, as well as economic, transformations.

New International Links and Involvements

After three decades of relative isolation, during which China had only minimal contact with the advanced nations of the non-Communist world and was involved in international organizations to a very limited degree, the new relationships that the Chinese are developing, especially with Japan, Europe, and the United States, are striking. Not only have contacts between leading Chinese and foreign officials and diplomats broadened significantly but many lower-level links are being established which may be even more important. New relationships of many kinds are developing between Chinese planners and technocrats and their counterparts abroad; between trade officials, bureaucrats, and plant managers and foreign businessmen, bankers, and traders; and between scientists, technicians, educational leaders, students, journalists, and other professional groups and comparable groups in foreign countries. The increasing flow of experts, students, and trainees abroad and of foreign experts, advisers, and students to China could have particularly great effects over time. The influx of foreign tourists into China also will have significant, and unpredictable, cultural and social results, broadening the horizons and raising the aspirations of many Chinese but creating resentments and evoking xenophobic reactions from others.

The scale on which these new contacts are developing should not be exaggerated. Compared with those among major non-Communist nations, they are still limited and probably will remain so. Chinese leaders doubtless will try to keep them under control, encouraging them for specific purposes directly related to China's development while trying to minimize undesired side effects, including agitation for political rights, the emergence of local elite groups linked to foreign countries, and the stimulation of unrealistic hopes for improved living conditions.

It is well to remember, also, that even extensive contacts between two societies do not necessarily determine long-term relationships, as history has repeatedly demonstrated. The contacts between China and the West before 1949 did not prevent—in fact, they helped to provoke—the anti-Western policies of the 1950s and 1960s, and China's close ties with the Soviet Union in the 1950s were replaced by intense hostility in the 1960s. While under certain conditions increased contacts can contribute to mutual understanding, a close linkage of interests, and cooperation, under different circumstances they can contribute to misunderstanding, friction, and conflict. No one can be certain, therefore, what the long-term effects of China's growing economic and other relationships with the non-Communist world will be. But there is little doubt that in the immediate future these relationships will involve the Chinese more deeply with many foreign countries.

The growth of China's foreign trade already has linked its economic interests to the world market to an extent unprecedented in the recent past. Global trends affecting the supplies and prices of capital goods and commodities now have a major effect on China's development program. Its interests are hurt when there are large increases in the prices of machinery and equipment and key commodities that it imports in sizable quantities, or when there are sudden drops in the demand for, or prices of, its major exports. China is greatly helped by increases in the world prices of export commodities such as oil. Recession or stagflation in the industrialized nations tends to lower demand for many Chinese goods in these countries and, through secondary effects, in the Third World nations as well. Any adverse trends affecting China's sales of textiles, other manufactured products, and crude materials reduce its capacity to earn the foreign exchange it needs to import essential capital goods, with unfavorable effects on its entire domestic economy.

In the 1950s and 1960s Chinese leaders may have hoped, for political reasons, to see a "crisis of capitalism" develop that would further worldwide revolutionary change. Today China's objective interests are best served by healthy economies in the industrialized capitalist nations as well as in the Third World. Stability and continued growth in the world economy assist China's development; instability and stagnation have damaging effects. It is now difficult for Chinese leaders to ignore these facts.

Increased trade is a double-edged sword, however, in its effects on China as on other countries. While Peking's leaders hope that imported capital goods and technology will foster faster growth at home, growing trade makes China more vulnerable to uncontrollable and unpredictable trends on markets, which complicates centralized planning. In recent years the Chinese at times have shown considerable skill in tailoring their import and export plans to fit changes in world prices, buying more of certain commodities when their prices have fallen and expanding exports of Chinese goods whose prices have risen. However, there are severe limits to their flexibility. Many imports are vital to their domestic economy, whatever their prices, and the bureaucratic nature of their economic system makes it difficult to adapt to changing world conditions.

The dramatic worldwide commodity price rises of the early 1970s, and the stagflation that hit the major industrial nations at about the same time, had adverse effects on China as it did on many other nations. The prices of many essential imports rose rapidly, while the prices and markets for many of China's exports (with the notable exception of oil) declined. These trends helped to produce large deficits in China's trade during 1973–75. Fortunately, however, from the Chinese point of view, because of the particular commodity mix of their exports and imports, the price rises in the early 1970s had less serious effects on their economy than on the economies of many developing countries. Actually, because China's overall "commodity terms of trade"[286] had improved during 1970–73 before dropping sharply during 1973–75, as of 1975 they were still better than in 1970.[287] Similarly, China's "income terms of trade"[288] also improved during 1970–73, then dropped in 1974–75, but were still substantially better in 1975 than in 1970. By the early 1970s China had become an oil exporter (albeit still a relatively small one), and the large increase in world oil prices helped to cushion the effects of other price increases. Also, in part because China's other exports are so diverse, their overall price level rose more during 1973–74 than the general price level of its imports. China therefore proved to be less vulnerable in the early 1970s to rapid changes than many other developing countries that were heavily dependent upon exports of a few primary commodities.[289]

Nevertheless, Chinese leaders now recognize that they no longer can insulate their economy from the effects of major trends affecting international markets and prices.[290] It is not only changes in world commodity markets that affect China's interests, but also changes in exchange rates. A decline in the value of the dollar, for example, benefits China if it is purchasing capital goods under contracts denominated in dollars, but it also tends to weaken China's reserve position since a large share of its reserves are in the Eurodollar market. In contrast, increases in the value of the yen can be damaging since so large a share of Chinese imports now comes from Japan. (Recently, they often tried to arrange for contracts with the Japanese to be designated at least partially in dollars rather than yen.) At present, China's currency, the yuan or RMB (renminbi), is not freely convertible, but in setting their official exchange rates, the Chinese try to ensure that cross rates with other major currencies are realistic so that prices, when defined in terms of RMB, take full account of the real values of the foreign currency in which they will be paid.[291]

Trends in world money markets have become increasingly important to the Chinese. Recently, they have been able to benefit from the state of financial liquidity that has existed in international finance, especially in Europe, which has made it relatively easy for them to obtain credits and loans on favorable terms. If money markets had been tighter, it is doubtful that the Japanese and Europeans would have offered such large loans on such favorable terms. If future trends make borrowing more expensive, this could complicate China's problems greatly.

China's purchases of foreign capital goods and search for credits have involved it increasingly in cooperative relationships with many of the largest and most powerful multinational corporations and private banks in the capitalist world. While some of these enterprises have shown flexibility in adapting to the requirements of the China market, the Chinese, on their part, have been compelled to modify many past practices to accommodate to the requirements of the international capitalist system. Step by step, they have moved to adopt new policies and procedures, now described by the Chinese simply as "normal international practices." The need to draft new laws and regulations to facilitate cooperation with foreign corporations probably has been one of the most compelling reasons the Chinese leadership has decided to give new emphasis, generally, to "socialist legality," which eventually could have significant political and social effects on the society as a whole.

China's expanding economic links abroad also have involved it increasingly, in new ways, with governmental economic agencies in many countries. The list of bilateral trade, credit, scientific, and technical agreements signed with such agencies in Japan, Europe, and the United States already is a long one, and most agreements require continuing cooperation for effective implementation. Some economic arrangements now being considered by the Chinese could involve complicated multi-lateral agreements with both private entrepreneurs and governments in several foreign countries. For example, a project reportedly has been discussed under which Britain would sell $600 million of coal mining equipment to China to help develop mines from which the Chinese would sell 3.5 million tons of coal a year to Hong Kong to help fuel a new $2 billion power station that ultimately might sell some of its electricity to Kwangtung Province in China.[292]

As China's need to earn foreign exchange has become more urgent, it also has stepped up its efforts to promote exports to the industrialized countries, which, in turn, have begun to control or limit imports of low-cost products from China, as from other developing nations. Although China has been granted most favored nation treatment by Japan, the EEC, and most recently the United States, since it does not belong to the international Multi-Fiber Agreement under the General Agreement on Tariffs and Trade (GATT), these countries have pressed it to agree to "orderly marketing" agreements designed to regulate and limit growth of imports of Chinese textiles.[293] This situation compels the Chinese to try to protect their interests by arguing their case more effectively to foreign legislatures and interest groups. Expanding economic ties inevitably leads to new linkages of many kinds with foreign societies.

Participation in International Organizations and Institutions

Chinese attitudes toward and relationships with various international organizations also have undergone major change. Since its seating in the United Nations in late 1971, China has been a member of most agencies affiliated with the United Nations (with the notable exception—until 1980—of the IMF and the World Bank) and has participated in the major UN-sponsored conferences on the environment, population, food, laws of the sea, technology transfers, commodity trade, and so on. However, until recently, it generally did not play very active roles in most UN operating programs.[294] While vocally backing the developing nations' demand for a "New International Economic Order," in the day-to-day operation of UN agencies the Chinese asked little for themselves and generally stayed uninvolved in most concrete programs designed to deal with global problems. Often, they voiced opposition to such programs.

Starting in late 1978, however, this began to change. The Chinese not only hinted that they were seriously considering applying for membership in the IMF and the World Bank, during 1978–79 they took the initiative, for the first time, to obtain technical assistance and credits from several UN-affiliated agencies and programs, including the United Nations Development Program (UNDP), the UN High Commissioner for Refugees Office, the Food and Agriculture Organization (FAO), the World Health Organization (WHO), and the UN Fund for Population Activities.[295] There were reports in 1979 that China might be considering membership in the UN Atomic Energy Agency; at least, Chinese diplomats were inquiring about the possible benefits of membership.[296] In addition, they became increasingly active in multilateral talks held under the auspices of the UN Conference on Trade and Development regarding international commodity agreements, in which they showed increasing pragmatism, adopting positions dictated more by China's own economic needs than by general North-South ideological issues.[297]

These trends culminated in Chinese moves to join the IMF and the World Bank. Although beginning in 1978 they had hinted that they might join, they did not take concrete steps in this direction for more than a year. Finally, in the fall of 1979 they made a definite decision to request seating after the U.S. Congress passed the U.S.-China trade agreement then awaiting approval.[298] This agreement was passed by Congress in January 1980, and the Chinese then moved rapidly; so too did the IMF and the World Bank. By April China was seated (replacing Taiwan) in the IMF; soon thereafter, in May, Peking replaced Taiwan in China's seat in the World Bank.[299]

It was not immediately clear how much the Chinese would be eligible to borrow from these institutions. In the IMF, several different formulas might be used to determine China's "quota." According to one analyst, if the existing China quota were used, China would immediately be eligible for more than $700 million and eventually as much as $2 billion to $3 billion or more. This analyst judged that if China were to obtain a $2.5 billion quota, it could draw $625 million "with minimal questions asked," and using various "credit tranches" it probably could draw another $2.5 billion.[300] In the World Bank, it would take some time to determine how much China could borrow, not only from the bank itself but also its "soft loan" agency, the International Development Association and the International Finance Corporation (IFC).

There is little doubt that the Chinese eventually will request sizable loans. Probably, they will be especially interested in concessionary IDA loans, which have long terms and low service charges, but they may find that regular World Bank loans are attractive too. Even though the interest charges on the World Bank's loans may be slightly higher than those of some alternative sources, the fact that they are not "tied" (that is, they can be used to make purchases anywhere, not just in one country, as is usually the case with loans guaranteed by export-import banks) is a major advantage.

In 1980 most available World Bank and IDA funds were already earmarked,[301] and considerable time will be required for specific loans to China to be arranged and approved. Since the World Bank operates on a project basis, its leading officials expected that it might take as long as eighteen months to work out specific loans. In the case of IDA, it appears that no significant amounts of funds for loans to China are likely to be available until mid-1983, when the next (the eighth) general "replenishment" is scheduled to occur. Nevertheless, World Bank officials indicated to the Chinese in mid-1980 that they were prepared to begin discussing and studying possible projects and privately stated that, once effective working relations with the Chinese have been established and concrete projects worked out, they anticipated that China could become one of the World Bank's largest borrowers and conceivably might borrow as much as $3 billion to $4 billion by the mid-1980s.[302]

China's entry into the IMF and the World Bank did more than open up important new sources of credit; the implications of the move were broader, both symbolically and in practical terms. Perhaps more than any other move in the period since Mao's death, it symbolized the decision of Peking's new leaders that China should become a more active participating member of the international community and economy. In practical terms, it meant that China would almost certainly further broaden its cooperative relations with international economic institutions generally. To obtain the potential benefits of IMF and World Bank membership, the Chinese will have to provide these institutions with much more data on the Chinese economy than it has been willing to release to date, and it will have to accept the fact that now Chinese policies will be closely scrutinized and evaluated by international agencies.

Whether the Chinese will now consider joining GATT is still unclear. As of mid-1980, they had not yet indicated an active interest in this possibility. However, they may well be weighing the pros and cons of such a move.[303] The advantage of joining GATT would be that they would automatically obtain the benefits of all reductions in tariffs and nontariff barriers resulting from GATT's multilateral negotiations and agreements. However, joining would also create new problems for Peking. Like the other Communist countries that have already joined (Poland in 1967, Rumania in 1971, and Hungary in 1974),[304] China, with its state trading system, would doubtless have to agree to make certain "reciprocal concessions" to GATT. At a minimum, it would probably have to agree, as Hungary did, to periodic GATT reviews of its trade.[305]

The most important consequence of China's joining GATT would be the general broadening of its links to global economy. The key question Peking's leaders will have to answer in making their decision will be whether or not the benefits, which would be substantial, would be outweighed by the possible costs and problems resulting from the further accommodations China would have to make to economic forces and trends beyond its borders.

In the period ahead, China's new policies are likely to impel it to become more active in many other international bodies, especially those whose policies and programs directly relate to Chinese economic interests. In addition to forums focusing on North-South relations, such as UNCTAD, UNDP, and United Nations Industrial Development Organization (UNIDO), these will probably include specialized agencies focusing on particular fields such as FAO, WHO, the International Civil Aviation Organization (ICAO), the International Telecommunications Union (ITU), the World Meteorological Organization (WMO), and the Intergovernmental Maritime Consultative Organization (IMCO), as well as the Economic and Social Council for Asia and the Pacific (ESCAP), formerly ECAFE.[306] In addition, China has started, and almost certainly will continue, joining a variety of nongovernmental organizations, especially those concerned with scientific and technical fields—groups it has shunned in the past.

China, the Third World, and Global Issues

In subtle ways, China's attitudes toward many of the issues now dominating North-South relations appear to be undergoing change. They could change further in the period ahead. In the early 1970s China's stand on most of these issues was fairly militant and to a considerable extent ideologically motivated. Peking's leaders viewed themselves as economic adversaries of the industrial countries, just as the leaders of many other developing countries did. They strongly criticized most economic proposals put forward by the advanced nations and insisted that there be a major redistribution of the world's income and wealth and basic structural changes in the international economic system.[307]

Some time ago the Chinese leaders' position began shifting, along with the positions of leaders of some other developing countries, and they started putting greater emphasis on the need for a "dialogue" between the developing countries and the developed nations. Peking placed special emphasis on the desirability of developing such a dialogue with the nations that Peking labeled "Second World" countries, the industrial nations in Western Europe and Japan.

During the years since Mao's death, officials have not reversed past positions or abandoned interest in North-South issues. As a relatively poor developing nation, China shares many common interests with other Third World countries, and it would benefit if many of the changes in North-South relations proposed under the rubric of the New International Economic Order could be achieved. Pragmatism reinforces ideology, therefore, in inducing China's leaders to support many proposals sponsored by other developing nations.

However, as China's economic and other ties with the industrial nations have grown, subtle changes have been discernible in its leaders' attitudes and statements. As early as 1977-78 China's press and propaganda coverage of major North-South issues declined noticeably,[308] and its rhetoric was more restrained.[309] Since 1979 this change has become steadily more obvious. There have been many other signs that, in moving toward essentially pragmatic foreign economic policies, the Chinese have increasingly recognized that changes in their real economic interests have complicated policy making and that today China's interests are not necessarily best served by unqualified support for all Third World positions or by confrontational methods of dealing with the economically advanced countries.

In the future, it seems likely that in some fields China's interests could diverge from those of many other developing nations and that over time this could have significant effects on China's concrete policies. China's interests in world trade in basic commodities provide a good example. Unlike many developing nations that depend heavily on the export of a few basic agricultural and mineral commodities, China's exports have been quite diversified. Like many industrial nations, it has been more an importer than an exporter of such commodities. According to UNCTAD statistics, for example, in the ten major commodities which that organization has identified as suitable for international agreements involving stockpile arrangements, China's imports in 1974–75 averaged $1.06 billion a year and its exports only $143.2 million a year.[310] Of the ten, China is a major importer of three (cotton, rubber, and wood); it also imports varying amounts of five others (sugar, copper, cocoa, coffee, and jute). Although it exports tea and tin, these products are not among its most important foreign exchange earners. The Chinese are now exporting significant amounts of petroleum and tungsten, but neither is included in UNCTAD's commodity program. China would pay a significant cost, therefore, if the prices of all these commodities were to rise substantially, while many other developing countries would benefit greatly. One participant in commodity negotiations involving the Chinese observed that now, more often than not, they mainly seem concerned with furtherance of their interests as consumers and importers, even though they continue rhetorically to support most Third World nations' positions dictated by the interests of countries wishing to maximize earnings from their commodity exports. The Chinese still do not wish to line up publicly with the West or the Soviet Union on commodity issues, and they "still make political statements in public, support for the Third World and all that," one observer remarked, "but where it really matters, when negotiating, they're in there as business people, bargaining hard and defending their interests."[311]

Over time the Chinese may confront an increasing number of other "contradictions" between their own economic interests and positions supported by numerous Third World nations. For years China's leaders enthusiastically endorsed Third World attacks on multinational corporations, and they may still feel that China's interests would be well served by proposed new codes of conduct that would impose restrictions on these corporations.[312] However, because they are now trying to induce many of these multinationals to undertake large-scale joint or cooperative ventures, Peking has moderated its criticism of them, and it may be less enthusiastic in the future about supporting some proposals aimed at seriously restricting these corporations' activities. The Chinese also have strongly supported majority Third World views regarding the need for an international code of conduct on technology transfers. In this field, too, the Chinese could benefit substantially, along with other developing nations, if the Third World could induce the industrial nations to be more accommodating and facilitate technology transfers in new ways, on a larger scale and at lower costs. However, now that the Chinese themselves are having increasing success in independent efforts to acquire new technology from the advanced nations through direct cooperation with their governments and multinational corporations, they may have doubts about endorsing and supporting efforts that might complicate their own programs.

One can speculate that in time the Chinese may conclude that some of their positions on law of the sea issues need reexamination.[313] In respect to control over territorial waters and economic zones, China's interests are well served by present trends, which increase the control of coastal states over adjacent waters. (So, too, it should be noted, are the interests of some of the most advanced countries, including the United States, even though many of the strongest pressures for larger zones and increased control have come from Third World countries.) However, if China's own shipping continues to expand, the Chinese eventually may question whether it really is in their interest to endorse control over straits by the nations bordering them; eventually they, like other maritime powers, may show greater concern about rights of free passage (which both the United States and the Soviet Union now stress).

Chinese positions on global environmental and international population issues already have changed significantly. Peking's past positions were strongly influenced by ideology, but China's new leadership recognizes the benefits of cooperative action, and in both fields, the Chinese have decided to become more actively involved in international efforts.[314]

Finally, in regard to world food problems, which will be discussed in detail later, China's objective interests call for more active participation in existing cooperative programs, but it remains to be seen whether they will see merit in proposals for new measures, such as creation of a world food reserve program to stabilize prices. To date, they have not, but in the context of their new overall policies, the possibility that they may change their views could increase.

These developments do not imply that the Chinese have altered all of their past positions on global issues. They do suggest, however, that China's present pragmatic, outward-looking economic policies are leading Peking to change its approach to some important international problems.

It seems likely that there will continue to be subtle changes in Chinese views on the relative importance of the Third World. Since the founding of the Chinese Communist regime, Peking's leaders have given high priority to relations with Third World countries, politically and psychologically, and over time they tended to identify China's interests increasingly with those of Third World countries. In the 1950s ideological, anticolonial, and revolutionary motives impelled them to do so. In the 1960s, when China was at odds with both of the superpowers, Peking tried to strengthen ties with Third World countries as part of its broad strategy of building opposition to both the United States and the Soviet Union. Gradually, the revolutionary component in its foreign policy declined, but China's identification with the Third World continued. Finally, in the early 1970s China openly labeled itself a Third World developing country, and it supported virtually every initiative of other developing nations in demanding basic changes in North-South relations.

There is every reason to expect that the Chinese will continue to have a strong interest in the Third World nations, will identify with them in some respects, and will coordinate policy with some of them on some issues. Not only will the Chinese have political motives for doing so, as the earlier discussion of trade patterns indicated, they have a practical interest in expanding economic ties with these countries.

Since the late 1960s, however, the major non-Communist industrial nations have been much more important than the Third World countries to China's crucial security interests, and in recent years, they have become far more important to China's economic interests as well. As Peking has increasingly tried to strengthen ties with Japan and the West, the relative importance of the Third World in China's overall policy unquestionably has declined. In 1979 the doctrine of "three worlds" virtually disappeared from the Chinese political lexicon; it was mentioned only once in passing in Hua Kuo-feng's speech at the National People's Congress in June.[315] Whether or not this trend foreshadows total abandonment of the doctrine, it reflects the change occurring in Peking's practical, objective interests, which inevitably affects its relations with all foreign nations.

China and the Industrial Nations

The most important recent trend in China's foreign economic relations clearly has been the great expansion of its ties with major non-Communist industrial nations and its increasing reliance on these countries for critically important imports of capital goods and technology, food, and industrial materials. This has had important effects on Peking's overall foreign policy. In the late 1960s the Chinese increased political links with these countries essentially for military-security reasons, in the hope that they would help to counterbalance and restrain the Soviet Union. However, the recent expansion of trade with these countries has made the economic dimensions of policy much more important than in the past and has strongly reinforced the trend toward cementing political relations with them.

Today the strongest and most important economic ties China has with any foreign nation are those with Japan. These ties have helped to create what in many respects is a special relationship between two countries. Some of the main features of this special economic relationship, as outlined and analyzed by a Japanese expert, deserve to be noted.[316] First, quantitatively Japan is far ahead of all competitors and probably will remain so. Over the seven years through 1979, two-way Sino-Japanese trade increased at an average annual rate of 29 percent. In recent years steel has been Japan's main export in this trade (in 1978 the Japanese exported 5.6 million tons to China, more than to any other country), but in 1979 this trade declined, at least temporarily, and the share of exports of machinery and equipment in Japan's total exports to China rose to 31 percent. Japan expanded sales of many other manufactured goods to the Chinese in 1979, including some consumer durables (especially television sets and tape recorders). Oil remained Japan's major import item from China (in 1979 it amounted to 7.6 million tons) but was declining proportionately (34 percent of Japan's imports from China in 1979, compared with 42 percent in 1977). Japan steadily broadened its purchases of raw materials and Chinese manufactured goods, some processed in China on consignment, and as a result Sino-Japanese trade has become less unbalanced.

This analyst predicted that by 1985 two-way Sino-Japanese trade could reach $20 billion and be roughly balanced. He estimated that exports of plants would increase each year by about $800 million through 1982, then drop, at least temporarily, and by 1985 Japan's sales of machinery and equipment to China, other than complete plants, could reach $2.9 billion. While not all Japanese would agree with all of these projections, they are plausible.

The analyst's explanations for Japan's unusual success in developing economic relations with China were particularly interesting. He attributed this success to five factors: (1) "history and culture"; (2) a "seven to eight year headstart" (compared with the United States); (3) "firm government support for China trade"; (4) "the way China trade is organized in Japan"; and (5) the unique capabilities and roles of Japan's "general trading companies" (Sogo Shosha). The importance of the first factor is debatable. "Geographical proximity" certainly is important, as the analyst noted, and he may have been right in saying that Japan's business leaders tend to be relatively "lenient," or flexible, in meeting Chinese demands, but it is difficult to judge to what extent Japanese businessmen have a "much better understanding of the Chinese." The other factors he discussed clearly set Japan apart from other countries dealing with China, however, and some of the facts he cited deserve special mention.

He noted the great importance that the Japanese place on all trade, compared with many other nations. Strong government support for China trade, he pointed out, started many years ago, even before normalization of diplomatic relations in 1972; so, too, did active China trade promotion by major Japanese corporations (often working through dummy corporations), each of which built up an in-house corps of China specialists. After 1972 the government rapidly concluded the intergovernment agreements necessary to facilitate Japan-China trade, including a trade agreement, air and maritime agreements, a shipping agreement, a trademark agreement, and others. In 1972 Japan began giving Export-Import Bank financing for sales to China, and by the end of 1979 the government had facilitated the extension of about $10 billion of credit offers to China. (This included all the government-supported or government-encouraged private bank credits as well as direct government credits.)[317]

The unique factors facilitating Japan-China trade analyzed by this expert have been organizational ones. He noted that several major Japanese organizations actively assist individual businesses engaged in China trade; they include JETRO, which provides information and analysis; the Japan-China Association on Economy and Trade, which assists its 406 member companies in numerous ways; and the Japan Association for the Promotion of International Trade, which is especially active in technical exchanges. Most important, Japan's huge "general trading companies" (especially the "Big Nine") advise, cooperate with, and provide expertise to numerous individual companies, and they are said to be involved in one way or another in about 80 percent of all Japanese trade deals with China. Many companies have developed special China sections or departments, with well-qualified, experienced specialists on their staffs. By mid-1980 more than 100 Japanese companies had established offices in Peking, and more than 500 Japanese were stationed in China, far more than any other country had. Two-way technical exchanges have been extensive; in 1979 more than 400 such delegations came from China and about 200 went to China. The Japanese have taken a very long-term view in developing China trade and have expended a great deal of effort, organizationally, as well as invested substantial sums, in gearing up to maximize its potential.

Despite the special character of Sino-Japanese economics, it is not likely that the result will be an alliance or even a close political entente. Sino-Japanese relations—political and security as well as economic—will continue to be complex and ambivalent. In all probability, the Japanese will continue to want what they used to call a policy of "equidistance"—and now often label "balance"—in dealing with Peking and Moscow, even if they tilt somewhat, as they are now doing, toward Peking. On their part, the Chinese will probably try to balance their ties with Japan by expanding relationships with Western Europe and the United States to avoid becoming overly dependent upon the Japanese.

Despite the importance both countries place on their ties, there is a great difference in their real economic significance from the perspectives of the two sides. For China, trade with Japan is now vitally important, accounting for one-quarter of its imports and almost that proportion of total trade. From Japan's perspective, the trade is less significant; in 1979, for example, it accounted for only about 3 percent of its total trade (3.6 percent of its exports and 2.7 percent of its imports).[318] Japanese projections of the likely percentage of China trade in total Japanese trade in 1985 vary greatly, from 5 to 10 percent.[319] Even if it reached the higher figure, it would not be vital to Japan. China trade is important to the Japanese, but their most crucial economic ties lie elsewhere, especially with the United States, the other industrial nations, and the oil-exporting countries. The facts of economic life will probably limit the degree to which the Japanese tilt toward China.

The Chinese, on their part, probably also will avoid any extreme tilt toward Japan. To limit dependence on the Japanese, they are likely to try to maintain some ceiling, perhaps between 25 and 30 percent of China's total trade. To the extent practicable, they can be expected to try to balance trade with Japan with increased trade with Western Europe and the United States. In military-strategic terms, China regards Western countries (especially the United States) as even more important than Japan because they provide the main global counterweights to the Soviet Union, and economic motivations now reinforce China's military and political motives for strengthening relations with both the EEC and the United States.

There is likely to be increasingly intense competition, at least in certain fields, in the years ahead between Japan and the major industrial nations. While there is no reason to expect that this competition will be fundamentally different from that in many other areas of the world, or that it will necessarily create uniquely serious tensions, it nevertheless could create some fairly complicated problems. At least some Japanese, who foresee increasing American and European competition in a market that they have dominated up to now, have recently shown growing concern about the possibility that competition for the China market could exacerbate existing strains in Japan's economic relationships with the other industrial powers, especially the United States. While some of these Japanese seem mainly to fear that U.S. competition will reduce Japan's opportunities, others appear more concerned that American resentment over Japanese dominance in the China market will grow and complicate U.S.-Japan relations. Privately, a few have urged that greater efforts be made to broaden U.S.-Japanese cooperation in support of major development projects in China, in part to minimize American resentments, in part to share the risks.[320] Increased cooperation along these lines, involving Europeans as well as Japanese and Americans, deserves serious consideration. However, it will be difficult to achieve, except perhaps in some of the very largest projects under consideration.

Trade with Western Europe has grown rapidly, both in absolute size and in relative importance in recent years, and by 1979 it accounted for roughly a fifth of China's total trade and close to a quarter of its imports. As in the case of Sino-Japanese relations, however, there is an important difference in the relative stake of the two sides in the trade. In 1978 China trade accounted for only a fraction of 1 percent (0.34 percent) of the total foreign trade of the European Community (EC includes the European Economic Community).[321] West European exports to China will rise in the next few years, but according to EC experts' calculations probably not to more than $10 billion, or over 2 to 3 percent of the EC's total exports.[322] Economically, Europe will continue to be much more important to China than China is to Europe. Nevertheless, broadened trade relations will reinforce to some extent the stake that West Europeans as well as the Chinese have in maintaining friendly political relations.

Until recently, the United States lagged far behind Japan and Europe in trade with China, but in the wake of normalization of diplomatic relations, American trade with the Chinese has grown rapidly, and in the period ahead it could catch up with that of Western Europe, though probably not with that of Japan. By 1979, although the United States bought less than 5 percent of China's exports, it provided almost 12 percent of its imports and accounted for over 8 percent of total Chinese trade. However, this still amounted to only a fraction of 1 percent of total U.S. trade.[323] According to U.S. Secretary of Commerce Juanita Kreps, Vice Premier Teng said to her in mid-1979 that "the U.S. share of their market must come to equal Japan's $6 billion annually."[324] But it does not seem likely that the United States will catch up with Japan because of Japan's many advantages, including proximity. Nevertheless, U.S.-China trade could grow to several billion dollars a year, and if it does, in this relationship as well as those involving Japan and Europe, trade will give both sides an increased stake in the relationship and will reinforce the political and strategic reasons both have for strengthening ties.

It is plausible that in the mid-1980s roughly 25 to 30 percent of China's total trade will be with Japan and that Western Europe and the United States may each account for about 15 to 20 percent. If the percentages are close to the lower figures in these ranges, China's trade with all the developed nations will probably be only slightly above what it now is as a percentage of its total trade. If they are close to the higher figures, however, the share of the developed countries in China's trade will be considerably higher than at present and trade with Third World countries as a whole proportionately lower. Whatever the exact figures in the near future, it is clear that China's trade relations with all the major industrial nations, already its most important foreign economic ties by far, are likely to become more important in the period ahead, and this trend probably will help to strengthen China's political relationships with these countries.

China and Asian Neighbors

One intriguing question about the future is whether China's present pragmatic approach to economic issues could lead it to consider new policies toward some of its smaller non-Communist neighbors. There is no way to answer this with certainty; however, one can say that it is now at least conceivable that economic motives could induce Peking to try to establish trade ties with certain regimes that it has so far shunned, and that over time this might lead to changes in its political approach to dealing with these regimes.

The most notable case in which economic interests have completely overshadowed politics in determining Peking's basic policies has been Hong Kong. Because of economic interests, Peking's leaders have carefully avoided actions that might upset the status quo, even though many Chinese must find the continued existence of an anachronistic capitalist, colonialist relic on China's doorstep embarrassing, politically and ideologically. Hong Kong's importance to China almost certainly will increase in the period ahead, even if Chinese exports to the colony do not increase as rapidly as exports elsewhere. The links now developing between Hong Kong and adjacent Kwangtung Province go far beyond trade. They are creating a symbiosis, with cross-border flows (many of them two ways) of water, fuel, labor, capital, and skills, which are intertwining their interests to a remarkable degree.[325] This situation will probably continue well into the twenty-first century, beyond the 1997 terminal date of the agreement leasing the so-called New Territories to Hong Kong. There is a good possibility, therefore, even though Peking insists that Hong Kong is its territory and must eventually be returned to China, that when the end of the New Territories lease approaches, the Chinese will consider new arrangements that will permit Hong Kong to continue functioning economically much as it does today. Because a Chinese political takeover or any actions that threaten Hong Kong's viability would have an adverse impact on China's own economic interests, Peking probably will avoid such actions.

Could Peking's economic pragmatism lead to comparable flexibility in policies toward Taiwan and South Korea as well? There is little doubt that significant economic relationships between the China mainland and Taiwan would benefit both. China could obtain relatively low-cost capital goods from Taiwan and could learn much from its managerial and production expertise. Taiwan could obtain needed raw materials, possibly including oil. Especially beneficial would be close economic cooperation between Taiwan and adjacent Fukien (Fujian) Province, which like Kwangtung, has been designated a special foreign trade area. Peking now strongly advocates the development of economic ties with Taiwan and asserts that even with reunification Taiwan could preserve its present economic and social system.[326] Taiwan's leaders fear, however, that Peking's motives may still be more political than economic and that trade and other contacts might weaken Taiwan's morale or undermine opposition to reunification. However, indirect trade between the two reportedly grew fairly rapidly during 1979, and it is possible that over time attitudes in Taipei as well as Peking will gradually change.[327]

The political and ideological conflict between Peking and Taipei is not likely to be settled for years, and there is little basis for believing that economic factors will alter Peking's determination to assert eventual sovereignty over Taiwan or Taipei's determination to avoid Communist control. Nevertheless, if economic links between the two regimes were to grow, first through Hong Kong or other intermediaries and later through direct trade and other contacts, the dynamics of their interaction could begin to change.

As its modernization program develops, Peking will probably see the economic as well as political reasons for promoting trade and other ties with Taiwan as increasingly compelling. Moreover, if such ties were to develop significantly, Chinese leaders might give increasing priority, as they have in the case of Hong Kong, to their economic interests, rather than viewing trade as a means to achieve political objectives. If so, this should reinforce Peking's present inclination to adopt a compromising approach to questions relating to the island's political future. It is at least possible that eventually leaders on Taiwan will conclude that the establishment of mutually beneficial economic ties with the China mainland, instead of increasing the threat of subversion to the island, might gradually create the basis for some kind of modus vivendi between Taipei and Peking, based either on a political reassociation with the mainland under conditions granting a high degree of real autonomy or on gradual moves toward some kind of separate status tolerable to Peking.

The case of South Korea, though different in many respects, has some similarities, and similar questions can be raised about whether economic factors might eventually influence China's policy. For several years South Korea has been eager to establish trade and other contacts with China, but Peking has been unresponsive, mainly because of its strong political ties to North Korea. Peking believes that it must avoid compromising its relations with Pyongyang to minimize the possibility that Moscow could increase its influence in North Korea.[328] On purely economic grounds, however, strong arguments can be made that China could benefit significantly from the development of economic relationships with South Korea as well as Taiwan. As is true in the case of

Taiwan, China could obtain some badly needed capital goods (ships for its growing maritime fleet, for example) as well as valuable planning and managerial expertise from South Korea, and the Koreans could buy needed raw materials. (The Koreans are concerned, however, about Chinese competition in third country markets for manufactured goods.[329])

Despite the potential economic benefits of such ties, however, one must assume that Chinese policy toward the Korean peninsula in the period ahead will continue to be shaped mainly by military-security and political considerations. If, however, the overall strategic context were to change—for example, if Pyongyang showed a willingness to develop a real political dialogue with South Korea, or if a limited detente between Peking and Moscow reduced the intensity of their competition in Korea—Peking might be strongly tempted to develop trade and other contacts with South Korea, probably, as in the case of Taiwan, indirectly at first. In fact, in 1980 there were credible reports that some indirect trade via Hong Kong had already begun to take place. If major trade were to develop, it not only would reflect political changes but would have significant political effects.

Competition with Third World Nations

The possibilities described above are partly speculative. More certain is the fact that China's need to expand exports of textiles and other low-cost manufactured products and desire to attract foreign investment, credit, and technical aid will put it into direct competition with other Asian developing countries, creating new frictions and strains in relations with them. China's drive to expand exports will involve intense competition for markets not only with the most successful, rapidly developing regimes near China, such as South Korea, Taiwan, Hong Kong, and Singapore, but also—especially in the field of textiles—with less developed Asian countries, including India, Indonesia, Bangladesh, and Sri Lanka.[330] Countries in the latter category will probably bear the brunt of Chinese competition. Countries that are economically and technically more advanced than China are in a better position to shift exports from labor-intensive commodities to more technically sophisticated goods. South Korea and Taiwan have begun to do this, as Japan did much earlier. However, like China, some larger, poorer countries in South and Southeast Asia have few options other than to try to increase exports of labor-intensive manufactured goods such as textiles during the period ahead. One can only speculate about the political effects of increased competition between China and these countries.

These countries are also worried, with justification, that China will siphon off credit, investment, and technical assistance that might otherwise flow to them. To an extent, this is almost certain to occur, especially two or three years from now when China draws substantial World Bank funds. This will create new problems in China's political relations with these countries.

Could substantial increases in China's oil exports eventually have significant effects on its relations with the Organization of Petroleum Exporting Countries? The answer is perhaps, but not necessarily. Peking has strongly supported OPEC's efforts to increase world oil prices. Originally its reasons were mainly ideological and political, but now they are economic as well. In pricing its oil exports, China has generally followed OPEC's lead and has benefited greatly from the rapid rise in world oil prices since the early 1970s. China has never shown any inclination, however, to join the OPEC cartel. Even though one cannot exclude the possibility that it might in the future, it seems more likely to continue maintaining independence of action. China will doubtless favor further increases in world oil prices. However, as it develops increasingly close, cooperative relationships with the major industrial powers, Peking's views are likely to be similar to those of leaders in the relatively moderate OPEC member countries, who favor continued price rises but are also aware that precipitate action might exacerbate inflationary and recessionary trends in the industrial nations, weakening their ability to counterbalance the Soviet Union and also endangering stability in the world economy, with adverse effects on all nations whose economies are linked to theirs.

If oil exports become crucial to Peking's entire modernization program in the second half of the 1980s, conceivably the Chinese on occasion may make some pricing decisions dictated wholly by their own interests without linking their prices directly to those of OPEC. In certain circumstances, it could become a competitor of some OPEC nations in trying to sell oil in Asian countries. Intense competition is not a high probability, however. In the 1980s, as the supply of oil becomes increasingly tight, prices will be largely dictated by decisions made in a few leading export nations (Saudi Arabia in particular), and generally China, which under the most optimistic assumptions can only become a middle-rank oil exporter, seems likely to continue following

OPEC's lead in its oil-pricing policy under most foreseeable circumstances.

Economic Relations with the Communist Bloc

Finally, China's new stress on foreign trade conceivably could have a significant impact on its relations with the Communist bloc countries in the period ahead. Its present trade with these nations (especially the Soviet Union) is now well below what it probably would be if based on economic considerations alone. Although Chinese trade with the bloc as a whole has risen recently, most of the increase has been with Eastern Europe. Trade with the entire bloc rose from $2.421 billion in 1977 to $3.086 billion in 1978 to $3.599 billion in 1979; trade with the Soviet Union rose from $334 million in 1977 to $500 million in 1978 but then dropped back to $355 million in 1979.[331]

In strictly economic terms, because of complementarities between China and the Soviet Union, greater two-way trade would be in the interest of both countries. China could buy more of certain kinds of capital goods that it needs from the Soviet Union—especially transportation, relatively unsophisticated machines, and replacement parts (which dominate the imports China now obtains from the Soviet Union)—and it could pay for them, and perhaps earn a surplus, by exporting more Chinese agricultural products, raw materials, and light manufactured goods to the Soviet Far East and Siberia.[332]

Possibly, in the period ahead, the Chinese may consider expanding this trade for pragmatic reasons. The fact that China could pay for increased imports of capital goods from the USSR relatively easily (which it cannot hope to do soon in its trade with any of the non-Communist industrial powers) could become an increasingly compelling reason to do so but only if there are changes in the political climate affecting Sino-Soviet relations. However, at some point the Chinese could decide to explore the possibility of a limited political detente with the Russians, in which case expanding trade would be a way to further the process.[333] If gradual steps toward a limited detente were to occur, the political constraints on trade would diminish, and there would be a high probability of some increase in Sino-Soviet trade, though probably not to anything like the level of Chinese trade with the major non-Communist industrial nations.

Conceivably, economic as well as strategic considerations may eventually impel Chinese leaders to consider the possibility of a limited

Sino-Soviet detente. Even though in their broad development program they are committed to modernizing China's military forces, they lack the resources to do so soon in any rapid, dramatic fashion. Because the operations against Vietnam in early 1979 required a sizable expenditure of funds and highlighted weaknesses in the Chinese military establishment, Peking had little alternative but to increase its military spending in 1979. But there is still no indication that the civilian-dominated leadership is considering any major shift of resources from civilian to military purposes. The cutback in targets for steel and other heavy industries in 1979 underlined Peking's determination to stress civilian needs, as did Hua's statement in his June 1979 speech to the NPC: "After producing military supplies of the required quality and quantity, the defense industries should also strive to turn out more products for civilian use, especially consumer durables."[334] China's inability to invest large sums in both basic economic development and military modernization at present creates obvious dilemmas for its leaders who are acutely aware of Soviet military superiority and still fear threats from Moscow. In this situation, it is possible that at some point Chinese leaders may favor steps toward a limited detente with the USSR in order to reduce the pressure to divert resources from civilian to military projects. Reduced tension in Sino-Soviet relations could lessen the need to invest huge sums immediately in military preparations in border areas adjacent to the Soviet Union.

There is little possibility that economic factors will become *the* major determinant of Peking's approach to relations with Moscow. As in the past, China's basic policies toward the Soviet Union, as toward all the major powers, will be determined above all by national security considerations. Even in economic policy, the Chinese are not likely to adopt a more flexible approach toward the Soviet Union unless they are convinced that this would be a sensible part of an overall strategy designed to cope with the Soviet threat as they see it, or unless they conclude that the Soviet threat has declined. Nevertheless, China's modernization program and greater stress on foreign trade may well, in time, influence its policy toward Moscow, strengthening the arguments in favor of both expanded economic relations and limited political detente.

Under China's present leaders, economic factors could have a greater general influence on Chinese foreign as well as domestic policy decisions than in the past, if current policies persist for a reasonable period of time. One cannot totally exclude the possibility of changes in China's priorities that could result in a slowing down, or even a reversal, of current trends. In the foreseeable future, Chinese interests are not likely to be so inextricably involved in global patterns of independence that the option of again turning inward will be foreclosed.[335] Nevertheless, the more China's international involvements grow, and the longer they last, the more China's leaders will see compelling reasons of national interest to continue active participation in the global economy and world community, and the greater the price will be if they consider returning to a policy of extreme self-reliance.

How far China moves down its present path will depend in large part on the success it achieves during the next few years in its modernization, the degree to which its new foreign economic policies support Peking's aims, and the domestic political effects of the changes now under way. It will also depend on the character of China's interactions with foreign powers and the kind of policies they adopt to deal with a more pragmatic, outward-looking China.

The World and China: Opportunities and Problems for the Industrial Nations

The importance of increased foreign trade for China's development is apparent. Although its importance for the rest of the international community may be less self-evident, from a global perspective Peking's new policies are potentially significant. Not only will they open up new trading and investment opportunities for the rest of the world, they will pose new policy issues, especially for the non-Communist industrial nations. There is a need for careful analysis of what policy responses will be most appropriate.

New Markets

The most obvious consequence of Peking's new policies is that during the next few years China should be a substantially larger market than in the past. To assess how significant this market may be, it is useful to view it in comparative terms to avoid exaggerating or minimizing its scale in global terms. If one evaluates it by calculating Chinese imports as a percentage of total world imports, it does not appear large. Recently, China's imports have been under 1 percent of the total imports of all countries outside the Communist bloc, which in 1978 amounted to $1.23 trillion.[336] Even assuming that Chinese imports grow more rapidly than world imports as a whole, by the mid-1980s they are not likely to be over 1 to 2 percent of the global total. It would be wrong to conclude from these figures, however, that China's imports are unimportant in world terms. While it is true that the industrial giants— Western Europe, North America, and Japan—all import much more, Chinese purchases are now approaching the levels of Western countries such as Norway, Denmark, Austria, and Australia, and they already exceed those of most developing nations. To obtain a balanced view of the international significance of the China market, it should be compared not just with the major trading nations but with other developing countries.

A regional breakdown of the total market of non-Communist nations[337] in 1978 shows that the imports of the major industrial countries totaled $837 billion (74 percent of the total); those of the oil-exporting LDCs totaled $101 billion (8 percent); and those of all other developing nations totaled $195 billion (16 percent). Calculated as a percentage of all other developing nations' imports (other than those of the oil-exporting countries), China's purchases amounted to between 5 and 6 percent of the total. In this context they do not seem so small.

A further breakdown of statistics on the imports of non-oil-exporting LDCs shows that the imports of those in Africa totaled $22 billion; those in the Middle East, $20 billion; those in the Western Hemisphere, $59 billion; and those in Asia, $88 billion.[338] Compared with some of these regional totals, China's imports of between $10 billion and $11 billion clearly were significant. Even among the oil-exporting LDCs, in 1978 only two imported much more than China (Saudi Arabia, $22 billion, and Iran, $18 billion, and since then Iran's have plummeted); the imports of two others were about the same as China's (Nigeria, $12 billion; Venezuela, $11 billion). Among all the other LDCs (excluding Hong Kong), there were only four that imported more than China in 1978, and of these, three were small Asian neighbors of China (all "Sinic" areas, influenced by Chinese culture if not populated by Chinese) that have been unusually successful in promoting trade-based growth (South Korea, $15 billion; Singapore, $13 billion; and Taiwan, $11 billion); the fourth was Brazil ($15 billion). Since then, moreover, Chinese imports have grown rapidly. As these figures show, China already is one of the most important markets in the Third World. (In 1978 its imports were about 40 percent larger than India's $7.4 billion.)

In the period ahead, China is likely to be one of the largest new markets for capital goods anywhere in the developing world, rivaled only by the largest oil-exporting nations. It already is one of the most important markets for commodities such as fertilizer, grain, and steel. Even though the China market is not likely to be the "bonanza" some uninformed optimists have hoped for, it is more important than certain analysts have suggested. It is understandably attractive to corporations searching for new outlets for their products. And any new market that will absorb billions of dollars of exports is significant to governments that face balance of payments problems, as a great many, including the U.S. government, now do.

Assisting China: Long-Term Implications

The significance of China's new foreign economic relations should not be judged solely in commercial terms. The possible effects on broader international relationships—including, in time, political relationships—could be equally important in the long run. Possible developments in this area pose some of the key questions about future policy.

Exports of capital goods to China, accompanied by foreign technical assistance and partially financed by foreign loans and credits, should, as Peking's leaders hope, support China's modernization and accelerate the buildup of its economic strength. This will strengthen the economic foundations for China's military power in the future. From a long-term perspective, what are the possible implications of this, not only for China's immediate neighbors but for the major powers that must deal with it? Should other nations assume that, from the perspective of their national interests, accelerated economic development in China is desirable and deserving of support, or should they be concerned about potential dangers that a stronger China might pose?

There are no simple answers to these questions; any judgments must be based on philosophical, historical, and political assumptions that are unprovable. Yet, implicitly or explicitly, leaders of other nations must assess the possible long-term consequences of aiding China's development unless they are prepared to turn a blind eye to the ultimate effects of current policies. At present, leaders in various capitals would give different answers to the questions. Those in Moscow, who are deeply disturbed that China, even though still comparatively weak, is strongly anti-Soviet, believe that China's development should not be assisted. Most leaders in the non-Communist industrial nations today feel that

China deserves help. Even leaders of the U.S. government, which for two decades embargoed all trade with China and tried to ostracize the Chinese from the world community, now maintain that it is in the U.S. interest for China to be "strong and secure."[339] Some leaders in Western Europe as well as in Japan support China's development even more strongly. The attitudes of leaders of many of the small neighbors around China are less clear, however; many have ambivalent feelings.

Probably no country should adopt a simple, unqualified position regarding the desirability of aiding the buildup of China's economic strength, since there can be no absolute certainty about what the eventual results will be. Moscow's leaders would do well to consider the possibility that a pragmatic China, developing successfully, could in time moderate its hostility toward the Soviet Union, and leaders in the non-Communist nations cannot totally exclude the possibility that a more modernized, stronger China eventually might become more assertive internationally in ways that could create new problems for the international community. It would be naive to assume that Chinese policies could never shift again.

Nevertheless, despite inevitable uncertainty about the policies China will pursue in the future, the soundest assumption for all the major powers—including the Soviet Union as well as the non-Communist powers—is that a leadership that succeeds in solving its most pressing problems and makes progress in economic development is less likely to pose major challenges to the international community in the years immediately ahead than a leadership that fails and encounters mounting domestic problems. It is also reasonable to assume that a cooperative attitude toward China's development efforts is likely to influence Peking's actions both at home and abroad in ways that are desirable and that a policy aimed at preventing or slowing China's growth would create hostile attitudes and lead to deteriorating relations and, in any case, would probably fail to prevent its modernization in the long run. China seems much more likely to pursue relatively moderate foreign policies if it has some success than if it feels increasingly threatened and insecure because of economic failure and weakness. Hua Kuo-feng's statement in 1979 that "China's socialist modernization requires an international environment of prolonged peace"[340] and Vice Premier Teng's statement in 1980 that "our strategy in foreign affairs, as far as our country is concerned, is to seek a peaceful environment for carrying out the four modernizations,"[341] deserve to be taken seriously.

These assumptions cannot be accepted without qualification, however, as necessarily valid permanently. They depend on other premises. The most important of these is that the main thrust of China's present development program is aimed at strengthening the country's civilian economy rather than building a powerful offensive military machine. Today it is reasonable to assume that the probable improvements in China's military capabilities in the period ahead will be essentially defensive and are not likely to enhance in any major way its capabilities to take aggressive military action abroad, and that the probability is low that China's leaders will pursue a broadly expansionist or militarily adventurist foreign policy. These assumptions will require periodic reexamination, however. If there is evidence in the future that China is embarking on a much larger program of militarization, or that its foreign policy is shifting toward increased militancy or territorial expansionism, policies designed to assist China's modernization will have to be reassessed.

Another question that deserves attention is whether or not the industrial nations' assistance to China's development will encourage greater and more constructive Chinese involvement in the global economy and international community. Judgments on this, like those on the consequences of helping to strengthen China, can only be tentative. Some argue that the roots of Chinese nativism are so deep that they will limit the ability of its leaders, whoever they are, to involve China constructively and permanently in the global community and that even if it moves in this direction now, in the long run cultural and ideological factors will work against full Chinese participation in cooperative international programs. Others question whether expanded Chinese international involvements are really desirable, since they doubtless will create new problems for the global community.

Such views cannot simply be dismissed. There can be no certainty about how far the Chinese will go in integrating their country into the existing network of international economic relations or exactly what the effects of increased Chinese participation will be. Nevertheless, on balance it is reasonable to assume that if other nations show a cooperative attitude toward China's new outward-looking policies and develop extensive trade and technological relations with China, this will encourage the Chinese to participate more constructively than they otherwise would in cooperative international programs, and that if this occurs, on balance the consequences will be highly desirable.

The basic trend in the world economy is toward increasing interdependence, and today broadly based cooperation is necessary to solve many international problems. In regard to some, including those relating to food and energy, China's noncooperation could cause serious problems. Therefore, even if China does not participate to the same extent, or in the same way, that the major industrial nations do, to the extent that its willingness to cooperate increases, this will be a net gain for the international community.

Broad questions such as these may appear to be only marginally relevant to the "real" policy issues facing leaders in other countries. Actually, however, they are important. Even if assumptions about them are not explicitly formulated or articulated, they will profoundly influence the specific policies pursued by the industrial nations toward China in the years ahead. Judgments about the desirability or undesirability of assisting China's development and of trying to draw the Chinese into more active participation in international cooperation must be the starting point for examining how other nations should respond to China's new policies. They do not, however, provide automatic answers to specific policy questions. Even if the non-Communist industrial powers base their policies on the premise that it is in their long-term interest to expand trade and economic cooperation with China, they will face complicated issues as they attempt to expand relationships with the Chinese.

Maximizing Prospects for Success

In selling capital goods and extending loans to the Chinese, political leaders as well as businessmen in the industrial nations cannot avoid hard questions about the chances for success of Peking's policies, the feasibility of specific projects, and the kinds of problems that may arise in the new economic relationships.

Foreign corporations cannot simply rely on Chinese judgments about whether the country's economic infrastructure is sufficient to support particular projects; whether the specific projects initiated are adequately coordinated and integrated; whether the Chinese possess, or can acquire, the minimum skills necessary to operate particular plants successfully; and whether the specific technology the Chinese wish to acquire is really "appropriate" for an economy such as theirs. The corporations themselves will have to make judgments on such questions. So, too, will the governments of the industrial powers in which the corporations are based.

Differences between Chinese and foreign views on such matters will inevitably create irritations and could create major strains in the new relationships. It will not be easy for governments to take these problems adequately into account in formulating official policies. In many respects, the main forces shaping the new economic and technological relationships with China are international market forces rather than official policies, and private entrepreneurs rather than governments. If foreign governments conclude that the Chinese are acquiring too much debt, buying inappropriate technology, or pursuing policies that involve too great a risk of failure, they can discourage the sale and financing of "too much," or the "wrong kind," of capital goods and technology through controls over sales of technology and the financing policies of their import-export banks. But they will probably feel under pressure to do what is possible to promote increased trade. Because businessmen from all the industrial nations will be competing for shares of the China market, even if governments doubt the wisdom of particular projects and question their prospects for success, they are likely to be inhibited from imposing restraints on their own businesses on the basis of un-provable, or at least debatable, judgments about possible risks in the future.

Nevertheless, governments should exercise what influence they can to try to ensure that the new relationships with the Chinese are viable and lasting. As economic and technological ties expand, it will become increasingly important to nations dealing with the Chinese that Peking's policies succeed. There are various things that governments can do to enhance the prospects that cooperative arrangements, even when carried out largely by private companies, have a reasonable chance to produce favorable results with few undesirable side effects. They can develop broader scientific and technical exchanges, give planning advice to Peking (when it is prepared to accept it) on realistic economic and technical options, and provide guidance to their own businessmen on effective ways of dealing with the Chinese, risks they should consider, and pitfalls they must try to avoid.

However, the plunge the Chinese are making into the international marketplace has created a new situation in which, for the first time since the Communists assumed power, their foreign economic relations are becoming linked to and dependent upon the success they can achieve in establishing effective working ties with private foreign businesses and corporations in the capitalist countries. Yet there is no doubt that if serious problems develop or major failures occur, they will have political-diplomatic repercussions. Whenever major problems or disputes regarding economic and technological relations arise, disillusioned or frustrated foreign businessmen will turn to their governments for help in dealing with the Chinese, and the Chinese will expect Western governments to help them deal with foreign companies against whom they have serious complaints. The ways that the industrial nations and China handle such questions could have significant effects on long-term political relationships.

Buying from China

Chinese efforts to increase exports rapidly will create friction in relations between the industrial powers and the Chinese, create complications in relations among these nations themselves, and inject issues relating to China trade into their domestic politics. As the industrial countries increase exports to China, Peking will exert growing pressure on them to facilitate larger imports from China. However, since low-cost imports from China, like those from other developing nations, will compete with vulnerable domestic industries, opposition will grow from labor unions and leaders in the industries affected. Other developing countries that export the same kind of products may try to exert what influence they can to prevent Chinese encroachments on their markets. Already the industrial nations are wrestling with the problem of what to do about Chinese textiles; many similar problems will arise as the Chinese increase exports of labor-intensive products. The task of the governments in the industrial nations will be to arrive at reasonable compromises among varied and conflicting interests. To promote two-way trade, they will have to allow for increasing imports from China. Yet, as they have in dealing with other developing countries, they doubtless will restrict imports to try to minimize "disruption" of markets and damage to their own industries and to placate internal opposition groups; otherwise the domestic political repercussions could be serious. They probably also will feel compelled to take into consideration the effects of growing Chinese exports on industries in other exporting LDCs such as South Korea, Hong Kong, and Taiwan. However, if the Chinese conclude that their exports are not being fairly treated by particular countries, they may restrict imports from them, and this could have adverse effects on general economic and political relationships.

The textile issue will pose some of the most difficult problems for all the industrial nations in the immediate future. The Chinese have a significant comparative advantage in textiles, which already constitute their largest category of exports, and they hope to expand textile exports substantially. However, they are at a disadvantage as relative latecomers in the highly competitive world market for textiles. For years, the industrial nations have had orderly marketing agreements setting quotas for the other LDCs that are large textile exporters. It will be difficult to absorb huge new Chinese exports without adjusting quotas for other nations. One possible approach, privately discussed, would be to adjust downward the textile quotas of certain countries, especially those that have export surpluses in their overall trade with the industrial nations and possess the technological and economic capability to increase exports of higher-quality products. However, this would be strongly resisted by the countries involved and by supportive groups in the U.S. Congress.

Technology Transfers

The most complicated and politically charged issues posed by the new economic ties that industrial nations are developing with China are those relating to sales of "high technology" that has possible military applications. The Chinese are eager to import high technology for sound economic reasons. To carry out their modernization plans, they urgently need equipment and knowledge relating to computers, electronics, integrated circuitry, aircraft engines, and satellites. However, they also desire such technology to enhance their military capabilities and lay the foundation for future modernization of China's defense forces. Even if purchased initially for civilian projects, many kinds of "dual use" technology have spinoffs that eventually can be used in military applications. For example, advanced computers required for modern steel mills may also help a country improve its ability to develop missiles.

In 1949 the Western industrial nations (joined in 1952 by Japan) established a Coordinating Committee (COCOM) that imposed strategic controls on technology sales to all Communist countries; in 1950 these controls were extended to cover China.[342] Since then, the non-Communist industrial powers have restricted technology transfers to these countries. However, from the start there has been some friction over controls because of different national perspectives and interests. The United States, which has borne the largest responsibility for maintaining the strategic balance with the Soviet Union (and until recently felt it had to "contain" China), generally has favored relatively tight restrictions, while Japan and West European nations often have argued for some relaxation of controls for commercial reasons.

During, and for some years following, the Korean War the COCOM nations (through their China Committee [CHINCOM]) imposed more extensive restrictions on trade with China than on trade with the Soviet Union. Starting in the second half of the 1950s, however, the European members of COCOM moved to reduce restrictions on China, and in 1957 the CHINCOM list was abolished. This eliminated the "China differential" for COCOM's European members, which thereafter applied essentially the same restrictions to China and the Soviet Union.

The United States continued its total embargo on China trade for a decade and a half thereafter. Then, when the "opening" of U.S.-China relations occurred during 1971-72, this policy changed. Washington abandoned the embargo, ended the China differential, and placed China trade on the same basis as trade with the Soviet Union.

Since then, as all of the non-Communist industrial powers have increased trade with China, pressure has grown to reduce restrictions still further. The trend has been toward creating a new "China differential" discriminating in favor of China instead of against it. Again, however, differences have emerged among members of COCOM. European nations have gone the furthest in selling "gray area" technology and even arms to the Chinese. In 1975, for example, the British sold to China the production rights of an advanced aircraft engine (the Rolls-Royce Spey), which the Chinese hope to use in military planes. More recently, the British, French, and others have shown an active interest in selling military aircraft and anti-tank and anti-aircraft missiles to the Chinese. In 1978, for example, the French offered to sell to China the Crotale, Milan, and HOT missiles, and in 1979 the British Prime Minister said his government had decided to sell Harrier fighter planes to the Chinese.[343] Soviet leaders sent strong warnings to the Europeans (and Americans) not to make such sales, and as of mid-1980 none had been consummated, although it was not clear whether this was due to Moscow's pressure or to Chinese indecision and lack of foreign exchange.[344]

The United States showed greater caution, in large part because of concern about possible Soviet reactions. Washington acquiesced to various European sales to China of high technology, including the Spey engine. It also made some ad hoc decisions authorizing direct U.S. sales of certain high technology items to China (such as the Daedalus Corporation's sale of sophisticated infrared scanning equipment in 1978).[345]

However, these were exceptions to general policy. Throughout 1978-79 U.S. leaders maintained that American policy would be "even handed" toward Moscow and Peking and that no weapons would be sold to either, although in late 1978 the U.S. Secretary of State revealed that Washington would not object to European sales of defensive arms to the Chinese.[346]

Toward the end of 1979, however, American policy began to change. Secretary of Defense Harold Brown, visiting Peking in January 1980, after the Soviet invasion of Afghanistan, announced that the United States henceforth would consider on a case-by-case basis sales to China of dual-use high technology that could have military applications; in January also, the Pentagon stated that, although the United States still would not sell lethal weapons to China, it now would be prepared to sell it military support equipment.[347] By mid-1980 a consensus in favor of a "China differential" discriminating in favor of Peking seemed to be emerging among the COCOM nations. There still were significant differences between U.S. and European policies, but as a group COCOM appeared to be moving toward a definite policy of relaxing certain restrictions on exports to China but not to the Soviet Union. (Conceivably, such a policy might be based on precedents set earlier in COCOM's policies toward Yugoslavia, Rumania, or Poland.)

The steps taken so far have raised as many questions as they have answered, however, and it is still unclear how far the non-Communist nations will—or should—go in selling either dual-use high technology or arms to China and what the consequences of alternative policies might be. Issues in this field will continue to pose complicated problems.

Many arguments can be made in favor of relaxing strategic controls on trade with China. The potential commercial advantages are obvious (these, more than anything else, are what have motivated the British, French, and other Europeans to consider sales of arms as well as high technology to the Chinese). Politically, such sales can help to strengthen ties with China. Economically, they should help China's development, which should increase stability in China and the prospects for moderate Chinese policies. Moreover, the arguments for denying advanced technology are much less convincing in the case of China than in the case of the Soviet Union. China is relatively weak militarily and, because its present technological level is comparatively low, there is less danger that it will be able rapidly to divert imported technology to military uses that could pose major threats to others. It can be argued that identical restrictions applied to both China and the Soviet Union would, in fact, discriminate against China because of China's economic backwardness and military weakness. It can also be argued that the huge discrepancy between Chinese and Soviet military power is a source of potential danger in East Asia and that as China's confidence in its defensive capabilities grows, the prospects for stability in the region should improve.

However, there are also many arguments in favor of caution about sales to China of weapons or high technology that can be easily used to improve its military capabilities. Chinese interests and policies toward many areas—including potential conflict zones such as those in Korea, Indochina, and the Taiwan strait—are by no means identical to those of the non-Communist powers, and Peking could make moves in these areas that would heighten dangers in the region. Moreover, sales of military-related high technology, and particularly sales of arms, could create an impression of closer military-security ties between the selling nations and China than in fact exist or at present the sellers desire. This would arouse apprehensions in China's smaller neighbors; over time, it could create anxiety even in Japan.

The greatest uncertainties about the consequences of arms sales to China relate to possible reactions of the Soviet Union. In recent years the Soviet Union has shown increasing concern, close to paranoia, about China and its new relationships with the non-Communist industrial powers.[348] The Russians know that China cannot soon catch up with them, economically or militarily, but they fear the emergence of an anti-Soviet coalition that would link China closely to all the major non-Communist powers; they believe that this would lead to broader, more active opposition to Soviet interests, and they suspect that the Chinese would be able to manipulate the other powers to their advantage. Moscow has opposed all sales of militarily useful high technology to China and has vehemently denounced all proposed arms sales because it has felt they would be steps toward, and symbols of, close strategic links between the industrial powers and China and would increase the likelihood of Peking's pursuing more assertive policies and the possibility of Western involvement in any future conflicts with the Chinese.

The policies of the non-Communist powers toward China obviously should not be determined in Moscow or designed simply to ease Soviet fears; in Asia as elsewhere, the problems the Russians face are to a large extent the consequences of their own policies. Yet it clearly is prudent to be sensitive to Soviet as well as Chinese anxieties, to consider

Soviet concerns, and to avoid provocations that could stimulate Soviet reactions to which it would be difficult to respond effectively. (Stepped-up Soviet intervention in Indochina during 1978-79 provides an example of the kind of Soviet reactions that are possible.)

It will not be easy to define technology transfer policies that respond to China's legitimate needs, strengthen relations with the Chinese, and encourage moderation on Peking's part, and at the same time avoid alarming China's neighbors and provoking Moscow to react in undesired ways. It is necessary, however, to try to do so. To minimize strains among themselves also, COCOM's members must coordinate their policies closely; if they decide to pursue differentiated policies in certain fields (for example, in arms sales), the differences should be based on clear understandings.

In general, a sound policy would be one that is permissive regarding sales to China of high technology whose uses are primarily civilian and therefore clearly more useful for Chinese economic development than for immediate military purposes, but restrictive regarding sales of technology that the Chinese appear to wish primarily for use in developing military items, especially offensive weapons. In light of China's present stage of development, the Western nations can be relatively relaxed about the possibility of technical spinoffs that may help the Chinese to improve their independent defensive military capabilities gradually. The Russians will doubtless continue to denounce all sales of such technology, but they are not likely to react in extreme ways.

Sales to China of military equipment, especially weapons, pose more sensitive questions, and there are good reasons for the non-Communist powers to pursue differentiated arms sales policies. Although the European nations cannot ignore the possible repercussions that such sales have on their relations with Moscow, limited sales by them of defensive weapons are not likely to provoke dangerous Soviet reactions, in part because Soviet leaders know that the West Europeans, distant from Asia, are not likely to develop military ties with the Chinese that could involve them directly in Asian conflicts. Arms sales to China by either the United States or Japan would be likely to stimulate stronger Soviet counteractions. Moscow would view such sales as a major step toward an overt alliance directed against them and might well react in ways designed to try to halt the trend, to counterbalance what it would perceive as an increasing danger, or to impose costs and demonstrate the vulnerability of one or more of the powers involved.

Neither the United States nor Japan need commit itself irrevocably to permanent restraint regardless of future Soviet policy. If Soviet assertiveness in East Asia were to continue increasing in ways that posed a growing military threat in the region, the reasons for restraint would diminish. At present, however, the arguments against American or Japanese arms sales to China are compelling. Under existing circumstances, they seem more likely to provoke than to deter the Russians, and to raise rather than to lower tensions in the area; the effects might well weaken rather than strengthen the security of China as well as others.

Even assuming that the COCOM nations generally agree on policies such as these, implementing them will involve major difficulties. No rules can provide clear guidelines for deciding all specific cases. There is no way of deciding once and for all the differences between "primarily civilian," "military related," and "strictly military" technology. Nor can the line between "defensive" and "offensive" weapons be sharply demarcated. Whatever basic policies are adopted, a large number of issues will have to be decided on a case-by-case basis.

Some continued friction among the non-Communist nations are probably inevitable. There will be strong competition in the China market, especially in the high-technology field, and differentiated policies, even in regard to arms sales, will be galling to businessmen in countries that have relatively restrictive policies. There is some danger that the effectiveness of COCOM itself could be eroded. To keep such problems within bounds, it will be necessary to strengthen the mechanisms within each industrial nation for dealing with these issues and essential to improve coordination within COCOM. For COCOM to work effectively, the criteria for restrictions will have to be refined and probably narrowed, but enforcement of agreed-upon controls should be tightened. In areas where differentiated policies are agreed upon, there will be a need to explain convincingly the basis and rationale for the differences.

Involvement in Global Problems

Problems relating to imports of low-cost manufactured goods from China and exports of high technology to China will pose many of the most complex immediate policy issues for the non-Communist industrial nations dealing with China; however, from a long-term, global perspective, other issues are likely to be equally or more important. In particular, how China's capabilities, needs, and policies will affect world food and energy problems will be matters of growing interest and concern to the entire international community. Already China is among the largest producers and consumers of both food and energy. In the period ahead Chinese interests and those of other nations will increasingly intersect in these crucial fields, and whether Chinese policies alleviate or exacerbate international problems in both areas could have far-reaching consequences.

In the discussion that follows, the interconnections between Chinese and global concerns relating to food and energy will be examined in detail. This will require a shift of focus. So far, the analysis has focused first on China's economic goals, problems, and potentialities and then on the implications for other nations. In analyzing food and energy, the discussion will start with an examination of issues facing the international community and then describe how Chinese interests and policies and those of other nations may relate to each other and interact in the period ahead.

III

China and the World
Food System

FOOD and agriculture pose basic problems for the international community. Feeding and improving the diet of a growing world population, managing the distribution of available food supplies, and reducing the present inequities in food consumption among rich and poor countries require international cooperation. So too do the problems of narrowing the gap between rich and poor in food consumption within poor countries, preventing extreme fluctuations in food prices, and ensuring against calamities in bad crop years.

Experts differ on probable trends in population and grain output. Even the optimists agree, however, that there will be fluctuations in supplies and prices and serious shortages could develop in some years, and that there is a need for an improved system to distribute food and manage grain reserves in order to stabilize prices and meet emergencies. They also agree that serious inequities in food distribution could cause political as well as economic problems and that more effective means are urgently needed to raise food output in the developing countries.

Feeding the world today requires huge international transfers of grain, as well as many other agricultural products, and both production and prices fluctuate as a result of changes in weather, market conditions, and political and social as well as economic factors. Many nations and numerous variables are involved, and the problems facing individual nations can be fully understood only in the context of the evolving world food system.

China has emphasized self-reliance and food self-sufficiency more than any other large nation, but it nevertheless has been unavoidably linked to the world distribution system for food and other products that affect the production and price of food. Its policies both affect and are affected by the world market for grain, other agricultural commodities, and manufactured goods essential to agriculture.

As one of the three largest producers of grain in the world (with the United States and the Soviet Union), China feeds more than one-fifth of the world's population. Whatever its direct linkages at any particular time with the global economy, it makes a significant contribution to the world food system simply by feeding such a large part of humanity, which it has been able to do with reasonable success during the past quarter century. Any disastrous failure in Chinese agriculture would either impose huge new demands on the world's limited food supplies or result in massive starvation or malnutrition which the rest of the world would find difficult to ignore.

Actually, China is linked to the world food system more closely than is generally recognized. Since the early 1960s it has been a major importer of grain and other agricultural commodities such as cotton. In some years it has been the largest grain importer among the non-industrialized developing nations, and in recent years it has been the world's largest importer of chemical fertilizers. Even though Chinese grain imports seem relatively small in relation to the country's total needs and domestic output, they have been vital to China—to meet critical shortages (especially in the early 1960s), to ensure supplies to China's major cities, to reduce the procurement burden imposed on peasants, to ease the strain on internal transport, and to free land to grow industrial and export crops. In years when China has been among the largest wheat importers in the world, its imports have had a significant influence on the worldwide availability and price of food. And, despite the Chinese leaders' desire until recently to insulate their society as much as possible from external influences, world market conditions affecting agricultural commodities have had a significant impact on China's economy.

China also is a major exporter of agricultural commodities, and its role as a supplier of rice is important to certain developing countries. This too must be considered in any assessment of China's role in the world food system.

China's future need for grain imports and ability to supply grain exports will depend above all on its agricultural performance at home. During the past quarter century, food output has kept ahead of population growth, which has been a notable achievement, but the margin of success has been thin. The Chinese have experienced severe shortages in some years and have not been able to make major improvements in diet.

China's most serious agricultural crisis since the Communist takeover occurred during 1959–61 following the Great Leap Forward, as a result of serious policy errors as well as bad weather. Since then, its leaders have given high priority to promoting agricultural growth, and in particular to increasing grain output. Abandoning the ideologically motivated "radical" policies that produced the post-Leap crisis, they have increased investments in agriculture, encouraged water conservation by traditional methods, applied more modern "inputs" (fertilizers, improved seeds, and so on), and started mechanization. As a result, grain output has risen significantly. They also have made a major effort to promote birth control, so as to limit the number of new mouths to feed. However, despite these efforts, they have had to continue importing grain to meet temporary shortages, build up depleted stocks, and support their broad social and political as well as economic objectives.

China's agricultural prospects in the next few years are difficult to assess with accuracy. Its present policies will have favorable effects. In particular the expansion of its fertilizer industry and new programs to develop improved seeds will continue to raise output. But it needs to modernize its agriculture rapidly, much more than in the past, to meet the growing demands placed on it for industrial and export crops in addition to food. In the 1960s grain output rose quickly as a result of increased use of modern inputs, but recently the rate of increase has fluctuated. Accelerating the rate will not be easy. Advanced agricultural development requires a complex mix of inputs and techniques that China still lacks. Unlike agriculture in many other developing nations, Chinese agriculture is already highly developed by traditional means, with relatively high per acre yields. Further development will require increasingly sophisticated and expensive modern methods.

China's ability to meet its future food needs will depend on many variables. One will be the ability of the government to make large investments in agriculture and in industries supporting agriculture, in the face of increasing competition for resources from China's civilian industries and military establishment; at some point very large investments in river control may be required. Equally important will be the regime's success in adapting rural institutions and implementing new incentive policies to spur increased production. Food output also will be influenced by how much of China's land and other resources has to be allocated to produce badly needed nonfood crops. Perhaps most important of all in the long run will be the regime's success in acquiring and disseminating new knowledge and modern techniques in agriculture. The Chinese have been successful in recent years in disseminating the knowledge they now possess, but the increasingly complex agricultural problems they will face in the future will require expanded and more successful efforts in agricultural research, education, and interchange with the international scientific community. China's food situation in the years ahead will also depend on trends affecting consumption patterns. Some of the questions most difficult to answer concern future trends in food demand. Today the average diet is still low in animal protein, and if China's development follows patterns elsewhere, there is likely to be increased pressure for an improved diet as China's per capita gross national product grows.

Whatever the long-term trends, food output will be greatly affected by year-to-year fluctuations in weather conditions, which will produce significant ups and downs in production. Moreover, some meteorological estimates of long-term weather trends raise troublesome questions about future agricultural prospects in North China.

All of these factors will help to determine China's food output and needs, and the demands it may place on world supplies of grain and the inputs its agriculture will require. No "great leap" that will suddenly solve China's food problems once and for all is in sight; the race between food and population will continue to be close. With effective policies, China should be able to keep up with rising demand for food, but with ineffective policies, it could experience serious shortages.

China is highly likely to continue to be a net grain importer. In fact, the size of its imports may grow. In bad years its demand could be very large. If major shortfalls in China coincide with bad years in other nations, such as the Soviet Union, the impact on world food supplies and prices could be great.

From China's perspective, its linkages with the global economy affect its entire economic situation and outlook. During 1973–74, for example, grain shortages in China compelled the Chinese to buy large quantities abroad at a time when they were unusually expensive because of world shortages caused by bad weather in 1972. Its problems were exacerbated by a worldwide rise in fertilizer prices, caused in part by the international oil crisis. Forced to use a large amount of its limited foreign exchange to import food, while still trying to purchase badly needed capital goods for industrial development, it accumulated significant balance of payments deficits that compelled it temporarily to slow down its overall development plan. China's need to import substantial quantities of grain has competed directly with its desire to accelerate industrialization. This has been true ever since the early 1960s and will continue to be true in the period ahead.

China's leaders, fully aware of the linkages between their national interests and the global food system, have had a good deal to say about world food problems. Despite their participation in the United Nations Food and Agriculture Organization (FAO) and the 1974 World Food Conference at Rome, however, in the past they did not take an active part in most international efforts to improve the world food system. During the period when the leaders stressed self-reliance, they blamed most world food problems on the policies of the developed capitalist nations and urged all countries, especially the developing nations, to strive for food self-sufficiency. They held up the Chinese approach to agricultural problems as a model for other developing countries, and its policies did have some influence on the policies in certain other countries. They argued strongly for increased cooperation among Third World nations to reduce dependence on the West, even though the Chinese ability to aid agriculture in other nations was limited. Although China clearly would benefit from many international programs, and also could make a useful contribution to them, during the 1960s and early 1970s its leaders avoided formal and active participation. Even after being seated in the United Nations, they declined to join major UN-sponsored bodies such as the World Food Council and publicly opposed the idea of creating internationally supervised food reserves.

Because of its vulnerability to the effects of world food shortages and price fluctuations, China has paid a price—although how large a one is debatable—as a result of its limited involvement in international cooperation to improve the world food system. The global community also has paid a price—also difficult to quantify—as a result of Chinese nonparticipation. It now appears, however, that in this as in other fields China's leaders may see the benefit of increased international contact and cooperation and the costs of isolationism.

Improving the global food system requires a wider international exchange of information, more effective programs to disseminate agricultural knowledge and techniques, and greater efforts to ensure the availability of needed inputs at reasonable prices. If it stays aloof from such programs, China will forgo the benefits it could obtain as well as the contributions it could make.

From a global perspective, there is a need for a new food reserve system to ensure adequate supplies in bad crop years and reduce price fluctuations which hurt the poor nations most. So far, China has indicated that it would not participate in any reserve system, and it has tried to solve its problems independently by relying on its own stocks and making long-term (generally three-year) agreements with its main foreign suppliers. Although it can be argued that China's maintenance of adequate reserve stocks alleviates the global supply problem and indirectly contributes to stabilization of world prices, China's nonparticipation in any new international reserve system could create real problems for China itself as well as for other nations involved in such a system. If the Chinese were to experience serious grain shortages at a time of world shortages, they might not be able to obtain the supplies they needed, or their sudden entry into the world market might have very disruptive effects on the system.

Both China and the global community would benefit substantially if China were to participate fully and constructively in all major cooperative efforts to deal with world food problems. In the past, Chinese leaders were reluctant to participate because of their commitment to self-reliance, their fear of compromising ideological and political values, and their desire to insulate China as much as possible from the vicissitudes of the world market. Nevertheless, even when China's radicals were in the ascendant, necessity forced China to involve itself to some extent, and in the period ahead its involvements probably will increase, although how much remains to be seen.

Whatever China's policies, they have to be taken fully into account by others concerned with the global food system. Policy makers in international organizations and other countries, including the United States, must consider how to involve China directly in cooperative efforts; in situations where the Chinese are not fully involved, whether there are ways to encourage them to pursue policies that parallel or support international efforts; and, if China's nonparticipation in international programs creates serious problems, what other countries should do about it.

Global Food Problems

To view China's problems and prospects in comparative terms, and to estimate how China may affect and be affected by global developments, it is necessary to examine trends worldwide as well as in China. No short discussion can deal adequately with the complexities of world food production and distribution, but certain facts need to be grasped in order to comprehend the global context in which China's situation must be analyzed. At a minimum, this requires an examination of trends in world population growth and food output, the geographical distribution of population and food production, regional variations in consumption and nutrition standards, and some of the major factors affecting output. In addition, it requires analysis of the international distribution of food, including trends affecting not only the volume of trade but also prices and food reserves. Statistics on these matters are cold and impersonal, but it should not be forgotten that the problems of poverty and inequity must ultimately be understood in human terms, although the numbers nevertheless are essential to any understanding of the dimensions of present world food problems and China's importance in relation to them.

Population Growth and Food Output

Concern about world food supplies has fluctuated over the years, swinging between pessimism and optimism as crops have varied, generally following the weather.[1] Ever since Malthus predicted that population increases would outstrip food supplies, alarmists have periodically forecast approaching disaster. In the years since World War II, there have been several waves of pessimism—in the late 1940s, early 1950s, mid-1960s, and, most recently, immediately following the grain crisis of 1972, when world production dropped, reserves dwindled, and prices skyrocketed. Periods of pessimism have generally been followed, however, by increased optimism—often resulting in complacency, at least in the developed nations—during periods of rising output.

If one takes a historical view of global trends, there is a basis for cautious optimism about the capacity to increase world agricultural production rapidly enough to keep ahead of population growth. Yet there is no basis for complacency. Global food output has been increasing faster than the world's population, but the margin of success has not been large—even when one focuses just on the global picture and ignores the wide discrepancies between the rich and the poor nations. Moreover, the future growth in the world's food supply will depend increasingly on petroleum and gas (for agricultural machines, fertilizers, and so on), introducing increased elements of uncertainty about the future.

Since the end of the eighteenth century, the total number of people in the world has multiplied spectacularly, by about four and a half times. During most of these two centuries the global food problem has, in one sense, been a population problem; the rapid proliferation of mouths to feed has meant that rapid expansion of food output has been required to avoid disaster. Until recently, the rate of population increase has been rising, largely because modern medicine and health measures have reduced worldwide death rates, though during the past few years there have been encouraging signs that the growth rate has started to decline.

Between 1930 and 1960 world population rose from about 2 billion to roughly 3 billion.[2] By 1970 it had reached 3.6 billion, and today it is well over 4 billion. Worldwide, the annual rate of increase, which was about 1.1 percent in 1930, rose to roughly 1.7 percent in 1960, and by the mid-1960s it was close to 2.0 percent. Then it began to decline slightly, and by the mid-1970s it had dropped to perhaps 1.7 or 1.8 percent.[3] Despite the recent drop, for any real per capita increase in world food availability to occur, output must increase by a rate close to 2 percent.

If the 2.0 percent rate of the mid-1960s had continued without major change, a rise in the world's population to about 7.8 billion by the end of this century would have been possible.[4] However, since fertility rates have begun, and probably will continue, to decline, it may not be that high. Nevertheless, the decline will be gradual, and the momentum of population growth will persist for many years because of the large numbers of women entering the childbearing age.[5] Some experts believe that even under very favorable conditions it will take at least four to five decades to halt significant population growth.

One UN estimate calculated that the global average population growth rate for the period 1970–2000 might be around 1.9 percent, and that by the year 2000 the world's population would total 6.4 billion.[6] This estimate probably overstated the likely growth rate, even though it appeared to underestimate China's population. More recent studies suggest that in the year 2000 the total may be somewhere near 6 billion. The United Nations recently has estimated that world population will reach 6.3 billion in the year 2000, but the World Bank has predicted that the figure will be 6 billion,[7] and the Population Reference Bureau has published a study predicting that it will be "only" 5.8 billion.[8]

There is no certainty, however, about when or at what level the world's population will ultimately stabilize. Robert S. McNamara, president of the World Bank, has warned, "Unless governments, through appropriate policy action, can accelerate the reduction in fertility, the global population may not stabilize below 11 billion. That would be a world none of us would want to live in."[9] There is no way that the world's population can be stabilized until some time in the twenty-first century. At the earliest this might occur between 2020 and 2025; probably it will be later. And the level at that time will be well above 6 billion.

Whatever estimates one accepts, the number of mouths to be fed inevitably will increase substantially in the period ahead. In 1978 alone, world population increased by 70 million, and by the year 2000 it may well be half again as large as at present. Over the long run, stabilizing the population will be a prerequisite to solving the world's food problems. During the next few decades, however, no foreseeable changes in population trends will obviate (though they obviously could ease) the task of feeding steadily rising numbers of people.

If this is the prospect for population growth, what is the outlook for production of food? In particular, what are the prospects for grain, which accounts for more than 70 percent of the world's crop area,[10] in direct consumption provides about 52 percent of mankind's energy intake, and converted to meat provides much of the rest.[11]

In gross terms, world grain production has kept ahead of population growth ever since the modern population explosion began. Despite an increase in population of four and a half times during the past two centuries, per capita consumption has risen, fairly spectacularly in the most advanced nations and at least marginally in the less developed nations.[12] Recently, when the population growth rate has risen, so has the rate of increase in food output.

According to statistics published by the U.S. Department of Agriculture (USDA),[13] total world output (of wheat, coarse grains, and milled rice) rose from an annual average of 851 million tons in the early 1960s (1960/61–1962/63) to 1.13 billion by the turn of the decade (1969/70–1971/72).[14] By 1976/77 it had reached a level of about 1.35 billion.[15] In roughly a decade and a half, it had increased by close to 60 percent—almost 3 percent a year (or, in terms of tonnage, by about 500 million tons, more than 30 million tons a year).[16] Then in 1977/78 output dropped 1 percent to 1.34 billion tons; in 1978/79 it rose almost 9 percent to 1.46 billion; and in 1979/80 it was estimated that it would again drop, by almost 4 percent, to 1.40 billion tons.[17] In three years the increase was only 3 to 4 percent.

The 3 percent rate of increase in global grain production since the early 1960s[18] has been about 1 percent more each year than the population growth rate. In one sense, this has been encouraging; however, it has left little to raise consumption levels; most has gone to feed new mouths.[19]

Looking ahead, it is no simple matter to predict future output or demand, taking into account possible increases in per capita consumption as well as population growth. There is no doubt that demand will continue to rise inexorably. In the early 1900s the world had to increase grain output by only about 4 million tons a year to meet rising demand. By the early 1950s the figure was roughly 13 million tons. Now it is considerably higher.[20] In 1978/79, grain consumption worldwide reportedly rose by 5.8 percent, or 77 million tons in one year.[21] The USDA has estimated that between the mid-1970s and 1985 world food demand probably will increase by 2.3 to 2.5 percent a year and will rise to between 1.50 billion and 1.55 billion tons.[22] At the World Food Conference in Rome in 1974, U.S. Secretary of State Henry Kissinger asserted that by the end of the century world grain production would have to be doubled to maintain present levels of per capita consumption and would have to reach 3 billion tons to achieve an adequate diet worldwide.[23]

Can grain output actually be increased fast enough to match what the USDA projects as likely demand? The answer is *probably* yes, according to many experts, assuming continued modernization of agriculture, expansion of acreage where possible, increased use of modern inputs to raise yields, reasonable price policies, and no prolonged period of abnormal weather.[24]

Optimists predict that grain production worldwide probably can be increased by 2 to 3 percent a year at least to the end of the century[25]— which would mean the food-population race would continue to be won by roughly the same margin as in the recent past. Specific USDA estimates of probable world production and demand show output in 1985 higher than demand, though perhaps by only 2 million tons a year in 1985.[26] (The USDA also estimates that by 1985 the United States alone might be able, if necessary, to increase its wheat output by at least one-third and its feedgrain production by one-half, which could probably meet any possible increase in world demand, at least in the period imme-diately ahead.[27] However, whether the United States alone would do so is by no means certain. And if the rest of the world were to become in-creasingly dependent on American supplies, how the poor countries would pay for their needs is unclear.)

The global outlook for population and food during the rest of this century does not justify apocalyptic predictions of disaster. But whether or not world food production continues to outpace increases in total population and rising per capita demand will depend on whether or not both the developed and developing nations pursue effective economic, political, and social policies that will increase food output and reduce population growth. Moreover, even if the global balance between food and population is not upset, there will continue to be enormous food problems worldwide. Gross statistics of global supply do not reveal these problems, many of which relate to the distribution of available grain.

Distribution of Population and Food

Today there is a huge food gap between the developed countries and most developing nations, and estimates of probable trends in population growth and food production in the rich and poor nations show that it is likely to widen in the period ahead. Already this gap poses moral and political as well as economic problems of major dimensions, and if it widens these problems will become increasingly serious.

The majority of the world's population lives in developing countries (including China), which face the greatest food problems. By 1970 these countries contained roughly 70 percent of all the people in the world (more than 2.5 billion out of the global total of 3.6 billion).[28] Ap-proximately 1 billion lived in the poorest thirty to forty countries— roughly the same number as in the well-fed developed nations.[29] By 1975 the developing countries contained almost 3 billion, or about 75 percent of the world total of 3.9 billion,[30] and the proportion living in the devel-oping nations will unquestionably continue to grow.

Between 1961 and 1973 the population growth rate in the developed countries as a whole dropped from 1.3 to 0.9 percent; however, the rate in the developing nations as a group actually rose between 1950 and the 1970s from about 2.0 percent to roughly 2.5 percent.[31] (As will be noted later, the rate in China was below the average for this group.) In 1973, of the total annual increase in world population of roughly 71 million, more than 61 million were in the developing nations (including China), and less than 10 million were in the developed countries.[32] Roughly 85 percent of the net *additions* to world population each year—now close to 75 million—are in the developing nations.

There is some encouraging evidence that fertility rates are beginning to decline in a number of developing nations; at least a few now appear to be undergoing the "demographic transition" that most of the developed world has already experienced.[33] Birth control and family planning programs should reinforce this trend. Even more important will be the effects of the economic and social changes accompanying development—increased urbanization, rising living standards, more widespread education, and the basic value changes accompanying such trends—which should help to reduce fertility rates further.[34] But at best it will take considerable time to close the gap between birth and death rates. In most developed countries the "demographic transition" took between fifty and one hundred years.[35] Some developing nations may now accomplish it more rapidly; conceivably a few might complete it in twenty to thirty years. But for most it will take longer.[36]

What does this mean for the world's population—and its distribution between the developed and developing nations—from now until the end of this century? The UN study cited earlier, which estimated that world population might increase at an average rate of 1.9 percent from 1970 to 2000, projected rates of 0.8 percent in the developed nations (including the Soviet Union and Eastern Europe) and 2.3 percent in the developing nations (including China).[37] If these were the actual rates, by the end of the century there would be more than 5 billion people in the developing nations (over one-fifth of them in China) and roughly 1.37 billion in the developed nations.[38] However, because of recent drops in fertility rates in some developing nations, the number in such countries in the year 2000 may be less than 5 billion, but almost certainly it will be at least 4 billion to 5 billion.

The growing food gap between rich and poor nations has been and will continue to be due in large part to the differences in rates of population growth; actually food output has been increasing somewhat more rapidly in the latter than in the former. Between 1954 and 1973, the annual average rate of increase in food production—2.8 percent globally—was roughly 3.0 percent in the developing countries as a group (China's rate was somewhat lower than this group's average) compared with 2.7

percent in the developed nations; however, because of more rapid rate of population increase in the poor countries (2.5 percent, compared with 1.0 percent in the developed countries) their average rate of per capita increase in food output was only 0.4 percent—less than one-third the 1.5 percent rate in the developed countries.[39] In 1979 it was estimated that during the 1970s total food production in the developing countries grew at a rate of 3.1 percent, but on a per capita basis it grew by only 0.7 percent.[40]

In the developed countries population increased only 22 percent during 1954–73, while food production rose 65 percent, producing a 33 percent increase in per capita food output.[41] In contrast, even though food production rose 75 percent in the non-Communist developing nations, their population increased 61 percent, so that the growth in their per capita food production was only 8 percent—starting from a much lower base. (In the same period China's grain output increased by about 60 percent and its population by close to 50 percent, so the growth in its per capita grain availability was also close to 8 percent.[42]) Averaged globally, the world's population had about one-fifth more food to eat in 1973 than in 1954, but the improvement was much greater in the rich countries than in the poor nations; in the latter, food consumption rose by less than one-tenth. Today the value, per capita, of food production in the developing nations is still less than one-fifth that in the developed countries.[43]

Demand for grain has been growing at a faster rate in the developing than in the developed nations, however. During the 1950s and 1960s the annual rate of increase in demand in the developing countries was about 3.5 percent or more (compared with about 2.5 percent in the developed nations); of this, 2 to 2.5 percent was attributable to population growth, however, and only about 1 percent or so a year to income growth.[44] Between 1977/78 and 1978/79, grain consumption increased 5.5 percent in the developed countries compared with 3.7 percent in the developing countries (not counting China).[45]

During 1969–71, according to USDA figures, the grain deficit (the difference between domestic grain production and demand) in the developing nations averaged 23.5 million tons a year (a figure which may be slightly too low because of a low estimate for China).[46] In 1978/79 it was 40 million tons.[47] If USDA predictions are valid, by 1985 the developing nations' annual deficit will be at least 50 million tons—and could even be close to 80 million[48] (the size of China's deficit is obviously a major factor determining the global total) while the surplus in the developed nations should be of roughly comparable size.

What these figures on population, grain production, and demand show is that in a fundamental sense the world food problem in the period immediately ahead will probably be less a problem of absolute shortages globally than a problem of unequal distribution between the rich and poor countries. (Moreover, *within* many developing countries, the inequality of food distribution will continue to be a serious problem.)

Nutrition

The meaning, in human terms, of the differences in food supplies between the rich and the poor countries becomes clear when differences in nutrition are examined. Nutritional sciences are still in their infancy, and the data for exact comparisons are lacking, but the general picture is clear.

In 1974 the FAO, using a standard of 1,900 to 2,000 calories per person per day as a basic measure for minimum protein/energy supply sufficiency (which is close to a minimum level of subsistence for moderate activity), estimated that 460 million people—roughly one-sixth of the population in the developing nations—were malnourished.[49] Actually, needs vary greatly according to climate, physical characteristics of the population, age, occupation, and other factors, and recent FAO publications give estimates of calorie requirements for particular countries that range between 2,200 and 2,700 per capita.[50] If these higher figures were used, estimates of the number of malnourished would be higher.

The USDA estimates that in the developed nations as a whole per capita daily consumption in the 1960s (1964–66), measured in calories, was 3,043, of which 1,127 came directly from grain, whereas in the developing nations it averaged only 2,097, of which 1,300 came directly from grain.[51] It estimates that the daily calorie intake in particular regions of the developing world were as follows: 1,969 (1,271 directly from grain) in East Asia and the Pacific, 1,975 (1,300 directly from grain) in South Asia, and 2,121 (1,589 directly from grain) in Southeast Asia. Other estimates of average per capita consumption of grain (direct or indirect) in all developing countries (excluding China) indicate an average of about 168 kilograms (370 pounds) in 1964–66 and 180 kilograms (395 pounds) in 1972–74—a 7 percent rise.[52] The *direct con-*

sumption of grain as food is roughly twice as much per capita in the developing nations as in the developed nations. Yet the *total* use of grain is three to four times as large in per capita terms in the developed countries as in the developing nations, and it is still growing more rapidly in the rich countries.

In 1964–66 the United States consumed an average of about 1,600 pounds of grain per capita (more than four times the average in developing countries); by 1972–74 this had risen to 1,850 pounds—a 15 percent increase.[53] The figures for the Soviet Union for those years were 1,105 and 1,435 pounds—a 30 percent increase. The *rates* of increase, as well as the absolute figures, have been much lower in the developing nations. Grain consumption has been growing in the developed nations because they now use very large amounts of grain to produce meat. In virtually all these countries, as per capita incomes have risen, meat consumption has soared. Improved diets call for more protein consumption, and increasing the use of meat is the preferred—though not the only— way to obtain more protein. In the United States, per capita consumption of all meat rose from 95.5 kilograms in 1961 to 113.9 kilograms in 1974.[54] The level in Western Europe is somewhat lower but increasing (it was 62.4 kilograms in 1961 and 81.2 kilograms in 1974). Per capita consumption of meat in Japan and Russia is also increasing. Since it takes (in the United States) roughly 2 pounds of grain to produce 1 pound of poultry, 3.5 pounds to produce 1 pound of pork, and 6.5 pounds to produce 1 pound of beef,[55] indirect consumption of grain has risen very rapidly while direct consumption of grain has actually tended to drop in the affluent countries. Per capita grain use in the United States now approaches one ton a year, but of this only about 150 pounds are directly consumed by humans. In contrast, in the developing nations meat consumption is low, and most grain is directly consumed.

Today, more than one-fourth of the world's grain (close to one-third if rice, which is not often used for feed, is excluded) is used to feed livestock and poultry.[56] Even Japan now uses more than one-third of its grain supply for feed (in 1976, 12.72 million tons out of 31.57 million), and the Soviet Union now uses more than a half of its grain supply in some years for feed (in 1972, 100 million tons out of 168 million).[57] The Soviet Union's increasing stress on meat production has been a major explanation for its large grain imports in recent years. Its leaders apparently have not wished to face the possible political repercussions of cutting meat consumption, although, as a result of the cut in U.S. grain exports to the Soviet Union after its invasion of Afghanistan, Soviet meat consumption may have to be reduced.

The increasing use of grain for meat in the developed countries has led some to suggest that one way to help solve the food problem in the developing nations would be to cut the consumption of meat among the affluent. Steps to limit meat intake in the developed countries would certainly be possible. (Norway has slowed the increase in consumption of beef and fatty meats by promoting the use of lean meats and fish, thus saving grain as well as improving health.[58]) But for many reasons it is unrealistic to view this as an effective way to solve the poor nations' problems. Cutting meat consumption in the rich countries will not solve the poor countries' problem of paying for the food they need; and expanding free aid—while essential in some cases—would make worse their problem of dependency.

Recent trends in consumption suggest that as per capita incomes increase in the future, there are likely to be growing pressures toward increased per capita use of grain both for the production of more meat and for direct consumption in the developing as well as the developed nations.

Fertilizers and Yields

Achieving faster growth of food production will require increasing both cultivated acreage and yields. Worldwide, there is still a great deal of uncultivated arable land (the USDA estimates that it may be almost as much as the land now planted).[59] However, much of this is in relatively sparsely populated areas, especially in Africa and Latin America. The potentialities for adding acreage are limited in many of the most heavily populated areas of the world where food problems are the greatest. In such areas, the primary task is to raise per hectare yields.

Average grain yields in most developing nations are still far below those in the developed nations. To cite a few examples, in 1972 the averages (for all grains) were 1.0 metric ton per hectare in Africa (which was roughly the worldwide per hectare average before World War II), 1.6 in Asia as a whole, 1.2 in the Philippines, 1.1 in India, and 2.1 in Indonesia. In contrast, the averages were 5.5 in Japan, 4.2 in France, 3.9 in the United States, and 3.8 in West Germany.[60] (China's yields, as will be indicated later, are higher than those in most developing nations but lower than those in many developed countries.) The potential for raising yields in the developing countries as a whole is still very great.

Much of the increase in global grain output in recent years has come from raising yields rather than just from expanding acreage. According to FAO figures, world grain acreage increased from about 665 million hectares in 1961 to roughly 698 million hectares in 1972, an increase of just under 5 percent;[61] in the same period, average per hectare yields for all grain crops worldwide rose by almost 29 percent, from 1.4 to 1.8 tons per hectare.[62] USDA figures show a rise of 7.6 percent in harvested grain area from the 1972/73 grain year (678.8 million hectares) through 1976/77 (730.6 million hectares), with average per hectare yields also rising 7.6 percent from 1.84 tons to 1.98 tons in the same period.[63] (The figures vary, of course, for different crops and areas.) Worldwide, one disturbing recent trend has been a slowing of the rate of increase in yields. From 1950 through 1971 world cereal yield per hectare grew at 2.4 percent a year, but since then the rate of increase has been about one-fourth of that.[64]

Here again, as in most aspects of the food problem, there are great contrasts between the developed and developing nations, as well as between particular countries. From 1960–62 through 1969–71 the average annual rise in grain yields in the developed countries was 2.8 percent (with output per hectare rising from 2.1 tons in 1961 to 3.1 tons in 1972).[65] In the non-Communist developing nations the rate of increase was only 1.9 percent (and output per hectare rose only from 1.1 tons in 1961 to 1.3 tons in 1972). This was the main reason that grain surpluses increased in the developed countries as a group while grain deficits grew in the developing nations. In the developed countries, even though cultivated acreage actually declined, because of increased yields total grain output rose at an annual rate of 2.7 percent—more than double the population growth rate of 1.1 percent and somewhat above the 2.5 rate of increase of demand.[66] In contrast, in the developing nations the rate of increase in output averaged 3.5 percent as a result of a 1.4 percent rate of increase in acreage and a 1.9 percent rate of increase in yields, but because this was below the 3.7 percent rate of increase in their grain consumption, their deficits rose. (In China, as the later discussion will indicate, recent increases in grain output have come almost entirely from rising yields, which have increased more rapidly than in most other developing countries.)

When one examines trends in yields, cultivated acreage, grain output, population growth, and consumption in some of the largest developing nations, the problem becomes clearer.[67] During the period from 1960–62 through 1969–72, in Indonesia the rates of increase were cultivated acreage, 1.3 percent; yields, 2.0 percent; grain output, 3.6 percent; population, 2.5 percent; and grain consumption, 3.7 percent; output failed to keep up with consumption. In India during the same period the rates of increase were cultivated acreage, 1.0 percent; yields, 2.0 percent; grain output, 3.0 percent; population, 2.6 percent; and consumption, 3.4 percent; output lagged considerably behind consumption.

Numerous factors influence yields, but a crucial one is the amount of fertilizer used. In many areas increased application of chemical fertilizers is the easiest way to achieve rapid production increases (although improved seeds, water control, and cultivation methods also are essential for best results). In a sense, each ton of fertilizer nutrient available, whether from domestic production or imports, can be viewed as the equivalent of several tons of grain. Although "fertilizer responses" depend on the conditions and amounts used, crudely speaking it is not unreasonable to consider each ton of nitrogen fertilizer nutrient (N) as equal to about eight tons of grain.

Globally, the use of chemical fertilizers—nitrogen, phosphate, and potash—has increased enormously over the past two decades, doubling between 1950 and 1960 and tripling between 1960 and 1973.[68] (China has been one of the countries that has increased fertilizer use most rapidly.) In 1962/63 world production of chemical fertilizers (in nutrient value) was 34.5 million tons; by 1978 it had roughly tripled and totaled (in nutrient value) almost 106 million tons (49 million nitrogen, 31 million phosphate, and 26 million potash).[69] The FAO estimated that world production *capacity* (including that in China) in 1976/77 was even higher —134 million tons—and that it would rise to 178 million by 1981/82.[70] The International Fertilizer Development Center has predicted that output could rise to 141.4 million tons in 1985.[71]

Here again, there are great contrasts between the developed and developing nations. In 1971/72 the developed nations produced almost 68 million tons of chemical fertilizers, consumed about 59 million, and exported almost 9 million.[72] The non-Communist developing nations produced about 6 million tons but consumed more than 10 million, and therefore had to import more than 4 million tons. (The "Asian planned countries"—mainly China—produced an estimated 3 million tons, consumed approximately 4.6 million tons, and imported roughly 1.6 million tons.) There is an urgent need for increased use of chemical fertilizers in the developing nations, where average yields generally are still less than half those in the developed countries and fertilizer output is much smaller.

Although opinions differ on whether probable supplies will meet likely demand, the FAO believes they probably will. One study by the World Bank questioned whether production increases in the developed nations would be as large as the FAO assumed, and it projected a shortage in the 1980s.[73] The World Bank recently has made more optimistic estimates, however. A recent study by the International Fertilizer Development Center predicts that in 1985 fertilizer output will exceed demand by 6 million tons.[74] However, even if future supply is adequate to meet demand, many of the poorest developing nations may have great difficulty purchasing the quantities they need.

Grain Trade

The varying rates of increase in food production and consumption in different areas of the world explain why food problems, which used to pose essentially domestic national issues, now are major international problems. Today huge international transfers of grain are required to meet the needs of countries with grain deficits.

World grain exports increased by roughly one-half in the decade between 1966/67 and 1976/77, from a little more than 100 million (metric) tons to more than 150 million tons.[75] The bulk of this trade was in wheat and coarse grains, and the proportion of coarse grain gradually rose; even though rice contributed close to 20 percent of world grain output, it accounted for only about 6 percent of world grain trade. By 1978/79 total grain exports exceeded 170 million tons, with world wheat exports totaling 71.3 million tons, coarse grain exports 89.5 million, and rice exports 11.7 million.[76] Today well over one-tenth of all grain produced in the world enters international trade.

Most major geographical areas of the world—both developed and developing—have become grain deficit areas, dependent on imports from just a few major suppliers.[77] This is a great change from only a few decades ago when the majority of nations grew most of the grain they consumed. At present, four countries—the United States, Canada, Australia, and Argentina—are the main suppliers of world grain exports. In some years the United States alone has provided almost two-thirds of the total, although in some the figure has been 50 to 60 percent. In 1974/75 the United States' *net* exports of wheat and coarse grains totaled 61.8 million tons; Canada's, 13.5 million; Australia's, 11.2 million; and Argentina's, 10.4 million.[78] The total net exports of the four were close to 100 million tons, compared with about 30 million tons twenty-five years earlier. In 1978/79, according to the USDA, the comparable figures were United States, 94.8 million tons; Canada, 16.1 million; Oceania, 15.4 million; and Argentina, 14.2 million.[79] The world's dependence on these countries—and above all on the United States—for food is greater today than its dependence on the Middle Eastern countries for oil.

Western Europe's net annual imports of grain now total about 16 million tons; Japan's are more than 23 million.[80] In the 1960s and early 1970s the Communist nations as a group became significant importers of grain and will continue to be. And the net grain imports of the non-Communist developing nations (excluding Argentina, the largest net exporter in the group) have risen greatly, from an annual average of 18.6 million tons in 1960/61 through 1962/63 to 57.6 million in 1978/79. (If Argentina is included, the figures for the group as a whole are lower: 13.4 million in 1960/61 through 1962/63 and 39.6 million in 1978/79.)

At present the grain purchases made by the developed market economies—Western Europe and Japan—do not pose serious international problems. From the U.S. point of view, in fact, such purchases are highly desirable as a major source of foreign exchange. Changes in their level of imports have generally been predictable, and both areas can pay for their needs with relative ease. From the 1950s until recently, Western Europe's net imports remained quite stable, at close to 20 million tons a year, but since 1977/78 they have dropped, and during the decade ahead they will probably average 10 million to 15 million tons per year. Japan's net imports have grown greatly in recent years as the country has become increasingly affluent, rising from less than 3 million tons in 1950/51 to more than 23 million in 1979/80; they may increase further in the decade ahead, perhaps to 30 million or more. Large as these imports are, because they have been predictable and have not involved major payments problems, they have not created any major difficulties.

In contrast, trends in grain purchases both by the Communist countries and by the developing nations do pose serious international problems, although the problems differ for the two groups of nations. In the case of the Communist nations—especially the Soviet Union—the erratic and unpredictable pattern of their grain purchases has had seriously disruptive effects on the world grain market, creating major problems for all others involved in the world food system, whether net exporters or net importers. In the 1950s and 1960s the Soviet Union was a net grain exporter in all but two years; usually it exported enough grain to meet the deficits of East European countries (generally between 5 million and 10 million tons a year). Since 1971/72, however, the Soviet Union has generally been a net importer, and the level of its total grain imports has fluctuated greatly, sometimes rising in a single year from a very low level to as high as 20 million to 30 million tons.[81] Eastern Europe continues to be a net importer, of roughly 8 million to 10 million tons in recent years, but its purchases have fluctuated less.

China—as will be discussed in detail later—also has been a net grain importer since the start of the 1960s. Although its demands on the world market have been smaller than the Soviet Union's and not as erratic, its net imports have nevertheless averaged about 4 million tons a year over the entire period 1961–76 and roughly double that, or about 8 million tons a year, during 1977–79.[82] Chinese purchases have also fluctuated substantially (though less than the Soviet Union's); annual grain imports have varied since 1960 from 2 million tons to more than 10 million tons. A major problem from the perspective of the world food system as a whole is how to cope with large, unpredictable purchases and reduce the disruptive impact these have on world supplies, reserves, and prices.

A different set of problems is created by the growing grain imports of the non-Communist developing nations. Already the *net* grain imports of these nations are more than 50 million tons a year, and their needs will almost certainly continue rising significantly in the period ahead. Continued population growth will increase their basic requirements inexorably, and any improvements in living standards will raise their food demands still further. Careful estimates indicate that even if grain output in the developing countries rises, as it probably will, the gap between their own production and their food demand is likely to increase steadily. According to several estimates, their net grain import needs could rise to as much as 85 million to 100 million tons a year by 1985; it is at least conceivable, according to one estimate, that they could eventually rise to 200 million tons.[83]

If the import needs of the deficit countries continue to grow in the years immediately ahead at the rate many analysts expect, will the major exporting countries have large enough surpluses to meet their needs? As stated earlier, the USDA believes that, in theory at least, they can. But one cannot be certain. It will depend on the policies that governments in both developed and developing countries pursue, and on how effectively the world trading system for food functions.

Prices

Doubts about the future focus not only on the adequacy of exportable grain supplies but also on payments problems and future trends affecting world food prices.[84] During the 1970s fluctuations of world prices created serious problems, and even if prices are more stable in the future, it is not clear how the developing nations will be able to pay for increasingly large grain imports.

Between 1955 and 1972 the world prices for grain and agricultural products generally remained relatively stable. Then between 1972 and 1974 they suddenly rose by between two and three times as a result of a special combination of circumstances. Because of bad weather, 1972 was the first year in more than two decades in which total world grain output dropped. At the same time, the Soviet Union, which experienced a large shortfall in cereal production, unexpectedly purchased huge quantities of grain. Then the effects of the world oil crisis on fuel and fertilizer prices exacerbated existing problems. This conjunction of events occurred after a period in which there had been unusually rapid economic growth globally, which had resulted in rising food consumption in many countries.

The FAO estimates that the worldwide costs of imports of grain by the developing nations jumped from $3.7 billion in 1971 to $12.4 billion in 1974—a 235 percent increase in cost for a 36 percent increase in the tonnage of their grain imports.[85] In 1971 developing nations paid, on the average, well under $100 a ton and in 1974 more than $200 a ton for all grain (more for wheat, less for coarse grains). The FAO also estimates that the cost of fertilizer imported by non-Communist developing nations rose from $533 million in 1971 to about $1.45 billion in 1974 (for 4.6 million tons of imports in 1971 and only slightly more, 4.9 million tons, in 1974).[86] In 1971 they paid a little more than $100 per ton for fertilizer, and in 1974 almost $300. In the same period oil prices skyrocketed.

It can be argued that this combination of factors in 1972–74 was extraordinary and probably will not recur soon. Prices for both grain and fertilizer peaked in 1974, then began declining in 1975; by late 1977 they had dropped greatly, falling, in real terms, to close to their pre-1972 level. Subsequently, however, they, and fertilizer prices as well, have risen again. Although the rise in 1979 was much less than in the early 1970s, it was characterized by the USDA as "sharp" and "dramatic."[87] The problems faced by many developing nations in paying for both grain and fertilizer imports remain extremely serious. The rising costs of the inputs—especially petroleum—used in producing both are likely to exert continued upward pressure on prices in the future.

Over time, how much strain the need to import increasing amounts of grain will impose on the developing nations will depend on the trend in their terms of trade, determined by the prices of their exports as well as their imports. At present it is by no means clear that this trend will move in their favor[88]—even though Third World countries are now pressing the developed nations to adopt policies that would help them in this respect.

Questions relating to price stability will continue to be of critical importance. Even if grain and fertilizer prices do not fluctuate as violently as in the first half of the 1970s, they will certainly experience ups and downs. Any large, sudden changes in international prices create problems for both deficit and surplus nations. Trends during 1972–74 highlighted how severe a strain any sudden price rises can impose on the developing nations. The fluctuations have caused different sorts of problems in the major exporting countries. One of the most troublesome has been the inflationary effects of rising world prices of basic commodities.

Domestic price policies also affect the world market. Both surplus and deficit countries face dilemmas in determining domestic price policies to take account of the interests of both their farmers, who need adequate incentives, and their nonfarming consumers, who are hurt by inflation, and in deciding how to balance their domestic and international interests and obligations.

Reserves

From a global perspective, a key question for the future is whether world grain reserves (stocks in addition to "working stocks" normally carried over from one year to the next) can be maintained at adequate levels. Without such reserves, price fluctuations are likely to be intensified, and if reserves fall to very low levels it might be impossible to meet —at any price—severe shortages caused by bad weather.

Calculations of existing and needed world reserves are not all identical. Generally, existing reserves are calculated by estimating start-of-year or year-end stocks and then subtracting the grain (working stocks) in the "pipeline," which in the exporting countries usually amounts to 10 percent or more of the previous year's consumption and exports. Some experts maintain that the world needs a reserve supply that is about two months above what is normally in the pipeline.[89]

During 1972–74 there was a precipitous drop in world reserves to dangerously low levels.[90] One study indicated that the world's grain reserves (mostly located in the United States) dropped from 180 million tons in 1961/62 to 130 million tons in 1966/67, rose to a peak of 208 million tons in 1969/70, and then dropped again to 123 million tons in 1975/76. (If the grain equivalent of idled U.S. cropland that could be put into cultivation fairly rapidly were added, the figures would be 261 million tons for 1961/62, equal to roughly 112 days of world grain consumption, and 123 million tons in 1975/76, equal to only 37 days' consumption.)[91]

Another study indicated that the "beginning stocks" of wheat and coarse grains in just the exporting countries were roughly 128 million tons (54 million tons of wheat and 74 million tons of coarse grains) in 1960/61 and then dropped to 49 million (20 million tons of wheat and 29 million tons of coarse grains) in 1974/75.[92] The USDA calculates that the world's "beginning stocks" of wheat totaled 72 million tons in 1960/61 (which was 30 percent of the world's annual consumption at that time) and 63 million tons in 1976/77 (17 percent of consumption), while stocks of coarse grain in those years totaled 96 million and 52 million tons (22 percent and 8 percent, respectively, of consumption).[93] In 1976/77 the world's "ending stocks" (stocks at year's end) of wheat, coarse grains, and rice rose impressively, according to USDA figures, by about 55 million tons, from 137 million tons in 1975/76 to 190 million tons in 1976/77; in 1977/78 they were about the same, 191 million tons, and then they soared in 1978/79 to 226 million tons.[94] The world entered the 1979/80 year with large stocks (18 percent above the previous year), which amounted to nearly 15.9 percent of world grain consumption, compared with an average of 16.3 percent in the early 1970s and a low of 11 percent in the mid-1970s. The uncertainty about world stocks was illustrated again, however, by predictions in mid-1979 that world grain output might fall by 2.5 to 8 percent during 1979/80, that Soviet imports would soar, and that as a result world carryover stocks might drop by 16 to 28 percent, which in tonnage would mean a drop from 229 million tons to between 168 million and 192 million tons, a level only slightly above the lows of the mid-1970s.[95] The Soviet Union's agricultural problems were the principal cause of such fears. It was predicted that in 1979 the Soviet grain crop might drop to between 170 million and 210 million tons, compared with 237 million in 1978, and that its grain imports could rise to 30.5 million tons.[96] These estimates were not far off the mark. Soviet grain output dropped to 179 million tons in 1979 (the lowest level since 1975); its imports rose to 30 million tons; and in 1979/80 world stocks again declined.[97] Preliminary estimates in 1980 indicated that at the end of the grain year, the world's ending stocks would have dropped by 11.5 percent to about 200 million tons, or 14 percent of world consumption.[98]

Recent trends have stimulated increased international concern about the problems of maintaining adequate world grain stocks and establishing some kind of international system to manage them. Several estimates have been made of needed or desirable world grain reserve levels. In 1974, the USDA estimated that world grain stocks of more than 80 million tons (29 million tons of wheat, 34 million tons of coarse grains, and 18 million tons of rice) would probably cover 95 percent of single-year grain output shortfalls globally (calculated on the basis of trends for the period 1960–73), but that, if possible substitution among grains was taken into account, 56 million tons might serve the purpose.[99] The USDA calculated that 25 million to 40 million tons would be needed to meet 68 percent of single-year shortfalls. To meet repeated shortfalls, however (and since the start of the 1970s there have been declines or stagnation in world output in 1972, 1974, and 1977, and probably in 1980), the needs would be greater. The FAO has estimated that a minimum safe level for world grain reserves would be somewhere between 66 million and 71 million tons (in addition to "working stocks," which it calculated at 12.5 percent of world consumption).[100] A Brookings Institution study estimated that the reserves of wheat and coarse grain necessary to meet shortfalls (covering risks up to 95 percent probability) would probably be 64.1 million tons (30.5 million tons of wheat and 33.6 million tons of coarse grains) in 1980.[101] (However, one Overseas Development Council study argued that wheat reserves should be the "pivot of any viable price stabilization scheme" and that "important stabilization achievements" would be possible with a wheat reserve of 15 million tons or conceivably less.[102])

At the World Food Conference in 1974, the U.S. government proposed that a world food reserve of 60 million tons be established; then it proposed a smaller reserve of 30 million tons, consisting of 25 million tons of wheat and 5 million tons of rice and excluding coarse grains. The recently established World Food Council has supported—as the World Food Conference did—the idea of a world reserve of 60 million tons, including coarse grains.[103] Among food experts there now is considerable support for establishing a reserve of about 60 million tons (which if added to a year-to-year carryover of 100 million tons or more of working stocks would be the equivalent of just under fifty days of the world's requirements), though some argue for a larger reserve of 80 million to 100 million tons, which they say is the amount that would have been required to keep grain prices reasonably stable during the recent food crisis.[104]

To date, the world's reserves have been nationally or privately managed, mainly in the United States and Canada. The establishment of an internationally supervised system has been discussed recently, especially in the International Wheat Council. No agreement has been reached, however, and even among those favoring such a system there is no consensus on how large the reserves should be, what they should consist of, where they should be located, who should own them, who should pay the costs of maintaining them, how they should be managed, or whether their acquisition and disposal should be based on quantitative or price criteria. These questions will not be resolved soon. Nevertheless, the arguments for establishing an international reserve system are strong, and whether or not an adequate reserve is established could be a major determinant of how manageable world food problems are in the period ahead.

Weather

Probably the least predictable factor affecting the world's food output always has been—and will remain—the weather, which is the main cause of sudden, short-term fluctuations in grain production.[105] Effective agricultural policies can reduce the adverse effects of bad weather but cannot eliminate them; in fact, in certain respects modernization can increase the risks of fluctuations in output caused by weather. Weather conditions are the major explanation for the most serious unanticipated shortfalls ("output below trends") and the actual declines in world production in some years.

Shortfalls frequently occur. For example, during 1960–73, there were seven shortfalls in world wheat output, the largest of which were in 1963, 1965, and 1972, when output was below trend by 20 million, 13.5

million, and 10 million tons, respectively.[106] The largest shortfalls in world rice production in this period were in 1965, 1966, and 1972, when they amounted to 7 million, 15 million, and 13 million tons, respectively. Coarse grain output fluctuated to an even greater extent, especially in the developed countries (due in part to weather and in part to changes in planted acreage); it was below trend by 20.7 million, 18 million, and 15.4 million tons in 1964, 1965, and 1970, respectively.

Certain large countries, including the Soviet Union, where much of the cultivated land is in high latitudes, and India, which is dependent on monsoons, are particularly vulnerable to weather changes. Soviet wheat output fell below trend by 20 million, 16 million, and 12 million tons in 1963, 1965, and 1972, respectively, and the shortfall was even greater in 1979 when grain output fell to 179 million tons, which was 48 million tons below plan and 58 million below 1978.[107] Indian rice production was below trend by 7.5 million in 1965, 8 million in 1966, and 5 million tons in 1972. (As will be indicated later, weather also has greatly affected China's output and was a major cause of output declines in 1954, 1960, 1968, and 1972 and stagnation in 1975–1977.)

Recent weather trends also raise the possibility that the world may have entered a period of climatic change that could create increased uncertainty about output.[108] Some experts maintain that during the past several years the number of droughts, floods, severe winters, and shifts in the monsoons has been unusual, and they are disturbed by the fact that in several years since the start of the 1970s bad weather has resulted in an actual decline in total world grain output—by more than 30 million tons (2.5 to 3 percent) in 1972/73, by close to 50 million tons (3 to 4 percent) in 1974/75, by a small amount in 1977/78 and, according to preliminary estimates, by over 55 million tons (almost 4 percent) in 1979/80.

If, in the period ahead, greater fluctuations in weather conditions occur, they could complicate the world's food problems greatly and would make the need for new forms of international cooperation—especially in establishing an effective system of global food reserves—even more urgent than at present.

Some meteorologists also have raised questions about the possibility of long-term climatic changes. No consensus on this has yet emerged, however. Some predict a global cooling during the rest of this century.[109] If there were a return to even a slightly cooler climate in the Western Hemisphere, perhaps comparable with that of the nineteenth century, it could have adverse effects on agriculture in northern Russia, much of China, and the Indian subcontinent. Other meteorologists believe, however, that, instead of cooling, the climate may actually warm up gradually as a result of increased carbon dioxide, nitrous oxide from fertilizers, and industrial dust particles in the atmosphere, a situation which could have adverse effects on grain output in North America, the largest surplus area today.[110]

Either a cooling or a warming might have far-reaching effects on world agriculture as it now exists. Although all predictions are speculative, it is impossible to ignore the possibility that there might be changes that could greatly magnify the world's food problems. However, long-term climatic changes, if they occur, would take place gradually, giving the world some time to adjust to them. In the years immediately ahead the variability and unpredictability of year-to-year changes in the weather will create the most serious problems.

Agricultural Development

In the long term, a basic requirement for solution of world food problems is accelerated agricultural development in the less developed nations.[111] The potential for such development clearly exists. In fact, modern scientific methods associated with what has been called the "green revolution" hold out the promise of doubling or tripling grain output in much of the world. But realizing this potential will not be easy.

One essential task will be to promote across-the-board modernization of agriculture in the developing nations—including China. This will require wider application worldwide of recently acquired scientific and technological knowledge, including a great increase in the use of new varieties of seeds (adapted to fit the conditions in particular localities), a substantial expansion of irrigation, large increases in the use of chemical fertilizers, and many other changes, most of which will require substantial investments.

It is easy to say that agriculture can be modernized everywhere, but the process will be difficult in many developing nations. In tradition-rooted societies there are innumerable impediments to change. Accelerated agricultural development will require more effective governmental policies resulting in major political and social as well as economic changes that will challenge, and be resisted by, those with vested interests in the status quo.

Developing nations attempting to carry out modernization of agriculture face many complex, interrelated tasks. To achieve success, governments in these countries will first need to give higher priority to agriculture in their overall economic development policies. They will need to alter traditional patterns of income distribution to raise living standards and create new incentives, especially among the poorest farmers. They will need to develop new industries—large and small—that serve agriculture and produce the inputs that modern farming requires. They also will have to develop the infrastructure of transportation, communication, and electrification that modernization requires.

In many countries governments may have to alter existing patterns of land ownership. Where the benefits from modernization are not widely shared, ordinary farmers have few incentives to produce more. Developing nations also will need to cultivate new attitudes favorable to innovation and experimentation. They will have to develop and train experts, and create new research institutions, to acquire and adapt modern agricultural science and technology to local needs. They will also need to raise literacy rates and expand rural education. And they will need to organize effective extension services to transmit new knowledge to the farming population.

In most developing countries only governments can provide most of the capital needed to carry out large-scale rural projects and ensure that there is adequate credit to permit farmers to use new inputs and try new methods. Governments also will need to adopt price policies, for both agricultural products and inputs into agriculture, that reinforce incentives to change. While shifting the urban-rural terms of trade in favor of agriculture and poor farmers, they will have to attempt to limit inflation in the cities and ensure that basic food supplies are available at reasonable prices. If they do not, the reaction of the urban population could undercut their efforts. This can be very expensive, and is easy only when overall growth is fairly high. Efforts to modernize agriculture also will have to be combined with effective programs to slow population growth. And governments will need to try to maximize employment opportunities, which in most developing countries means promoting labor-intensive methods, and prevent mass migration to the cities. They will also have to develop new marketing mechanisms involving both rural and urban areas. In short, many changes in both institutions and attitudes will be required for development strategies to succeed in creating the foundation for modernizing agriculture and raising simultaneously per hectare yields and per farmer productivity.

One fundamental goal of most developing countries is to achieve greater self-reliance and minimize their dependency on foreign nations; and in most cases they are not likely to succeed in modernizing agriculture unless they do show a determination to be more self-reliant. The most difficult decisions facing them involve essentially domestic problems.

Yet most developing countries cannot avoid some degree of dependency, especially during the early stages of agricultural modernization. They must make up their grain deficits while they strive to increase their own output and try to obtain the knowledge and modern inputs required for modernization. Short-term dependency during the development process should not be disturbing *if* the developing countries devise sensible strategies to cope with their problems in the context of a world system that inevitably will involve a substantial degree of interdependence among all nations, rich and poor, for the foreseeable future. If, however, developing countries pursue policies that result in steadily increasing dependence, the problems facing the world food system eventually could become overwhelming. The problems will remain manageable only if leaders and governments in *both* the developing and developed nations genuinely understand them and pursue policies that effectively cope with them.

China's Food Problems and Prospects

Although most discussions of world food problems pay little attention to China, it looms large if one views these problems from a global perspective. China is the largest developing nation in the world, and it produces close to one-sixth of the world's grain and feeds roughly 23 percent of the world's population.[112] Its rice output was roughly 36 percent of the global total in 1978/79, its coarse grain output 11 percent, and its wheat output 12 percent.[113] It already is the fourth largest producer of chemical fertilizer in the world and probably soon will be the third.[114] By the late 1960s it rated between tenth and twentieth globally in the value of its total trade in agricultural commodities.[115] In 1978/79 its wheat imports were the largest in the world and accounted for 11 percent of total world wheat imports; in 1979 its rice exports were 10 percent of the world total (over the years they have varied between 10 and 20 percent).[116] In recent years China also has been the world's largest importer of chemical fertilizers. These statistics should make it clear that China cannot be ignored in any analysis of the global food situation.

Agricultural Development: Problems and Policies

China's agricultural problems are similar in many respects to those in other developing countries. However, the sheer scale of its problem of feeding more than one-fifth of the world's population sets it apart from other nations; only India is comparable in this respect. The man/land ratio in China also makes it a special case; while many developing countries have substantial tracts of unused arable land, the Chinese put their best agricultural areas to use long ago.

China's past success in developing agriculture by traditional methods makes solving present and future problems more difficult in many respects than in countries whose traditional agriculture is more backward. According to one experienced student of Chinese agriculture, "Under long-term population pressure, the Chinese raised prescientific agriculture to the highest levels attained by any people. In the 1930s, yields per acre for major crops except cotton, corn, and potatoes were higher in China than they were in the United States."[117] Now, however, as a leading economic analyst of China's agriculture points out, "There are no obvious and gross inefficiencies in Chinese farming that could be quickly overcome," and therefore "the problems that Chinese agriculture will have to face over the coming decade differ markedly from those in other less developed countries."[118] This analyst concludes, "At no time since 1945 have increases in Chinese farm output been achieved with ease, but there is reason to believe that future increases will require even greater effort" including "new breakthroughs . . . in basic agricultural sciences," and "the harnessing of the irrigation potential of China's northern rivers."[119]

For more than 2,000 years Chinese leaders have recognized the crucial importance of food production to the country's political and social stability.[120] After achieving power in 1949 through a long struggle based in large part on peasant rebellion the Communists placed very high priority on both revolutionary change and agricultural development in rural China. They immediately began to carry out land reform and to try to raise farm output, which was at a low point after years of war and civil conflict.[121]

Between 1950 and 1952 they implemented the most extensive land redistribution program in history. They also initiated many other programs, based largely on mobilized labor, to promote agricultural production. Output rose rapidly to pre-1949 levels. How much of the increase was due to the regime's land reform and other revolutionary policies is difficult to estimate. Redistribution of land doubtless improved incentives for many poor peasants. The regime's unprecedented organizational control in the countryside also facilitated the mobilization of millions of people to improve irrigation and build public works in rural areas. However, rapid social change in the countryside also disrupted the credit system and weakened many elements in the traditional agricultural system, and it had adverse effects on the incentives of many peasants who had been among China's best—those labeled "rich peasants." Whatever the negative impact that disruption of the old system had, however, it was more than counterbalanced by the restoration of order and normal transportation and communication, as well as by the positive effects of many of the regime's new policies, and at first production rose fairly rapidly.

When China embarked on its first Five Year Plan in 1953, its leaders shifted their attention to the country's urban sector. Following the Soviet model, they called for rapid industrialization and allocated the bulk of investment to urban areas. Only 6.2 percent of planned state investment for the period 1953–57 was earmarked for agriculture, most of it for water control projects; actual state investment in agriculture during the first plan period finally amounted to 8.2 percent of total investment.[122] China's leaders hoped that farm output would increase sufficiently to meet the country's needs mainly as a result of institutional changes and local investment, without large inputs by the state.

As the first plan progressed, however, it became evident that agricultural growth was lagging behind the leader's hopes and the country's needs. In the first two years of the plan period, the rate of increase in grain output (less than 2 percent each year) was actually less than the rate of population growth.[123] Recognizing that new measures to speed agricultural growth were required to prevent a slowdown in overall development, China's leaders, in particular Mao Tse-tung (Mao Zedong), decided to carry out further institutional change in the countryside through collectivization.

Steps toward collectivization had begun immediately after land reform, but originally it had been conceived of as a gradual process leading in stages from individual farming to mutual aid teams, and then to so-called lower producer cooperatives in which peasants retained land ownership, before finally moving toward full collectives, called higher producer cooperatives in China at that time.[124] Then in 1955, despite opposition from other Chinese leaders, Mao suddenly decided to push through rapid collectivization, and by late 1956 the countryside had, for all practical purposes, been fully collectivized, with minimum overt peasant opposition, at least compared with the Soviet Union's experience.

The lag in China's farm output continued, however, and over time the leadership increasingly realized that without faster agricultural growth, it would be impossible to achieve their ambitious industrial and overall economic goals. In 1957 the rate of increase in grain output (just over 1.5 percent) was again below the rate of increase in population, and the lag in agriculture was one major factor impelling China's leadership in late 1957 to reassess their entire economic development strategy and to abandon the Soviet model.

In early 1958 China's leaders adopted radical new economic policies and embarked on the Great Leap Forward and communization program. The essence of their new approach was the idea that they could accelerate growth in both agriculture and industry primarily by an unprecedented mobilization of labor, increased local as well as central investment, and a further institutional transformation in agriculture.[125] For a brief period there was an extraordinary effort in China. In agriculture, the peasants were organized along semimilitary lines. New and inadequately tested labor-intensive techniques, including close planting and deep plowing, were introduced. Huge numbers of small-scale irrigation and other public works projects were initiated. The regime encouraged the peasants to build small plants throughout the countryside, especially to contribute to agricultural output. The immediate result was a leap forward in both agriculture and industry. Grain output jumped to a new high (good weather was a major factor).

Success was short-lived, however. The communes as originally conceived simply did not work. Some of the agricultural innovations were misapplied, and many of the new small rural factories were not viable. The peasants reacted negatively to the reduction of incentives and to overwork, and the entire economy was badly disorganized.

The Great Leap and communization program, plus three years of bad weather starting in 1959, produced a major crisis in China's agriculture and in the economy as a whole.[126] Grain output fell drastically;

by 1960 it was below that of 1952, even in absolute terms—which meant, of course, that it was much lower (by about one-fifth) in per capita terms. China experienced the Communist equivalent of a great depression, and there was widespread malnutrition.

Beginning in 1961–62 the regime, guided then in its day-to-day operations by leaders other than Mao, backtracked.[127] Moving away from many of the basic ideas that had motivated the Great Leap, Peking (Beijing) in effect abandoned the original commune concept, and, while retaining the name, returned to a form of rural organization similar to the pre-1958 collectives. Most important, the leadership reexamined its fundamental economic priorities, including the relative priorities of agriculture and industry.

Beginning in 1961–62 Peking's leaders adopted a policy assigning a higher priority to agriculture than previously.[128] In some respects it was an "agriculture first" policy. Investments in rural areas were increased, and higher priority was assigned to industries serving agriculture. Pragmatic considerations now tended to outweigh Mao's ideological predispositions. To meet critical food deficits, China began in 1961 to import grain from abroad on a sizable scale. From 1963 on it also steadily increased imports of chemical fertilizer.

The real modernization of agriculture in China—involving greater investments in rural areas, increased supply of modern inputs to peasants, and greater efforts to promote scientific methods—began in the early 1960s. Previously the regime's accomplishments had resulted mainly from an intensification of traditional techniques, primarily labor-intensive programs, which had produced modest increases in output. Efforts to spur agricultural growth through greater mobilization of labor and further intensification of traditional methods continued, and probably will persist in the years ahead.[129] But in the early 1960s China's leaders recognized that increased application of labor without more effective use of modern scientific methods has diminishing returns, and consquently from that time on they placed increasing stress on modern inputs and methods.

In the early 1960s they started introducing some new high-yield rice seeds and began expanding domestic fertilizer output.[130] Special emphasis was placed on increasing production in selected "high and stable yield" areas (mainly those with favorable soil and water control conditions, which had the greatest potential for rapid increases in yields). State investments at that time tended to be concentrated in such areas, especially in rice growing regions in the South, and these areas achieved the greatest progress.[131] As a result of the new policies, by 1966 grain output had recovered to, and thereafter surpassed, the previous 1958 peak in absolute terms. Because of population growth, however, it remained considerably below the 1958 level in per capita terms throughout the 1960s—and, in fact, until the late 1970s.

The general economic strategy that the regime adopted in the early 1960s, which gave higher priority to agriculture, and the broad lines of Chinese agricultural policies defined at that time had considerable continuity thereafter, although certain aspects were given greater or lesser emphasis at various times. Efforts to increase the output of chemical fertilizers were speeded up in the second half of the 1960s, especially through the construction of small factories; by 1971 these were producing as much as China's large chemical fertilizer plants. However, in the early 1970s China's leaders shifted emphasis back to large plants producing higher-quality nitrogen and purchased abroad thirteen of the world's largest ammonia-urea complexes.[132]

During the 1960s they organized an effective system of agro-technical and extension services throughout China's countryside. At the start, agricultural scientists as well as the peasant "masses" played important roles in this system. Then, during the Cultural Revolution, measures to combat elitism badly disrupted China's scientific establishment dealing with agriculture and other fields. Only recently has the damage done at that time begun to be repaired.

In the 1960s, also, special emphasis was placed on rural small-scale industries. This time the program was more rational and viable than the one pushed during the Great Leap. Small plants began producing increased quantities of fertilizer, agricultural tools, machinery (including irrigation pumps), cement, and other inputs for agriculture and the rural economy in general. In the early 1970s this policy received even greater emphasis, and the regime also called for accelerated efforts to mechanize agriculture.[133]

In the early 1970s China's agricultural planners shifted attention from rice-growing areas in the South, where yields were already high, to wheat areas in the North, where yields had lagged.[134] With improved irrigation (especially through increased use of tube wells and electric pumps) and greater applications of fertilizers, wheat output rose significantly. While increasing the use of modern inputs where possible, the regime also continued trying to improve agricultural areas everywhere, relying to a large extent on traditional labor-intensive methods, especially for the leveling of land and improvement of water control.

All of these efforts produced results, and output of food increased substantially. However, China's rate of agricultural growth, which was slower than in many other developing countries, clearly lagged behind what the regime had hoped for and needed.

Nevertheless, Peking's policies aroused considerable interest internationally in the "Chinese development model," especially as it relates to agriculture.[135] Actually, China has pursued several development "models" over the past three decades. However, during the 1960s and early 1970s China did evolve a set of policies that was distinctive and definitely set it apart from most developing nations. What impressed foreign observers most was Peking's emphasis on egalitarianism and rural services.

The commune (or collective) system, particularly after the early 1960s when farm management was decentralized to the production team level and some personal incentives were restored, provided the main organizational instrument for carrying out the regime's agricultural policies.[136] Even though the communes were by no means optimally efficient in increasing agricultural output, from the early 1960s on they proved to be viable, and working through them, the regime did achieve some notable successes. While increasing output, the regime prevented the widening of differences in wealth, characteristic of so many other developing countries, and ensured that income was distributed on a relatively egalitarian basis even though the urban-rural gap as well as significant differences among rural groups persisted. It eliminated old forms of exploitation by landlords and moneylenders, although a sizable portion of what peasant families produced still went to the communes and the state. After recovery from the post-Leap depression, the regime was able to ensure a minimal standard of consumption for most Chinese, in rural as well as urban areas, in part by rationing grain and other basic commodities.

The communes facilitated mass mobilization of labor for production, made possible increased local investment for collective purposes, and provided a mechanism for expanding agro-technical extension services that facilitated dissemination of some new farming techniques and encouraged wider use of modern inputs into agriculture. Rural education and training, as well as simple health services, were greatly expanded, although the quality remained low in most places. The development of rural small-scale industry and expansion of large-scale industry serving agriculture provided increased quantities of modern inputs for agriculture.

During the 1960s, also, the regime started a serious program of nation-wide birth control. It also restricted population migration, limiting the flow of peasants to the major cities, and, in fact, transferred millions of urban residents to the countryside. It also had notable success in controlling inflation. And, gradually, it altered the rural-urban terms of trade, narrowing to some extent the existing urban-rural gap.

A New Program: 1978–79

The policies of the 1960s and 1970s by no means "solved" China's agricultural problems, however, and the pragmatic leaders who succeeded Mao fully realized this. With remarkable frankness, they admitted that China had made progress only on a treadmill, that in a basic sense the life of the average Chinese in rural areas had improved little since the 1950s, and that the egalitarian policies of the previous decade and a half had seriously weakened incentives. They recognized that faster agricultural growth was urgently required to support their modernization program. During 1978–79 Chinese leaders deliberately publicized facts about problems that for many years had been carefully concealed. In official statements they revealed that although population had increased by more than 300 million from the late 1950s to the late 1970s, the area of cultivated land had actually dropped (due to diversion of land to industrial and other uses) and that per capita distribution of foodgrain was no higher than it was in 1957 (in some statements they said it was about the same; in others they said that it was lower than in 1957).[137] Per capita farm incomes in 1977 still averaged only a little over 70 yuan a year, Peking stated, and it admitted that about 100 million people, or more than one-tenth of China's population, did not have enough to eat.[138]

Starting in 1978 China's leadership began to outline a new strategy and set of policies designed to cope with this situation, and thereafter they steadily raised the priority given to agriculture in their overall plans. While in theory an "agriculture first" policy had been adopted in the early 1960s, in reality state investment in rural areas had remained relatively low. Now the regime decided to do more to support agriculture.

At first, in his 1978 report on China's modernization, Hua Kuo-feng (Hua Guofeng) set grandiose goals:[139] make all grain-deficient areas self-sufficient by 1980, increase agricultural output 4 to 5 percent a year during 1978–85, reach a grain output target of 400 million tons by 1985, achieve 85 percent mechanization by 1985, and so on. Many of these initial targets were quite unrealistic, however; the leadership had not devised feasible ways to achieve them, nor had they yet made the hard decisions on reallocating resources that would be required to accelerate agricultural development.

Study of agricultural policies continued throughout 1978, and by year-end China's leaders produced a comprehensive statement on agricultural goals and policies, and the leadership finally decided to allocate substantially greater resources to agriculture. In December 1978 at the Eleventh Central Committee's Third Plenum, the Party adopted a document titled "Decisions of the CCP [Communist Party of China] Central Committee on Some Problems in Accelerating Agricultural Development (Draft)."[140] This draft was then distributed throughout the country for discussion and trial implementation.

The Third Plenum declared that "the whole Party should concentrate its main energy and efforts on advancing agriculture as fast as possible."[141] It decided to raise the state purchase prices for grain and some key cash crops quite dramatically. Not long thereafter, when Peking's decisions on economic "readjustment" were announced in mid-1979, it was revealed that the allocations of state investments to agriculture were to be increased significantly, rising in 1979 to 14 percent of all state investments (compared with 10.7 percent in 1978).[142] A few months later, in September 1979, the Fourth Plenum of the Central Committee formally adopted the "Decisions" on agricultural development, and since then Chinese publications have described this document as the "programmatic statement" that will "guide our agricultural development in the new period of socialist construction."[143]

The policies and targets outlined in the "Decisions" are notable in many respects. The document called for much greater use of material incentives and market forces, raising rural living standards, and diversifying agriculture, as well as for scientific and technical modernization; in addition, it promised greater stability and continuity of policy.

Special stress was placed in the "Decisions" on the need to give greater decision-making authority to communes, and especially to their small production teams, concerning choice of crops suited to local conditions, "self-management" methods, and distribution of net income. The importance of private plots, rural free markets, and peasants' sideline production was underlined. Incomes in farming as well as industrial areas, the "Decisions" made clear, should henceforth be based on work, not political, ideological, or other considerations.

The draft "Decisions" promised substantially increased investment in agriculture and major price changes to improve further rural China's terms of trade. During the next few years (the draft said five to six years, the final document three to five years), investments in agriculture would rise to about 18 percent of all state investments in construction, and overall expenditures to support agriculture and the communes would increase to about 8 percent of total state expenditures. Farm loans with low interest and long terms (ten, fifteen, or even twenty years) would be doubled by 1985, it promised. The state purchase prices for agricultural commodities would be immediately raised (in the case of grain by 20 percent for quota grain and 50 percent for above-quota grain), and there would also be significant reductions in the prices of manufactured goods needed by peasants. (These steps were carried out during 1979, even before the "Decisions" were officially adopted.) In addition, the "Decisions" promised, grain procurement quotas would not be increased; for a "relatively long period," it said, they would be based on the level of 1971–75, and some reductions and exemptions might be made.

The "Decisions" called for much greater diversification of agriculture, increased specialization, and more attention to animal husbandry, aquatic products, and forestry. The draft stated that by 1985 the number of domestic animals should be increased by 30 percent, meat production should be doubled, and output of aquatic products should be increased by 40 percent. The program called for changing China's "national diet" by increasing the availability of animal foods. The "Decisions" also called for building a large shelter belt stretching from northwest to northeast China and for afforestation in many other areas. Rural industry should continue to be promoted energetically, it said, with the aim of raising the value of output of commune and brigade enterprises to over 50 percent of the total income of communes by 1985, an increase of almost 80 percent above 1978 (when reportedly such enterprises accounted for 28 percent of all commune units' income).

The program also outlined varied policies to increase the production and use of chemical fertilizers; to develop better seeds; to expand irrigation, electrification, and mechanization; and to train better-qualified cadres and larger numbers of agricultural scientists and technicians. The draft stated that China's chemical fertilizer output should surpass 80 million tons (gross weight) by 1985 (with a better balance among nitrogen, phosphorus, and potassium). Better seed production bases and a network of seed companies were called for. The draft also set a reclamation target of more than 8 million hectares by 1985 (with land reclaimed by communes and brigades to be exempted from state purchase quotas for five years). A land law would be drafted, it said, in part to prevent illegal use of agricultural land. The program also called for increased mechanization, but exactly how much or how fast was not wholly clear; the original draft talked of achieving 80 percent mechanization by 1985 (slightly below the original goal set in 1978), but later statements were less specific.

It was evident from the "Decisions" that a special and increasingly important role was envisaged for state farms (owned and managed by the government) as a main source for obtaining "commercial grain." The draft stated that until 1985 state farms could keep and use their own profits, and that it was expected that by then commercial grain procured by the state would have been tripled. The program called for energetic efforts to develop agricultural export products, promising specific allocations of foreign exchange to help. A special commission under the State Council would be established, it said, to assist the most backward rural areas in the northwest, southwest, and mountain, frontier, and minority areas. The "Decisions" also stated that there should be a readjustment in the distribution of industry supporting agriculture within two to three years, expansion of the rural road system so that by 1985 all communes would be served by vehicles, and the development of new small towns (in county and commune seats and near large cities) to absorb population from villages. It also urged more effective birth control measures in rural as well as urban areas.

The program outlined in the "Decisions" was very ambitious, but it took greater account of realities than either the policies pursued in the 1960s and early 1970s or the initial plans announced by Hua in 1978. However, it still was only a general program that had to be translated into feasible concrete plans and actions. The State Council and its commissions and ministries—in particular the State Agricultural Commission and State Planning Commission—were instructed to draw up more specific year-to-year and long-term plans. The "Decisions" warned against trying to do everything at once. At first efforts should be "concentrated," the document said, and "farm machinery, money, and materials for agriculture should go to key areas." It stated that "in the first few years" the focus should be on areas with one-fifth of China's population to ensure that they would achieve a substantial increase in production and would then "serve as an example for the rest of the country."

These "Decisions" provide a broad framework for Chinese agricultural policy during the period ahead, but they do not provide ready answers to key questions about what China's actual food prospects are likely to be. To try to judge these prospects, it is necessary to examine each of the most important factors that will affect China's agricultural output and food–population balance.

Population Growth

In China, as in many other developing areas, the most basic food problem is simply to keep up with population growth. Analysis of China's record and prospects logically can start, therefore, with population estimates. One immediately confronts difficult problems in assessing China's performance, however, because of the absence of any reliable official series of population statistics covering the years from the late 1950s until very recently.[144]

There has been only one comprehensive national census in China (or at least only one made public). It indicated that in 1953 China had a population of 583 million.[145] The Chinese continued to publish national population data throughout the 1950s, but stopped at the end of the decade. It is not surprising, therefore, that there are substantial differences of opinion about actual demographic trends in China during the 1960s and 1970s. Nevertheless, plausible estimates have been made on the basis of information about population in particular provinces and other scattered statistics, as well as data on population policy.

Until quite recently, Chinese officials generally described the country's population as being about 800 million, and some Western estimates were not much above that figure, but this was clearly too low, as subsequently published figures have shown. In 1975 Premier Chou En-lai (Zhou Enlai) said that China's population had increased by 60 percent since 1949, implying that by then it had grown to about 880 million.[146] His statement indicated that the annual growth rate for the entire period was about 1.9 percent, which implied that despite ups and downs the rate had dropped gradually over time from around 2.2 percent to perhaps 1.8 percent by the early 1970s. But the actual size of the population was almost certainly higher than Chou implied, and in late 1977 Chinese officials began using the round figure of 900 million, first in private conversations with foreigners and then in official publications.[147] From 1976 on, new figures on particular provinces also were released, showing that the population in many had risen substantially. By early 1977 the published provincial figures added up to about 920 million (and for some provinces the figures appeared to be out of date and therefore too low).[148] The new data supported the views of foreign analysts who had estimated that China's total population already was somewhere in the middle 900 millions. Finally, in June 1979 the Chinese stated officially that the country's population (excluding Taiwan) was close to 947 million in 1977 and in 1978 had grown 1.20 percent to more than 958 million.[149] And in 1980 they claimed that in 1979 it grew 1.17 percent to almost 971 million.[150] (The specific figures given, however, showed that population rose 12.83 million, from 958.09 million in 1978 to 970.92 million in 1979, indicating an increase rate of 1.34 percent, well above the 1.17 percent rate officially cited. There was no explanation for this discrepancy.)

Among the most thorough estimates available on China's population for the entire period since 1949 are those prepared by John S. Aird of the Foreign Demographic Analysis Division of the U.S. Department of Commerce. In estimates made in early 1978, he constructed three different "models" based on different assumptions. The conservative "low model" (which I have used throughout this study) indicated that between mid-1952 and mid-1978 China's total population (excluding Taiwan) had grown from 570 million to 964 million (roughly 6 million above Peking's official figure for 1978), an increase of 394 million, or 69 percent, which indicated an average annual rate of growth over the entire period of roughly 2 percent.[151] (See table 3-1.)

The rate of natural increase has varied considerably from year to year, however, due to changing economic conditions, national policies, and other factors. Aird's "low model" indicated that from a fairly high level (varying between 2.1 and almost 2.6 percent) during much of the 1950s, the rate dropped well below 2 percent in the early 1960s, rose again to between 2 and about 2.2 percent during 1963–71, then dropped in the 1970s (with ups and downs), reaching 1.7 percent in 1978. Aird projected a fairly rapid decline as China's birth control program produces results, to below 1.4 percent in 1980, under 1.2 percent by 1985, and between 1 and 1.1 percent by the end of the century.

However, the official Chinese figures indicate that by 1978 the rate of natural increase already had dropped to 1.21 percent (12 per thousand) and despite the seemingly conflicting data on 1979 this suggests that the effects of China's birth control efforts have been greater than many Western analysts have believed. It is possible, however, that Peking's figures for 1977–79 may be low because of undercounting, and that the rate of increase actually is higher than it calculates. If so, the figures for 1977 and 1978 may eventually have to be revised again when China carries out a new census, in 1981 or 1982. Nevertheless, there is no doubt that China's current birth control program, using both positive incentives and negative sanctions, is more likely to slow the country's rate of population growth than any of the regime's past efforts. China's first moves toward a birth control program began soon after the 1953 census, but the issue of population policy was still highly controversial, ideologically and politically, and in the late 1950s during the Great Leap the program was, in effect, shelved. However, efforts were renewed in the early 1960s and have continued ever since, with only brief setbacks during the Cultural Revolution and in the 1976–77 period.[152] Over time, birth control has been given increasing emphasis, and during 1978–79 drastic new measures were adopted. Today there is no doubt that China's program is the most energetic and effective anywhere in the developing world.

For many years the Chinese have produced and distributed free contraceptives on a large scale.[153] They also have facilitated abortions and sterilization. Most important, they have used their impressive organizational and propaganda skills to induce the population to restrict births, exerting strong social pressures to this end. Specifically, they have vigorously promoted late marriages and pressured women to plan and limit the number of children they will have.

In 1979 they adopted and began to implement experimentally a program that offers rewards to families having only one child and imposes penalties on those having more than two. Under this program, the one-child family is defined as the norm—or, at least, the goal—for the entire society; no other nation has ever attempted to do this.

Substantial economic benefits are offered to families that, after having one child, pledge to have no more.[154] In some places one-child families are promised a subsidy of 5 yuan a month for fourteen years, or fourteen years of free health services, and free education from nursery school through secondary school, plus higher pensions and other benefits. Parents are encouraged to undergo sterilization after their first child to ensure that they can fulfill their pledge. If, however, they are not sterilized and have another child, they must pay back all the subsidies or benefits previously received. If they have a third child, economic penalties

TABLE 3-1. *China: Estimated and Projected Population (U.S. Government Estimates)*
Thousands of persons as of July 1

Year	Population	Vital rates per thousand persons			Year	Population	Vital rates per thousand persons		
		Natural increase	Births	Deaths			Natural increase	Births	Deaths
1949	537,918	12.0	45.4	33.4	1967	781,410	21.2	34.1	12.9
1950	547,364	13.5	45.4	31.9	1968	798,397	21.8	34.3	12.5
1951	558,096	15.1	45.3	30.2	1969	816,102	22.1	34.0	11.9
1952	569,904	18.0	45.2	27.2	1970	834,235	21.9	32.9	11.0
1953	582,603	22.5	45.0	22.5	1971	852,114	20.5	30.8	10.3
1954	596,015	23.0	43.8	20.8	1972	869,090	18.9	28.7	9.8
1955	610,006	23.4	42.8	19.4	1973	885,049	17.5	26.9	9.4
1956	624,559	23.8	42.1	18.3	1974	900,055	16.1	25.0	8.9
1957	639,258	22.8	40.7	17.9	1975	914,662	16.0	24.5	8.5
1958	653,500	21.3	39.6	18.3	1976	930,000	16.5	25.5	9.0
1959	667,064	19.8	38.7	18.9	1977	946,716	19.7	27.5	7.8
						(947)			

Year	Population			
1960	680,019	18.7	38.0	19.3
1961	692,436	17.5	38.0	20.5
1962	705,405	19.6	37.6	18.0
1963	719,510	20.0	37.0	17.0
1964	734,033	20.0	35.6	15.6
1965	749,310	21.2	34.7	13.5
1966	765,190	20.7	34.3	13.6
1978	964,250 (958)	17.0 (12)	24.5	7.5
1979	979,922 (971)	15.2	22.4	7.2
1980	994,298	13.9	20.8	6.9
1985	1,057,849	11.5	18.0	6.5
1990	1,119,442	11.4	18.0	6.5
1995	1,186,355	11.6	18.3	6.7
2000	1,254,797	10.6	17.6	7.0

Sources: The 1977–79 figures in parentheses are based on State Statistical Bureau data (Taiwan's 17 million subtracted from the SSB totals); see Foreign Broadcast Information Service, *Daily Report—People's Republic of China*, June 27, 1979, p. L20, and April 30, 1980, p. L10. The estimates for 1949–52 are from Central Intelligence Agency, *China: Economic Indicators*, Reference Aid ER 77–10508, October 1977, p. 8. Estimates and projections for 1953 on are from John S. Aird, "Population Estimates and Projections for the People's Republic of China," April 1978, processed, pp. 40–41. There are three "models" or series of estimates for 1953–78 in this source; the series in this chart are from the low model (mid-year July 1 figures). The intermediate model indicates a population of 1,003,855,000 and a natural increase rate of 2.04 percent for 1978. The high model indicates a population of 1,038,794,000 and a natural increase rate of 2.29 percent for 1978. Although Aird thought the intermediate model was probably the "best guess model," the low model is the most plausible, and therefore I use its estimates throughout this study. Aird has already slightly modified the above figures (for his series as adjusted in late 1978, see Joint Economic Committee, *Chinese Economy Post-Mao*, 95 Cong. 2 sess. [Government Printing Office, 1978], p. 465) and plans to revise them again. Until the Chinese publish a complete series, any Western estimates can only be approximations.

are imposed. In some places special excess-birth charges are levied, and both the father and mother have 10 percent of their wages deducted for fourteen years (in rural areas, it may be 10 percent of their work points). For each additional child, another 5 percent is deducted. In addition, they are penalized in many other ways. For example, they may be denied extra housing space, have to pay higher prices for grain rations, lose bonuses, and have to pay for all medical services.

This population control program is unquestionably one of the most comprehensive and draconian ever attempted anywhere. Peking's present leaders, recognizing that China's modernization cannot succeed without effective birth control, appear strongly committed to a tough policy, however, and they express optimism that it will work. For example, Vice Premier Chen Mu-hua (Chen Muhua) stated in an article in 1979 that she expected that "by 1985 no one will have a third child," and that by then a large number will have only one.[155]

During 1979–80 Peking worked on a national birth control law based on the local experiments under way. However, there was evidence of resistance and opposition to codifying such strong measures in a national law. Not only would a one-child pattern have far-reaching effects on individual families, but it would also profoundly change the entire society.

The population growth targets that Peking has set for China are extraordinarily ambitious and probably will be achievable only if the new one-child family program works. Chinese leaders now state that their aim is to reduce population growth to 0.5 percent in 1985 and zero percent in the year 2000.[156] It is problematic whether or not such targets are attainable, even if the new policies are implemented. Hua Kuo-feng himself pointed out in his 1979 National People's Congress (NPC) report that throughout the 1980s and 1990s, the number of persons of marriageable age will rise significantly, and Chen Mu-hua admitted that achievement of Peking's stated goals would be a "herculean task" because "people under 21 now constitute one-half of the nation's population and they will get married and have children before the end of this century."

Many of the greatest uncertainties center on China's vast rural areas and huge peasant population. There is little doubt that Peking's birth control programs to date have had their greatest impact on urban areas; the new program will face the largest obstacles in the countryside, where traditional attitudes and values, especially the desire for sons, still encourage parents to have several children.[157]

In 1978 John Aird (in his low model) predicted a steady decline in China's rate of natural increase between now and the end of the century, but only to about 1.06 percent, with birth and death rates in the year 2000 at 17.6 and 7.0 per thousand, respectively, which would fail to reach Peking's target. Aird's estimates indicated that at the end of the century China's population would total close to 1.25 billion.[158] It is too early to know whether the predictions of Western demographers or the projections of Chinese planners provide the best clues to how much China's population actually will grow in the period ahead. Probably, the announced Chinese targets will prove to be too ambitious. However, if Peking is able to carry out its present program effectively, the rate of population increase should drop more than Western analysts have predicted. But because of China's huge population base and age structure, the momentum from past growth will continue, even under the most optimistic assumptions, and for many years there will be large increases. In 1978 and 1979, despite the declining rate, population increased by 11 million and 13 million, respectively. If one makes optimistic projections, annual increases in the period ahead might drop to between 5 million and 10 million a year. It could well continue to be between 10 million and 15 million a year, however. In sum, in China as in other developing nations, although effective measures can eventually bring population growth under control, there is no way to halt the process immediately. Feeding an expanding population will continue to pose enormous problems for China for several decades, even if it achieves unprecedented success in birth control. It will be an extraordinary achievement if the Chinese are able to stabilize their population before it reaches 1.2 billion.

Grain Output

As China's population has grown, so too has its agricultural output, but increases in grain production have barely kept up with the growing number of mouths to feed.

The U.S. government estimates that between 1952 and 1973 China's total agricultural output (in 1957 yuan) rose from 42.79 billion yuan to 81.20 billion yuan,[159] and that, with 1957 as a base year, the index of agricultural growth rose from 83 in 1952 to 148 in 1976.[160] These figures indicate that, for the period as a whole, the average annual rate of agricultural growth in value terms exceeded population growth, but only by a small margin. Moreover, growth has not been steady and consistent. The rate of growth was highest in the immediate post-1949 years when agriculture recovered rapidly from the lows of the civil war period. It was slower during the initial years of China's first Five Year Plan period, rose at the end of the 1950s, and then dropped precipitously during 1959–61. Thereafter, it rose again, and by 1964 was slightly above the 1957 level. From the mid-1970s on, output continued to rise but at varying rates. For the entire period 1952–76, the rate of overall agricultural growth was between 2 and 3 percent.[161] The rate for food alone was a little over 2 percent. This was slightly below the global average; worldwide, food production increased from 1954 through 1973 at a rate of 2.8 percent, or 0.8 percent per capita. (In the developing nations as a whole, the rate was about 3.0 percent, or 0.4 percent per capita.)[162]

The growth of China's production of grain, the foundation of the population's diet, followed a similar pattern.[163] According to U.S. government estimates, "grain" output (including both soybeans and tubers) rose rapidly from 111 million tons in 1949 (an abnormally low level) to 161 million tons in 1952, and then increased gradually, with ups and downs, to 283 million tons in 1977.[164] From 1952 through 1977 the level of production rose by 122 million tons, or 76 percent. (See table 3-2.) The average annual rate of increase was about 2.3 percent.[165]

During the final two years of the Maoist era and the first year thereafter, grain output stagnated; it was 284 million tons in 1975, 285 million in 1976, and 283 million in 1977.[166] But in the next two years grain output rose rapidly. In 1978 it jumped 7.8 percent to almost 305 million tons.[167] Then in 1979, according to the State Statistical Bureau (SSB), it rose by more than 27 million tons, or almost 9.0 percent, to more than 332 million tons.[168] There is some reason to question, however, whether this figure was comparable to previous years' figures. Less than a month before the SSB's report, a Vice Minister of the State Planning Commission, Li Jen-chun (Li Renjun) had told the NPC Standing Committee that grain output in 1979 had been only 324.9 million tons, which he said represented a 15.1 million ton rise (implying that 1978 output had been 309.8 million, or 5 million tons higher than the SSB's figure); this indicated that the increase during the year could have been less than 5 percent.[169] These discrepancies are difficult to explain. While there is good reason to believe that the regime's new price and incentive policies as well as technical policies had favorable effects on output, it is possible that the SSB's figure for 1979 also reflected some changes in statistical methods or coverage. In any case, the goal set for 1980 was more modest. Li Jen-chun said the target was to raise grain production by 10.85 million tons

TABLE 3-2. China: Grain Output, 1952-78

Millions of metric tons

Year	Amount	Year	Amount
1952	161	1965	194
1953	164	1966	215
1954	166	1967	225
1955	180	1968	210
1956	188	1969	215
1957	191	1970	243
1958	206	1971	246
1959	171	1972	240
1960	156	1973	266
1961	168	1974	275
1962	180	1975	284
1963	190	1976	285
1964	194	1977	283
		1978	305

Sources: For 1952–76, Robert Michael Field and James A. Kilpatrick, "Chinese Grain Production: An Interpretation of the Data," *China Quarterly*, no. 74 (June 1978), p. 380; and Henry J. Groen and James A. Kilpatrick, "China's Agricultural Production," in JEC, *Chinese Economy Post-Mao*, p. 649. These figures are also used in CIA, *China: Economic Indicators*, p. 11. For previous CIA estimates, see 1976 source cited in note 163. The figures for 1977–78 are the official Chinese claims. The State Statistical Bureau's "Communique on Fulfilment of China's 1978 National Economic Plan" reported that grain output in 1978 was 304.75 million tons, which was 7.8 percent above the 1977 level of 282.75 million tons; see FBIS, *Daily Report—PRC*, June 27, 1979, p. L14.

(which would represent only a 3.34 percent increase over what he had said 1979 output was, and even less of a rise, 3.27 percent, if one uses the SSB's output figure for 1979).[170] Some reports in 1980 suggested that, because of poor weather during the winter of 1979–80, grain output might actually decline in 1980, perhaps by as much as 3 percent.

If one judges the SSB's grain production figure for 1979 to be valid, the increases in 1978–79 raised the long-term rate of growth for the twenty-seven-year period 1953–79 to 2.7 percent. If, however, the rate is calculated for the twenty-one years from the peak year of the 1950s (1958) through 1979, it is lower, 2.3 percent. But for 1971–79 it is 3.5 percent. But if output in 1980 does drop by about 3 percent, this would lower the 1971–80 average to 2.8 percent.

Trying to use past rates to predict the future is difficult at best. It almost certainly would be unrealistic to project the rates of 1978–79 into the future. The target set for 1980 may provide a better clue to future rates, but conceivably even it may too high. Performance in 1980 is a reminder that output can drop as well as rise as a result of the weather. Careful analysis of the agricultural problems China faces suggests that, even assuming the regime's new policies are successful, it will not be easy to raise the long-term rate of growth in grain output very dramatically.

In many respects, the total increase in grain output has been impressive.[171] Even the 2-plus percent annual rate during the quarter century from 1952 through 1977 was four times the long-term rate of increase in grain production in China from the late fourteenth century to the mid-twentieth century and about double the rate in the half century before the Communist takeover.[172] However, if population growth is taken into account, the performance was less impressive. During 1952–77 the increases in production kept just ahead of the growing population.

The increasing rate during the 1970s, achieved at a time when the rate of population growth dropped substantially (to perhaps 1.2 percent), has been encouraging. However, the year-to-year fluctuations since the start of the 1970s are much less reassuring. Grain output increased by a modest 1.2 percent in 1971, dropped by 2.4 percent in 1972, and increased by an impressive 10.8 percent in 1973. Increases during 1974 and 1975, 3.4 percent and 3.3 percent, were good and steady. But in 1976 output rose only 0.35 percent, and there was an apparent drop of 0.70 percent in 1977. The 7.8 percent and 9.0 percent increases reported in 1978 and 1979 again gave cause for optimism, but the regime's reduced target and generally poorer performance in 1980 showed that Peking's planners did not believe such high rates were sustainable. The recent fluctuations have made it difficult to discern any clear pattern or trend that can be confidently projected into the future.

The gross figures, moreover, do not reveal per capita trends. If one simply divides the official estimates of China's grain output by estimates of its population, per capita "grain" output (including tubers and soybeans) increased from 299 kilograms (659 pounds) in 1957 to 332 kilograms (732 pounds) in 1977 and 342 kilograms (754 pounds) in 1979, an increase of 43 kilograms (95 pounds), or 14 percent in twenty-two years (just over one-half percent a year).[173] From recent Chinese statements, it is clear that even these do not reveal real consumption. In 1978, not only did Hu Chiao-mu (Hu Qiaomu) state that "per capita grain distribution only matched that of 1955," but the public version of the "Decisions" on agriculture asserted that "per capita grain output was only equivalent to that of 1957" (the draft "Decisions" said that "the national average amount of food grains per person was slightly less than in 1957").[174]

While it is not clear exactly what calculations lay behind these statements, it is apparent that the official gross figures do not reveal the amounts of grain actually available for consumption. That figure is difficult to calculate. Even to begin to get an idea of what amount of grain—in the conventional sense—has been available for consumption, one must separate out the figures for output of rice, wheat, and coarse grains (subtracting the figures for tubers and soybeans) and then translate the rice figures from paddy (unmilled rice, in which output figures are presented) to milled, consumable rice.[175] If one does this for 1952 and 1976, the figures show that per capita output of consumable grain was 198 kilograms (437 pounds) in 1952 and 215 kilograms (474 pounds) in 1976; the increase in roughly a quarter century was only 17 kilograms (37 pounds). In 1952, output amounted to 1.2 pounds of grain per person per day; in 1976 it was about 1.3 pounds. Some analysts, in constructing "food balance sheets," have tried to calculate "extraction rates" for wheat and coarse grains to estimate consumable quantities; one used the following rates for China: wheat, 75 percent; corn, 80 percent; and other cereals, 60 to 80 percent.[176] Doing this reduces the figures further, of course.

Even these figures do not show the amounts of grain available for actual consumption. To estimate this, it would be necessary to subtract estimates of spoilage, losses in processing and transport, and the amounts used for seed, feed, and other purposes. It is impossible to do this for China with accuracy, but it is probable that it would lower the figures for consumable grain considerably.

Nutrition

Various attempts have been made to estimate per capita grain consumption (direct and indirect) in different areas and countries. One attempt, made by the Development Assistance Committee of the Organization for Economic Cooperation and Development (OECD), estimated that in China during 1972–74 per capita grain consumption averaged 430 pounds a year, which was somewhat more than the estimated average for all other developing nations (395 pounds), but just over two-thirds that in Japan (620 pounds) and less than one-fourth that in the United States (1,850 pounds).[177] The Chinese themselves apparently believe that per capita grain consumption is below what they consider a

minimum for a healthy population. One Chinese study in the 1950s estimated that the country's per capita grain requirement was between 275
kilograms (606 pounds) and 300 kilograms (662 pounds) of grain a
year.[178] A few sample surveys in China in the 1950s indicated that actual
consumption averaged about 250 kilograms (551 pounds) per capita.[179]

Gross figures on per capita grain consumption are of only limited
value in judging the nutrition in China or elsewhere. More relevant are
figures on a population's overall caloric intake and the proportion of calories provided by grain. Such estimates are difficult to make, however,
and the margin for error is great when data are limited. Nevertheless,
various attempts to make such estimates have been made. The FAO has
estimated, for example, that in the mid-1960s (1964–66) the per capita
daily intake of calories in China averaged 2,045, of which 1,383 (68 percent) came directly from grain.[180] This placed China slightly below the
average figure for all developing nations, which the FAO estimated was
2,097 calories (1,300 directly from grain), and far below the average for
the developed nations, which was 3,043 calories (1,127 directly from
grain).

One of the most ambitious attempts to construct a detailed food balance for China indicated that daily per capita availability of food for
consumption in China amounted to 2,073 calories in 1957 and 2,070 calories in 1974, and in both years over 70 percent was accounted for by
grain for direct consumption.[181] While the author of the study was
aware of the difficulty of making accurate estimates, he nevertheless
concluded that "China's per capita food energy supply in the mid-1970s
was, at best, only marginally better than two decades ago."[182]

Scattered data on rationing in China support this conclusion. There
has been no significant rise in rations of grain or other food staples over
the past quarter century; the grain ration normally has averaged 30 to
40 catties (15 to 20 kilograms) a month.[183] Through relatively equitable
distribution of available grain supplies, the regime has maintained minimal consumption standards, and there appears to have been some improvement in the supply of vegetables and certain subsidiary foods (although vegetable oils and soybean products, including bean curd, often
have been in short supply). But the consumption of grain and overall
intake of calories have risen little, if at all, remaining close to minimal
standards. The "meat revolution" that has occurred in more affluent
countries has not yet begun in China. The FAO has estimated that in

1964–66, of the average per capita intake of 2,045 calories in China, only 134 calories—less than 7 percent of the total—came from meat. The author of the detailed food balance for China mentioned above estimated that in 1974 only 4 percent of the average Chinese caloric intake came from meat.[184] A recent U.S. government study, based on refugee and traveler reports, indicated that actual consumption in China in 1979 averaged 1,936 calories and 45.1 grams of protein per day.[185]

All of these estimates indicate that China has just been able to keep up with population growth and maintain minimal nutrition standards, and that substantially improving the Chinese level of nutrition remains a task for the future.

The frankness with which Peking's leaders have acknowledged this fact during the past two years is remarkable. Not only have they stated that more than one-tenth of the population has "inadequate food grain supplies,"[186] but they have published figures on meat production that show that in 1979, even though total meat output was 24.1 percent above 1978, it still amounted to only 10.624 million tons, or about 11 kilograms (24 pounds) per person per year.[187] The emphasis now placed on improving the national diet, by increasing the availability of meat and other plant foods as well as grain, has potentially far-reaching implications for China's food-population balance in the period ahead.

Land

Various factors have influenced—and will continue to influence—the size and rate of growth of China's food output. One of the most basic is the availability of land. Expanding cultivated acreage is an obvious way to expand food output, and, as stated earlier, the possibilities for doing this are still great in many developing countries. In China, however, the potential is relatively small.

In the five and a half centuries between 1400 and the Communists' rise to power, the amount of land cultivated in China steadily rose, and probably accounted for more than half of the total rise in grain output, which increased at an average rate for the entire period of about 0.5 percent a year.[188] Because of war and other factors, however, the amount of cultivated land dropped significantly in the late 1930s and 1940s. Then during the first decade after 1949 it rose again, largely through restoration of land neglected during the war and civil war. By 1958 China's cultivated area may have been about 10 percent above that in 1948.

Since then, however, there has been relatively little added to cultivated acreage, and a considerable amount has been shifted to industrial
and other uses. During the Great Leap, perhaps 4 million hectares were
withdrawn from cultivation, and although subsequently there has been
some new sown land (perhaps as much as 12 million hectares), even
more has been withdrawn from cultivation.[189] Some years ago the total
amount of cultivated land in China was estimated to be 107 million hectares (264 million acres),[190] but in late 1979 the Chinese themselves indicated that it was under 100 million. This means that the total now is less
than it was in the late 1930s. Even though cultivated land constitutes
only about 11 percent of the country's area, it is close to the total that is
arable under existing circumstances. (In the United States the amount of
land under cultivation in 1964 amounted to 156 million hectares [386
million acres], which constituted roughly 20 percent of the country's
area.)[191]

At present there is only about 0.10 hectare (close to 0.04 acre) of cultivated land per person in China (compared with about 0.80 to 0.90 hectare in the United States, 0.32 in India, and less than 0.06 in Japan).[192] The
amount of cultivated land per member of the farming population is
somewhat higher but still very low; according to one estimate, in twelve
heavily populated provinces in central and south China it is less than 0.15
hectare, and it probably is less than 0.20 nationwide (compared with
more than 15 hectares in the United States, 0.48 in India, and 0.24 in
Japan).[193]

In 1978 Chinese planners set as their target the opening of 8 million
hectares of new arable land by 1985,[194] but they are not likely to achieve
this. Limited amounts of new land could be opened up for cultivation in
underpopulated areas in the northeast, the northwest, and some coastal
areas. Some of these areas lack sufficient water, however, and the cost of
trying to irrigate arid land is extremely high. Recently there have been
signs of new reclamation efforts, especially in Heilungkiang (Heilongjiang) and coastal provinces, but the costs will be high and productivity
may be low. The Chinese also are continuing to make major efforts to
improve existing land through leveling and terracing. However, none of
these efforts is likely to increase China's arable land substantially or rapidly.

China's land shortage makes its problems of increasing food production more difficult than in most developing nations. Although some addi-

tions probably will be made to the cultivated area in the years ahead, as in recent years these will be counterbalanced—and conceivably may continue to be more than counterbalanced—by urban, industrial, and other encroachments. To increase its output of grain and other crops, China must rely primarily on land now in use.

Grain and Other Crops

In theory, China might be able to increase its grain output by transferring land from other agricultural uses to the cultivation of rice, wheat, or coarse grains. In certain brief periods this has been done on a limited scale. However, at present there is little potential for doing so. In fact, current policies call for shifts of some land to other edible and industrial crops such as oilseeds and cotton, which are essential to maintain even minimum standards of food and clothing and, since Peking has pledged to raise living standards, have received increasing emphasis. The land allocated to these crops is already inadequate to produce what China needs to clothe as well as feed its population. There has been no significant rise since the mid-1960s of typical rations of cotton cloth, which have averaged a little more than three yards per person per year in the South and about double that in the North, or of the ration of vegetable oil —essential for cooking in China—which has fluctuated between four and eight ounces a month, close to the absolute minimum needed.[195]

The case of cotton, which still provides the raw material for most Chinese clothing, illustrates the problem.[196] Actually, total cotton output has risen impressively. Production, which totaled 1.3 million tons of ginned product (6 million bales) in 1952, rose to 2.4 million or 2.5 million tons a year (more than 11 million bales) during 1973–74. However, it then dropped to 2.0 million tons in 1976, and during 1978–79 it was 2.2 million tons. This increase has been the result of steadily rising yields, which more than doubled from 234 to 495 kilograms per hectare between 1952 and 1975. China is now the second or third ranking producer of ginned cotton in the world—after the Soviet Union and (at times) the United States—and between 1972 and 1979 its production of cotton cloth rose from 3.8 million to 12.2 million linear meters.

Yet China's need for cotton to produce textiles—both for internal use and for export—has risen, even without significantly increased domestic cloth rations, faster than domestic output. As a consequence, China in recent years has had to import large and increasing amounts of raw cotton. During 1971–77 its cotton imports averaged just over 250,000 tons a year; then they rose to over 500,000 in 1978 and over 600,000 tons in 1979.[197]

Despite China's great—and increasing—need for cotton, cultivated cotton acreage was believed to be less in 1978 than it was in 1952 (4.400 million hectares compared with 5.576 million hectares in 1952). The problem obviously could have been alleviated if land could have been shifted from grain to cotton (some was shifted in the 1950s; cotton acreage was at its peak—6.256 million hectares—in 1956), but since the 1950s the regime has felt the need for more grain to be even more urgent than the need for more cotton. It is now trying to cope with the problem of obtaining sufficient textile raw materials not only by importing large amounts of cotton but also by expanding production of synthetic fibers (which use petroleum and gas rather than land). This will help, but China's need for more domestically produced cotton keeps growing not just to meet needs at home but also to produce textiles for export (to earn badly needed foreign exchange).

The situation relating to soybeans (and all oilseeds) is comparable in some respects. Soybean acreage has actually declined from 11.679 million hectares in 1952 to 9.200 million in 1978,[198] and yields have not increased very much (they were 815 kilograms per hectare in 1952 and 1,141 kilograms in 1978). Consequently, estimated output in 1978 was only marginally above that in 1952 (10.5 million tons compared with 9.5 million tons), and remained well below the 1959 peak of 11.5 million tons. As a result, even though China is still the second or third largest producer of soybeans in the world (after the United States and possibly Brazil), it has suffered serious domestic shortages, and in recent years it has become one of the world's largest importers of soybeans. During 1973–79 annual imports averaged almost 300,000 tons a year, and in 1974 they were over 600,000 tons and in 1979 almost 600,000 tons.[199] (In contrast, before World War II China was the world's largest soybean exporter, selling between 2 million and 3 million tons a year in the years from 1925 through 1934.)[200]

In sum, China's land shortage creates serious problems affecting all the crops that the country needs for internal food consumption, industrial use, and export. It is not easy for China, as it is for some countries, to shift the use of land. Peking's present emphasis on the need to increase output of cash crops as well as grain creates severe dilemmas in decisions on land use. However, in 1980 a leading Chinese economist stated that to diversify agriculture, grain acreage would be reduced to less than 80 percent of China's cultivated land.[201] This will be extremely difficult to do. If it is done, it may solve some problems but will create others, and will add to the uncertainty about the adequacy of future grain supplies.

Yields

China's ability to increase food production in the years ahead will depend above all on its success in increasing per acre yields through improved water control, multiple cropping, increased use of fertilizers and pesticides, development of better seeds, and other steps to raise the scientific level of farming. China has major assets which will facilitate the process of agricultural modernization, including the time-tested skills of its farmers and the regime's organizational talents. Yet it faces formidable obstacles particularly because, as noted earlier, its yields are already comparatively high.

Although even in the pre-Communist period China's yields were already among the highest of all countries using traditional agricultural methods, the present regime has steadily raised yields. The USDA estimates that between 1952 and 1975 average yields per sown hectare of all "grain" in China (including tubers, converted to "grain equivalent," but not soybeans) rose 45 percent (from about 1.38 tons to 2 tons); rice yields, USDA estimates, rose by 47 percent (from 2.4 to more than 3.5 tons), wheat yields by 89 percent (from 0.74 to about 1.4 tons), and the yields of other grains by 34 percent (from 1.0 to 1.37 tons).[202] These figures show that China has done much better than most countries, since average yields of all grains worldwide only rose from about 1.4 tons per hectare in 1961 to between 1.8 and 1.9 tons in the years since 1971, and average rice yields in all the developing countries only rose from about 1.5 tons per hectare during most of the 1960s to 1.8 tons in 1970 (and have since fallen).[203] Not only are China's overall grain yields above the world average, its rice yields in particular are fairly impressive, being about double those in the developing nations as a group.

Even so, yields in China are still well below those in the most advanced developed nations. In the United States, for example, in the late 1960s (1967–71 average) average rice yields were 5 tons per hectare (more than 40 percent higher than China's in the mid-1970s), and U.S. coarse grain yields were 3.9 tons (almost triple China's).[204] Despite China's more extensive irrigation and far greater inputs of labor, yields in the

United States are much higher because of its modern scientific (and capital-intensive) methods. So too are methods in Japan. In 1975 Japan's irrigated rice yields averaged 4.81 tons per hectare, and its wheat yields were 2.69 tons per hectare.[205] There still is a potential for increasing yields in China, therefore.

Water Control and Cropping Practices

Water control has a long history in China, which today has more irrigated land than any other nation.[206] Some historians have described China as a "hydraulic society" and have explained the rise of the Chinese state in terms of the need for public works in the field of water conservancy. Huge irrigation systems such as those built in Kuan Hsien (Guanxian) on the Chengtu (Chengdu) Plain more than two millennia ago are, in fact, among the agricultural wonders of the world. In this tradition the Communists have expended enormous effort since 1949 to improve and expand China's water control facilities, and their accomplishments have been impressive.

It is estimated that in the 1930s about 26.5 million acres, or 27 percent of China's cultivated land, were irrigated; in South China especially, irrigation was very extensive and already covered more than two-thirds of the rice land.[207] Subsequently the irrigated area declined as a result of neglect and destruction, and in 1952 irrigation may have covered only about 20 percent of China's agricultural land. Since then, however, it has risen steadily, to a new peak.

Chinese leaders have encouraged construction of many different types of irrigation, drainage, and other water control projects, to combat droughts, floods, and waterlogging. During the first years of their regime they placed special stress on large conservation projects such as those on the Yellow and Huai (Huai) rivers. These projects produced real benefits, but construction was slower and more costly than had been hoped. Subsequently, greater emphasis was placed on smaller projects. In the 1960s improvement of water control in "high and stable" yield areas, especially in South China, were the focus of attention and investment. In the 1970s special efforts were made in North China—where yields are lower and the needs greatest—to improve water control through construction of irrigation and drainage canals and tube wells.

By 1973, according to some estimates, 44 million hectares were irrigated, an increase of 66 percent compared with the 1930s,[208] and recent

Chinese statements indicate that half of their cultivated land is now irrigated.[209]

The rapid expansion of tube wells and electric irrigation pumps provides one index of the scale of effort in recent years. Between 1965 and 1974 the number of tube wells in China rose from about 100,000 to 1.3 million, an increase of thirteen times.[210] The production of powered irrigation equipment is estimated to have increased from 1.15 million horsepower in 1965 to 7 million in 1975. In the same period, according to U.S. estimates, the total horsepower of China's inventory of such pumps rose by about 250 percent, from about 8.5 million horsepower to roughly 43 million horsepower; and the capacity of rural hydroelectric plants that helped to power them rose from 0.3 million to 3.0 million kilowatts.[211] Recent Chinese claims are even higher; according to the State Statistical Bureau, in 1979 China had 71.22 million horsepower of rural drainage and irrigation machines.[212]

Improvement of water control has been one very important explanation of the rise in grain output in China in recent years. Water control has reduced the impact of droughts and floods and has made possible increased multiple cropping, and in some areas intensive intercropping. Many fields in China now produce two crops; some produce three or even four. The USDA estimates that at the start of the 1970s the *sown* area in China totaled about 150 million hectares (about 40 percent higher than the figure for cultivated area), giving it a cropping index of 140, one of the highest in the world.[213] Today it is doubtless higher.

While improved water control has helped China greatly in the past to raise per hectare yields, the high cropping index already achieved means that the potential for further progress in this respect has limits—and will be increasingly difficult and expensive. Some potential for further expansion and improvement clearly exists, and visitors to China are impressed by the regime's continuing efforts to build and improve canals and wells. These improvements are important. As modernization of agriculture progresses, simple antiflood, antidrought measures will not suffice; use of improved seeds and more chemical fertilizers and pesticides requires increasingly precise control of amounts of water and the timing of its flow in irrigation and drainage. Much can still be done by relatively simple methods. Chinese officials claim, for example, that half of the farmland in key provinces in North China—Hopeh (Hebei), Honan (Henan), and Shantung (Shandong)—can ultimately be irrigated by wells.[214] But there are limits. There is uncertainty, for example, about whether a large increase in the number of tube wells may affect the water table, reducing the amount of underground water available.

Because of the limits to what can be done by traditional methods and small-scale projects, improvement of water control may not have as much effect on yields in the period immediately ahead as it has had in the recent past. Over the long run, China will doubtless have to increase its investment in large-scale—and expensive—river control schemes. Taming the Yellow River and controlling both its flow and silting doubtless will be on Peking's agenda. The Chinese have been working on this for years, however, and the task has proven to be difficult, slow, and costly. Even if they allocate increased funds and labor to the task, it may take decades to do what is needed.

In the longer term, the Chinese will try to make progress in the more difficult task of tapping the flow of the Yangtze (Yangzi) River, which has twenty times the flow of the Yellow River, to irrigate North China. This will be a huge undertaking, probably taking several decades to complete. During 1978–79 the Chinese indicated that they were seriously studying how best to harness the Yangtze.[215] If they can accomplish this eventually, it will help enormously to solve China's long-term problems. However, major success may not be possible until the twenty-first century.[216]

In sum, although improving water control will continue to be extremely important, in the near future it alone will not produce large increases in yields rapidly.

Labor and Machines

Past increases in yields in China have depended fundamentally on the intensive application of labor to agriculture. The care with which Chinese farmers cultivate their fields has always awed foreign observers, many of whom have observed that much agriculture in China is more like gardening than extensive farming as now practiced in the West.

Despite the Chinese commitment to modernize agriculture, moreover, much farming appears to have become more rather than less intensive in recent years. Ever since 1949 peasants have been mobilized on an unprecedented scale to improve the land, build water projects, and cultivate farms collectively. The organization of the peasants into communes has greatly facilitated the full mobilization of the rural labor force, including women. And the rural labor force has steadily grown as a result of natural population increases and the regime's policy of limiting migration to the cities and transferring millions of urban residents to the countryside. In 1978 the Chinese stated that the country's rural population totaled 800 million and the rural work force 300 million.[217] In sum, over 80 percent of China's population still lives in rural areas, and the majority of adult rural residents are still engaged in agriculture.

Chinese agricultural policies have made full use of the country's rural population. The labor intensity of China's agriculture is such, in fact, that even though by most standards the country unquestionably is over-populated, its agriculture needs all the labor it can get to sustain and increase yields by current methods. The need for labor to build water control projects and carry out increasingly intensive hand-transplanting, weeding, application of fertilizers and pesticides, and intercropping has grown in recent years. And the spread of multicropping has required increasingly large numbers of farmhands to harvest and sow crops rapidly during critical periods. Often Chinese communes have experienced temporary farm labor shortages and have had to draw on labor from the cities and from rural industries for help.

Some further intensification of farming by labor-intensive methods is possible, and until recently the regime held up one brigade—Tachai (Dazhai)—as a model of how this can be done.[218] But there are limits to how much per hectare yields can be increased this way, and in 1980 Tachai was denounced as a fraud.[219] Moreover, increasing labor intensity will not solve another basic problem: the need to increase labor productivity. One of the dilemmas the Chinese face is that although solving their food problem clearly requires raising per hectare yields, improving the welfare of the population requires increasing labor productivity. The marginal productivity of much of China's agricultural labor force is already low (as Teng Hsiao-ping's [Deng Xiaoping's] 1978 statement that per peasant output in China is currently about one-fiftieth the U.S. figure pointed out).[220] The productivity of future farm laborers may be even lower. At some point, additions to the agricultural labor force may not increase productivity sufficiently to feed the added farm workers.

The Chinese have long discussed mechanization of agriculture. Although at times it has been a subject of heated debate, steps to mechanize some farm operations have been accelerated in recent years. Between 1966 and 1976, according to Western estimates, the total number of tractors in China (measured in standard 15 horsepower units) increased from 154,000 to almost 1.2 million, of which 971,000 units were large tractors and 216,000 garden tractors.[221] (In 1970 the United States used about 5 million tractors on its farms.[222]) Officially, the Chinese now say that in 1979 the country had 667,000 large- and medium-size tractors and 1.67 million hand tractors.[223]

Efforts to mechanize many agriculture-related activities through the introduction of relatively simple and low-cost machines has been strongly emphasized for several years. In 1978 China's leadership gave major priority to this task and asserted that the country's agriculture should be "basically" mechanized by 1980.[224] (It is not wholly clear what "basically" mechanized means; it almost certainly does not mean anything like the mechanization in Western nations.) Since the reassessment of 1979, however, the pace and scope of the mechanization program has been slowed, and Chinese officials now stress the need to be selective and take local conditions into account.[225] But they nevertheless are continuing efforts to expand the use of machines in China's farming.

In many respects, increased agricultural mechanization is clearly desirable, but it can only help solve some of China's problems, and it will create new ones. Over the long run, to raise the per capita productivity of the country's entire population China must not only mechanize but also reduce the proportion of its population engaged in agriculture and transfer many farm laborers to industry and other occupations in rural areas as well as in the cities. (Current policy calling for development of small towns to absorb labor released from farming makes good sense, but it will not be easy to create new jobs rapidly enough to absorb large-scale transfers soon.) In the short run, some released labor probably can be absorbed in work groups doing agriculturally related tasks, and some in commune industries. However, in the long run, unless huge numbers of new industrial jobs are created, mechanization of agriculture could create serious unemployment problems.

It remains to be seen, moreover, what effects mechanization will have on per hectare yields in China. In some respects it should have a favorable impact. For example, it should facilitate increased multiple cropping by speeding up operations during critical periods, and also make possible improved tillage. For a limited period labor released from some tasks by machines can be used for other useful agriculturally related tasks. And some mechanization, especially where farming is relatively extensive (for example, in the Northeast), should increase efficiency in ways that could raise yields. However, mechanization also could have unfavorable effects on per hectare yields in some areas in China, especially in the South where farming is most intensive, where there is complicated intercropping, and where present cultivation methods rely on hand operations that will be difficult to replace with machines.

Basically, mechanization seems more likely to help China solve its long-run problem of increasing labor productivity than to solve its urgent problem of rapidly increasing the productivity of the land, raising per hectare yields, and expanding total grain output to feed its growing population.

Fertilizer

Increased use of chemical fertilizers has been one of the main explanations for the rapid rise of worldwide grain crop yields since World War II, and in China chemical fertilizers probably have been the most important single factor in the rise of yields since China embarked seriously on agricultural modernization in the 1960s.[226] It will continue to be one of the best ways to achieve rapid increases in food output in the immediate future.

The Chinese always have recognized the importance of fertilizing their fields, and for centuries their use of large amounts of organic fertilizers—"night soil" and "green manure"—was a key reason for their success using traditional methods. But until recently China used very little modern chemical fertilizer, and it still uses less than many countries whose modernized agriculture produces higher yields.

During the 1950s Chinese planners did not pay great attention to chemical fertilizers. In 1952, just before China's first Five Year Plan started, the country produced only 39,000 tons and imported about 40,000. By 1957, the last year of the plan, it was still producing only 159,000 and importing 270,000.[227] (All of these and the following fertilizer figures, unless otherwise stated, are in terms of primary nutrients rather than in bulk fertilizer weights, which would be much higher.) China's big push to increase the use of chemical fertilizers began in the 1960s and continues today. Its total annual "supply" (including domestic production and imports) has risen spectacularly, from 710,000 tons in 1960 to roughly 9 million tons in 1977—an increase of more than ten times.

Most of this increase has resulted from the expansion of China's own production, in both large and small plants. Between 1960 and 1977 domestic output of all chemical fertilizers rose from 495,000 tons to 7.24 million tons. By 1979 it had risen to 10.65 million tons (8.82 million nitrogenous, 1.82 million phosphate, and 16,000 potash).[228] Small plants scattered throughout China's countryside played a unique role in this industry; in 1975 they accounted for over 60 percent of China's output. Special stress has been placed on nitrogen fertilizer, which already by 1977 accounted for between 4.5 million and 5 million tons of the domestic fertilizer output, making China the third largest world producer of this fertilizer after the United States and the Soviet Union. In 1978 nitrogen fertilizer accounted for almost 83 percent of domestic fertilizer production.

Domestic production has not kept up with demand, however, and China's imports of chemical fertilizer also have increased greatly. They rose from 215,000 tons (nutrient value) in 1960 to 1.55 million tons in 1972 and 1.52 million tons in 1973. During 1974–76 they varied between 1 million and 1.2 million tons, but in 1977 they rose again to 1.52 million tons.[229] In 1978 they soared to 2.17 million tons and in 1979 dropped only slightly, to 1.72 million tons.[230] (To give some idea of the relative scale of these imports, the total imports of chemical fertilizers by all non-Communist developing nations in 1970/71 was just under 4 million tons.)[231] From 1967 through 1977 China imported a total of more than 14.6 million tons of fertilizer nutrient. If one calculates, crudely, that each ton of nutrient was the equivalent of perhaps eight tons of grain,[232] the 1.5 million to 2.0 million tons of fertilizer that China imported per year in the early and late 1970s were in effect a substitute for imports of 12 million to 16 million tons of grain. The increasing priority the Chinese recently have given to fertilizers is highlighted by the fact that in the six-year period 1971–76, they devoted almost $1.5 billion of scarce foreign exchange, an average of almost $250 million a year, to pay for fertilizer imports.[233] This was close to one-half of what China spent on grain imports ($3.5 billion) and about one-fifth of what it spent on machinery imports (almost $7.5 billion) in the same period. During 1978–79 it spent even more on fertilizer imports—roughly $500 million a year.

In late 1972, following a bad crop, Chinese planners made a major decision to undertake a crash program to build big, sophisticated fertilizer plants. Thereafter, they contracted with foreign firms (including the U.S. Kellogg Corporation) to purchase thirteen enormous urea-ammonia complexes—twenty-six plants—to produce nitrogen fertilizer.[234] Buying so many plants—in effect, importing the basis for a whole new industry—instead of simply obtaining one or two prototypes, was atypical of Chinese practice at that time and underlined the urgency Peking felt about the need to increase fertilizer use.

These plants are changing the nature of the industry in China, raising the quality as well as the quantity of its output. Most of the small plants, which accounted for 58 percent of China's domestic nitrogen output in 1975, produced ammonium bicarbonate, a volatile, poor-quality fertilizer with low nutrient content and short storage potential;[235] plants producing such fertilizer seem destined to be less important in the future. When all of the new large plants (which will cost China more than $650 million) are in full operation, they will have added about 3.5 million tons (in nutrients) of nitrogen fertilizer to China's capacity, which is close to the total of all nitrogen fertilizer produced in China in 1975.

Although China has placed highest priority on nitrogen fertilizer, it has also increased its output of phosphates,[236] from 150,000 tons (of phosphorus) in 1960 to almost 2.5 million tons in 1977. It is now the fourth largest producer of phosphates in the world. However, it has only begun to produce potassium (the output, in nutrients, in 1977 was 275,000 tons). And in the past it imported relatively little of either phosphate or potassium (in 1974, for example, the figure in nutrients was 40,000 tons for the former and 190,000 for the latter),[237] although this has begun to change.

Today China's use of chemical fertilizer is far higher than in most developing nations. In 1977, according to Chinese figures, it averaged 64 kilograms of nutrient per cultivated hectare; according to Western estimates it amounted to more than 43 kilograms (in nutrients) per hectare of sown land,[238] compared with less than 5 kilograms at the start of the 1960s. In 1978 use of chemical fertilizers rose almost 40 percent, to 89 kilograms of nutrient per cultivated hectare. And in 1979 it rose by over 20 percent, to 109 kilograms per hectare. If one assumes that one ton of chemical fertilizer nutrient might produce about eight tons of grain, the increased use of these fertilizers (with necessary complementary inputs of water and seeds) could account for perhaps 50 million tons of the 78 million by which China's 1975 grain production exceeded that of the late 1950s peak, in 1958.[239] It doubtless accounted for a large share of the rise in grain output in 1978 and 1979.

Chinese use of organic fertilizer also has risen as a result of more energetic collection, and the increase in China's population of hogs. Mao once called the hog a "fertilizer-factory," and the increase from 115 million head in 1957 to 280 million in 1976 and to 320 million in 1979 has significantly boosted China's supply of organic fertilizer, which now may be between 50 and 75 kilograms per cultivated hectare, and in some places more.[240] If so, China now uses, on the average, 150 kilograms or more of all fertilizers, organic and chemical, per *cultivated* hectare. The amount per *sown* hectare (taking into account multiple cropping) is lower (perhaps by about one-third; a second crop on a field needs fertilizing but not as much as the first). Such averages conceal major place-to-place differences; some land in China doubtless receives much less than this, and some considerably more. Nevertheless, by any standard, China obviously is now a very large fertilizer user.

These figures help to explain why China's yields are higher than in many other developing nations. If China now uses 150 kilograms or more per hectare, this is more than the 75 to 150 kilograms (for chemical fertilizer alone) which is the recent average for all industrial nations (the U.S. average is about 90).[241] Its use of chemical fertilizers alone is now comparable with the average in the industrialized nations.

However, use is still well below that in certain countries that have very high yields. According to U.S. government estimates, in 1975/76 the Netherlands used 754 kilograms of chemical fertilizers per hectare; Belgium, 513; Ireland, 407; East Germany, 373; Japan, 317; and North Korea (in 1974/75), 284.6.[242] The Chinese clearly could raise their fertilizer use much higher, therefore, and the country's leaders are determined to do so. Teng Hsiao-ping is reported to have said some years ago that China eventually needs 60 million to 70 million tons of chemical fertilizer (presumably he meant in bulk weight, which in nutrients might be, roughly, between 12 million and 14 million tons),[243] and in 1978 Peking reportedly set 80 million tons (perhaps 16 million in nutrients) as a production goal for 1985,[244] which would be close to three times China's 1975 output and would provide more than 150 kilograms per cultivated hectare.

Increased use of fertilizers will be essential for China to meet its food needs in the years ahead. However, even under ideal conditions, continued applications cannot produce steady, proportionate rises in grain output. When fertilizer use reaches a certain point, the "yield response" —that is, the number of kilograms of increased grain output from each added kilogram of fertilizer—declines. One study of fertilizer use in rice cultivation in forty countries showed, for example, that the yield response averaged 19.5/1 for the first fifty kilograms of nitrogen nutrient, 8.2/1 for the second fifty kilograms, and 6.4/1 for the third fifty kilograms.[245]

TABLE 3-3. *China: Fertilizer Yield Ratios, 1965–75*

	Increase or decrease over previous year				
Year	Chemical fertilizer used (millions of metric tons)	Percentage increase or decrease	Grain output (millions of metric tons)	Percentage increase or decrease	Yield ratio[a]
1965	0.635	42.76	0	0	...
1966	0.484	22.83	21	10.82	43/1
1967	0.159	6.11	10	4.65	63/1
1968	0.365	13.21	−15	−6.66	...
1969	0.430	13.75	5	2.38	12/1
1970	0.708	19.90	28	13.02	40/1
1971	0.554	12.99	3	1.23	5/1
1972	0.674	13.98	−6	−2.44	...
1973	0.941	17.13	26	10.83	28/1
1974	−0.342	−5.31	9	3.49	...
1975	0.608	9.98	9	3.27	15/1

Sources: Fertilizer figures were calculated from data in CIA, *China: Economic Indicators*, p. 12. Grain figures were calculated from data in Field and Kilpatrick, "Chinese Grain Production," p. 380. The ratio is calculated by comparing the increase or decrease in fertilizer use each year with the increase or decrease in grain output for the same year.
a. Based on actual increases or decreases (grain/fertilizer). Figures are rounded.

An examination of the data on China's chemical fertilizer use and grain output in recent years shows erratic year-to-year fluctuations. From the figures, it is difficult to correlate fertilizer use and grain output. However, they suggest that there has been a decline over time in the yield ratio.

The fluctuations shown in table 3-3 demonstrate that there is no simple, direct, dependable link between the amount of fertilizer used and the amount of grain produced.

In 1965 there was no increase in grain output despite a huge increase in fertilizer use. In 1968 and 1972 there were drops in grain output despite substantial rises in fertilizer. And in 1974 there was a significant rise in grain output despite a decline in use of fertilizers. The calculated ratios for particular years vary widely from 63/1 to 5/1.

The year-to-year fluctuations highlight the fact that a great many variables influence the size of any grain crop, and some—especially the weather—clearly have a greater impact on output in any particular year than the amount of fertilizer used. Longer-run trends provide a better clue to the impact of chemical fertilizers on grain output, although even these can give only a crude indication of the correlation. The data

TABLE 3-4. *China: Yield Ratios, Long-Term Trends, Selected Periods,
1961–75*

	Increases over previous period		
	---	---	---
Period	Chemical fertilizer used (total of annual increases in millions of metric tons)	Grain output (total of annual increases in millions of metric tons)	Yield ratio, grain/fertilizer
1961–65	1.410	38	27/1
1966–70	2.146	49	23/1
1971–75	2.435	41	17/1

Source: Calculated from grain output and fertilizer use in sources cited earlier. The fertilizer figures used are nutrient, not bulk, figures. (Since 1975 the ratio has fluctuated greatly, with almost no increase in grain output despite fertilizer increases during 1976–77 but with substantial increases in 1978–79. The yield ratio in 1979 was probably around 18/1.)

for three five-year periods from 1961 to 1975 are as shown in table 3-4.[246] For the fifteen-year period from 1960 through 1975, the figures indicate a yield ratio of about 21.4/1. But over time it appears to have declined, when one compares the three five-year periods, from 27/1 to 23/1 to 17/1.

There are several possible reasons for a decline. As stated earlier, on the basis of experience elsewhere one should expect that when the amount of nitrogen fertilizer used reaches a certain point there will be a lower yield response. In the case of China, moreover, it is possible that a large proportion of chemical fertilizer was at first used on "high and stable yield" areas, but now as chemical fertilizer is being used more widely on fields with less favorable conditions (for example, fields with poorer water control), the yield responses may be lower. Perhaps the low-quality ammonium bicarbonate produced by China's small nitrogen fertilizer plants (which still supply close to half of what China uses) has resulted in lower yield responses. Conceivably, also, the effectiveness of the increase in nitrogen fertilizer use has been reduced by a lack of an optimal mix of fertilizers. Some studies indicate that for chemical fertilizers to have the greatest effect, three major types (nitrogen, phosphates, and potassium) should generally be mixed in a ratio of about 100/50/33.[247] The balance between nitrogen and phosphate in the chemical fertilizers used in China appears to be reasonable at present, but the Chinese have used relatively little potassium; for example, the ratio (based on the availability of each of the three, from domestic production and imports) was 100/40/6.5 in 1975/76.[248] The Chinese obtain substantial amounts of nutrients similar to those that potash supplies from organic fertilizer. Nevertheless, they have begun to recognize their need for more potassium and have started importing larger quantities. One analyst predicts that in the future, imports of nitrogen will decline but imports of potash will rise, perhaps to as much as 2 million tons a year.[249]

Increased use of chemical fertilizers clearly will continue to help raise yields in China, but how much is uncertain. It will depend on how effectively fertilizers are combined with a better mix of new seeds, improved water control, effective pesticides, control of plant diseases, and generally more scientific methods of cultivation. Fertilizers are no panacea; they produce optimal results only if broadly based agricultural modernization occurs. At present it is difficult to predict exactly what yield responses to expect from further increases in the use of chemical fertilizers in China. The possibility that response ratios might decline significantly adds uncertainty to any attempt to judge future prospects.

Seeds and Science

Together with improved water control and increased fertilizer use, the introduction of high-yield seeds has been an important factor in the rise in yields in China as elsewhere in recent years. The potential for further improvement in plant varieties is great. Short-stock, disease-resistant, high-yield seed varieties have been one of the keys to the "green revolution" in India and several other Asian countries since the late 1960s. In India, for example, during the second half of the 1960s the average rate of increase in grain output was 3.3 percent a year, a result of the use of new seeds combined with a great increase in fertilizer use and improvement of water control.[250] (From 1950 to the mid-1970s India's rate of increase in grain output was 2.8 percent, somewhat higher than the long-term rate in China.)[251]

China has begun its "green revolution," but it has by no means completed it. Starting in the late 1950s the Chinese developed a number of high-yield rice and wheat varieties and began to use them in the early 1960s. It is estimated that by 1973 improved rice seeds were used on 6.7 million hectares.[252] Some high-yield winter wheat seeds also were introduced in the 1960s and others in the early 1970s, and their use has gradually spread. In addition, some of the famous high-yield rice and wheat seeds developed in the Philippines and Mexico have been adapted for use in China. In 1977 the Chinese began production of a new hybrid rice ("male-sterile F_1 hybrid") which they have claimed represents "a major breakthrough"; by 1978 it was used on 4.3 million hectares.[253] The Chinese have also developed some new corn and sorghum hybrids.

Western observers have differed, however, in their judgments on China's achievements to date in developing new seeds. A delegation of American plant scientists visiting China in 1974 concluded that some of the new varieties used in China have "high genetic yield potential."[254] Some reports have suggested that under optimal conditions certain new Chinese varieties could produce up to two or even three times the per hectare yields of previously used seeds. One group of Western agricultural scientists visiting China in 1977 concluded that "China is in the forefront of the world's research on winter wheat"; yet many observers have noted that China's plant scientists still lag in many aspects of sophisticated seed research, and some have maintained that most of China's plant breeding until very recently consisted mainly of seed selection and relatively simple methods of crossing and hybridization.[255]

China's success in developing better seeds—and using them effectively—will greatly influence its agricultural prospects in the period ahead. In fact, the general progress China makes in basic agricultural sciences may prove to be the critical factor affecting their ability to solve their long-term food problems. No one input—whether water, fertilizers, or seeds—can provide the solution. In modern scientific agriculture, the mix of all these factors and the methods with which they are used in cultivation determine yields.

In modernizing its agriculture, China has one important advantage compared with most developing nations. With great organizational skill, the Communists have developed what may be the most widespread and effective institutional structure for agricultural extension services in any developing nation. At every level, down to commune subunits, extension personnel, agro-technical stations, and demonstration plots are used to educate peasants, test new methods, and solve local production problems.[256] Since the early 1960s this network of institutions has spread knowledge throughout China.

The problem that China now faces is to develop new knowledge, adapted to varied regional and local conditions. "Where in the early 1960s there was a considerable backlog of new technology waiting on government actions to supply the required inputs, there is no comparable backlog today," asserts one of the best analysts of China's agricultural economy; "new breakthroughs are required in the basic agricultural sciences in China."[257]

China still faces a serious problem because for roughly a decade, from the mid-1960s almost to mid-1970s, the Cultural Revolution had an extremely adverse effect on advanced research and training. Under attack from China's radicals who mounted a major assault on "elitism," many types of basic research came to a virtual halt, scientists were sent to the countryside, and training institutions and processes were disrupted.

A distinguished group of American agricultural scientists visiting China in 1974 came to the following conclusion:

> China has been remarkably successful in farm application of [its] accumulated knowledge. . . . However, if the nation is to continue to improve agricultural yields and production, a dynamic, production-oriented and much more sophisticated fundamental research effort will be required. . . . It appears that during the last several years little of the needed fundamental agricultural research has been done . . . much Chinese agricultural research is currently stagnant. . . . China must develop for each crop or major problem a critical mass of highly talented research people.[258]

Since the death of Mao, a major effort has been initiated to expand and upgrade research, including basic research, in all major scientific fields including agriculture.[259] It will take time, however, to create a new generation of competent agricultural scientists and to undertake the research needed to increase China's yields rapidly enough to meet China's needs.

Incentives

Another very important variable that will help to determine China's ability to solve its food problems will be the motivation of its peasants. Profound changes have occurred in the incentive structure affecting peasants since the Communist takeover. Before 1949 Chinese agriculture was based on private ownership of land, as it had been for two millennia. The desire to own land and to advance one's family's fortune through private effort provided a strong motivation for millions of China's peasants. Yet for millions of others who owned no land, incentives were minimal. Many paid huge land rents, were saddled with debt, suffered from price changes manipulated by others, and saw little prospect for escaping poverty.

After 1949 land reform and then collectivization changed the situation fundamentally. For many, the loss of ownership of their land weakened family-based traditional incentives. The incomes of individuals became linked to the performance of nonfamilial groups, and severe limits were imposed on how much anyone could advance personal or family fortunes.

However, some new kinds of incentives have been built into the collective system. The communes provide a degree of security that millions of peasants formerly lacked. A commune's success is important to its members, since the welfare of individuals and families depends not only on the workpoints each can earn but also on the overall success of their production teams (and brigades and communes). Communes also provide collective as well as individual benefits, including education and health facilities and other services. In addition, each peasant household can earn additional income from its small "private plots" (which families can use but do not own) and "sideline occupations" (handicrafts, for example), part of which can be sold at local "free markets."

However, although the incentive system built into China's collective system has been workable since the restoration of private plots and free markets in the early 1960s and the decentralization at that time of most farm management and income distribution decisions to the production teams, it clearly has not been optimal. China's peasants are still strongly motivated by a desire to advance their individual and family interests. One evidence of this is the care and investment they lavish on their private plots, often at the expense of collective activities. The small plots are in many respects the most productive tracts of land in China (partly because many are used mainly to produce vegetables and pigs but partly because peasants are strongly motivated to maximize their output), and they produce a disproportionate share of peasant families' incomes.[260] There has been an inevitable tension between collective and private interests. Radically inclined leaders in China almost always have favored increased collectivism and a cutback of private activities. However, more pragmatic leaders have insisted that at least minimal private incentives be retained, and in 1975 the right to farm private plots was written into the country's new constitution.[261]

Periodically, some Chinese leaders have favored increasing private incentives still further. This was true, for example, during China's agricultural crisis in the early 1960s. At that time there were some proposals —apparently approved by Teng Hsiao-ping who then, as now, was playing a large role in shaping policy—to return control of farm management to individual families, which would have amounted to virtual abandonment of collectivization; this occurred experimentally in limited areas.[262]

Perhaps the most dramatic recent change in agricultural policy, especially since the readjustment of 1979, has been the tremendous stress placed on the need to increase peasant incentives.[263] Chinese leaders have emphasized in an unprecedented way the importance of free markets and private plots and the need to give the small production teams greater decision-making authority. During 1979 a large-scale increase in private trade in agricultural products was observable. However, the economic costs of even small steps to raise peasant incomes are large, and competing demands on the country's limited resources restrict the amount of funds the regime can devote to raising incentives in agriculture. Even the significant increase in funds allocated to agriculture in 1979 were relatively small amounts when translated into per capita terms. Moreover, because the commune system has many advantages, most Chinese leaders probably will oppose steps that might weaken or undermine it. Nevertheless, there is likely to be further experimentation with the incentive structure to try to stimulate peasant productivity.

One of the principal means by which Peking can increase peasant incentives without fundamentally altering the commune system is to use tax and price policy to change the terms of trade between agricultural and industrial products, so as to give the rural population as a whole an increased share of total national output. Use of tax and price policy to do this is not new. Since the 1950s the government has tried gradually to improve peasants' terms of trade. It has kept the land tax fairly low, and the tax has declined as a proportion of agricultural production. In the 1950s it varied between 10 and 13 percent of farm output; now, according to some claims, it is only 5 or 6 percent.[264] The use of price policy has been an even more important instrument to redistribute income. One index of prices, with 1952 as a base (100), shows that by 1973 the index figure for prices of farm and sideline products had risen to more than 160, while the index of prices for all industrial goods sold in rural areas had risen much less (it was 114 in 1971), and the index for industrially produced means of production sold in rural areas had dropped by 1973 to perhaps 50.[265] According to one recent Chinese claim, between 1952 and 1977 the state's purchase prices for farm products increased by 68.8 percent, while the sale prices of chemical fertilizers, pesticides, and farm machinery dropped 48 percent.[266]

According to another, during the first twenty-nine years of the People's Republic "the purchase price of agricultural products" doubled, while "the retail price of industrial products" increased only 28 percent.[267] This shifted the rural-urban terms of trade to a degree; in fact, these price adjustments were the main explanation for the limited rise in per capita peasant incomes that occurred.

However, the urban-rural income gap has continued to be large, and the majority of communes and peasants have remained very poor, with only limited prospects for improvement in their living standards. The decision to make dramatic increases in state purchase prices for agricultural products in 1979 was one of the most important steps taken by the leadership in its economic "readjustment," and it clearly had an immediate impact on peasant incentives, helping to explain the good performance of agriculture during the year. The claimed 13.5 percent rise in "the average income of a peasant" in 1979 was quite impressive.[268] However, even with this increase, the average peasant's income (84 yuan) remained very low; it still was only 12 percent of the average wage of an urban worker (which rose over 9 percent in 1979 to 704 yuan).[269]

Because four-fifths of the population live in rural areas, the Chinese government has no alternative but to extract a great deal from the peasantry, whether directly or indirectly (for example, through the profits of state industries and commercial enterprises) to help finance the state's operations and the country's development. There are no easy ways to raise peasants' productivity rapidly, and the limits to Peking's ability to allocate resources to increasing peasant incomes are severe. Nevertheless, Chinese leaders will continue doing what they can to enhance peasants' incentives to encourage greater productivity, and the degree to which they succeed will be a major factor influencing future output.

Per Capita Demand

One of the greatest causes of uncertainty about China's ability to meet its food needs in the future is the difficulty of predicting trends in per capita food demand. As indicated earlier, while the Chinese have been able to assure a fairly adequate minimal diet to most of the population in recent years, they have done so by rationing basic staples strictly, and as a consequence there has been no significant improvement in the general level of food consumption during the past quarter century, despite the fact that per capita GNP has risen gradually.

In virtually all other countries, as per capita GNP has risen, average food consumption also has increased. This has been most dramatic in the industrialized countries; in Japan and the Soviet Union, for example, there have been large increases in per capita demand for grain in recent years, partly because of rapidly rising meat consumption and the growing need for feedgrain. Even in many developing countries, per capita demand for grain has grown substantially. According to USDA estimates, grain consumption in India, for example, increased between 1960–62 and 1969–71 by 3.4 percent a year (when the population growth rate was 2.6 percent), and in the same period in Indonesia the average annual rate of increase in grain consumption was 3.7 percent (compared with a population growth rate of 2.5 percent).[270] Neither of these countries has distributed food in the egalitarian way that China has, so variations in consumption within each country have been greater, with some of the population badly malnourished and some eating well; nevertheless, their overall food demand has risen steadily.

During most of the period since 1949 the leadership in China has held down consumption, concentrating its efforts on equitable distribution; it has not permitted increases in personal income to be used to improve food consumption to any significant degree. Per capita GNP is still low in China, but it has more than doubled in the last quarter century. While most of the increase has been reinvested in development, a portion has gone to increased consumption of goods and services; yet there has been little increase in consumption of basic food staples.

Over time, pressure for increased consumption has grown, and Peking's present policies, calling for an improvement in the national diet, including greater consumption of meat, are the leadership's response to pent-up pressures. The new policies, instead of eliminating the problem, however, may raise aspirations, increase demand, and result in additional pressure for an improved diet. Rises in both peasant and worker incomes will probably have this effect; so too will new urban growth, which is likely to increase again as the pace of industrialization in China picks up, even if continued efforts are made to restrict the flow of people to the cities. It is possible, also, that in the atmosphere now prevailing in China, the food control system could be loosened, and while the regime's success in rationing staples so strictly for more than two decades has been remarkable, it may not be able to continue doing so indefinitely.

While trying to improve living standards gradually, increase incentives, and spur productivity, the leadership doubtless will continue to try to keep consumer pressures under control. It may attempt to channel most increased spending into manufactured consumer goods—the output of which it is now expanding—and continue to limit increases in food consumption. Even if it tries to do this, however, some of the increases in consumers' incomes and demand will result in pressure for increases in food for consumption.

It is hard to see how China could experience a "meat revolution" comparable with that in countries such as the Soviet Union and Japan; probably the Chinese economy simply could not support such a development. But there clearly will be some increase in meat consumption, and this is likely to increase the country's need for feedgrain significantly.

In many developing countries, an increase of 1 percent in average per capita income has resulted in roughly an 0.8 percent increase in per capita demand for food.[271] If this had occurred in China in the period from the 1950s to the early 1970s, food demand would have grown by several percent a year. Such growth was inhibited for more than two decades by rationing of a kind that few other countries have been able to maintain except during wartime. It probably will be increasingly difficult to maintain rationing of this kind without modification.

Because China's population is so large, even small increases in per capita food consumption will increase the nation's food needs by millions of tons. If, for example, average per capita demand for grain (whether for direct consumption or for use as feed for animals) were to increase by even 1 percent a year, national grain requirements automatically would increase at close to half the average rate at which grain production actually increased between the 1950s and early 1970s. If there were a major explosion of food demand in China, the result could be a nightmare for the country's leaders. This may not occur, assuming that the regime's organizational controls remain reasonably effective, and the leadership will try to prevent it from happening. However, some increase in per capita food consumption is likely, and even a modest increase could widen the gap between domestic production and domestic supply of grain and increase China's need to import grain. In sum, trends in food demand could have as much and possibly more effect on China's future food balance than trends in population and production, and predicting future demand is in some respects more difficult than predicting output.

Reserves

Whatever the long-term trends in demand and supply of grain in China, there are certain to be significant fluctuations in production due to changes in the weather, which remains the most important single variable affecting year-to-year output in China as elsewhere. The tremendous ups and downs in the late 1950s and early 1960s were noted earlier. The fluctuations continue to be substantial, as table 3-5 indicates.

Because of such variations, China must maintain substantial reserves of grain to have any degree of real food security. Reserves have a long tradition in China, where the idea of maintaining an "ever-normal granary" originated centuries ago, and the present Chinese leadership clearly realizes the importance of reserves. In the early 1970s Mao made "store grain everywhere" one of the basic slogans of the regime, reserves being necessary to prepare for the danger of war as well as the risk of natural calamities.

Although the Chinese Communists always have maintained reserves, there are no reliable data on their stocks. However, fragmentary information provides clues to their size. Apparently, in a four-year period during China's first Five-Year Plan in the 1950s close to 2.5 million tons were allocated to reserves each year, totaling just under 10 million tons, which probably was close to 5 percent of total marketed grain during the period.[272]

The national agricultural plan formulated during 1956–57 proposed that the target for reserves should be an amount equal to one to two years' needs. Collectives were urged to store stocks equivalent to their needs for three to eighteen months. In 1957, also, two Chinese economists advocated building up national state stocks to a level of 35 million to 50 million tons. China may not have reached that level in the 1950s; one analyst has estimated that by the end of 1958 state reserves may have totaled 20 million to 25 million tons.[273]

Whatever the reserves were at that time, they almost certainly dropped to a very low level during the "three bad years" from 1959 through 1961. However, subsequently they were rebuilt, and in late 1970 Premier Chou En-lai stated that China's "state grain reserves" totaled 40 million tons.[274] Chinese officials now assert that some reserves are held at all levels, including the national, provincial, commune, brigade, team, and individual household levels, but they have given no fig-

TABLE 3-5. *China: Annual Changes in Grain Output and Population, 1965–78*

	Increase or decrease in grain output compared with previous year		
Year	Metric tons	Percentage change	Percentage population increase
1965	0	0.0	2.08
1966	21	10.8	2.12
1967	10	4.7	2.12
1968	−15	−6.7	2.17
1969	5	2.4	2.22
1970	28	13.0	2.22
1971	3	1.2	2.14
1972	−6	−2.4	1.99
1973	26	10.8	1.84
1974	9	3.4	1.70
1975	9	3.3	1.62
1976	1	0.4	1.68
1977	−2	0.7	1.83
1978	22	7.8	1.20

Sources: Data for 1965–76 were calculated from grain and population statistics in tables 3-1 and 3-2; 1977–78 data are from SSB Communiqué, FBIS, *Daily Report—PRC*, June 27, 1979, pp. L13, L20. The 1977 figure for percentage increase in population may be too high because the population estimate for 1976 (a U.S. government estimate) may be too low.

ures on their size.[275] However, a foreign scholar recently has estimated that China's food reserve may be just under 50 million tons.[276] The fluctuations of annual output doubtless affect their year-to-year size. Probably reserves were depleted during 1975–77 but then built up again during 1978–79.

There is no clear answer to the question of how large a grain reserve China "should have" to achieve food security. Rice does not store as well as wheat and coarse grains, so one would not expect reserves to be as large as they might be if wheat and coarse grains dominated China's food supply. If the Chinese were to maintain a one month supply (roughly the level of world reserves of grain in 1976, though many considered this to be a dangerously low level), it now would require between 20 million and 30 million tons. A two or three month supply now would require roughly between 55 million and 85 million tons.

If China had a reserve equivalent to a two or three month supply, it probably could meet its minimum needs in most poor years. It is by no means certain, however, that it can maintain such a level in the period immediately ahead. Nevertheless, it probably will feel under pressure to build up its reserves to the extent possible, in part by imports. In calculating China's future grain needs, therefore, its need to build or replenish reserves must be taken into account, although at present there is no way to determine exactly what the amounts required might be.

Prospects

So many factors will affect China's output and demand for grain and other foodstuffs that it is impossible to make accurate predictions about the future. The present leadership's recognition that raising agricultural output is China's "main problem" reflects a new realism, and the decision to increase investment in the rural sector was an important one. However, the limits on China's ability to shift resources to agriculture was highlighted by the fact that the 32 percent planned rise in state (central) agricultural capital construction during 1979 amounted, in monetary terms, to less than 1.4 billion yuan and raised agricultural investments in the central budget only to 5.6 billion yuan. Even the estimated 7.8 billion yuan total for all agricultural capital construction investment in 1979 amounted to less than 10 yuan per person of China's rural population.

Peking's strong commitment to carry out comprehensive agricultural modernization through the development and increased use of better seeds, fertilizers, and pesticides and improved water control and methods of cultivation is of immense long-term significance. However, while improvements in all of these areas can have important payoffs over time, none is likely to have miraculous immediate effects. The likelihood that the fertilizer–yield ratio will decline, necessitating use of larger quantities to achieve needed results, has been noted. A 1979 study of Chinese agriculture suggests that this may be symptomatic of a broader problem. In general, the study concluded, both "factor productivity" (that is, the amount of inputs of all sorts that must be used to achieve increases in output) and farm labor productivity (the value added per farm worker) have been stagnating or even declining rather than rising in China.[277] If this is correct, increasing output may be more expensive in the future.

The effort China is now making to train thousands of agricultural scientists and technicians and to improve their "system of agro-scientific research and agro-technical popularization" will be crucial to agricultural modernization in the long run. But this is not the kind of effort that is likely to produce quick, dramatic results. It will take years to develop skills, acquire new knowledge about sophisticated methods, and raise the technical level of the mass of ordinary peasants.

Peking's program for the steady spread of certain kinds of agricultural mechanization, which the Chinese themselves now recognize is no panacea and have wisely modified and slowed down, makes good sense, especially in terms of the long-term objective of increasing worker productivity. However, what the immediate effects on land yields will be is problematic. While in some places increased productivity should increase per hectare output, in others it could decrease land productivity in the short run.

Peking's decision to diversify agriculture and promote greater specialization clearly should, in time, result in increased efficiency and productivity, and it will increase the availability not only of meat, vegetables, and fruits but also of cash crops needed for industry and export. However, if significant amounts of land and other resources are shifted from grain production to other crops, the growth of grain output could be slowed. Peking hopes that state farms and "large commodity grain bases" will rapidly expand their output of grain, but whether they will fulfill the leadership's hopes remains to be seen.

The regime's unprecedented stress on improving the national diet and its commitment to increasing production of pork, poultry, and other meat dramatizes Peking's determination to try to raise living standards and provide better incentives for both the rural and urban population. However, this could escalate demand for grain. Even if animal husbandry is developed rapidly in frontier grasslands, there will be greater need for feedgrains to supply commercial pig and chicken farms, especially in suburban areas, and throughout the countryside peasants may use more feed. According to one estimate, the production of meat required 3.3 times as much land as the production of grain with equivalent food value[278] (although perhaps in China it may be somewhat lower). As urbanization progresses, as it probably will as industry grows, the demand for foods other than grain probably will rise significantly. A Japanese economist specializing in China has estimated that Chinese urbanites tend to eat two to three times as much meat as persons living in rural areas.[279]

In late 1978 Peking made the major decision to spur increased productivity, taking dramatic steps to improve peasant incentives by granting local groups more autonomy in production decisions, allowing market forces greater play, and above all raising state purchase prices for agricultural products. Peking's decision may have more immediate favorable effects on farm output than almost any other aspect of its new agricultural policies. However, it will be difficult to keep raising prices indefinitely, and the policy inevitably involves risks. Continuous price rises will feed inflationary pressures, and there is a danger that hopes and expectations for improved living standards may surpass what it is realistically possible to achieve.

In light of the basic facts of China's agricultural situation and the multiplicity of problems it faces, it would be extremely difficult for it to achieve an average annual rate of increase in grain output close to the 4.4 percent target, which was set in 1978 for the period through 1985, even though, because of the large rises in 1978–79, this would only require a 3.1 percent rise during 1980–85. In early 1980 some Chinese indicated that the regime already had adjusted this target. The head of Peking's Economic Research Institute, for example, reportedly stated that the 400 million ton output target originally set for 1985 had been pushed back to 1979 or 1980,[280] which implied that the regime now expected the average annual rate of growth during 1980–85 to be only around 2 percent or even less. This probably would be too pessimistic a projection.

What is plausible is that despite the fact that in some respects the problems of increasing grain output may grow in the period ahead, China's present realistic, pragmatic policies should be able to produce an average rate of increase in grain output of 2 to 3 percent, and if the new policies are extraordinarily successful the rate might be above 3 percent. However, it is also likely that demand for grain, for both indirect use (in meat) and direct consumption, will also increase at least as rapidly as grain production. If so, China's grain deficit is likely to rise.

A study made in 1979 by a leading Chinese-American specialist on China's agriculture attempted to estimate trends in both grain output and grain supply in China through the year 2000.[281] The author calculated high, low, and medium possibilities. In his medium estimate for the year 2000, which he regarded as most plausible, he projected China's grain output at 524 million tons, its grain demand at 538 million tons, and the resulting deficit at 14 million tons. If one accepts the official output figure of 332 million tons in 1979 as correct, an annual average rate of 2.2 percent in grain output would result in 524 million tons output in the year 2000. The author estimates that grain demand may increase at an average annual rate of 3.0 percent, which is lower than historical rates in areas such as Taiwan and Japan, and that the income elasticity of demand for grain might be 0.60, which, although higher than in China's past experience, would be below that in many developing nations.

No estimate of what China's food situation will be five, ten, or twenty years in the future can be more than an informed guess. However, the best guess is that while China's agriculture will be steadily modernized and grain output will continue to grow at a respectable rate, per capita demand also probably will rise, very possibly at a faster rate than production, and the increase in overall demand may well surpass that of domestic supply. If so, China's grain deficit will increase, and its grain import needs will also push upward in the years ahead.

China and World Food Trade

To understand China's present linkages with the world food system, it is necessary to examine briefly its overall trade in agricultural commodities, and then to analyze in detail its grain trade. Even though China is a continental-size nation with one of the smallest levels of per capita trade of any major nation, it nevertheless is an important trader in many agricultural commodities. This should not be surprising in view of the fact that it is the world's largest agricultural nation.

In 1969 China ranked fourteenth in the world as an exporter and nineteenth as an importer of agricultural products.[282] Its exports of agricultural goods were very diversified, but in about a dozen products it ranked among the world's five largest exporters and accounted for at least 5 percent of total world exports; these included rice (10 percent), pigs (27 percent), silk (34 percent), unshelled eggs (21 percent), and tung oil (36 percent). Its largest imports of farm products included wheat, rubber, cotton, and sugar; China accounted for 7 percent of world imports of wheat (and was the fifth largest wheat importer in the world), 8 percent of world imports of rubber, 2 percent of cotton, and 1 percent of sugar imports.[283]

Until recently most of China's foreign exchange earnings came from exports of farm products. In 1935–39 such products accounted for two-thirds of China's total exports.[284] The proportion dropped in the 1960s, but then it rose again, and in 1972 agricultural exports totaled $1.2 billion and constituted 51 percent of all Chinese exports.[285] In 1973 exports of nonagricultural products surpassed those of agricultural commodities, and this has remained the pattern ever since. However, in 1975 foreign sales of agricultural commodities, totaling close to $2.3 billion, still accounted for 41 percent of China's foreign exchange earnings.

Although agricultural imports have constituted a smaller percentage of China's total imports, they have been sizable nonetheless. In the second half of the 1950s they averaged about $200 million a year; in the 1960s the figure rose to more than $500 million annually;[286] and in the 1970s it has been considerably higher. Between 1972 and 1974, when world prices skyrocketed, agricultural imports rose sharply in value terms and constituted close to one-third of China's total imports. In 1972 they amounted to $633 million (30 percent); in 1973, $1.25 billion (32 percent); and in 1974, $1.64 billion (28 percent).[287] In 1975–76 they dropped temporarily, but since then they have risen again.

Even though imports of foodstuffs averaged about 18 percent of China's total imports during the period 1967–74,[288] China remained a net exporter of foodstuffs. In 1976, for example, it earned $1.95 billion from exports of food while spending only $560 million to import food—and therefore it had a net balance of almost $1.40 billion in food trade.

In 1977 its food exports totaled $2.03 billion, its imports of food $1.12 billion, and its net earnings in food trade $910 million.[289] This provides a basis for China's claim that it is self-sufficient in food. Yet in a fundamental sense, this claim is misleading. Most of China's main food exports (apart from rice, which will be discussed below), including live animals, meat, eggs, tea, fruits, and vegetables (much of which goes to Hong Kong) are not staples, while the bulk of its food imports consists of what is the most basic of all staples for a poor country, grain.

Grain Imports

In the immediate pre-Communist years, China normally was a net importer of grain. During 1935–39 it imported, on an average, 1.03 million tons of grain a year (generally including more than half a million tons of rice and close to 400,000 tons of wheat and flour).[290] Then after 1949 its situation appeared to change remarkably, and it became a net grain exporter for the first time in the modern period. From 1950 through 1960 China's imports of grain exceeded 150,000 tons only in one year, while its rice exports steadily rose from 20,000 tons in 1950 to a peak of about 1.6 million tons in 1959 before dropping to 712,000 tons in 1969 and averaging over 400,000 tons a year during the second half of the decade.[291]

This favorable situation lasted for a decade, but then it changed fun-

TABLE 3-6. *China: Grain Trade, 1961–79*

Millions of metric tons

Year	Imports of grain (1)	Exports of rice (2)	Grain imports minus rice exports (3)	Grain imports minus all grain exports (4)
1961	5.601	0.444	5.157	5.033
1962	5.122	0.578	4.544	4.544
1963	5.617	0.640	4.977	4.755
1964	6.294	0.784	5.510	5.221
1965	6.024	0.753	5.271	5.007
1966	5.814	1.264	4.550	4.311
1967	4.354	1.198	3.156	3.042
1968	4.393	0.967	3.426	3.357
1969	3.939	0.811	3.128	3.108
1970	4.963	0.986	3.977	3.930
1971	3.128	0.924	2.204	2.092
1972	4.642	0.899	3.743	3.597
1973	7.642	2.142	5.500	5.432
1974	6.790	1.985	4.805	4.652
1975	3.459	1.440	2.019	1.813
1976	2.061	0.900	1.161	0.993
1977	6.937	0.800	6.137	6.100
1978	9.437	1.200	8.237	n.a.
1979	10.933	1.00	9.933	n.a.

Sources: For 1961–70, all figures are from Frederick M. Surls, "China's Grain Trade," in JEC, *Chinese Economy Post-Mao*, p. 655. For 1971–79, figures on grain imports and rice exports are from CIA, *China: International Trade Quarterly Review, Fourth Quarter 1979*, Research Paper ER CIT 80-003, May 1980, p. 32. Column 3 figures are my calculations. Column 4 figures are from Surls, "China's Grain Trade," p. 655. The difference between column 4 and column 3 is due to Chinese exports of coarse grain, usually between 100,000 and 200,000 tons a year. Figures are rounded.
    n.a. Not available.

damentally in 1960 as a result of the post-Great Leap crisis in China. Ever since then, China has been a sizable net importer of grain, and during 1977–79 imports reached unprecedented levels.

Chinese grain imports since 1960 are shown in table 3-6. During 1961–66 China imported an average of 5.75 million tons of grain (mostly wheat) a year. The average dropped somewhat during 1967–72 to 4.24 million tons a year, and it appeared as if China's reliance on imports might decline or even end. However, during 1973–74 grain imports rose again sharply, averaging around 7 million tons a year. In the next two years they dropped sharply, to about 3.5 million tons in 1975 and 2 million tons in 1976. Since then, however, they have soared, rising to new highs, almost 7 million tons in 1977, 9.44 million tons in 1978, and 10.99 million tons in 1979.[292] In the nineteen years starting with 1961, when China began sizable foreign purchases of grain, through 1979, these imports totaled more than 107 million tons—an average of 5.64 million tons a year (and, as will be indicated below, *net* grain imports averaged more than 4 million tons and probably close to 4.5 million tons a year).

The cost of imported grain has also risen greatly since the start of the 1970s. Whereas the value of China's grain imports was only $280 million in 1970, it rose to $1.180 billion in 1974 (16 percent of the cost of China's total imports), and in 1975 it amounted to almost $680 million (9.3 percent of imports).[293] In the following four years, the figures rose from $300 million in 1976, to $655 million in 1977, to $960 million in 1978, and to $1.370 billion in 1979, when again they were 9.3 percent of total imports.[294] The average annual cost since the late 1960s has been well over $500 million and in the three years since Peking has adopted new economic policies it has averaged roughly $1 billion a year.

If one considers fertilizer imports to be, in one sense, a substitute for grain imports, the figures obviously would be higher. In the ten-year period 1968–77, China's fertilizer imports (excluding phosphate rock) averaged 3.72 million tons a year in bulk form—or, converted crudely at five to one, close to 0.75 million tons of nutrients—and they cost a total of $2.51 billion, or an average of $250 million a year.[295] Assuming that one ton of fertilizer nutrients may be equal to roughly eight tons of grain, annual average fertilizer imports were the equivalent of about 6 million tons of grain. If fertilizer imports are added as "grain equivalent" to actual grain imports, China in the decade 1967–76 imported the equivalent of more than 11 million tons of grain annually at an average annual cost of more than $750 million.[296] These figures have continued to rise. By 1979, China's imports of 1.720 million tons of fertilizer cost $480 million.[297] When the same eight to one formula is used for calculating the grain equivalent of fertilizer, and this is added to grain imports, in 1979 China imported the equivalent of almost 25 million tons of grain at a cost of close to $2 billion.

Grain Exports

Until recently the Chinese have underplayed their need for foreign grain, explaining that their grain trade is simply an economically rational exchange of high-priced Chinese rice for lower-priced foreign wheat. It is true that China has become a significant rice exporter as well as a wheat importer. In the late 1930s China's net imports of rice were sizable (averaging close to 700,000 tons a year during 1934–38). However, in the 1950s it became a net exporter, selling sizable amounts from 1955 on.[298] Calculated for five-year periods, China's rice exports averaged almost 180,000 tons (of milled rice) a year during 1950–54, close to 1 million tons a year during 1955–59 (the peak was 1.57 million tons in 1959), roughly 725,000 a year during 1960–64 (the peak was about 1.17 million in 1960), and a little under 1 million tons during 1965–69 (the peak was over 1.2 million in 1966). During 1971–79 they averaged over 1.250 million tons a year, with a high of 2.142 million tons in 1973 and a low of 800,000 tons in 1977. The average during the most recent three-year period, 1977–79, has dropped somewhat, to 1 million tons a year.

Net Grain Trade

The Chinese are correct when they point out that they have been selling rice at fairly high prices and buying wheat at considerably lower prices. But their grain trade has not been merely an exchange of rice for wheat. Ever since 1961 the Chinese have been a large *net* importer of grain.[299] Their rice exports have paid for only a part of the costs of their grain imports, and they have had to expend a great deal of scarce foreign exchange to obtain needed wheat. Recently they also have been importing sizable amounts of corn.[300]

During the first half of the 1960s (1961–65), China's *net* annual imports of grain averaged almost 5 million tons a year. During 1966–70 it dropped to just over 3.5 million tons a year. During 1971–76 it was erratic, dropping to about 2.1 million tons in 1971, rising to almost 5.5 million tons in 1973, then dropping to under 1.0 million tons (the lowest in a decade and a half) in 1976. After that, however, China's *net* grain imports steadily rose, to over 6.0 million tons in 1977, over 8.0 million in 1978, and close to 10 million in 1979. From 1961 through 1979 China's net imports of grain averaged close to 4.5 million tons a year, and now are more than double that.

In dollar terms, the net cost of China's grain trade (the costs of imports minus receipts from exports)[301] averaged $270 million a year during the period 1961–69, dropped to $170 million in 1971, then rose to $465 million in 1974. In 1975, for the first time since 1961, China actually made a small net profit from its grain trade because it temporarily cut wheat imports drastically and profited from soaring rice prices. But this situation was short-lived. China is again paying much more for its grain imports than it receives from its rice exports. By 1978 what it paid for grain imports ($960 million) was more than half a billion dollars more than it earned from grain exports ($360 million), and in 1979 the $1.370 billion it paid for grain imports probably was close to $1 billion more than it earned from rice exports. The cost of grain imports creates a serious problem because it uses up foreign exchange that otherwise could be used to pay for imports of plants, machinery, and raw materials for its industrial development program.

Not long ago some analysts were predicting that China might become a net grain exporter by 1980.[302] It now seems highly likely, however, that China's grain imports will continue to rise. In late 1978 Vice Premier Li Hsien-nien (Li Xiannian) stated that China would import "something over 10 million tons of foreign grain per year," 5 million to 6 million of which would be purchased annually from the United States during the next few years.[303] During 1978 and early 1979 it signed new three-year agreements with Canada, Australia, and Argentina that called for annual grain imports from these countries totaling 5 million to 6 million tons a year.[304] In early 1979 USDA officials estimated that China's grain imports would soon rise to more than 12 million tons.[305] Probably in the years immediately ahead, Chinese grain imports will average somewhere between 10 million and 15 million tons. Predicting longer-run trends is more difficult. But it is certainly possible that as per capita demand for food in China rises, imports could rise further, perhaps to a level of 15 million to 20 million tons. (Sino-American grain trade is discussed in part V.)

The Importance of Grain Trade to China

At first glance, China's total grain imports, even in recent years, seem relatively small in relation to its population's total needs. From the mid-1960s to the mid-1970s total grain imports amounted to between 2 and 3 percent of China's domestic production.[306] In 1979 the figure was just a little over 3 percent. However, the importance of imported grain becomes clear when compared with the amount of grain actually marketed within China. Unlike more developed nations, China does not have a highly commercialized agricultural economy. Most grain in the country stays in the communes where most Chinese live. A large percentage of the grain that does leave rural areas does not move very far; only a small amount crosses provincial boundaries.

From the government's point of view, however, the grain that does move—that is, "commercial grain" (which the Chinese sometimes call "commodity grain")—is extremely important. Collected by the state through a land tax in kind and a system of "planned purchase and supply" (involving compulsory sales at government-set prices), this grain is required to feed China's urban population and military forces; to make up deficits in backward areas, calamity-stricken localities, and regions producing industrial crops; and to meet industrial and export needs.

Until recently statistics on commercial "commodity" grain were as scarce as those on most other aspects of Chinese agriculture, but it was possible to make plausible estimates of the amounts involved. In the 1930s perhaps 25 to 30 percent of China's total grain output entered the market (at that time through private commercial sales, the land tax, and rent in kind to landlords),[307] and it has been estimated that in 1952 about 28 percent[308] and in the mid-1950s somewhere between 23 and 34 percent[309] of grain output was collected (through the land tax and compulsory sales); in volume commercial grain probably totals somewhere between 40 million and 60 million tons, perhaps close to 50 million tons, or just about 30 percent of total output. The figure doubtless dropped in the early 1960s, but rose again thereafter. Now it reportedly varies from just under to just over 50 million tons. According to official Chinese figures, state taxes and purchases collected about 48 million tons of grain in 1978 and over 52 million tons in 1979,[310] or less than 16 percent of output. As noted earlier, the Chinese are now determined to increase the amount of marketable grain greatly, but it will not be easy to do.

The significance of grain imports is obvious when these facts are taken into account. Measured as a percentage of "commodity" grain in China, imports in the 1960s and much of the 1970s may have totaled at least 5 to 10 percent, and perhaps more, of total grain collected by the state. In 1979, grain imports were more than 20 percent of the grain procured domestically by the state, and during 1977–79 wheat imports amounted to one-seventh of domestic production in the country.[311]

If the regime imported less grain, it could, of course, try to meet its needs by extracting more from China's peasants. Or it could reduce rations, either nationally or in certain localities. But doing either would be risky, politically as well as economically. Popular resistance might well make such moves impossible.[312] In any case, official policy is now moving in the opposite direction, toward increasing peasant incentives and raising living standards.

When grain imports are compared with the amount of grain that moves across provincial boundaries, their importance looms even larger. Interprovincial transfers in China appear—from the fragmentary data available—to be surprisingly small, not just because of transportation difficulties but also because of provincial resistance to large-scale grain requisitions. One Chinese source published in the late 1950s stated that in the "last few years" more than 5 million tons of grain had moved between provinces each year, probably most of it originating in Heilungkiang, Kirin (Jilin), and Szechwan (Sichuan).[313] Another estimate placed the figure at 8.7 million tons in 1955–56, with Szechwan providing the largest supplies, Hunan (Hunan) and Kiangsi (Jiangxi) next, followed by Hupeh (Hubei) and Kirin.[314] Perhaps the amount is larger now, but not necessarily, since until recently the regime has encouraged local grain self-sufficiency. If one assumes that annual interprovincial transfers in recent years may have been between 5 million and 10 million tons, China's annual imports of grain may in some years have been roughly equal to internal transfers.

Finally, China's grain imports are of special importance in relation to the problem of supplying its larger cities, especially its three leading cities, Peking, Shanghai, and Tientsin (Tianjin), all of which have provincial status administratively and are of particular importance politically. Feeding these cities poses large problems. Although their suburbs and adjacent areas supply some of their needs, much of the grain they require comes from imports. According to one rough estimate, by the late 1960s these three cities alone needed as much as 3 million to 3.5 million tons a year of grain from abroad.[315] Imports now probably provide a large share of the grain needed to feed these metropolitan centers.[316]

As all of these figures show, China's imports are of far greater importance to the regime and the country than one might conclude from the fact that they amount to only about 3 percent of national production. Without imports, China would have to try to reduce consumption by about 3 percent, and its leaders would face serious problems if they tried to do this. Or they would have to increase extractions from the peasantry and expand transfers to supply major cities and other deficit areas, which could have an extremely adverse effect on their entire economic program. They probably would not try to do it unless there was no alternative.

The Importance of China's Grain Trade to the World

Although China's grain trade is more important to it than to its trading partners, in a global perspective it is clear that China's trade is very important to the world food system in terms of both supply and demand.

World trade in rice is relatively small compared with trade in wheat and coarse grains, and China's exports constitute a surprisingly large percentage of total world rice exports. In the period 1975–78, for example, Chinese exports averaged 10 percent (and varied between 6 and 19 percent) of all rice exports in the world.[317] During 1979–80 the figure was between 9 and 10 percent.[318] In recent years China has usually been the third largest rice exporter in the world, after the United States and Thailand (though in some years Pakistan and Burma have exceeded China's level). Over the past quarter century Chinese rice exports have been important to a variety of countries and areas, especially Hong Kong, Sri Lanka, Vietnam, and Indonesia.

From the point of view of those concerned with the dependability and price stability of wheat supplies in the world food system, China's imports also are very important. During the grain years 1977/78 through 1979/80, China's imports accounted for 10 percent of total world wheat imports; in 1977/78 and 1978/79, its wheat imports exceeded those of any other nation.[319]

Three large countries have contributed most to the uncertainty—and the fluctuations—that have characterized world grain trade in recent years. By far the most important has been the Soviet Union, whose purchases have fluctuated most unpredictably. The impact of India and China on the world market has been considerably less; nevertheless they too have made large grain purchases that have been difficult to predict. It has been widely recognized that until recently India has posed special problems for the global food system, but less attention has been devoted to China. This is in part because China has been able to pay for its grain needs, while India, in many years, has needed sizable amounts of food aid; but both have imposed large demands on the available world supplies.

During the entire period 1965/66 through 1977/78 China purchased *more* wheat and coarse grains on the world market than India did. In those twelve years India purchased an annual average of 4.63 million tons, compared with China's 5.12 million tons.[320] In the 1960s, during 1965/66 through 1967/68, India bought more—around 8 million to 9 million tons, compared with China's 5 million or 6 million tons. From 1969/70 through 1974/75, however, China usually bought considerably more each year than India did. During 1975/76 and 1976/77 India again purchased roughly double what China bought but then in the 1977/78 grain year

India became a net exporter. (An unusual series of three good monsoons helped it build up stocks sufficient to meet shortfalls for several years.) Since 1977–78 China's wheat imports have been significantly larger than India's were even at their peak levels in the mid-1960s.

Today, therefore, it is essential to take China fully into account in any international programs designed to stabilize world food supplies and prices and increase global food security. The necessity to do so, moreover, will increase greatly if Chinese imports rise to the level of 15 million to 20 million tons a year, which, as indicated earlier, is at least within the realm of possibility.

China's Interests, Needs, Attitudes, and Policies

Objectively speaking, China's interests are now directly linked to the world food system in important ways. Because grain imports are vitally important to it, it needs dependable access to sources of grain supply, mainly from the United States, Canada, and Australia. During 1978–1979, 37 percent of China's grain imports came from the United States, 30 percent from Canada, 26 percent from Australia, and 6 percent from Argentina.[321] Denial of any of these sources would have serious consequences for China; whatever increases the dependability of its access to them serves Chinese interests.

Greater stability of world grain prices also would serve China's interests. The sudden rise in the price of wheat—and fertilizers—starting in 1973 put a serious burden on its foreign exchange resources. However, the Chinese are ambivalent about grain prices. They are partially protected from the impact of rising wheat prices because they export rice; generally rice prices have risen at the same time as wheat prices, sometimes even more rapidly. Yet for China, as for other countries, unpredictable price fluctuations create great uncertainties and make planning difficult. Moreover, what it earns from its rice exports now falls far short of covering the costs of its wheat imports. The Chinese can be seriously hurt, therefore, by sharp rises in wheat prices. A world food reserve system that helped to stabilize prices unquestionably would benefit the Chinese as well as others.

There are other important interests that now link China to the world system. Like other nations, it needs as much information as possible in order to plan sensibly. To cope with changes in the weather it needs all the meteorological information it can get. Information about the Eurasian land mass (especially the Soviet Union), where most of North China's weather originates, and the Pacific, where the monsoons and typhoons affecting South China originate, is most important to it. Today, obtaining such information requires close links with the worldwide meteorological network.

China also needs, for planning purposes, all the market information it can get. To follow developments that could affect world supplies and prices, China needs data on crop conditions elsewhere—and on government policies that may affect output—especially in the principal exporting nations (most of all, those in North America) but also in the largest importing countries (such as the Soviet Union).

Access to reasonably priced world supplies of many other agricultural commodities, including cotton, soybeans, and rubber, as well as to numerous agriculture-related products, such as fertilizers, agricultural machinery, and plants producing inputs to agriculture, also is very important to China. The availability of these products directly affects China's agricultural situation.

Finally, China needs scientific and technical knowledge from the international community, especially from the most highly developed countries, to upgrade its agricultural sciences. Its need for the best available technical knowledge about new seeds, fertilizers, pesticides, ways of combating plant diseases, and cultivation methods is urgent. Even though not all techniques developed elsewhere are usable in China, importing knowledge is essential for the rapid modernization of Chinese agriculture.

China's objective needs long have argued in favor of its active participation in cooperative international efforts to solve world food problems. However, in this field as in others, Chinese leaders criticized most major proposals for international cooperation throughout the 1960s and the first half of the 1970s. Viewing world food problems in the context of struggle between the developing and developed nations, they denounced the "exploitation" of the poor by the rich and urged all developing nations to strive for food self-sufficiency and an end to dependence on the advanced countries.

In many respects, China's stress on self-reliance made sense. Increased food production in all developing countries clearly is needed to solve global food problems. Yet the Chinese were reluctant to acknowledge that, in the years immediately ahead, most countries will not be able to avoid relying on a few advanced countries for essential grain supplies and for new knowledge needed to increase their own food output. An unavoidable interdependence exists in the world food system, and unpredictable fluctuations in grain supplies and prices have adverse effects on both the developed and developing nations.

China's views on world food problems at that time were articulated in a speech made by Hao Chung-shih [Hao Zhongshi], Vice Minister of Agriculture and Forestry, at the United Nations World Food Conference in Rome on November 7, 1974.[322] He defined the issues essentially in terms of North-South struggle.

The current world food problem is mainly an urgent problem of numerous developing countries. On the food problem, there has always been an acute struggle between colonialism, imperialism, and particularly the superpowers, which practice plunder and control, and the developing countries which fight against their plunder and control. This is an extremely important aspect of the present struggle . . . to smash the old international economic order and establish a new one. . . .

Hao blamed politics more than economics for the food problems in developing countries:

At present, many developing countries are short of food grains. . . . Some people attribute this primarily to bad weather and natural disasters. Others attribute it primarily to the rising prices of fertilizers and so on and so forth. But all of these are only superficial, partial and temporary factors, and do not constitute the fundamental cause. Historical facts and present-day life fully prove that the food problem confronting developing countries is mainly the result of plunder and control by colonialism, imperialism, and the superpowers [which] forced on them a lopsided single-product economy and the exchange of unequal values and extorted superprofits from them. . . . Since World War II, one of the superpowers has been dumping large quantities of its "surplus" food into the developing countries. This has seriously damaged the food production and exports of [these countries], forcing more and more countries to live on food imports. . . .

He also denied that population growth was a key aspect of the problem:

. . . the superpowers still pick up the long-discredited Malthusian theory of population and assert that the developing countries' "food shortage is the result of over-population.". . . This fallacy . . . is surely being spread with ulterior motives. . . .

His primary prescriptions were self-reliance and cooperation among the developing countries:

The developing countries have great potentials for developing agriculture and increasing food production. So long as a country works unremittingly in the light of its own specific features and conditions and advances along the road of independence and self-reliance, it is fully capable of solving its food problem. . . . Of course, self-reliance by no means implies self-seclusion or refusal of foreign aid. We have always held that, on the basis of mutual benefit and exchange of goods, all countries can acquire the food they need through trade and make up for one another's economic and technological deficiencies so as to develop their national economy and food production. Economic cooperation and mutual aid among the developing countries, in particular, have broad prospects and are of lasting significance.

In describing China's food policies, he in effect held them up as a model for others:

China is a developing socialist country. From our experience we have become keenly aware of the importance of developing agricultural production and solving the food problem. . . . In agricultural production, we act on the principle of taking grain as the key link and ensuring all-round development, i.e., make a rational arrangement of grain crops and economic crops as well as forestry, animal husbandry, sideline occupations and fishery, so as to meet the multiple needs of national construction and the people's livelihood. . . . Throughout the countryside we have launched the mass movement of "in agriculture, learn from Tachai.". . . We are earnestly carrying out the "Eight-Point Charter for Agriculture": soil improvement, use of fertilizer, irrigation, better seed strains, close planting, plant protection, better farm implements and field management, adopting scientific agriculture in a big way, and are engaged in farmland and irrigation building far and wide, thus wresting good harvests for years running. Now the basic food situation in China is that the state, the collective and the commune members all have some grain reserves. The living standard of the Chinese people is not yet high. A further rise in our standard of living calls for the continued efforts of our entire people. However, we have ensured the supply of the basic means of subsistence, stable food prices and adequate food for everyone.

Discussing China's grain trade, he underplayed its importance:

China has also imported some foodgrains from the world market, but China does not rely on imports for feeding her population. The main purpose of our imports is to change some food varieties. In about three years from 1972 up to now we have imported over two billion U.S. dollars' worth of grain, mainly wheat. In the same period, we have exported grain, mainly rice, valued at the same amount. Therefore, China's food imports and exports in the past three years strike a rough balance in value. . . . Our rice exports are largely for supply and aid to Third World countries . . . the price of rice would further rise, causing even greater difficulties to many rice consumer countries if China should stop exporting rice. . . . Our contribution to solving the world food problem is yet very small. It is our hope that . . . we shall be able gradually to change this state of affairs.

Finally, Hao spelled out principles that he said should govern any approach to solving world food problems:

We hold that the developing countries, in order to solve their food problem, must adhere to the principle of independence and self-reliance . . . gradually changing the situation of relying on imported foodgrains. . . .

We hold that deep sympathy and concern should be given to those developing countries in acute food difficulties, and that it is necessary to render them timely and effective aid in all forms. The developed countries should shoulder the main responsibility in this regard. The developing nations can support and aid one another on a voluntary basis. . . .

We support the reasonable demand of the developing countries for the transfer of agricultural technology from developed countries. . . .

We hold that international trade should be based on the principles of equality, mutual benefit and the exchange of needed goods. We support the demand of the developing countries for food imports at fair and reasonable prices. We support their reasonable demand for improved trade terms. . . .

. . . . We support the full right of the developing countries . . . to take part in all decision-making on food. . . .

Hao's speech was a prime example of the ideological component that until recently dominated Chinese thinking and rhetoric regarding world food problems. Yet in their actual policies, even before the post-Mao policy changes, the Chinese generally were fairly pragmatic, and economic considerations usually took precedence over political objectives in their food policies. However, their approach was essentially national and unilateral, and they resisted efforts to involve China more extensively in international cooperation or multilateral action.

The Chinese attempted to assure their access to needed grain, first of all by developing good relations with the main grain exporting nations, especially Canada and Australia. Although there is no evidence that food was a significant factor influencing China's decision in the early 1970s to reopen contacts with the United States, once ties were established, the United States became an important alternative source of grain supply, and eventually food became a key element in the new Sino-American relationship.

The Chinese did not simply rely on year-to-year negotiations to assure access to grain; in the early 1970s they decided to sign medium-term agreements with major suppliers. In late 1973 they signed three-year agreements with Canada, Australia, and Argentina which committed China to buy (and the three countries to supply) specified quantities of grain between then and the end of 1976.[323] When these initial agreements expired, new ones were signed with Canada and Australia,[324] and then in 1979 new ones were concluded with all three countries.[325] Finally, in 1980—as noted in part V—China also signed a major grain agreement with the United States.

However, China, like all countries, has remained vulnerable to world price fluctuations that it cannot control. Within the limits of its capabilities, it has attempted to adjust its import and export plans to take advantage of price changes. In 1973, for example, when its wheat imports reached record levels, it also raised its rice exports to a peak level—almost 2 million tons, which was more than double the level of previous years—because of the unusually high price of rice in the world market. However, its ability to adjust its sales and purchases in response to price trends is limited; both its vital domestic need for adequate grain supplies and foreign exchange limitations have restricted its flexibility. In 1974, despite continued high rice prices on the world market, it was compelled to cut back rice exports to under a million tons. During 1972–74 it was compelled to buy record quantities of wheat at peak prices. Thereafter, although it would have benefited from building up its stocks at lower prices, because of foreign exchange shortages it cut back wheat imports during 1975/76 to the lowest level in a decade and a half.

The Chinese also have paid a price, as have others, for inadequate two-way flows of information. In varied ways, it is true, they have been able to obtain a good deal of information about world market conditions and the factors affecting world supplies and prices, since data on the crop prospects and agricultural policies in the major exporting countries are available in published sources; also, the steady improvement in China's commercial representation abroad has increased the Chinese capability to collect needed information. However, until recently they did not obtain the kind of information that can come only from close cooperative ties, and they remained unwilling to provide complete statistical information about Chinese agricultural conditions, even to UN agencies to which they belong, despite the fact that they themselves would clearly benefit from increased sharing of information about world conditions and trends.

Very soon after Mao's death, however, there began to be signs of change in Chinese attitudes and policies in this as in other fields. During 1978–79, as Peking shifted to highly pragmatic outward-looking policies, most of the old rhetoric about world food problems was abandoned, and gradually the Chinese started to expand their international contacts relating to agriculture and, step-by-step, increased their involvement in some cooperative programs.

One of their first steps was to agree to participate fully in the world-wide weather information network. Gradually over the years, they had developed links with the World Meteorological Organization's (WMO) reporting system, but until recently they provided less than complete information about China's weather. In the fall of 1977, however, they signed a meteorological cooperation agreement with the Japanese that called for rapid and full weather reporting to be fed into WMO's world-wide weather-watch through a regional center in Japan.[326]

From 1977 on, China also rapidly expanded scientific exchanges with foreign countries in the agricultural field. For almost a decade during and immediately after the Cultural Revolution, China's contacts with the international scientific community in this as in other fields had been reduced to a bare minimum. The adverse impact on research and training in China was serious, and in certain respects basic agricultural sciences in China had stagnated. The Chinese decided to try to catch up as quickly as possible. During 1976–77 they hosted almost fifty foreign agricultural delegations and sent about twenty abroad.[327] Many of these led to on-going exchanges; for example, the Chinese began exchanging germ plasm (seeds) with a number of countries—a move that is of great importance to the development of basic agricultural sciences.

The semiofficial (so-called facilitated) exchanges between China and the United States relating to agriculture during 1978 showed the range of Chinese interests as they broadened their international contacts. Delegations sent to the United States included ones focusing on insect control, plant photosynthesis, agricultural mechanization, fruit growing, animal feeding, and fertilizer development; and the Chinese invited American delegations of specialists concerned with plant studies, water conservation, insect control, rural small-scale industry, and the growing of fruit, wheat, and vegetables.[328] A large number of FAO-sponsored visitors have also gone to China.[329]

In 1979 the Chinese initiated exchange programs with the U.S. Department of Agriculture. Plans for 1980 called for broadening and deepening these exchange relationships. Delegations scheduled to visit the United States during the year included ones specializing in agricultural education, cotton germ plasm, biological pest control, agricultural economics and statistics, tractor testing, soil tillage equipment, forestry management, grain storage and handling, soil and water management, medicinal plants, and agricultural research in cotton, peanuts, soybeans, and animal parasitology.[330] An even larger number of American delegations, also extremely varied, were scheduled to visit China. These U.S.-China exchanges were only a part of China's broadening international cooperation in agriculture.

The Chinese also rapidly developed important relationships with a number of world-renowned agricultural specialists and research institutions, such as Norman Borlaug and the International Maize and Wheat Improvement Center in Mexico, and they became active participants in organizations such as the International Rice Research Institute in the Philippines.[331]

In 1973 China joined—or, as it put it, "resumed" membership in—the FAO and ever since then it has participated in the international and regional meetings held under its aegis, including the World Food Conference in 1974.[332] In addition to attending the biennial meetings of the FAO conference (from 1973 on, the chief Chinese delegate was one of its three vice chairmen), starting in 1973 China's representative was one of the forty-two members of FAO's executive council, and its assessed contribution has amounted to a sizable 7.01 percent of the organization's budget. During the Maoist period, however, China argued that FAO should keep its budget low and reduce activities not directly related to the task of helping Third World countries. The Chinese decided not to maintain a permanent, separate mission at FAO (relying instead on their embassy personnel in Rome to provide liaison), and as of early 1977 there were no Chinese on the FAO secretariat's staff. China played a relatively inactive role in FAO, therefore; its "operational behavior" was described by one observer as "passive and self-consciously devoid of political controversy," and it acted "more like an observer than an active member."[333] Now, however, this is changing, and for the first time the Chinese seem likely to consider much more active involvement in many cooperative international activities relating to world food.

The International Community and China

Because of its size and growing linkages with the world food system, the policies China pursues and the success or failure of its efforts inevitably will have a significant impact on the international community. What basic attitudes should underlie the approach of other nations in dealing with China in regard to food problems? Broadly speaking, the rest of the world not only should applaud Chinese efforts to solve their agricultural problems but also should develop effective programs to assist them. To the extent that China can feed its own population, it will make an important contribution to achieving a global balance between food and population. In general, the international community should encourage the Chinese to be as self-supporting as possible, since the more China can approach self-sufficiency, the less likely it is to impose an increasing burden on the world food system.

However, the international community should recognize several facts: China is and will continue to be dependent on the global food system in many ways; its future grain trade will have significant effects on world supplies and prices; and unpredictable fluctuations in its purchases will complicate international problems. Because of these facts, it should be recognized that greater Chinese involvement in cooperative international programs that help to solve world food problems will be highly desirable, and in some cases Chinese involvement may be essential for effective international action.

From the perspective of other nations, it is important for planning purposes to obtain more complete and up-to-date information than is yet available on China's general agricultural policies and performance, on its crop prospects at any particular time, on the weather conditions likely to affect its agricultural output, and on the domestic reserve stocks it has to draw upon if it suffers shortfalls. Planners determining policies elsewhere also need to obtain advance information about China's plans for buying wheat—and selling rice—on the world market.

Those of all nationalities concerned with agricultural development, especially in the developing nations, need to have a greater understanding of Chinese agricultural policies. This is necessary to judge which Chinese experiences and policies might be relevant and possibly transferable to other areas (examples of potentially important areas in this respect are their experience in regard to small-scale rural industries serving agriculture, their extensive use of organic fertilizer, their labor-intensive intercropping, and their innovative agricultural extension services). Even experts in the advanced countries, where agricultural science is far ahead of China's, would benefit from increased contacts with China (to exchange germ plasm, for example); although in most respects they have more to teach the Chinese than to learn from them, they could profitably study China's labor-intensive methods. Private international organizations dealing with agriculture and food problems also would unquestionably benefit from more active Chinese participation in their research activities.

Finally, a continuing effort should be made to encourage the Chinese to become full and active participants in all international programs concerned with world food problems, under the United Nations, the World Bank, and related organizations, and in all important intergovernmental forums dealing with food problems, such as the World Wheat Council.

The structure of international organizations that has been developed to deal with world food problems in recent years is extensive. Some organizations were established in the 1950s and 1960s under the FAO (which itself was set up in 1945 as the first permanent specialized agency under the United Nations). Many have been organized recently, in the wake of the food crisis of the early 1970s and following the World Food Conference of 1974, which gave added impetus to international cooperation in this field.[334] The World Food Conference adopted a resolution calling for the eradication of world hunger by 1985, and it discussed a wide variety of problems relating to food production in the developing countries, improvement of nutrition, and food aid, and it proposed creation of an international system of food reserves. Several new international organizations were proposed to deal with these problems.

Today there are several important international organizations or groups dealing with world food problems—apart from FAO. The World Food Council, established by the UN General Assembly in 1975 (with representatives from thirty-six countries), is responsible for monitoring the global situation and major UN programs in the food field. The International Fund for Agricultural Development (IFAD), financed by voluntary contributions from the OECD and the Organization of Petroleum Exporting Countries (OPEC) members (with an initial capitalization target of more than $1 billion), is designed to provide aid to increase output in the poor countries. The Consultative Group on Food Production and Investment in Developing Countries, operating under the joint auspices of the World Bank, the FAO, and the UN Development Program, encourages investment in developing nations to support small farmers, raise yields, produce fertilizers, and grow crops for local use rather than for export. The Global Information and Early Warning System on Food and Agriculture monitors crops worldwide so that all countries can better adjust their policies on production, trade, prices, and consumption. In addition, several other international organizations or groups deal with specialized problems; these include the World Wheat Council, the International Fertilizer Supply Scheme (under the FAO), and the Consultative Group on International Agricultural Research (and, associated with it, the International Food Policy Research Institute). Now is the opportune time to try to persuade China to become an active member of all these organizations, since this would serve both its interests and those of the international community.

China cannot be expected to play a significant role in programs dealing with international food aid (especially grant aid). The developed countries, particularly the United States plus the OPEC nations, will have to carry the main burden in this field. On occasion, China has sent small donations to help other countries suffering calamities and may do so again, and its own bilateral aid programs have included, and probably will continue to include, projects related to agriculture.[335] However, in the foreseeable future China is no more likely to be a significant donor of agricultural and food aid than it is to be a large food aid recipient.

But it is reasonable to try to induce it to play active roles in many other kinds of programs. There would be clear advantages to the Chinese as well as others if they were to join the major international planning and monitoring organizations, especially the World Food Council. Full Chinese participation in organizations concerned with research and international exchanges of information also would be to everybody's—including China's—advantage. Their publication of some national statistics since mid-1979 has been a major step toward greater openness, and now they should be urged to publish complete data on agriculture and other economic sectors.

One of the areas in which Chinese willingness or unwillingness to participate will be especially important is that related to world food reserves. Since the World Food Conference, when UN leaders proposed an international reserve system, discussion of the idea of a system of nationally held but internationally coordinated reserves has continued, mainly in the World Wheat Council and at the FAO, but progress toward establishing the system has been slow. In fact, in 1979 negotiations on the issue broke down, at least temporarily.[336] If and when a reserve system finally is established, however, the question of China's participation will immediately come to the fore. It is important to involve it in discussion of the issues long before then. The Chinese frequently have stated that they cannot be expected to accept international agreements resulting from negotiations in which they have not participated. Efforts should be made now, therefore, to start involving the Chinese.

It is widely recognized that Soviet involvement would be necessary for the success of any world food reserve system because of the huge and unpredictable purchases it periodically makes. If the Russians were to refuse to participate, it probably would be necessary to limit their freedom to procure grain from the participating nations.[337] Even though China's purchases have been smaller than those of the Soviet Union and the fluctuations in its trade less extreme, its participation also probably would be necessary, and certainly highly desirable, for a reserve system to succeed. If China's general level of grain imports rises significantly, its membership clearly will become essential.

The kind of bilateral agreements by which both the Soviet Union and China and their major grain trading suppliers have attempted to introduce some regularity into their grain trade do not really solve the problems that an international grain reserve might. This already has been demonstrated in the Soviet case. Despite the 1975 U.S.-Soviet agreement (in which the Russians promised to purchase at least 6 million tons of grain a year from the United States for five years, and Washington assured Moscow that at least 8 million tons a year would be available to it), until the United States imposed special restrictions following the Soviet invasion of Afghanistan, Moscow still could purchase unlimited amounts of grain on the world market if and when it felt it to be necessary. In 1977 and 1979 it suddenly did increase its purchases, which had the same kind of destabilizing effects on supplies and prices that its earlier purchases had.[338] Bilateral agreements have some value, and they will be useful so long as no international reserve system exists. But the aim of the United States and other nations playing major roles in the world food system still should be to establish a reserve system and to convince the Chinese as well as the Russians that it is in their interest to participate.

To date China has shown no interest in discussing such a possibility. However, if and when progress is made toward establishing a reserve system, it will be necessary to make it clear to the Chinese—as well as to the Russians—that nonparticipation on their part will not be allowed to prevent the establishment of the system, and that if they do not participate, they will have to be excluded from its benefits, which could mean that in times of tight supply they would be "residual purchasers" of grain on the world market, able to obtain what they need only after the needs of participating nations had been met. Conceivably, if the Chinese were to demonstrate convincingly that even without joining an international reserve system they would maintain an adequate national grain reserve and would pursue policies that would parallel international efforts and help to stabilize the world market, their participation might not be essential. However, unquestionably it would be preferable to involve them directly.

There clearly should not be any punitive action directed against China unless it were to attempt to disrupt cooperative efforts organized by others. Even if China stays out of such cooperative programs, the international community should provide whatever assistance it can to help China increase its food production and meet its national needs. Nevertheless, the Chinese should be made to understand that if they prefer to act unilaterally rather than cooperatively, they will face increased risks; the world cannot be expected to exempt them from the obligations that international cooperation demands of others or from the problems that noncooperation might create for them. There is now a much firmer basis for optimism, however, that Chinese leaders will see that it is genuinely in their long-term interest to participate in multilateral cooperative efforts to solve international food problems, and leaders in other nations should work persistently to persuade the Chinese that this is the case.

IV

China and the World
Energy System

ENERGY problems pose challenges to the international community that are as great as, and in some respects more complex than, the world's food problems. Modern societies require energy to fuel their machines just as they need grain to feed their people, and today most nations rely at least partially on energy purchased abroad. The heavy dependence of the advanced industrial countries on oil imports makes these countries vulnerable to disruptions of international trade. Moreover, oil—the principal source of primary energy now traded in the world market—is currently being depleted at a rapid rate. New ways must be found to meet the escalating global demand for energy before shrinking oil supplies become so costly that economic growth is threatened.

In the interim, while the transition to a new mix of energy sources takes place, vigorous efforts must be made both to conserve the available supplies and to expand the global supply of all forms of energy.[1]

In the two centuries following the start of the Industrial Revolution, the world depended above all on coal to fuel its economic growth. After World War II, however, world dependence shifted rapidly to oil. In 1967, for the first time in history, the global community consumed more energy from oil than from coal. By 1975 liquid fuels provided 44 percent of all primary commercial energy used in the world, while solid fuels accounted for only 33 percent.[2] In a basic sense, oil has become the lifeblood of the international economy.[3] By the mid-1970s more than one-third of the primary energy produced in the world was traded internationally, and most of this consisted of crude petroleum and products derived from it.[4]

The crisis of 1973–74—when for a brief period, Arab oil exporters embargoed sales to certain areas and cut back their overall production, and the world price of oil quadrupled—shocked the international community into a realization of the seriousness of the energy problems that lie ahead. The drop in Iranian oil exports and rise in world oil prices in 1979 following the revolution in Iran had a similar psychological effect. These developments forced leaders in both the developed and developing nations to recognize not only the immediate problems caused by many nations' vulnerability to cutoffs of energy supplies and the worldwide impact of higher energy costs, but also the long-run dangers created by the steadily rising demand and shrinking supplies of major fuels, oil in particular.

Questions about the future of oil are now high, therefore, on today's agenda of international problems. Experts differ, however, in their judgments about the size of the world's petroleum reserves, as well as about probable future trends in demand, supply, and prices. There is no certainty about the exact time when the global "need" for oil will surpass global production "capabilities," that is, when at given prices demand exceeds supply, or when the transition to a nonpetroleum energy base must be completed if severe economic disruption is to be avoided. There *is* broad agreement, however, that although oil will continue to be the dominant fuel in the international economy in the period immediately ahead, its dominance cannot last more than several decades. The global need for oil may surpass the readily available supply in the 1990s and possibly even in the 1980s.[5] It is now widely recognized, therefore, that alternative energy sources must be developed rapidly, and on a large scale, and that energy consumption patterns must be substantially changed within the next few years. Otherwise, the world could face the prospect of major dislocations, stagnation, and, at worst, chaos in the global economy. In light of these facts, developments relating to the production and consumption of oil and other major sources of energy worldwide are extremely important to all concerned with basic international problems.

Until recently, scant attention was paid to China in relation to oil or broad energy problems. In global terms, China produced relatively little primary energy, its per capita consumption of commercial energy was among the lowest anywhere, and it played no important role in world energy trade.[6] Although the Chinese exported small amounts of coal and imported some oil, the quantities were not significant internationally. It was generally believed, moreover, that China did not possess oil resources sufficient to make it even a potentially significant participant in international energy trade.

Within the past few years, however, it has become clear that it is impossible to ignore China in analyzing the global energy situation. Both the production and consumption of energy in China have been rising at a remarkably rapid rate. Even though in per capita terms it still ranks low internationally, by the mid-1970s China had become, in gross terms, the third largest energy consumer in the world, after the United States and the Soviet Union, and at least the fourth largest energy producer after these two superpowers and Saudi Arabia (conceivably it may already be third, or close to it).[7] Globally, China by 1975 ranked third in output of coal, tenth in petroleum, and perhaps eleventh in natural gas.[8]

Recent international interest in China's possible relationships with the world energy system has focused above all on oil. Since the late 1950s new discoveries of sizable oil reserves in China have made it clear that, contrary to past assumptions, China does have resources to become a major producer, and its oil output has increased rapidly during the past decade and a half. By 1978 it was the eighth largest oil producer in the world; conceivably it might become the fifth largest before very long.[9]

The question of greatest interest to observers outside China is whether or not the Chinese can become large-scale oil exporters in the years ahead. China started to export oil in 1973, and has exported several million tons of petroleum annually since then.[10] However, so far the amounts have been relatively small. Recently, China's petroleum exports of around 15 million tons have been just about 1 percent of world oil exports.[11] Compared with the sales made by the oil giants, China's exports do not appear important; in 1978, Saudi Arabia exported more than 400 million tons.[12]

Yet even at their present level, China's exports of oil are not insignificant. It is true that a few countries dominate the world oil export market; United Nations statistics show that by 1975 three countries accounted for more than one-half of all world oil exports, and nine countries accounted for over four-fifths.[13] This situation has not basically changed. However, countries exporting smaller amounts account for roughly one out of every five tons of oil traded internationally. Therefore, no nation whose oil sales are in the millions of tons can be regarded as unimportant. As of 1975 there were only sixteen countries whose net exports of crude petroleum totaled more than 5 million tons; among them China ranked fifteenth.[14] In 1978, according to UN statistics, there were twenty-three countries whose exports exceeded 5 million tons; among them, China ranked twentieth, but Central Intelligence Agency (CIA) figures on China placed it seventeenth.[15]

While even China's current oil exports are not unimportant, the possibility that the Chinese could export substantially increased amounts in the years ahead has aroused international interest. Some analysts have predicted that the Chinese will be able to export several tens of millions of tons a year in the 1980s, which would clearly make China a significant oil exporter, rather than a minor one as at present. If China could export oil on that scale, it obviously would become increasingly important in relation to the world's energy supplies, and this could have very significant implications for China's overall relationship to the world economy in the period ahead.

There is no certainty, however, that China will become a significant oil exporter. To make realistic judgments about what is in fact possible, it is necessary to assess a variety of factors that will influence China's capabilities and determine both its domestic energy supply and its capability to export energy in sizable quantities. How one judges China's prospects for becoming a major oil exporter depends on answers to some difficult questions concerning China's total energy situation and energy policies. What energy resources does China have—not only of oil, but of coal, natural gas, and other energy resources? How rapidly can they —and will they—be exploited? In a capital-scarce economy, will adequate investment funds be available? In China's future energy development, what mix of energy forms is likely? At what rate is domestic demand for energy—and for particular types of energy—likely to grow? How will China's overall economic strategy and development policies affect the country's structure of energy demand as well as the sources of its supply? How efficient will the Chinese be in using their energy; will their "energy/GNP elasticity coefficient" be high or low?[16]

Only if one correctly assesses likely trends in total energy supply and demand in China can one realistically analyze the prospects for oil, which requires asking another set of difficult questions. What rate of increase in oil output is possible, with China's present known oil reserves? What are the geologic prospects for adding to these reserves? Is China likely to develop its offshore oil as well as its resources onshore rapidly, on a large scale? Will it have the required capital and technology?

Judgments on these and related questions are required to estimate China's possible future role in the world oil market. Will China have a significant amount of exportable oil, that is, a surplus over domestic demand, and if so, how much of a surplus? How hard will it push exports? What are its marketing prospects? More broadly, how are its future policies affecting oil likely to fit into its overall economic policies at home and abroad?

On the basis of the information now available, there can be no certainty about China's future as an oil exporter, only a range of possibilities; what actually takes place will be determined by numerous variables. There is little doubt that, in theory, China might produce increasing amounts of oil, and that if its leaders focus on the goal of increasing exports with little concern for other priority objectives, China's sales of oil abroad could be increased substantially. However, Chinese leaders will face many dilemmas—and will have to make hard choices—in determining basic energy policies in the context of overall development priorities. Whether or not China in fact becomes a significant oil exporter in the 1980s will depend on many decisions its leaders must make in the next few years.

China has several options; none is without costs. If it puts a large share of its investment capital into development of the oil industry, it will obviously have less for investment in other priority industries, some of which, including steel, are essential to support the oil industry as well as other priority economic activities.[17] The extent that China increases domestic oil consumption will limit the amount available for export. Yet stressing rapid development of coal as well as oil could limit the resources China has available to invest in the oil industry. If China has to rely primarily on its onshore oil reserves, the rate of increase in oil output will probably remain low. Yet if it exploits offshore oil on a large scale, development costs and the need for foreign technology will be large.

Unless the rate of increase in China's energy output outpaces the growth of domestic demand for energy, exporting large amounts of oil could create domestic energy shortages that would slow overall economic growth at home.[18] But if China cannot export oil in significant quantities, it may encounter serious foreign exchange shortages that could severely limit its ability to import the technology that is badly needed to accelerate China's overall economic growth, including oil development. Large-scale exploitation of offshore oil could lead, in time, to substantially increased output. But in the meantime, it will also require greatly expanded imports of foreign equipment and know-how.

The problems that China's leaders face in determining and implementing their energy policies in the period ahead are complex, therefore. The policies they pursue will not only help to determine whether or not China becomes an important oil exporter, but they will also have a major influence on the kind of general relationships that China develops with the international community in the years ahead.

Global Energy: Trends and Problems

The potential international importance of China's energy situation and prospects, and its possible future roles in the world energy system, are best understood in the context of trends that have profoundly changed the global energy picture in recent years. Since the oil "crunches" of 1973–74 and early 1979, most informed persons worldwide recognize that the world faces serious energy problems. However, relatively few understand in detail the long-term trends that have been transforming the global energy system, and the implications of these trends for the future. These long-term trends are clear if one examines statistics for the half century between 1925 and 1975. China's potential importance in the world energy system is increasing because of these trends.

Skyrocketing Energy Consumption

The economic growth of modern—and modernizing—economies since the eighteenth century has depended fundamentally on "primary commercial energy," that is, energy derived from coal, petroleum, natural gas, hydroelectricity, and, most recently, nuclear electricity.[19] These energy sources were used very little, or not at all, in earlier years when "traditional energy" sources, such as wood, wastes, and animal and human energy, filled most human needs.[20] With the exception of hydroelectricity and nuclear electricity, these are all nonrenewable fossil fuels.

The appetite of modern machines for energy from these sources has been voracious, and consumption has increased spectacularly in recent decades, especially during the past half century or so. Between 1925 and 1975, the total annual consumption of primary commercial energy, worldwide, more than quintupled, from less than 1.5 billion tons to 8 billion tons of "coal equivalent," or CE (table 4-1).[21] (To compare, or aggregate, energy from different energy sources, it is necessary to use some standard unit. Coal equivalent, which is used in UN statistical compilations, will be used in this discussion.)

Traditional energy sources are still widely used in less developed

TABLE 4-1. *World Consumption of Commercial Energy, 1925–75*
Millions of metric tons of coal equivalent

Area	1925	1950	1965	1975
World	1,484	2,490	5,220	8,003
Developed nations	...	1,863	3,269	4,635
Non-Communist developing nations	...	137	387	778
European and Asian Communist nations	...	490	1,564	2,590
North America	749	1,187	1,913	2,576
United States	718	1,114	1,783	2,350
Western Europe	517	575	1,057	1,468
Japan	31	46	178	402
European Communist (Eastern Europe and Soviet Union)	81	447	1,222	1,965
Soviet Union	25	287	836	1,411
Eastern Europe	55	160	374	554
Africa	14	41	88	158
Latin America (including the Caribbean area)	25	63	168	311
Middle East	...	8	42	127
Non-Communist developing Asia ("Far East," excluding Japan)	30[a]	51	150	402
Communist Asia (mainly China)	24	43[b]	341	625
China	...	43[b]	316	570
Oceania	16	29	62	101

Sources: The figures for 1925 are from Joel Darmstadter and others, *Energy in the World Economy, A Statistical Review of Trends in Output, Trade, and Consumption since 1925* (Johns Hopkins Press, 1971), p. 10. (Hereafter Darmstadter, *Energy*.) Figures from 1950–75 are based on Economic and Social Affairs Department, United Nations, *World Energy Supplies, 1950–1974*, Statistical Papers, Series J, no. 19 (UN, 1976), pp. 2–9, 43, 79, 93, 111 (hereafter UN, *WES 1950–74*), and *World Energy Supplies 1971–1975*, Statistical Papers, Series J, no. 20 (UN, 1977), pp. 2–9, 19, 27, 31, 37 (hereafter UN, *WES 1971–75*).
a. Includes Middle East.
b. UN, *WES 1950–74*, gives a figure of 43.495 for all Communist Asia and 43.025 for China; its figures for North Korea and Mongolia are only 0.381 and 0.089, respectively. The figure for North Korea seems implausibly low.

countries, where they are of vital importance to rural populations. In fact, according to one rough estimate, the amount of energy from traditional sources now used each year may total about 2.25 billion tons of coal equivalent, globally equal to about 28 percent of the total primary commercial energy consumed in 1975.[22] However, the modern sources of energy, classified as primary commercial energy, are the sources that are crucially important internationally.

Not only did the world's consumption of primary commercial energy increase enormously in absolute terms from 1925 through 1975, but until recently the rate of increase rose fairly steadily. During the quarter century from 1925 through 1950, the average annual rate of increase in total energy consumption worldwide was 2.1 percent; consumption rose by 66 percent in twenty-five years, from about 1.5 billion to 2.5 billion tons CE.[23] During the next quarter century, from 1950 through 1975, the rate of increase was 4.8 percent—more than double that of the earlier period—and total consumption rose by about 220 percent, from 2.5 billion to 8 billion tons CE.[24] In per capita terms, average consumption of commercial energy worldwide increased at an average annual rate of 1.0 percent from 1925 through 1950, rising from 785 to 1,003 kilograms CE per person, and at a rate of 2.9 percent from 1950 through 1975, rising from 1,003 to 2,028 kilograms CE per person.[25]

Unequal Distribution

As in the case of food, statistics on global energy consumption show important overall trends, but they do not reveal the huge differences in energy consumption between various areas and countries. These differences are even greater in the case of energy than in the case of food consumption. A relatively small number of industrialized or industrializing nations has consumed—and continues to consume—a huge proportion of the world's total energy (table 4-2). Before World War II, North America and Western Europe were the only really high energy consumers, but since the war they have been joined by Japan, the Soviet Union, and Eastern Europe, while the less developed nations have lagged far behind.

In percentage terms, the figures are startling. In 1925 North America and Western Europe consumed close to 85 percent of total primary commercial energy used that year (the United States alone consumed close to one-half).[26] Japan consumed only 2.1 percent, the Soviet Union 1.7 percent, and Eastern Europe 3.7 percent. The rest of the world, including all developing nations, consumed only 7.3 percent. (The figure for the developing nations alone was about 6.1 percent.)

Fifty years later, in 1975, North America, Western Europe, and Japan together accounted for 56 percent of world energy consumption (the share of the United States alone was 29 percent) while the Soviet Union and Eastern Europe together consumed 25 percent of the total.[27] In absolute figures, the United States in 1975 accounted for 2.35 billion tons CE; Western Europe, 1.47 billion; Japan, 0.402 billion; the Soviet Union, 1.41

TABLE 4-2. *World Energy Production and Consumption of Commercial Energy, 1975*

Millions of tons of coal equivalent

Area	All energy	Solid fuels	Liquid fuels	Natural gas	Hydro-electricity and nuclear electricity
		Production			
World	8,555	2,640	4,035	1,658	221
Non-Communist developed	3,188	1,091	901	1,032	165
Non-Communist developing	2,593	146	2,265	152	30
European Communist	2,129	888	752	470	20
Asian Communist[a]	645	516	118	5	7
		Consumption			
World	8,003	2,623	3,526	1,633	221
Non-Communist developed	4,635	1,106	2,322	1,043	165
Non-Communist developing	778	154	475	199	30
European Communist	1,965	849	630	467	20
Asian Communist[a]	625	514	99	5	7

Source: Based on UN, *WES 1971–75*, pp. 2–9.
a. UN figures. (My analysis of China uses CIA figures.)

billion; and Eastern Europe, 0.554 billion. Recently, China has joined the group of nations whose gross energy consumption is very large—it now exceeds that of Japan—even though it remains low in per capita terms. Altogether, the developed nations (non-Communist and Communist) used about 6.6 billion tons CE, or more than four-fifths of the world total in 1975; 58 percent was consumed in the non-Communist developed countries and 25 percent in the Soviet Union and Eastern Europe (table 4-3).[28]

By 1975 the share of the world's energy consumption accounted for by all the developing nations (non-Communist and Asian Communist) had risen to 7.5 percent (table 4-3) (compared with about 6.1 percent in 1925 and roughly 7.2 percent in 1950). Yet all of these nations together, representing the majority of the world's population, still consumed only 1.4 billion tons CE, less than one-fifth of the global total of 8 billion.[29]

Per Capita Energy Consumption

Figures on per capita consumption highlight the stark contrast between different areas and countries. To take two extreme cases, per cap-

TABLE 4-3. *World Energy Production and Consumption, 1975*
Percent

Area	All energy	Solid fuels	Liquid fuels	Natural gas	Hydro-electricity and nuclear electricity
			Production		
Non-Communist developed	37.26	41.33	22.33	62.24	74.66
Non-Communist developing	30.31	5.53	56.13	9.17	13.57
European Communist	24.89	33.64	18.64	28.35	9.05
Asian Communist[a]	7.54	19.55	2.92	0.30	3.17
			Consumption		
Non-Communist developed	57.92	42.17	65.85	63.87	74.66
Non-Communist developing	9.72	5.87	13.47	7.29	13.57
European Communist	24.55	32.37	17.87	28.60	9.05
Asian Communist[a]	7.81	19.60	2.81	0.31	3.17

Source: Based on UN, *WES 1971–75*, pp. 2–9.
a. UN figures. (My analysis of China uses CIA figures.)

ita energy consumption in the United States in 1975 was 10,999 kilograms CE, whereas in India it was 221 kilograms CE.[30] The average American consumed almost fifty times as much commercial energy as the average Indian!

Globally, per capita energy consumption averaged 2,028 kilograms CE in 1975. However, while it was 6,094 kilograms in the non-Communist developed nations and 5,412 kilograms in the European Communist nations, it was only 402 kilograms in the non-Communist developing nations. There are significant differences among the developing nations, however. In parts of Latin America and the Middle East per capita energy consumption averaged well over 1,000 kilograms CE in 1975; the lowest levels still are in developing African and Asian nations.[31] China's per capita energy consumption has risen to a level significantly above that of the developing nations as a whole, but it is still well below the global average and far below the level in the developed countries, including the European Communist nations.

Energy Consumption Growth Rates

Important trends in global energy use are revealed by rates of change as well as by absolute figures; past rates of growth in energy consumption are not just of historical interest. Although it is not possible to predict future consumption simply by projecting past rates ahead, since

TABLE 4-4. *World Consumption of Commercial Energy, by Type and Region, 1975*

Millions of tons of coal equivalent; percent

Area	Total energy consumption	Solid fuels	Liquid fuels	Natural gas	Hydro-electricity and nuclear electricity
Non-Communist developed	4,635	1,106 (23.86)	2,322 (50.10)	1,043 (22.50)	165 (3.56)
Non-Communist developing	778	154 (19.79)	475 (61.05)	119 (15.30)	30 (3.86)
European Communist	1,965	849 (43.21)	630 (32.06)	467 (23.77)	20 (1.02)
Asian Communist[a]	625	514 (82.24)	99 (15.84)	5 (0.8)	7 (1.12)

Source: UN, *WES 1971–75*, pp. 2–9. Percentages, shown in parentheses, are my calculations, based on figures given in the source.

a. UN figures. (My analysis uses CIA figures.)

many factors could modify them, nevertheless, they highlight problems that the international community has only recently begun to confront realistically.

Analysis of the growth in total energy consumption during the half century 1926–75 and in two subperiods—1951–75 and 1966–75—shows that the growth rate rose steadily until the mid-1960s, when it began to drop, but remained well above the average rate for the half century as a whole.

During the entire half century 1926–75 the average annual rate of increase worldwide was 3.4 percent.[32] During the quarter century 1951–75 it was even higher, 4.8 percent. During the decade 1966–75 it dropped somewhat but was still very high, 4.4 percent. Some decline occurred in all areas except the Middle East and Africa; however, the drop in the global rate was due mainly to declining rates in the major industrial nations.

The slowdown in the growth in energy consumption in the major industrial countries has been significant, since these countries consume so much of the world's total energy output. However, rates of increase in the developing nations have remained high—recently they have been about double those in the major developed countries—which suggests that even though these countries start from a low base, they will place increasing demands on the world's energy resources in the period ahead.

During 1966–75 the average annual rate of growth in energy consumption in the non-Communist countries was 3.5 percent in the developed nations and 7.2 percent in the developing nations. In the Communist world—if one uses UN figures—the rates were 4.9 percent for the developed (European) Communist nations and 6.3 percent for the developing (Asian) Communist countries.[33]

There were significant differences within these broad groups. For example, among the industrial countries, the rate in the United States was 2.8 percent (compared with 3.0 percent for 1951–75), while in Japan it was 8.5 percent (compared with 9.1 percent in 1951–75).[34] Among the developing countries, the 1966–75 rate was 6.0 percent in Africa but 11.7 percent in the Middle East.[35] Despite these differences, however, the figures highlight important facts. The advanced industrial countries still dominate world energy consumption and will continue to do so in the years immediately ahead. However, the rate of growth in energy consumption in the developing nations is now considerably higher than that in the developed countries, and the requirements of these nations will rise substantially in the period ahead. China is no exception. In recent years, the rate of growth in its energy use has been one of the highest in the world, well above that in most developing nations. Many analyses of world energy problems written by Westerners focus almost entirely on the problems of the industrialized nations. No analysis is adequate unless it takes account of the growing needs and problems of the developing nations, including the world's largest developing nation, China.

Energy and Economic Growth

Energy use does not take place in a vacuum; growing consumption is linked to overall economic growth. Greater use of energy both stimulates and reflects economic development. The relationship between overall economic growth and increases in energy consumption can vary substantially, but there is an important correlation between them. This is evident if one compares figures on rates of increase in energy consumption with estimates of rates of overall economic growth.

One set of U.S. government estimates indicates that (in constant 1974 dollars) annual gross national product (GNP) growth worldwide in the period 1967–75 averaged 4.1 percent a year, 3.6 percent in the developed countries and 6.1 percent in the developing nations.[36] Another U.S. government source (using market prices) indicates that the worldwide rate of growth in GNP during 1966–75 averaged 4.6 percent a year, 4.2 percent in the non-Communist developed nations, 6.2 percent in the non-Communist developing nations, and 4.3 percent in the European Communist nations.[37] These rates were fairly close to the growth rates in energy consumption.

In analyzing past rates of growth in energy use, in a sense one is simply assessing general economic growth. Until recently, high energy use and economic development have gone hand in hand; low energy use has reflected low levels of economic development. However, while overall development and energy consumption have been linked, rates of increase in energy consumption have tended to be higher in newly industrializing developing nations than in mature industrial societies; in the latter there has been a decline in the energy output ratio in recent years.

Energy specialists use the term "energy/GNP elasticity coefficient" to express the relationship between increases in energy consumption and increases in GNP. Some studies of past periods have shown that globally the ratio was frequently around 1.00, that is, roughly a 1 percent increase in energy consumption was required for—or at least accompanied—a 1 percent increase in GNP.[38]

But there have been significant differences between countries—both developed and developing—and within particular countries at various times, which have reflected differences in economic structures, stages of development, and the efficiency or inefficiency with which energy has been used.[39] Here too, as in so many other economic indicators, there have been notable differences between the developed and the developing countries as groups. In the period 1951–65 the coefficient worldwide was 1.06, but in the non-Communist developing nations it was 1.67, while in the non-Communist developed nations it was 0.85.[40] In general, countries in the early stages of development require more energy for each increment of GNP growth than advanced industrial countries do. China fits this pattern; in fact during some years it appears to have had an exceptionally high energy/GNP elasticity coefficient, although the figure has dropped recently.

Shifts in Energy Sources

The shifts in sources of energy supply during the modern period have been just as striking as the overall growth in energy consumption. The first great change was that from traditional resources—wood, crop residue, dung, vegetable waste, and human and animal energy—to coal, which took place as a result of the Industrial Revolution. Following World War II there was another dramatic shift, from coal to oil, and then there was a major increase in the use of natural gas.

There were many reasons for the shift to oil. An obvious one was the discovery of large oil deposits, especially in the Middle East, which could be exploited relatively cheaply. However, there were other important reasons. Oil is a convenient fuel, easily transportable, and until recently was relatively inexpensive. Moreover, as new industries geared to liquid hydrocarbon fuels developed—especially the automotive and petro-chemical industries—oil became essential. Much of the industrial development in the years since World War II has been based on cheap oil.

In 1925 solid fuel (coal and lignite) was still dominant, accounting for more than four-fifths (83 percent) of all primary commercial energy consumption worldwide.[41] Liquid fuel (mainly oil) was a poor second, accounting for only 13 percent; the shares of natural gas and hydroelectric power were only 3 percent and 1 percent, respectively.

The balance began to shift during the next quarter century, when consumption of liquid fuel increased at an average annual rate of over 5 percent.[42] Yet solid fuel was still dominant in 1950, when it accounted for three-fifths (61.53 percent) of world energy consumption.[43] Liquid fuel's share had risen, however, to over one-fourth (26.96 percent) and that of natural gas had grown to almost one-tenth (9.79 percent). The share of hydropower was still very small—1.68 percent.

Then petroleum achieved a position of clear dominance during the next quarter century. From 1950 through 1975, liquid fuel consumption grew at a rate of 6.9 percent, compared with 2.2 percent for solid fuel.[44] By 1975 liquid fuel accounted for more than two-fifths (44 percent) of world energy consumption, solid fuel for a one-third (33 percent), and natural gas for one-fifth (20 percent).[45] The share of hydropower was still relatively small, under 3 percent. (In fact, the rate of growth of hydropower—as well as natural gas—surpassed that of oil, but from a relatively low starting point, and although its importance in producing electricity has grown, its share of total energy use is destined to remain relatively small.)[46]

The shift to oil has taken place not only in the industrial nations, but in the developing countries as well. In the 1960s this process started to occur in China, too; however, China continued to rely more heavily on coal than most countries do, and in the past ten years it has taken steps to slow down the shift to oil.

Oil will continue to be the dominant fuel worldwide in the years immediately ahead. However, it is now clear that this position cannot be maintained indefinitely. At probable rates of consumption, oil resources are likely to decline to a relatively low level in several decades—almost certainly before the mid-twenty-first century.

New Patterns of Dependence

In energy, as in food, one of the most striking developments during the years since World War II has been the emergence of entirely new patterns of international dependence and interdependence. In the 1920s most areas and countries in the world—including Western Europe and Japan, which today are crucially dependent on energy imports—produced most of the energy they consumed.[47] By the start of the 1950s, although the situation had been altered slightly, there had been no dramatic change, and the energy deficit of the industrial countries as a whole was still small.[48]

Since then, however, enormous changes have occurred, and the pattern now is very different. The major industrial nations—and a majority of developing nations as well—today are heavily dependent on large energy imports, mainly oil, from a relatively small number of exporting nations. By 1975 Japan produced less than one-tenth of its energy needs, Europe only a little more than two-fifths, and the United States less than nine-tenths.[49] Although the less developed countries as a group now have a large energy surplus, this is entirely due to surpluses in a few oil exporting countries. Most developing countries are now heavily dependent on energy imports; although the quantities they import appear small compared with the imports of the industrial giants, they are crucial to economic growth in the developing nations.

The increase in world energy trade during the half century 1925–75 was extraordinary. In 1925 world exports of all types of energy totaled only 214 million tons CE—more than two-thirds of which was solid fuel —and this amounted to roughly one-seventh of total world energy consumption.[50] By 1950 energy exports had more than doubled, to 502 million tons CE, which was one-fifth of world consumption.[51] By 1975 energy trade had increased almost six times compared with 1950, in absolute terms, and had almost doubled as a percentage of world energy consumption. Most of the increase was accounted for by oil. World energy exports totaled 2.939 billion tons CE in 1975, which was about 37 percent of total world energy consumption. Liquid fuel exports (roughly 1.4 billion tons liquid, or more than 2 billion tons CE) were thirty times as large as a half century earlier and now accounted for 72 percent of all international energy trade.[52]

As a result of these trends, the developed industrial nations in the non-Communist world became extremely dependent on imports from major oil exporting countries—especially a few countries in the Middle East, Africa, and Latin America and, above all, those in the Arab world. As a group these industrial countries used close to three-fifths of the world's energy in 1975 but produced only a little more than one-third of it.[53] Although in 1975 they were roughly self-sufficient in coal and natural gas, each of which accounted for one-fifth to one-fourth of their energy consumption,[54] more than half of the energy they used consisted of oil.[55] These countries accounted for about two-thirds of global oil consumption, although they produced only a little over one-fifth of the world's oil output.

To date, the Communist countries as a group have maintained self-sufficiency in energy; in fact, they still have a small surplus.[56] Coal has continued to be their dominant energy source—in 1975 it accounted for more than two-fifths of energy consumption in the European Communist nations and about two-thirds in China—but the importance of oil, and natural gas as well, has been growing.[57] Among the Communist nations, however, those in Eastern Europe became very dependent on energy imports from the Soviet Union.

By 1975 the non-Communist developing nations as a group produced more than 30 percent and consumed less than 10 percent of the world's energy, and, therefore, had a huge surplus.[58] However, it is no longer meaningful to regard these nations as one group, at least in terms of energy. Among them, about a dozen oil-exporting nations belonging to the Organization of Petroleum Exporting Countries (OPEC) have become the primary suppliers of energy to the rest of the non-Communist world.[59] The developing nations that do not produce oil have become heavily dependent, along with the industrial countries, on imports from OPEC members. In fact, to meet their energy needs, the non-Communist developing countries as a group now depend even more heavily on oil than the major industrial nations do. By 1975 oil provided more than three-fifths of their total primary commercial energy needs.[60] The only major region within the non-Communist developing world in which oil provided less than three-fifths of all energy used in 1975 was Asia, and even there it was close to one-half.[61]

The Oil Era

The present period in world history might well be labeled the oil era. By 1975 not only had petroleum become the dominant fuel within most countries, but it accounted for more than 70 percent of world energy trade. When one examines international problems relating to energy, of necessity the focus must be on oil.

The first commercial use of petroleum in the modern period began a little more than a century ago, when wells were drilled in Rumania and the United States.[62] However, use of oil did not spread widely until the twentieth century, and the oil era really is a post-World War II phenomenon. In 1950 total world production of crude oil was only 520 million tons.[63] By 1975 it had quintupled to 2.65 billion tons (more than 19 billion barrels, or roughly 53 million barrels a day).[64] The rates of growth (calculated from UN figures) for production of crude oil and consumption of energy petroleum products from 1950 through 1975 were extremely high, 6.7 percent and 6.9 percent, respectively.[65]

Oil Consumption

At first oil consumption was highly concentrated, but during the past three decades it has spread rapidly worldwide. In 1950 the United States accounted for almost two-thirds of all consumption of petroleum products in the world.[66] Then, from 1950 through 1975, while consumption of energy petroleum products in North America increased at an average annual rate of 3.7 percent, in Western Europe it increased at a rate of 10.4 percent, and in Japan it rose at an astounding rate of 22 percent.[67] The European Communist nations also became large users of petroleum products during this period; from 1950 through 1975 their consumption increased at an annual rate of 10.2 percent.[68] The growth of oil consumption in the non-Communist developing countries was slower but still fairly rapid; from 1950 through 1975 the rate of increase was 7.5 percent a year.[69]

Until the late 1960s China played only a minor role in the global oil picture. Since then, however, it has followed the path trod by so many others and has consumed as well as produced increasing amounts of oil. The rate of increase in its oil consumption has been one of the most rapid experienced by any nation.

In short, reliance on oil has become virtually a worldwide phenomenon. By 1975, although North America was still the largest world consumer (table 4-5), using 737 million tons of energy petroleum products (one-third of world consumption), Western Europe consumed 526 million tons (more than one-fifth of the world total) and Japan 193 million tons (just under one-tenth of world consumption).[70] The European Communist nations in 1975 consumed 410 million tons (close to one-fifth of the global total).[71] And the developing nations—non-Communist and Communist—consumed 373 million tons.[72]

Even though oil consumption has increased almost everywhere, the gap between the developed and developing nations continues to be huge, reflecting the general economic gap between rich and poor nations. Energy petroleum products consumed in 1975 by all developing nations—non-Communist and Communist—were only about one-sixth of the global total, even though these countries contain the bulk of the world's population, and per capita consumption of oil in these countries was, on the average, approximately one-tenth of that in the developed nations.[73] Nevertheless, the developing nations too have become very dependent on oil.

The Concentration of Oil Production

While petroleum has now become an essential source of primary energy throughout the world, production today of exportable oil is concentrated in relatively few areas, especially in the Third World. Worldwide, the rate of increase in the production of crude oil was 6.7 percent from 1950 through 1975. However, while it was 2.7 percent in the developed non-Communist countries, it was 8.4 percent in the non-Communist developing countries, and 10.9 percent in the Communist nations as a group.[74] By 1975, of the total of 2.65 billion tons of crude oil produced in the world, more than 1.5 billion tons were produced in developing nations and just over a half billion tons each in the developed non-Communist countries (537 million tons) and the Communist nations (591 million tons).[75]

By 1975 twenty-three "countries" (to treat the European Economic Community [EEC] as a single unit) each produced more than 10 million tons of crude oil, and sixteen of them were net exporters.[76] Among the twenty-three, four were giants: the Soviet Union, the United States, Saudi Arabia, and Iran. The two largest producers were the Soviet Union (491 million tons) and the United States (413 million tons). However, the United States was a large net importer (203 million tons), while the Soviet Union was a sizable exporter (93 million tons gross, and about 87 million tons net), mostly to its Communist neighbors.[77] The two next largest producers were Saudi Arabia (352 million tons) and Iran (268 million tons).[78] Both were huge exporters.

In 1975 nine other countries each produced between 50 million and 125 million tons: one was China (which in 1975 produced 80 million

TABLE 4-5. *World Petroleum, 1950 and 1975*
Millions of metric tons

Area	Year	Production of crude petroleum	Imports of crude petroleum	Exports of crude petroleum	Apparent supply of crude petroleum[a]	Apparent consumption of energy petroleum (refined)[b]	Apparent per capita consumption of energy petroleum (kilograms)
World	1950	520.412	139.014	140.647	517.780	433.433	175
	1975	2,046.838	1,431.158	1,409.244	2,658.990	2,284.459	579
Non-Communist developed countries	1950	274.926	78.085	5.783	347.690	346.891	600
	1975	536.639	1,080.693	41.045	1,584.502	1,501.771	1,974
Non-Communist developing countries	1950	201.490	59.997	134.388	125.638	49.963	46
	1975	1,519.406	273.849	1,265.146	516.157	308.167	159
European Communist countries	1950	43.794	0.932	0.476	44.250	36.446	136
	1975	510.793	76.610	94.353	493.325	409.735	1,129
Asian Communist countries	1950	0.202	...	...	0.202	0.133	...
	1975	80.000	0.006	8.700	65.006	64.786	73
North America	1950	270.614	36.231	4.705	302.478	294.277	1,772
	1975	482.988	244.554	31.230	696.275	737.174	3,116
United States	1950	266.708	24.880	4.705	287.538	278.561	1,829
	1975	413.090	203.124	0.290	615.547	664.634	3,111

Western Europe	1950	3.982	39.774	1.078	42.802	44.547	147
	1975	27.850	582.727	9.629	609.950	526.140	1,442
Japan	1950	0.293	1.233	...	1.526	1.282	15
	1975	0.606	225.855	0.001	224.740	192.862	1,738
Soviet Union	1950	37.878	0.337	0.300	37.915	32.439	180
	1975	491.000	6.499	93.070	404.429	337.153	1,325
Eastern Europe	1950	5.916	0.562	0.176	6.335	4.007	...
	1975	19.800	70.111	1.283	88.806	72.582	...
China[c]	1950	0.202	...	...	0.202	0	0
	1975	80.000	...	8.700	65.000	60.280	73
Asian non-Communist developing countries	1950	11.534	5.828	6.744	10.430	8.457	13
	1975	87.252	81.527	61.946	106.020	81.358	72
Africa	1950	2.670	0.060	0.007	2.667	8.068	37
	1975	239.374	33.661	219.892	52.609	44.844	112
Middle East	1950	85.841	6.999	55.461	37.221	3.599	59
	1975	975.609	26.348	883.739	113.632	50.880	424
Caribbean–Latin American (CAM)	1950	95.697	44.023	71.617	66.828	16.686	243
	1975	178.074	101.011	90.053	182.991	73.270	517
South American (OAM)	1950	5.964	3.343	0.564	8.724	15.116	162
	1975	43.997	46.852	9.516	80.555	72.600	408

Sources: UN, WES 1950–74, pp. 193–227, 280–335, and WES 1971–75, pp. 62–71, 92–103. Crude petroleum does not include natural gas liquids.

a. Production plus imports minus exports and additions to stock.
b. Consumption of refined products (the best indicator of consumption).
c. These UN estimates for China are different from CIA estimates; see tables 4-12 and 4-14.

tons according to the UN estimate or 77 million tons according to the CIA estimate). The others were Venezuela (122 million tons), Iraq (111 million tons), Kuwait (105 million tons), Nigeria (88 million tons), the United Arab Emirates (80 million tons), Libya (72 million tons), Canada (70 million tons), and Indonesia (64 million tons). All except Canada produced more than their needs and were net exporters.

Another ten countries produced between 10 million and 50 million tons in 1975. They were Algeria (45 million tons), Mexico (36 million tons), Qatar (21 million tons), Argentina (21 million tons), Australia (20 million tons), Oman (17 million tons), Rumania (15 million tons), and Gabon, Trinidad, and the EEC (about 11 million tons each). (Of these, however, only five—Algeria, Mexico, Qatar, Oman, and Gabon— were net exporters; the others continued to buy more than they sold, the EEC on a huge scale.)

As these figures show, if judged solely by its gross oil output, by 1975 China already had become a middle-rank oil power, but its production remained far below that of the four largest producers.

Oil Trade

As the oil era has developed, the majority of nations in the world have become increasingly dependent on a few oil exporters for crucial supplies. According to UN figures, of the total world production of 2.65 billion tons of crude petroleum in 1975, 1.41 billion tons, or 53 percent, were exported.[79] Eleven countries each exported more than 40 million tons. However, the net sales by these major exporters ranged from 41 million to 328 million tons.[80] Saudi Arabia exported more than 300 million tons, Iran more than 200 million, and Iraq more than 100 million (table 4-6); these were the world's oil exporting giants. Eight of the eleven were middle-rank oil exporters, each selling between 40 million and 100 million tons (the Soviet Union, Venezuela, Kuwait, Nigeria, United Arab Emirates, Libya, Indonesia, and Algeria). The net exports of most other exporting countries were 10 million tons or less (with the notable exception of Qatar, an OPEC member, which exported 21 million tons, and Oman, not an OPEC member, which exported 17 million tons).

In 1975 the thirteen members of OPEC (Saudi Arabia, Iran, Venezuela, Iraq, Kuwait, Nigeria, United Arab Emirates, Libya, Indonesia, Algeria, Qatar, Gabon, and Ecuador) dominated the world market, accounting for 1.2 billion tons—or 85 percent of the total;[81] the Middle Eastern nations were clearly the dominant members. While one mem-

TABLE 4-6. *Petroleum Production and Exports of Significant World Producers, 1950-75*

Millions of metric tons

Area	1950 production of crude petroleum	1965 production of crude petroleum	1975 production of crude petroleum	1975 exports of crude petroleum	1975 imports of crude petroleum
Soviet Union	37.878	242.888	491.000	93.070	6.499
United States	266.708	384.946	413.090	0.290	203.124
Saudi Arabia[a]	26.649	109.550	352.394	328.194	0.479
Iran[a]	32.259	94.126	267.623	233.720	0
Venezuela[a]	77.897	182.409	122.150	76.718	0
Iraq[a]	6.584	64.474	111.168	103.218	0
Kuwait[a]	17.190	118.457	105.232	90.942	0
Nigeria[a]	0	13.538	88.440	84.908	0
United Arab Emirates[a]	0	13.558	80.457	80.376	0
China	0.202	10.000	80.000	8.700	0
Libya[a]	0	58.492	71.533	69.177	0
Canada	3.906	39.868	69.898	30.940	41.430
Indonesia[a]	6.673	23.950	64.116	48.833	0
Algeria[a]	0.003	26.025	45.057	40.992	0
Mexico	10.155	16.540	36.456	5.500	0
Qatar[a]	1.636	10.961	21.102	20.695	0
Argentina	3.357	13.672	20.773	0.016	2.117
Australia	0	0.333	20.159	0.185	7.706
Oman	0	0	17.016	17.064	0
Rumania	5.047	12.571	14.590	0	5.085
Gabon[a]	0	1.264	11.375	10.472	0
Trinidad	2.919	6.913	11.216	6.835	7.895
European Economic Community	2.120	15.566	10.603	1.113	475.754

Source: Based on UN, *WES 1950-74*, pp. 193-227, and *WES 1971-75*, pp. 62-71.
a. Members of OPEC. (Ecuador is also a member of OPEC but produced less than 10 million tons in 1975.)

ber in Asia exported roughly 49 million tons (Indonesia), two in Latin America exported 84 million tons (Venezuela 77 and Ecuador 7), and four in Africa exported 205 million tons (Nigeria 85, Libya 69, Algeria 41, and Gabon 10), the six Middle Eastern members of OPEC exported a total of 857 million tons—three-fifths of total world exports. One nation alone—Saudi Arabia—exported 328 million tons—more than 23 percent of world exports in 1975—and the other two oil exporting giants, Iran and Iraq, sold 234 million and 103 million tons, respectively. Some of these figures had increased by 1978 (table 4-7).

TABLE 4-7. *Petroleum Production and Exports of Significant World Producers and Exporters, 1977–79*

| Area | Production of crude petroleum (excluding natural gas liquids) | | | | | | Exports of petroleum (including refined products) | | | |
| | 1977 | | 1978 | | 1979 | | 1977 | | 1978 | |
	Thousands of barrels a day	Millions of tons	Thousands of barrels a day	Millions of tons	Thousands of barrels a day	Millions of tons	Thousands of barrels a day	Millions of tons	Thousands of barrels a day	Millions of tons
World	59,610	2,981	60,190	3,010	62,370	3,119	...	...	...	...
United States	8,180	409	8,700	435	8,525	426	...	...	...	...
Canada	1,320	66	1,315	66	1,495	75	...	...	...	...
Mexico	980	49	1,215	61	1,460	73	...	...	...	...
Venezuela	2,240	112	2,165	108	2,355	118	1,963	98	1,930	97
United Kingdom	770	39	1,080	54	1,570	79	...	...	...	...
Iran	5,665	283	5,240	262	3,035	152	4,986	249	4,685	234
Iraq	2,350	118	2,560	128	3,435	172	2,309	115	2,415	121
Kuwait	1,785	89	1,895	95	2,215	111	1,938	97	2,060	103
Saudi Arabia	9,015	451	8,065	403	9,245	462	8,993	450	8,135	407

Abu Dhabi	1,650	83	1,445	72	1,465	73	1,643	82	1,425	71
Algeria	1,100	55	1,160	58	1,135	57	1,065	53	1,165	58
Libya	2,065	103	1,985	99	2,065	103	2,034	102	1,945	97
Nigeria	2,085	104	1,895	95	2,305	115	2,044	102	1,835	92
Indonesia	1,685	84	1,635	82	1,590	80	1,473	74	1,370	69
Soviet Union	10,700	535	11,215	561	11,470	574	3,120	156	3,250	163
China	1,875	94	2,080	104	2,120	106	226	11	285	14

Sources: Production figures are from National Foreign Assessment Center, Central Intelligence Agency, *International Energy Statistical Review*, ER IESR 80-008, April 23, 1980, p. 1. Export figures are from NFAC, CIA, *Handbook of Economic Statistics, 1979*, Research Aid ER 79-10274, August 1979, p. 137. Figures are rounded. (Chinese exports were not included but are given here for comparison with the major exporters; see table 4-14 for details.) Export figures for some countries are not in this table because they were not in the sources cited. Figures are available in UN sources but are not included here because they are not precisely comparable; see United Nations, International Economic and Social Affairs Department, *World Energy Supplies, 1973–1978*, Statistical Papers, Series J, no. 22 (UN, 1979), pp. 126–35, 158–72 (hereafter UN, *WES 1973–78*). For slightly different, and more complete, CIA statistics on producers, see NFAC, CIA, *International Economic and Energy Review*, ER IESR 80-002, May 15, 1980, p. 8.

On the importing side, the number of buying countries is much larger; in fact, virtually all countries in the world now need some oil. Yet in quantitative terms, there is a great concentration of demand as well as supply in world crude oil trade. By 1975 the three major industrial areas of the world—North America, Western Europe, and Japan—together imported a total of more than a billion tons (Western Europe, 583 million tons; North America, 245 million; and Japan, 226 million), which accounted for three-quarters of total world imports.[82]

The 1973 Oil Crisis and Subsequent Trends

The present patterns of energy dependence and interdependence emerged over a quarter century, but not many people understood their full economic and political implications until the early 1970s. Then, the oil crisis of 1973–74 shocked the world into a realization of the vulnerability of the existing energy system. This crisis, precipitated by the Arab-Israeli War of October 1973, was a watershed, resulting in major changes in the configuration of international economic and political power.[83] The immediate shock came when, in reaction to the war, the Arab oil countries declared an embargo on sales to some areas; many cut back their production, using oil as a weapon to try to achieve certain political goals, and all OPEC members suddenly raised their prices for oil, increasing the prevailing world price level approximately four-fold.

In reality, however, the seeds of change had been planted much earlier.[84] From the start, the development of oil resources throughout most of the world had been carried out by a few Western companies, which monopolized the required capital, technology, and skills. Over time, these companies made agreements with most of the governments in areas where large oil reserves were believed to exist, which made possible the sale of oil at prices highly advantageous to the Western companies and to consumers in the industrial nations. Ultimately, eight major companies—five American (Exxon, Standard Oil of California, Mobil, Gulf Oil, and the Texas Company) and three European (the Royal Dutch Shell Group, British Petroleum, and the Compagnie Française des Pétroles)—controlled most of the world's major known reserves outside of the United States and Soviet Union and dominated the international oil system at every stage, from exploration to production, refining, transportation, and marketing.[85]

By the 1940s some of the less developed countries where oil development had occurred began to show mounting dissatisfaction with this situation and started to work actively for changes. One of the first was Venezuela, which in the early years of the decade pressed hard for a greater share of oil profits.[86] Gradually, the oil companies felt compelled to make concessions and to give larger shares of the oil receipts to the governments involved. They continued, however, to make large profits and kept oil prices low, to the advantage of Western consuming countries but not of the countries where the oil was located. When the companies took steps toward lowering the "posted prices" on the basis of which they paid taxes and royalties, these governments organized to resist this trend.[87]

Change was inevitable, in part because in the postcolonial era nationalism had steadily grown in the oil-producing countries, and their leaders now were determined to end foreign control of their most important resource. In 1960 a group of these countries formed OPEC, which became the main instrument for pressing to obtain a greater share of oil receipts and to increase local control over production. Step by step, OPEC's members extracted concessions from the oil companies. By 1972 the governments in some countries began to take control of oil properties, while in others they negotiated new participation agreements.

Since the 1973 crisis, the transfer of control has been close to total,[88] and today the major oil companies no longer own or control most production facilities in the OPEC countries, nor do they decide how much oil will be produced or what the sale prices will be. The companies now simply work for the governments in those countries, under conditions set by local political leaders rather than by the companies themselves. The companies provide technology, production, and management expertise and handle the worldwide distribution of the oil produced. They still make sizable profits, but local governments now receive the largest share of the receipts.

The 1973–74 crisis not only accelerated and highlighted the shift of power from the oil companies to the OPEC members' governments, it signaled fundamental changes in the structure of the global economic system. The willingness of some producing countries to use oil as a political weapon profoundly disturbed political leaders in the industrial countries, and the sudden, spectacular increase in international oil prices had an economic impact that was alarming.

In the industrial countries, the oil price increase added significantly to already difficult problems of recession and inflation and increased their balance of payments problems enormously. Most developing nations publicly applauded OPEC's action[89] because they too desired greater control over foreign companies and a larger share of foreign companies' profits. OPEC seemed to many to provide a model for cartels to control the output and prices in other basic commodities (although, in fact, it is unlikely that the model can be widely applied).[90] The 1973–74 crisis provided a major stimulus, therefore, to the so-called North-South dialogue on a wide range of economic issues and on many relationships that the less developed countries (LDCs) wished to see changed. China strongly backed OPEC's actions and increasingly identified itself with Third World positions on international economic issues during that period.

Actually, however, many non-oil-producing developing nations were hit harder by the oil price rise than were the developed countries (DCs) because they were less able to adjust to the new situation.[91] While most of the dollars earned by OPEC members flowed to investments and money markets in Western nations, the non-OPEC developing countries encountered increasing difficulties paying for oil. By 1976 they purchased about 150 million tons (net), costing close to $15 billion—five times their oil bill in 1973.[92] Certain OPEC members took steps to alleviate the strain imposed by their price increases and extended aid to some developing countries (though mainly to certain Arab and African states). Many developing countries, however, suffered seriously from the skyrocketing costs of not only oil but also oil-based products, such as chemical fertilizers, at a time when the costs of many other basic commodities they needed, such as food, also rose.[93] The LDCs' debt burden rose rapidly.[94]

Despite widespread outrage in the developed nations about the new oil prices, some Western analysts maintained that the new price level was tolerable and reflected the true scarcity value of oil more nearly than pre-1973 prices.[95] But it clearly created major economic strains affecting both DCs and LDCs. For a period of time, oil prices tended to stabilize, at close to $13 a barrel, mainly because Saudi Arabia and a few others held the line.[96] However, the effects of the crisis reinforced inflationary and recessionary trends in most nations.

When, during 1976–78, global oil output rose significantly and prices temporarily stabilized, the earlier sense of alarm eased. By 1978, in fact, oil supplies clearly exceeded demand globally (see table 4-8); temporarily, there was even concern about a new "oil glut";[97] and the real price of oil declined. However, there was continuing uneasiness about the pos-

TABLE 4-8. *World Production and Consumption of Commercial Energy, 1978*

Millions of tons of coal equivalent

Area	All commercial energy	Solid fuels	Liquid fuels	Natural gas	Hydro-electricity and nuclear electricity
		Production			
World	9,332	2,784	4,557	1,735	257
Non-Communist developed	3,271	1,069	982	1,040	179
Non-Communist developing	2,868	125	2,524	180	39
European Communist	2,356	923	897	507	28
Asian Communist	837	667	153	7	11
		Consumption			
World	8,755	2,803	3,959	1,737	256
Non-Communist developed	4,953	1,115	2,560	1,099	179
Non-Communist developing	936	140	625	132	39
European Communist	2,046	883	636	499	28
Asian Communist	821	665	139	7	11

Source: UN, *WES 1973–78*, pp. 2–3, 34–35, 38–39.

sibility of another cutoff of oil supplies, especially if there were to be a new Arab-Israeli conflict, and concern about longer-range problems also steadily increased.

One of the major uncertainties was what the Arab OPEC members would do with the huge dollar surpluses they were accumulating. In dollar terms, the value of the world's oil trade rose enormously. From 1972 to 1975, for example, the cost of the world imports of oil rose from $26.8 billion to $117.0 billion. As a percentage of total world imports, oil increased from 6.9 to 14.4 percent.[98]

The countries accumulating the largest dollar surpluses from this oil trade were a few large Arab exporters—especially Saudi Arabia but also Kuwait, the United Arab Emirates, and other countries with small populations. The total of these surpluses held in other countries grew rapidly. By the end of 1977 OPEC's net external assets totaled $155 billion,[99] and it was predicted that in time, the surpluses held by these countries could amount to several hundreds of billions of dollars.[100] Although the "recycling" of Arab dollar surpluses was more orderly than many believed possible, it was uncertain whether this could continue to be the case indefinitely. Moreover, most of the dollars found their way into investment and currency markets of the major industrial nations, and while this eased the problems of the Western nations, it did not help the non-oil-producing developing countries. There was continuing concern, also, because the Arab countries could if they wished, for either economic or political reasons, transfer large sums between countries in a way that could seriously damage the industrial economies.

After the 1973 crisis, such fears moderated briefly as leaders in some OPEC member countries, such as Saudi Arabia, demonstrated that they recognized the existence of a new kind of interdependence. With most of their dollar holdings in the major industrial nations, these countries could not ignore the danger of destabilizing trends which could diminish the value of these holdings.

The renewed tendency toward complacency in the industrial nations, apparent during 1976–78, proved to be short-lived, however. It was shattered again in late 1978 and early 1979 by another "oil crisis." The principal immediate cause this time was revolution in Iran and the upheaval there accompanying the overthrow of the shah. In response to the drop in Iranian oil exports, several oil-producing countries, most notably Saudi Arabia, temporarily increased their output, which helped to ease the immediate supply problem. However, in mid-1979 the OPEC nations announced another sharp price increase, raising the world oil price to more than $20 a barrel on the average, which greatly complicated the world's problems of coping with inflation, recession, and balance of payments deficits. (OPEC prices increased 60 percent in the seven months between December 1978 and July 1979.) By mid-1980 the average price of crude oil worldwide was about $30 a barrel and was expected to keep rising.

Trends ever since the first oil crisis in 1973 have clearly demonstrated that there is no basis for complacency about the global energy situation. These trends have highlighted the fact that in the period ahead energy problems are certain to become more, not less, serious (even if, as is possible, there is another temporary respite for a year or two).

The brief stabilization of oil supplies and prices during 1974–78[101] was due in part to a slowdown in the economic growth in the major industrial nations (Organization for Economic Cooperation and Development [OECD] countries), which averaged 2.5 percent annually in that period, compared with almost 5.0 percent in the previous five years. Even though the energy/GNP ratios also dropped in these countries (in 1978, according to one estimate, the ratio was 94.4 percent of the 1973 figure) as a result of conservation efforts and steps to increase efficiency, it was clear that any significant rise in the GNP growth rate in the industrial nations would again bring about a rise in energy consumption. Despite slower GNP growth in this period, energy consumption continued to grow. By 1978 the energy "supply" (production plus net imports) in the major industrial nations had risen to 5.640 billion tons CE[102] (75.2 million barrels a day [b/d], or 3.760 billion tons of oil equivalent [OE]). Of this, 2.978 billion tons CE (39.7 million b/d, or 1.985 billion tons OE) came from oil, and their imports (net) accounted for 64.74 percent of their total oil supply (1.285 billion tons OE, or 25.7 million b/d, or 1.928 billion tons CE). The continued growth of U.S. oil imports was particularly striking. Whereas Japan's crude oil imports increased less than 3 percent from 1975 to 1978 (from 4.539 million to 4.662 million b/d), and West Germany's by under 6 percent (from 1.807 million to 1.913 million b/d), U.S. crude oil imports increased by 52 percent (from 4.105 million to 6.232 million b/d) in the same period.[103]

The impact of the Iranian revolution dramatized once again the vulnerability of worldwide supplies of oil to political disruptions; this was underlined, moreover, by subsequent hints made by Nigeria, Libya, and others that they, too, might consider using oil exports again as a political weapon to retaliate against countries pursuing policies that they disapproved.[104] In addition, overall trends affecting energy supplies in general, as well as oil output in particular, highlighted the fact that even without political disruptions, world energy supplies will become increasingly tight in the period ahead (particularly if and when the overall growth rate in the major industrial countries begins to rise again).

In a few areas, significant additions to the world's oil supplies have come on stream in recent years, for example, from Alaskan and North Sea production and from increasing production in some developing countries such as Mexico. However, many factors make the outlook for the near future generally a pessimistic one. Alaskan North Slope output already is believed, by some, to be reaching a plateau, and overall U.S. oil production now is expected to start to decline; proved oil reserves in the United States outside of Alaska have recently fallen. While British and Norwegian North Sea production is giving the economies of these countries an important temporary shot in the arm, North Sea oil output is expected by many analysts to peak in the 1980s. Mexico's reserves are now believed to be large (25 billion to 30 billion barrels, or roughly between 3.5 billion and 4 billion tons), but the Mexicans are deliberately exploiting their oil slowly (production in 1980 is expected to be about 100 million tons, or 2.0 million b/d), in order to prolong the period they can rely upon it. Moreover, output increases in the Soviet Union, the world's largest oil producer, have slowed ever since the mid-1970s, and output could peak soon; if so, the USSR itself may have little to export, and the East European nations may have to turn increasingly to Middle East nations as sources of supply (a few already have begun to do so).[105]

Perhaps most important of all, the major OPEC oil producers in the Persian Gulf now seem unlikely to increase their oil output to any large extent in the period immediately ahead (except possibly to ease serious world shortages temporarily, as the Saudis did in 1979).[106] Iranian output probably will remain well below its earlier peak level (production in 1979 was 3.035 million b/d, compared with 5.240 million b/d in 1978; some believe it will eventually stabilize at between 3 million and 4 million b/d, or 150 million and 200 million tons a year). Most of the other large Persian Gulf producers have made it clear that for varied economic, social, and political reasons, including an understandable desire to conserve their oil resources for longer use, they now intend to try to maintain ceilings on output, in many cases below present capacity. The Saudis, for example, are now reluctant to produce more than 8.5 million b/d, or 425 million tons a year. The leaders in Kuwait, Abu Dhabi, and other countries also are inclined to limit their output. It is very possible, therefore, that OPEC oil production will not increase much above its present level during the next few years.

These trends have made it evident that the effects on the international system resulting from recent energy developments, and from those affecting oil in particular, will be far-reaching and in a basic sense are irreversible. As a result, the search for alternatives to crude oil has, of necessity, accelerated. There is no question that in time many other energy sources—including synthetic fuels, solar, thermal, and wind energy, and perhaps eventually energy from fusion, as well as significantly increased use of coal, natural gas, and (probably, despite current opposition in many quarters) nuclear energy—will gradually replace oil. This change *must* occur, because if it does not, the world economy eventually will enter a period of major crisis. However, the change will at best take time. During the difficult transition period, world trends affecting the supply and demand of oil will continue to be a primary determinant of the economic health and potential for growth of the entire global economy.

The Future of Oil

No one knows exactly when world oil "supplies" will drop below the world "demand" or "need."[107] All estimates must be based on complex calculations of likely supply and demand, and there are as many unknowns as knowns that must be considered. No disagreement exists, however, about the fact that the total supply of oil in the world is limited and steadily shrinking.

In 1977 a leading oil expert, M. King Hubbert, formerly of the U.S. Geological Survey, estimated that the proven, recoverable crude oil reserves in the world as of January 1, 1976, totaled roughly 78 billion tons (567 billion barrels).[108] From the start of the world oil industry until 1976, according to his calculations, cumulative oil output had totaled more than 46 billion tons (339 billion barrels). Therefore, all the oil discovered up to 1976—the sum of past production and remaining known reserves—amounted to 124 billion tons (906 billion barrels). Adding to these figures his estimate of possible future discoveries of recoverable oil, Hubbert concluded that, worldwide, "ultimate production" (that is, the total amount that will ultimately be found and considered recoverable added to that already discovered and used) will probably amount to around 274 billion tons (2 trillion barrels). Of this, he estimated, oil in the non-Communist countries will account for about 193 billion tons (1.41 trillion barrels)—of which the Middle East alone will account for 82 billion tons (598 billion barrels)—while that in the Communist nations will probably be about 65 billion tons (472 billion barrels). (To these specific estimates, Hubbert then added his estimate of possible future discoveries, unattributed to any area.) He concluded that future production of oil (after January 1, 1976) might total about 228 billion tons (1.66 trillion barrels).

There are some variations in estimates of known oil reserves in the world, but they are not great. (Some of the differences are due to differences in definitions of "proved" and other terms.) In 1977 the CIA put the total of the world's "proved and probable" reserves in 1976 at close to 91 billion tons (665 billion barrels)—with roughly 82 billion tons (600 billion barrels) in the non-Communist world and close to 9 billion tons (65 billion barrels) in the Communist nations.[109] A study by a leading group of international oil experts, the Workshop on International Energy Strategies, endorsed oil industry estimates which indicated that at the end of 1975 proved world reserves of crude oil totaled roughly 90 billion tons (658 billion barrels)—76 billion tons (555 billion barrels) in the non-Communist nations and 14 billion tons (103 billion barrels) in the Communist nations.[110] Generally in recent years estimates of known recoverable reserves have varied from a little less than to a little more than 80 billion tons (though the figure has sometimes been more than 90 billion tons when probable reserves have been included, as in the CIA figure cited).[111]

There also has been a fairly strong consensus that the total of the world's ultimate recoverable oil is probably close to Hubbert's estimate of 2 trillion barrels (around 274 billion tons). (Hubbert cited eight other estimates made by experts from 1971 on that ranged between 1.8 trillion and 2 trillion barrels or between 247 billion and 274 billion tons.[112]) These figures suggest, it should be noted, that recoverable reserves discovered in the future will exceed all the reserves found to date. If this estimate proves to be wrong, the world's oil supply will, of course, become very tight even sooner than most experts predict.

There are a few specialists who challenge the conventional wisdom and argue that more, rather than less, new oil than now projected is likely to be discovered in the future and that, therefore, estimates of the world's total ultimately recoverable oil should be larger than most recent estimates. One expert, in particular—Bernardo F. Grossling of the U.S. Geological Survey—has argued strongly that recent estimates have grossly underestimated the size of likely recoverable reserves in many Third World countries, where exploration to date has not been extensive. He has asserted that ultimate oil recovery in Africa, Latin America, and parts of Asia may turn out to be at least double—and perhaps three or more times—the size indicated by current estimates and that projections of the world total supply, therefore, should be a good deal higher than Hubbert's.[113] It remains to be seen whether this view is justified— although the World Bank has been sufficiently impressed by analyses such as Grossling's to launch a major program to find and produce new oil in non-OPEC Third World countries.[114] However, for the present, it is doubtless wise to base estimates of future oil supplies on the conservative consensus views.

If one accepts Hubbert's estimates as valid, what they mean, simply stated, is the following. If one were to assume that world production of crude oil will remain at roughly 3 billion tons a year (slightly above the mid-1970s level but slightly below the level in mid-1979), the total of proved and recoverable reserves known as of early 1976 would last twenty-six years. There are certain to be significant new discoveries, however, and if they total roughly what Hubbert predicts (that is, if, at the start of 1976 the world still had 274 billion tons remaining to be discovered and exploited), production at the rate of 3 billion tons a year would last ninety-one years, or until the mid-twenty-first century.

It is clear, however, that oil production and consumption will not remain indefinitely at around the 3 billion ton level of recent years but will continue to rise, probably very substantially. (And, already in 1979, consumption increases exceeded new oil discoveries.[115]) Rates of growth in oil demand probably will slow, but total demand still will go up and up. Hubbert calculated that from 1880 to 1973 world oil production increased at an average rate of 7 percent a year, doubling every ten years, and that the oil produced in the world during the period 1960–70 almost equaled all oil consumed from the start of oil production (in the 1850s) to 1960.[116] (In the six-year period 1960–65 global oil consumption was only a little less than the total in the previous ten years.)[117] Even if the pace of increase slows, as it probably will, the rise in future oil demand will be fairly large in absolute terms. Key questions for the future are exactly how rapidly and by how much demand will rise, and what the relationship between future demand and future supply will be.

Many attempts have been made to estimate likely trends in both the supply and the demand for oil in the years ahead. All have tried to assess a wide variety of factors: the size of present oil reserves, the rate of discovery of new reserves, the likely amount of ultimate oil recovery, the possible worldwide rate of GNP growth, the likely energy/GNP elasticity coefficient, the probable rate of growth in overall demand for energy, the possible increases in the production of energy other than oil, and therefore the likely demand for oil (which often is simply calculated as a residual—that is, the difference between total energy demand and non-oil energy supplies). Such estimates generally also have been based on calculations about the consequences of oil cost and price trends, the possibilities for increasing oil production, the likely rates of depletion (the reserve/production [R/P] ratio), and possible increases in oil recovery rates (the percentage of known oil deposits that can be extracted economically). As this list of factors indicates, so many variables are involved that the margin for possible error is large in any estimate. Yet the differences in estimates have not been as great as one might have expected. The conclusions reached by a few leading experts provide at least a general idea, therefore, of what the probable future of oil will be.

One fairly pessimistic projection was made in 1977 by CIA energy analysts.[118] These analysts made global projections, but the main question on which their analysis focused was how long OPEC exporters will be able and willing to meet the import needs of the major industrial nations. Analyzing first the economic prospects for the OECD countries (the major industrial powers that consume most of the world's energy), they estimated that the rates of GNP growth between 1981 and 1985 would be 4 percent in the United States, 3.5 percent in OECD Europe, and 6 percent in Japan. According to calculations in this study, total world energy demand (for all commercial energy, not just for oil) would by 1985 reach 5 billion tons of oil equivalent, a figure 40 percent above 1976, and the authors estimated that by 1985 the oil import needs of the OECD countries would be 2.7 billion to 2.8 billion tons (54 million to 56 million b/d).

Calculating that the GNP growth rate of the non-Communist, non-OPEC developing countries would average 4.5 percent until 1985, they estimated that their oil import needs would be 150 million to 200 million tons (3 million to 4 million b/d) by the mid-1980s. And they estimated that by 1985 the Communist nations—mainly the Soviet Union—might be net importers of 175 million to 225 million tons (3.5 million to 4.5 million b/d) (instead of, as recently, net exporters to the West). Altogether, according to the CIA's 1977 estimates, by 1985 the entire world other than the OPEC nations would require 2.34 billion to 2.56 billion tons (46.8 million to 51.2 million b/d) of oil from the OPEC nations (compared with 1.5 billion tons [30 million b/d] in 1976)—in addition to other sources of supply—to meet their needs.

On the supply side, CIA analysts calculated that by 1985 OPEC nations other than Saudi Arabia might produce between 1.38 billion and 1.47 billion tons (27.6 million to 29.4 million b/d), only marginally above their recent output level, and that world demand for Saudi Arabian oil could rise to between 950 million and 1.15 billion tons (19 million to 23 million b/d) in 1985—roughly double Saudi Arabia's current sustainable capacity. Although, theoretically, the Saudis could produce that much by then, the CIA analysts predicted that for understandable economic and other reasons, they would be reluctant to do so. The CIA concluded, therefore, that by 1985 world oil supply would fall considerably short of global needs and that, in anticipation of this, sharp price rises probably would occur in the early 1980s. (Although in 1977 some other specialists disagreed with the CIA's judgment that the Soviet Union is likely to become a sizable oil importer by 1985,[119] in 1979 CIA specialists strongly reaffirmed their judgment, again predicting that the European Communist bloc as a whole would become net oil importers in the 1980s.)[120]

In their later analysis in 1979, projecting trends through 1982,[121] CIA estimates were somewhat different but still pessimistic. Its analysts calculated that by 1982 the oil available for importation by OECD nations might be 23.1 million b/d (1.155 billion tons), that the imports of other developed nations might total 0.9 million b/d (45 million tons), and that those of the non-OPEC developing nations would be 2.6 million b/d (130 million tons), while by 1982 the Communist nations as a whole might be net importers of about 0.7 million b/d (35 million tons). They also estimated that by 1982 the OPEC nations might produce 30.2 million b/d (1.510 billion tons) of oil and export 27.3 million b/d (1.365 billion tons). Concluding that the total energy available to the industrial countries would increase only slowly in the early 1980s and that there would be little increase in available supplies of oil, they predicted low growth rates, partly because of the energy supply constraints, unless there is much greater—in fact unprecedented—improvement in conservation and in the efficiency of energy use. They predicted that energy needs in the OECD countries might exceed readily available supplies if their average GNP growth rate is above 2 percent—and certainly if it is above 3 percent—unless the OPEC nations are willing to export more than is now predicted.

Hubbert, whose figures on reserves were cited earlier, calculated that unless there are unexpected developments, total world production of oil will rise to a peak of perhaps 5 billion tons a year in about the mid-1990s and thereafter will decline and approach zero sometime between 2050 and 2075. By the third quarter of the twenty-first century, he estimated, the world will be without significant supplies of crude oil for all practical purposes.[122]

Another expert, John H. Lichtblau of the Petroleum Industry Research Foundation, predicted in 1977 that if past rates of increase in oil demand were to continue, an oil crisis would be inevitable as early as the mid-1980s. He judged that what actually is likely is that oil demand (and GNP) will grow at somewhat lower rates than in the recent past but that, even so, oil needs in the non-Communist world are likely to surpass the amount of oil available at prices that are nonprohibitive by 1990 and that supply constraints will increase and major price rises will occur before then.[123]

The OECD itself estimated in 1977 that the energy demand of its members would grow at an average rate of 3.1 percent and that if so, these countries will require 5 billion tons of oil equivalent (101.9 million b/d) of all forms of energy by 1985. At that time, according to OECD calculations, they would still rely on oil for about 2.5 billion tons (50.3 million b/d), or about half of their total energy needs (49 percent, compared with 51 percent in 1974), and would need to import (net) about 1.75 billion tons (35 million b/d) of oil.[124] OECD estimated that worldwide the oil available for export in 1985 (1.76 billion tons from OPEC members, 190 million tons from other non-Communist nations, possibly 100 million tons from the Soviet Union, and up to 60 million tons from China) might still exceed (though only barely) the world's oil import needs (including 1.75 billion tons needed by OECD, 210 million tons needed by other non-Communist countries, and 120 million tons needed by Eastern Europe). However, it predicted that a gap between demand and supply would develop soon thereafter.

A very detailed analysis of the future of oil was prepared in 1977 by the Workshop on Alternative Energy Strategies (hereafter called the Workshop) mentioned earlier.[125] The Workshop concentrated its analysis on the non-Communist world and focused primary attention on the major consumers in OECD and the major suppliers in OPEC. It projected a range on plausible futures.

First, the Workshop calculated what demand and supply theoretically could be, under different assumptions. It estimated rates of GNP growth at high and low levels. (The high was 5.2 percent per year for the period 1976–85 and 4 percent from 1985 to 2000; the low was 3.4 percent per year from 1976 to 1985 and 2.8 percent from 1985 to 2000—well below actual recent rates.) It also estimated the possible effects of high and low prices. (At one extreme, the assumption was that real energy prices would remain constant to the year 2000, which was very unrealistic; at the other extreme, the assumption was that a 50 percent increase would occur between 1985 and 2000—even this was clearly overoptimistic.) Combining different variables, the study projected possible rates in oil demand growth, ranging between lows of 2.5 percent from 1976 to 1985 (and 1.8 percent from 1985 to 2000) and highs of 3.6 percent from 1976 to 1985 (and 2.6 percent from 1985 to 2000). (These, too, may be optimistic and in any case are below rates in the recent past.) It calculated that the rate at which additions to proven reserves are discovered between 1975 and 2000 could vary from a low rate of 1.37 billion tons a year to a high rate of 2.74 billion. It also judged that the recovery rate from wells (recently just under 30 percent worldwide) might rise to about 40 percent. And it assumed that the maximum realistic R/P ratio globally would be 15/1. (The actual global average ratio recently probably has been just under 30/1, although in different places it has varied from just over 10/1 to well over 40/1.)[126]

Combining different assumptions and estimates of the effects of these key variables, the Workshop made several projections of when world oil needs would exceed supply. In one, they predicted that the critical year would be 1990, when production would peak at 3.6 billion tons, thereafter declining to 2.5 billion in 2010 and 1 billion in 2025. In another, it predicted that this would not occur until 1997, when production would reach a maximum of 4.3 billion, thereafter declining to 4 billion in 2000 and 1.5 billion in 2025.

All of these theoretical projections—which placed the peak years of oil supply between 1990 and 2000—were based on the assumption that the OPEC members, especially Saudi Arabia, would be indefinitely willing to deplete their reserves at a high rate. However, the Workshop judged (undoubtedly, correctly) that, in fact, this is highly unlikely and that OPEC members' output will be well below their theoretical capacity. Because of this, the Workshop concluded, production in OPEC, and the world, would probably peak by at least 1990 (and this also may have been too optimistic).

What all of these studies, despite their differences, suggest is that although global oil supply probably will meet world needs, at rising but still tolerable prices, for a few years to come, at some point between 1985 and 2010—most plausibly, perhaps, around 1990—rising world demand and lagging world supply will create a critical situation; the price of oil will rise sharply, and the use of petroleum will decline. Oil could virtually disappear as a significant energy source at least by the middle of the twenty-first century.

This is the global context in which China's emergence as a major oil producer—and as a possible exporter of increased amounts of oil—must be examined. During the next decade or two, and possibly as early as 1985, long-term trends could create an oil crisis of much more fundamental and lasting significance than the crises that occurred in the 1970s.

The seriousness of the crisis will depend in large part on how rapidly, in the next few years, the world can develop energy sources other than oil and can increase the efficiency with which all energy is used—in short, how successfully and rapidly it can make the transition to a new kind of world energy system. The ease or difficulty with which this transition occurs also will be influenced, however, by the ability and willingness of major oil producers to keep up or expand their oil exports during the transition years. The most important questions in this respect obviously concern the future capabilities and policies of Middle Eastern oil giants such as Saudi Arabia. But any new additions to world oil supplies during this period, from old or new oil exporters—including China—could be significant.

China's Energy

Modernization and economic growth have been accompanied by rap-idly rising consumption of primary commercial energy in China, as else-where.[127] Since the Communist takeover, as both industrialization and agricultural modernization have occurred, the country's need for energy has soared. The Chinese have given high priority, therefore, to industries producing energy in their development plans, placing special emphasis starting in the 1960s on oil. Since the early 1960s, they have been able to meet their escalating energy needs and have had a small exportable sur-plus. However, they also have confronted serious energy bottlenecks, and by the late 1970s energy issues posed some of the most difficult and important questions for China's entire development program.

Even in the context of a world in which energy consumption quin-tupled between 1950 and 1975, the rapid growth of China's energy con-sumption in recent years has been remarkable; from 1952 through 1978 estimated consumption of energy in China (according to CIA data) in-creased almost fifteen-fold (table 4-9).[128] In 1950, despite being the most populous nation on earth, China ranked only tenth in total energy con-sumption, using less energy than Poland and Canada. Today it ranks third, in gross terms (though it still ranks fairly low in per capita con-sumption).[129]

China's development as an energy producer has been even more im-pressive (table 4-10). Only a few other major countries have been able

TABLE 4-9. *China: Consumption of Primary Energy, by Sector, Selected Years, 1952–78*

Year	Total	Industry construction	Agriculture	Transport	Residential-commercial
		Millions of metric tons of coal equivalent			
1952	42	11	*	5	26
1957	96	36	1	9	50
1965	196	95	6	15	80
1970	293ª	168	12	17	96
1975	471	292	30	24	125
1976	492	305	33	25	129
1977	558	345	36	28	149
1978	626	387	40	32	167
		Percent			
1952	100	26	*	12	62
1957	100	38	1	9	52
1965	100	48	3	8	41
1970	100	57	4	6	33
1975	100	62	6	5	27
1976	100	62	7	5	26
1977	100	62	6	5	27
1978	100	62	6	5	27

Source: NFAC, CIA, *China: A Statistical Compendium*, ER 79-10374, July 1979, p. 10. These estimates were made prior to the revised estimates of production and supply included in tables 4-10 and 4-11. They should be regarded as rough estimates that will require adjustment downward. (Total consumption may be roughly several million tons less in recent years than this table shows, but the distribution by sector is probably close to correct.)
* Negligible
a. The original, by mistake, had 273 instead of 293.

to meet their own energy needs in this period of rapidly rising demand. (The only other notable case is the Soviet Union.) For the Chinese to have done so has been a significant achievement. In the process, China has risen from eleventh to either fourth or third in its ranking among world energy producers.[130]

The fact that China is now a net exporter of energy is remarkable, even though the volume of its energy exports is still relatively small. Among the other major powers, only the Soviet Union now has a surplus of energy to sell abroad. During the next few years, China's ability to expand its oil and coal exports could be important both economically

TABLE 4-10. *China: Production of Primary Energy, Selected Years, 1952-79*

Year	Raw coal (millions of metric tons)	Crude oil (millions of metric tons)	Natural gas (billions of cubic meters)	Hydroelectricity (billions of kilowatt-hours)
1952	66.5	0.4	*	n.a.
1957	130.7	1.5	0.7	n.a.
1965	232.2	11.4	1.1	13.2
1970	327.4	30.1	3.8	26.8
1975	478.0	77.1	9.2	46.7
1976	483.0	86.8	10.2	47.4
1977	550.0	93.6	12.5	48.3
1978	618.0	104.1	13.7	45.9
1979	635.0	106.2	14.5	50.6

Sources: The figures for coal and oil through 1978 are from NFAC, CIA, *China: A Statistical Compendium*, p. 9. The 1979 figures for coal, oil, and natural gas are from State Statistical Bureau Communiqué, in Foreign Broadcast Information Service, *Daily Report—People's Republic of China*, Department of Commerce, National Technical Information Service, April 30, 1980, p. L2. The figures on hydroelectricity are CIA estimates as of mid-1980, obtained orally from the CIA, July 25, 1980 (they exclude output of small hydroelectric stations with a capacity under 500 kilowatts). The figures for natural gas from 1952 through 1978 are from NFAC, CIA, *Electric Power for China's Modernization: The Hydroelectric Option*, Research Paper ER 80-10089U, May 1980, p. 23.
n.a. Not available.
* Negligible.

and politically, not only to the Chinese themselves but also to the entire global community.

Consideration of the possible international implications of China's future energy policies requires prior analysis of likely trends in energy production and energy consumption within China. A logical starting point is an examination of the growth to date of the major Chinese industries producing energy (see table 4-11). Oil is the resource with the greatest international significance, but before trying to judge China's oil export potential, it is necessary to look at the growth, problems, and prospects of each major energy source in China.

Coal

Coal has been used as a fuel in China longer than in Europe or elsewhere. As early as the fourth century, coal was used for smelting iron.[131] When Marco Polo visited China in the thirteenth century, he expressed amazement about the "black stones" that burned.[132]

However, until about a hundred years ago, coal mining in China was

TABLE 4-11. *China: Supply of Primary Energy Including Net Imports, Selected Years, 1952–79*[a]

Coal equivalent

Year	Total	Coal	Oil	Natural gas	Hydro-electricity
		Millions of metric tons			
1952	50	48	2	*	*
1957	110	103	5	1	1
1965	197	177	17	1	2
1970	300	246	46	5	3
1975	477	355	104	12	6
1976	499	360	119	14	6
1977	560	409	128	17	6
1978	624	458	142	18	6
1979	637	470	142	19	6
		Percent			
1952	100	96	4	*	*
1957	100	94	5	under 1	under 1
1965	100	90	7	under 1	1
1970	100	82	15	2	1
1975	100	74	22	3	1
1976	100	72	24	3	1
1977	100	73	23	3	1
1978	100	73	23	3	1
1979	100	74	22	3	1

Sources: The coal equivalent figures for coal and oil for 1952 through 1978 are from NFAC, CIA, *China: A Statistical Compendium*, p. 10. I calculated the 1979 figure for coal at the same conversion rate the CIA uses for 1975 through 1978 (1 ton of raw coal equals 0.74 ton CE). I calculated the 1979 oil CE figure as the same as 1978 since the supply (crude oil production minus crude oil exports) is roughly the same. (The conversion rate is somewhat more than 1.5 tons of CE per ton of oil.) I have calculated the CE figures for natural gas and hydroelectricity using the following conversion rates: 1,000 cubic meters of natural gas equal 1.332 tons CE, and 1,000 kilowatt-hours of electricity equal 0.125 ton CE. The annual totals of CE and percentage figures are my calculations.

* Negligible.

a. Data for coal, oil, natural gas, and hydroelectric power are expressed in terms of coal equivalents (calorific value of 7,000 kilocalories per kilogram); minor fuels such as peat and fuelwood excluded.

limited to small mines employing primitive methods, and the quantities of coal used were small. The Industrial Revolution led to widespread use of coal in Europe, but for many years thereafter China, despite its long history of using coal in small quantities, continued to rely for its energy mainly on traditional fuels and human and animal power.

Large-scale modern mining of coal in China began largely as a result of foreigners' initiatives.[133] From the late nineteenth century on, however, coal use developed steadily, and gradually some large mines were opened, with Western help at Kailan (Kailuan) in North China and with Japanese help in the Northeast (Manchuria).

The growth of modern transportation and new industries after World War I stimulated increased output of coal. Production grew steadily, from 16 million tons in 1926 to 21 million tons in 1931, 34 million tons in 1936, and 58 million tons in 1942, thereafter declining as a result of war and civil conflict.[134] Coal mining was one of the first large-scale modern industries in China, and as such it played an extremely important role in the small but dynamic modern sector of the economy; in most years between 1912 and 1949 it accounted for one-fifth or more of total net value added in China's modern industry.[135]

In the first half of the twentieth century coal achieved overwhelming dominance as the primary fuel for China's economic development, as it had in the early stages of modern development in Europe, the United States, and many other areas. In fact, coal became virtually the only important source of modern commercial energy; as late as 1952 it provided 96 percent of China's primary energy[136] (although for the economy as a whole, traditional forms of energy probably exceeded coal in total energy contribution until several years later).

When the Communists assumed power in 1949, China's coal output was about 32 million tons (well below its previous peak), roughly two-thirds of which came from large mines and one-third from small pits.[137] The new regime, of necessity, gave high priority to restoring old mines and expanding the industry. In the ensuing years, output grew impressively. By 1951 coal output was close to its previous peak, and during China's first Five Year Plan period production doubled, rising from more than 66 million tons in 1952 to almost 131 million tons in 1957. Following the ups and downs of the economy as a whole, coal production skyrocketed as a result of the Great Leap, surpassing 230 million tons in 1958 and 300 million tons in 1959, then plummeted in the depression that followed, reaching a low of 170 million tons in 1961 before starting a long climb upward. It was not until 1970, when production reached 327 million tons, that output surpassed its 1959 level. Since then, however, it has continued to rise steadily, reaching 483 million tons in 1976, 550 million tons in 1977, 618 million tons in 1978, and 635 million tons in 1979.[138]

The structure of the coal mining industry has changed significantly during these years.[139] In the 1950s, before the Great Leap, expanded output came mainly from large mines. The output of small mines was fairly constant—about 10 million tons a year—and their share of China's total coal production dropped to less than one-tenth (compared to close to one-third in 1949).

Then, starting at the time of the Great Leap Forward, China's leaders put increasing stress on small-scale local industry, and the output of small coal mines rose rapidly. By 1976, according to a Western estimate, their output totaled about 148 million tons, or roughly one-third of national coal production, and recent Chinese figures show that now small mines account for close to half.[140] The quality of coal produced by these mines generally is low, and many mines are inefficient and wasteful. Nevertheless, small mines have made a major contribution to China's energy supplies during the past two decades.[141] They have required relatively small amounts of capital and have resulted in significant savings in transport costs.[142]

Coal continues to be China's dominant source of primary energy. However, since the early 1960s—when greater efforts to develop other fuels began—its share of China's total energy output has dropped, as it had earlier in most major developed countries. By 1979, China obtained almost one-fourth of its energy from other sources (mainly oil), and coal's share of the nation's total energy supply had dropped to about 74 percent—compared with close to 100 percent thirty years earlier.[143] Nevertheless, coal continues to be more important in China than in any other large nation. It probably still fuels more than two-thirds of China's industry[144] and accounts for close to three-fourths of the electricity provided by large power plants in China.[145] Coal still runs almost all of China's railways and serves the energy needs of the mass of Chinese, especially in urban centers. As of the mid-1970s, according to one estimate, perhaps 56 percent of all the coal produced in China was used in industry, 25 percent in households, about 9 percent for the generation of electricity, and 6 percent for transportation.[146]

Technologically, although coal mining in China has been gradually modernized since 1949, prevailing methods still lag fairly far behind those used in advanced industrial nations. Mechanical mining accounted for only a tiny percentage of China's coal output three decades ago—only 4 percent in 1950 according to one estimate.[147] The percentage has risen since then, and today probably most of the output in China's large mines is mechanized to some degree, but most of the small mines producing roughly half of China's coal are still primitive. Soon after 1949 the regime decided to shift, in most large mines, from room and pillar mining to the more efficient long wall method, which now predominates.[148] However, in the 1960s and early 1970s the pace of modernization in coal mines slowed, and technological improvement lagged, in part because the regime gave high priority to other energy sources such as oil in its investment policies. As a result, the rate of increase in coal production declined during the mid-1970s, and the industry was plagued with problems, especially after 1973.[149]

In the period from 1952 through 1979 the annual average rate of increase in raw coal output was 8.7 percent.[150] However, the rate declined in the early 1970s before rising again. From 1970 through 1976 the average annual rate was 6.7 percent, significantly below the long-term average. Fluctuations since then have created uncertainties about the near future. Immediately following the confusion of Mao's final years, coal output rose impressively, by almost 14 percent in 1977 and over 12 percent in 1978. However, it then dropped to under 3 percent in 1979.

Because of coal's importance to the economy as a whole, the recent drop in production has been disturbing. The Chinese now fully recognize that they must continue to rely on coal as the country's main energy source. Acknowledging that the industry is a weak link in the economy, they have initiated a major effort to increase the level of mechanization in coal mining and to introduce more advanced technological processes.[151] In 1978 they stated that their goal would be to double output in the next ten years, which would require an average annual rate of increase of well over 7 percent a year.[152] However, more recent statements indicate that at least some Chinese realize that this will be difficult to do and that this target already has been reduced. In fact, in private conversations some Chinese express concern that during the next year or two coal output could stagnate—or even decline—before output picks up again.

China's theoretical potential for increasing coal output is enormous. Long before the Communists came to power it was known that the country's coal reserves are among the largest in the world; in the pre-1949 period they were conservatively estimated at between 200 billion and 300 billion tons.[153] By the late 1950s, after further geological exploration, some Chinese claims put the figure as high as 9 trillion to 10 trillion tons.[154] Western experts are more conservative, but even their estimates are now high. One recent survey of world resources lists China's coal reserves at about 1 trillion tons—300 billion "measured" and 700 billion "indicated and inferred."[155] U.S. government sources currently estimate that China's total coal resources are probably about 1.5 trillion tons—which puts China roughly on a par with the United States and the Soviet Union—and that "proved" reserves are at least 80 billion tons.[156] A more conservative Chinese estimate in 1980 put the figure at 600 billion tons.[157] Conceivably, China may have close to one-fifth of the world's "probable recoverable" coal.[158] There is no doubt that China's resources can sustain a high level of output for almost the indefinite future; unlike oil, coal is not in danger of being depleted soon. Even if China had "only" 80 billion tons of recoverable coal, it would be able to produce at the present level for more than 125 years.[159]

The country's coal problem is not due to any shortage of resources, therefore, but to insufficient investment in the industry—which competes for scarce capital with many other industries—and lack of modern technology to speed up production. In the recent past the coal industry has received considerably less capital investment or new technology than competing industries such as oil. To meet China's urgent needs, investment in coal will have to be increased.

The problems facing China's coal industry are numerous. A great deal of the equipment used today, even in the country's best, large coal mines, is obsolete. Much of it has been overused and, at a minimum, needs replacement;[160] what is really needed is more modern and efficient equipment. China's small mines face a variety of problems. The relatively low caloric content of much of the coal the small mines produce imposes severe limits on its use.[161] Without the benefit of economies of scale, moreover, production costs in these mines often are high. And few of the small mines have any beneficiation facilities to clean and process coal. China's plant facilities for preparation of coal (including beneficiation) from large mines have increased significantly in the past quarter century, but, according to one estimate, by 1975 they could handle only 133 million tons of coal; although this was almost twenty-seven times the figure for 1949, it meant that China's coal preparation capacity still could handle less than one-third of the nation's total output.[162]

The location of China's coal reserves creates other problems. North China is believed to have about 70 percent, and Shansi (Shanxi) Province alone close to 50 percent, of China's identified deposits.[163] The country's largest mines have been developed in the North and the Northeast; transporting coal to other regions, especially in the South, has posed major problems and involved large costs. In recent years the Chinese have made a deliberate effort to open new mines—especially small and medium ones—in the South, with some success,[164] but output is still geographically concentrated.

Large coal mines in China are generally administered by bureaus, which control all the mines in a particular locality; a small number of these bureaus—most are in the North and Northeast—still produce a disproportionate percentage of China's coal.[165] In the mid-1970s, at least eight bureaus, including those of Kailan (Kailuan), Tatung (Datung), Fuhsin (Fuxin), Fushun (Fushun), and four others, each produced 10 million to 20 million tons or more a year. Seven others produced 5 million to 9 million tons each; at least fourteen produced 2 million to 4 million tons; but about sixty produced only between 0.5 million and 2 million tons.

The concentration of large mines in the North, where the best coal reserves are located, creates serious transportation problems. As China's coal industry gradually is dispersed, as will eventually happen when some of the best existing mines begin to exhaust their richest and most easily exploitable seams, the production costs of some coal mining could well rise and there will have to be large new investments in the country's transportation network. China will then have to place greater emphasis on coal development in more remote areas such as the Northwest, where a large percentage of China's "probable resources" (more than half, according to Soviet experts) is located.[166] This may, however, be some years in the future.

In the period immediately ahead, China urgently needs to raise the output of coal, mainly from mines in the North and Northeast, but it is difficult to predict the rate of increase. One CIA study estimated that between 1977 and 1985 the average rate could be between 6 and 7 percent a year.[167] If, starting from output of 635 million tons of raw coal (470 million tons CE) in 1979, the annual increase did average 6 to 7 percent, 1985 output would total between 900 million and 953 million tons of raw coal, and, assuming that the ratio between high-quality output from large mines and low-quality output from small mines remained the same, this would equal 666 million to 705 million tons of standard coal (with 7,000 kilocalories per kilogram). To judge from China's performance in 1979–80, this estimate seems too optimistic.

Some analysts believe that China will have difficulty achieving such rates of increase in coal output and that future growth could be slower than in the past.[168] However, if China steps up its investments in the coal industry and carries out a major program of technological modernization, after the present "readjustment" a rate of 6 or 7 percent or even slightly higher is possible. Unquestionably, a substantial modernization effort will be required, and investment in the coal industry will have to receive higher priority in overall development plans than it did in the late 1960s and early 1970s, when Chinese leaders definitely favored the oil industry. During that period, Chinese leaders fostered unnecessary conversions from coal to oil in power plants and began a general shift to oil that followed a pattern set in many other countries. Until recently, some experts predicted that China would continue to give much higher priority to oil than to coal.[169]

Yet at least since 1978 Peking's leaders have recognized the necessity to foster rapid coal development at the same time that they try to accelerate exploitation of oil. They have not only slowed down the shift from coal to oil in domestic use but have actually started converting some plants using oil back to coal. No matter how large China's oil reserves prove to be, its coal resources are much larger, and from a long-run perspective it is clear that China must try to stretch out the use of available oil resources.

Large-scale expansion and modernization of coal output will not be cheap, and substantial capital will have to be invested in new transportation facilities as well as in new mines. Nevertheless, because even modernized coal mining is more labor-intensive than oil or gas production, it should have cost advantages. Modernization of Chinese coal mining will require sizable imports of foreign capital and technology, but because the technology required in the coal industry is less complex than that required for oil or gas, the needed equipment and technology from abroad probably will require less foreign exchange.[170] In any case, the importance of coal to many key industries—including iron, steel, and railway transportation—as well as for urban household and commercial use in China, makes it essential to give primary attention to this industry. Although there are some unavoidable disadvantages in relying heavily on coal—including high transport costs and pollution problems—fairly rapid expansion of coal output will be one prerequisite for success in China's modernization program. It will also be essential if China is to earn the foreign exchange it needs to import essential capital goods and technology. Not only do the Chinese now hope to increase their coal exports, especially to Japan, but production of enough coal to meet a large share of China's domestic energy needs will be a prerequisite for releasing any significant amount of China's oil for export. If coal output lags, most of China's oil will have to be used at home.

China's urgent need for increased output of both coal and oil has long posed difficult dilemmas for Peking's leaders, who for many years have debated the relative priority they should give—in allocating investments, skills, and foreign exchange—to further development of China's oldest and still dominant coal producing industry and to its fastest developing (until recently) and vitally important new oil producing industry.

From the start of the 1960s until recently, oil was unquestionably the glamour industry in China, specially favored in investment policy, and the "Taching [Daqing] model" was held up as an example for others to follow.[171] However, during 1978 it became evident that Peking (Beijing) had decided that a major effort also had to be made to increase coal output as rapidly as possible. In his speech to the National People's Congress (NPC) in early 1978 Hua Kuo-feng (Hua Guofeng), in describing large new projects scheduled for construction during the period 1978–85, mentioned eight major coal mines as well as ten oil and gas fields.[172] By early 1978 Chinese officials stated in private discussions with visiting foreigners that China would "mainly concentrate" on coal because it is China's "most reliable and ample" fuel.[173] At about the same time, China's top leader in the field of science and technology stressed that coal would be China's main energy source for a "fairly long time"; he also discussed the need to build power stations at coal pits and proposed developing coal "gasification, liquefaction, and multipurpose utilization."[174] And, as noted earlier, it was revealed that China's long-term target was to double coal output in ten years and then to double output again between 1987 and the end of the century.[175]

During 1978 the Chinese began to import sizable amounts of coal mining equipment and discussed with the Germans, British, Americans, and others possible projects requiring foreign cooperation or assistance that were variously estimated to involve ultimate costs of $4 billion to $6 billion. Great stress was placed on the need to modernize and mechanize coal mining in both old and new mines. In the fall of that year, the Chinese press reported that Kailan, Tatung, and fifteen other major coal mines had begun to mechanize mining fully, in part with imported equipment, and that one hundred new mines were being designed or constructed "according to what is required for fully mechanized mining."[176] However, plans also called for continued operation and development of small coal mines. In 1978, the Chinese said, 1,168 of China's 2,000-plus counties had small coal mines, which accounted for 276 million tons of output, or 45 percent of China's total output.[177] Chinese planners called for steps to raise the technical and management level of these mines, even though they now placed highest priority on developing large new mines and increasing the level of mechanization in them.

By mid-1979 some Chinese statements suggested that in the immediate future increasing coal output should have highest priority, even above oil, while exploration of new petroleum resources is pushed. At the NPC meeting in June, China's leaders called specifically for power plants using oil to be converted back to the use of coal "as soon as possible."[178] About the same time, the New China News Agency asserted: "In the campaign to increase production of coal, oil, electric power, and transportation, coal is the key link, and only when coal production is ensured can steady progress be made in power generation and can all other production plans be properly arranged."[179]

The 13 percent average annual increase in coal output during 1977–78 (despite the 1976 disaster that crippled Tangshan [Tangshan], one of China's key coal areas) was very high by historical standards. It is possible that a sizable proportion of the increases came from small mines producing low-quality coal, but even if this was the case the rise was remarkable.

Then, much to the surprise of most outside observers, Peking announced plans for 1979 that called for almost no quantitative increase in coal output; the year's target was set at 620 million tons, only a fraction of 1 percent over 1978. In light of the tremendous emphasis placed on the importance of coal, this was startling. The apparent explanation was that after the large output increases in 1977–78, the regime had decided to concentrate, at least for a brief period, on improving existing mines, building new ones that would add to future capacity, mechanizing, and (probably) shifting emphasis to large mines as well as upgrading small ones. The plan for 1979 called for completing at least twenty-seven large mines that would add 14.2 million tons of capacity to the industry.[180]

The actual rise in coal output in 1979—an increase of 2.8 percent to 635 million tons—was above the plan but considerably below the rate required to achieve the regime's long-term goals. However, Peking reported that during the year new mines completed actually added 39.93 million tons to China's production capacity (this new capacity amounted to over 6 percent of the total output in 1979, and if, as seemed likely, most consisted of large mines, it may have added 12 or 13 percent to China's big mine capacity).[181] It was also reported that during the year, 14.9 billion tons of new coal reserves were "verified."[182]

To sustain the economic growth rates that China hopes to achieve in its modernization program, it must make a major effort to speed up the rate of increase in its coal output, above all for domestic use but also for export, and to release oil for export. Oil may continue to be China's glamour industry in the field of energy, but coal will continue to be the energy "workhorse" on which the economy depends most of all. Striking an optimal balance between coal and oil in allocation of attention, skills, investment resources, and foreign exchange for technical improvements will not be easy, but over the long run the success China achieves in this respect will help to determine not only whether it can meet its own energy requirements but also whether it can become a significant energy exporter.

Natural Gas

Natural gas has been the source of considerable confusion to analysts of China's energy situation in recent years. The existence of substantial reserves in China has been known, and fragmentary data on production have indicated that development and consumption increased from the 1960s on. But until 1979 relatively little reliable, detailed information about actual output was available, and Western analysts greatly overestimated Chinese production. The CIA, for example, in a 1977 study made an estimate that was close to four times China's actual output.[183]

There is little doubt that China's reserves of natural gas are large. Most estimates have ranged between 500 billion and 600 billion cubic meters, and one recent U.S. government estimate was 700 billion.[184] (Roughly speaking, this is probably the energy equivalent of about 620 million tons of oil.)[185] If correct, it means that China's natural gas reserves are extremely important (even though they are smaller than the estimated reserves in some other countries that are large oil producers),[186] and it is possible, moreover, that the estimates for China's reserves will be raised after further exploration.

Before 1949 China produced only negligible amounts of natural gas. Serious development began during the first Five Year Plan period. Thereafter, the rate of increase was fairly rapid. For the entire period from 1952 through 1979 output increased about twenty times, at an average rate of almost 15 percent a year.[187] From a production level not much above zero in 1952, output rose to about 700 million cubic meters in 1957, then jumped to 3.8 billion in 1970. In the 1970s it almost quadrupled, reaching 14.5 billion cubic meters in 1979 (equal to just under 20 million tons CE or just over 13 million tons OE).[188]

One of the most notable facts about both production and consumption of natural gas in China to date has been its geographical concentration. Although reserves have been found in several parts of the country, some in association with oil and some in separate fields, the largest and most easily exploitable deposits discovered so far have been in one province, Szechwan (Sichuan). U.S. government analysts have estimated that about 80 percent of China's output is produced there. (Some estimates have placed the figure even higher, at 90 or even 95 percent.)[189] Within the province there are about 1,000 kilometers of pipelines to distribute the gas.[190] However, since there are no gas pipelines out of the province, output must be consumed locally.

Natural gas has become very important in this one province. It provides fuel for many industries, including iron and steel, provides feedstock for chemical fertilizer plants and other petrochemical factories, and substitutes for gasoline in public buses.[191] A large amount, also, is consumed in household and commercial use. In the opinion of some observers, however, a substantial amount probably is wasted because of inefficient handling and transport.[192] Rough estimates indicate that of the natural gas now consumed in all of China—which means primarily Szechwan—about half is used in industry and construction (including a small amount in electric generation) and about half in residential and commercial use.[193]

Even though Szechwan is China's most populous province, with close to one-tenth of the national population (its population, close to 100 million, is larger than that of all but a few countries in the world), the concentration of both output and use of natural gas in this one area means that China has not yet begun to realize the national potential of natural gas as a fuel. It could be much more important if deposits were developed more extensively elsewhere, or if Szechwan gas were transported to other areas. In recent years natural gas has accounted for only about 3 percent of China's national supply of primary commercial energy.[194] It doubtless could supply much more.

In shaping their energy policy, Chinese leaders may in time see compelling reasons both to broaden the geographical base and to expand the use of natural gas nationally.[195] It is a convenient and relatively cheap and clean fuel (which minimizes pollution problems), all of which are reasons why its use has increased rapidly in recent years in many economically advanced nations. China's need for natural gas will certainly grow, moreover, as chemical fertilizer and petrochemical industries expand.[196] According to one estimate, perhaps close to 5 billion cubic meters a year of China's present output already are used in these industries, and demand could rise greatly in the future.[197]

The Chinese have discussed the possibility of building a natural gas pipeline that would link Szechwan to the coast, and reportedly the French and the Germans have expressed interest in the idea.[198] Although this would be a large and costly undertaking, it could contribute significantly to the national energy supply.

Development of facilities to produce liquefied natural gas (LNG) is another possibility. This, too, would be costly and would require major foreign technical assistance, but it not only would expand the possible uses of China's natural gas domestically, but also would open up new possibilities to export energy. The Chinese have discussed this idea with the Japanese, who are said to have shown interest in building a pilot LNG plant in North China, close to the Takang (Dagang) oil field (near the coast), to produce 150,000 tons a year. Reportedly, the Chinese would like to see a plant with a larger capacity built.[199] However, in the immediate future, cost factors may argue for piping gas rather than developing LNG on a large scale.

It is clear that natural gas has great unexploited potential. Even though it already has become the third most important commercial fuel in China, its share of China's national energy supply remains less than one twenty-fifth that of coal and only about one-seventh that of oil—and it has become important only to the one-tenth of China's population that lives in one remote province.

The logic of the situation would seem to call for a major effort to expand natural gas output and develop pipelines to distribute it more widely throughout the country. However, as in so many areas relating to energy policy, China's leaders in considering the possibility have to make difficult choices. Expanding natural gas output, building pipelines, constructing LNG plants, and developing the extensive infrastructure necessary for wider use of gas would—like the further development of both coal and oil—require large investments and new imported technology. Nevertheless, increased production and use of natural gas would be of great advantage, not simply because it would add to China's overall supply of energy, but also because it would give Chinese leaders greater flexibility in deciding how and where to use their oil. Increased production of natural gas would, among other things, increase the supply of feedstock for petroleum industries and enhance China's prospects for exporting a significant amount of either oil or natural gas in the form of LNG. However, there has been little evidence so far that Chinese planners are placing special priority on natural gas development, and today there is considerably less attention given to this fuel than to coal and oil in Chinese discussions of energy problems.

U.S. government analysts have projected an increase in China's natural gas output between now and 1985 at rates comparable with actual gas output growth in the past—that is, somewhere between a low of 10 percent and a high of 20 percent a year.[200] This would result in output in 1985 anywhere between, roughly, 25 billion and 43 billion cubic meters (or 34 million to 58 million tons of coal equivalent). Despite the relatively low priority assigned to development of gas, these estimates probably are plausible. However, they mean that natural gas will remain a fuel of only secondary importance in the national energy picture. For gas to become more important nationally than at present, the Chinese would have to invest much more in the industry, find new resources, and at some point build pipelines to transport Szechwan gas to other areas.

Hydroelectricity

In popular writing, hydroelectricity receives a great deal of attention in discussions of power sources. However, although it is extremely important in electricity production, in very few nations does hydropower account for more than a small fraction of total primary energy. Typically, it ranges from under 1 percent to as high as 3 percent.[201] In 1975, according to UN statistics, hydropower in the United States accounted for about 15 percent of all electricity, but it provided only 1.8 percent of all primary energy; in the Soviet Union the comparable figures were 12 percent and under 1 percent.[202] The role of hydroelectricity in China is similar; it provides only a tiny fraction of total energy supply but it provides a major share—just under or just over one-fifth—of the country's electricity.

China has a huge potential for development of hydroelectricity. One study estimated that it has 1,600 large rivers carrying almost 2.8 thousand cubic kilometers of water a year (more than the rivers of any other country except the Soviet Union and Brazil) and has 8.5 percent of the world's hydroelectricity potential.[203] Theoretically, according to this estimate, China could develop a capacity of about 540 gigawatts.[204] The Chinese themselves have estimated their potential to be 600 gigawatts.[205] But much of this potential is in remote areas, and large hydroelectric schemes require enormous investments. Most is likely to remain unexploited, therefore, for the indefinite future. A CIA study, which states that "China leads the world in hydropower resources," estimates that 145 to 220 gigawatts are now economically exploitable.[206]

Starting from a very low base, China's hydroelectricity output has increased rapidly in recent years. U.S. government estimates and recently published official Chinese figures indicate that between 1952 and 1979 it rose at an average annual rate of between 14 and 15 percent, from 1.3 billion to 50.6 billion kilowatt-hours, and the share of hydroelectricity in China's total production of electricity increased from 18 to about 20 percent.[207]

One interesting development since the late 1960s has been the construction in Chinese rural areas of thousands of small hydropower stations. By 1976 China had built between 50,000 and 60,000 of these,[208] and the number has continued to grow. Most are tiny; the capacity of the majority is probably under 100 kilowatts, and the average is believed to be 60 kilowatts. Yet they provide some electricity for lighting and small machines used in homes, fields, and factories in rural areas that never before had access to electric power. Today they probably total about 88,000 and produce more than two-fifths of China's total hydroelectric output (but much less—about one-tenth—of China's total electric output).[209]

Even though the rate of growth in hydroelectricity output in China has been impressive, its contribution to China's total primary energy supply remains small. In 1979 hydroelectricity still accounted for less than 1 percent of China's total primary commercial energy output. The estimated hydroelectric output of 50.6 billion kilowatt-hours in 1979 was equal, roughly, to 6.33 million tons CE, or 4.20 million tons of oil.[210]

Even though hydroelectric power provides only a small fraction of China's total primary energy needs, the development of the electric power industry as a whole will be crucial to China's modernization during the period ahead. Hydroelectricity appears destined to play a growing role in China's electric industry; however, because of the long lead time needed to complete large hydro projects, the results of efforts started now will not be felt fully for some years to come.

The growth of total electricity production over the past thirty years has been quite dramatic. From 1949 through 1979 output increased over sixty-five times, at an average annual rate of almost 15 percent, from 4,300 million to 256,550 million kilowatt-hours; per capita electric use increased from 8 to 256 kilowatt-hours a year.[211] By 1979, according to CIA estimates, installed capacity in China totaled about 50.5 gigawatts, of which 34.8 gigawatts were in thermal plants and 12.8 gigawatts in hydroelectric plants. By early 1979 it was estimated that China had a total of about 90,000 electric power plants of all sizes. However, only a few hundred were "large" (with more than a 24 megawatt capacity). The CIA estimated that about 88,000 small hydro plants in rural China had an aggregate capacity of roughly 5 gigawatts, just under one-tenth of the country's total electricity generating capacity.

Despite the impressive overall growth of the industry, however, China has suffered serious electric shortages in recent years. Inefficiency and waste have been contributory causes. The Chinese now state that in 1979 they increased output by 40 million kilowatt-hours by improving and restoring idle or inefficiently used capacity. They also assert that 10 billion kilowatt-hours still could be saved annually by reducing line losses, especially in rural areas. Current policy places great stress, therefore, on conservation and improved efficiency.

However, continued rapid growth in electricity capacity is required to support the country's modernization program, and Peking recognizes this. As of late 1979 fifty-five large power plants with a capacity of 18 gigawatts were under construction; additions to existing plants totaling 8 gigawatts were being built; and perhaps 3.5 gigawatts of new small hydro plants were under construction. But the Chinese still have to confront hard choices about the kinds of power plants to build in the near future. Peking's leaders clearly intend to rely on a mix of thermal plants and large and small hydroelectric plants in the foreseeable future. In thermal plants, they will depend principally on coal (and, as already noted, they now are switching plants using oil back to coal). There is little prospect of using much natural gas for electricity in the next few years. One key unanswered question, however, is how much effort to put into building large hydro plants during the next few years.

According to the recent CIA estimates, plants in existence and under construction may sustain a GNP growth rate of only about 3 percent in the near future and thus to make possible a 5 to 7 percent GNP growth, China will need to add at least 5.7 to 10.8 gigawatts, and possibly as much as 16.0 to 21.2 gigawatts, to China's capacity between now and 1985, beyond what it now has in operation or under construction. This clearly will require an acceleration of present construction efforts. Because most large hydro plants will require foreign assistance and take five to ten years or even longer to come into operation, new thermal plants using coal will be critically important during the next few years. However, to meet China's needs in the late 1980s and 1990s, there are strong arguments in favor of starting now to build new hydroelectric projects, including some very large ones.

During 1978–79 Chinese officials and the Peking press began to give a great deal of publicity to plans to expand output of hydroelectric power.[212] Fang Yi (Fang Yi), in his outline plan for science and technology, emphasized the increased need for "large hydroelectric power stations."[213] Soon thereafter, Peking officials began discussing with leaders from several countries, including the United States, possible technical cooperation and aid for hydroelectric projects. This subject was an important item on the agenda of U.S. Department of Energy Secretary James Schlesinger's talks in China in 1978, and in 1979 Vice President Walter Mondale signed a protocol in Peking on U.S. assistance for developing hydroelectric power in China (the U.S. government classified China as a "friendly" nation to make it legally possible for American government agencies such as the Army Corps of Engineers and Bureau of Reclamation to provide aid to China on such projects on a reimbursable basis). According to press reports in 1979, the Chinese were considering building about twenty large new power-generating hydroelectric dams; some optimistic reports stated that the United States might assist on a dozen or so of them, each of which, it was said, might cost as much as $1 billion.[214]

All of these developments indicated that as part of its overall energy policy, China hoped to expand hydroelectric output significantly. However, large new projects will not be simple undertakings, and debates on how much to invest immediately in large hydro plants that will take considerable time to complete have continued. Apparently, plans formulated in 1978 called for work on several huge and costly projects, including twenty hydro stations of at least 1 gigawatt each, but reportedly in mid-1979 some of these were postponed while others remained under discussion.[215]

It is still premature to estimate how rapidly Chinese hydroelectric output will grow in the next few years; the rate could be 10 percent or more.[216] If so, although hydroelectricity's share of China's total output of primary energy would still remain under 1 percent, it would gradually become increasingly important in China's electricity supply.

Secondary Sources of Energy

China's leadership today shows strong interest not only in the major conventional fossil fuels and hydropower, but also in every possible source of energy, from sophisticated nuclear power plants to simple devices using solar energy and traditional fuels. Some low-technology, fairly simple devices already are significant supplementary sources of energy, especially in rural areas, but most nonfossil sources of energy requiring advanced technology are still in experimental stages. In China, as elsewhere, they are not likely to be of more than marginal importance in relation to China's total energy needs for a fairly long time to come.

China has begun to take steps toward developing a nuclear power program, but only haltingly.[217] As late as 1976 Chinese officials stated to Westerners that no decision to build any nuclear plants had yet been made.[218] However, in early 1978 Chairman Hua Kuo-feng, in his major policy statement to China's National People's Congress, asserted that China definitely planned to build nuclear power plants; Fang Yi then called for rapid progress in building such plants.[219] It appeared that a policy decision must have been made sometime in early 1977 to proceed with the development of nuclear energy.

China possesses most of the technical know-how to begin such a program. However, to move rapidly to develop nuclear power would require imported technology, and starting in the early 1970s the Chinese began serious "window shopping" in advanced industrial countries for nuclear technology.[220] It appeared that by late 1978 they had decided to purchase two 900 megawatt Framatome nuclear power plants from the French at a cost of $2 billion or more.[221] But shortly thereafter, in May 1979, they apparently decided not to go ahead with the purchase. It appeared that nuclear power had lost out, probably mainly on cost grounds, to coal, hydropower, and oil.[222] At the NPC in June 1979, although priority was given to fuels and power, the main focus was on coal, oil, thermal electricity, and hydroelectricity; nuclear power was virtually ignored.

The Chinese have not totally abandoned interest in nuclear power, however. They continue to give high priority to relevant research in high-energy physics. They also have discussed seriously the possibility of purchasing from the United States a 50 gigaelectronvolt proton synchrotron—which would be the fourth largest in the world—for the Institute of High Energy Physics in Peking (at a possible cost of about $100 million).[223] They also have shown interest in nuclear fusion.

In 1980, moreover, there was evidence of continuing debate on whether to go ahead with the construction of at least one nuclear power plant in China. Japanese news reporters revealed that Kwangtung (Guangdong) Province had formulated plans to build a commercial nuclear power plant in Shumchun (Shenzhen), on the border with Hong Kong, and that negotiations with foreign manufacturers were under way.[224]

In light of China's abundant resources of coal, hydropower, and oil and the enormous capital costs of nuclear power, it does not seem likely that China will embark on any major nuclear power program in the foreseeable future. It is possible, however, that at some point, perhaps before very long, the Chinese may build one or two plants, partly to acquire the scientific and technological knowledge required for larger-scale development in the future, and partly to enhance China's international prestige. But nuclear power production will not supply a significant portion of China's energy needs during the 1980s. (Even in the United States, nuclear power provided less than 1 percent of all primary energy in 1972; moreover, in 1977 the Federal Energy Administration estimated that by 1985 it would provide only between 11 and 14 percent,[225] and in the wake of the "Three Mile Island incident" in 1979 even this figure may be too optimistic.) Development of nuclear power on a large scale in China, if it occurs, will probably be in the 1990s or in the twenty-first century.

Among the most interesting energy developments in China during recent years have been those involving simple rural energy sources, at the opposite end of the technological spectrum from nuclear power. China has led the world, for example, in the development of village biogas tanks, which use human and other wastes to produce methane gas (as well as solid fertilizer) useful for household lighting, cooking, and other purposes.[226] Although some of these anaerobic digesters have a production capacity up to 100 cubic meters of gas, most are single-family units with a 6 to 10 cubic meter capacity.[227]

A program to build these tanks was begun in the early 1970s in Szechwan Province, and since then the program has spread to many other parts of the country; by 1980 China had more than 8 million pits, and they will doubtless be developed further.[228] One Western analyst estimates that if they were developed to the maximum extent possible, theoretically they could produce as much as 58 billion cubic meters of gas a year—several times China's total natural gas output in 1975![229] It is not likely that their capacity will approach that level, but clearly they already are a useful supplementary source of energy in rural areas, and their use will probably continue to spread.

The Chinese also have been experimenting for some time with other unconventional power sources.[230] They have shown special interest in geothermal possibilities. Reportedly, more than 2,500 geothermal sites have been identified in numerous areas, but especially in China's Southwest. China put its first small geothermal power station into operation in 1970 (with a capacity of 86 kilowatts), and now eight are functioning (the largest reportedly having a capacity of 3 megawatts). The Chinese have developed solar water heaters, which already are in use in a number of areas, and have done research on or experimented with various kinds of solar collectors.[231] They also have built an experimental solar thermal power station. The potential of wind also interests them, and they have constructed several experimental wind energy conversion systems. In addition, four Chinese institutes have experimented with magnetohydrodynamic power, converting coal gas to plasma. Although this research is slow and expensive, it is potentially important because it could expand China's uses of its vast resources of coal. (The one area of possible importance in which the Chinese have shown relatively little interest to date is ocean systems using tides and thermal energy conversion.) Use of most of these unconventional energy sources is still in a very early stage in China. These sources will not contribute significantly to the country's energy supply in the 1980s, but they could gradually become much more important thereafter.

Many traditional sources of energy also still are important in China. Even though they are not included in statistics on primary commercial energy, they nevertheless continue to supply substantial amounts of the country's energy, especially in the countryside.

Several attempts have been made to estimate the energy contribution of wood, crop residues, and other vegetal wastes in China. One study concluded that in the mid-1950s they may have supplied the equivalent of 50 million to 60 million tons of coal annually.[232] Another analyst calculated that in the mid-1950s China burned about 36 million cubic meters of firewood a year, equivalent to perhaps 9 million tons of coal, and that it probably uses more now.[233] According to one estimate, China may also have used as much as 114 million tons of crop residues a year in the 1950s, equivalent to perhaps 30 million to 40 million tons of coal, plus undetermined amounts of other vegetal materials.[234]

A study by another specialist gave even higher estimates. The author concluded that at the start of the 1970s traditional vegetal sources of fuel in China may have contributed an amount of energy equivalent to as much as 70 million to 80 million tons of coal a year (45 million tons from wood and 33 million tons from crop residues).[235] (He also estimated that animate sources contributed more than 90 million tons of coal equivalent, 30 million or more from animals, and twice that from humans.) If correct, these estimates suggest that the energy provided by all traditional vegetal sources may have totaled about 20 to 25 percent as much as the total amount of primary commercial energy produced in China at that time.

There is no way of knowing whether these estimates are close to correct. Nevertheless, it is evident that in China, as in other developing nations, traditional energy sources still play much more important roles than in economically advanced nations. As China develops industrially, the use of traditional fuels probably will decline, with commercial fuels being substituted for them. Some people believe that this process has been under way for some time in China and has contributed to the rapid increase in demand for commercial energy in recent years. However, it is difficult to know exactly to what extent this has occurred to date.[236] Conceivably, the frugality of the Chinese people, as well as the regime's desire to avoid waste, will ensure continued use of traditional fuels on a sizable scale for a long time, even as the use of modern sources of energy expands.

Oil

Although China's economy depends most of all on coal, during the past three decades petroleum has emerged as the country's second most important energy source. It has become critically important for China's entire modernization program, and Peking's success or failure in sustaining the growth of its oil industry may have more important implications for its broad foreign economic policy and general international relations than any other aspect of the Chinese energy situation.

Oil (as well as gas) has been known in China for more than two millennia; in fact, Tzuliuching (Ziliujing) in Szechwan, where seeps occurred at ancient salt wells, may have the oldest hydrocarbon fields in the world.[237] The development of the modern oil industry is very recent, however, and of the world's large oil producers, China is the newest.

The first modern commercial oil fields in China were discovered in West China—in Tushantzu (Dushanzi) in Sinkiang (Xinjiang) in 1897 and in Yenchang (Yanchang) in Shansi in 1907—but they did not lead to any large-scale production.[238] Until recently, the conventional wisdom was that China had no large reserves. A leading Western geographer specializing on China wrote as late as 1952 that no major oil fields were ever likely to be discovered there.[239] In the mid-1930s the Chinese government estimated that the oil reserves in China proper (excluding the Northeast, then under Japanese control) amounted to only about 300 million tons[240] (2.227 billion barrels).[241] The U.S. Geological Survey in that period estimated China's total reserves to be just under 450 million tons (3.274 billion barrels).[242] The oil actually extracted from China's few operating wells was barely a trickle before 1949. It is estimated that between 1907, when Yenchang opened, through 1948, the last year of Nationalist rule on the mainland, only forty-five wells were put into operation, and their cumulative output in four decades totaled a mere 2.78 million tons.[243]

The Growth of Oil Production

Soon after the Communist takeover, the Chinese government, with Soviet assistance, began intensive prospecting. New discoveries were soon made, mainly at first in the Northwest and Southwest—in Sinkiang, Szechwan, and Tsinghai (Qinghai) provinces. While important, none of the new fields located in the regime's first decade were huge. Oil production increased, but only slowly, and the level of total output remained low. Production did not surpass 1 million tons until 1956, and in 1959 it was still under 4 million tons.[244]

The situation changed radically at the start of the 1960s. Some of the exploration begun earlier, with Soviet help, suddenly paid off, and within a few years several large new fields were discovered in North and Northeast China—first Taching in the Northeast (which immediately became, and has remained, China's largest operating field), then Shengli (Shengli) in Shantung (Shandong) Province, and subsequently Takang in Hopeh (Hebei), near the coast. These fields established an entirely new base for rapid expansion of China's oil output.[245]

Following the Sino-Soviet split and the Soviet Union's withdrawal of its technicians from China in 1960, the Chinese urgently strove to achieve oil self-sufficiency to free themselves from dependence on oil imports from the USSR, for military and political as well as economic reasons. Although previously they had acquired considerable technological know-how from the Russians, now they were essentially on their own,[246] and they began a crash program of development.

Discovered in 1959, Taching went into operation in 1960.[247] Peking poured large amounts of money and labor into its development, and it soon became a national showplace. Starting with an output of less than 1 million tons in its first year, production rose at an extraordinary pace, reaching almost 18 million tons in 1970 and 43 million tons in 1976 (table 4-12). In 1976 this field accounted for 52 percent of China's oil production, and by year-end it had produced 54 percent of the nation's cumulative output since 1949.[248] It was not surprising that Mao Tse-tung (Mao Zedong) urged all Chinese industry to emulate its performance.

The second large new field, Shengli, went into operation in 1962.[249] Although its development has been slower and more erratic than Taching's, by 1975 it produced 15 million tons, about one-fifth of the national total. The third large field, Takang, which was close to Shengli, produced 4 million to 5 million tons in 1975.[250]

These three fields have dominated China's oil industry since the start of the 1960s; by 1975 they accounted for four-fifths of total national output. But intensive exploration and development efforts have continued throughout the country, and by the mid-1970s China had at least thirty operating fields, fourteen of which probably produced half a million tons or more annually; the most important of these besides the three major fields are Chienchang (Qianjang) in central Hopeh, Panshan (Banshan) in Liaoning (Liaoning), Fuyu (Fuyu) in Kirin (Jilin), Lenghu (Lenghu) in Tsinghai, and Yumen (Yumen), Tushantzu, and Kolamai (Kelamayi) in Sinkiang.[251]

Total national production of oil has soared. Whereas production was less than 1 million tons a year annually through 1955, and was still only 3.7 million in 1959, it is estimated that production surpassed 11 million tons in 1965, was 30 million tons in 1970, and reached almost 87 million tons in 1976.[252] (These figures include small amounts of shale oil and liquefied coal.)[253] Official figures published by Peking indicated that oil output reached 93.64 million tons in 1977, 104.05 million tons in 1978, and 106.15 million tons in 1979.[254]

The rate of increase in China's oil output was spectacular by any standard. During the period from 1950 through 1976 output increased 434 times (!) at an average rate of almost 26 percent a year.[255] Between 1960 and 1976 (a more meaningful period to examine) the average annual rate of increase in production was over 19 percent—or five to six times the rate of increase in coal output in that period.[256]

In the early 1970s the rate of increase in oil output rose further; the world oil crisis may have stimulated China's leaders to put even greater stress on oil, for export as well as domestic consumption. For the period 1970–75 the average rate of increase was 21 percent—higher than the long-term rate since 1960.[257] However, since then the annual rate has dropped disturbingly. Although in 1975, it was still close to 15 percent, thereafter it dropped to under 13 percent in 1976 and to 8 percent in 1977. After rising, briefly, to 11 percent in 1978, it plunged to 2 percent in 1979. In 1980 some reports indicated that oil output might not grow at all during the year and that conceivably it might even decline for a short time in the early 1980s.

The long-term rate in China's growth in oil output from 1960 through 1979—over 17 percent—clearly was most unusual; few countries have surpassed it over any prolonged period of time. (For comparative purposes, the long-term rates—from 1950 through 1976—in two major producers were as follows: in Saudi Arabia the average rate was 11.2 percent from 1950 through 1976, although from 1969 through 1976 it was 14.9 percent; in the same twenty-six-year period the rate in the Soviet Union was 10.6 percent but dropped to 6.7 percent in 1970–76.)[258] However, the rapid decline in the rate recently raises very serious questions about the future. Several years ago some analysts began to question whether China could long sustain a rate near 20 percent, and many were inclined to believe that it was likely to be nearer 10 to 15 percent. Now it is evident that in the near future, at least, it will probably be well below that; a major effort over several years may be required to restore the oil growth rate to that level.

The slowdown in oil output in 1979 was not entirely unanticipated; the rate of increase was just about what the plan for the year had called for (1.9 percent).[259] But when he stated the year's low targets for both oil and coal, the head of China's State Planning Commission warned that "tension in fuel and power supplies will continue for a fairly long period."[260] Peking has decided to concentrate its immediate efforts on new exploration to discover additional energy sources and on conservation, and it has attempted to formulate a multifaceted, long-term ap-

TABLE 4-12. *China's Crude Oil Production, by Field, 1949–76*
Millions of metric tons

Year	National	Taching	Shengli	Takang	Yumen	Kolamai	Tsaidam[a]	Residual
1949	0.121	...	...	...	...	...	...	0.121
1950	0.200	...	...	...	...	...	...	0.200
1951	0.305	...	...	...	...	...	...	0.305
1952	0.436	...	...	...	0.143	...	...	0.293
1953	0.622	...	...	...	0.198	...	...	0.424
1954	0.789	...	...	...	(0.239)	...	...	0.550
1955	0.966	...	...	...	0.414	...	...	0.552
1956	1.163	...	...	...	0.533	...	...	0.630
1957	1.458	...	...	...	0.755	0.05	...	0.653
1958	2.264	...	...	...	1.002	0.25	0.03	0.982
1959	3.7	...	...	...	1.337	(0.239)	(0.044)	2.080
1960	5.1	0.792	...	...	1.700	(0.226)	(0.058)	2.324
1961	5.186	(1.022)	...	...	1.600	(0.214)	(0.072)	2.278
1962	5.746	(2.726)	0.046	...	(1.303)	0.201	(0.085)	1.385
1963	6.360	4.427	(0.321)	...	(1.006)	(0.307)	(0.099)	0.200
1964	8.653	(5.765)	0.596	...	(0.709)	(0.416)	(0.113)	1.054

Year								
1965	10.961 [11.374]	7.106	0.735	...	0.412	0.523	0.127	2.058
1966	14.074	8.776	2.0	...	(0.414)	(0.473)	(0.135)	2.276
1967	13.9	(9.045)	(2.625)	0.20	(0.416)	(0.423)	(0.144)	1.046
1968	15.2	9.297	(3.250)	(0.34)	(0.417)	(0.373)	(0.152)	1.371
1969	20.377	12.830	(3.875)	0.48	0.419	0.323	0.160	2.290
1970	28.211 [30.129]	17.666	4.5	0.96	0.490	0.384	0.165	4.046
1971	36.700	22.136	6.5	(1.64)	0.544	0.503	0.180	5.197
1972	43.065	25.550	8.45	(2.33)	0.620	0.604	0.320	5.191
1973	54.804	28.298	9.50	3.00	0.676	0.725	0.442	12.163
1974	65.765	34.668	11.02	3.74	0.710	1.036	0.530	14.121
1975	74.261 [77.060]	40.072	14.90	4.34	0.785[b]	1.065[b]	0.582[b]	12.517
1976	83.608 [86.760]	43.093	...	...	...	...	...	...
Total	503.994	273.209	68.318	17.030	16.842	8.335	3.438	...
	3.679 bb	1.994 bb	0.499 bb	0.124 bb	0.123 bb	0.063 bb	0.024 bb	...

Source: CIA, *China, Oil Production Prospects*, ER 77-1003OU, June 1977, p. 9. These estimates are useful mainly for a general indication of the distribution of output. The estimated national totals are now obsolete. For recent official Chinese figures and revised CIA estimates of total output, see table 4-10. The national figures in brackets are revised CIA estimates, in NFAC, CIA, *China: A Statistical Compendium*, p. 9. Parentheses indicate linear interpolation; bb = billion barrels. All figures are U.S. government estimates.

a. Actually consisting of three separate fields.
b. Regression analysis, 1969–74.

proach to energy development. In oil, it has finally decided that it should extend efforts to offshore as well as onshore resources in a big way. The degree of success it achieves in implementing this new energy development program will be a major factor in determining the success of its entire modernization. Oil is only one element in its energy program, but it will be a crucial one.

China's Oil Reserves

The future role of oil in China's modernization obviously will depend fundamentally on the size of its reserves. Although more is known now than a few years ago about these reserves, the data available still are limited. Geological surveying of the country is far from complete. A top Chinese official stated in early 1978 that prospecting had covered less than one-tenth of the country's depositional basins.[261] Moreover, only part of the knowledge about onshore reserves that the Chinese themselves have accumulated has been publicly revealed. Serious surveying of most offshore areas started only in 1979. Outside estimates have had to be based in large part, therefore, on geological analogies, with relatively little supporting data to date from drilling.

Estimating reserves requires difficult judgments not only on how much oil may be underground in particular areas but also on how much will be recoverable. A large portion of China's reserves appears to be in continental (lacustrine) deposits—usually in scattered and highly faulted formations that are both hard to identify definitely without drilling and often difficult and costly to exploit.[262] (One American expert believes that because of the nature of the deposits in China, although conceivably its hydrocarbon resources could be as large as those in the Middle East, only a fraction of them are likely ever to be recoverable.)[263]

China's total petroleum reserves include liquid crude oil deposits both onshore and offshore. (In the long run, China's shale oil deposits also could be important, but because of the costs of extraction, oil from shale is not likely to play a major role in the industry during the next two decades.)[264] One of the first comprehensive estimates of China's reserves by a Westerner was made by an American oil specialist, A. A. Meyerhoff, who had access to Soviet data. His figures, revised as of 1975, have generally been considered to be among the best. Meyerhoff estimated that China's recoverable onshore reserves of crude oil (proved, probable, and potential) may total 5.42 billion tons (39.6 billion barrels)

—or 6.2 billion tons (45.2 billion barrels) if one adds a conservative estimate of reserves in the shallow waters of the Pohai (Bohai) Gulf, off the North China coast (where the reserves are in effect an extension of the onshore deposits).[265]

The U.S. Geological Survey also has studied China's oil reserves, and as of 1976 its preliminary conclusion was that China's onshore reserves may total 4.6 billion tons (33.6 billion barrels).[266] CIA analysts have cited a "private study" (without identifying it specifically) that in 1977 they believed was the best to date, reporting that preliminary results of the study suggest that China's onshore reserves could be anywhere between 5.62 billion and 9.32 billion tons (41 billion to 68 billion barrels) but are probably closer to the lower figure.[267] This study estimated that as of 1977 the total of reserves already discovered in China amounted to 2.19 billion tons (16 billion barrels) and that the undiscovered potential could total 3.42 billion to 7.12 billion tons (25 billion to 52 billion barrels). Some estimates are lower than these, however, in part because of different criteria used. Tatsu Kambara, of the Japanese Petroleum Development Corporation, for example, has estimated that "proved and probable" reserves in known oil fields in China as of 1973 probably were between 1.2 billion and 1.8 billion tons.[268] But a few estimates are considerably higher. For example, the Japan External Trade Organization (JETRO) reported one estimate indicating that China's potential onshore reserves, including those in the Pohai Gulf, could total 10.5 billion to 13.5 billion tons (76.65 billion to 98.55 billion barrels)—4.5 billion tons on land and 6 billion to 9 billion in the Gulf.[269] Although conceivably such estimates could prove to be valid, the data available so far do not support them.

Estimating China's offshore reserves has been more difficult in many ways than estimating those onshore. Very little drilling has been done to date (reportedly, as of 1978 only about 200 tests had been made throughout the entire Yellow Sea and East China Sea areas).[270] Nevertheless, there have been various attempts to make rough estimates. A UN-sponsored survey made in the late 1960s in areas off the China coast first stimulated serious interest in the possibility that large reserves might be located in the region. The report resulting from that survey stated that there is a "high probability" that the continental shelf between Taiwan and Japan might be "one of the most prolific oil and gas reservoirs in the world."[271] However, all of the estimates made public so far have of necessity been fairly speculative, and they have varied considerably.

The private study mentioned above, which was cited by the CIA, conservatively estimated that China's potential offshore reserves might total a quarter-billion to a half-billion tons (2 billion to 3 billion barrels),[272] but Meyerhoff estimated that they could total 4.11 billion tons.[273]

One study by an American oil company executive estimated, on the basis of all exploration and studies done up to 1978, that on the entire Asia continental shelf area there "may" be an "undiscovered potential" of roughly 5 billion to 9 billion tons (37 billion to 66 billion barrels).[274] Of this total, he calculated between 2 billion and almost 3.3 billion tons (15 billion to 24 billion barrels) could be in areas off China's east coast, in the Yellow Sea, East China Sea, Taiwan Basin, and Ryukyu Basin (not including the Pohai Gulf, which the study estimated could have 0.4 billion to 0.8 billion tons), areas that the Chinese claim (but do not fully control). In the South China Sea area, the study estimated, there could be a total of between 2.6 billion and 4.9 billion tons (19 billion to 36 billion barrels). However, some parts of this general area, while claimed by China, are actually controlled by others; moreover, certain sectors would be very difficult to develop, since the water is extremely deep and beyond the reach of current technology. In early 1980 still another study estimated that China's offshore oil reserves could total 4 billion to 7 billion tons.[275]

The CIA asserts, correctly, that the necessary data for reliable estimates of China's offshore reserves have not been available, but CIA analysts nevertheless have made general estimates, on the basis of the best data available, of the total of China's oil reserves, including both onshore and offshore oil. In the opinion of these analysts, China's potential ultimately recoverable liquid oil reserves probably total at least 5.5 billion tons (40 billion barrels) and conceivably could be as large as 13 billion to 14 billion tons (100 billion barrels).[276] The fact that these analysts give considerable credence to a study estimating offshore oil reserves alone to total between 5.6 billion to 9.3 billion tons suggests that they think the likely total is above the minimum figure but not necessarily as large as the maximum. Meyerhoff, as of 1977, concluded that the most realistic estimate is 9.5 billion tons (69.51 billion barrels)—5.40 billion tons offshore and 4.11 billion onshore.[277]

On the basis of all these estimates, it is reasonable to assume that China's "known" reserves (in fields already found) amount to at least 2 billion tons, that its potential onshore reserves could total 5 billion to 6 billion tons, and that (if one takes an optimistic view) its offshore reserves could prove to be of comparable size. Until the results of new surveying and exploration now under way are known, these estimates are the best available. Assuming they are close to correct, they indicate that China's reserves must be considered to be among the very important oil resources in the world. (Although estimates of reserves in other areas may not be exactly comparable, as of January 1976 Africa was estimated to have reserves of just over 7 billion tons, North America more than 5 billion, and Latin America about 4 billion.[278] It is very possible that China's reserves may prove to be in the same general class as those in these areas.) There is no present basis for believing that China's recoverable oil reserves will prove to be comparable with those in the Middle East, where the reserves, as of the start of 1976, were estimated to total 45 billion tons,[279] but they undoubtedly are of a size that will make China significant in the global oil picture.

As stated earlier, Hubbert estimated world oil reserves as of 1976 to be 78 billion tons. China's already discovered reserves of about 2 billion tons amount to less than 3 percent of Hubbert's estimate of known world reserves. But if one accepts optimistic estimates that China's reserves might total 13 billion to 14 billion tons (or around 100 billion barrels)—which implies that as much as 11 billion or 12 billion tons remain to be found—China's still-to-be discovered reserves conceivably might total between 7 and 8 percent of the total reserves that Hubbert estimated still may be found throughout the world (150 billion tons).

Within the next few years, knowledge of what oil reserves China actually has should increase rapidly. During 1977–79 Peking greatly stepped up its own exploration. In fact, as suggested earlier, it appears to have given highest priority—probably for at least the three-year period 1979–82—to discovering new oil reserves rather than to maximizing output from known deposits.[280] Even though there is less grandiose talk now than in 1978 about developing ten new oil fields of the size of Taching,[281] a great effort is under way to discover new oil resources. Some significant finds have been reported recently in North China and the Northwest as well as in the Taching area of the Northeast.[282] In 1978 a *People's Daily* (*Renmin Ribao*) editorial called for a five-fold increase in drilling, which it termed the "key link" in the current program to develop China's oil industry.[283]

Most important, in 1979 Peking decided—as will be discussed further below—to contract with many of the world's leading oil corporations to start intensive surveying of offshore areas all along the China coast.

This effort began in 1979 and should start to reveal during 1980–81 the extent of China's offshore oil resources.

The Location Problem

As stated earlier, three major oil fields in the North and Northeast have to date dominated China's oil production, producing more than 70 percent of China's total cumulative output in the period 1949–76.[284] However, according to one estimate (made in 1977) only about 550 million tons (4 billion barrels) of the 2-plus billion tons of the already discovered oil reserves in China are located in the North and Northeast, while most of the rest (almost 1.4 billion tons or 10 billion barrels) is in the remote West.[285] According to another estimate, the probable recoverable reserves at Taching (which in 1976 produced about 43 million tons and from 1960 through 1976 had accounted for an estimated 273 million tons of China's cumulative output) may at the start have totaled only 600 million to 800 million tons.[286] If this estimate is correct, Taching's reserves already may have dropped below 500 million, possibly even below 300 million.

The implications of such estimates, if they are valid, are sobering. They suggest that, even assuming that Taching's annual output declines, as some expect, the mainstay of China's oil industry could approach exhaustion during the next decade or two unless its reserves prove to be substantially larger than estimated. In fact, the known reserves in most of the already discovered fields in the entire North and Northeast (if they total only 550 million tons) conceivably could be exhausted in twenty years.[287] It is virtually certain, of course, that some new reserves will be discovered in this area, in existing fields as well as in new ones. In fact, in 1978 several new fields were reportedly discovered in both Northeast and North China, and in 1979 the New China News Agency stated that experts thought optimistically that Taching's reserves were 25 percent larger than previously estimated.[288] However, even if one assumes that optimistic estimates of undiscovered reserves in currently developed areas are correct and that new resources can be rapidly discovered and exploited, if fields in these areas continue to be called upon to provide four-fifths of China's production (about that of the recent past), the known oil in China's North and Northeast conceivably could be mostly used up in the 1990s.[289]

Nationally, the prospects are brighter. Even assuming that the reserves in all China's known fields total only about 2 billion tons, production at roughly the present level could continue for twenty years, and if new discoveries eventually confirm that China's national reserves total 5.5 billion tons, or perhaps even double that, production at the present level could continue for fifty-five to one hundred years. Obviously, however, China's oil production will rise eventually, so no calculations such as these reveal how long China's oil will last. There is no way, at present, to estimate this accurately. Nevertheless, such calculations, crude as they are, do suggest that unless estimates of China's oil reserves are revised upward substantially, the oil era in China, as elsewhere, is likely to be a relatively short period. China clearly has sufficient oil to be an important producer for some years, but it is probable, even if one takes a relatively optimistic view, that China's oil will approach depletion in a period of decades, not centuries. Because China is a latecomer in oil production, however, the end of the oil era in China may come later than in certain other areas of the world.

In the short term, if China's oil industry were to rely only on already discovered deposits, it could face a serious problem within a decade or two as a result of the depletion of the major known reserves in the North and Northeast. This is why the Chinese are now compelled to devote much greater effort to the discovery and exploitation of undeveloped oil reserves—both the onshore deposits in China's far West and offshore deposits along its coast. The private study cited by the CIA[290] estimated that of China's already discovered reserves of 2.19 billion tons (16 billion barrels), about 1.37 billion tons (10 billion barrels)— two and a half times the amount in the North and Northeast—are in the far West. However, the country's "estimated undiscovered petroleum" is believed to be more equally distributed, with possibly 1.78 billion to 3.56 billion tons (13 billion to 26 billion barrels) in the North and Northeast and 1.37 billion to 3.01 billion tons (10 billion to 22 billion barrels) in the far West. Both of these areas will continue to be important for several decades, therefore.

Nevertheless, in the near future, as the major existing fields are gradually depleted, there will be increasing pressure to accelerate the discovery and development of new reserves elsewhere.[291] It will take time to identify major new fields, however, especially in areas still relatively unexplored (though some recent reports indicate progress in this respect),[292] and it will take several years to get large new fields into operation (it took between five and ten years for China's major existing fields to get into full, large-scale production).[293]

China's long-term hopes for oil development were first revealed publicly in very euphoric official statements. In early 1977 a top Chinese leader revealed for the first time that the regime hoped to have in production by the end of the century ten more fields the size of Taching, which seemed to imply plans to increase capacity by about 400 million to 500 million tons.[294] And in 1978 a vice minister of the Petroleum and Chemical Industry Ministry in China stated that Peking already had selected fifteen locations for oil development, each of which will eventually have a capacity for producing 20 million tons a year, implying plans for opening up new capacity totaling at least 300 million tons a year.[295] Optimistic targets of this sort reflected the unrealistic euphoria of the time. Since 1979, it is clear, the targets have been scaled down, although Peking has not yet made any definitive statements on what its long-term oil production plans now call for. What is clear, however, is that Chinese leaders now realize that to come even close to achieving their hopes, they must broaden the geographical base of their oil industry and speed up development of their offshore reserves as well as their onshore resources.

China's existing onshore fields are very well located. They are close to some of China's major industrial centers, and pipelines link them to ports, so that it is relatively easy to supply other important consuming areas within China—and foreign buyers as well. In contrast, the reserves in China's West are far away from most potential consumers, whether within China or abroad. Large-scale oil development in western China will be more costly than in the North and Northeast, and transport costs will be high. Moreover, it will involve strategic disadvantages, since the area is close to the Sino-Soviet border. There will be many arguments in favor of giving priority to the development of offshore oil. Even though the development of offshore fields is technologically more difficult, and in some areas may be more costly than development of onshore fields, transport of the product will be relatively easy, since the oil can be moved by tankers. In developing its offshore oil capabilities, China will face complex problems. It will be compelled to import a great deal of costly foreign equipment and technology, and in some regions it may eventually have to confront difficult issues created by unresolved territorial disputes and conflicting claims regarding the Asian continental shelf. But the advantages of exploiting offshore deposits clearly outweigh the disadvantages.

In the period ahead, China's oil production will depend not only on the number of fields it can discover and exploit but also on the rate at which it is willing to deplete its proven reserves. Although, worldwide reserve/production (R/P) ratios vary greatly, from well over 40/1 to about 10/1, the average worldwide ratio is estimated to be just under 30/1 (in 1975 it was 46.22/1 in the Middle East and 10.71/1 in the United States).[296] In China annual oil output has been about one twenty-fifth of estimated proven reserves nationally in recent years,[297] but if, as some estimates indicate, the remaining proven reserves in the North and Northeast have dropped to half a billion tons or less, then the R/P ratio in this area in the mid-1970s may have been close to 10/1 (or even 8/1), which indicates a high rate of depletion.[298] The recent slowdown in the rate of increase in output of Taching may have been due in part to greater use of techniques which increase the ultimate recovery and reduce the rate of depletion (R/P ratio).[299]

The question of how rapidly to deplete known fields will probably be a major issue in China in the period ahead. The country's rising demand for energy may argue for extracting as much oil as possible, as soon as possible. However, if China is to maximize the amount of oil that it will be able to obtain from the ground over the long run, and if it wishes to prolong the period during which it will have significant amounts of oil to use, it may have to restrict the rate of depletion. Conceivably, the fairly drastic slowdown in the growth in oil production may be attributable in part to recognition of this problem.

Requirements for Development

Whatever development strategy China chooses, large investments will be required for oil development. During the decade and a half from 1960 until the mid-1970s, the Chinese poured capital into the oil industry—to some extent at the expense of other basic industries. It is difficult to estimate how much China has invested to date in its oil industry, but it undoubtedly already has amounted to billions of dollars.[300] Future development will require billions more. According to an estimate made in 1976, to achieve an annual output of 335 million tons by 1985, China would have to invest about $4.5 billion a year.[301] However, the payoff in profits from investments in oil will probably also be large. One study estimates (on the basis of the difference, crudely calculated, between the per ton production cost of oil and its per ton sales price within China) that by 1975 the profit from Taching alone had exceeded $6 billion.[302] And the chief geologist engineer at Taching in 1978 claimed that the "accumulated funds" given by Taching to the state in eighteen years were 16.4 times higher than the total amount of state investment there.[303]

While it is difficult to make a realistic estimate of exactly how much China must invest to develop its oil, it is clear that not only will investment costs be high, but they will rise as China develops new offshore reserves as well as onshore deposits in the West. According to one U.S. estimate, Chinese offshore oil construction and production efforts in the next few years could generate $50 billion of business for foreign firms.[304]

Developing new oil production requires much more than finding and exploiting new fields. An extensive, and expensive, infrastructure must be built to move and use the output. A large oil-producing country needs adequate pipelines, railways, tanker ships, trucks, railway cars, storage facilities, and plants to build oil equipment and sophisticated instruments. It requires special high-quality steel for pipelines and many types of equipment. It needs to build, or adapt, many varieties of factories to use the oil produced. And for all of this it must train new kinds of scientists and technicians. Since 1949—and especially since 1960—the Chinese have made significant progress in these respects. However, as its oil industry develops, they will need to do much more, and the costs of developing the supporting infrastructure, as well as opening oil fields, will be high.

By mid-1976 China had close to 5,500 kilometers of pipeline either built or started (3,500 kilometers completed and 2,000 under construction),[305] with pipes of diameters varying from 20 to 61 centimeters. Although the Chinese have themselves manufactured some of the pipe needed, they also have had to import large amounts, especially pipe with larger diameters, since most Chinese-made steel cannot stand the high pressures in large pipes. From 1968 through 1975 China imported about 328,000 tons of pipe from Japan—probably close to the amount China itself produced.[306]

The most important pipelines in China connect its largest fields in Northeast and North China with major refineries, industrial cities, and ports. In fact, 3,700 of the 5,500 kilometer total are in the North and Northeast. Because of the high wax content of the oil from major fields in these regions, many of the pipelines require special heating facilities to keep the oil moving.[307] The longest pipeline elsewhere in the country is a 1,100 kilometer link between Tsinghai and Tibet, the main significance of which is military and strategic rather than economic. If oil is to be further developed in western China, a great deal more pipeline will be required in that region.

Gradually, the Chinese have developed port facilities for handling oil, both for shipment to various parts of China and for export. Since the mid-1970s it has had six ports with a capability to handle some oil.[308] So far, however, only one, a new port at Lu Ta (Dairen–Port Arthur), can handle tankers with a capacity up to 100,000 tons (fairly small by international standards), and none can handle supertankers. Further development of port facilities clearly will be required.

China also has started to build its own tankers, but its fleet is still limited, and the ships the Chinese themselves build are small. Most of them built in the 1950s and 1960s had a capacity of less than 5,000 deadweight tons, and were for coastal use. Since then, they have begun building ships with a 10,000 deadweight ton capacity or larger, and in 1976 they constructed one of 50,000 deadweight tons.[309] What China now needs, however, are tankers that are considerably larger—100,000 deadweight tons and above—to cut transport costs.

As oil output increases, so too will the Chinese need for refining capacity. Since 1949 the Chinese have greatly expanded their refinery facilities. Particularly since the late 1960s, new refineries have been built at a rapid rate, about half of them at major oil fields and half near large consuming cities. Between 1965 and 1975 the country's total refining capacity is estimated to have increased from 13.6 million to 66.5 million tons.[310] By 1975 China had forty-four refineries, including twenty-seven catalytic crackers.[311] Few countries other than the United States and the Soviet Union have invested so much in these expensive, sophisticated cracking facilities. The Chinese have had to do this because the characteristics of much of their oil necessitate fairly complex processing to break its components into usable form. Not only does most of China's oil (like that from continental deposits elsewhere) have a high wax (paraffin) content (though it is low in sulfur), it is generally a high-gravity crude with a large percentage of residuum from primary distillation, requiring expensive cracking to extract its components—gasoline, kerosene, diesel fuel, naphtha, feedstock for petrochemical plants, and so on.[312]

However, even though the growth in China's refining capacity has been impressive, it has not kept up with the increase in the country's crude oil output, and the situation has been tight in recent years. This may be one reason for the decision in the mid-1970s to use some crude oil directly in power plants in China. Probably some oil also has been stored for military and other purposes, although concrete data on this are lacking.[313] It is apparent, however, that if China's oil output continues to rise, so too must its refining capacity—unless it exports a much larger percentage in the form of crude oil. (Conceivably, if construction of new refining capacity were to lag a great deal behind output, this fact alone could argue for a substantial increase in exports of crude oil, although the Chinese doubtless will try to avoid such a situation and will determine how much to export on other grounds.)

Past Energy Consumption

The discussion so far has focused on China's production of energy. To assess China's energy situation and prospects, it is equally important to examine trends in its energy consumption. Actually, many analyses of "energy balances" start with an examination of demand rather than supply, for a very logical reason. Energy demand is not simply a function of domestic energy output (in some countries, high energy demand occurs even when there is virtually no domestic energy production). Rather, the growth of demand reflects overall economic growth and has a dynamic of its own. As a country's economy expands, its need for energy tends to rise—no matter how much it produces itself. When it cannot meet its demand from domestic production, it imports energy if it can—usually in the form of oil—to make up the difference.

China is one of the few large countries in which the economy's growing energy needs and domestic energy production have been fairly closely balanced in recent years. Although immediately after 1949 it had an energy deficit, very soon thereafter its energy production surpassed its consumption. This has been true ever since, and for some years China has been a net energy exporter.

However, the rate of increase in China's consumption of energy has been high, and consequently, despite the impressive increase in its production, its "surplus" has been small, and, in fact, domestic energy supplies have been very tight. There are many reasons to believe that energy consumption in China will continue to rise at a fairly rapid rate. The key question is, exactly how rapidly, in comparison to energy output? Some overly optimistic estimates, made several years ago, of China's potential as an energy exporter focused mainly on its production record and gave inadequate attention to demand trends. Recently, more pessimistic estimates have paid greater attention to factors likely to affect future domestic consumption. Whatever judgments one makes about China's energy situation in the future must be based on realistic calculations about possible trends affecting demand as well as production.

The rate of increase in China's total consumption of primary energy during the past quarter century has been one of the fastest anywhere in the world.[314] CIA analysts estimate that, expressed in terms of coal equivalent, the country's energy consumption rose from 42 million tons in 1952 to 492 million tons in 1976—an increase of more than ten-fold.[315] The rate of increase in Chinese energy consumption averaged 10.8 percent a year from 1952 through 1976, or 9.0 percent from 1957 through 1976; then in 1977 China's apparent energy consumption rose over 13 percent to 558 million tons CE, and in 1978 by over 12 percent to 626 million tons CE.[316]

A high rate of increase in energy consumption is not surprising in light of China's GNP growth. Nevertheless, the rate has been unusually high by international standards. There have been some other countries whose rates of growth in energy consumption have been comparable and, in a few cases, even higher. The rate in the Soviet Union, for example, was 10.4 percent from 1925 through 1950, although it dropped to 6.6 percent from 1950 through 1975.[317] The rate in Japan, which had been only 1.6 percent from 1925 through 1950, rose to 9.1 percent in the years from 1950 through 1975.[318] Thailand's rate from 1950 through 1975 was over 14 percent, and Indonesia's was 7.3 percent.[319] China's rate is by no means unprecedented, therefore; but this should not obscure the fact that since the 1950s its rate has been one of the highest in the world. (India's, by comparison, was only 5.4 percent from 1950 through 1975.)[320]

There have been many reasons for the high rate of increase in China's consumption of energy. A basic one has been the growth in its GNP, and especially in its industrial output, but this has by no means been the only one. China's energy/GNP elasticity coefficient also has been high—that is, it has consumed relatively large amounts of energy in relation to its GNP growth. CIA analysts have estimated that during 1953–57 the elasticity coefficient was 2.45, which was extraordinarily high, and that although it dropped thereafter, it was still a high 1.74 during 1958–65.[321] Subsequently, the situation improved, and according to this study, the elasticity coefficient was 1.46 during 1966–70. Apparently, it rose sharply in the mid-1970s, to 1.88 in 1975 and 2.47 in 1976, partly as a result of political turmoil in those years. However, a recent CIA study estimates that in the period 1970–78 the elasticity ratio was probably around 1.4.[322] (Another analysis of past rates of growth in both GNP and energy in China, using a different methodology, indicated that from 1949 through 1974, 1.83 kilograms of CE were required for each one dollar increase in GNP.)[323]

Even if one ignores the energy/GNP ratio in China in earlier years, it is clear that the pattern of growth that has occurred since the early 1950s has required comparatively large amounts of primary energy, for many reasons. The Chinese until recently have placed great emphasis on basic heavy industries that are large consumers of primary energy. (Almost all Communist countries are relatively heavy users of energy, partly for this reason.) Electric power generation and the production of iron and steel, coal, and cement all require large amounts of energy; some CIA statistics indicate, in fact, that these four industries alone may have used about two-thirds of China's industrial energy in the late 1950s.[321] In recent years, also, China has developed a variety of new industries, such as those producing chemical fertilizers and petrochemicals, which are heavy energy users. In addition, since the early 1960s the use of energy in agriculture has increased rapidly—for pumps, electric motors, tractors, and other agricultural machinery. Also, the growth of rural small-scale industry—producing fertilizer, cement, electric power, iron and steel, and farm machinery—has imposed new demands on China's energy supplies, and many rural uses of energy may have been relatively ineffi-cient[325] if measured by the contribution to GNP of each unit of energy expended.

Since the 1950s, as the basic structure of China's economy has changed, so too has the pattern of its energy consumption as well as pro-duction. In 1952 it is estimated, almost two-thirds (62 percent) of China's primary commercial energy was consumed in the residential-commercial sector and just over a quarter (26 percent) in industry and construction; transport used 12 percent, and agriculture only a negli-gible amount.[326] By 1978 industry and construction probably consumed almost two-thirds of the total (62 percent) and the residential-commer-cial sector only 27 percent; the agricultural sector consumed 6 percent, and transport 5 percent. The rate of increase in energy consumption from 1957 through 1978 was 12.0 percent in industry and 19.2 percent in agriculture, compared with only 6.2 percent in transportation and 5.9 percent in the residential-commercial sector. (Basic changes in the struc-ture of China's energy supply paralleled these changes in consumption patterns. As the earlier discussion indicated, of China's total energy supply, measured in standard coal equivalents, in 1952 coal provided 96 percent and oil only 4 percent, and the contributions of both natural gas and hydroelectricity were negligible.[327] But by 1978, while coal still provided 73 percent, the share of oil had risen to 23 percent and that of natural gas to 3 percent, although hydroelectricity still provided only about 1 percent.)

Although structural changes in the economy partially explain China's high energy/GNP elasticity coefficient in the past, another major explanation has been the wasteful, inefficient ways in which the Chinese often have used their energy. The downward trend in the energy/GNP ratio from the 1960s on (except for the 1975–76 period) suggests that over time some progress was gradually made toward more rational and efficient use of the country's available energy supplies. However, the tremendous emphasis that Chinese leaders themselves placed during 1978–79 on the need for improved conservation measures to save energy indicated that there was still a great deal of unnecessary wastage and numerous opportunities for improving the efficiency of energy use.

Statistics on 1979 indicate that Chinese efforts to use their available energy more effectively already have produced results. Even though total energy production and consumption increased by only a little under 3 percent during the year, Chinese statistics indicated that national income rose by 7 percent and that gross industrial output rose by 8.5 percent, and the CIA estimated that GNP increased during the year by 5.4 percent.[328] It is difficult to fully understand the significance of these figures, which suggest a sudden major improvement in China's energy/ GNP elasticity coefficient. Taken at face value, the figures show a dramatic drop in the energy/GNP ratio to a very low level—perhaps close to 0.5.

Conceivably, these figures are misleading to some degree. China's total energy supply rose rapidly during the previous two years (over 12 percent in 1977 and over 11 percent in 1978), and perhaps there were some stocks, especially of coal (the output of which rose almost 14 percent in 1977 and over 12 percent in 1978), which were carried over and used in 1979. The relative increase in better-quality coal from some large mines (which probably increased production by close to 5 percent in 1979, even though overall coal output rose by less than 3 percent) also may have made the use of coal more efficient. More important, the shift of emphasis from heavy industry to light industry and agriculture probably helped to some extent to increase the average GNP output per unit of energy used (although the effects of this trend may be more apparent during the next few years than at present).

None of these factors adequately explains the apparent great improvement in the energy/GNP ratio in 1979, however. The most important explanation, therefore (unless somehow the figures are basically misleading), probably is that the regime's energetic conservation measures and efforts to rapidly improve the efficiency of energy use—for example, by closing some energy-inefficient plants—must have had some fairly quick and remarkable effects. Even so, it is difficult to understand how this could reduce the energy/GNP ratio so much—from close to 1.5 to only a little over 0.5—unless the waste and inefficiency of energy use previously were much worse than had been generally recognized.

It is doubtless premature to reach any final conclusion even about what really occurred during 1979 and certainly about what the likely trend in the energy/GNP ratio will be in the future. Basic trends of long-term significance may not become clear until two or three years from now. Nevertheless, present evidence points to a significant increase in efficiency in energy use in 1979, which was encouraging, at a time when there was a substantial decline in energy production, which was discouraging. However, the strict—perhaps draconian—conservation measures, which apparently made possible continued high industrial and GNP rates of growth in 1979 despite declining energy output, obviously cannot be expected to produce comparable results indefinitely, since there are limits to what can be achieved by energy-saving measures. By 1980 there was evidence that the extremely tight energy situation resulting from very slow energy growth was having an adverse effect on industrial and GNP growth. According to some reports, quite a few industrial plants were operating below capacity.

Factors Affecting Future Demand Trends

It is virtually impossible to predict energy demand trends in the period ahead with any accuracy. Despite the apparent increase in the efficiency of energy use in 1979, a number of factors could operate not only to increase China's overall energy consumption but also to raise the energy/GNP ratio again in the future. Even though light industry and agriculture will probably continue to receive high-priority attention in the immediate future, to achieve their ambitious modernization plans the Chinese in time clearly must substantially expand the output of many basic industries that are heavy users of energy. They also must further develop modern transportation, which will also raise the demand for energy. (Conceivably, greater regional specialization of industry will lead to more interregional trade, further increasing energy demand in the transportation field.) Certainly, any significant modernization of China's military forces, if it occurs, will add to the country's need for energy. So too will increased agricultural mechanization.

Probably there also will be pressures for increased personal consumption, especially in urban areas, requiring larger allocations of energy for household use. Although the regime doubtless will continue trying to limit personal consumption of energy, because of its promises to raise living standards it will find it difficult to ignore completely the pressures that may result from hopes it has aroused.[329]

In China, as elsewhere, as the economy and society are modernized, a continued increase in the level of per capita consumption of energy seems inevitable—especially to fuel industrial and agricultural growth but to some degree for household use as well. Even though China is now the third largest consumer of energy in the world, it still ranks very low in per capita consumption. In 1952, when per capita consumption of energy worldwide averaged 1,085 kilograms CE and was only 147 kilograms CE in all non-Communist developing nations, it averaged just 74 kilograms CE in China.[330] However, by 1975 China's per capita consumption of energy had risen to about 515 kilograms CE per person, compared with more than 2,000 kilograms CE worldwide and just over 400 kilograms CE in all developing nations. By 1978 the figure for China had risen to more than 650 kilograms CE per person. Per capita energy consumption in China is now higher, therefore, than the average in all developing countries and is well above that in countries such as India, Indonesia, Egypt, Nigeria, and Zaire.[331] However, it is still lower than in many developing countries, including Chile, Brazil, Lebanon, Turkey, South Korea, and Malaysia, and it does not begin to compare with that in the advanced industrial nations.

China's Future Energy Balance

Although it is a safe prediction that China's energy consumption will continue to rise, in both absolute and per capita terms, it is no simple matter to predict how much and how fast.

A standard (albeit crude) method for calculating future energy demand is to estimate (1) the likely rate of growth in GNP and (2) the probable energy/GNP elasticity coefficients, and then to estimate the rate of growth in energy demand on the basis of these two indicators. A more complex method is to try to estimate (1) probable rates of growth of energy demand in particular sectors of the economy and (2) the future shares of each sector in the GNP and energy demand of the total economy, and then to aggregate these sectoral estimates.

A 1977 U.S. government study that attempted to project the growth of demand for energy in China used both of these methods.[332] Instead of making definite predictions, the study defined a range of possibilities.[333] The CIA analysts who wrote the study hypothesized that China's GNP growth rate in the period ahead would be somewhere between 4 and 8 percent a year. They calculated that if the country's energy/GNP elasticity coefficient continues at about the level of the late 1960s and early 1970s (that is, close to 1.5), GNP rates of 4, 6, or 8 percent would be accompanied by growth rates in energy demand of 5.9, 8.8, or 11.8 percent, respectively. (The authors of the study were inclined to believe that Chinese leaders would probably aim at a GNP growth rate of about 6 percent.)

In their sectoral analyses, the authors estimated that between 1977 and 1985 the rates of growth in energy demand might be between 10 and 13 percent in industry, 15 and 20 percent in agriculture, 4 and 6 percent in transportation, and 3 and 5 percent in the residential-commercial sector. (Their preferred "medium" projections were industry, 11.5 percent; agriculture, 17.5 percent; transportation, 5.0 percent; and the residential-commercial sector, 4.0 percent.)

Based on an aggregate of these estimates, the study projected overall rates of increase in total energy demand ranging between a low of 8.1 percent and a high of 11.2 percent in the period 1977–80 and between a low of 8.4 percent and a high of 12.0 percent in the period 1981–85. (The preferred medium estimates were for rates of growth in total energy demand of 9.8 percent during 1977–80 and 10.4 percent during 1981–85, resulting in consumption of 722 million tons CE of all energy in 1980 and 1,182 million tons in 1985.)[334]

To construct China's probable energy balance, the authors then estimated the range of possible growth rates in China's total energy production and supply between 1977 and 1985. They calculated that in this period the supply of coal could increase at a rate between 6 and 7 percent a year, oil between 10 and 20 percent, natural gas between 10 and

20 percent, and hydroelectricity between 6 and 10 percent. (The medium estimates, considered most likely, were coal, 6.5 percent; oil, 15 percent; natural gas, 15 percent; and hydroelectric power, 8 percent.) From an aggregate of these sectoral estimates, the study projected rates of growth in China's total energy supply that ranged between 6.8 and 11.3 percent in the period 1977–80 and 7.7 and 13.7 percent in the period 1981–85 (with the medium rates being between 9.0 and 10.4 percent). (All of these projections assumed a continuing shift from coal to oil, with oil accounting for between 29.3 and 41.5 percent of supply in 1985; the medium estimate was that oil would account for 35.5 percent of China's total energy production in 1985.)

These projections suggested that although under certain conditions China could have a sizable energy surplus in the future, it also would be possible, despite large increases in output, for it to have a deficit (under certain conditions a fairly large one) due to rapidly increasing domestic demand. The figures showed that if China's energy supply were to grow at the highest possible rates projected, the country could have an energy surplus in 1985 ranging between 108 million and 432 million tons CE (equal to 72 million to 288 million tons OE),[335] depending on how fast demand were to rise. The highest of these figures (based on an unlikely combination of a very high rate of growth of energy supply and very low rate of growth of energy demand) was not really plausible, but an estimate that then appeared to be at least theoretically possible was the one indicating that if China's energy supply were to grow at a high rate and its energy demand at only a medium rate, by 1985 it theoretically could have an energy surplus of 262 million tons CE (equal to about 175 million tons of oil).

The study's estimates also showed, however, that if the growth rate of energy surplus were low, China could have an energy deficit in 1985 ranging between 75 million and 399 million tons of CE (equal to roughly 50 million to 266 million tons OE), depending on how fast demand were to increase. Among the most disturbing of the study's estimates were those indicating that if China's energy supply were to grow at only a medium rate, it would have an energy surplus only if the rate of growth in energy demand were low (under such circumstances China's surplus in 1985 could be 139 million tons CE equal to about 93 million tons of oil). If both energy supply and demand were to grow at a medium rate, the study calculated, China still could have an energy deficit in 1985, perhaps amounting to 31 million tons CE (21 million tons OE). If demand were to grow at a high rate while supply grew only at a medium rate, the deficit could be as high as 185 million tons CE.

On the basis of all of these calculations, CIA analysts concluded in this 1977 study that China's oil exports might not be very large in the period ahead.[336] They assumed, doubtless correctly, that Chinese leaders will export some energy, to earn badly needed foreign exchange; but they concluded that large exports of oil might result in energy deficits that would slow China's overall rate of growth.[337]

This study highlighted many of the variables that will affect China's future energy balance, and its conclusions were sobering. However, it also indicated how difficult it is to make accurate predictions; the authors were unable to forecast trends accurately even for the relatively brief 1977–80 period. Developments during this period compound the problems of forecasting.

During 1977–78, China's energy production was significantly higher than most analysts had projected (mainly because of the very high rate of increase in coal production; the rate of increase in output of oil dropped to below what most observers had expected). So too was the level of China's energy consumption, and the apparent energy/GNP ratio remained high. However, in 1979, the rate of growth in energy production dropped to a level far below any previous projections, and the energy/GNP ratio appeared to improve more dramatically than anyone predicted it could.

On the basis of the data currently available, it seems probable that the trends that emerged in 1979 will continue not only in 1980 but at least through China's readjustment. But no one can really say whether trends in 1977–78 or trends in 1979–80 are a better basis for long-range predictions. In a rapidly changing situation, probably no past period provides a good basis for accurately predicting future trends. Neither the data available nor the methodological state of the art provides a basis for confident forecasts.

What is clear is that to achieve their modernization goals, the Chinese, once the present "readjustment" slowdown is over, will have to accelerate the growth of energy production again and at the same time continue to work to improve efficiency in energy use. This is what they hope their present energy program will accomplish during the next few years, but what they actually can achieve will depend to a large degree on how effectively their new policies can be implemented.

What seems probable, however, is that following the current readjustment period, the new policies now being gradually instituted in China will result eventually in an increase in energy output and probably an energy/GNP ratio lower than that of most of the 1960s and 1970s. But it is impossible to know precisely how rapidly energy production can be increased or how effectively energy demand can be controlled and energy efficiency improved. The future, therefore, is in many respects open ended. During the 1980s China, at worst, could encounter serious energy deficits that would slow its own growth and severely limit its energy exports. However, it is still conceivable that it could have significant energy surpluses permitting growing energy exports. Which of these alternative outcomes results will depend on how successful Peking's new policies prove to be, and it will have profound effects both on China's domestic modernization and on its foreign relations.

China and World Energy Supplies

To date, China has been the least involved of all major nations in the world's energy system through trade. Only one other large nation—the Soviet Union—has been able to meet its essential needs in recent decades from its own output, and, unlike China, it has played an international role of considerable significance in recent years as an exporter of oil and coal to Eastern Europe and, more recently, as a supplier of oil and natural gas to Western Europe.[338] China has neither exported nor imported energy on any large scale, although its small energy trade has always been very important to its own economy.

In the 1930s China's total consumption of energy was very small, and so too was its energy trade. It imported all of the oil and oil products that it needed, but the total was well under a million tons a year. However, it was a net exporter of coal, which was a valuable foreign exchange earner.

China's exports of coal totaled roughly 1.4 million tons in 1936 and then rose steadily in the 1930s to more than 4.8 million in 1940.[339] During the same period, however, China also imported between 0.5 million and 2 million tons of coal a year (561,000 tons in 1936; 2 million tons in 1940). Its net coal exports thus varied from a little less than 1 million tons to about 3 million tons. These coal exports were not large in international terms. Worldwide, total exports of solid fuels—coal and lignite (expressed in terms of standard coal equivalent)—generally were between 125 million and 150 million tons a year during that period,[340] so that China's coal exports in the late 1930s generally were only 1 or 2 percent of the world's total. Even though they were larger than those of any other developing nation, in the context of total world energy trade China's coal exports did not loom large.

China's use of oil was extremely limited in the pre-1949 period. Nevertheless, several types of petroleum products were important to its economy, including gasoline and diesel oil for vehicles and kerosene for lighting, especially in rural areas ("oil for the lamps of China," as it was described by an American novelist of the time). Kerosene was the most important, and expensive, oil product that the Chinese bought abroad. In 1936 they imported 104 million gallons of kerosene, as well as 46 million gallons of gasoline and 313,000 tons of diesel oil, costing, respectively (in the "Chinese National Currency" dollars of the 1930s), CNC $40 million, $22 million, and $16 million.[341]

China's Recent Trade in Energy

In the early 1950s, immediately after the Communist takeover, the level of China's imports of oil and oil products was roughly comparable with the prewar level; the total was 143,000 tons in 1949 and only slightly higher—281,000 tons—in 1950 (table 4-13). But thereafter, as China's industrial development accelerated, the level steadily rose.[342] In 1952, just before the start of the first Five Year Plan period, China imported 608,000 tons; by the end of that period in 1957, the total was 2.69 million tons, and in 1959 it reached 3.93 million tons. During the 1950s China's payments for oil and oil products accounted for a significant (though not huge) proportion of its total import bill. In the early 1950s oil generally amounted to 3 or 4 percent of the value of total Chinese imports; from 1956 through 1960, it was 5 to 6 percent; and during 1961–62, it rose to 7 or 8 percent, before dropping to a low level in the mid-1960s.

At the start, China obtained all of its oil and oil product imports from the Soviet Union. The bulk consisted of refined products rather than crude oil. For example, of the 3.0 million tons imported from the Soviet Union in 1959, 2.4 million tons were refined oil products and only 636,000 tons crude oil. From 1955 on, however, the Chinese began to buy from other Communist countries, mainly Rumania and later Albania. Then, following the Sino-Soviet split, Chinese oil imports from

TABLE 4-13. *China: Imports of Crude Petroleum and Petroleum Products, 1949–74*

Thousands of tons

Year	Soviet Union	Others	Total	Imports as percent of domestic crude oil production
1949	143	...	143	119
1950	281	...	281	141
1951	733	...	733	236
1952	608	...	608	138
1953	834	...	834	135
1954	904	...	904	114
1955	1,589	278	1,867	192
1956	1,732	1,005	2,737	236
1957	1,803	891	2,694	183
1958	2,507	733	3,240	143
1959	3,048	882	3,930	106
1960	2,963	912	3,875	75
1961	2,928	456	3,384	63
1962	1,856	1,144	3,000	50
1963	1,408	1,600	3,008	43
1964	505	1,805	2,310	27
1965	38	974	1,012	10
1966	40	440	480	4
1967	7	181	188	1
1968	8	361	369	2
1969	10	649	659	4
1970	...	661	661	3
1971	...	353	353	1
1972	...	382	382	1
1973	...	385	385	1
1974	...	1,095	1,095	2

Sources: Vaclav Smil, *China's Energy: Achievements, Problems, and Prospects* (Praeger, 1976), p. 121. Soviet data from Ministerstvo Vneshnei Torgovli (or Ministry of Foreign Trade), Union of Soviet Socialist Republics (MVT SSSR), *Vneshnyaya torgovlya SSSR Statisticheskii sbornik 1918–1966* (Moscow: MVT, 1967); MVT, *Vneshnyaya torgovlya 1966–1970* (Moscow: MVT, 1967–72). "Others" data compiled from estimates made by A. A. Myerhoff, "Developments in Mainland China, 1949–68," *American Association of Petroleum Geologists Bulletin*, vol. 54 (August 1970), p. 1569; and by B. A. Williams, "The Chinese Petroleum Industry: Growth and Prospects," in Joint Economic Committee, *China: A Reassessment of the Economy*, 94 Cong. 1 sess. (GPO, 1975), app. B, table 1, p. 262.

the Soviet Union rapidly declined, while those from other Communist sources rose and by 1963 surpassed those from the Soviet Union. (In monetary terms, China's bill for Soviet oil rose to a peak of between $110 million and $120 million a year during 1959–61; and oil imports as a proportion of China's total imports from the Soviet Union, by value, reached their highest level during 1961–63, when they were roughly one-third of the total.)

The years 1958 through 1963 were the peak period for China's imports of oil and oil products; during these years they averaged 3 million to 4 million tons annually. Although these figures do not appear enormous, compared with the oil imports of most other developing nations at that time they were sizable. (However, by 1960 India imported more —5.7 million tons of crude oil and 1.5 million tons of petroleum products—and by 1974 India's imports of crude and products had risen to 14.6 million and 3.7 million tons, respectively.)[343] Clearly, China's energy imports were vitally important to it, both economically and militarily, in the 1950s. Throughout the decade, China's imports of oil and oil products were larger than its own output.[344] In fact, during 1955–57 —the last three years of the first Five Year Plan period—China's imports of these commodities were almost double the quantity that it produced itself.

This situation rapidly changed in the early 1960s, when, after the Sino-Soviet polemics of 1960, the Russians withdrew their technicians from China, the Chinese gradually cut their Soviet ties and stressed self-reliance, and Peking pushed China's own oil development at Taching and elsewhere. Chinese imports of oil and oil products steadily declined. By 1965 they amounted to only 1 million tons, and by 1967 they were less than 200,000 tons. They rose again briefly during 1969–70 to more than 650,000 tons a year, but then they stabilized at a level of between 300,000 and 400,000 tons a year in the early 1970s (although in 1974 they jumped, briefly, to 1 million tons). The last year in which China imported any significant amount of oil from the Soviet Union (roughly 500,000 tons) was 1964. Thereafter, Chinese imports of Soviet oil products dropped to a low level, and after 1969 they were ended.

In the mid-1960s China achieved essential self-sufficiency in oil. Whereas in 1960 its imports of oil and oil products still were 75 percent as large as its own domestic production, the figure dropped to about 50 percent in 1962, then to 10 percent in 1965.[345] By 1970 the figure was only 3 percent, and since then it has never been more than 1 to 2 percent. Imports of unrefined crude oil virtually ended in 1960; since then China has imported only special types of oil products.

Therefore, although strictly speaking China remained a net importer of oil and oil products until 1973 (when it sold its first million tons of crude oil abroad and imported only 385,000 tons of oil products), it has been essentially self-sufficient since the mid-1960s. In 1965 its own oil production surpassed 10 million tons for the first time, and in 1966 its imports of oil products dropped to well under 1 million tons for the first time since the 1950s.[346]

Then in 1973 China emerged on the world market as an oil exporter.[347] Despite the fact that its oil exports that year were small, international interest was immediately aroused, in part because the Arab embargo and oil crisis later that year made all sources of petroleum important. Several basic factors probably influenced Peking's decision to start exporting oil in 1973. In that year Chinese oil output reached about 55 million tons and appeared to be outpacing the country's domestic refining capacity and demand. Moreover, in the wake of China's Cultural Revolution, as leaders such as Chou En-lai (Zhou Enlai) attempted to put China on a new economic course, requiring increased imports of foreign plants and technology, the Chinese began to search for new ways to earn foreign exchange. And the quadrupling of world oil prices in late 1973 suddenly made oil exports extremely valuable as a potential earner of foreign exchange.

In conversations with the Japanese, the Chinese soon began to talk about remarkably high oil export targets, on occasion indicating that they wished to sell as much as 50 million tons of oil a year to Japan by 1980.[348] These discussions of targets may have sincerely represented what Chinese leaders thought at that time might be possible, or they may have simply represented an attempt by Peking, for political as well as economic reasons, to try to arouse Japanese interest in Chinese oil and discourage Tokyo from helping the Russians develop oil in Siberia. In any case, such statements helped to stimulate very unrealistic hopes abroad. Before long many organizations and individuals outside China were predicting that by 1980 China would become a large—perhaps even a huge—oil exporter. One Chinese-American (not an oil expert, but a person with good contacts in the Chinese leadership) predicted that China would be exporting 225 million tons by 1980![349] Even some Japanese predicted that by 1980 China's oil exports would total 100 million tons or more,[350] and a number of estimates made by reputable specialists and responsible organizations placed the 1980 figure at about 50 million tons.[351] All of these projections proved to be wildly over-optimistic.

Today, China's sales of petroleum and petroleum products abroad are only a little more than 16 million tons a year. Starting with exports of 1.9 million tons in 1973, the Chinese increased sales abroad to 5.6 million tons in 1974 and then to 10.5 million tons in 1975 (table 4-14).[352] In 1976 the level dropped to 9.6 million. However, since then the level has risen significantly, to 11.3 million tons in 1977, 14.3 million in 1978, and 16.3 million in 1979. (Exports of crude oil alone rose to 8.8 million tons in 1977, 11.9 million in 1978, and 12.5 million in 1979 [table 4-15].[353]) The bulk of these exports have gone to Japan, which bought 1.03 million tons in 1973, 3.96 million in 1974, 7.93 million in 1975, 6.17 million in 1976, 6.75 million in 1977, 7.77 million in 1978, and 7.73 million in 1979. In addition, the Chinese have sold increasing quantities to Hong Kong (42,000 tons in 1973, 1 million tons in 1978), to the Philippines (103,000 tons in 1974, 1.20 million tons in 1978), to Thailand (19,000 tons in 1973, 300,000 tons in 1978), and, surprisingly, to Rumania (233,000 tons in 1975, 1 million tons in 1978). China has also exported oil to Vietnam and North Korea (it has had pipeline links to both). Exports to Vietnam probably have now ended, but China still exports about 1 million tons a year to Korea.

Although the rise in China's oil exports from less than 2 million tons in 1973 to more than 16 million tons in 1979 was not unimpressive, it fell far short of many predictions made in the mid-1970s. The most basic reason was the rapid growth in domestic energy demand which created a tight energy supply situation within China. Another was the decline in the rate of increase in Chinese oil output after 1975. Still another was the accelerating shift from coal to oil in China in the mid-1970s, resulting in an increase in oil's share of China's energy supply from 15 percent in 1970 to a peak of 24 percent in 1976.

In some years, China also encountered marketing problems abroad. After their initial enthusiasm in the wake of the 1973-74 oil crisis about the possibility of a new source of oil opening up in China, some Japanese became less interested in Chinese oil once the world oil supply situation temporarily eased.[354] To import much larger amounts of Chinese oil, Japan will have to adapt old refineries and build new ones, at considerable cost, because of the wax content of Chinese oil. (In recent years Japan has expanded its refinery capacity to handle a different kind of

TABLE 4-14. China: Commercial Exports of Petroleum and Petroleum Products, 1973–79 [a]

Year	Total	Japan	Philippines	Thailand	Rumania	Hong Kong	Other
1973	38,000 b/d	20,596 b/d	0	379 b/d	0	841 b/d	16,184 b/d
	1.90 mmt	1.03 mmt	0	0.019 mmt	0	0.042 mmt	0.809 mmt
1974	112,000 b/d	79,348 b/d	2,050 b/d	845 b/d	0	6,613 b/d	23,144 b/d
	5.60 mmt	3.96 mmt	0.103 mmt	0.042 mmt	0	0.331 mmt	1.157 mmt
1975	210,000 b/d	158,510 b/d	8,288 b/d	1,148 b/d	4,660 b/d	13,124 b/d	24,270 b/d
	10.50 mmt	7.93 mmt	0.414 mmt	0.057 mmt	0.233 mmt	0.656 mmt	1.214 mmt
1976	192,000 b/d	123,426 b/d	11,320 b/d	5,845 b/d	9,120 b/d	12,277 b/d	30,062 b/d
	9.60 mmt	6.17 mmt	0.566 mmt	0.292 mmt	0.456 mmt	0.614 mmt	1.531 mmt
1977	225,900 b/d	134,900 b/d	16,920 b/d	6,113 b/d	9,849 b/d	18,342 b/d	40,000 b/d
	11.30 mmt	6.75 mmt	0.846 mmt	0.306 mmt	0.492 mmt	0.917 mmt	2.000 mmt
1978	285,400 b/d	155,400 b/d	24,000 b/d	6,000 b/d	20,000 b/d	20,000 b/d	60,000 b/d
	14.27 mmt	7.77 mmt	1.20 mmt	0.300 mmt	1.00 mmt	1.00 mmt	3.000 mmt
1979	325,000 b/d	154,500 b/d	n.a.	n.a.	n.a.	n.a.	n.a.
	16.25 mmt	7.73 mmt					

Sources: For 1973–76, see CIA, *China: Economic Indicators*, ER 78-10750, December 1978, p. 43. (For figures on exports just of crude oil, see CIA, *China: Economic Indicators*, ER 77-10508, October 1977, p. 41.) For 1977–79, see CIA, *International Energy Statistical Review*, ER IESR 80-008, April 23, 1980, p. 27, which was used in compiling the figures for 1977–79. "Other" includes North Korea, Vietnam, and Brazil. The figures under "other" are my calculations (the difference between totals and the sum of figures for specified areas); the actual figures probably are slightly different. The sources give rounded figures for both the "total" and "other" columns.

n.a. Not available.

a. Million metric tons (mmt) values are based on a conversion rate of 1 million barrels a day (b/d) of oil equal 50 mmt. The totals include exports to North Korea and other areas.

TABLE 4-15. *China: Breakdown of Exports of Crude Petroleum and Petroleum Products, 1978–79*

Exports of crude petroleum, 1978		Exports of petroleum products, 1978		Exports of crude petroleum, 1979		Exports of petroleum products, 1979	
Barrels a day	Millions of tons	Barrels a day	Millions of tons	Barrels a day	Millions of tons	Barrels a day	Millions of tons
238,000	11.9	48,000	2.4	250,000	12.5	75,000	3.75

Source: Robert Michael Field, CIA, May 20, 1980. The 1979 figures are preliminary estimates.

crude oil, Arabian light.) A substantial investment will be required, therefore, to gear up to handle much larger amounts of Chinese oil, and there have been disagreements in Japan over who should pay the costs. As long as adequate amounts of oil were available from the Middle East and elsewhere, it was easier and cheaper to use than Chinese oil. However, the Japanese government and leading businessmen in industries such as iron and steel who wish to expand exports to China have, from the start, been strong advocates for expanded Japanese imports of Chinese oil. The government is interested because, as a matter of long-term policy, they wish to diversify Japan's sources of energy as much as possible, and the business leaders are interested because they realize that sizable oil imports from China will promote overall trade expansion. Generally, until very recently, Japanese oil companies have been considerably less enthusiastic because of the prospect of higher refining costs, although this attitude now appears to be changing.

China's policy on pricing has also at times created problems. If the Chinese had shown greater flexibility in bargaining over oil prices, they probably would have been able to arouse more enthusiasm in the 1970s among potential buyers, especially Japan.[355] In practice, they proved to be hard bargainers. For both political and economic reasons, not only has Peking strongly supported all OPEC price increases, but they have followed OPEC's lead (although it is not always easy to determine exact equivalences in pricing oil, in light of the varying characteristics of different types of oil, different transportation costs, and so on). Except for a few instances in which China has sold small quantities to Southeast Asian nations at so-called friendship prices,[356] it generally has not tried to use price concessions to create any special incentives to buy Chinese oil.

Political disputes in China also impeded the growth of China's oil exports during 1973–76. In the debates between the country's top radicals and its more pragmatic leaders, differences on oil policy symbolized the broader issue of whether to stress self-reliance or to increase China's international economic intercourse. The radicals not only opposed oil exports but took concrete steps to slow exports of oil and actively promoted increased domestic use of it (for example, in power plants) in ways that limited the amount available for export.[357] The oil trade that did develop in the mid-1970s was in spite of the radicals' obstructionism.

Since the purge of the radicals in 1976, there have been no political obstacles in China to increased exports of oil, however, and each event increasing uncertainty about the Middle East has aroused greater foreign interest in Chinese oil. Now Peking's leaders strongly assert that they regard increased exports of oil (and coal as well) as extremely important to help pay for what China needs to buy from abroad.[358] As early as 1977 Vice Premier Teng Hsiao-ping (Deng Xiaoping) emphasized, both publicly and privately, Peking's determination to increase oil exports. In one interview at that time, for example, he stated, "We are preparing to export more oil products, and we can do that. . . . To introduce technology to China from other countries, we must export more, and oil will be the main product. . . . But it must be increased step by step."[359] The key question now is not whether China *wishes* to export oil, but how much it will be *able* to export.

In early 1978 the Sino-Japanese trade agreement set targets for exports to China's main oil market for the years through 1982. It was, in essence, an agreement for the exchange of Chinese energy—mainly oil, but coal as well—for Japanese technology, plants, construction materials, and machines.[360] Its specific targets for the five-year period 1978–82 called for gradually increasing Chinese crude oil exports to Japan, to 7 million tons in 1978, 7.6 million in 1979, 8 million in 1980, 9.5 million in 1981, and 15 million in 1982. During 1978–79 actual Chinese oil exports to Japan were close to these targets. The two sides also agreed in 1978 that in 1981 they would decide on how much oil (and coal) China will export to Japan during 1983–85, indicating that the amounts would be "increased gradually." In 1980, however, some Chinese had already begun to tell the Japanese that Peking might have difficulty fulfilling its oil export commitments to Japan even in 1980–82.

Although from the start Japan has been the largest customer for China's oil, one significant trend during 1977–79 was Peking's move to broaden its oil markets. In 1976 only 34 percent of total Chinese oil exports went to countries other than Japan; since then this figure has steadily risen, to 40 percent in 1977, 46 percent in 1978, and (according to preliminary estimates) 52 percent in 1979.[361] In 1979 oil exports to the Philippines, Hong Kong, and Rumania reportedly in each case surpassed the 1 million ton level, and oil became the second largest Chinese exchange earner in its trade with the United States (after textiles but ahead of agricultural goods).[362] China also continued its oil exports to Thailand, increased such exports to North Korea, and began selling oil to several other countries, including Brazil and Italy.[363]

While oil is now by far China's most valuable energy export commodity, recently the Chinese have gradually increased their exports of coal as well. Since 1949, they have generally exported about 1 million to 2 million tons a year, most of it to Communist neighbors. Although this level has been considerably below that in peak power years, in most years since 1949 the Chinese have earned roughly $100 million a year (sometimes slightly more) from coal exports.[364] (In 1977, for example, coal exports totaled $95 million, of which $60 million was earned from coal sales to other Communist countries.)

Recently, however, it has become clear that sometime during 1978–79 the Chinese decided to try to expand coal exports in a major way in the near future. At the same time, the Japanese began to show increased interest in Chinese coal. As in the case of oil, Japan clearly will be China's major market.

To date Japanese purchases of Chinese coal have not been very large, but since 1978 they have been rising. In 1976 and 1977 they totaled 322,000 and 491,000 tons, respectively, but then they jumped to 772,000 tons in 1978 and 1.4 million tons in 1979. (Of the 1.4 million in 1979, which cost the Japanese $69 million, coking coal accounted for 749,000 tons, anthracite for 402,000 tons, and steaming coal for 256,000 tons.)[365] The long-term Sino-Japanese trade agreement signed in 1978 called for significant increases in Chinese coal exports to Japan, setting targets of 300,000 to 500,000 tons in 1978, 650,000 to 700,000 tons in 1979 (a figure that was greatly exceeded), 1.5 million to 1.6 million tons in 1980, 2.5 million to 2.7 million tons in 1981, and 3.5 million to 3.7 million tons in 1982.

Then in 1978 the Chinese and Japanese began discussing possibilities for joint coal development and much larger Chinese coal exports to Japan. In 1979 they made rapid progress toward agreement, and the final details of a cooperative program were agreed on in early 1980.

Five major Japanese corporations (Mitsui Mining, Mitsubishi Coal Mining, Sumitomo Coal Mining, Taiheiyo Coal Mining, and Matsushima Coal Mining) cooperated in reaching the agreement, under which the Japanese will provide technology and services to help develop possibly as many as twelve coal mines in China, the majority of them in Shantung and Shansi provinces.[366] Of these, eight that are scheduled to be completed between 1984 and 1986 should have a combined output capacity of 19.5 million tons; these will receive financial support from Japan's Export-Import Bank. The others, still unscheduled, include two proposed production-sharing ventures (to build mines that together would produce 8 million tons of coal) and two joint ventures (one for a coal mine to produce 3 million tons and another for a huge coal project in Inner Mongolia that might produce 10 million to 20 million tons and possibly be completed by 1990). The Japanese now say that they hope to increase their imports of Chinese coal to 15 million tons a year by 1985 (part of it to come from these new mines), and reportedly the Chinese have promised to consider exports to Japan of at least 10 million tons a year by then.

To enhance the prospects that China will increase its coal exports to Japan, the Japanese also have promised major support for the building of Chinese railways and ports of particular importance to the facilitation of coal exports. Following Premier Ohira's trip to China in mid-1980, at which time he announced a decision to provide concessionary Japanese government loans for development projects in China, especially for exploitation of oil and coal, it was revealed that the first six projects decided upon by the Chinese included four coal-related ones in North China—two major port development projects, at Shihchiuso (Shijiusuo) and Chinhuangtao (Qinhuangdao), and two railways, from Yenchou (Yanzhou) to Shihchiuso and from Peking to Chinhuangtao—each of which is intended above all to encourage larger coal exports.[367] (The other two projects were for a large hydroelectric plant in central China and a railway in South China.) Although, in theory, companies from any country can bid for these projects even though they will be financed by Japan, the Japanese probably will receive most if not all of the contracts because, as they themselves state, they "have a considerable lead as they possess exact information about the projects."[368]

China's Future Energy Export Prospects

It obviously is extremely difficult to predict exactly how much energy China will be able to export during the 1980s. There now can be no doubt that the Chinese hope and plan to increase both oil and coal exports substantially in order to earn badly needed foreign exchange to help finance increased imports of capital goods and technology. Even though they themselves state that their present "tight" energy situation will persist for some time, they are proceeding with programs that clearly are designed to expand energy exports. As China's development program progresses, moreover, the need for foreign exchange will increase, which will add to the pressures to increase oil and coal exports. However, how much energy China actually will be able to export will depend in large part on trends affecting its domestic energy production and needs. No one, even in China, can really know what achievements will be possible by the middle or late 1980s because they will depend on the success of policies only now being implemented. Nevertheless, it is very possible that China will gradually increase its exports of both oil and coal—even if this causes difficulty at home—because expanded energy exports will be virtually a prerequisite for financing what it urgently needs from abroad for its modernization program. The key question is not *whether* it will increase energy exports but by exactly *how much.*

Despite the many uncertainties, various attempts have been made to estimate the possible level of Chinese oil exports in the 1980s. They vary considerably. In its 1977 study cited earlier, the CIA hedged, concluding that depending on the circumstances, China in 1985 might in theory export close to 300 million tons of oil, but that actually it might have very little exportable surplus.[369] A number of other estimates made at about the same time were less equivocal, but they varied in their degree of optimism or pessimism. One specialist on Chinese energy estimated that the highest possible export levels that China could be expected to achieve, under favorable conditions, might be about 50 million tons of oil in the mid-1980s and approximately 80 million tons in 1990.[370] Another suggested that China's oil exports might reach a peak of about 40 million tons in 1985 but then decline thereafter to 20 million tons in 1990 because of rising domestic demand.[371] Still another analyst, who earlier had been very optimistic about China's prospects both for oil production and for oil exports, concluded that even though there was (in his opinion) better than a fifty-fifty chance that China's oil production would reach the 400 million ton level by 1990 (which now appears very unlikely), the Chinese probably would consume most of it and have little left for export.[372]

All of these estimates were made before China's new modernization programs had become clear and before it became evident that the Chinese had decided to turn their attention in a serious way to offshore oil and would launch a major program to develop offshore resources with foreign help. Since then, there have been a number of new estimates; at least some of them have been cautiously optimistic.

In 1979 a leading specialist on Chinese energy concluded that, under optimistic assumptions, China's exports of all kinds of energy (mainly crude oil but also petroleum products, coal, and possibly some LNG) might rise in the 1980s to a peak of 135 million tons OE a year and continue at a fairly high level through the 1990s; however, he judged it to be more likely that they would peak at 50 million to 75 million tons OE sometime between the middle and late 1980s and then decline in the 1990s.[373] In early 1980 another specialist, taking into account both the sudden drop in China's onshore oil production in 1979 and its stepped-up efforts to start development of offshore oil, predicted that China's crude oil exports would rise very little between 1980 and 1985 but then would rise significantly and reach at least 50 million tons and possibly more by 1990 (and that two-thirds of this would be from offshore fields).[374] This estimate, which was labeled "conservative," seems plausible, and the analyst making it doubtless was correct in underlining the fact that the size of the increases in China's oil exports during the 1980s will depend to a large extent on its success in new development efforts offshore and in stressing that the main effects of most offshore oil development will not be felt until the second half of the 1980s.

Very few estimates have been made of China's probable coal exports during the 1980s, but until recently it has generally been assumed that they would not increase to much more than 5 million tons a year (mainly to Japan) by the mid-1980s. It now appears possible, however, that during the second half of the 1980s they could rise to a substantially higher level, conceivably to between 15 million and 20 million tons a year. As in the case of oil, very large increases probably will not be possible until the late 1980s.

Key Variables Affecting Export Prospects

It is *possible* that China will be able to increase its exports of oil to around 50 million tons or more a year and its exports of coal to between 15 million and 20 million a year toward the end of the second half of the 1980s, but it is by no means *certain*. The key variables will be domestic rather than international. To achieve such export levels, the Chinese will have to accelerate their own production of energy of all kinds.

To expand oil output, they must step up their efforts to discover and exploit oil in areas other than the North and Northeast; this will require increased attention to the oil in China's far West, despite the locational disadvantages and the higher costs involved. (Some Western oil experts recently have visited Sinkiang, but the visits have not yet led to any concrete new projects for cooperative energy development there.) Most important, expansion will depend on the success in current efforts to discover and exploit China's offshore oil. Expansion of the infrastructure required to process, transport, and use oil also will be required on a large scale. The Chinese will have to increase their efforts to build refineries, pipelines, tankers, ports, and other transportation facilities.

In the immediate future the Chinese ability to expand oil production may depend on their willingness to deplete existing wells at a fairly rapid rate. From a long-term perspective, however, it would be desirable for them to slow the rate of depletion in existing fields in order to increase the amount of oil ultimately recoverable while they develop new fields. The size of China's oil supply in the near future will be significantly influenced by how the Chinese decide to balance these short- and long-term considerations.

Although oil development must receive high priority in China, no policy that concentrates on oil alone could possibly succeed. What will be required is a broad and balanced energy policy that emphasizes the development of many energy sources. The speed with which China can increase the output of coal will be of critical importance. Accelerating the growth of coal output will require increased mechanization of the extraction and processing of coal, especially in China's largest mines. In coal, as in the case of oil, China now must develop many areas that have been unexploited to date, and it must build numerous additional railway links to distribute output. In addition to opening new large mines, the Chinese will need to increase the efficiency and improve the quality of the output of thousands of scattered small mines. To facilitate the distribution of energy derived from coal, they probably will be impelled to build at least some large new thermal power plants at major coal pits. They also must expand China's electric grids on a national basis—though this will be costly and take many years to complete. They probably also should at least consider building some facilities for the liquefaction and gasification of coal.

A balanced energy policy in China eventually will require expanded output and use of natural gas. The building of pipelines to distribute gas from Szechwan to other parts of the country, although expensive, would help. But the Chinese also need to make a major effort to discover and exploit natural gas in other parts of the country. Eventual development of facilities to produce LNG may also be desirable, since it can be exported as well as used domestically.

China must try to accelerate development of its hydroelectric potential. It also should attempt to maximize the use of traditional fuels, further expand the use of simple energy sources such as biogas, and develop geothermal, solar, and other new sources to the extent possible. It probably will not make sense, however, for China to invest large sums in nuclear power in the foreseeable future; with limited investment resources, it can better use its funds to develop coal, oil, natural gas, and other secondary energy sources. Faster expansion of the production of all major sources of primary energy will require large-scale investment and technical assistance from abroad.

China's energy policy cannot succeed just on the basis of increased production. The Chinese must try to keep the growth of domestic energy demand under control. Any increase in energy efficiency and reduction in the country's energy/GNP elasticity coefficient will have the same effect as increasing energy output. Although some planned industrial projects and agricultural mechanization will work to increase the ratio, if priority continues to be given to technical improvements that are energy conserving and to more effective administration to help prevent waste and promote conservation, China should be able to use its energy more efficiently than in the past, as recent trends indicate.

To increase its exportable surplus of oil, specifically, the Chinese will have to check the shift from coal to oil that has occurred in most developing nations and stress greater use of coal and, possibly, natural gas. Because of oil's convenience and versatility, there doubtless will be increasing pressure to expand the uses of oil. A number of the regime's modernization policies, including agricultural mechanization, will work in this direction. However, measures to limit domestic oil consumption, in order to maximize the exportable surplus, will be essential if China is to achieve its broad goals.

Chinese Policy Trends

If one evaluates recent trends in Chinese policy in light of the desiderata outlined above, Peking's leaders must be given high marks for steps they have proposed since 1977 to evolve a rational approach to their energy problems. John Deutsch, director of the Office of Energy Research of the U.S. Department of Energy (who accompanied Secretary James Schlesinger on a trip to China in the fall of 1978), summed up his judgments on these policies by stating, "The Chinese have a remarkably impressive blueprint for where they intend to go in the whole energy area by 1985, and then by the end of the century."[375]

The full scope and precise nature of Peking's energy policies may not become completely clear until it publishes its first "energy act," which Hua Kuo-feng in mid-1979 stated would be enacted "as soon as possible." However, numerous aspects of Chinese policies already have been spelled out in a series of official statements since 1977 and have become clear from concrete actions taken by Chinese officials.

The first indication of the direction of the new energy policies came in 1977 when the official Chinese press attacked the previous policies of the radicals, who had opposed both oil exports and the importation of foreign technology for the development of Chinese resources and had fostered an accelerated shift from coal to oil, especially in Shanghai (Shanghai) and the Northeast.[376] Not long thereafter, in early 1978, Hua Kuo-feng, in his report outlining China's "ten year" plan, made it clear that Peking had decided to give very high priority to the development of the fuel and power industries—especially oil, coal, and electricity—and in doing so to rely heavily on foreign technology and expertise.[377] It was a striking fact that of the 120 "large-scale projects" which Hua said would be built in China during the next few years, 48—two-fifths of the total—were to be in the field of power and fuel; they included ten oil and gas fields, eight coal projects, and thirty power stations.

Shortly thereafter, Fang Yi, head of China's State Scientific and Technological Commission, discussed China's new energy policies in considerable detail, calling for a broad research program designed to develop diversified energy resources and to increase the efficiency of energy use in China. His outline of priority tasks remains one of the most important succinct summaries published to date. In it, he stated:[378]

We must make big efforts to accelerate the development of energy science and technology so as to carry out full and rational exploitation and utilization of our energy resources.

We have our own inventions in the science and technology of the oil industry, and in some fields we have caught up with or surpassed advanced levels in other countries. We must continue our efforts to catch up with and surpass advanced world levels in an all-round way. We should study the laws and characteristics of the genesis and distribution of the oil and gas in the principal sedimentary regions, develop the theories of petroleum geology and extend oil and gas exploration to wider areas; study new processes, techniques and equipment for exploration and exploitation and raise the standards of well drilling and the rate of oil and gas recovery; and actively develop crude oil processing techniques, use the resources rationally and contribute to the building of some ten more oilfields, each as big as Taching.

China has extremely rich resources of coal, which will remain our chief source of energy for a fairly long time to come. In the next eight years, we should mechanize the key coal mines, achieve complex mechanization in some of them and proceed to automation. The small and medium-sized coal mines should also raise their level of mechanization. Scientific and technical work in the coal industry should center around this task, with active research in basic theory, mining technology, technical equipment, and safety measures. At the same time research should be carried out in the gasification, liquefaction and multipurpose utilization of coal and new ways explored for the exploitation, transport, and utilization of different kinds of coal.

We must push up the power industry as a pressing task. We should take as our chief research subjects the key technical problems in building large hydroelectric power stations and thermal power stations at pit mouths, large power grids and super-high-voltage power transmission lines. We must concentrate our efforts on comprehensive research in the techniques involved in building huge dams and giant power-generating units, and in geology, hydrology, meteorology, reservoir-induced earthquakes, and engineering protection which are closely linked with large-scale key hydroelectric power projects.

New sources of energy should be explored. We should accelerate our research in atomic power generation and speed up the building of atomic power plants. We should also step up research in solar energy, geothermal energy, wind power, tide energy and controlled thermonuclear fusion, pay close attention to low-calorie fuels, such as bone coal, gangue and oil shale and marsh gas resources in the rural areas.

Attention should be paid to the rational utilization and saving of energy, such as making full use of surplus heat, studying and manufacturing fine and efficient equipment for this purpose, lowering energy consumption by every means and particularly coke consumption in iron smelting, coal consumption in power generation and energy consumption in the chemical and metallurgical industries.

Although Fang Yi's statement underlined the fact that Peking had adopted very ambitious goals calling for a diversified program of energy development, like many Chinese leaders in statements made in 1978 he revealed relatively little about the problems and dilemmas facing China in the energy field. In this area, as in many others, Peking had not yet sorted out its priorities or faced up to the difficult choices it had to make. Fang discussed the need to develop oil, coal, electricity (both thermal and hydroelectric), nuclear power, and all other energy sources with little indication of relative priorities (except, perhaps, in the order in which he listed them, although he did say that coal would remain China's "chief source of energy for a fairly long time to come"). For example, he stressed that China should "speed up the building of atomic power plants" while accelerating development of all the other major sources of energy. And, while he discussed energy conservation and the need to increase the efficiency of energy use in China, these items were listed last among the tasks he outlined.

By mid-1979, however, when Chinese leaders outlined the country's policies for the "readjustment period," it appeared that they had confronted fairly realistically many of the problems facing China.[379] In these reports, they placed even greater stress than they had in 1978 on the priority that should be given to energy policy in general in their development program, but, although they still called for both accelerated development of diversified energy sources and conservation of energy, they gave a clearer sense of priorities than they had previously for the period immediately ahead.

They indicated clearly that top priority must be given to coal, oil, and hydroelectricity. In coal and oil, emphasis in the immediate future will be on discovering new resources, adding capacity, and modernizing the industries, with significant infusions of foreign equipment and technology, rather than on trying immediately to maximize production or rapidly to raise rates of increase in output in the short run. While oil will continue to have high priority, in 1979 Peking's leaders raised the priority given to coal. They also stressed the need to slow down the rate of increase in domestic oil consumption, in part by switching back to coal many plants, including power plants, that earlier had shifted to oil, and they showed new concern about depleting existing oil fields too rapidly. They placed especially high priority on the need to discover and develop new fields, both onshore and offshore.

The development of natural gas did not appear to be given very high priority, however, although conceivably this issue is still being debated. It is possible to argue that natural gas deserves higher priority. By mid-1979 the Chinese seemed to have decided, sensibly, to postpone developing nuclear power, although this too may be a subject of continuing debate, as recent hints about the possibility of purchasing at least one foreign nuclear plant indicate.

By mid-1979 the Chinese clearly had decided to accelerate the development of hydroelectricity, which makes very good sense so long as they do not divert so much of their investment resources to large, long-term hydro projects that the near-term development of oil and coal is hampered. The Chinese also continue to push the development of biogas in rural areas, the use of all traditional fuels, and the development of other nonfossil fuels; this, too, is sensible, even though the short-run potential of such fuels is limited in relation to China's overall energy needs.

One of the most striking aspects of current Chinese policy is the tremendous emphasis that has been placed on conservation, and on the need to take all possible steps to increase energy efficiency. Peking's energy program adopted in 1979 calls for a national system for distributing energy that will give priority in the allocation of fuel and power to efficient enterprises (and in many cases will deny supplies to inefficient factories) and to enterprises producing for export. This program should help China to get through the present period of tight energy supplies while it accelerates its efforts to discover and develop new resources. Successful implementation of the plan, especially the proposed changes affecting the distribution of power, will depend to a considerable degree not only on the "unified regulations concerning the allocation and supply of electricity," which Hua in mid-1979 said would soon be enacted, but also on the speed with which China can, as its leaders now say they intend to do, create national as well as regional power grids under the control of the Ministry of Power Industry. Peking has made it clear that all of these policies are designed not only to ensure that China will be able to meet its essential domestic needs for fuel and power but also to increase its ability to expand exports of both oil and coal.

These policies will not resolve all of the problems and dilemmas that China faces in the energy field, and the tension between energy supply and energy demand doubtless will continue for some time. Chinese leaders obviously will have to make more hard choices in the future. Nevertheless, Peking's current energy policies in general appear sensible and realistic. If these policies can be successfully implemented, China's capacity both to meet its domestic needs and to increase energy exports should gradually improve, and it could conceivably export 50 million tons or more of oil, and 15 million to 20 million tons of coal, by the late 1980s. However, if China's overall domestic energy program falters, the country's oil and coal exports doubtless will fall considerably short of these theoretically possible levels. If Peking's new energy policies were to clearly fail, China might have no surplus energy to export; at worst, it might even have to consider importing energy again, in which case the success of its entire modernization program would become uncertain.

The Importance of Energy Exports to China

Stated bluntly, the degree of success that China achieves in increasing its exports of energy in the 1980s will be one of the key determinants—conceivably the key determinant, in many respects—of its ability to increase overall trade with the major industrial nations, to import badly needed capital goods and technology, and therefore to carry out its entire modernization program.

Already oil exports are very important in relation to China's balance of payments, and during the next ten years they should become increasingly so because they represent the easiest and surest means for China to earn large amounts of foreign exchange to pay for essential imports.

Even in the brief period since 1973, oil exports have become one of China's principal earners of foreign exchange. According to CIA statistics, in 1973 the Chinese earned only $80 million from their export of crude oil and petroleum products.[380] In 1974 the figure jumped to $525 million. In 1975 it was $910 million and in 1976, $840 million. Since then, it has steadily risen, in 1977 to $1.015 billion, in 1978 to $1.220 billion, and in 1979 to an estimated $2.887 billion.[381] The sale of crude oil accounted for most of these earnings ($425 million in 1974, $760 million in 1975, $665 million in 1976, $795 million in 1977, $985 million in 1978, and an estimated $1.853 billion in 1979), but income from the sale of refined products also greatly increased (from $100 million in 1974 to $150 million in 1975, $175 million in 1976, $230 million in 1977, $235 million in 1978, and an estimated $1.034 billion in 1979).

As a percentage of China's total foreign exchange earnings (from exports alone), oil and petroleum products amounted to less than 2 percent in 1973, rose to 8 percent in 1974, then stayed at 12 to 13 percent during the next five years (13 percent in 1975; 12 percent in 1976; and close to 13 percent in 1977, 1978, and 1979).[382] The only category of exports that earned more foreign exchange than oil and petroleum products during 1975–78 was textiles, including both fibers and products (which in 1978 totaled $2.4 billion).[383] However, in 1979, because of rapid oil price rises, the value of China's exports of crude oil and petroleum products appeared to be catching up with textiles. They will become more important in the period ahead, because oil prices are likely to continue rising more rapidly than textile prices. Since most of China's oil sales are to industrial countries, they earn valuable hard currency, which many of its textile exports to developing nations do not, and today there is little doubt that China can easily find markets for any oil that it wishes to sell, while it probably will encounter growing resistance to increased sales of its textiles in many countries.

The theoretically possible rise in China's earnings from oil was discussed in part II, with hypothetical examples of what it conceivably might earn under different circumstances from oil exports in the period ahead.[384] Already Chinese oil earnings are close to $3 billion a year. Even if the volume of oil exports increases only gradually during the first half of the 1980s, continued price increases could raise its oil earnings to more than $5 billion. If by the end of the 1980s China can export 50 million tons a year of oil and oil products, and if the price of oil rises to around $50 a barrel (or roughly $365 a ton), which is plausible, the Chinese then could be earning more than $18 billion annually from oil exports. The share of oil in China's total foreign exchange earnings should in time grow, therefore, and in the second half of the 1980s oil sales could well pay for at least one-fifth to one-fourth of China's import bill and possibly more. This is why China's success or failure in oil development will be so crucial to the country's entire modernization program. Even during the first half of the 1980s, the Chinese, in deciding how much they can prudently borrow from abroad to finance imports of capital goods and technology, will clearly be influenced by their leaders' estimates of oil export prospects in the late 1980s.

Coal exports also will be important, for similar reasons, although considerably less so than oil, because the per ton value of coal is much less than that of oil and is not likely to rise so much. In 1978 China's coal export earnings began to rise above the level of previous years (when the figure had averaged around $100 million) to $120 million. Then in 1979, according to preliminary CIA estimates, earnings jumped to around $200 million.[385] If China can raise its coal exports to around 5 million tons a year by 1985, and then to 15 million to 20 million tons a year by the end of the 1980s, even at the present average export price for China's coal (apparently about $50 a ton in sales to Japan in 1979), the Chinese could be earning more than a quarter of a billion dollars from coal exports in the mid-1980s and close to a billion dollars a year by the 1990s. Coal prices certainly will rise, moreover, so that China's potential coal earnings could be greater than these figures suggest. Coal also is likely to become an increasingly valuable foreign exchange earner for China, therefore, although its potential importance obviously does not compare with that of oil.

The International Importance of China's Oil Exports

The potential importance of China's oil to the international community also should be readily apparent. China's ability to meet its own needs constitutes, in and of itself, a significant contribution to the world energy system, reducing the strain on the available world supplies, just as China's ability to meet most of its own food needs eases the strain on the world food system. If China's huge population had to depend heavily on the world energy market, the impact on world supplies and prices could seriously exacerbate existing problems. Actually, there is little possibility, under any foreseeable circumstances, that China will become a very large purchaser of foreign supplies of energy. If domestic demand for energy in China began to surpass domestic supply by any large margin, although Peking's leaders could resort to imports, before long they would probably have to take steps to reduce the country's rate of economic growth in order to restore a balance, rather than become dependent on large-scale energy imports. Economic necessity—especially foreign exchange problems—would dictate this; China simply would have no way to pay for large energy imports.

But China's potential importance in the energy field derives less from the fact that it is able to meet its own needs than from the possibility that under favorable circumstances it might become an increasingly important exporter at a time when world supplies, especially of oil, will become progressively tighter. The contribution that China can make during the next five years to global energy supplies, through the export of limited amounts of oil and lesser amounts of coal, will doubtless continue to be relatively small. From a broad international perspective, its role in the immediate future, therefore, will remain minor—though not insignificant, since any addition to the world's supply of exportable energy now has some importance, and to a few countries, such as Japan, the value of Chinese oil and coal will grow even in the first half of the 1980s. However, if during the second half of the 1980s its annual oil exports rise to 50 million tons, China would become a real factor in the world energy picture. The size of its oil exports then would approach the amounts that Indonesia and Algeria have in some recent years contributed to the world market.

If, as many Western analysts believe, most of the major OPEC exporters decide to limit the growth of their exports during the period ahead, the importance of *all* of the world's middle-rank exporting nations will grow. As of the late 1970s there were only eight nations that could be classified in this category—that is, countries selling between 40 million and 100 million tons of oil a year. From what it known at present, only two other nations appear likely to join their ranks within the next few years: Mexico and China. In sum, if China is able to export 50 million tons or more a year during the second half of the 1980s, it clearly will become one of the world's important middle-rank oil exporters, and the addition of several tens of millions of tons of Chinese oil, at a time when the adequacy of global oil supplies will at best be problematic, will be a development of considerable international importance.

Offshore Oil and Foreign Technology

China's prospects for becoming a middle-rank oil exporter within the next decade will depend above all on its success in developing its *offshore* oil resources fairly rapidly (its onshore oil resources in the West clearly will take longer to develop), and this will depend fundamentally on the nature and scope of the foreign economic and technical assistance that it can obtain in the near future. Without extensive foreign cooperation, offshore oil development inevitably will be slow, and China probably will remain at best a minor oil exporter during the 1980s. With large-scale foreign help, however, there is a very good possibility that its offshore oil can be developed in the 1980s. This will require the Chinese to establish unprecedented foreign ties, and it will create certain forms of interdependence between China and other nations that could have far-reaching political as well as economic implications. As of mid-1980, although many uncertainties remained, major steps already had been undertaken to push toward large-scale offshore oil development, as rapidly as possible, with close foreign cooperation, and these steps give cause for considerable optimism about offshore oil production prospects, especially from the mid-1980s on.

Some Chinese leaders, including Chou En-lai (Zhou Enlai), started showing interest in offshore oil in the late 1960s and early 1970s. Although at that time Peking's top radicals were still opposing any involvement of foreign personnel in Chinese oil development, Peking began to purchase some oil equipment abroad and also to build certain equipment itself. From 1972 on, the scale of China's purchases of oil equipment from a variety of foreign sources—American, Japanese, Canadian, French, British, and others—steadily increased.[386] These purchases included a wide range of items: rigs, seismic surveying systems, offshore drilling and down hole equipment, special computers, steel bits, blowout preventers, well logging equipment, diving compressors, sonars, oil supply boats, numerous types of instruments, steel pipe, and tankers. One source estimated that by mid-1976 the value of China's oil equipment purchased abroad already totaled $400 million (this figure included tankers).[387] Another source estimated that (not counting tankers) by early 1977 China had purchased about $340 million of petroleum equipment abroad (and that by then it had developed a sizable industry producing its own oil equipment).[388] By 1978, according to a variety of estimates, China had acquired eleven jack-up rigs, three drill ships, and one high-technology, semisubmersible rig.[389] Purchasing activity was further stepped up during 1978, and by the end of that year the total of China's purchases made during the previous twenty-six months had risen to over $500 million—more than in the entire period from the late 1960s through mid-1976.[390]

Throughout these years, however, the Chinese continued to pursue what might be labeled a modified do-it-yourself approach. They purchased foreign oil equipment very selectively, and in limited quantities, apparently with the primary aim of obtaining prototypes of basic items that they could then copy, adapt, and manufacture themselves. The Chinese also purchased a few sophisticated components that they knew they could not hope to produce themselves in the near future, and they paid for these imports with foreign exchange, not oil. Peking still gave no evidence that it was prepared to establish close cooperative arrangements of a long-term nature with foreign companies. It continued, in short, trying to be as "self-reliant" as possible under the circumstances.[391]

If the Chinese had persisted in this strategy, they doubtless could have acquired, very gradually, the equipment and know-how necessary to develop a significant capacity for offshore oil development and eventually would have gotten production under way. But the process clearly would have been slow. As of 1978, after several years of effort, they had barely begun serious offshore exploration and had only experimented with offshore production. Their main activities were confined to the Pohai Gulf, which is the easiest area in which to work (since the average depth of the water is only about 60 feet) but is not likely to be the most rewarding one in the long run. In the Pohai, they had built a few small platforms close to shore. They also had done some preliminary surveying in the Yellow Sea (where the water also is relatively shallow, averaging about 125 feet) and in a few other places close to China's shores. But not only had their exploration been minimal, the results had been very limited.

Estimates made at that time, by some foreign analysts, of China's near-term potential for offshore production and exports of oil clearly were too optimistic. One estimated, for example, that even if China continued to pursue a relatively self-reliant development strategy, it might be able to produce close to 150 million tons a year of offshore oil by 1985 and perhaps as much as 200 million tons by 1990—and that by then offshore oil should account for roughly half of China's total oil production.[392] In early 1978, another analyst, while somewhat more realistic, also considerably overestimated the speed with which China's offshore oil could be developed. He calculated that if China continued relying mainly on its own technology, its offshore oil output might reach around 50 million tons (1 million b/d) by 1985, and that if China embarked on an all-out effort relying heavily on foreign technology, offshore output by 1985 might amount to "several times that amount."[393] The author of this study predicted that the Chinese probably would pursue a "middle-of-the-road" policy, making only selective imports of foreign technology, but that nevertheless their offshore oil output could reach close to 140 million tons a year (1 billion barrels a year) in the early 1980s. All of these estimates suggested that large-scale offshore output might start almost immediately instead of five years or more in the future.

While foreign analysts were making these optimistic predictions, the Chinese themselves apparently were in the process of reassessing their energy situation, and they concluded that development of their offshore oil would be unacceptably slow without large-scale foreign assistance. Sometime during early 1978 they decided that they must initiate a crash program aimed at rapid development of offshore oil, which they hoped would be done with large amounts of foreign assistance.

In mid-1978 Peking began to invite foreign oil companies to send representatives to China to begin discussions about conducting detailed seismic surveys of all China's major offshore areas.[394] Within a few months, the trickle of foreign oil companies negotiating with the Chinese became a flood. By the fall numerous American companies were negotiating, including Exxon, Phillips Petroleum, Pennzoil, Standard Oil

(Indiana), Union Oil of California, Mobil, and Atlantic-Richfield, as were many Japanese and West European companies, including the Japan National Oil Corporation, Idemitsu Kosan, the Japanese Petroleum Exploration Corporation, British Petroleum, ENI (Italy), ELF Aquitaine (France), Deminex (West Germany), Saga Petroleum (Norway), the Royal Dutch Shell Group, and others.[395]

Talks continued through the winter and spring of 1978–79. Then in mid-1979 the Chinese signed a series of agreements for seismic exploration along the China coast which involved a large percentage of the major—and many minor—international oil companies.[396] The terms were favorable from the Chinese point of view. Several major areas, or blocks, were delineated for seismic surveys,[397] and one or more major companies were designated as the principal "operators" for surveying each area. In addition, many other companies were invited to be "participants" (who also could receive the survey data and make bids on the basis of the results). The foreign oil companies involved agreed to conduct the seismic surveys at their own expense within their designated areas and to submit the analyzed results to the Chinese within about twelve months.

Thereafter, intensive seismic surveying was soon initiated along almost all of the China coast.[398] In the Pohai Gulf, off North China, a Japanese consortium led by the Japan National Oil Corporation (and reportedly also including the Japan Arabian Oil Company, Idemitsu Kosan, Japanese Petroleum Exploration Corporation, Mitsubishi, Mitsui, and Teikoku) is surveying and exploring 24,500 kilometers in the southern and western portions of the Gulf. Under an agreement reached on April 27, 1979, and supplemented by later agreements in December and in subsequent months, the Japanese will pay for the exploration costs, estimated at $120 million (although if no commercial deposits are found, the Chinese will share exploration costs). The two sides then will share development costs, estimated at about $1 billion, with the Chinese paying 51 percent and the Japanese 49 percent. Ultimately, production will be shared according to a formula that will give the Chinese 57.5 percent of the output and the Japanese 42.5 percent (in fact, the first 15 percent will go to the Chinese, and the remaining 85 percent will be divided equally). These, at least, have been the terms publicly reported, but some American oil experts doubt that they are yet firm and final.

In regard to the northern part of the Pohai Gulf, two French companies (ELF Aquitaine, which is 60 percent government owned, and CFP-Total, which is 40 percent government owned) reached agreement in

1979 (ELF Aquitaine's protocol was signed on April 22) for seismic and geological surveying of two areas of 2,000 and 2,100 kilometers, and this was soon started. The French then began negotiating for later exploration and development rights, which will probably only be decided, however, after the Chinese have thoroughly analyzed the survey results. Several other companies are "participants" in this area, including British Petroleum, Petro Canada, and Japan National Oil Corporation, but the French clearly have the inside track.

In the Yellow Sea, surveying has been divided into two spheres that are assigned primarily to the British and French. ELF Aquitaine is the operator that surveyed 60,000 kilometers between Shantung Province and Korea, and British Petroleum is the operator that surveyed 30,000 kilometers between Shanghai and Shantung (the British agreement was signed on June 8). In addition, about thirty companies are participants and sharing the surveying costs; they include Exxon, Phillips Petroleum, ELF Aquitaine, Shell Oil, and Union Oil.

American companies have been the main operators in the surveying of most of the South China Sea, just off the China coast, from south of Taiwan to south of Hainan. Six major blocks were soon designated in this region on the basis of agreements signed in mid-1979. In addition to the major operators, a large number of other companies—not just American—then signed on as participants with access to the seismic data (and, like the principal operators, got the right to analyze the data that was to be sent to the Chinese and have the option to participate in the eventual bidding for exploration and developing rights). The principal operators for the six major blocks, from north to south, are Phillips Petroleum, Chevron/Texaco, Exxon, Mobil, Arco (Atlantic-Richfield), and Amoco. Their agreements were signed between March and July 1979. On March 19 the Chinese signed a contract with Arco for surveying an area south of Hainan. In mid-June, they signed contracts for surveying areas stretching from Taiwan south to the Arco area; these were with Exxon and Mobil on June 5, Phillips Petroleum on June 8, Chevron/Texaco on June 9, and Amoco on July 10. On July 4 the Chinese notified fifty-five other foreign companies that they could participate in the four South China Sea areas that had been agreed to up to that date, if within sixty days they expressed a serious intention of doing so and if they then formally agreed to participate within another thirty days. In mid-July they invited twenty foreign companies to consider participating in the Amoco area. (Later, the deadline for signing on as participants was extended to December 1979.) The American companies that decided to participate in these South China Sea blocks included Cities Service, Hunt-Sedco, Murphy Oil, Occidental, Pennzoil, Shell, Texas Eastern, Union Oil (California), and Allied Chemical's Union Texas Asia Offshore. The foreign company participants include Ampol (Australia), AGIP (Italy), Cliff Oil (United Kingdom), Deminex (West Germany), Hispanoil (Spain), INA (Yugoslavia), and the Royal Dutch Shell Group.

Under most of the documents finally signed, the participating foreign companies have agreed to bear the surveying costs (with the operating company mainly responsible but receiving some payments from other participating companies). In most instances, the operating companies promised they would give the analyzed results of their surveys to the Chinese twelve months after the start of their work—that is, by late 1980—and the participating companies also agreed to give their interpretations of the data to the Chinese no later than eight months after they have received all of the processed data. China would then soon start its own analysis. Thereafter, Peking promised, it would open the bidding for contracts for actual exploration and then production, starting within twelve months from the time it received the analyzed data from the foreign companies, although there has been some slippage in all of these deadlines.

The Chinese have made no definite promises that any of the principal companies involved, even if they are the major operators in surveying particular areas, will necessarily be awarded the final contracts for exploration and development; all participating companies will be given a chance to bid. However, it is highly likely that the major surveying companies will have a large advantage when the final bidding occurs, unless others obviously outbid them.

As these facts indicate, the Chinese have shown extraordinary skill in the initial stage of their effort to obtain major assistance from the world's leading oil companies in developing China's offshore oil. By 1980 several dozen oil companies from all over the world were involved, and since then they have conducted one of the most extensive and intensive oil surveying operations in history, at their own expense. The surveying costs are by no means negligible; according to one estimate, they could total $10 million to $20 million for each major area.[399]

China's future oil prospects—and, in fact, general economic prospects of its broad modernization program—during the decade ahead may depend to a significant degree, as stressed earlier, on the results of these efforts. Most of the seismic surveys were completed before late 1980, and the Chinese received geological base maps shortly thereafter. There now is to be a period of some months during which the Chinese themselves study the data and decide what they wish to do.

Ultimately, they may decide to undertake some development work themselves. Throughout 1978–80 they continued their own explorations close inshore, and they reported some new discoveries, for example, in the Pearl River Delta. By 1980 they also had acquired at least sixteen offshore rigs (eleven jack-ups, of which seven are in operation, three drill barges, one catamaran barge, and one semisubmersible).[400] In addition, five new jack-ups are under construction in China.

However, the Chinese now clearly recognize that they still lack an independent capability for most operations. Moreover, even in the use of equipment in their possession, they have had periodic accidents which demonstrate their need for technical assistance in operating most of the sophisticated technical equipment.[401] They now plan to contract for foreign development in most areas. Although they may hold back certain blocks for future Chinese development, starting in 1981 they probably will sign a number of contracts, first for exploratory drilling, and later for actual production, with a variety of major oil companies. And they probably will press for development as rapidly as possible.

As of 1980 it appeared that the Japanese, French, and British were likely to play the major development roles in the North, in the Pohai Gulf and Yellow Sea areas, and that the Americans probably would take the lead in the more difficult—but perhaps eventually more rewarding—South China Sea areas.

If no major unexpected delays are encountered, exploratory drilling could be carried out during 1981–82, and (assuming, of course, that significant oil deposits are discovered) planning and preparation for actual development could take place during 1982–84. Actual production might start in 1984 and get under way on a significant scale during 1985–86,[402] and offshore oil output could increase quite rapidly thereafter.

This is a plausible timetable, but there still are uncertainties that could delay the process. The timetable assumes, to begin with, that the exploratory drilling during 1981–82 will locate major deposits of commercial oil. This seems highly likely. In fact, an expert working for one of the American oil companies involved privately speculated, after completion of his company's survey, that oil deposits in at least some of the South

China Sea areas might be "comparable to those in the Gulf of Mexico." However, if this assumption proves to be wrong, the entire program could be aborted or greatly delayed, which could have profoundly adverse effects on China's entire modernization program.

Assuming that significant oil resources are discovered, there still will be hard bargaining over precise terms and arrangements between the Chinese and the foreign oil companies. Development costs probably will be high, and decisions must be made on how they will be shared. Estimates vary, but in 1980 one informed source calculated that just exploratory drilling, prior to any production, could cost $200 million to $300 million in each major area.[403] Discussions during 1980 between the Chinese and foreign oil companies were not easy, and on many technical and economic issues significant differences of opinion emerged. It remained to be seen whether agreements acceptable to both sides could be reached in the near future.

Chinese bureaucratic politics also may complicate matters at each stage in the process. During 1979 the lines of authority often seemed blurred between the China Oil and Natural Gas Exploration and Development Corporation (a subsidiary of the Petroleum Corporation, under the Ministry of Petroleum) and the China Geological Exploration Corporation (under the recently reconstituted Ministry of Geology). Because of its economic and political importance, the development of oil is likely to continue to be affected by intense competition within the Chinese government, possibly complicating the problem of reaching agreements with foreign companies and causing delays. During 1980 several leaders who have long been key figures in onshore oil development in China appeared to lose some prestige and status in the Chinese hierarchy, which suggested that oil policy continued to be a controversial matter in Peking.

Exactly what kind of cooperation agreements China ultimately will be prepared to sign with various foreign oil companies remains unclear. The Sino-Japanese agreement concerning the Pohai Gulf area provides one model, but agreements for other areas may differ somewhat. The Chinese may well consider various Brazilian, Indonesian, Algerian, and Norwegian models, or variations of them, before deciding on what formulas to apply in individual cases. In certain instances, especially in dealings with American companies, the Chinese will have to devise new tax formulas acceptable to the foreign companies (enabling them, for example, to avoid double taxation). Dealing with many of the Western countries also will be different from dealing with the Japanese because the Western foreign governments will be much less involved.

Whatever the difference, however, most agreements probably will require the foreign companies to cover the exploration costs (with a sharing of costs if no commercial oil is discovered), will call for a sharing of subsequent development costs, and will spell out some formula for product sharing, specifying an agreed-upon ratio, so that the foreign companies will receive all or most of their payments in oil. The Chinese can be expected to be hard bargainers in negotiations on all these issues (they constantly accuse international oil companies of earning excessive profits). However, the huge foreign multinationals dealing with the Chinese have long experience in the field and possess a great deal of leverage, since they have the know-how and will be asked to put up large investment funds and undertake considerable risk. Development costs will be high— much higher than for surveying or exploration—for both the foreign corporations involved and the Chinese. One recent estimate is that development costs could range between $500 million and $3 billion (and possibly more) for each of the major fields along China's coast (with the South China Sea fields being most expensive because of the deepest waters).[404] Reaching agreements certainly will not be a simple matter, therefore. However, because rapid exploration of China's offshore oil is so important to the Chinese, and because it could become very profitable for the major oil companies, there is reason to be fairly optimistic that within the next two or three years active programs will be under way to get oil production started in at least several of China's major offshore areas, that they will be in production by the mid-1980s, and that thereafter China's offshore oil output will steadily rise and become increasingly important to China and a factor of growing significance on the world market.

Conflicting Territorial Claims

Many economic and technical problems will have to be solved if China is to realize its offshore oil potential. But these probably will be handled skillfully enough to permit the start of oil development in the near future. However, in the long run, development could be complicated by an extraordinarily complex tangle of disputes involving China and all of its maritime neighbors. The history of conflicting claims regarding the entire continental shelf in Asia, and of disputes over certain island groups in the region, has been analyzed in detail elsewhere and will not be repeated here.[405] However, some understanding of the international political complications that these past conflicts could create is necessary for any realistic assessment of the long-run prospects for future offshore oil development in Asia.

Until the late 1950s the Chinese showed relatively little interest in the waters and shelf adjacent to China and gave only slight attention to law of the sea issues. However, in 1958—during the offshore islands crisis that year (which occurred soon after the Geneva Law of the Sea Conference)—Peking asserted a twelve-mile claim in defining its territorial waters. But then its interest in maritime issues was again dormant during most of the 1960s.

It was only in the late 1960s, following a UN-sponsored survey of the Asian continental shelf that indicated the probability of large oil resources in the area, that both China and its neighbors began to show strong interest in continental shelf issues. Japan, South Korea, and Taiwan all began at that time to assert specific shelf claims—Japan on the basis of the "median line" principle, Taiwan on the principle of "natural prolongation of the continental territory" (which the World Court had recently used in settling certain North Sea cases), and South Korea on the basis of a mixture of these two principles. Ultimately, these three regimes delineated a total of seventeen concession blocks (thirteen of which overlapped) and signed contracts with a number of foreign oil companies to begin exploration.

From the start, China denounced all of these claims and actions. In 1970–71 its warnings deterred Japan, South Korea, and Taiwan from developing a cooperative approach among themselves, and in 1974, when Japan and Korea decided to sign an agreement for joint development in specified shelf areas, Peking's strong verbal attack resulted in a long delay in Japanese ratification. When Japan finally did ratify the agreement (it went into effect in 1977), Peking declared it to be "illegal" and "null and void."[406]

The legal principle on the basis of which Peking has opposed exploration or exploitation of most of the shelf by its neighbors has been the "natural prolongation" principle. The Chinese indicated their acceptance of this principle in a working paper that they submitted to subcommittee II of the UN Seabed Committee in 1973. In that paper they stated, "By virtue of the principle that the continental shelf is the natural prolongation of the continental territory, a coastal State may reasonably define, according to its specific geographical conditions, the limits of the continental shelf under its exclusive jurisdiction beyond its territorial sea or economic zone. The maximum limits of such continental shelf may be determined among states through consultations."[407]

Applying this general principle when denouncing the Japanese-Korean agreement in 1977, the Chinese stated bluntly, "The East China Sea continental shelf is the natural extension of the Chinese continental territory. The People's Republic of China has inviolable sovereignty over the East China Sea continental shelf. It stands to reason that the question of how to divide those parts of the East China Sea continental shelf which involve other countries should be decided by China and the countries concerned through consultations."[408]

It now appears, therefore, that the claim to sovereignty which China now makes regarding the entire continental shelf is a sweeping but still very general one. If, in practice, the Chinese were to try to assert this claim fully, they could, in theory, apply it to most of the shelf in Asia. (In the case of Japan, for example, China could try to claim the shelf right up to the "Okinawa Trough," just off Japan's coast.)

Actually, China's real position remains ambiguous in many respects. Despite the extensive nature of its general claim, China never has defined it in specific terms; moreover, all of its major statements have asserted that conflicting claims between neighbors should be settled by negotiation—or, as the Chinese put it, by "consultation." But to date the Chinese have showed no willingness to negotiate settlements of the shelf disputes, and their strong opposition to almost all activity on the shelf by others has slowed exploration, even in areas much closer to their neighbors' shores than to their own.

The most potentially explosive ocean issues in the region focus on certain island groups where oil is now believed to be located. One is the Tiaoyutai (Diaoyutai)/Senkaku group of uninhabited islands on the southern tip of the Ryukyus, north of Taiwan. Both Japan and China (as well as Taiwan) have asserted claims to these islands, and neither has shown any willingness to compromise sovereignty over them. For the moment, everyone concerned seems prepared to lay the issue aside, so long as none of the others push it, in order to avoid clashes that could be dangerous. However, although the Japanese presence is stronger in the area, in 1978 China demonstrated that it was not prepared to let the islands go to Japan by default when it sent armed fishing vessels into the area, putting on a limited show of force. (Peking later claimed that the incident was accidental, but this did not appear to be convincing to many

Japanese.) It will be extremely difficult—and risky—for anyone to start oil development in this particular region until some agreement on rights can be reached.

The conflicting claims to certain islands in the South China Sea are even more complicated, involving China, Vietnam, Taiwan, and the Philippines. In 1974 China and South Vietnam both attempted to assert control over the Paracels; the result was a brief but intense military clash, with Peking emerging the victor. Since then, China has substantially strengthened its presence and is building a full-fledged harbor there. However, Vietnam continues to claim sovereignty over the islands.

The Chinese also claim the Spratlys, although actually these islands, 300 nautical miles to the south of the Paracels, are in others' hands (Vietnam, Taiwan, and the Philippines all occupy certain islands within the group). The Philippines, with foreign help, has begun some prospecting in the area and located oil at Reed Bank; the Chinese have protested but to date they have not taken any hostile counteractions (in fact, they have continued to try to improve overall relations with the Philippines—and to sell it Chinese oil). It is questionable, however, whether significant oil development can take place in either the Paracels or Spratlys area unless and until there is a settlement of existing disputes, which seems unlikely in the near future. The U.S. government has warned American oil companies that they cannot expect U.S. protection if they operate in any of the most sensitive disputed areas on the Asian continental shelf.

The development of offshore oil could be considerably complicated, and in some areas delayed, by these disputes. Currently, the greatest dangers lie in the Gulf of Tonkin and in the South China Sea area south of Hainan to the Paracels and Spratlys.[409] However, if most of the conflicts remain latent, they will not necessarily obstruct efforts to develop oil in the majority of the shelf areas, including all of those near China's coast, most of which are not claimed by any of its neighbors. With the exception of areas near Hainan, these are the areas to which the Chinese are now giving priority in their efforts to get exploration and exploitation under way.

In the long run, the willingness of foreign oil companies, and their home governments (especially the United States), to become deeply involved in assisting the Chinese in their offshore oil development probably will be contingent on Peking's showing restraint in dealing with these shelf and island disputes. If the Chinese were to try to assert actual control over the entire continental shelf, or if there were to be major military clashes over the Tiaoyutai/Senkaku islands or even the Paracel and Spratly groups, foreign corporations and governments probably would become greatly concerned and increasingly cautious, and they might decide to disengage. It is possible, though, that partly because of this the involvement of foreign companies in Chinese offshore oil development will impose significant new constraints on Chinese actions regarding the disputed areas.

Conceivably, increased foreign involvement in oil development in the entire region, in cooperation not only with the Chinese but with others as well, could eventually lead to tacit if not explicit understandings that might remove some of the present obstacles to oil development throughout the area. As the pace of Chinese offshore oil development is stepped up, the incentives for China's neighbors also to increase their efforts with foreign help will grow. Presumably, their efforts would be in areas clearly on their side of a hypothetical median line between themselves and China. Whether the Chinese would acquiesce to such a development cannot be predicted with absolute confidence; however, it is possible that they would feel compelled to do so, since if they actively tried to prevent others from developing oil, the result could create a conflict—or a threat of conflict—that might end the willingness of foreign oil companies to cooperate in China's own oil program.

However, there is no question that until the shelf and island disputes in the region are resolved, or at least effectively shelved for a long period of time, they will continue to complicate efforts to develop offshore oil and will pose dangers of potential conflicts that could be very destabilizing regionally. If delineation of the shelf by official agreements is to occur, it almost certainly will have to be based on acceptance by China, as well as its neighbors, of the median line for setting ocean boundaries. Perhaps eventually China will be willing to negotiate shelf issues on this basis. It is also possible, however, that, instead, China will simply choose to leave the issues unresolved for the indefinite future.

Because the political and legal problems involved in these situations are so complex, the arguments for not trying immediately to resolve seemingly irresolvable issues may be strong. Consequently, China, as well as the other countries involved, may prefer in practice to continue tacitly living with the status quo, yet trying to avoid open conflict. Even though competing claims to Asian offshore oil areas will continue to create strain in the period ahead, it also is possible that the strong desire to develop offshore oil actually could prove to be a deterrent to conflict.

After oil development has gotten well under way, it will involve not only the Chinese but other Asian nations as well in new and complex webs of relationships with many industrial countries, creating new patterns of mutual interdependence.

The International Community and China's Oil

From a global perspective, China's development of oil unquestionably is in the broad interest of the international community. As the world's oil supply diminishes, *all* new sources of oil will become increasingly important. If, as is likely, in the 1980s the global supply becomes increasingly tight, the fact that China may be able to sell several tens of millions of tons of oil on the world market could make a difference to the global economy. There is little likelihood that China will emerge as another Saudi Arabia, but if it can export 50 million tons or more of oil a year, the world energy system will be a clear beneficiary.

Oil will become increasingly important to China itself over time as an earner of foreign exchange, and the new foreign economic relationships required for rapid offshore oil development could create particularly strong mutual interests linking it with the major non-Communist industrial powers. Moreover, to the extent that increased Chinese oil exports make possible greater general participation by the Chinese in international trade, this should reinforce the existing trend toward Chinese acceptance of the realities of international interdependence. Over time, this realization should have desirable general effects on China's foreign policy and international relationships. Even though one should not expect China suddenly to involve itself in cooperative international efforts to the extent that the world's major trading nations do, oil development should create new links of potential long-term importance. Obviously, it would be unrealistic and naive to believe that economic interests will override basic security and political concerns; nevertheless, expanded economic ties, perhaps particularly in the oil field, could well have major effects on broad policy, probably of a moderating sort.

Other nations should be prepared, therefore, to provide major assistance to China as it attempts to accelerate its oil development, especially offshore. The initial responses of foreign oil companies to China's efforts to get surveying of coastal areas under way indicate that many are eager to participate in Chinese oil development, if Peking is flexible enough to make it commercially attractive to them. These companies themselves should be prepared, however, especially when, after the exploration phase, they negotiate production contracts, to show flexibility to try to bridge the existing political and cultural gaps. In considering concrete arrangements for cooperation, foreign companies should be sensitive to the special political as well as economic problems that Peking's leaders face.

The governments in the non-Communist industrial powers will, in time, have to confront a variety of important policy issues relating to oil development in China. Difficult decisions will have to be made, for example, on how far to go in authorizing export to China of particular technology items that are important not only in oil development but potentially in military-strategic uses. Some of the most difficult decisions regarding trade controls during the next few years will relate to computers and other equipment needed for oil exploration and development. It is possible that the Chinese decision to rely heavily on foreign assistance in both exploration and development of oil could make it somewhat less urgent from their viewpoint to obtain such sensitive technology themselves immediately. But they almost certainly will continue to believe that it is essential to obtain the most sophisticated technology available from abroad eventually, in order to build up China's independent capabilities. Even though policy on the sale of oil-related equipment will merely be one facet of a much broader policy problem, it is likely to be particularly important, and particularly difficult, both because some of the technology involved is so sophisticated and potentially useful militarily, and because oil is potentially so important internationally as well as in relation to Chinese interests.

Perhaps more than any other aspect of China's evolving new foreign economic relations, the development and export of oil could have important, broad foreign policy implications of great long-term significance. Oil and politics are almost inevitably linked, and already have been even in China's case. The Chinese initiatives in first pushing for large oil exports to Japan during 1973–74 may have been motivated in part by a desire to forestall Japanese cooperation with the Russians in developing Siberian oil and gas and to try to induce Tokyo to tilt politically toward Peking rather than Moscow. Increasing oil sales to Japan in the period ahead could clearly be a significant factor tending to broaden and strengthen Sino-Japanese relations. Similarly, increasing U.S.-China cooperation in oil development should help not only to expand bilateral trade but also to strengthen Sino-American political relations.

China's oil development could affect many of its international political relationships over time. The Chinese could decide, for example, to increase their oil exports to certain Southeast Asian nations, and perhaps to other Third World countries as well, to help strengthen economic and political ties with them. Conceivably—although one can only speculate on this at present—oil eventually could become a significant factor in relations between China and Taiwan in the future. The trade in oil that could develop between them could help to open the door to other relationships. As emphasized already, conflicting claims to continental shelf areas and offshore islands in potential oil areas will continue for many years to influence China's relations with most of its neighbors—Japan, South Korea, Vietnam, and others. While conflicting claims could create serious strains, it is also possible that if foreign oil companies expand cooperative programs not only with the Chinese but also with other Asian nations near China, the potential for conflict that now exists in the area might be gradually defused.

In the broadest terms, if one takes an optimistic view, China's offshore oil development, with the cooperation of many foreign companies, and its increasing export of oil in the 1980s, should reinforce Peking's present proclivities to be more outward looking, more inclined to give priority to economic interests rather than ideological and revolutionary goals, and more inclined to participate constructively in cooperative international programs. However, if one takes a pessimistic view, the possibility cannot be excluded that the politics of oil could become a destabilizing factor throughout the region. The ultimate outcome will depend on many future policy decisions, made in Peking, in the capitals of its neighbors, in the power centers of the major industrial nations, and in the boardrooms of many international oil companies.

V

U.S.-China Relations: The Economic Dimension

SIGNIFICANT economic ties are now developing between Americans and Chinese. Even though the United States remains behind Japan and Western Europe in the China trade, U.S.-China relations have rapidly acquired a new economic dimension that should grow and not only help to shape the character of bilateral relations but also influence the general nature of regional relationships.

This economic dimension is strikingly new. Economics had little to do with the hostility and conflict that developed between the two countries in the 1950s and 1960s or with the initial decisions to reestablish contacts in the early 1970s. Sino-American relations were determined mainly by political, ideological, and strategic considerations.[1] These factors will remain crucially important; there is little doubt, in fact, that leaders in both Washington and Peking (Beijing) will continue to focus primary attention on national security issues, viewed in broad geopolitical terms. However, the expansion of U.S.-China economic relations and the parallel development of scientific, technical, educational, and intellectual links are beginning to create a pattern of relationships that could, in time, create deeper and stronger ties between the two countries. In many respects, trade and other economic links are at the cutting edge today in the development of U.S.-China relations, and the success or failure of the two countries in their efforts to build lasting economic ties will have a major influence on long-term political and strategic relationships.

Some of the policy issues that new economic relations with China pose for all the non-Communist industrial powers were discussed earlier.[2] Many of these are especially important with respect to U.S.-China relations, and some could be particularly difficult for Washington to handle because of the complexities of the factors influencing U.S. foreign policy and the responsibilities and problems that confront the United States as an economic and military superpower whose actions inevitably have a wide impact on both the international economy and the global strategic balance. In the U.S. case, economic and strategic relationships are inevitably intertwined.

The Basic U.S. Stake in Sino-American Relations

Although it is not possible here to discuss all of the strategic, political, and other factors that influence U.S.-China relations, before examining the new economic ties between Washington and Peking a few comments are necessary on the basic U.S. stake in Sino-American relations and on the evolution of ties between the two countries in recent years.[3]

Since the late nineteenth century, the interests of the United States as a Pacific power have been intimately linked to the degree of stability or instability existing in East Asia; developments in China, or international competition centering on China, have been primary determinants of regional trends. To a large degree, U.S. policy toward and relations with China have shaped relationships in the rest of East Asia.

For roughly two decades after the Communist takeover of China, U.S.-China confrontation, based on Washington's perception of a "China threat" as well as Peking's sense of threat from the United States, provided the prime driving force for American policies toward both Northeast and Southeast Asia. The "China threat" provided the main motivation for a huge American investment in building an alliance system and base structure in Asia, maintenance of large American military forces in the region, U.S. participation in two costly local wars in Korea and Vietnam, and American involvement in a series of tense military crises.

During the past decade, as a result of the Sino-Soviet conflict and the development of friendly U.S.-China relations, the situation has fundamentally changed. The U.S.-Japan alliance remains the cornerstone of U.S. policy in East Asia, but no longer is its principal raison d'être the presumed threat posed by China; now its main purpose is to meet the challenge created by Soviet power and ambitions and to protect American as well as Japanese economic interests throughout the region.

Since the start of the 1970s, detente in both Japanese-Chinese and American-Chinese relations has created a new pattern of relationships among these powers. For the first time in this century, Washington enjoys friendly relations with both Peking and Tokyo, and improved relations among all three have significantly reduced the causes of conflict in East Asia. Stability in the region has become increasingly important to American interests, moreover, because today U.S. trade with East Asia exceeds its trade with any other region in the world. For economic as well as security reasons, therefore, the United States now has a large stake in continued friendly relations with Tokyo and Peking, which require a strengthening of U.S. ties with China as well as maintenance of the American alliance with Japan. Any breakdown of the existing pattern could have effects that would be costly to U.S. interests.

However, while the new relationships among the United States, Japan, and China have contributed to East Asian stability in certain respects, they have not eliminated other causes of instability. There is a continuing danger of conflict deriving from a combination of unresolved local conflicts in both Northeast and Southeast Asia, continuing big power competition, and serious tensions between the Soviet Union and the other major powers.

Soviet policy has become increasingly assertive in the region in recent years. Moscow's increased activity has been motivated in part by long-standing Russian nationalist ambitions. It also, however, has been fueled by the Sino-Soviet conflict and, as new ties have developed among China, the United States, and Japan, by fear of an anti-Soviet coalition composed of these powers linked to the West European nations in NATO. In the eyes of Soviet leaders, recent trends have raised the specter of hostile "encirclement" and highlighted the perils of a possible two-front war.

On its part, since the 1960s Peking has been almost totally preoccupied in its foreign policy with what it sees, with good reason, as a major Soviet threat to China. Acute fear of the Soviet Union was, in fact, what impelled the Chinese leadership to decide in the late 1960s to improve relations with the non-Communist powers. Current Soviet policies have reinforced Chinese hostility toward Moscow as well as increased the apprehension of the other major powers, leading all of them to take new steps to strengthen their defenses.

Today the Russians continue, as they have for some years, to invest large resources in the steady buildup of their military power, both conventional and nuclear, with the aim of achieving a position of strength that they hope to translate into increased international political influence. Increasingly, they have tried to project their power and influence abroad into situations of local instability and conflict, and when Moscow used its own forces on a massive scale against Afghanistan, an Asian neighbor, it raised the apprehension of leaders in all the other major powers.

When Washington and Tokyo initially moved to improve relations with Peking, they did not define their goals as anti-Soviet, despite their perception of a Soviet threat. U.S. leaders asserted that the aim of U.S. policy was to improve relations with both China and the Soviet Union and to work toward a stable equilibrium among all the powers in the hope that eventually this would check the arms race and restrain all powers from exploiting local conflict situations. However, Washington did emphasize that any external threat to China would be dangerous and should be prevented, and after Moscow invaded Afghanistan, Washington's announcement that certain types of military equipment would be sold to China raised new questions about the kind of relationship that might develop in the future.

Present U.S. relations with China represent an enormous change from the situation in the 1950s and 1960s, and generally the change has been favorable to U.S. interests. However, the intrinsic problems of consolidating bilateral U.S.-China ties and the complexities of multilateral interactions among the big powers in East Asia have created difficult new policy problems. Although the United States has a strong interest in strengthening relationships with China, its interests also argue for the avoidance of steps that could result in increased tension, polarization, and destabilization of big-power relationships in the region. A central issue for U.S. policy toward China in the period ahead is how to evolve economic and security policies that will both consolidate U.S.-China ties and enhance regional stability.

The Evolution of Overall U.S.-China Relations

When the U.S. government began to explore the possibility of contacts with the Chinese in the late 1960s, it asserted that it opposed external threats to China but had no intention of manipulating either Moscow or Peking against the other. Immediately after the Sino-Soviet border clashes in 1969, well before any real detente in U.S.-China relations had occurred, Secretary of State William Rogers stated in April, "We do not think it wise to attempt to exploit" the Sino-Soviet dispute; "our best posture is to attempt to have more friendly relations with both the Soviet Union and Communist China."[4] During the months that followed, top U.S. leaders showed genuine concern about a possible Soviet attack on China, which they believed could profoundly alter the international balance.[5] In September Under Secretary of State Elliot L. Richardson, asserting that "long-run improvement in our relations [with China] is in our national interest," declared that the United States "could not fail to be deeply concerned . . . with an escalation of this quarrel [between China and the Soviet Union] into a massive breach of international peace and security."[6] He also stated, "We do not seek to exploit for our own advantage the hostility between the Soviet Union and the People's Republic." The U.S. intent, he declared, was "to pursue a long-term course of progressively developing better relations with both." A few months later, in July 1970, U.S. officials rejected a Soviet feeler about a possible agreement on "joint action" to deter or punish any other nuclear power (meaning China) that might take "provocative actions."[7]

Both President Richard Nixon and National Security Adviser Henry Kissinger viewed the opening of direct contacts with China in 1971–72 in broad geopolitical terms and believed that it inaugurated a new period of "triangular diplomacy."[8] The Shanghai communiqué signed by Nixon and Premier Chou En-lai (Zhou Enlai) in 1972 reflected this. In the communiqué the two countries stated, "Both [countries] wish to reduce the danger of international military conflict; neither should seek hegemony in the Asia-Pacific region and each is opposed to efforts by any other country or group of countries to establish such hegemony; and neither is prepared to negotiate on behalf of any third party or to enter into agreements or understandings with the other directed at other states."[9] This, in effect, constituted a pledge by both countries not only to minimize their own conflicts and improve bilateral relations, but also to oppose, in parallel if not jointly, any efforts by other nations (meaning the Soviet Union) to "establish hegemony" anywhere in the world. At the same time both stated that U.S.-China agreements or understandings would not be "directed at other states."

In the period between the Shanghai (Shanghai) communiqué and final normalization of U.S.-China relations, American officials made many statements that highlighted the importance of China in U.S. policy and reiterated Washington's commitment to improve relations with Peking. However, during the slowdown in the process of normalization between 1973 and 1978, some American leaders' statements also noted the limits of Sino-American relations and continuation of important differences.

Secretary of State Kissinger declared in June 1975 that the new U.S.-China relationship already had become a "durable feature of the world scene" which "serves our respective interests and the broader interests of peace and stability in Asia and around the world."[10] In September he made an even stronger statement along similar lines: "There is no relationship to which the United States assigns greater significance."[11] Yet, in the next month, while in Peking, Kissinger stated, "The differences between us are apparent." "Our task," he said, "is not to intensify those differences . . . [but] to advance our relationship on the basis of mutual interests. . . . Each country must pursue a policy suitable to its own circumstances. The United States will resist hegemony. . . . But [it] will also make every effort to avoid needless confrontations, when it can do so without threatening the security of third countries."[12] During his trip to Peking in December, President Gerald Ford reiterated that "the normalization of relations would be in the mutual interests of our peoples and would contribute to the development of a more secure international order," adding that "we have a mutual interest in seeing that the world is not dominated by military force or pressure, what in our joint statements we have called hegemony."[13] He also emphasized, however, that "in pursuing our objectives, each of us will, of course, determine our policy and methods according to our differing perceptions of our respective national interests."

From the start of the Carter administration, official statements placed even greater stress on the importance of China in U.S. policy than the Nixon administration had, at least during 1974-76. "We see the American-Chinese relationship as a central element of our global policy, and China as a key force for global peace," Carter declared in May 1977.[14] In June Secretary of State Cyrus Vance asserted that "China's role in maintaining world peace is vital. A constructive relationship with China is important, not only regionally, but also for global equilibrium."[15] A good U.S.-China relationship "will threaten no one," he declared. "It will serve only peace." When Vance returned from his November 1977 trip to China, during which he had tried but failed to move the process of normalization forward, he stated, "I believe deeply it would be a great mistake for the United States to provide arms to either the People's Republic of China or to the Soviet Union."[16]

Despite the rhetorical stress the Carter administration placed on relations with China, it made little progress toward normalization of relations during 1977; in practice, it gave higher priority to other foreign policy issues. However, in the late spring of 1978 Carter decided to try to speed up and complete the normalization process; this was immediately reflected in official U.S. statements. In March Assistant Secretary of State Richard C. Holbrooke repeated the now-standard position that China had a "vital role to play in maintaining peace in Asia and in the world" and reiterated that China policy had become a "central part of our foreign policy."[17] He also stated, "Consolidating a constructive relationship with China is an essential element in our effort to promote a prosperous, peaceful, and secure Asia." He added, "We intend to move toward full normalization of relations."

The visit to Peking of National Security Adviser Zbigniew Brzezinski in May 1978 marked the beginning of an active diplomatic effort to find a basis for normalization of relations, and thereafter American officials increasingly emphasized parallel concerns shared by Washington and Peking. While in Peking, Brzezinski declared that "a secure *and strong* [emphasis added] China is in America's interest,"[18] and he underlined the importance of common strategic interests:

Our commitment to friendship with China is based on shared concerns and is derived from a long-term strategic view. . . . We recognize—and share— China's resolve to resist the efforts of any nation which seeks to establish global or regional hegemony. . . . We approach our relations with three fundamental beliefs: That friendship between the United States and the People's Republic of China is vital and beneficial to world peace; that a secure and strong China is in America's interest; that a powerful, confident, and globally engaged United States is in China's interest.[19]

Although Brzezinski asserted that the United States "does not view its relationship with China as a tactical expedient," the verbal sideswipes he made at the Soviet Union during his trip—for example, in his denunciation of countries that dispatch "international marauders" abroad[20]— evoked immediate charges that Washington was trying to play a "China card" against Moscow and was tilting toward Peking. After Brzezinski's trip both President Carter and Secretary of State Vance attempted to counter such charges. In June Carter declared once again, "We are not trying, nor will we ever try, to play the Soviets against the People's Republic of China, or vice versa."[21] Two weeks later, in July, Vance repeated earlier denials that Washington had any intention of selling arms to Peking. "Our policy simply stated," he asserted, "is that we do not and will not supply arms to either."[22] On the following day Carter declared that " 'Chinese card' is not a term used by my administration. The United States seeks to improve its relations with both the Soviet Union and the People's Republic of China."[23] Apparently, U.S. officials' rhetoric in Peking was intended to convince the Chinese of the advantages of "normalization" of relations, while the rhetoric in Washington was designed to calm some of the fears of opponents of "normalization." A few months later, however, Secretary Vance revealed that although the United States itself would not sell arms to China, it would not try to prevent its allies from selling the Chinese defensive military equipment. He stated, "Insofar as other nations are concerned, this is a matter which each of them must decide for itself."[24]

Frequently the tone of Brzezinski's and Vance's statements differed, and this reflected real differences within the U.S. government on China policy, even though in part these were differences in style.[25] However, there was as yet no decision to tilt unambiguously toward Peking or to develop any military relationship with the Chinese. Official U.S. policy continued to call for "balance" (Brzezinski's phraseology) or "even-handedness" (Vance's term) in relations with both China and the Soviet Union.

The actual negotiations on normalization of relations initiated following Brzezinski's visit to Peking, while stimulated by a growing perception of parallel strategic interests, focused to a large extent on bilateral issues, particularly on the Taiwan problem, which from the start had been the major obstacle to establishment of full diplomatic ties.[26] The agreement that was finally reached, and announced in December 1978, was based on mutual compromise.[27] The United States reiterated that it did not challenge Peking's claim to Taiwan and accepted Peking's claim to be the sole legal government of China, but it indicated once again that it opposed any military action against Taiwan and intended to continue the substance of its relations with Taiwan, including sales of defensive military equipment to it, on an unofficial basis. Washington agreed, however, to terminate the U.S. mutual defense treaty with Taiwan and cut formal diplomatic ties with Taipei. Peking's major compromise was to acquiesce to U.S. military sales to Taiwan.

The joint communiqué on normalization issued simultaneously in Washington and Peking on December 15, 1978, stated:[28]

The United States of America and the People's Republic of China reaffirm the principles agreed upon by the two sides in the Shanghai communiqué and emphasize once again that:

Both wish to reduce the danger of international military conflict.

Neither should seek hegemony in the Asia-Pacific region or in any other region of the world and each is opposed to efforts by any other country or group of countries to establish such hegemony.

Neither is prepared to negotiate on behalf of any third party or to enter into agreements or understandings with the other directed at other states.

The reiteration of these "principles," in language drawn from the Shanghai communiqué, underlined the fact that Washington and Peking recognized a common interest in opposing Soviet expansionism (that is, "hegemony") but also recognized that the new U.S.-China relationship was a limited one, not an alliance aimed at Moscow.

President Carter, commenting on the importance of normalizing relations with Peking and the necessity to cut formal ties with Taiwan, talked about expanded commercial and cultural relations, not military ties.[29]

We do not undertake this important step for transient tactical or expedient reasons. In recognizing the People's Republic of China, that it is the single Government of China, we are recognizing simple reality. But far more is involved in this decision than just the recognition of a fact.

Before the estrangement of recent decades, the American and the Chinese people had a long history of friendship. We've already begun to rebuild some of those previous ties. Now our rapidly expanding relationship requires the kind of structure that only full diplomatic relations will make possible.

The change that I'm announcing tonight will be of great long-term benefit to the peoples of both our country and China—and, I believe, to all the peoples of the world. Normalization—and the expanded commercial and cultural relations that it will bring—will contribute to the well-being of our nation, to our own national interest, and it will also enhance the stability of Asia.

The strategic premise that underlay the decisions made in Washington and Peking appeared to be that strengthened political and economic relations, even without military ties, would serve the geopolitical and security interests of both nations.

During the year following establishment of diplomatic relations, Washington and Peking moved rapidly to strengthen economic as well as politicial ties. Leaders of the two countries continued to have wide-ranging discussions of global issues of the kind initiated by President Nixon and Secretary Kissinger in their meetings with Mao Tse-tung (Mao Zedong) and Chou En-lai during 1971–72. What was really new during 1979, however, was that both countries stepped up efforts to expand concrete economic, scientific, technical, scholarly, and other links.

High-level contacts between officials in the two governments concerned with economic affairs multiplied rapidly, U.S.-China trade grew significantly, and major progress was made toward creating the legal and institutional framework necessary for long-term economic relationships.

While leaders in both countries obviously believed that closer economic relations would serve the political and security interests of both nations, the development of economic ties acquired a dynamic of its own. Having initiated their new modernization program, the Chinese had strong economic reasons for expanding relations with the United States. U.S. leaders also placed increasing stress on the practical benefits of economic ties.

In August 1979 Vice President Walter Mondale visited Peking. While there he made an important speech at Peking University (the first public speech made by any American official in China in more than three decades).[30] In his speech he summed up U.S. policy toward China as it had developed up to that time and defined the premises the Carter administration believed should underlie U.S. China policy in the 1980s. Mondale declared that "a strong and secure *and modernizing* [emphasis added] China is . . . in the American interest in the decade ahead."[31] The addition of the word "modernizing" was significant; it indicated official U.S. support for China's modernization program. Washington was now prepared not just to develop trade with China but to give it some other kinds of economic assistance. Mondale placed great emphasis on economic cooperation, linking it to the broad political and security interests of the two countries. In his speech he declared:[32]

We must press forward now to widen and give specificity to our relations. The fundamental challenges we face are to build concrete political ties in the context of mutual security, to establish broad cultural relations in a framework of genuine equality, and to forge practical economic bonds with the goal of mutual benefit . . . what we accomplish today lays the groundwork for the decade ahead. The 1980s can find us working together—and working with other nations—to meet world problems. Enriching the global economy, containing international conflicts, protecting the independence of nations—these goals must also be pursued from the perspective of our bilateral relationship. The deeper the relationship, the more successful that worldwide pursuit will be.

Mondale also stated that "the closeness of your development goals to our own interests will provide the basis for our continuing economic cooperation." Elaborating on this, he declared:

In trade, our interests are served by your expanding exports of natural resources and industrial products. And at the same time your interests are served by the purchases you can finance through these exports. As you industrialize, you provide a higher standard of living for your people. And at the same time our interests are served—for this will increase the flow of trade, narrow the wealth gap between the developed and the developing world, and thus help alleviate a major source of global instability.

He also stressed the need for broader international economic cooperation in the cause of creating a world at peace and in "equilibrium."

In a world that hopes to find new energy resources, peace is essential. In a world that aims to eliminate hunger and disparities in wealth, global equilibrium is vital. In a world that is working to eradicate communicable diseases and to safeguard our environment, international cooperation is crucial.

What Mondale called for, in short, was increased economic cooperation, bilaterally and internationally, in the context of close political relations, and he announced several concrete U.S. economic moves (which will be discussed later) to promote such cooperation. But he also strongly identified U.S. national interests with China's defensive security interests, stating, "Any nation which seeks to weaken or isolate you in world affairs assumes a stance counter to American interests." This raised the level of U.S. political support for China's efforts to deter threats to its security.

We know that we live in a dangerous world. And we are determined to remain militarily prepared. . . . We will ensure that our investment in security is equal to the task of ensuring peace. . . . And despite the sometimes profound differences between our two systems, we are committed to joining with you to advance our many parallel strategic and bilateral interests.

At the same time, however, Mondale reiterated the often-repeated position that the United States viewed U.S.-China relations in essentially nonmilitary terms and was not contemplating an anti-Soviet coalition or alliance. "Sino-American friendship is not directed against anyone," he said, using what by now was standard phraseology; and he declared, "We do not have nor do we anticipate a military relationship."[33]

The Vice President's trip was a landmark in the development of post-normalization U.S.-China relations. One observer called his speech "perhaps the most important event in U.S.-China relations since the Shanghai Communiqué";[34] another labeled it "a touchstone for U.S.-China relations for the next decade."[35] An American official described the trip more modestly as an attempt to put "some muscle on the skeleton of normalization."[36]

During 1979 the economic dimension of U.S.-China relations became more important than ever. Both Washington and Peking pledged to strengthen economic ties, in part for practical reasons and in part because economic cooperation was viewed as the most practical and feasible means to cement overall relations rapidly. Positive steps were taken to lay the foundations for economic cooperation, and trade grew quickly. The development of new economic ties was intrinsically important, but it was linked inevitably to broader security issues. Mondale had stated that the United States did not intend to develop a "military relationship" with the Chinese. However, questions about whether or not to sell China technology and equipment of potential military use were unavoidable. Even though the Carter administration had repeatedly stated that policy toward Peking and Moscow would be evenhanded in this respect, as U.S.-China relations improved, pressure within the government for greater permissiveness in licensing sales to China increased.

Not long after Mondale's trip events impelled the United States to move toward greater flexibility in dealing with the Chinese, and immediately following the Soviet invasion of Afghanistan it was announced that Washington was prepared to authorize sales to China of "dual use" high technology and certain types of military support equipment. This marked the start of another phase in the development of U.S.-China relations. It constituted a clear, albeit still limited, tilt toward China and opened the door to new kinds of economic and security relations. However, it was not immediately clear, and in fact still remains uncertain, how far this door will be opened. Some of the key questions about the direction of future U.S.-China policy will center on this issue.

The Development of U.S.-China Trade, 1972–77

Between the opening of U.S.-China contacts in 1971–72 and the full normalization of relations in 1978–79, two-way trade grew, but it fluctuated erratically for a variety of reasons, both economic and political.[37] The Nixon administration began in the early 1970s to dismantle the embargo that for more than two decades had blocked all economic transactions between the United States and China. However, at the start few Americans were sanguine about the prospects. The conventional wisdom, within both the U.S. government and the American business community, was that Sino-American trade would increase only gradually and was likely to remain relatively small. Actually the growth immediately after the opening was, to almost everyone's surprise, quite rapid; in percentage terms it was spectacular. From nothing in 1970, trade sky-

TABLE 5-1. *U.S.-China Trade, 1971–79*

Millions of U.S. dollars

Year	Total U.S.-China trade	China's exports[a]	China's imports[a]	China's trade balance with the United States
1971	5.0	5.0	...	+5.0
1972	95.9	32.4	63.5	−31.1
1973	805.1	64.9	740.2[b]	−675.3
1974	933.8	114.7	819.1[b]	−704.4
1975	462.0	158.3	303.6	−145.3
1976	337.3	201.9	135.4	+66.5
1977	374.5	203.0	171.5	+31.5
1978	1,145.1	324.1	821.0	−496.9
1979	2,315.4	591.4	1,724.0	−1,132.6

Sources: The figures for 1971 through 1977 are from the U.S. Department of Commerce, in Joint Economic Committee, *Chinese Economy Post-Mao*, 95 Cong. 2 sess. (Government Printing Office, 1978). The figures for 1978 and 1979 are from National Foreign Assessment Center, Central Intelligence Agency, *China: International Trade Quarterly Review, Fourth Quarter 1979*, Research Aid ER CIT 80-003 (May 1980), pp. 7–8. (For slightly different figures from the International Monetary Fund, see ibid, pp. 9–12.) For CIA figures for 1971–77 giving imports c.i.f. and exports f.o.b., see Central Intelligence Agency, *People's Republic of China: Trade Handbook*, A ER 75-73 (October 1975), p. 10, and ER 76-10610 (October 1976), p. 15; and *China: International Trade, 1976–77*, ER 77-10674 (November 1977), p. 10, and *China: International Trade, 1977–78*, ER 78-10721 (December 1978), p. 12.

a. The figures for China's imports and exports during 1971–77 are f.a.s. (free along side) for exports and "customs value" for imports (which is close to f.a.s.). For all practical purposes one can consider both to be f.a.s. (which differs little from f.o.b.).

b. Includes some shipped via third countries and not reported as going to China.

rocketed to almost $1 billion in 1974. Two-way trade rose from $5 million in 1971 to $95.9 million in 1972, to $805.1 million in 1973, to $933.8 million in 1974 (see table 5-1).[38]

One explanation for this rapid increase was that Peking made a deliberate effort to redirect some trade toward the United States to try to accelerate the process of normalizing political relations. Another reason was Peking's need to import large amounts of grain at a time when global supply was tight. China's exports to the United States grew slowly, and the balance was overwhelmingly in the United States' favor.

From zero in 1971, China's imports from the United States rose to $63.5 million in 1972, then leaped to $740.2 million in 1973 and $819.1 million in 1974. Agricultural commodities were by far the largest portion. In 1972 grain alone accounted for 95 percent of the total.[39] In 1973 agricultural commodities constituted 81.7 percent (wheat, 41.5 percent; corn, 19.1 percent; soybeans, 7.5 percent; and cotton, 13.6 percent);[40]

in 1974 they made up 79.9 percent (wheat, 28.6 percent; corn, 11.7 percent; soybeans, 16.9 percent; and cotton, 22.7 percent).[41]

During 1972–74 the United States suddenly became China's second largest trading partner, after Japan. The U.S. share of China's imports rose from 2.8 percent in 1972 to 15.8 percent in 1973 and 12.7 percent in 1974. While the U.S. percentage in 1974 was still well below Japan's 27.9 percent, the U.S. share rose above Canada's 6.8 percent and West Germany's 6.4 percent.[42] China's exports to the United States started to rise, but compared with imports they remained small. From $5.0 million in 1971 they rose to $32.4 million in 1972, $64.9 million in 1973, and $114.7 million in 1974.[43] They remained under 2 percent of China's total exports (1.0 percent in 1972, 1.3 percent in 1973, and 1.8 percent in 1974). In 1974 the United States still ranked only eleventh among China's export markets.[44] (Markets ahead of the United States were Japan, 19.0 percent; Hong Kong, 13.4 percent; Malaysia and Singapore, 6.9 percent; West Germany, 2.6 percent; France, 2.5 percent; Indonesia, 2.3 percent; Soviet Union, 2.1 percent, United Kingdom, 2.1 percent; Rumania, 2.0 percent; and Australia, 1.9 percent.[45])

Then in 1975 China virtually cut off its imports of grain from the United States (though it continued to buy U.S. cotton on a sizable scale). As a result, total Chinese imports from the United States fell precipitously, to $303.6 million, only a little more than one-third of the 1974 figure. Although exports to the United States increased to $158.3 million, two-way trade was cut by more than half, dropping to $462.0 million. In 1975 the U.S. share of China's imports dropped to 4.5 percent, and its rank among nations selling to China dropped to sixth (below not only Japan, which had 32.1 percent of the China market, but also West Germany with 8.1 percent, Canada with 5.9 percent, France with 5.9 percent, and Australia with 4.8 percent). In 1975 the United States' rank as a market for China rose to fifth, but it still accounted for only 2.2 percent of China's total exports.[46]

One fundamental reason for the great drop in China's purchases from the United States was the improvement in its domestic grain supply. Another was Peking's growing concern about rising trade deficits and its shortage of hard currency. Because of the large deficit in China's overall foreign trade (which increased from $150 million in 1973 and $760 million in 1974),[47] Peking's leaders decided to retrench and cut the large deficit in trade with the United States.

While economic factors were the main explanation for the sudden drop in Chinese imports from the United States, politics also played a role. In Peking major debate between China's radicals and pragmatists was in full swing, which unquestionably had adverse effects on trade. Moreover, during 1974–75 it was evident that the process of normalizing U.S.-China relations had slowed, and the Chinese began stressing privately that only after the completion of normalization could the full potential of U.S.-China trade be realized.[48]

The large decline in U.S.-China trade in 1975 underlined the fact that even though the United States had suddenly become one of China's major trading partners during 1973–74, no stable basis of long-term trade relations had yet been achieved. U.S. exports to China, consisting predominantly of agricultural products, were subject to violent fluctuations and even total cutoffs; whereas in 1974 the United States had supplied almost 35 percent of China's grain imports, in 1975 it sold almost none. Even though American exports of manufactures to China doubled, from just over $100 million in 1974 to a little over $200 million in 1975, the United States still supplied only a small share of China's total imports of such goods—4.8 percent in 1975, compared with 3.5 percent in 1974—and the Chinese continued to look to Japan and Western Europe as their main sources of industrial plants and equipment.[49]

Following the cutoff of China's grain imports from the United States in 1975, which reduced the Chinese deficit in U.S.-China trade to a manageable level, under $150 million, trade between the two countries was stagnant during 1976–77. Overall two-way exchanges declined to $337.3 million in 1976 and in 1977 rose only slightly, to $374.5 million. China's imports from the United States continued to drop rapidly, reaching $135.4 million in 1976 before rising marginally to $171.5 million in 1977. Exports to the United States rose somewhat, to $201.9 million in 1976 and $203.0 million in 1977, which meant that for the first time since 1971 China actually achieved small surpluses in its American trade. But the increases were not sufficient to encourage Peking to increase its purchases of American products significantly, and overall two-way trade remained low.

The rate of increase in U.S.-China trade in 1977 (about 11 percent) was below that of China's total trade (13 to 14 percent).[50] The modest increase that did occur was mainly due to a small rise in Chinese imports of agricultural products; exports to the United States grew very little. Even though China had not yet resumed purchases of U.S. grain, three of its top five imports from the United States in 1977 were agricultural:

soybean oil ($28 million), raw cotton ($18 million), and soybeans ($14 million); the other two were vehicles ($29 million) and synthetic fibers ($19 million).[51] No other commodity exceeded $10 million. Exports to the United States were more varied. The leading ones were feathers ($19 million), cotton fabrics ($17 million), basketwork ($11 million), fireworks ($10 million), bristles ($9 million), antiques ($8 million), and carpets ($7 million).[52] Gradually, however, textiles were becoming the most important category of China's exports in its trade with the United States as in its worldwide trade. In 1977 the value of textile items among China's twenty-five leading exports to the United States (cotton fabrics, garments, raw silk, gloves, socks, and others) totaled between $40 million and $50 million, or between one-fifth and one-quarter of all Chinese sales to the United States.[53]

U.S.-China trade still did not appear to be of very great importance, however, even to China, to say nothing of the United States. In 1977 the Chinese did not look to the United States for the imports of greatest importance to them—whether manufactured goods or grain—and imports from China were of minor importance to the United States. In 1977 the United States accounted for only 2.6 percent of China's imports and 2.5 percent of its exports,[54] and trade with China accounted for only a little over one-tenth of 1 percent of total U.S. trade.[55]

Big Jump in Trade, 1978–79

Then, in 1978, the picture changed again rapidly. U.S.-China trade boomed and suddenly became more important than at any time since 1949, not only to China but potentially to the United States as well.

The main reason for the rapid increase was the sudden jump in China's overall trade resulting from its new modernization program and outward-looking foreign economic policy. In 1978 total Chinese trade rose, in dollar terms, by close to 40 percent.[56] However, the growth rate of U.S.-China trade greatly surpassed that of China's total trade. It suddenly tripled, rising (according to U.S. government estimates) from $375 million in 1977 to $1.145 billion in 1978.[57] In 1978 the United States was China's fourth largest trading partner, after Japan ($5.021 billion), Hong Kong ($2.312 billion), and West Germany ($1.314 billion).

In 1978, as in 1973–74, China again turned to the United States for badly needed grain imports, but additional considerations, both economic and political, influenced Peking's trade policy. Because of their new modernization program, Chinese leaders showed increased interest in the United States as a source of needed plants, equipment, and technology as well as agricultural goods, and as U.S.-China political relations began to move forward during 1978, the Chinese made a special effort to expand U.S.-China trade. Even though only a few of the numerous discussions initiated with major U.S. corporations during 1978 resulted in agreement, those that did (for example, those involving purchases of American airplanes, helicopters, and trucks during 1978–79) began to broaden the base for U.S. exports to China. China also stepped up its efforts to promote exports to the United States, and these rose significantly, though not fast enough to prevent the trade balance from swinging against China again.

As in 1973–74, the most important single factor explaining the spectacular jump in overall U.S.-China trade in 1978 was Peking's decision to resume large-scale buying of grain from the United States. In 1978 Peking's purchases of U.S. agricultural commodities of all kinds increased almost nine-fold, rising from $64 million in 1977 to more than $573 million in 1978; in 1978 they accounted for roughly two-thirds of total Chinese imports from the United States (if one adds U.S. grain that went to China via Canada, the figure is higher).[58] Significantly, Chinese purchases of American manufactured goods more than doubled in the same period, rising from $87 million in 1977 to $193 million in 1978; almost half of the manufactured goods total in 1978 consisted of machinery and equipment (oil and gas equipment alone totaled $46.5 million). Imports of U.S. semimanufactured goods for use by Chinese industry also rose significantly (these included $44.3 million of polymer fibers).[59] Although the rise in Chinese exports to the United States was slower, it was not unimpressive. The increase was roughly 60 percent, from $203 million in 1977 to $324 million in 1978. Over 70 percent of Chinese sales to Americans in 1978 consisted of manufactured goods, led by textile products, tin, basketwork, and antiques. Agricultural exports, led by leathers, down, essential oils, bristles, cashew nuts, tea, and raw silk, also increased.[60]

In 1978 the United States again became one of China's top trading partners. It was the third largest source for China's imports and, according to CIA figures, accounted for 8.4 percent of total Chinese purchases abroad. However, the total of U.S. sales to China ($818.2 million according to the Commerce Department, $864.6 million according to the

CIA) was still far behind the exports to China of Japan ($3.074 billion), Western Europe as a whole ($2.340 billion), or Germany alone ($995 million).[61] In 1978 the United States was the fourth largest market for Chinese exports. The $324 million of goods that China sold to the United States was far below its sales to Hong Kong ($2.249 billion), Japan ($1.948 billion), or Western Europe ($1.262 billion), but they were roughly the same as its exports to Singapore ($326 million) and slightly larger than its sales to West Germany alone ($319 million).

Despite some increase in China's exports to the United States in 1978, the huge jump in its imports resulted in another large Chinese deficit in U.S.-China trade, totaling $497 million, which as a percentage of total two-way U.S.-China trade amounted to 48 percent.[62] The problem this posed was not unique to U.S.-China trade. In 1978 China had large deficits with most countries that were major sources of its imports of industrial goods and grain. (As a percentage of its two-way trade, its trade deficit with Western Europe as a whole was 30 percent; with West Germany, 51 percent; with Japan, 22 percent; with Canada, 68 percent; and with Australia, 55 percent.) These deficits were sustainable only because China's surplus of $3.156 billion in trade with Hong Kong and the developing nations (plus a surplus of $26 million in trade with other Communist countries) almost made up its total $3.491 billion deficit in trade with all non-Communist developed nations in 1978. Consequently, its overall foreign trade deficit was only $297 million.[63] Peking may or may not tolerate large deficits in the period ahead and finance them in part by foreign borrowing if this is necessary to obtain imports essential for its modernization program. But clearly, the large Chinese deficit in U.S.-China trade in 1978 posed problems that could not be ignored, and in dealing with the United States, Peking began exerting pressure for action (such as the granting of most favored nation status) that would encourage larger U.S. imports of Chinese goods.

The trends started in 1978 continued in 1979, and China's trade with the United States and the rest of the world continued to rise rapidly. Two-way U.S.-China trade doubled to $2.315 billion, with Chinese imports rising 110 percent, to $1.724 billion, and exports increasing 82 percent, to $594 million.[64] The United States once again became China's second largest source of imports, providing 11.7 percent of the total (much less than Japan's 25.0 percent but more than West Germany's 10.1 percent), and it rose to third as a market for China's exports, accounting for 4.4 percent of the total (compared with 22 percent for

Hong Kong and 20.7 percent for Japan). Agricultural goods still dominated China's imports from the United States, totaling $1 billion (57.9 percent), but the Chinese also bought larger quantities of machinery ($166 million) and metals and metal products ($202 million). Textile fibers and products were China's main exports to the United States, totaling $202 million, or 34 percent of the total. The most interesting new development was the sale of Chinese petroleum and petroleum products in the United States, totaling $96 million, which exceeded agricultural goods and was surpassed only by textiles.[65] Exports of Chinese manufactured goods also grew, with machinery sales increasing to $166 million. As of early 1980 it appeared that this trade would continue growing, and the National Council for U.S.-China Trade (NCUSCT) predicted that two-way trade would rise to $2.5 billion to $3.0 billion in 1980, with Chinese imports increasing to $1.8 billion to $2 billion and its exports to $700 million to $900 million.[66] Although these estimates seemed optimistic at the time, they were in fact low.

Despite the rapid growth of U.S.-China trade during 1978–79, from the American perspective the total was still small. Even a two-way trade of more than $2 billion was under 1 percent of total U.S. foreign trade. Nevertheless, the rate of growth was impressive, and it appeared possible that by the mid-1980s two-way U.S.-China trade could rise to a level that would be significant for the United States as well as extremely important to China. Earlier[67] it was estimated that by the mid-1980s total two-way Chinese foreign trade might rise to around $50 billion or more a year and that if one were to make an optimistic projection of the U.S. share, it could account for as much as 15 to 20 percent of this, or somewhere between $7.5 billion and $10.0 billion. In 1979 Secretary of Commerce Juanita M. Kreps made a somewhat more conservative estimate, calculating that by 1985 two-way U.S. -China trade might total between $4.5 billion and $5.0 billion (and for the 1978–85 period as a whole total around $20 billion), but as of early 1980 the NCUSCT estimated that by 1985 total U.S.-China trade conceivably could rise to about $8 billion.[68] These estimates, however, were too low. In 1980 U.S.-China trade jumped to about $4.5 billion.[69]

There is no guarantee that U.S.-China trade will continue to rise at such a rate, however. China's growing deficit with the United States ($1.1 billion in 1979 and probably between $2 billion and $2.5 billion in 1980) and other problems could hold back growth. Whether the potential that exists is realized will depend in part on Chinese policy. However, it will also depend on whether or not the U.S. government and the business community take the necessary steps to establish a sound institutional and economic basis for expanded and lasting economic ties with China. If not, the United States could lose out in competition in the China market in the long run.

Broadening Economic Links, 1972–79

The growth of U.S. trade with China from 1972 through 1980 was in many respects surprising. After more than two decades during which relations between the two countries had been totally cut, American business had little experience or knowledge of the special problems of trading with the People's Republic of China, which businessmen from Japan and Western Europe had started accumulating in the 1950s. Moreover, even though American businessmen legally were able to deal with China on the same basis as with the Soviet Union and most other Communist countries once the U.S. embargo on China trade was ended, the legal and institutional framework for trade with China remained inadequate. Because of unresolved questions concerning U.S. claims against China for American property taken over by the Peking regime in its early days, and Chinese assets frozen in the United States, normal economic ties were still impossible. Any Chinese property brought to the United States was subject to legal attachment by any American claimant against the Chinese.[70] Moreover, there were no intergovernmental agreements covering a wide range of matters relating to trade. It was still impossible to establish normal banking relationships, to have direct two-way transportation links, or to develop most of the other ties usually regarded as essential for normal trading relationships. Problems of this sort were less of an obstacle to bulk sales of agricultural commodities than to more complicated economic transactions, but they hindered U.S.-China trade in general.

Major progress toward creating an adequate legal and institutional framework for U.S.-China trade proved to be impossible until the normalization of diplomatic relations. Although negotiation on the assets-claims issue had begun soon after Nixon's opening to China and at first had appeared to make progress, by 1974 they were bogged down. The Chinese made it clear in that period that it would be fruitless to try to resolve most trade-related issues requiring intergovernmental agreements until after full normalization of diplomatic ties.

In spite of all obstacles, however, both the Americans and the Chinese took steps gradually to broaden economic contacts and promote trade ties. The establishment of liaison offices in Peking and Washington in 1973 permitted the exchange of commercial experts qualified to explore trade possibilities, and they began to engage in trade promotion. In the United States a group of leading private businessmen organized with government encouragement the NCUSCT in 1973, and it established direct ties with Peking's China Council for the Promotion of International Trade (CCPIT) and began efforts to promote trade.[71] The U.S. Department of Commerce gradually strengthened its capacity to assist Americans interested in China trade possibilities.

The pace of developments was relatively slow at the start, however. The NCUSCT sent its first delegation to China in 1973, but the CCPIT did not reciprocate until 1975.[72] Then not only the CCPIT group but four other trade-related Chinese delegations visited the United States, and about the same time American corporations were invited in significant numbers to present technical seminars in China.

Thereafter the frequency of group exchanges, as well as the flow to China of individual American businessmen representing large and small corporations, increased steadily. In 1976 four Chinese trade groups visited the United States, and in 1977 six more groups arrived. In 1977 nine U.S. trade delegations went to China, and in the fall the number of American businessmen attending the semiannual Canton Trade Fair rose to between 700 and 800. Then in 1978 there was a quantum jump in two-way contacts. Large numbers of American businessmen, including representatives of many of the largest U.S. corporations, made business trips to China; many initiated negotiations on possible contracts and cooperative arrangements. The flow of Chinese trade representatives and technical missions to the United States also increased greatly: in early 1978 about twenty Chinese delegations visited the United States, most of them technical or trade related; by late 1979 the number had risen to almost sixty delegations a month.[73]

All these contacts were important. They began to build the personal and organizational links essential in international trading relationships. By late 1978 such contacts had resulted in several significant contracts between large U.S. corporations and the Chinese, and negotiations were in process on many more that related to possible sales of U.S. plants, machinery, equipment, and technology. Even after the Chinese slowed the pace at which they were contracting for capital goods imports in early

1979, serious negotiations involving many American corporations continued, and gradually some produced results. Most notable in terms of their potential importance for future U.S.-China economic relations were the contracts signed in 1979 by American oil companies for seismic surveys of offshore oil resources. The NCUSCT in early 1980 estimated that during 1979, of $7.4 billion worth of contracts signed by the Chinese, $1.1 billion were with U.S. corporations.[74]

By 1979, for the first time since the Communist takeover in China, a large number of major U.S. corporations were becoming actively involved in exploring the China market, competing against corporations from Japan and Western Europe. This greatly increased the possibilities for active U.S. participation in the market for capital goods and technology in China. Previously U.S.-China trade had been dominated by agricultural commodities, while sales of capital goods and technology had been dominated by the other industrial nations. Even as late as 1977, of China's total imports of manufactured goods from the West, 61.5 percent came from Japan, 15.8 percent from Germany, 19 percent from other West European countries, and only 2.9 percent from the United States.[75] Although a few American corporations (including Boeing and Kellogg-Pullman) had penetrated the Chinese market, it was only in 1978–79 that sizable numbers of companies became involved and U.S. sales of machinery, equipment, and technology began to grow. According to one estimate, manufactured goods accounted for nearly 30 percent of U.S. exports to China in 1979, and it was predicted that this might rise to almost 50 percent in 1980.[76]

Institutionalizing Scientific and Technological Ties, 1978

During 1978, after Brzezinski's trip, exchanges between American and Chinese governmental officials concerned with economic matters and scientific, technical, and scholarly cooperation, began to take place on an unprecedented scale. Frank Press, the President's Science Adviser and Director of the Office of Science and Technology Policy in the White House, led a distinguished fourteen-member delegation to Peking in July.[77] Described by some as the most prestigious delegation of its kind ever sent abroad by the United States, it included the heads of numerous American government agencies such as the National Aeronautics and Space Administration (NASA). In October Secretary of Energy James

Schlesinger headed a thirty-five-man delegation which discussed cooperation in a wide range of energy-related fields, including hydroelectric power, coal, oil and gas, high-energy physics, and renewable energy sources.[78] Chou Pei-yuan (Zhou Peiyuan), acting chairman of China's Science and Technology Association, visited the United States in October, met with a U.S. delegation headed by Richard C. Atkinson, director of the National Science Foundation, and reached an understanding on exchanges of students and scholars under which between 500 and 700 Chinese would study or conduct research in the United States during the academic year 1978/79, and a smaller but significant number of Americans would study or do research in China.[79]

In November Secretary of Agriculture Robert Bergland visited China and reached an understanding on agricultural exchanges. Cooperation was called for in agricultural technology, economic information, science, and education; trade in agricultural products and exchanges were proposed in a wide variety of fields.[80] From November through January Jen Hsin-min (Ren Xinmin), director of the Chinese Academy of Space Technology, led a delegation to the United States whose members reached an understanding in principle on cooperation in space technology with a group headed by Robert A. Frosch, administrator of NASA; the understanding called for broad cooperation in civilian space matters and development of China's broadcasting and communication system, including the probable Chinese purchase of a U.S. satellite broadcasting and communications system with the space satellite to be launched by NASA, and a ground station capable of receiving information from NASA's Landsat remote sensing satellites.[81]

These high-level official contacts in 1978 clearly helped to create a climate of opinion favorable for normalization of political relations. Then when the U.S. and Chinese governments announced on December 15 that diplomatic ties would be formalized as of January 1, 1979, added momentum was given to the process of expanding and institutionalizing economic, scientific, and technical cooperation. When Vice Premier Teng Hsiao-ping (Deng Xiaoping) made the first state visit to the United States by any Chinese Communist leader, he was accompanied by Fang Yi (Fang Yi), the Politburo member heading China's scientific and technological establishment. Teng visited Atlanta, Houston, Seattle, and Los Angeles as well as Washington, and in each place met leading businessmen and visited major plants. He (and President Carter) called for expanded trade and for economic, scientific, and technical cooperation; the

U.S. press reported his visit with headlines such as "Teng's American Business Trip."[82] On January 31, just before Teng left Washington, U.S. and Chinese leaders signed a spate of new agreements.[83] Apart from a cultural agreement and an agreement on consular relations, most agreements concerned expanded cooperation in economic, scientific, and technical fields. A formal "umbrella" agreement on science and technology signed by Carter and Teng called for cooperation in agriculture, energy, space, health, environment, earth science, engineering, and other areas and for broad educational and scientific exchanges of students, scholars, and information. It provided for the establishment of a Joint Commission on Scientific and Technological Cooperation (the first meeting of which was held in January 1980). Accompanying this agreement was a letter from Frank Press to Fang Yi which included, as annexes, under-standings already reached on exchanges of students and scholars, agricultural exchanges, and cooperation in space technology, formalizing these understandings and giving them added weight. Schlesinger and Fang signed an implementing accord on cooperation in high-energy physics, calling for establishment of a bilateral committee to deal with this field.

Creating a Framework for Broader Economic Relations, 1979

The understandings reached during 1978, culminating in the official agreement on cooperation in science and technology in January 1979, broadened scientific and technological ties that would assist the development of economic relations, and during 1979 significant intergovernmental as well as private exchanges increased in all fields covered by these understandings. However, prior to normalization of political relations major obstacles to normal economic relations remained. To provide a sound framework for economic relations it was necessary first of all to solve the long-standing assets and claims issue, then to conclude a general trade agreement, and then to reach a variety of other official agreements.

During the year following normalization of diplomatic ties, both countries gave high priority to the task of removing existing barriers to trade. At the beginning the U.S. government envisioned a step-by-step process starting with a solution to the assets and claims problem, then proceeding to an agreement on trade in textiles, followed by negotiation of a general trade agreement, after which would come agreements on maritime and aviation links and other matters.[84] Early negotiation of a textile agreement was considered desirable, and perhaps essential, in order to gain congressional support for a broad trade agreement. As things worked out, initial efforts to reach a textile agreement failed, and the Carter administration had to alter its priorities, or at least its schedule of negotiations. Nevertheless, by the end of 1979 Washington and Peking had made major progress toward removing past barriers to trade and creating a framework for expanded economic ties. In addition to concluding an agreement settling the claims issue, they signed a trade agreement promising most favored nation (MFN) treatment for China, and the U.S. government took initial steps to facilitate provision of government credit to help finance U.S.-China trade. Each of these agreements solved major problems; however, the negotiations also raised new issues.

Agreement on the Assets-Claims Issue

The origins of the assets-claims problem can be traced to the period of Communist takeover in China and the Korean War. Immediately after 1949 the new government had taken over a substantial amount of American (and other foreign) property in China, and after the outbreak of the Korean War the U.S. government had frozen all assets in the United States owned by the Peking regime and by Chinese on the mainland.[85] The frozen assets totaled an estimated $80.5 million, and the U.S. government calculated that certified legitimate private claims of U.S. corporations and individuals on the new Chinese regime amounted to $197 million.[86] Until settlement of this issue, any Chinese-owned property brought into the United States would be subject to attachment by American organizations and individuals with claims against Peking.

When Secretary of the Treasury Michael Blumenthal led a delegation to China in February 1979, his priority aim was to settle this issue.[87] He was compelled, however, as U.S. negotiators on the issue had been for some years, to operate under constraints rooted in American domestic politics. Soon after the negotiations on the problem had started in the early 1970s, the Chinese had indicated a willingness to pay a certain amount on the American claims—roughly the amount of the frozen assets they already had been able to collect outside the United States—and to transfer the assets blocked in the United States to the U.S. government. However, U.S. negotiators felt they could not accept this amount because it would have provided so little to U.S. claimants that Congress probably would have rejected it. In previous cases involving claims on Communist regimes, Congress had insisted on settlements providing sufficient funds to pay a minimum of roughly forty cents on the dollar to American claimants, and U.S. negotiators had insisted that the settlement be large enough for Congress to accept. During the talks the Americans also had mentioned pre-1949 Chinese government bonds, but Peking was not inclined to take any responsibility for them. (There were hints that some people in the Chinese bureaucracy may have objected to *any* payments to the United States.) For several years there had been no movement toward resolution of these issues.

When Blumenthal resumed the negotiations, both the Americans and the Chinese quickly showed that they now had the will to reach an agreement. It was the Chinese who made the largest concessions. In a document initialed (though not finally signed) while Blumenthal was in Peking they agreed to a formula under which Peking would pay an amount equal to the value of Chinese assets that the U.S. government had frozen, which the U.S. government would then distribute to pay American claimants about forty-one cents on the dollar.

The procedures agreed upon were highly advantageous to the United States, and potentially quite costly to China.[88] Instead of simply authorizing the U.S. government to collect and use the frozen Chinese assets to pay American claimants, the Chinese agreed to make cash payments to the U.S. government totaling $80.5 million, starting with an installment of $30 million on October 1, 1979, to be followed by annual payments of $10.1 million each year thereafter through 1984. This meant that the Chinese themselves would have to try to collect the frozen assets. For a variety of reasons they were unlikely to be able to collect anything like $80.5 million. No information was publicly available on where many of the assets were located. Moreover, the ownership of some assets was almost certain to be contested in U.S. courts. It was possible that the Chinese would recover only a fraction of the total (some informed observers estimated that they might collect only $15 million to $20 million); much of the $80.5 million the Chinese pledged to pay probably would have to come, therefore, from their own budget rather than from the frozen assets. It was also likely that to collect as much as they could the Chinese would have to become involved in prolonged litigation in U.S. courts (especially if they decided to try to collect part or all of the back interest on the assets held by banks since 1950).

It is not clear that the Chinese fully understood the problems they would face in trying to collect the frozen assets. Moreover, they were soon dismayed to learn that the U.S. government might not give them as much help in locating and recovering the assets as they expected. In the agreement the United States had made a general statement promising help; however, thereafter some American officials maintained that the U.S. government was prevented by law from revealing information gathered on a basis of confidentiality, even about who the holders of the assets were. It finally required a high-level decision within the U.S. bureaucracy to enable American officials to give the Chinese such assistance.

Despite the problems, the agreement on the assets and claims issue, formally signed in May,[89] was an important step forward that made it possible for the two governments to move on to discussion of questions that were intrinsically more important. However, it highlighted for the Chinese some of the difficulties, deriving from congressional and bureaucratic politics as well as legal constraints, of dealing with the United States. It is almost certain also that litigation in the process of recovering the frozen assets will be a source of continuing frustration and an irritant to the Chinese for some years to come.

The Trade Agreement and MFN

The necessity to reach agreement on the assets and claims issue was dictated mainly by U.S. domestic considerations, and the Chinese were willing to accept a solution disadvantageous to themselves because they recognized it was required to move on to more important problems. At the top of their list was the need to reach a general trade agreement that would grant them most favored nation treatment.[90] Without this, many Chinese exports to the United States would continue to be subject to tariffs much higher than those imposed on most other nations. The U.S. government also was eager to reach such an agreement, but for different reasons; it was necessary to provide U.S. businessmen with patent, trademark, and copyright protection and generally to regularize U.S.-China commercial relations.

When Washington and Peking agreed upon a visit to China by Secretary of Commerce Juanita Kreps in May, a principal objective of both sides was the conclusion of a general trade agreement. Preparation for the visit began early in 1979. Before Kreps arrived in Peking the two governments had exchanged drafts, and an advance delegation of U.S. officials had begun negotiations. Once again, however, the Chinese were confronted with some of the special problems of dealing with the American government. The U.S. Trade Act of 1974 specified a long list of requirements for such an agreement, far exceeding those most governments require.[91] The initial draft submitted to the Chinese was a long and complex document that went even further than the Trade Act required and included provisions dealing with virtually every question that the Americans ideally would have liked to include, even though the Chinese preference in trade agreements has tended toward relatively short, simple documents. On being presented with the U.S. draft, the Chinese are reported to have said that they had never seen and certainly had never signed anything like it.

When Secretary Kreps arrived in Peking and herself saw the Chinese reaction, she set members of her delegation to work to reexamine the draft and eliminate nonessentials, although the requirements of the Trade Act, including those regarding "market protection" and emigration policy (the latter required by the so-called Jackson-Vanik amendment), had to be met. A revised draft was then discussed with the Chinese.

The negotiations were not easy, and when Kreps was scheduled to leave Peking, no final agreement had been reached (although she was able to sign the assets and claims agreement that had been initialed by Blumenthal). Some of her staff stayed behind, however, to try to iron out the remaining differences, and as it turned out they were able to do so fairly rapidly. Reportedly, Vice Premier Teng intervened to overcome some of the problems,[92] which underlined the importance Peking placed on the matter, and just before Kreps left China from Canton (Kwangchow or Guangzhou) she initialed the resulting agreement. It was signed formally two months later, in July.[93] (Some American officials used Vice President Mondale's upcoming trip to China as an excuse to delay signing it, but there was strong pressure on both sides to reach final agreement first, since it was clear that little would be accomplished on his visit if this hurdle had not been surmounted.)

By far the most important provision of the trade agreement from the Chinese point of view was the reciprocal granting of MFN treatment (article I, section 1), substantially lowering the U.S. tariffs on imports from China and making many Chinese goods more competitive in the U.S. market. The Chinese had a sense of urgency about obtaining MFN treatment because they hoped to be able to increase considerably their sales in the United States. (They may also have had a political motive: to achieve a symbolic victory in obtaining MFN before such treatment was again given to the Soviet Union.) It remained to be seen, however, what the actual effects of MFN treatment would be. Estimates by American analysts varied. The tariff reductions would be significant; for example, the tariff on cloth shirting would drop from 17 percent to 9.51 percent, on textile yarn and thread from 45 percent to 10.5 percent, on woven cotton fabrics from 15.7 percent to 8.7 percent, and on clothing and accessories from 58.2 percent to 21.8 percent. Tariffs on many other goods would be cut by up to half, and in some cases by more.[94] However, it was not clear how much these tariff reductions would affect Chinese sales. Not only was it virtually certain that quantitative restrictions would be imposed by the United States on many textile products, but it was also uncertain how much price elasticity there was in U.S. demand for Chinese products.

Nevertheless, several studies did indicate that the effect on Chinese exports to the United States could be significant. One study estimated, for example, that if China had enjoyed MFN treatment in 1976, its exports to the United States that year would have been about 30 percent higher than they actually were.[95] Another calculated that MFN status should result in an increase of roughly 25 to 30 percent in Chinese sales to the United States during 1980–82.[96] A third concluded that the impact of MFN treatment on U.S. demand in 1975 might have resulted in 50 to 90 percent higher Chinese sales, and that even though the price elasticity for many commodities China now sells to the United States may be low, the impact on future Chinese exports of other light manufactured goods might be more substantial.[97] Therefore, even though it was impossible to predict exactly the effects of MFN treatment, it seemed likely to give an important boost to Chinese exports and consequently to two-way trade.

Although the Chinese considered the granting of MFN treatment as most urgent, the agreement included other provisions that would be valuable to China in the long run.[98] One clause made China eligible for "official export credits on the most favorable terms appropriate" (article V, section 2), a general statement that required further U.S. action to become operative but nevertheless was important. The agreement also stated that the United States and China would "take into consideration in the handling of their bilateral trade relations, that, at its current state of economic development, China is a developing country" (article II, section 3). Classifying China formally as a "developing country" opened the door to the future possibility of granting China duty-free treatment under the so-called Generalized System of Preferences (GSP), which the

United States and other industrial nations have done for many less developed countries (LDCs). The trade agreement also made it possible (article V, sections 3 and 4) for the Bank of China to operate branches in the United States as well as for American bank representatives to function in China.

From the U.S. perspective many provisions were important. The agreement called for effective protection of patents, trademarks, and copyrights (article VI). (According to the Trade Act of 1974, U.S. trade agreements with Communist countries must have patent and trademark protection not less than that specified in the Paris Convention and copyright protection not less than that afforded by the Universal Copyright Convention.)⁹⁹ The agreement also provided for mutual exchanges of information (article VII); the settlement of disputes through "friendly consultations, conciliation, or other mutually acceptable means," and, if these are unsuccessful, through "arbitration" (article VIII); arrangements for trade promotion and reasonable treatment of businessmen and trade representatives (article III); and the establishment in both countries of official government trade offices (article IV).

One of the most important clauses from the U.S. (especially the congressional) point of view was the provision for unilateral action when "market disruption" is threatened (the Trade Act of 1974 also requires this). The agreement (article VII) stated that when problems cannot be solved by consultation, either party "may take such measures as it deems appropriate," and that in an "exceptional case where a situation does not admit any delay," either party may take "preventive or remedial action provisionally."

The conclusion of the trade agreement was the most important step taken up to that time toward regularizing U.S.-China economic relations. However, the executive act of signing it did not end the process; on the U.S. side it was still necessary to obtain congressional approval, which required surmounting several hurdles. One was the provision contained in the Jackson-Vanik amendment that forbids trade agreements granting MFN treatment to Communist countries that restrict emigration; it required that the President must certify that such countries' emigration policies are acceptable. Although aimed at the Soviet Union, the wording of this amendment made it applicable to China as well. However, U.S. officials made it clear that the President was prepared to grant the necessary waiver to China because Chinese leaders, including Teng Hsiaoping, had given adequate assurances about their policies toward emigration.[100] According to some reports Teng had stated that as many Chinese as wished to leave the country would be allowed to do so, even if they numbered in the millions (which is hardly what other nations desired); during 1978–79 there was a large flow of Chinese emigrants to Hong Kong, and some relatives of Chinese-Americans joined them in the United States.[101] Even though certain congressmen indicated they might raise questions about the precise nature and form of the Chinese assurances and try to insist that the President provide Congress with a written statement or documentation on the matter, from the start it seemed likely that this hurdle could be surmounted.

Another issue that created problems both within the Carter administration and in Congress was the question of whether or not the United States should proceed to grant MFN status to China before it could also accord it to the Soviet Union, since such a move might look like a definite tilt toward China, compromising the idea of evenhanded treatment of Peking and Moscow that Washington had said was the aim of U.S. policy. In principle, the Carter administration favored granting MFN status to both countries at or about the same time.[102] However, even though for some time Moscow had allowed increased numbers of Jews to emigrate, it still refused to give explicit assurances about its emigration policy, and without this the President could not hope to grant a waiver and obtain congressional acceptance of it.

The issue boiled down, therefore, to the question of whether the U.S. government, after successfully negotiating the trade agreement with China, should tell Peking that implementation would have to be postponed. There was considerable debate within the Carter administration on the MFN issue, and there was a short delay in sending the Chinese agreement to the Congress for approval. However, by this time the development of U.S.-China trade had a momentum of its own, and it would have been extremely difficult to tell the Chinese that the United States was unwilling or unable to follow through because the Soviet Union was unwilling to give assurances, as China had already done, on emigration policy.

Throughout most of 1979 it appeared likely that some congressmen would attempt to block or delay the U.S.-China agreement. Some were particularly concerned, as were certain members of the executive branch, with the problem of maintaining a balance in relations with Peking and Moscow, particularly at a time when U.S. relations with Moscow were deteriorating. Early in 1979 several leading congressmen strongly urged parallel action to grant MFN status to both China and the Soviet Union. In January 1979 Representative Charles A. Vanik, cosponsor of the original amendment on emigration, came out in favor of parallel action,[103] and in February Senator Adlai E. Stevenson proposed modifications of the Jackson-Vanik amendment itself that might make possible moves to grant MFN status to both Peking and Moscow.[104] However, Senator Jackson and others opposed all such moves and favored going ahead to grant MFN status to China alone, which ultimately was done. (As long as the Jackson-Vanik amendment is on the books, it should be noted, it will require renewal of the presidential waiver for China every year; this means the United States could unilaterally end the trade agreement at almost any time, even though its formal term is for three years with renewals for similar periods.)

The Carter administration was also concerned about possible opposition to the U.S.-China trade agreement from congressmen representing the main textile-producing states. In fact Secretary Kreps reportedly indicated in May that the administration might not be able to send the trade agreement to Congress until a separate textile agreement had been signed.[105]

These and other considerations (such as Congress's crowded calendar and preoccupation with other issues) meant that even though Secretary Kreps initialed the trade agreement in May, Washington was unable to tell Peking how soon it would be implemented, and the Chinese were not happy about the possibility of delay.[106] Once again they learned about the complexities of dealing with the political and bureaucratic factors affecting U.S. policy. They lost no time, however, in demonstrating their single-mindedness in pursuing high-priority objectives; immediately they started to exert pressures publicly and in conversations with U.S. visitors for rapid implementation, with some effect on U.S. policymakers.[107]

The signing of the assets-claims agreement and conclusion of a trade agreement were the most important developments affecting U.S.-China economic relations during the first half of 1979, but there also were others of significance. During her visit to China in May Secretary Kreps and officials concerned with science, technology, and economics in the two governments signed five protocols calling for cooperation in the fields of management of science and technology and scientific and technological information, marine and fishery sciences, metrology and standards, atmospheric science and technology, and the exchange of trade exhibits.[108] In May NASA administrator Frosch led a delegation that continued discussions on cooperation with China's embryonic civilian space program, and Postmaster General Benjamin F. Bailer's visit produced agreement on direct mail exchanges.[109] In June Secretary of Health, Education, and Welfare Joseph Califano headed a delegation to China, and the visit produced a protocol on cooperation in medicine and public health (a joint health committee was established) as well as an understanding on further exchanges in education.[110] Broad scholarly and cultural exchange programs, which had been under way on a modest scale for some years under the sponsorship of U.S. organizations such as the Committee on Scholarly Communication with the People's Republic of China and the National Committee on U.S.-China Relations, developed further, qualitatively as well as quantitatively. By 1980 more than 5,000 Chinese, a sizable proportion with Chinese government support but also many others, were studying or doing research in the United States, and 100 to 200 American scholars and students (roughly 50 of them with U.S. government support) were at work in China. In addition, the flow of Chinese technical delegations to the United States kept rising, and China began to reciprocate the flow of U.S. cabinet-level leaders to China with ministerial-level trips to the United States. The most notable of these were the visit in May of China's Minister of Finance, Chang Ching-fu (Zhang Jingfu), who held broad-ranging discussions with American business leaders as well as government officials, and the May-June visit of Chinese energy specialists led by Vice Premier Kang Shih-en (Kang Shien).[111] Step by step these developments broadened and strengthened the basis for economic as well as scientific, technical, and cultural cooperation between the two countries.

The Textiles Problem

Not everything went smoothly during early 1979, however. On the textile issue, which was one of the most politically sensitive trade problems in the United States and one of the most important commercial questions for China, the two countries deadlocked, and as a result the U.S. government unilaterally imposed restrictions that were distasteful to the Chinese.[112] The issue involved a serious conflict of interests. The Chinese felt it essential to maximize exports of textiles to the United States. They saw, correctly, a great opportunity to sell more cloth and apparel in the American market because of China's comparative advantage based on low labor costs. Moreover, they believed it imperative to earn more foreign exchange this way to pay for increased imports from

Americans. The Carter administration, however, felt it essential to impose restrictions on imports of textiles from China as well as other countries because of the weak competitive position of the American industry, the formidable strength of the domestic textile lobby (strongly supported by both business and labor), and the administration's vulnerability to retaliation by the lobby that could endanger other basic objectives of broad U.S. foreign economic policy. Domestic political considerations had a greater influence on the U.S. stand on textile imports than on any other issue in the evolving U.S.-China economic relationship.

For years the United States has set limits (as have most other industrial nations) on imports of textile products from virtually all the main LDC exporters, mostly under an umbrella Multi-Fiber Agreement worked out in connection with the General Agreement on Tariffs and Trade (GATT).[113] Since China, not being a member of the GATT, was not a party to this agreement, the U.S. textile industry was alarmed by the prospect of an uncontrolled flow of Chinese textiles into the United States. Moreover, in late 1978 and early 1979 textile issues became closely linked to even more important issues in broad U.S. foreign economic policy. When the so-called Tokyo Round of negotiations among the major trading nations, which had been under way for several years (trying to promote trade by reducing tariffs and other restrictions), finally produced an agreement, the U.S. government began lobbying vigorously to overcome domestic protectionist opposition to it in order to obtain congressional approval. Opposition from the textile lobby was one of the main potential obstacles. In 1978 the United States had a $6 billion deficit in overall textile trade, and the industry pressed strongly for steps to reduce it.[114] The administration, through Robert S. Strauss, the President's special trade representative, felt compelled to make major concessions to the industry's leaders to overcome their opposition to the GATT agreement. Although Strauss ultimately was successful in mobilizing sufficient support to obtain congressional approval, one of the prices paid was a pledge to U.S. textile interests in January 1979 that restrictions would be imposed on textile imports from China as well as from other LDCs.[115] Washington felt that it was politically imperative, therefore, to put the negotiation of a textile agreement fairly high on its agenda of economic issues to discuss with China, even though the Chinese might have preferred that it not be on the agenda at all.

Informal talks with the Chinese regarding textiles began in August 1978. Then from January 1979 on they were pursued by the United

States with increasing vigor.[116] In April, even before formal signing of the assets-claims settlement or negotiation of the trade agreement, the U.S. government sent a delegation to China to try to reach an agreement.[117] It failed. Then in May Strauss himself went to China to try again, but he too failed, even though he warned the Chinese that in the absence of an agreement, the United States would have to impose quotas unilaterally.[118] On May 31 Washington did just that. On five categories of Chinese textile product exports—cotton work gloves, cotton blouses, men's and boys' cotton shirts, cotton trousers, and synthetic fiber sweaters—specific limits were set for the next twelve months based on the level of Chinese exports of these items to the United States during the year that had ended February 28. These quotas covered the bulk of China's exports of apparel to the United States, although they did not affect cotton print cloth or many other textile items.[119] The Chinese had good reason to be unhappy about the U.S. action, even though they accepted it and some Chinese recognized that it would be preferable to an agreement that imposed even wider restrictions.

As in the case of most complex issues involving real conflicts of interests, there were compelling arguments on both sides. The U.S. textile industry's arguments carried added weight because Chinese textile exports to the United States were, in fact, rising rapidly. By early 1979 China reportedly was second only to Hong Kong in sales of cotton textiles to the United States[120] and had become the sixth largest supplier of textiles of all kinds (including synthetics and wool) to the American market.[121] Textiles, including garments, became the largest category of Chinese exports to the United States, and during the first quarter of 1979, despite high tariffs, they rose sharply (perhaps in part because Peking anticipated the imposition of restrictions). In that period sales of Chinese cotton trousers to the United States increased by 108 percent, men's and boys' shirts by 94 percent, women's and girls' knit shirts and blouses by 71 percent, and work gloves by 84 percent.[122] China had become the largest "uncontrolled" supplier of textiles to the U.S. market. It was inevitable that the U.S. textile lobby would insist on steps to ensure "orderly growth"—and a slowdown in the rate of growth.

From the Chinese perspective, however, they had no alternative but to press to maximize textile exports to the United States, especially in view of the large Chinese deficit in overall trade with the Americans. Moreover, as a latecomer in the field China faced special problems. Under the GATT Multi-Fiber Agreement the industrial nations had in effect divided up the existing market, allocating pieces of the pie to each of the major LDC exporters. Not being a party to this agreement, China had a legitimate fear that it might not be allowed to obtain a fair share of markets already penetrated by other LDCs, since it would be difficult if not impossible for the industrial nations to reduce the level of their imports from Hong Kong, Taiwan, South Korea, and other areas in order to increase imports from China.

Despite the rapid rate of growth of Chinese textile exports to the United States and its rise to number six among such exporters, China remained far behind the leading LDC textile exporters. In May 1979 one of China's Vice Ministers of Foreign Trade complained that "our exports of textiles comprise only a little more than 1 percent of total U.S. textile imports."[123] The Chinese also rightly pointed out that their imports of U.S. raw cotton were larger than Chinese sales of textiles to the United States. During 1978, for example, although China's textile exports to the United States increased to $120 million, its purchases of U.S. cotton increased even faster, rising from under $18 million in 1977 to over $157 million in 1978.[124] Peking asked how the Americans could expect to increase exports to China significantly unless they were prepared to import more from China. When the Chinese indicated they found the U.S. position on textile imports difficult to understand, it was not simply a bargaining argument. Undoubtedly they did find it baffling that the U.S. government would give priority to protecting the interests of one particular American industry rather than promoting the interests of those wishing to increase exports to China, and to favoring those desiring to restrict imports rather than those wishing to expand overall U.S.-China economic relations.

Following Strauss's failure to achieve an agreement and Washington's imposition of unilateral quotas, negotiations continued, and it was quite clear that some agreement ultimately would be reached since the Chinese were under great pressure to agree. The quotas imposed in May, which froze the levels for a one-year period, had no provisions for further increases, and any formal agreement probably would provide for at least some annual growth; consequently, even an agreement setting limits below what the Chinese would like would be better than none.

The fifth round of U.S.-China talks on textiles, held in Washington in April-May 1980, also resulted in failure, and the U.S. government announced that the quotas would be extended at existing levels for another year.[125] The official Chinese news agency reported that the chief Chinese negotiator "described the quotas as discriminatory and said they would be detrimental to the development of friendly relations and trade relations" and "ran counter to the spirit of the Sino-U.S. Agreement on Trade Relations," pointing out that despite the rise in Chinese textile sales they still accounted for only 3 percent of U.S. textile imports in 1979.[126] About a month later U.S. officials privately stated that an agreement based on mutual compromise was near, but it was clear that, if so, it would impose limits well below what the Chinese would like to obtain.

Disagreement over textiles will be a continuing major issue in U.S.-China economic relations. In some respects, it is surprising that it did not have more adverse effects on trade in 1980; the fact that it did not reduce the momentum of broadening economic ties in other fields testified to the pragmatism of the Chinese in adapting to realities, however unpleasant. As overall economic relations grow in the future, China's need to expand textile and other manufactured goods exports to the United States will increase, however, and it is certain that textile issues in particular will continue to cause friction and misunderstandings that could be serious.

"Friendly Nation" Status

Despite the failure to reach a textile agreement in 1979—in fact, perhaps to some extent *because* of that failure—the Carter administration turned its attention to other ways in which the United States could assist China economically. In the interim between the visit by Secretary Kreps in May and the planned trip by Vice President Mondale in August, Washington made several important decisions regarding proposals or offers Mondale would make to the Chinese, both to strengthen bilateral relations and, it was hoped, to encourage greater U.S.-China cooperation on broader international problems.

While in Peking, in addition to making general statements that went further than any previous ones in stressing parallel American and Chinese interests and pledging general U.S. support for Peking's development goals, Mondale announced several specific U.S. moves designed, as he put it, "to give specificity to our relations" and "forge practical economic bonds."[127]

Before Mondale left for Peking, the U.S. government finally decided to decouple the granting of MFN status to China from issues concerning U.S.-Soviet relations and to proceed without further delay to try to obtain congressional approval for the U.S.-China trade agreement. In

China Mondale announced that the Carter administration would send the agreement to Congress for approval before the end of the year and that it would not be "linked to any other issue."[128] Soon thereafter the administration acted on this promise, and in late January 1980 both the Senate and House voted approval. Although there was some debate in the House, the final vote was 294 to 88. In the Senate there was little debate, and the vote was 74 to 8. The Soviet invasion of Afghanistan, which figured prominently during the debate in the House, undoubtedly hastened congressional approval.[129]

Equally important, during the week before Mondale's trip Secretary Vance and the Agency for International Development (AID) certified China officially to be a "friendly nation" in U.S. eyes, which was a bureaucratic prerequisite (under the Foreign Assistance Act of 1961) for making China eligible for assistance from U.S. government agencies "on a compensatory basis."[130] Only one other Communist country, Yugoslavia, had been so certified in the past. This opened the door to a wide range of possible cooperative projects on a paid basis involving U.S. government organizations.[131] While in China Mondale took the first step toward developing cooperation of this sort. Following up discussions started by Secretary Schlesinger, he signed a protocol on cooperation to develop China's hydroelectric power, which, it was anticipated, might ultimately involve the U.S. Army Corps of Engineers, the Department of the Interior's Bureau of Reclamation, the Department of Energy, and the Tennessee Valley Authority.[132]

These actions—the move to obtain final approval of the trade agreement without linking it to MFN status for the Soviet Union, the decision to treat China officially as a "friendly country," and the steps taken to initiate intergovernmental cooperation in the energy field—were economically important. They also had considerable political significance, highlighting the importance that Washington placed on the need to consolidate friendly relations with Peking.

Export-Import Bank Credits

Finally, while in Peking Mondale announced that the United States was prepared both to extend government economic credits to China and to seek authorization for U.S. government guarantees (or insurance) for American investments in China. Specifically, he stated that the United States would establish Export-Import (Ex-Im) Bank credit arrangements for the Chinese, permitting loans on a case-by-case basis up to a total of $2 billion over a five-year period, and added, "If the pace of development warrants it, we are prepared to consider additional credit arrangements."[133] He also promised that the administration would seek the necessary congressional authorization to make possible Overseas Private Investment Corporation (OPIC) guarantees for U.S. investments in China.

Implementation of Mondale's promise of Ex-Im Bank credits would require follow-up action to put it into effect.[134] The 1968 enabling legislation for the Bank prohibited loans to Communist countries unless the President declared such loans to be in the national interest. As of late 1978 four other Communist countries—Yugoslavia, Poland, Rumania, and Hungary—were eligible for Ex-Im Bank loans (the Soviet Union once had been eligible, before passage of the Jackson-Vanik amendment, but no longer was).

The Carter administration planned to act on the promise of Ex-Im Bank credits to China after congressional passage of the trade agreement and after resolution of one remaining legal complication. Washington considered the Peking government to be liable under U.S. law for repayment of about $26 million in claims arising from Ex-Im Bank loans made to the Chinese Nationalist regime on the mainland of China before the Communist takeover,[135] because when the Communists assumed power they took control of the assets purchased with these loans. However, the Chinese refused to acknowledge any liability for them. This issue had to be dealt with in some way. During 1979 it was not clear how the hurdle could be surmounted, but there was confidence that it would be somehow resolved. Later the Export-Import Bank did so simply by handling the problem as a bookkeeping issue.

It is quite possible that the Chinese will wish to draw upon U.S. Ex-Im loans if and when they become available. They first indicated their desire for such loans in early 1979,[136] and their active solicitation of credits from export-import banks in Japan and Western Europe during 1978–79 provided evidence that they were considering this kind of financing.[137] While visiting the United States in May, Chinese Finance Minister Chang Ching-fu met with Ex-Im Bank President John L. Moore, Jr., and they discussed the legal problems posed by the old bank claims.[138] In subsequent discussions the possibilities of future loans for aircraft purchases and for mining, steel, and hotel projects reportedly were raised.

It remains to be seen, however, whether or not the Ex-Im Bank will have funds to fulfill Mondale's promise and can offer the Chinese terms competitive with those it can obtain elsewhere. In 1979 the Bank requested direct lending authority for fiscal year (FY) 1980 (October 1, 1979, through September 30, 1980) of $4.1 billion,[139] but Congress delayed approving this amount, so the Bank had to operate on the basis of a "continuing resolution" authorizing the same amount as in FY 1979, $3.75 billion. In view of the many demands on its limited funds, it was clear that larger congressional authorizations would be required to make possible loans to China of the amount Mondale promised.

In recent years Congress has increased the Ex-Im Bank's funds. Its direct lending authority rose from $700 million in FY 1977 to $2.872 billion in FY 1978 and $3.75 billion in FY 1979 (and the total of its credit and loan guarantees rose to $7.38 billion in FY 1978). By the fall of 1978 the bank's outstanding loans totaled more than $26 billion (of which 29.9 percent, or $7.9 billion, were in Asia, the largest exposure being in South Korea, which had almost $766 million in Ex-Im loans outstanding).

Then in late 1978 its charter was amended to increase its total loan, guarantee, and insurance authority from $25 billion to $40 billion; and in debates in Congress in 1979 on what lending authority to authorize for FY 1980, the House proposed $4.1 billion, as requested; the Senate proposed $6 billion; and a $5 billion compromise was discussed. However, as of June 1980 no final action had been taken. The Bank was still operating on the basis of the $3.75 billion continuing resolution; and with three months of the fiscal year still ahead, only $75 million of that was still uncommitted, and the Bank had made more than $2 billion in preliminary commitments out of its nonexistent FY 1981 budget.

Despite the upward trend in Ex-Im Bank authorization, it still plays a much smaller role in financing U.S. trade than comparable Ex-Im institutions do in other industrial countries. In FY 1978 the U.S. Ex-Im Bank's total of $7.38 billion in loans and guarantees financed only about 6 percent of total U.S. exports; the comparable figures for other selected countries were 37 percent for Japan, 35 percent for the United Kingdom, and 33 percent for France.[140] And by late 1979, of the total credits offered to China by institutions in Japan and Europe, more than $13 billion had backing by government export-import banking agencies—more than six times what Mondale had promised the U.S. Ex-Im Bank would loan.[141] While the promise Mondale made was important, it did not come close to matching those already made by other industrial nations (although according to some reports the U.S. Ex-Im Bank would be authorized to extend $2 billion in credit guarantees on private loans to China in addition to $2 billion in direct Ex-Im loans, which would help). It remains uncertain, therefore, how much the Ex-Im Bank will actually be able to loan to finance trade with China.

It is also uncertain whether U.S. banks—either government or private—will in practice be able to match the terms offered the Chinese by banks in other industrial nations. In 1978 an amendment to the 1945 Export-Import Bank Act authorized it to match the "rates and terms and other conditions" of its competitors, even, if necessary, providing loans at rates below the Organization for Economic Cooperation and Development (OECD) guidelines which set a minimum of 7.25 percent for official medium-term credits to developing countries.[142] In FY 1978 the average rate for Ex-Im Bank credits dropped to 8.25 percent, compared with 8.53 percent in FY 1977, and in 1979 it gave a few loans at even lower rates. However, most of the Japanese and European loans offered to China during 1978–79 had interest rates ranging between 7.25 and 7.50 percent, some were as low as 6.25 percent,[143] and the Japanese offered concessionary government loans at 3 percent.

To date, American bank offers have not been competitive. During 1979 a number of leading U.S. private banks established formal banking relations with China, but by year-end they had extended no significant loans to China. The first of any significance offered by an American bank to the Chinese was one in early 1979 from Chase Manhattan for initial work on a trade center in Peking; it amounted to only $30 million, and it was subsequently postponed—at least temporarily—by the Chinese.[144] The second, extended in May by the First National Bank of Chicago to the Fukien Provincial Investment Enterprise, was for a mere $8 million to be used to buy coastal ships;[145] as of the end of 1979 it was still the only medium- or long-term loan actually made by an American bank to the Chinese since the U.S.-China opening. Even though American banks have played a major role in lending to other LDCs, by the end of 1979 they had not yet seriously joined the competition in lending to China.

One reason undoubtedly was that the Americans were latecomers on the scene. But there were also more fundamental reasons for the U.S. lag. One was the willingness of Japanese and European bankers to offer easy terms to the Chinese arising in part from the greater liquidity in their countries than in the United States.[146] In addition, they took the

China market more seriously than Americans did, regarded its long-term potential as important, and were prepared to extend large loans at relatively low interest rates (in many cases low even by comparison with what they offered to other LDCs) in order to develop trading relations that could be significant for many years. They were ready to take a longer-term view than Americans. It remains to be seen whether American banks will follow their lead. If not, this undoubtedly will tend to limit the development of U.S.-China economic relations in the period ahead.

OPIC Investment Guarantees

The fourth major promise that Mondale made in Peking was that the Carter administration would seek congressional authority to grant OPIC guarantees and insurance for American investments in China.[147] As in the case of the offer of Ex-Im Bank credits, this was an important move, but its possible effects could not be judged immediately.

OPIC is a self-sustaining U.S. government agency (operating under the guidance of the Secretary of State), established in 1961, mainly to provide political risk insurance to U.S. companies investing in "less developed" but "friendly" nations. Its insurance covers loss of investments due to expropriation, war, revolution, or insurrection as well as from inconvertibility of currencies. OPIC can write insurance contracts for up to twenty years at comparatively low premium rates for projects that it considers sound, and it will guarantee commercial loans of up to $50 million. It can also make modest loans (up to a maximum of $5 million) directly to smaller firms (with annual sales of $110 million or less) to help finance foreign investment. The coverage given by OPIC is restricted to developing countries with a per capita income (in 1975 dollars) of $520 or less.

Until 1979 eligibility for investment guarantees would have been irrelevant to China since there was virtually no foreign investment in the country, but Peking's adoption of a foreign investment law that year and the strong interest that the Chinese subsequently have expressed in attracting foreign investment make it potentially important. A number of major U.S. corporations have shown initial interest in the possibility of investing in Chinese projects; the availability of OPIC guarantees could be a key variable influencing their decisions.

Both executive and legislative action will be required to implement

Mondale's promise. The first is a determination by the President that extending OPIC guarantees to investment in China would be "important to the national interest." Congress must also decide to exempt China from the prohibition affecting Communist countries contained in the 1961 act. This will not be difficult to do; it already has been done for Yugoslavia and Rumania simply by the addition of one sentence to title IV of the OPIC legislation. Some in Congress may question the advisability of doing the same for China, but there is good reason to believe it will go through.

Assuming that these steps are completed soon, what then will be required is negotiation of a bilateral U.S.-China agreement on procedures for consultations regarding the suitability of projects, payments, and arbitration of disputes. In light of Peking's eagerness to attract foreign investment this should not pose any great difficulties, so it is possible that OPIC guarantees on American investments in China will be in place before long.

Such guarantees alone will not guarantee large-scale American investments in China in the period ahead. This will depend on many factors, especially Peking's ability to create conditions genuinely attractive to foreign investors. It will also depend on the seriousness with which American businessmen view opportunities in China and their ability to compete successfully with businessmen from Japan and Europe. Nevertheless, government guarantees for U.S. investment in China could be an important factor enhancing the prospects for broader and deeper U.S.-China economic ties.

1980: Steps to "Complete Normalization"

By the end of 1979, only a year after the decision to establish formal diplomatic ties, the United States and China had made major progress toward creating the necessary legal and institutional framework for developing "normal" economic relations. To complete the process, however, several additional steps were required. The prospects appeared good that these could be taken fairly expeditiously.

The priority task on the American side was to carry out effectively the promises Washington already had made. This required passing legislation making OPIC guarantees possible, taking concrete action to ensure that

Ex-Im Bank credits are available, and reaching an agreement on textiles that will facilitate an orderly but substantial growth of Chinese exports in the United States.

In addition, U.S.-China agreements in two other fields—aviation and maritime affairs—were needed. American and Chinese officials discussed a possible maritime agreement at some length during 1979.[148] In the talks differences emerged, but they were of a practical kind, and there was good reason to believe that they could be resolved fairly rapidly. The principal point of contention concerned cargo sharing. The Chinese, not surprisingly, desired an agreement that would allow them to carry as much of the two-way trade as possible in Chinese ships. Reportedly, the United States argued for an arrangement ensuring that U.S.-flag ships could carry one-third of the bulk cargo in the trade.[149]

The problems of reaching an aviation agreement were not very different. Although the United States and China long had been eager to start regular air service and China had authorized a number of U.S. charter flights, inauguration of regular service required an intergovernmental agreement.[150] Under pressure from several major American airlines that had filed route applications with the Civil Aeronautics Board, the U.S. government drafted and sent a model aviation document to the Chinese in early 1979. The Chinese were slow in responding, however, because of reservations about a number of its provisions.[151] Reportedly, the main issue concerned whether the United States should be authorized to have one or more air carriers with regularly scheduled flights to China. In dealings with other countries—most of which have only a single international air carrier—the Chinese had not previously authorized more than one international air carrier for any country, and they wished to treat the United States the same way (their preference was said to be Pan Am).[152] But the United States, with a long tradition of multiple international carriers, strongly urged more than one. Washington had been subjected to heavy pressure from major U.S. airlines, including Trans World Airlines and Northwest Orient Airlines as well as Pan Am, to insist on this.*

*After intensive, accelerated negotiations during the first seven months of 1980, the United States and China signed three economic agreements (plus a new consular agreement) in September 1980, when Vice Premier Po Yi-po (Bo Yibo) visited Washington to attend the first meeting of a new U.S.-China Joint Economic Commission. (For the texts of all four agreements, see *Department of State Bulletin*, vol. 80, no. 2044 [November 1980], pp. 1–25.) Most important was a textile agreement. However, although it was described privately by a U.S. official as "a compromise

Issues for the Future

Without a doubt, as economic relations expand, new issues are certain to arise. Some will pose difficult problems for both countries. Each country will be confronted with the questions of how far it wishes to go in expanding ties, cooperating, and compromising with the other and what the political and strategic implications of particular moves will be. The issues likely to arise will not be viewed from exactly the same perspective or be given the same priority in the capitals of the two countries, and they will reveal some conflicts of interest as well as important common interests.

While it is not possible to predict exactly what the agenda of issues will be during the next few years, some can be readily identified. From the U.S. point of view an agreement relating to energy will deserve study and very serious consideration. Whether or not the United States should grant China further tariff concessions under the so-called General System of Preferences will probably become an issue before long. The United States also may desire to discuss a possible general trade agreement that sets overall quantitative targets similar to those Japan and several West European countries already have signed. Before long, also, Washington doubtless will have to confront the question of whether to

---

about halfway between what the Chinese government and the U.S. textile industry desired," it left the Chinese far from completely satisfied. The civil air transport agreement permitted both sides to designate one airline immediately to start two-way U.S.-China service and allowed for the addition of a second designated airline within two years. The maritime transport agreement affirmed "the interest" of each side in "carrying a substantial part of its foreign trade in vessels of its own flag" and also stated that "both Parties intend that their national flag vessels will each carry equal and substantial shares of the bilateral trade." At the signing ceremony, President Carter proclaimed that, with these agreements, "the normalization of relations between the United States of America and the People's Republic of China is at last complete" (ibid., p. 1). This was an overstatement, since some of the issues discussed above remained to be fully resolved, and various other questions, to be discussed below, remained on the agenda for the future. However, the signing of these agreements in September did represent a climax in the Carter administration's effort to complete, before the end of 1980, the building of a structure of intergovernmental accords, on the basis of which economic relations can be further expanded in the years ahead. (Before the Carter administration ended, one further step was taken to implement an earlier promise. On October 30, Ambassador Leonard Woodcock and Vice Foreign Minister Chang Wen-chin [Zhang Wenjin] signed an OPIC agreement in Peking. See Department of State, Bureau of Public Affairs, "Two Years of U.S.-China Relations, *Bulletin Reprint,* January 1981.)

consider concessional aid to China. Finally, questions relating to the transfer of high technology will pose the most difficult problems because of the political and military sensitivity, as well as economic importance, of the issues involved.

Agreements on Grain and Energy

Trade in grain is of such importance to both countries—and is likely to remain so even if trade relations broaden—that it will be in the interest of both countries to ensure that trade is conducted on a stable, dependable basis. American interests require efforts to minimize disruptions that create unstable farm conditions and inflationary pressures at home, and because of the United States' responsibility for trying to ensure the availability of world food supplies at reasonable prices, American interests would be well served by a system of internationally supervised grain reserves, with China as an active and cooperative participant. However, since there is now little prospect that such a system can soon be created, the United States should consider the pros and cons of various types of bilateral grain agreements and induce the Chinese to discuss them.

At a minimum, it would be desirable from the point of view of both Americans and Chinese to conclude a short-term agreement comparable with those that China has signed with its other major grain suppliers—Canada, Australia, and Argentina—which would set minimum amounts China would be committed to buy and the United States would promise to sell over a stated period of time (perhaps three years, as in the agreements China has signed with others). Without an agreement of this kind U.S.-China grain trade could be subject to unpredictable, large-scale fluctuations in the future as in the past.

It is obviously in the U.S. interest to sell grain to China on a sizable scale. This does not mean, however, that Washington should encourage increasing Chinese dependency on the world food market. In broad terms, U.S. long-term interests will be served best if countries such as China are as agriculturally self-reliant as possible; hence the United States should actively assist China in its high-priority efforts to increase its own agricultural output. Nevertheless, since it is probable that China will continue to import large and possibly increasing amounts of food, the United States should try to ensure that it will continue to be one of China's major suppliers. The foreign exchange earned will be important to the U.S. balance of payments as well as to the incomes of American farmers. China now is the largest LDC buyer of U.S. grain, and because of the embargo placed on grain sales to the Soviet Union at the start of 1980 in retaliation for its invasion of Afghanistan, China's relative importance in the world grain market has increased (even though it is still not comparable in this respect to Japan and Western Europe). It is obviously in the U.S. interest that the China market be dependable. On their part, the Chinese have a vital interest in ensuring for themselves adequate sources of supply and predictable prices, which is why they have signed three-year agreements with other major grain suppliers. It should not be difficult to persuade the Chinese that their long-term interests would be served by an agreement with the United States that would give U.S.-China grain trade the same degree of stability. (One sign of an increasingly cooperative attitude on China's part regarding its grain trade with the United States was that soon after the announcement of the reduction of U.S. grain exports to the Soviet Union, Peking indicated a willingness to consider increasing its grain purchases from the United States.)[153]

If China's grain imports rise substantially in the future and fluctuate more than in the past, it may become desirable (especially from the U.S. point of view but conceivably from the Chinese perspective as well) to consider a more comprehensive agreement along the lines of the one that has regulated U.S.-Soviet grain trade in recent years. This kind of agreement would level out year-to-year fluctuations by ensuring minimum purchases by China in its good crop years and guaranteeing a certain level of U.S. sales to China in any year, and also allowing the United States to set maximums, if necessary, in years of unexpectedly high demand.*

For the future, another area in which some sort of broad intergov-

*During the second half of 1980, U.S.-China negotiations concerning a possible bilateral grain agreement proceeded without any publicity. In early October it was announced unexpectedly that the two countries had been negotiating such an agreement for two months, and not long thereafter, on October 22, it was signed. The agreement was precisely the kind of bilateral accord suggested above. It committed the Chinese to purchase (and the Americans to supply) 6 million to 8 million metric tons of American wheat and corn annually for the next four years. It specified that between 15 and 20 percent of the purchases should be corn. No special mechanisms were established (the sales are to be through regular commercial channels), no special credit arrangements were revealed, and no upper limit on Chinese purchases was set, although it was agreed that if China wished to purchase more than 9 million tons of American grain in one year, it would first have to consult with the U.S. government. See Seth S. King, "U.S. Signs Agreement to Sell China 6 to 8 Million Tons of Grain a Year," New York Times, October 23, 1980.

ernmental agreement may become desirable at some point is the field of energy. Concrete links in this field have begun to develop, and they are likely to become increasingly important. Strong mutual interests exist in expanding cooperation in this field. The rapid development of all energy sources is vitally important to China's entire modernization program, and access to American technology and know-how, particularly for offshore oil development, could be a critically important overall economic success. It also is in the U.S. interest to help China to increase its energy output, so that it can not only meet its domestic needs but also, perhaps, expand its exports of oil and coal. Because world interdependence in energy is now so great, any increase in global supplies is important—particularly to the United States since it is the world's largest energy consumer and importer—even if the new energy available goes mainly to countries other than the United States.

Developments during 1978–80 laid an initial foundation for cooperation in this field. The discussions started by Secretary Schlesinger and the protocol signed during Vice President Mondale's visit opened the door to intergovernmental cooperation in many energy-related fields, with particular emphasis at the start on hydroelectricity. The contracts that the Chinese signed in 1979 with major U.S. oil companies for offshore seismic surveys and discussions with other American corporations about possible contracts in the field of coal development seemed to be precursors of significant private sector involvement, which in the long run could be even more important, especially in the field of oil, than U.S. government assistance. (In intergovernmental discussions with the U.S. Department of Energy, the Chinese focused first on cooperation in high-energy physics, then cooperation in research in the fields of nuclear physics and magnetic fusion; however, neither area will be as important to U.S.-China commercial relations as fossil fuels in the years immediately ahead.)

With these beginnings there may not be any necessity for a broad intergovernmental agreement in the near future. Yet as relations in the energy field expand, the possible benefits of such an agreement should be carefully examined. Extensive cooperation on energy development would create new, mutually beneficial economic relationships, but such cooperation also could create situations involving critical national interests on both sides, raising complex problems affecting the two countries' political and economic interests. The U.S. government will have to make difficult decisions in the period ahead regarding the licensing of critical technology for energy projects, since many will require dual-use high technology with possible military applications. If large-scale U.S. investments are involved, which is possible, U.S. companies will desire supportive governmental action to minimize the risks. The Chinese, in considering major commitments involving American corporations, will want to have some assurance that these will not be undercut either by corporate decisions or by changes in U.S. policy. If the U.S. government provides support that facilitates large-scale energy projects, it can justifiably expect some assurances that mutual benefits will result. For example, in return for its facilitating major offshore oil projects (by licensing the needed technology), Washington (as well as the U.S. corporations involved) should require Peking to make firm commitments concerning the amount of oil it will make available for export. In any large-scale projects serious differences or disputes might arise, and methods of consultation on problems and mechanisms for solving disputes involving the two governments as well as the American corporations directly involved perhaps should be agreed upon. While conceivably all problems that arise in the future might be settled on an ad hoc basis, the time may arrive when a general agreement, and possibly the establishment of a joint intergovernmental body to regulate or oversee cooperative efforts in the energy field, will deserve serious consideration.

Preferential Tariffs (GSP)

The granting of MFN status, by removing discriminatory tariffs on Chinese exports to the United States, should boost China's sales in the U.S. market and therefore encourage two-way trade, but this alone will not put China on an equal footing with many other developing countries that enjoy the benefits of preferential tariff treatment granted by industrial nations under the General System of Preferences (GSP). This system, adopted by most leading industrial nations in response to a proposal by the United Nations Conference on Trade and Development (UNCTAD), permits duty-free entry of certain goods from developing nations. Since the start of 1976 the United States has granted GSP treatment to 140 developing nations or territories, and it is estimated that in 1978 GSP treatment affected about $5.25 billion of U.S. imports, roughly 3 percent of total U.S. imports.[154]

In discussions with Secretary of Commerce Kreps in May 1979, Peking officials reportedly indicated that China wished to be considered for GSP treatment by the United States. In October 1978 they already had been granted such treatment by Australia and New Zealand.[155] In the following month they requested Japan to do the same, and the matter was taken under active consideration in Tokyo. During 1978 China also negotiated with the European Economic Community (EEC) for GSP treatment. In December 1979 Prime Minister Masayoshi Ohira, during his state visit to Peking, informed the Chinese that Japan would make China eligible for GSP, "with necessary adjustments," starting in April 1980.[156] It appeared likely that the EEC would follow suit.[157]

The Chinese request to be treated, by the United States as well as others, like other non-Communist developing countries in this respect was another notable example of the new pragmatism motivating Peking's leaders. Few if any foreign observers would have predicted even a year or two earlier that Chinese leaders would request the special tariff treatment accorded to less important developing nations, if for no other reason than national pride.

To date the U.S. government has given no public indication that it is considering granting the Chinese GSP treatment. Not only are there still legal barriers—as will be noted below—to taking this step; doing so would in many respects be a major step, politically and psychologically as well as economically. It would underline the fact that in economic terms Washington is prepared to treat China fully as a developing nation, even though it is also a Communist-ruled country and a major power.

China obviously is, in fact as well as in the rhetoric of its leaders, a developing nation; and in the trade agreement signed in 1979, the U.S. government formally recognized this fact. In a variety of ways, moreover, American leaders already have indicated that current U.S. policy is based on the premise that not only is China now a "friendly" nation but also that its success in its modernization is desirable in terms of U.S. interests (with the unstated caveats that China remains friendly and non-expansionist and that its development is aimed primarily at civilian goals rather than at a major military buildup). If these premises of U.S. policy are valid and genuinely accepted, they logically argue for granting the Chinese GSP treatment.

In many respects this move would not be a radical new departure; it would simply carry one step further the effects of granting China MFN status and facilitating U.S. government assistance on a compensatory basis. The concrete, immediate effects might not be very dramatic. According to one study, although MFN status might increase Chinese ex-

ports to the United States by as much as 30 percent, adding GSP preferences might add no more than 4 percent to that figure.[158] Even this
amount would help to promote increased trade, however, and the long-
run effects might be greater. U.S. labor organizations can be expected to
object in this case as they have in others, because of deep-rooted fears
of giving special duty-free treatment to any developing nation that has
low labor costs.

Some of the major objections to granting GSP treatment to China
may be based mainly on political considerations. To grant GSP treatment
to China the President will have to certify that China is not "dominated
or controlled by international communism."[159] If this were to be interpreted strictly to include all Communist-ruled countries, China obviously
would not be eligible. However, if the phrase is interpreted to mean "not
supportive of Moscow-dominated international activities," China clearly
will qualify. Since this was essentially what U.S. officials did in certifying
China as a "friendly nation," this issue should not pose any real barrier.
Another basic question is whether the United States should make a
move that would so clearly differentiate its policies toward the two Communist powers. Washington should not permanently abandon the aim of
achieving some sort of balance in dealing with Peking and Moscow.

However, there is no reason to accept the proposition that even a
policy aimed ultimately at balanced relations must be applied equally
and mechanically to all issues. In shaping U.S. policy it is necessary to try
to distinguish between acts that the Soviet Union would consider major
provocations and that would be likely to evoke possibly dangerous, even
military, Russian responses and acts that simply support a policy aimed
at expanding normal relations with China and against which Moscow can
have no legitimate reason for taking strong counteractions, no matter
how much it may dislike them in general terms. Granting China GSP
treatment belongs to the latter category.

The arguments in favor of considering GSP treatment for China outweigh any arguments against it. However, whether or not this becomes
feasible will depend on China as well as the United States. Even though
U.S. law (the Trade Act of 1974)[160] gives the President considerable
discretionary power in deciding whether or not to grant GSP treatment
to particular countries, he is barred from granting it to any nation that
does not belong to both the IMF and GATT. Since China is not a member of GATT, the question is moot for the present. However, the United

States should be prepared to grant China GSP treatment if it joins GATT; if Washington indicates that this is its intention, Peking may be encouraged to take this step.

An "Umbrella" Trade Agreement

Another question that may arise in the period ahead, possibly before some of those already discussed, is whether or not the United States and China should consider signing a long-term, intergovernmental, "umbrella" agreement that would set overall targets for two-way trade for a period of several years. As noted earlier, China has already signed such agreements with Japan, France, and the United Kingdom, and it might be favorably disposed to consider a similar agreement with the United States. Such an agreement would be quite different from the U.S.-China trade agreement signed in 1979, which established a framework for trade, not quantitative targets.

The "umbrella" trade agreements that China signed in 1979 with other nations did not create absolute commitments on the part of either China or the other countries involved; they merely defined general targets. How much actual trade will develop will depend on the total of actual contracts signed. Nevertheless, the setting of overall targets can be of some importance.

From Peking's perspective agreements of this sort are useful because they set targets for both imports and exports, and therefore promote *two-way* trade, ensuring that the countries that are China's major sources of imports will try to increase imports from China. From the point of view of the other countries involved, such agreements are potentially valuable because the setting of targets helps to ensure that Chinese officials will give serious attention to purchases from these countries. Even though there is no guarantee that either side in such agreements will, in fact, reach the targets, the agreements ensure bilateral trade promotion by both sides.

The tradition of pluralistic entrepreneurship and the relatively loose links between government agencies and private business in the United States (especially in comparison with Japan but even in comparison with West European nations) are likely to argue against an agreement of this sort between the United States and China. One can also question whether or not there is a danger that such an agreement might raise some Americans' expectations to unrealistic levels. Yet there also may be arguments in favor of such an agreement. Even though it is difficult to judge the extent to which specific Chinese trade decisions are influenced by umbrella agreements of this sort, it is plausible that Chinese officials may give preference (though not necessarily automatically) to imports from the countries involved. To the extent this is true, agreement between the United States and China would at least reduce the disadvantages that American businessmen might otherwise have in dealing with the Chinese in competition with the Japanese and the Europeans. If nothing else, it would be of some symbolic significance, as another sign of the determination of both Washington and Peking to expand their economic ties.

Concessional Aid

U.S.-China economic relations to date have developed entirely on a pay-as-you-go basis, and none of the further steps under consideration would change this. The Chinese have not formally requested, and the United States has not offered, grant aid or credits on concessional terms. However, if present trends continue the question of whether the United States should consider giving concessional assistance to China, as it does to numerous other developing nations, is likely in time to become a live policy issue. One recent development increases the likelihood that this will occur, namely, Japan's decision in 1979 to extend substantial government credit to China on concessional terms.

The Japanese have led the way in the competition for China trade at every stage, and to maximize their share of the China market they have frequently been more willing than others to go beyond normal commercial and financial practices. Even some of the loans offered by Japanese private banks to China during 1979 can be regarded as semiconcessional— their interest rates are not only lower than most offered by European banks, but also lower than the rates the Japanese set on most loans to other LDCs (which has made some Japanese bankers uneasy).[161] While visiting Peking in December 1979, Prime Minister Ohira offered the Chinese a government line of credit amounting to about $200 million (in yen) for fiscal year 1979 at 3 percent interest to be used to finance six large railway, port, and hydroelectric projects.[162] (Reportedly, the Japanese government actually committed a total of about $1.5 billion, which it was prepared to extend in a series of low-interest loans for these projects over a five- to eight-year period.) It was said that the Chinese could use these credits for purchases from other countries, but Japanese industrialists stated that they expected 70 to 80 percent of the funds to be used to buy Japanese equipment.[163]

Chinese leaders have shown skill and shrewdness in the way they have encouraged the major industrial nations to compete against each other. Whenever one of China's major trading partners agrees to take action going beyond what others have done, subtle pressures are exerted on others to follow suit. It would not be surprising, therefore, if the Japanese decision to extend concessional government loans to China induces some West European governments to do the same, and in time the U.S. government will probably feel under similar pressure, particularly if U.S. trade with China lags behind that of other industrial nations.

The fact that Japan or European countries take certain actions does not automatically mean that the United States should do so, and there are reasons for caution about initiating any plan for large-scale concessional aid to China. The funds available to the U.S. government for concessional aid are limited, and most of what is available probably should go either to non-Communist countries with which the United States has had long and close associations or to the most desperately poor nations of the so-called fourth world. The sheer size of China's needs is sobering and argues against starting large concessional aid programs without careful consideration of their possible long-term implications. China could prove to be a "bottomless pit," capable of absorbing almost all the aid funds available—and more. Clearly, the initiation of large-scale concessional aid to China, whether by the United States, other industrial nations, or institutions such as the World Bank, could alter the present overall patterns of aid from the developed to the developing nations in ways damaging to smaller and poorer nations.

Furthermore, if large-scale concessional aid is given to China, although its immediate impact on the attitudes of the current leadership in Peking would doubtless be favorable, it could become in the future a special target of nationalistic, xenophobic individuals and groups in China, and could reactivate, more than any purely commercial relationships would, opposition from Chinese who still fear dependence and argue for "self-reliance."

On balance, probably the wisest course for the United States to pursue in the near future is to continue efforts to expand U.S.-China economic ties mainly on a pay-as-you-go commercial basis. However, U.S. policy in this respect should not be rigid. Even now there are good reasons to consider concessional aid on a modest scale for specific purposes. For example, giving aid to support training programs for the Chinese, in either the United States or China, would certainly be feasible and justifiable, and there would be compelling reasons to donate aid for humanitarian purposes if China encountered major disasters. The more difficult question will be whether or not to consider giving concessional aid to help build China's economic infrastructure, as Japan is now doing. Despite the already-cited reasons for caution, a case can be made for providing such aid for Chinese development in certain key fields—above all, those relating to energy and food. However, there is little basis for believing that the U.S. Congress and public would soon support large-scale concessional aid even in these fields. The most realistic assumption, therefore, is that Americans will have to develop bilateral economic relationships with China essentially on a commercial basis, basing most economic transactions on careful estimates of China's capacity to finance its development.

Technology Transfer Issues

The most sensitive issues that the new economic relationships between the United States and China pose for policy makers in Washington are those relating to transfers of high technology. While none of the major industrial nations can ignore the problems, the issues are particularly complex for the United States because of the unique nature of the triangular relationship among the United States, China, and the Soviet Union. Linkages between technology transfers, military cooperation, and broad geopolitical and military-security issues are inescapable. More than any other aspect of U.S.-China relations, policy in this area has potentially far-reaching implications for overall U.S. relations with both Peking and Moscow as well as with other nations in East Asia.

Understandably the Chinese wish to import advanced technology, including a good deal of "high technology," to carry out their modernization plans; they need advanced equipment and knowledge relating to computers, electronics, integrated circuitry, aircraft engines, satellites, and many other high technology fields. However, they also desire high technology to enhance their military capabilities and to lay the foundation for gradual modernization of their defense forces. Many kinds of "dual use" or "gray area" technology can be used—or at least carries knowledge that can be used—in military applications, even if that technology is purchased initially for civilian economic projects. For example, some equipment needed for offshore oil exploration can also be used to increase a country's anti-submarine warfare capabilities, and some highly sophisticated computers clearly enhance a nation's ability to build improved long-range missiles.

The United States has strong economic reasons for promoting sales of technology, especially high technology, to China.[164] Worldwide, American producers have been losing their competitive edge in many industrial products as countries such as Japan and West Germany have improved their positions, but it continues to hold a lead in many high technology items, including computers and aircraft. The United States, to help solve balance of payments problems, needs to promote exports of such technology.

A recent study of technology trade worldwide highlighted the importance of high technology exports, especially from the U.S. point of view.[165] According to this study, in 1976 high technology accounted for 10.9 percent of the total exports of fifteen leading non-Communist industrial countries, 12.6 percent of their exports to all Communist countries, 14.0 percent of their exports to the Soviet Union, and 10.0 percent of their exports to China. The percentage of high technology exports in U.S. worldwide trade was higher, and even though it was lower in trade with all Communist countries, it was relatively high in trade with China. In 1976 high technology exports accounted for 17.2 percent of total U.S. exports, 9.3 percent of exports to all Communist countries, 9.0 percent of exports to the Soviet Union, and 16.9 percent of U.S. exports to China.

Within the U.S. government in recent years there has been almost continuous debate over strategic controls among executive agencies as well as within the Congress.[166] While the Department of Defense has generally favored fairly restrictive policies, many officials in the Department of State and the Department of Commerce stress the benefits of expanded technology exports on both economic and political grounds, with strong support from important segments of U.S. business.

For several years a reassessment has been under way to review policy on high technology sales to all Communist countries, but many key questions have yet to be authoritatively resolved. However, during 1978–79 a consensus appeared to be emerging that the licensing process should be simplified and speeded up, that a "critical technologies" approach should be followed, and that efforts should be made to narrow the list of equipment covered by export restrictions but to tighten controls over restricted items. Those favoring such an approach (such as the authors of the so-called Bucy Report, prepared for the Department of Defense) have called for concentrating attention on restricting transfers of what they call "revolutionary" technology and have placed greater stress on the need to restrict transfers of "know-how" than on prohibiting the sale of "hardware."[167]

While general policy affecting all transfers of high technology has been under review, the question of what restrictions to apply to China has received increasing attention; and as U.S.-China political relations have improved and economic ties with China have expanded (and U.S.-Soviet relations have deteriorated), pressure to relax restrictions on sales of high technology to the Chinese has increased.

There are some obvious arguments in favor of relaxing controls on high technology sales to China. Not only is China now officially regarded as a nonhostile country (since 1979, a "friendly" country), but there has been a growing perception of parallelism in important U.S. and Chinese interests, especially on the basic problem of checking the expansion of Soviet power. However, there is continuing uncertainty about what the long-run implications would be of increased U.S.-China cooperation that could contribute to a major improvement in China's military capabilities, especially for U.S.-Soviet and Sino-Soviet relations, but also for relations with other Asian nations.

As relations between China and the United States have improved, Moscow's anxiety about the trend has steadily mounted. Even though they have had no valid reason for opposing normalization of U.S.-China diplomatic ties, the Russians have warned that expanded economic, scientific, and technical ties between the West and China (to say nothing of arms sales) will help China develop its military capabilities and make it a threat in the future. Most of all they have feared that transfers to China of high technology with obvious military applications will prove to be precursors of close U.S.-China military ties.

Consistently suspecting the worst about the motivations of leaders in Washington as well as those in Peking, the Russians have discounted all American claims that U.S. policy toward China is not specifically directed against Moscow. Warning Washington not to try to play a "China card," they have stepped up their efforts to "encircle" China, politically and militarily, most notably during 1978–79, by signing a treaty with Vietnam that greatly increased their commitment to the Hanoi regime, which Moscow then backed in its invasion of Cambodia.

During 1978–79, although the Carter administration stated repeatedly that it intended to maintain balanced relations with Moscow and

Peking and therefore would bar arms sales and apply the same restrictions on high technology exports to both of them, there was really no consensus in Washington on how the United States should deal with China in the context of the U.S.-China-Soviet Union triangle, or whether in practice the United States should apply exactly the same restrictions on technology transfers to Peking and Moscow. Some members of the Carter administration, including National Security Adviser Brzezinski, believing that improvement of U.S. relations with China could be a useful lever to exert pressure and impose new restraints on Moscow, tended to favor greater flexibility in technology transfers to China than to the Soviet Union. Others, including Secretary of State Vance and key individuals in the State Department, favored steps to improve overall U.S.-China relations, but believed that even the appearance of playing a "China card" could be dangerous because it might trigger destabilizing Soviet reactions; they opposed significant deviations from "evenhandedness" in technology transfer policy, as in other policy fields.

During most of 1978–79 such differences remained largely below the surface, and there was no significant change in the Carter administration's basic policy. The Chinese complained repeatedly during this period about the denials or delays that their requests for specific dual-use high technology items encountered, and in a few instances Washington decided, on an ad hoc basis, to license certain equipment for sale to China but not to the Soviet Union.

Then gradually the situation changed. Small steps were taken to establish military "contacts" with the Chinese, exchange military attachés, and initiate conversations on military matters. Increasingly during 1979, as U.S. officials stressed the existence of parallel security interests between the United States and China, they began talking about the need for some sort of "security relationship" with Peking, even in the absence of direct military ties. In the fall of 1979 (at the time of the mini-crisis over the Soviet military presence in Cuba) it was announced that Secretary of Defense Harold Brown planned to visit Peking in January 1980.

When Brown's trip was first planned it did not appear to have very far-reaching objectives, even though it was anticipated that his trip would result in broadened military contacts, that he would discuss basic geopolitical issues and security problems with military leaders in China and underline parallel American and Chinese interests, and that the

United States would use the trip to indicate some increased flexibility regarding sales of high technology to China. However, at first American officials tended to downplay the trip. They emphasized, with some justification, that the military-related developments in U.S.-China relations during 1978–79 involved no more than minimal security and military contacts of a kind any major power should establish with all other major powers. For years, it was pointed out, Washington and Moscow had exchanged military attachés and developed significant contacts relating to security affairs. (They also noted that the Soviet Minister of Defense recently had been invited to visit the United States but had turned down the invitation.)

In late December 1979, when the Soviet Union launched a major invasion of Afghanistan, the Brown trip assumed greater significance. This was the first time Moscow had used its own military forces to impose its will on a Third World country, which, though adjacent to the Soviet Union, was far removed from the Soviet sphere of influence in Eastern Europe. Whatever Moscow's motives in making this move, American leaders viewed it as a violation of tacit ground rules they believed had constrained big power behavior ever since World War II. In response, Washington imposed a variety of sanctions on the Soviet Union, one of which was a halt, "until further notice," to all sales of high technology to the Russians (it was said that future policy would be decided after a thorough review, which almost certainly would result in a more restrictive policy).[168]

President Carter, saying that the Russian invasion of Afghanistan had changed his basic views about the Soviet Union, called the crisis potentially the most serious since World War II. Some analysts proclaimed the end of detente and a return to the cold war. Whether or not they were correct, the triangular relationship among Washington, Moscow, and Peking was profoundly affected. Just before Brown left for Peking, a U.S. official asserted that the trip marked the end of "President Carter's preference for an 'evenhanded' approach in relations with Peking and Moscow."[169] Another official said that the invasion of Afghanistan gave the trip a "new dimension" and stated that "the Soviets have forced us and the Chinese into a posture in which we both see the world in the same way."[170] He noted that closer security ties with China were viewed by some U.S. officials as a principal way for Washington to respond to Soviet actions in Afghanistan. On his arrival in Peking Brown himself declared that if jointly threatened, the United States and China could respond with complementary actions.[171] He had come to China, he said, to "exchange views" on how Americans and Chinese "might facilitate wide cooperation on security matters"; such cooperation, he stressed, "should remind others that if they threaten the shared interests of the United States and China, we can respond with complementary actions in the field of defense as well as diplomacy." The Afghanistan crisis, he asserted, was an example of a situation in which "the United States and China find it in the self-interest of each of us to concert parallel responses to the world situation."[172]

Brown's discussions in Peking covered a wide range of topics that had earlier been put on the agenda. In addition, there was extensive discussion of Afghanistan and of possible ways to increase aid to Pakistan. However, at the end of his trip Brown told U.S. reporters that although there was a "growing convergence of views" on Afghanistan and the Soviet Union, there had been no specific agreements on how to respond to the Soviet invasion or on the coordination of Chinese and U.S. aid to Pakistan.[173] Both countries, he said, would act independently to help strengthen other nations in the area.[174]

The most concrete change in policy revealed immediately was that affecting sales of high technology to China. On the basis of an American decision made at the highest level in Washington before his departure for China, Brown announced that the United States would sell China a Landsat-D satellite ground station. Brown also said Washington henceforth would be receptive to Chinese requests to buy dual-use high technology equipment such as computers that could have military applications.[175]

The Brown trip signaled a new stage in the development of U.S.-China relations. One official on the trip stated that "evenhandedness" was "frayed."[176] Even though Brown and others in his party stated that the United States had not changed its policy of not selling arms to China,[177] some U.S. officials indicated privately that they did not rule out the possibility of making such sales in the future.[178] When members of Brown's party maintained that Washington still intended to pursue a balanced relationship with China and the Soviet Union, it was unconvincing, since they also asserted that "balance" did not mean "identity"; protestations of evenhandedness now had a somewhat hollow ring.[179]

However, it was not clear how much American and Chinese views did in fact "converge" or what statements about "complementary" and "parallel" actions really meant. Brown acknowledged that the Chinese still opposed the stationing of U.S. troops in South Korea as well as sales of American arms to Taiwan.[180] He also emphasized that China did not wish to buy large amount of arms abroad because doing so would make it too dependent on foreign suppliers.[181] Significantly, the Chinese appeared cautious about the idea of "coordinated" responses to Soviet actions.[182] Just after Brown left Peking, when he was visiting Chinese military installations elsewhere, a correction was made of the official translation of remarks Vice Premier Teng had made to him: Teng had suggested not an "alliance" against Moscow but that all countries should "unite" against the Soviet Union.[183] New China News Agency reports on the trip quoted Brown extensively as calling for "coordination" and "cooperation" in security matters, but Chinese statements talked only of "converging views," "parallel actions," and the need for each country to strengthen its "own defense capabilities" to cope with the new threats.[184]

Brown's trip did make it clear that Washington had decided to be more flexible in its policy on sales of high technology items to China. The fact that this policy shift was revealed at a time when U.S.-Soviet relations had reached a new low increased the psychological impact of the decision. The one new U.S. action announced by Brown in Peking was the sale of a Landsat-D ground station to China. A sale of some kind of Landsat station had been discussed with the Chinese for many months. In itself it had little strategic significance since the direct military utility of such stations is not significant. Images from such satellites are useful mainly for surveying crops and mineral resources; their resolution is not sufficient to be of great military use. (The United States has sold Landsat stations to several non-Communist nations.) While their sophisticated computers and taping systems will help China develop technology which will have military as well as civilian uses in the long run, there will be few immediate military spinoffs. The information obtained from the station will be controlled by the United States,[185] and, in line with U.S. general policy governing sales of Landsat stations, the U.S. government has insisted that the Chinese agree to make available to any interested country all data received and to allow site visits by American technicians.

Although the announcement of the Landsat decision itself was not significant militarily, it was the precursor of steps that went further. In late January 1980, just after Brown's trip, the U.S. government revealed that it was prepared to sell nonlethal military support equipment including early warning radar, communications gear, and trucks to the Chinese.[186] In March, at about the time of a visit to Washington by Vice

Foreign Minister Chang Wen-chin (Zhang Wenjin), the Department of State's Munitions Control Newsletter published a longer list of items that could be considered "on a case-by-case basis" for licensing, including certain aircraft and helicopters, airborne equipment, flight simulation devices, radar, navigation, and instrument flight trainers, search radar systems, fathometers and underwater telephones, telemetering equipment, aerial cameras, and photointerpretation and photogrammetry equipment.[187] In May, when Vice Premier Keng Piao (Geng Biao), the Secretary-General of the Chinese Communist Party's Military Affairs Commission, visited the United States (returning Brown's trip), he was told that the United States was also prepared to license the building of plants to manufacture computer circuits and transport helicopters in China and that concrete procedures had been worked at to implement the policies on dual-use technology transfers and the sale of support equipment.[188]

The rhetoric surrounding these moves appeared designed deliberately to warn Moscow of the possibility of closer U.S.-China security ties, without specifying how far the United States might go. In June Assistant Secretary of State Richard Holbrooke stated that between Washington and Peking a "serious dialogue on international security matters is now taking place in an atmosphere of friendship and candor" but that Washington had "only just begun" to address the "momentous issue" of what U.S. "hopes and objectives should be in the 1980s."[189] Holbrooke asserted that "the famous triangular diplomacy of the early 1970s is no longer an adequate conceptual framework in which to view relations with China." Because of the "increasingly complex interplay among power centers such as Japan, the Association of South East Asian Nations, India, the Organization of Petroleum Exporting Countries, and Western Europe," he said, "relations with China are not a simple function of our relations with the Soviet Union." Noting that Mao Tse-tung had told American leaders in 1973 that they "must not attempt to stand on China's shoulders to strike at the Soviet Union," he stated that U.S. and Chinese "perspectives and our policies may be parallel from time to time; but they will rarely be identical"; hence, "in the absence of frontal assaults on our common interests, we will remain—as at present—friends, rather than allies." Reiterating Washington's intention to "assist China's drive to improve its security" by selling it "carefully selected items of dual-use technology and defensive military support equipment," he stated, "We do not sell arms to China, or engage in joint military planning arrangements with the Chinese" because the "current international situation does not justify our doing so."

By mid-1980 it was apparent that the U.S. government had jettisoned its "evenhanded" posture of 1978–79 and was prepared to develop certain kinds of cooperative security relationships with the Chinese but not the Russians. However, it still was not clear how far such relationships might develop. Some U.S. officials emphasized that existing relationships were still very limited, pointing out that even Moscow has been willing to sell helicopters, transport planes, and trucks to the Chinese despite the hostility characterizing Sino-Soviet relations. Privately they indicated that they regarded the existing level of security relationships with China as "about right," that they did not view the moves made in the first half of 1980 as merely first steps toward much broader and closer military ties, and that they did not plan to move toward actual arms sales. However, Holbrooke's speech and other official statements clearly left the door open to further steps.

In the period ahead, the question of whether to stabilize U.S.-China security relationships at their present level or to move step by step toward closer military ties will be a continuing, critically important issue.

It obviously is possible to imagine circumstances in which the attraction of forging stronger military ties with China might be compelling. If the Soviet Union were to continue escalating its expansionist activities, if the polarization between Moscow and the other major powers were to increase further, and if the major Western nations, Japan, and China were to see a mounting military threat, the arguments for closer military cooperation might be very strong.

However, despite the clear need to develop effective strategic policies to prevent further Soviet expansionist moves, the international situation has yet to reach a point of irreversible polarization, and the objective of the major powers should be to try to prevent such a polarization. One aim of U.S. policy should be to work to achieve conditions that will make possible a renewal of some cooperation between Washington and Moscow, to strive for a more stable equilibrium among all of the major powers, and to restore a tolerable balance in U.S.-Soviet relations. As long as this remains an objective, U.S. policy should not foreclose the possibility of improving relations with the Russians.

Under existing circumstances, any crude attempt to play a "China card," implying the existence of a U.S.-China military alignment directed against Moscow, could result in increased dangers. It might provoke Moscow more than deter it. No U.S. sales of high technology and military support equipment can have more than a marginal effect on China's defense capabilities during the next few years. One contingency study made by the Department of Defense in 1979 estimated that procurement of sufficient military goods and services from the United States to give China a "confident capability" to defend itself against any Soviet conventional attack probably would cost between $41 billion and $63 billion, including $8.78 billion to $13.38 billion for high priority systems.[190]

One cannot totally exclude the possibility that under certain circumstances the Soviet Union might be tempted to respond with military actions, possibly around China but conceivably even against China itself. There is little likelihood that if this were to occur the United States could help China effectively defend itself. The United States doubtless would, as it has in the case of Afghanistan, respond with diplomatic and economic moves and perhaps even with military aid, but it is not likely that this would prevent Moscow, with greatly superior forces on China's borders, from taking effective punishing action. There is some danger that the United States might arouse unrealistic Chinese expectations about possible assistance, leading to disillusionment in the future, which could undermine the basis for good long-term U.S.-China relations. Perhaps recent Chinese caution can be interpreted as an indication that Peking leaders do not have illusions and may realize that excessive provocation of Moscow could pose new threats to their security.

The Chinese will probably continue to be cautious in developing certain types of relationships with Americans and will try to ensure that they are not "used" by the United States. It is also important for Washington to avoid creating situations in which it could be used by China. Under certain circumstances, future Chinese leaders might conclude, or at least hope, that steps implying increases in U.S. military support give them increased freedom to take foreign policy actions that Washington would oppose. If, for example, U.S. policy, even inadvertently, encouraged Peking to launch another invasion of Vietnam, the consequences might be dangerous; at worst, such an attack could lead to a Sino-Soviet military confrontation under conditions that would pose great dilemmas for Washington.

Even assuming that the probability is low that "worst case" contingencies of this sort will occur, continued movement toward closer U.S.-China military cooperation could involve sizable costs and risks. It could increase the polarization between Moscow and the other major powers, heighten tensions in both U.S.-Soviet and Sino-Soviet relations, and make it more difficult to restore tolerable relations with the Russians in the future.

Equally important, a significant increase in U.S.-China military ties, much beyond the level now evident, could create new questions and anxieties in the minds of leaders in many other Asian countries, including Japan and most of the medium and small powers in Northeast and Southeast Asia. These powers have, in general, strongly applauded the recent steps toward improvement in U.S.-China political and economic relations, viewing them as positive developments in relation to peace and security in the region. If, however, U.S.-China military ties were expanded greatly, and it appeared that Washington were pushing and supporting a major Chinese military buildup or moving toward a quasi-alliance, leaders in many other Asian nations, including Japan, might have serious doubts about the long-run consequences for them. Such a trend could have adverse effects on U.S. relations with these countries and impel some of them to reexamine their policies and consider options that Washington would prefer them to forgo.

In light of all these considerations, what policy should the United States pursue? First of all, it should continue to bar U.S. arms sales to China, and it should avoid rhetoric that is likely to heighten Soviet fears, alarm U.S. allies, and mislead the Chinese. However, the United States should actively facilitate and try to maximize the sale of equipment and know-how that will assist China's economic modernization. In making case-by-case licensing decisions on specific items of dual-use high technology, Washington in general should approve items clearly desired by the Chinese for civilian economic needs and should speed up the process of authorizing them. However, on particularly sensitive items that could have important military applications, the United States should require end-use statements from the Chinese and obtain their agreement to allow on-site inspections (which since 1979 they have been willing to consider).[191]

In making decisions on transfers of technology to China, the United States can legitimately take into account China's relative military weakness, technological backwardness, and lesser ability to divert technology to military applications threatening to others. However, the United States should make it clear that it will continue to show restraint. Leaders in Washington should scrupulously avoid the temptation to use such sales for anti-Soviet political or psychological purposes. Attempts to use technology sales to China for such purposes, or to exert political leverage on Moscow, are likely to be counterproductive.

More broadly, the United States should do what it can, difficult as it may be, to indicate convincingly to Moscow as well as to Peking and others that its decisions regarding high technology sales to China are not intended to be symbolic signals of step-by-step moves toward close U.S.-China military relations designed to threaten the Soviet Union. It should consistently maintain the position that although the United States will act in parallel with China where common interests justify doing so, it will not try to promote any anti-Soviet military coalition permanently hostile to Moscow. It should try to demonstrate that although it is determined to continue strengthen'ng relations with China, the United States will strive to achieve an international equilibrium and avoid long-term polarization of the world into permanently hostile camps, and recognizes that mutually tolerable U.S.-Soviet relations are necessary to achieve these goals. U.S. leaders legitimately can emphasize that whether or not this becomes possible will depend in large part on Soviet restraint. However, they should recognize that it will require U.S. restraint as well.

Washington should make it clear to Peking that it understands Peking's security concerns and desire to improve its defense capabilities gradually and will not try to obstruct Chinese purchases of defensive arms in Europe or elsewhere. However, it should stress that a premise underlying U.S. policy is that the greatest direct contribution the United States can make to China's security as well as to regional stability under existing circumstances is a strengthening of U.S.-China political relations and increased economic cooperation rather than arms sales or formation of an anti-Soviet coalition. U.S. policy on the sale of dual-use high technology to China should be consistent with this premise.

Even if such an approach is adhered to, many licensing decisions on specific high technology items will continue to be difficult. Moscow will probably continue to denounce all U.S. sales of dual-use high technology to China, but this should not deter Washington from authorizing the sale of items that will help China's economic modernization even if they gradually enhance Peking's ability to improve its defense capability in the long run. However, the United States should avoid sales that imply closer U.S.-China military relations than in fact exist and that are unnecessarily provocative to Moscow. Trying to maintain these distinctions will not be easy, but it is necessary to try, to ensure that expanded U.S.-China ties have stabilizing rather than destabilizing effects regionally.

Interactions of Chinese and Americans

The future course of development of U.S.-China economic relations will obviously depend in part on broad economic, political, and military-strategic trends. However, the success or failure of efforts to build a sound economic relationship between the two countries will also be influenced by the chemistry of Sino-American personal interactions. As contacts between Americans and Chinese grow, personal, institutional, and social relationships will have a major impact on the character of overall relations.

Even though, as was argued earlier, China's current turning outward could be not just another swing of the pendulum but rather a watershed in the recent history of China leading to much greater and more lasting Chinese involvement in the global economy, in light of past history it is impossible to say that the Chinese have resolved once and for all the dilemmas that they have faced for more than a century in trying to come to terms with the outside world. As Chinese contacts with foreigners have proliferated, the effects have been exhilarating for many Chinese, especially intellectuals and urban youth; but many are ambivalent about the consequences. Some are doubtless actively opposed to recent trends, fearing that Western influence will have a corrupting influence on Chinese society and that China will again become dependent on foreign powers and conceivably subservient to them.

In light of the fact that ever since the middle of the nineteenth century the catalytic "impact of the West" on China's domestic policies and external relationships has repeatedly resulted in periods of reaction, one cannot deny that this pattern could be repeated. The explosion of contacts with foreigners and influences from abroad since Mao's death has been sudden and fairly extreme, and the new policies have not been in effect long enough to judge what the long-term impact on Chinese society will be.

The nature of the impact will unquestionably be affected by the character of personal interaction of Chinese and foreigners. At best, foreigners dealing with the Chinese could have a constructive influence and help to inject into China the kind of dynamism that Peking's present leaders now believe is essential to achieve their goals. At worst, they could be the cause of growing resentment and friction that eventually could create a backlash.

Even though the United States has been a latecomer on the scene, since 1978 there has been a remarkable expansion of contacts of many kinds, on many levels, between Americans and Chinese. In late 1979 a Chinese scholar holding a high position in Peking's research establishment commented that a veritable "Americamania" had developed in some Chinese cities; he reported widespread uncritical enthusiasm about things American, especially among youth, but he also pointed out that it was based on an almost total lack of any real knowledge of the United States.[192]

The recent multiplication of personal contacts has gone well beyond those of an official or semiofficial sort. On the American side the new relationships have begun to involve, in significant numbers, American scientists, technicians, professionals, intellectuals, scholars, students, and businessmen; on the Chinese side the impact has steadily widened, especially in major urban centers. In the long run the intellectual and cultural effects could be profound, and the personal interactions clearly will help to shape the character of overall U.S.-China relations. American businessmen—and others who become deeply involved in economic relationships with the Chinese—will play a key role in this respect.

As businessmen become more deeply involved, their interaction with Chinese society will become increasingly complex, and this will create problems. In the late nineteenth and early twentieth centuries, although foreign businessmen—Europeans, Japanese, and Americans—helped plant the seeds of modernization in China, their attitudes and behavior also stimulated the nationalism, anti-foreignism, and anti-imperialism that led to their ultimate expulsion. In the 1950s Soviet advisers and experts gave crucial assistance to the Chinese as they started their industrialization drive, but in less than a decade the Chinese had rejected the Soviet economic model, and resentment against arrogant or patronizing attitudes added venom to the clashes of national interest that produced the Sino-Soviet conflict. These precedents should not be forgotten by foreigners now attempting to build new economic relationships with the Chinese.

The situation now, of course, is different in some basic respects. The nationalist, xenophobic reactions in the late nineteenth and early twentieth centuries were due in part to the legal structure of special rights imposed on China from the 1840s on. The "concessions," "spheres of influence," and "extraterritorial rights" resulting from treaties the Chinese regarded as "unequal" gave foreigners a privileged status, legally as well as economically and socially. But Chinese resentment was not due to the "unequal treaties" alone; the attitudes and behavior of many foreigners—perhaps especially businessmen—helped to stimulate anti-foreign feelings. These businessmen in China constituted a special elite group, living lives of obvious privilege. Only a few bothered to learn the Chinese language or to try to understand the country's society and culture. Most lived in enclaves, separated to a large degree from ordinary Chinese. Conspicuous consumption was the rule rather than the exception. In personal dealings with Chinese many were insensitive, even arrogant. Often they worked through intermediaries—the "compradores"—which limited the range of their own contacts with the society.

Now there is no legal structure granting foreigners a special status, and clearly none will be re-created. More than in the past, also, most foreign businessmen dealing with China recognize that they must adapt to the requirements of the Chinese as well as vice versa. Yet one cannot help but be struck by similarities to the past. The majority of foreign businessmen dealing with the Chinese now, as then, know little about China's society, culture, or politics—or even its basic economic system—and even fewer know the Chinese language.

Once again foreign businessmen, with a superior knowledge of technology, are trying to develop extensive relationships with the Chinese without adequate knowledge of the complex forces shaping the society. Only a minority of these businessmen appear to recognize that some understanding of China in a broad sense may be crucially important to the success of efforts to establish lasting and significant economic relationships. Many appear to operate on the assumption that trade and technology transfers involve problems that are essentially technical, culturally neutral, and apolitical. In actuality, the export to China of foreign goods and technology, to say nothing of foreign managerial concepts and organizational methods, may have far-reaching effects on the status and relationships of different groups within Chinese society, on the distribution of power within the country, and on social values and political attitudes that are subjects of intense domestic debate in China.

Some foreign businessmen dealing with China believe that, when presented with a specific problem, they can rapidly provide an answer based on experience in their own societies. They tend to be impatient when serious obstacles, rooted in local social and political as well as economic conditions, complicate their efforts. Many are interested mainly in short-run goals—in the "quick fix" and immediate profits—rather than in adapting what they offer so that it will be integrated and absorbed into Chinese society and be viable in the long run.

Ironically, for their own reasons China's leaders continue to treat foreigners in ways reminiscent of the past. Despite a lack of special legal status, foreigners again enjoy a privileged status. As in the past, they are usually confined to special enclaves, and the regime provides them with preferential treatment in housing, food, and transportation. Special stores give them access to goods not available to most Chinese.

There are probably several reasons for this special treatment. Despite their decision to open China again to contacts with the West, Peking's leaders still desire to control and limit the interactions between Chinese and foreigners. They also wish to show China's best face and minimize exposure to unaccustomed discomforts inevitable in a poor society. Yet the effect on many ordinary Chinese is to revive past images of foreigners as a privileged class, uniquely affluent and isolated from Chinese society. Even though the old legal privileges no longer exist, and despite the fact that much of the past arrogance of foreigners is gone, the special treatment given foreigners risks evoking nationalist and xenophobic responses, especially from Chinese who are skeptical about present policies or believe that their interests are adversely affected by current trends. The interaction between privileged foreigners and dissatisfied Chinese has often been explosive, and it could be again.

In fact, there already have been some public expressions of resentment against the special treatment accorded to foreigners that are doubtless just the tip of an iceberg. In late 1979 the *People's Daily* carried an article that dealt frankly with the problem as related to tourism.[193] The author stated that China has a tradition of hospitality and should receive foreigners "enthusiastically and with due courtesy," but this should be "confined to a reasonable limit." He stated:

It is rather common that anything dealing with "foreigners" is considered to be exceptional, places where foreigners go are often turned into zones that are out of bounds for others. In these places signs forbidding the entry of Chinese people have been put up and this makes one feel disgusted. In some places where foreigners shop, eat, and tour or [are] on their way to the airport, Chinese people are invariably shunned or driven away. Some people handle their countrymen very roughly in the presence of foreigners as if their countrymen were slaves. .... Chinese people are frequently refused entry to exhibition halls or other places of interest because foreigners are visiting there. On some passenger trains, the dining cars are often closed to the travelling public so that a few foreigners can eat.

The author summarized his views as follows:

The masses are in favor of taking good care of and making things convenient for foreign friends. However, the masses will not be satisfied with anyone who rides roughshod over others in the name of providing service to foreigners. It is necessary to receive guests politely. Nevertheless, the masses cannot allow others to show respect for foreigners by belittling and humiliating our compatriots.

By early 1980 there were signs of efforts to counter the current "Americamania." One example was a speech sharply criticizing the United States made by an American-educated university administrator in Peking to a meeting of Communist Youth League members. "The American people are good," he said, "but the American government and the capitalists are imperialists. We don't want to entertain any illusions."[194] The speech debunked U.S. society:

We saw that all Americans have cars, workers have cars, and they also have nice houses . . . but this is only one side of the coin. The other side is that wealth in America is unevenly distributed. Capitalists lead a life of debauchery and waste. .... Most of the workers are very nervous and worried. .... The United States also has great unemployment, and in the American social system there are family problems. If the mother goes to a son's house to eat, she must also give money. I'm not joking in the least.

Generalizing about the United States, the speaker said,

It oppresses and exploits domestically. Abroad it is expansionist, grabbing many colonies. Does the United States have colonies? On the surface, it doesn't appear to have any. But in reality it is neo-colonialist.

Attitudes such as these are part of the reality that foreigners dealing with China must take into account.

Despite the long history of U.S.-China contacts before the Communist takeover, as latecomers in post-1949 China American businessmen have less experience in dealing with the Chinese than others. Japanese and European businessmen started trading with the People's Republic in the 1950s, but there were no similar American contacts before 1972, and they have become extensive only since 1977. The Americans, therefore, are "playing catch up," a fact which creates special problems and dilemmas. To try to compete with Japanese and Europeans, some feel, understandably, that they must think big and act fast. However, excessive haste and overly ambitious undertakings could lead to serious problems and increase the risk of failure. American businessmen, as well as others, need to take a long view. To build viable, lasting relationships with the Chinese, patience is required to create a basis for mutual confidence gradually. While this is true of most international economic relationships, it is particularly so in dealing with the Chinese.

In major development projects, foreign businessmen will have to show more than ordinary flexibility and adaptability. They will need to consider how advanced technology and foreign management methods can be modified to work in a "socialist" Chinese setting. The natural tendency of many businessmen is simply to transplant what they know, intact, into a new setting. In the first burst of activity in China's modernization program, some Chinese technocrats appeared similarly simplistic and unrealistic, hoping that advanced technology and foreign methods of operation could rapidly be grafted onto the Chinese economy. What will be required, however, are complicated mixtures of modern and traditional methods, of high and low technology, of labor-intensive and capital-intensive approaches, and of "socialist" and "capitalist" modes of operation. Foreign businessmen, like China's own planners, administrators, and technical experts, will have to experiment to find viable mixtures.

American businessmen involved in cooperative arrangements, joint ventures, and direct investment in China will need to be particularly knowledgeable about and sensitive to Chinese economic, social, and political realities in order to succeed, especially if they participate in the management of enterprises. They will have to understand the nature of Chinese bureaucratic institutions; the relationships between Party authorities, government officials, and enterprise personnel; and the interactions of management and labor. Despite the strong commitment of China's present leaders to improve management methods and raise labor productivity, efforts to change old practices will encounter serious obstacles—from bureaucrats resistant to any changes, from Party cadres who fear a loss of influence, and from elements in the workforce whose interests will be adversely affected. Foreign businessmen will be compelled, along with Chinese favoring change, to cope with such obstacles. They will also have to learn the special importance of personal relationships in China. The new investment law and other economic regulations now emerging from the top levels of the Peking regime are essential to help create the minimal legal framework for economic cooperation between foreigners and Chinese as well as for more regularized operational procedures throughout the Chinese economy, but they will not suddenly transform old patterns of behavior based on tacit codes and values and on personal relationships rather than on legal norms. Foreign businessmen will have to acquire knowledge of these patterns and of existing webs of personal relationships to function successfully.

Another area in which Americans as well as other foreign businessmen will be called upon to show unusual flexibility is in devising ways to finance projects. While the Chinese intend to import sizable amounts of foreign technology, it has become increasingly clear since the "readjustment" of 1979 that they intend, to the extent possible, to solve their payments problems by arranging compensation, barter, and comparable arrangements under which the foreign costs of projects can be repaid in the goods they produce. To compete effectively in the Chinese market, American businesses will have to be prepared to consider varied types of repayment schemes.

They will also have to give adequate attention to developing effective training programs. China's present leaders are not interested in relationships that create a permanent dependency on foreign personnel or nations. While determined to upgrade their economy with foreign knowhow, their aim is to acquire an independent capacity to deal with their problems. Business organizations planning significant involvement in China must therefore think in terms of finite rather than open-ended periods of involvement and build into their proposals programs designed to train Chinese personnel on the job, in the United States or in Chinese institutions. They also will need to consider means to help the Chinese improve their research capabilities. Relationships between foreign businesses and the Chinese need not be brief, but foreign businesses must be prepared to adapt their roles as the Chinese absorb new skills and improve their capabilities.

Foreign businessmen will need to recognize the desirability of careful phasing in the way they get involved as well as the way they eventually reduce their involvement. Starting with large-scale, long-term, irrevocable commitments is unwise in most cases, from the point of view of the foreign businessmen as well as the Chinese. After reaching general understandings on long-term objectives, generally the most prudent approach will be to plan projects in stages, set limited and attainable goals for each stage, and agree that at the completion of each stage both sides will evaluate the results, problems, and prospects before setting further goals.

Matters of style also will affect the extent to which American businessmen operate effectively in China. To succeed, Americans will have to be activists in some respects, pressing for actions essential for the success of projects undertaken; but at the same time they will have to avoid arrogance and be sensitive to Chinese cultural predispositions and personal relationships. In general, they will probably have greater chances of long-term success if they maintain a relatively "low posture."

The prospects for lasting American business relations with the Chinese will also depend in part on whether or not U.S. corporations develop American personnel with real knowledge and expertise not only about effective ways of negotiating with the Chinese and the technical problems of implementing specific projects, but also about China's broad modernization plans and the social and cultural factors that will affect their success. Long ago most large Japanese corporations seriously interested in major operations in China recognized the need to have on their payrolls persons with broad expertise on China, including knowledge of the Chinese language. Few American corporations have yet done this. Some, wisely, have drawn upon the knowledge of qualified Americans of Chinese origin; these Chinese-Americans can play a special role in future U.S. business relations with China. However, American businesses seriously interested in long-term involvement in China will need to develop a broader basis for interpreting, analyzing, and dealing with China. They will need to ensure that some persons in the mainstream of their company operations acquire in-depth knowledge of China. They will also have to learn how to draw more effectively on the knowledge about China that exists in U.S. government agencies and academic institutions (which, on their part, will have to make a greater effort than in the past to communicate their knowledge effectively to businessmen and also learn from them).

Whether or not U.S. businessmen learn to deal successfully with the Chinese will affect more than the balance sheets of the corporations involved; the prospects for forging lasting economic links between the United States and China will be greatly influenced by the interactions between American businesses and the individuals and institutions with which they deal in China, and success or failure in broadening economic ties will have a major impact on overall U.S.-China relations.

Prospects, Benefits, and Risks

Peking's new foreign economic policies, which have opened the door to greater trade and broader Chinese participation in the international economy, have significant political as well as economic international implications that U.S. policy should fully consider. U.S.-China economic ties are still in an early stage of development, but under favorable circumstances they could become increasingly important in the period ahead. The United States should now pursue policies that maximize the prospects for growing and lasting economic links with China, the benefits of which could be substantial.

The most apparent, though not necessarily the most important, benefits will be those resulting from any increase in U.S. sales abroad, which not only assist American agriculture and industry, but also help the U.S. balance of payments. The potential of trade with China should not, of course, be exaggerated. However, with serious effort on both sides, the present volume of close to $4.5 billion a year could be doubled, tripled, and conceivably quadrupled in the years ahead. Even though this would still amount to no more than 1 to 2 percent of total U.S. foreign trade, it would not be unimportant. Apart from trade with Western Europe, Canada, and Japan, most American trade is widely distributed, and few countries account for very large percentages. For example, even though U.S. exports to China, though expected to exceed $3.5 billion in 1980, appear very small compared with sales to the advanced industrial nations (in 1978 U.S. exports to the EEC, Canada, and Japan were $32.1 billion, $28.4 billion, and $12.9 billion, respectively),[195] they look more significant, even today, if compared with exports to other developing nations. In 1978 U.S. sales to all non-Communist developing nations in the Far East totaled $11.0 billion and those to all the rest of Asia and Africa except for the Middle East amounted to only $4.8 billion.

In several commodities, moreover, China trade is likely to be considerably more important than the overall figures suggest. This is true, for example, of trade in grain, of which the United States is the world's largest exporter; in oil, of which it is the world's largest importer; and in high technology items, which are of special importance in U.S. trade. Already China is the largest buyer of grain among the developing countries, and it clearly is in the American interest to provide a large share of its needs. If by the late 1980s China can become a middle-rank oil exporter, which American assistance in offshore oil development could help to make possible, this too could be important from the U.S. point of view. And if China continues to be one of the largest markets for high technology in the developing world, the United States will clearly benefit from increased sales of such technology to the Chinese.

The potential political benefits of increased U.S.-China trade and economic cooperation could be as great as or greater than the economic ones. Expanding economic relations should help strengthen political ties with China in the period ahead. Even though closer economic links cannot guarantee friendly political relations, on balance they will enhance the prospects for good overall relations. To the extent that U.S. cooperation, both private and governmental, helps Peking achieve its developmental goals, this should contribute to political stability in China, increase the chance that Peking will continue to pursue pragmatic, growth-oriented policies at home, and reinforce the trend toward more moderate, cooperative Chinese foreign policies.

In addition, it could encourage Peking to cooperate more than in the past with the United States and others in dealing with global economic problems. From the U.S. perspective, this would be of special importance in relation to food and energy problems, but it might also help to induce Peking to adopt more cooperative approaches to other international problems. This would certainly be in the U.S. national interest. In the long run, increased Chinese involvement in responsible roles in the increasingly interdependent global community could prove to be the most important result of current trends in Chinese policies, and Washington should view its economic cooperation with China as a means to work toward this end.

For all of these reasons it is highly desirable that the United States pursue a very active policy aimed at increasing trade and expanding other forms of economic cooperation with China. In light of the difficulties the Chinese face and the competition Americans will encounter in the Chinese market, this will not happen automatically. To realize the potential for strong economic ties between the two countries that now exists, the U.S. government and American businessmen, scientists, technicians, scholars, and others will have to give adequate attention to certain prerequisites for success.

First, it will be essential to complete the process of establishing a sound legal and institutional basis for long-term economic relations. Notable progress has been made in this respect, but more needs to be done. Second, both U.S. government agencies and private American banks should give more attention to financing than they have so far to make the United States more competitive. Without adequate U.S. credit the Chinese may feel compelled to rely primarily on others.

Third, the United States will need to increase imports from China. In the near future this will mean permitting more labor-intensive, low-cost, Chinese manufactured goods to enter the United States. This will not be easy, but it is necessary if there is to be a significant growth in two-way trade. As an alternative to protectionism, Washington should be prepared to give more effective aid through means other than tariffs and quotas to domestic industries adversely affected by low-cost, labor-intensive imports. In time, U.S. imports of natural resources from China should grow, and every effort should be made to encourage this.

Fourth, the United States should make a major effort to sell technology, plants, equipment, and know-how to the Chinese. To help promote such exports, U.S. policy on the sale of high technology to China must be flexible in permitting the sale of dual-use items desired primarily for civilian development, even though for strategic reasons it should restrict items primarily of military value. Defining broad technology transfer policy and making specific decisions on licensing particular items will pose difficult problems. The aim, however, must be to encourage increased exports of technology to China while restricting sales that imply closer U.S.-China military ties than actually exist—or than either Washington or Peking currently desires—and avoiding unnecessary provocation of Moscow.

Finally, the American business community, with U.S. government support, must take seriously the potential of the China market and develop the knowledge and expertise necessary to deal effectively with the Chinese and compete successfully in the China market. Failing this, Americans will probably lose out in the long run to the Japanese and West Europeans. This might not be disastrous in terms of American national interests, but if it occurs the United States would forgo important benefits. It certainly would not contribute in any positive way to broad U.S. political and economic objectives.

Even assuming that the above prerequisites for success are fulfilled, developing broader U.S.-China economic ties will involve unavoidable risks. Success will depend on many political and economic variables. Any of a number of events or trends could have adverse effects on the process, and, at worst, some could derail it.

One variable will be the success of the Chinese in maintaining reasonable political stability at home, implementing their modernization policies, and creating conditions that attract greater foreign involvement. Peking as well as Washington will have to take further steps to improve the legal and institutional framework for cooperative relations, including passage of new laws and regulations relating to foreign investment, taxes, labor practices, and other matters of concern to foreign business.

The process of developing U.S.-China economic ties also will inevitably be affected by the general political climate in the region. Outbreaks of conflict in the Taiwan Strait or other disputed offshore areas, in Korea or Vietnam, or in Sino-Soviet border areas could shake the confidence of foreign governments and businessmen, reducing their willingness to support China's economic development and commit resources to cooperative ventures.*

*During the latter half of 1980, several developments revived the "Taiwan problem" as a political issue that conceivably could again complicate and possibly could set back, at least temporarily, U.S.-China relations. Steps taken or statements made both by the Carter administration and by candidate Ronald Reagan and others associated with his campaign created anxiety in Peking that the understandings embodied in the Shanghai Communiqué of early 1972 and the agreement on normalization of late 1978 might—from their perspective—be ignored or violated on the American side in ways which, they indicated, could compel China to respond in a retaliatory way. In June, when it was revealed that the U.S. government had authorized American companies to discuss possible sales of more sophisticated aircraft, the so-called FX, to Taiwan (see Associated Press, "U.S. to Let Firms Discuss Sale of FX Jet to Taiwan," *Washington Post*, June 13, 1980), Peking protested. At about the same time, when Reagan and others linked to him called for raising the status of U.S. relations with Taiwan, making them more "official," there was an even stronger Chinese response (see, for example, Fox Butterfield, "Chinese Criticize Reagan on Taiwan," *New York Times*, June 16, 1980, and James P. Sterba, "Reagan Revives Dormant Topic of Taiwan Ties," *New York Times*, August 24, 1980). The Chinese protested again in October, when the Carter administration granted "nonofficial" Taiwanese representatives many privileges similar to those accorded to official diplomats (see "China Says U.S.-Taiwanese Accord Threatens Washington-Peking Ties," *New York Times*, October 10, 1980), and in early January, when it was reported that leading figures from Taiwan had been invited to attend Reagan's inauguration (see Don Oberdorfer, "People's Republic Rips Invitation of Taiwanese," *Washington Post*, January 15, 1981). About the same time, when there were reports that the Dutch had decided to sell Taiwan two submarines, Peking threatened to reduce the level of Sino-Dutch diplomatic ties—a move clearly designed to be a signal to Washington as well as to the Dutch (see James P. Sterba, "China Attacks U.S. on Dutch-Taiwan Deal," *Washington Post*, January 19, 1981). By early 1981 Chinese leaders

While dangers of this sort are real, they are probably no greater—and may well be less—than dangers in other critical areas such as the Middle East, where the governments and businessmen of the major industrial powers already are deeply involved, economically as well as politically and strategically. The potential benefits of economic ties with China make the risks tolerable so long as these ties can be developed in the context of friendly bilateral relations and a regional climate that discourages major conflict.

The strengthening of U.S.-China economic ties should help to cement political ties and also contribute gradually to the development of "a secure and strong China," which, as U.S. leaders recently have stressed, would support broad U.S. aims both in East Asia and globally. If such ties help to draw China gradually into more extensive and constructive involvement in the international community, they will serve a historic purpose, bringing to a new stage the long search, begun in the nineteenth century, for a basis for long-term, friendly, and mutually beneficial relations between China and the West.

---

unquestionably were worried about future U.S. policy toward Taiwan, and high-ranking Chinese visitors in the United States stated privately that they viewed 1981 as a period of some uncertainty in U.S.-China relations, not just because of the change of administration but specifically because of the possibility of changes in U.S. ties with Taiwan. Clearly, the new Reagan administration confronted some delicate and difficult policy decisions and the problem of restoring confidence in the probability that Washington would continue to work effectively to strengthen U.S.-China relations. If it decided to act promptly to reaffirm the agreements and understandings on which "normalization" had been based, this probably could be accomplished fairly quickly. However, failure to act quickly could result in a significant slowdown or setback in the process of consolidating and expanding economic as well as political and strategic ties with Peking.

Appendix

TABLE 1. *China: Estimated GNP (U.S. Government Estimates, July 1979)*

Year	GNP (*billions of 1978 dollars*)	Year	GNP (*billions of 1978 dollars*)
1949	59	1965	185
1950	72	1966	210
1951	84	1967	202
1952	99	1968	204
1953	105	1969	226
1954	110	1970	263
1955	120	1971	281
1956	130	1972	294
1957	138	1973	332
1958	164	1974	344
1959	156	1975	368
1960	152	1976	368
1961	120	1977	398
1962	131	1978	444
1963	148		
1964	164		

Source: National Foreign Assessment Center, Central Intelligence Agency, *China: A Statistical Compendium*, Reference Aid ER 79-10374, July 1979, p. 3.

TABLE 2. China: Selected Economic Indicators (U.S. Government Estimates, July 1979)

Indicator	1952	1957	1965	1970	1975	1976	1977	1978
Agricultural production index (1957 = 100)	84	100	101	126	148	148	144	156
Total grain (million metric tons)	161	191	194	243	284	285	283	305
Cotton (million metric tons)	1.3	1.6	1.6	2.0	2.4	2.3	2.0	2.2
Hogs (million head)	93	146	168	226	...	...	292	301
Industrial production index (1957 = 100)	48	100	199	316	502	502	574	651
Electric generators (thousand kilowatts)	29.7	312.2	800	2,300	...	...	3,181	4,838
Machine tools (thousand units)	13.7	28.3	45	70	90	85	...	...
Locomotives (units)	20	167	...	...	...	...	293	521
Freight cars (units)	5,792	7,300	...	...	...	...	6,396	16,950
Trucks (units)	0	7,500	...	...	...	...	125,400	149,100
Electric power (million kilowatt-hours)	7,300	19,300	62,000	107,000	187,000	203,460	223,400	256,550
Coal (million metric tons)	66.5	130.7	232.2	327.4	478	483	550	618
Crude oil (million metric tons)	0.436	1.458	11.374	30.129	77.060	86.760	93.64	104.05
Crude steel (thousand metric tons)	1,349	5,350	12,220	17,800	24,000	20,500	23,740	31,780
Chemical fertilizer (thousand metric tons)	194	803	7,600	14,000	28,800	26,320	36,357	43,663
Cement (thousand metric tons)	2,860	6,860	16,280	26,500	46,900	48,600	55,650	62,240
Timber (thousand cubic meters)	11,200	27,870	...	...	...	...	49,670	51,620
Machine-made paper (thousand metric tons)	371.8	913	...	...	...	...	3,770	4,390
Cotton cloth (billion linear meters)	3.8	5.0	5.8	8.5	9.7	9.0	10.2	11.0
Processed sugar (million metric tons)	0.5	0.9	1.5	1.8	2.3	...	1.8	2.3
Bicycles (thousand units)	80	806	1,792	3,640	5,460	...	7,430	8,500

Source: NFAC, CIA, *China: A Statistical Compendium*, pp. 3, 6, 8, 9. This source also updated figures on other sectors of the economy.

TABLE 3. *Romanizations of Chinese Names and Terms Used in This Volume*

PERSONAL NAMES[a]

Modified Wade-Giles	Full Wade-Giles	Pinyin
Chang Ching-fu	Chang Ching-fu	Zhang Jingfu
Chang Chun-chiao	Chang Ch'un-ch'iao	Zhang Chunqiao
Chang Ko	n.a.	Zhang Ke or Zhang Ge or Chang Ke or Chang Ge
Chang Wen	Chang Wen	Zhang Wen
Chang Wen-chin	Chang Wen-chin	Zhang Wenjin
Chao Tzu-yang	Chao Tzu-yang	Zhao Ziyang
Chen Fang	n.a.	Chen Fang or Zhen Fang
Chen Hsi-lien	Ch'en Hsi-lien	Chen Xilian
Chen Kuo-tung	Ch'en Kuo-tung	Chen Guodong
Chen Lieh-min	Ch'en Lieh-min	Chen Liemin
Chen Mu-hua	Ch'en Mu-hua	Chen Muhua
Chen Yun	Ch'en Yün	Chen Yun
Chen Yung-kuei	Ch'en Yung-kuei	Qian Yonggui
Cheng Tzu-hua	Ch'eng Tzu-hua	Cheng Zihua
Cheng Wei-ming	n.a.	Zheng Weiming or Cheng Weiming
Chi Teng-kuei	Chi Teng-k'uei	Ji Dengkui
Chi Ti	Chi T'i	Ji Ti
Chi Wei	n.a.	Qi Wei or Ji Wei
Chiang Hsueh-mo	Chiang Hsüeh-mo	Jiang Xuemo
Chiao Kuan-hua	Ch'iao Kuan-hua	Qiao Guanhua
Chien Hsueh-shen	Ch'ien Hsüeh-shen	Qian Xueshen
Chien San-chiang	Ch'ien San-ch'iang	Qian Sanqiang
Chin Chih-po	n.a.	Jin Zhipo or Jin Chipo or Jin Zhibo or Jin Chibo or Qin Zhipo or Qin Zhibo or Qin Chipo or Qin Chibo
Chin Feng	n.a.	Jin Feng or Qin Feng
Chin Ming	Chin Ming	Jin Ming
Chin Shih-huang	Ch'in Shih-huang	Qin Shihuang
Chin Wen	Ch'in Wen	Qin Wen
Chin Yen	n.a.	Qin Yan or Jin Yan
Chin Yi-wu	n.a.	Qin Yiwu or Jin Yiwu
Ching Wen	n.a.	Qing Wen or Jing Wen
Chou Cheng	Chou Cheng	Zhou Zheng
Chou Chin	n.a.	Zhou Jin or Zhou Qin or Chou Jin or Chou Qin
Chou Ching-hua	Chou Ching-hua	Zhou Jinghua
Chou En-lai	Chou En-lai	Zhou Enlai
Chou Hsun	Chou Hsün	Zhou Xun
Chou Pei-yuan	Chou P'ei-yüan	Zhou Peiyuan
Chu Chin-ping	n.a.	Zhu Jinping or Zhu Qinping or Chu Qinping or Zhu Jinbing or Zhu Qinbing or Chu Qinbing or Chu Jinping or Chu Jinbing

TABLE 3 (*continued*)

Modified Wade-Giles	Full Wade-Giles	Pinyin
Chu Chin-shih	n.a.	Chu Jinshi or Zhu Jinshi or Zhu Jinshi or Qu Jinshi or Zhu Chinsi or Qu Chinshi
Chung Chin	n.a.	Zhong Qin or Zhong Jin or Chong Qin or Chong Jin
Chung Shih	n.a.	Zhong Shi or Chong Shi
Fang Hai	Fang Hai	Fang Hai
Fang Yi	Fang Yi (or Fang I)	Fang Yi
Feng Lan-jui	Feng Lan-jui	Feng Lanrui
Fu Chung-li	Fu Ch'ung-li	Fu Chongli
Hao Chung-shih	Hao Chung-shih	Hao Zhongshi
Hsiang Chun	n.a.	Xiang Jun or Xiang Chun or Xiang Qun
Hsiao Han	Hsiao Han	Xiao Han
Hsing Chung	Hsing Chung	Xing Zhong
Hsu Ti-hsin	Hsü Ti-hsin	Xu Dixin
Hsueh Mu-chiao	Hsüeh Mu-ch'iao	Xue Muqiao
Hu Chi-wei	Hu Chi-wei	Hu Jiwei
Hu Chiao-mu	Hu Ch'iao-mu	Hu Qiaomu
Hu Shih	Hu Shih	Hu Shi
Hu Yao-pang	Hu Yao-pang	Hu Yaobang
Hua Kuo-feng	Hua Kuo-feng	Hua Guofeng
Huan Hsiang	Huan Hsiang	Huan Xiang
Huang Ching-lin	n.a.	Huang Qinglin or Huang Jinglin
Huang Hua	Huang Hua	Huang Hua
Jen Chiu	Jen Ch'iu	Ren Qiu
Jen Hsin-min	Jen Hsin-min	Ren Xinmin
Jen Lo-sen	Jen Lo-sen	Ren Luosen
Jen Min	Jen Min	Ren Min
Jou Shui	Jou Shui	Rou Shui
Jung Yi-jen	Jung Yi-jen (or Jung I-jen)	Rong Yiren
Kang Shih-en	K'ang Shih-en	Kang Shien
Kao Lu	Kao Lu	Gao Lu
Keng Piao	Keng Piao	Geng Biao
Ku Ming	Ku Ming	Gu Ming
Ku Mu	Ku Mu	Gu Mu
Kuo Chi	n.a.	Guo Ji or Guo Qi
Kuo Chi-tsu	n.a.	Guo Jizu or Guo Jicu or Guo Qizu or Guo Qicu
Li Chang	Li Ch'ang	Li Chang
Li Chiang	Li Ch'iang	Li Qiang
Li Chih-sheng	n.a.	Li Zhisheng or Li Chisheng
Li Hsien-nien	Li Hsien-nien	Li Xiannian
Li Hsin	Li Hsin	Li Xin
Li Hung-lin	Li Hung-lin	Li Honglin
Li Jen-chun	Li Jen-chün	Li Renjun
Li Lieh	Li Lieh	Li Lie

TABLE 3 (continued)

Modified Wade-Giles	Full Wade-Giles	Pinyin
Li Teh-sheng	Li Teh-sheng	Li Desheng
Li Yung-chi	Li Yung-chi	Li Yongji
Liang Hsiao	Liang Hsiao	Liang Xiao
Lin Chu-wen	Lin Chu-wen	Lin Zhuwen
Lin Piao	Lin Piao	Lin Biao
Lin Teh-ming	Lin Teh-ming	Lin Deming
Liu Shao-chi	Liu Shao-ch'i	Liu Shaoqi
Lo Yuan-cheng	n.a.	Luo Yuancheng or Luo Yuanzheng
Lu Ting-yi	Lu Ting-yi	Lu Dingyi
Mao Tse-tung	Mao Tse-tung	Mao Zedong
Ni Chih-fu	Ni Chih-fu	Ni Zhifu
Niu Keng	Niu Keng	Niu Geng
Ou-yang Hui-yun	Ou-yang Hui-yün	Ouyang Huiyun
Peng Chung	P'eng Ch'ung	Peng Chong
Peng Teh-huai	P'eng Teh-huai	Peng Dehuai
Po Yi-po	Po Yi-po (or Po I-po)	Bo Yibo
Shen Ko-ting	n.a.	Shen Keting or Shen Keding or Shen Geting or Shen Geding
Su Hsing	Su Hsing	Su Xing
Su Shao-chih	Su Shao-chih	Su Shaozhi
Sun Ching-wen	Sun Ching-wen	Sun Jingwen
Sun Yeh-fang	Sun Yeh-fang	Sun Yefang
Sung Jen-chiung	Sung Jen-ch'iung	Song Renqiong
Teng Hsiao-ping	Teng Hsiao-p'ing	Deng Xiaoping
Tien Sang	T'ien Sang	Tian Sang
Tsou Ssu-yu	Tsou Ssu-yü	Zou Siyu
Tsung Lin-chung	Ts'ung Lin-chung	Cong Linzhong
Tung Chih-min	T'ung Chih-min	Tong Zhimin
Tung Tai	Tung T'ai	Dong Tai
Tung Yuan	n.a.	Dong Yuan or Tong Yuan
Wan Li	Wan Li	Wan Li
Wang Chen	Wang Chen	Wang Zhen
Wang Jen-chung	Wang Jen-chung	Wang Renzhong
Wang Tung-hsing	Wang Tung-hsing	Wang Dongxing
Wei Ching-sheng	Wei Ching-sheng	Wei Jingsheng
Wei Min	Wei Min	Wei Min
Wei Yu-ming	Wei Yü-ming	Wei Yuming
Wu Chia-lin	Wu Chia-lin	Wu Jialin
Wu Teh	Wu Teh	Wu De
Yang Teh-chih	Yang Teh-chih	Yang Dezhi
Yao Wen-yuan	Yao Wen-yüan	Yao Wenyuan
Yao Yi-lin	Yao Yi-lin (or Yao I-lin)	Yao Yilin
Yeh Chien-ying	Yeh Chien-ying	Ye Jianying
Yu Chiu-li	Yü Ch'iu-li	Yu Qiuli
Yuan Pao-hua	Yüan Pao-hua	Yuan Baohua

TABLE 3 (*continued*)

CHINESE PLACE NAMES

Postal form, or modified Wade-Giles	Full Wade-Giles	Pinyin
Canton	Kuang-chou	Guangzhou
Chengtu	Ch'eng-tu	Chengdu
Chienchang	Ch'ien-chang	Qianjang
Chinwangtao	Ch'in-huang-tao	Qinhuangdao
Chitung	Chi-tung	Jidung
Fuhsin	Fu-hsin	Fuxin
Fukien	Fu-chien	Fujian
Fushun	Fu-shun	Fushun
Fuyu	Fu-yü	Fuyu
Hangchow	Hang-chou	Hangzhou
Heilungkiang	Hei-lung-chiang	Heilongjiang
Honan	Ho-nan	Henan
Hopeh (or Hopei)	Ho-pei	Hebei
Hsisha	Hsi-sha	Xisha
Huai	Huai	Huai
Huatung	Hua-tung	Huadong
Hunan	Hu-nan	Hunan
Hupeh (or Hupei)	Hu-pei	Hubei
Kailan	K'ai-luan	Kailuan
Kansu	Kan-su	Gansu
Kiangsi	Chiang-hsi	Jiangxi
Kiangsu	Chiang-su	Jiangsu
Kirin	Chi-lin	Jilin
Kolomai	K'o-la-ma-yi	Kelamayi
Kwangtung	Kuang-tung	Guangdong
Lenghu	Leng-hu	Lenghu
Liaoning	Liao-ning	Liaoning
Liuchiahsia	Liu-chia-hsia	Liujiaxia
Nansha	Nan-sha	Nansha
Panshan	Pan-shan	Banshan
Paoshan	Pao-shan	Baoshan
Peking	Pei-ching	Beijing
Pohai	Po-hai	Bohai
Shanghai	Shang-hai	Shanghai
Shantung	Shan-tung	Shandong
Shansi	Shan-hsi	Shanxi
Shengli	Sheng-li	Shengli
Shensi	Shan-hsi	Shaanxi
Shihchiuso	Shih-chiu-so	Shijiuso
Shumchun	Shen-chen	Shenzhen
Sinkiang	Hsin-chiang	Xinjiang
Szechwan	Szu-ch'uan	Sichuan
Tachai	Ta-chai	Dazhai
Taching	Ta-ch'ing	Daqing
Taipei	T'ai-pei	Taibei

TABLE 3 (continued)

Postal form, or

modified Wade-Giles	Full Wade-Giles	Pinyin
Takang	Ta-kang	Dagang
Tangshan	T'ang-shan	Tangshan
Taochuan	T'ao-ch'uan	Taoquan
Tatung	Ta-t'ung	Datung
Tiaoyutai	Tiao-yü-t'ai	Diaoyutai
Tientsin	T'ien-ching	Tianjing
Tsinghai	Ch'ing-hai	Qinghai
Tsinghua	Ch'ing-hua	Qinghua
Tsunyi	Ts'un-yi	Cunyi
Tushantzu	Tu-shan-tzu	Dushanzi
Tzuliuching	Tzu-liu-ching	Ziliujing
Whangpoo	Huang-p'u	Huangpu
Yangtze	Yang-tzu	Yangzi
Yenchang	Yen-ch'ang	Yanchang
Yenchou	Yen-chou	Yanzhou
Yumen	Yü-men	Yumen

OTHER CHINESE TITLES, WORDS, AND TERMS

Modified Wade-Giles or
commonly used

romanized form	Full Wade-Giles	Pinyin
Cheng-jen	Ch'eng-jen	Chengren
Chi-shih Nien-tai	Ch'i-shih Nien-tai	Qishi Niandai
Chieh-fang Jih-pao	Chieh-fang Jih-pao	Jiefang Ribao
Ching	Ch'ing	Qing
Ching-chi Yen-chiu	Ching-chi Yen-chiu	Jingji Yanjiu
Han-yu	Han-yü	Hanyu
Hsia Fang	Hsia Fang	Xiafang
Hsia Hsiang	Hsia Hsiang	Xiaxiang
Hsin-hua She	Hsin-hua She	Xinhua She
Hungchi	Hung-ch'i	Hongqi
Jen-min Jih-pao	Jen-min Jih-pao	Renmin Ribao
Jenminpi	Jen-min-pi	Renminbi
Kung-jen Jih-pao	Kung-jen Jih-pao	Gongren Ribao
Kuoyu	Kuo-yü	Guoyu
Kwangming Daily or Kwang-Ming		
Jih-pao	Kuang-ming Jih-pao	Guangming Ribao
Li-shih Yen-chiu	Li-shih Yen-chiu	Lishi Yanjiu
Luan	Luan	Luan
Ming Pao	Ming Pao	Ming Bao
Pinyin	P'in-yin	Pinyin
Pu-tung hua	P'u-t'ung hua	Putonghua
Ssu-ching	Ssu-ch'ing	Siqing
Ta-kung Pao	Ta-kung Pao	Dagong Bao
Tang	T'ang	Tang
Ti	T'i	Ti

Table 3 (*continued*)

Modified Wade-Giles or commonly used romanized form	Full Wade-Giles	Pinyin
Tung-chih	T'ung-chih	Tongzhi
Tzu-chiang	Tzu-ch'iang	Ziqiang
Tzu-li keng-sheng	Tzu-li keng-sheng	Zili gengsheng
Wei jen-min fu-wu	Wei jen-min fu-wu	Wei renmin fuwu
Yang Wu	Yang-wu	Yangwu
Yuan	Yüan	Yuan
Yung	Yung	Yong

a. This list includes only names of public figures or authors in China itself; surnames are listed first, according to standard Chinese usage. (Chinese abroad, whose surnames are given last according to Western usage, are excluded.) In cases in which neither the Chinese characters nor the full Wade-Giles romanizations are available, it is impossible to know the correct pinyin forms, so all the possibilities are given.

Notes

THE general policies on romanization of Chinese (and Japanese and Korean) names and terms followed in this study were described in the Note on Romanization at the start of this volume. In these notes, however, the surnames of Chinese-American authors, or other Chinese authors writing for publications outside China, are given last rather than first, since this is the practice such authors almost universally follow; the romanization of their names follows the forms they themselves have chosen, no matter how idiosyncratic the forms may be. For Chinese authors writing in English-language journals published in China itself before 1979, when names were romanized in modified Wade-Giles, if neither the original Chinese characters nor full Wade-Giles romanizations are now available, it is impossible to know what the correct pronunciation of their names, and therefore the right pinyin form, should be. In the notes, I have given in parentheses two possible pinyin forms for such names; in appendix table 3 I provide all the possibilities.

Introduction

1. For historical background on Sino-American interactions and the impact of the West on China, see John K. Fairbank, *China's Response to the West* (Atheneum, 1963), and *The United States and China* (Harvard University Press, 1955); Mary C. Wright, *The Tung-chih* [Tongzhi] *Restoration, 1862–1874* (Atheneum, 1966); Joseph R. Levenson, *Confucian China and Its Modern Fate* (University of California Press, 1965); Warren I. Cohen, *America's Response to China* (Wiley, 1971); and Thomas A. Metzger, *Escape from Predicament: Neo-Confucianism and China's Evolving Political Culture* (Columbia University Press, 1977). The disintegration of China's traditional system started well before the impact of the West, as historians such as Frederic Wakeman, Jr., and Albert Feuerwerker have stressed, but Western influence accelerated it.

2. On China's traditional approaches to foreign relations, and its nineteenth century search for ways to deal with the West, see John K. Fairbank, *Trade and Diplomacy on the China Coast* (Harvard University Press, 1953); John K. Fairbank, ed., *The Chinese World Order: Traditional China's Foreign Rela-*

tions (Harvard University Press, 1968); and Immanuel C. Y. Hsu, *China's Entrance into the Family of Nations: The Diplomatic Phase, 1858–1880* (Harvard University Press, 1960).

3. For an interesting analysis of Chinese leadership groups, categorized in terms of their approach to modernization and attitudes toward the outside world, see Michel Oksenberg and Steven Goldstein, "The Chinese Political Spectrum," *Problems of Communism*, vol. 23, no. 2 (March–April 1974), pp. 1–13.

4. Levenson, "Ti and Yung—'Substance' and 'Function,'" in *Confucian China and Its Modern Fate*, pp. 59–78.

5. Many typical press statements of the period can be cited from the New China News Agency (NCNA). An article on February 14, 1953, titled *"Jen Min Jih Pao* [Renmin Ribao] Editorially Hails Sino-Soviet Treaty Anniversary," in *Survey of China Mainland Press*, no. 513, American Consulate-General, Hong Kong, February 13–17, 1953, pp. 13–14 (hereafter *SCMP*), stated, "To industrialize our country, the primary issue before us is to learn from the Soviet Union. . . . We must set going a tidal wave of learning from the Soviet Union on a nationwide scale, in order to build up our country . . . 'follow the path of the Russians' [a quote from Mao]." An article on July 30, 1953, titled "Chinese Communist Party Sends Greetings to Communist Party of the Soviet Union on 50th Anniversary of Its Founding," in *SCMP*, no. 621, July 30, 1953, p. 19, asserted, "The Chinese Communist Party has been founded and developed on the model of the Communist Party of the Soviet Union." On August 13, 1953, an article titled "Sino-Soviet Friendship Association Organs at Various Places Study How to Intensify Work," in *SCMP*, no. 632, August 15–17, 1953, p. 24, stated that the main task of the association was to intensify publicity on "Sino-Soviet friendship and learning from the Soviet Union."

6. It is difficult to judge the extent to which the shift of China's trade, from non-Communist to Communist bloc nations, resulted from Peking's own choice or was forced on China by Western trade restrictions during the Korean War. Both factors undoubtedly were involved. In any case, whereas in 1950 China's trade with non-Communist nations was more than double its trade with the bloc, by 1951, immediately after the major non-Communist nations imposed wartime restrictions, China's trade with bloc countries exceeded its trade with all other nations. Thereafter bloc trade steadily rose as a percentage of China's total trade, through 1959, after which it began to drop; see table 2-1.

7. For my analysis of the causes of the split, see A. Doak Barnett, *China and the Major Powers in East Asia* (Brookings, 1977), pp. 20–87. For numerous other sources on it, see ibid., pp. 340–41.

8. At a Party meeting held in December 1965, on the eve of China's Cultural Revolution, Mao Tse-tung (Mao Zedong), stressing the need to protect China's distinctiveness and to restrict borrowing from abroad to functionally useful "techniques," stated, "Toward the end of the Ching [Qing] Dynasty, some people advocated 'Chinese learning for substance and Western learning for application.' 'Substance' is like our general line which cannot be changed. . . . The 'substance' of Western learning cannot be applied . . . only the tech-

niques of the West can be applied"; see "Talk at the Hangchow [Hangzhou] Conference," December 21, 1965, in *Current Background*, no. 891, American Consulate-General, Hong Kong, October 8, 1969, p. 51.

9. For varied views on the "Maoist model," see A. Doak Barnett, *Uncertain Passage: China's Transition to the Post-Mao Era* (Brookings, 1974); Michel Oksenberg, ed., *China's Development Experience* (Academy of Political Science, Columbia University, 1973); Donald S. Keesing, "Economic Lessons from China," *Journal of Development Economics* (Netherlands), vol. 2 (March 1975), pp. 1–32; E. L. Wheelwright and Bruce McFarlane, *The Chinese Road to Socialism* (Monthly Review Press, 1970); Suzanne Paine, "Balanced Development: Maoist Conception and Chinese Practice," *World Development*, vol. 4, no. 4 (1976), pp. 277–304; Neville Maxwell, ed., *China's Road to Development* (Oxford: Pergamon, 1976); Werner Klatt, ed., *The Chinese Model* (Hong Kong University Press, 1965); and John G. Gurley, "Maoist Economic Development: The New Man in New China," *The Center Magazine*, vol. 3 (May–June 1970), pp. 25–33, and *China's Economy and the Maoist Strategy* (Monthly Review Press, 1976). Numerous other sources are cited in Patricia Blair, ed., with an essay by A. Doak Barnett, *Development in the People's Republic of China: A Selected Bibliography*, Occasional Paper 8 (Overseas Development Council, December 1976).

10. The "little red book" of quotations from Mao (first published in 1964 by the General Political Department of the army), which became a key symbol of the Cultural Revolution, had a section (21) on "Self-Reliance and Arduous Struggle" with quotations from Mao on self-reliance dating back to 1945; *Quotations from Chairman Mao Tse-tung* (Praeger, 1967), pp. 110–14. The summarization by Lin Piao [Lin Biao] of the essence of Mao's revolutionary strategy, in "Long Live the Victory of People's War," issued in September 1965, had a section titled "Adhere to the Policy of Self-Reliance," in which he argued that self-reliance had been basic policy since the war years of the 1930s and 1940s; see the text in A. Doak Barnett, *China after Mao* (Princeton University Press, 1967), pp. 231–36. Actually, however, the concept was not stressed during most of the 1950s but was revived in the late 1950s and then received enormous emphasis in the 1960s. Clearly, the intellectual roots of the term, tzu-li keng-sheng (zili gengsheng), can be found in China's past, and, in fact, it is reminiscent of the nineteenth century slogan "self-strengthening," or tzu-chiang (ziqiang).

11. During 1960–62, following the Great Leap Forward, Liu Shao-chi (Liu Shaoqi), Chen Yun (Chen Yun), Teng Hsiao-ping (Deng Xiaoping), and others undertook a major adjustment of economic policies (labeled China's "new economic policy" by many analysts outside China) which set precedents for some of the policy changes made during 1977–79; see Parris H. Chang, *Power and Policy in China* (Pennsylvania State University Press, 1975), pp. 128 ff.; and Byung-joon Ahn, *Chinese Politics and the Cultural Revolution: Dynamics of Policy Processes* (University of Washington Press, 1976), pp. 48 ff. In 1961 Mao himself said that China's approach should be one of "seeking truth from reality" (a slogan revived early in the post-Mao period). In fact, however, the policy changes during 1961–62 moved steadily away from what

Mao favored, until he began taking steps in late 1962 to halt the trend. Most policy changes in the early 1960s focused on domestic issues. However, some leaders favored a more moderate and outward-looking foreign policy. These probably included the then-chairman of the Peking government, Liu Shao-chi, although he denied certain later accusations to this effect, which were leveled at him by China's radicals; see Lowell Dittmer, *Liu Shao-chi and the Chinese Cultural Revolution: The Politics of Mass Criticism* (University of California Press, 1974), pp. 98, 107, 225, 236–37. There is reason to believe that Premier Chou En-lai (Zhou Enlai) favored more outward-looking policies at that time, as he did during most of his long career.

12. Alexander Eckstein, "China's Trade Policy and Sino-American Relations," *Foreign Affairs*, vol. 54, no. 1 (October 1975), pp. 134–54, described the beginnings of "China's new international economic policy" during 1971–72; he concluded that major changes started in late 1972.

13. See discussion in part II, pp. 123 ff.

14. See sources cited in part I, note 2.

15. See part II, pp. 125 ff.

16. See Communiqué, Third Plenum, 11th Central Committee of the Chinese Communist Party, December 22, 1978, in Foreign Broadcast Information Service, *Daily Report—People's Republic of China*, Department of Commerce, National Technical Information Service, December 26, 1978, pp. E4–E13.

17. This emphasis began during 1977. See, for example, the speech by Chairman Hua Kuo-feng (Hua Guofeng), on May 9, 1977, at the National Conference on Learning from Taching [Daqing] in Industry, in which he stated that China must "continue the revolution in the realm of the superstructure to make it harmonize with the economic base, continue the revolution in the realm of relations of production to make them harmonize with the development of the productive forces, make big efforts to carry out technical innovations and technical revolution and develop productive forces rapidly"; see *Peking* [Beijing] *Review*, no. 21 (May 20, 1977), p. 8.

18. See part II.

19. Barnett, *China and the Major Powers in East Asia*, p. 254.

20. Ibid., pp. 48–52, 193–97, 227–30.

21. China's new relationships with non-Communist industrial nations, its deemphasis of world revolution, and its perceptible downgrading of the importance of the Third World in its policies, discussed in part II, all testify to this.

22. Samuel S. Kim, *China, the United Nations, and World Order* (Princeton University Press, 1979), makes this clear, but he also describes China's growing activity in international organizations in recent years. William R. Feeney, "The Participation of the PRC in the United Nations," in Gene T. Hsiao, ed., *Sino-American Détente and Its Policy Implications* (Praeger, 1974), pp. 103–34; and John G. Stoessinger, "China and the United Nations," in ibid., pp. 97–103, also discuss China's gradually expanding activity in the United Nations.

23. See part III, pp. 309–15 and note 158.

24. After the United States, the Soviet Union, Japan, West Germany, and France (in 1978); National Foreign Assessment Center, Central Intelligence Agency, *Handbook of Economic Statistics, 1979*, Research Aid ER 79-10274, August 1979, pp. 1, 10.

25. After those of the United States and the Soviet Union; see Arms Control and Disarmament Agency, *World Military Expenditures and Arms Transfers, 1966–75*, ACDA Publication 90, December 1976. The latest figures in this source are for 1975. Ruth Leger Sivard, *World Military and Social Expenditures, 1976* (Leesburg, Va.: WMSE Publications, 1976), p. 15, lists China as fourth (after West Germany), but her figure for China is too low.

26. See NFAC, CIA, *Handbook of Economic Statistics, 1979*, pp. 128–29.

27. As of 1976; see CIA, *Handbook of Economic Statistics, 1977*, ER 77-10537, September 1977, p. 78. In a table of estimates of "proved" reserves in 1978, NFAC, CIA, *Handbook of Economic Statistics, 1979*, p. 131, lists China third in coal, ninth in oil, and fifteenth in natural gas. For a definition of "primary energy," see part IV, note 2.

28. See K. P. Wang, *The People's Republic of China: A New Industrial Power with a Strong Mineral Base* (Department of the Interior, U.S. Bureau of Mines, 1975); and "China's Mineral Economy," in Joint Economic Committee, *Chinese Economy Post-Mao*, 95 Cong. 2 sess. (Government Printing Office, 1978), pp. 370–402.

29. See CIA, *Handbook of Economic Statistics, 1977*, pp. 91, 93, 94, 96, 99, 103, 106, 108, 124. Most figures given are for 1976 (but a few are for 1975).

30. See NFAC, CIA, *Handbook of Economic Statistics, 1979*, pp. 113, 118, 120, 121, 123; the figures are for 1978, except in the cases of radio receivers and trucks and buses (which are for 1975). Since this source lacks estimates for Chinese mainline diesel locomotives, the ranking in this case is based on 1975 figures in the 1977 handbook, p. 119.

31. See the discussion in part II.

32. Based on International Monetary Fund, *Direction of Trade, Annual 1971–77* (IMF, 1978), pp. 2, 4, 6.

33. It was just over 0.5 percent; my calculation from ibid.

Part I

1. For background on China's economy and development, see Alexander Eckstein, *China's Economic Revolution* (Cambridge University Press, 1977), and *China's Economic Development: The Interplay of Scarcity and Ideology* (University of Michigan Press, 1975); Dwight H. Perkins, ed., *China's Modern Economy in Historical Perspective* (Stanford University Press, 1975); Allen S. Whiting and Robert F. Dernberger, *China's Future, Foreign Policy and Economic Development in the Post-Mao Era* (McGraw-Hill for the Council on Foreign Relations, 1977); Audrey G. Donnithorne, *China's Economic System* (London: Allen and Unwin, 1967); Nai-Ruenn Chen and Walter Galenson, *The Chinese Economy under Communism* (Chicago: Aldine, 1969); Alexander Eckstein, Walter Galenson, and Ta-chung Liu, eds., *Economic*

Trends in Communist China (Aldine, 1968); Jan S. Prybla, *The Political Economy of Communist China* (International Textbook Co., 1979); Chu-yuan Cheng, *Communist China's Economy, 1949–1962, Structural Changes and Crisis* (Seton Hall University Press, 1963); and Yuan-li Wu, *The Economy of Communist China: An Introduction* (Praeger, 1965). Specialized studies on the economy, especially in the 1950s, that provide baseline data (and analyses of growth) important for later analyses include Ta-chung Liu and Kung-chia Yeh [K. C. Yeh], *The Economy of the Chinese Mainland: National Income and Economic Development, 1933–1959* (Princeton University Press, 1959); Yuan-li Wu, *The Economic Potential of Communist China* (Stanford Research Institute, 1963); Alexander Eckstein, *National Income of Communist China* (Free Press, 1961); Dwight H. Perkins, *Market Control and Planning in Communist China* (Harvard University Press, 1966); and Choh-ming Li, *Economic Development of Communist China* (University of California Press, 1959). Collected statistics for the 1950s are in Nai-Ruenn Chen, ed., *Chinese Economic Statistics: A Handbook for Mainland China* (Aldine, 1967); and State Statistical Bureau, *Ten Great Years* (Peking [Beijing]: Foreign Languages Press, 1960).

Since the second half of the 1960s the best collections of descriptive and analytical studies on current trends in the Chinese economy (containing contributions by both leading scholars and government specialists) have been periodic volumes published by the Joint Economic Committee (JEC) of the U.S. Congress. These include *Chinese Economy Post-Mao*, 95 Cong. 2 sess. (Government Printing Office, 1978), vol. 1; *China: A Reassessment of the Economy*, 94 Cong. 1 sess. (GPO, 1975); *People's Republic of China: An Economic Assessment*, 92 Cong. 2 sess. (GPO, 1972); and *An Economic Profile of Mainland China*, 2 vols., 90 Cong. 1 sess. (GPO, 1967). Some of the best comprehensive current reports on the Chinese economy are in *Far Eastern Economic Review* (Hong Kong) and *China Business Review* (originally *U.S.-China Business Review*). A useful bibliography is Patricia Blair, with an essay by A. Doak Barnett, *Development in the People's Republic of China: A Selected Bibliography*, Occasional Paper 8 (Overseas Development Council, December 1976). Chronologies of major developments appear in each issue of the *China Quarterly* (London). Two useful Japanese studies (in English) that contain data comparable to (though not identical with) data in U.S. studies are Japan External Trade Organization, *China, A Business Guide: The Japanese Perspective on China's Opening Economy* (Tokyo: JETRO, 1979); and Japan Economic Research Center, *A Study on Japan-China Economic Relations* (Tokyo: JERC, 1979). For the sake of consistency, however, I generally have used U.S. statistical data.

2. Domestic policy debates and processes in China are analyzed in A. Doak Barnett, *Uncertain Passage: China's Transition to the Post-Mao Era* (Brookings, 1974); Parris H. Chang, *Power and Policy in China*, 2nd ed. (Pennsylvania State University Press, 1978); Lowell Dittmer, *Liu Shao-ch'i* [Liu Shaoqi] *and the Chinese Cultural Revolution: The Politics of Mass Criticism* (University of California Press, 1974); Richard Baum, *Prelude to Revolution:*

Mao, the Party, and the Peasant Question, 1962–66 (Columbia University Press, 1975); Richard Baum and Frederick C. Teiwes, *Ssu-Ching* [Siqing]: *The Socialist Education Movement of 1962–1966,* China Research Monograph 2 (Center for Chinese Studies, University of California, Berkeley, 1968); Stuart R. Schram, ed., *Authority, Participation, and Cultural Change in China: Essays by a European Study Group* (Cambridge University Press, 1973); Byung-joon Ahn, *Chinese Politics and the Cultural Revolution: Dynamics of Policy Processes* (University of Washington Press, 1976); Roderick Mac-Farquhar, *The Origins of the Cultural Revolution,* vol. 1: *Contradictions among the People, 1956–1957* (Columbia University Press, 1974); Franz Schurmann, *Ideology and Organization in Communist China* (University of California Press, 1966); John M. H. Lindbeck, ed., *China: Management of a Revolutionary Society* (University of Washington Press, 1971); and Richard H. Solomon, *Mao's Revolution and the Chinese Political Culture* (University of California Press, 1971). Ideological aspects of the debates are analyzed in Stuart R. Schram, *The Political Thought of Mao Tse-tung* [Mao Zedong], rev. ed. (Praeger, 1969); Benjamin I. Schwartz, *Communism and China: Ideology in Flux* (Harvard University Press, 1968); Chalmers Johnson, ed., *Ideology and Politics in Contemporary China* (University of Washington Press, 1973); James Chieh Hsiung, *Ideology and Practice, The Evolution of Chinese Communism* (Praeger, 1970), and *The Logic of "Maoism," Critiques and Explication* (Praeger, 1974); and Frederick Wakeman, Jr., *History and Will: Philosophical Perspectives on Mao Tse-tung's Thought* (University of California Press, 1973). Stuart R. Schram, ed., *Chairman Mao Talks to the People: Talks and Letters, 1956–1971;* and Jerome Chen, ed., *Mao* (Prentice-Hall, 1969), are collections of Mao's statements that give revealing insights into his views on key issues. Valuable additional material on Mao may be found in Joint Publication Research Service (JPRS), "Miscellany of Mao Tse-tung Thought, 1949–1968," pt. I, JPRS 61269-1, February 20, 1974, and pt. II, JPRS 61269-2, February 20, 1974. The official (edited) versions of many of Mao's major statements are in the five published volumes of *Selected Works of Mao Tse-Tung* (Peking: Foreign Languages Press); volume 5 (1977) deals with the years 1949–57. For a collection of articles on economic issues mainly reflecting the "radicals'" views, see Gordon Bennett, ed., *China Finance and Trade: A Policy Reader* (Sharpe, 1978). For general background on the basic political system and political processes which have shaped ideological and policy debates, see Lucian W. Pye, *The Spirit of Chinese Politics* (MIT Press, 1968), and *China, An Introduction* (Little, Brown, 1972); and James R. Townsend, *Politics in China* (Little, Brown, 1974).

3. On the post-Great Leap policies, see Chang, *Power and Policy in China,* chap. 5; Ahn, *Chinese Politics and the Cultural Revolution,* pp. 137–57; Dittmer, *Liu Shao-chi and the Chinese Cultural Revolution,* pp. 246–67; and Thomas Fingar and Genevieve Dean, "Recent Policy Trends in Industrial Science and Technology: An Overview," paper prepared for the Workshop on the Development of Industrial Science and Technology in the PRC, Bermuda, January 1979. On the first steps toward a new policy in the early 1970s,

see Alexander Eckstein, "China's Trade Policy and Sino-American Relations," *Foreign Affairs*, vol. 54, no. 1 (October 1975), pp. 134 ff.

4. This statement is not simply made with the benefit of hindsight. For my earlier predictions, see A. Doak Barnett, *China after Mao* (Princeton University Press, 1967); *Uncertain Passage;* "The Policy Context," chap. 1 in Organization for Economic Cooperation and Development, *Science and Technology in the People's Republic of China* (Paris: OECD, 1977); and "Round One in China's Succession: The Shift toward Pragmatism," *Current Scene* (Hong Kong), vol. 15, no. 1 (January 1977).

5. *Peking Review* (later *Beijing Review*), no. 1 (January 1, 1965), p. 6; this formulation was later revived and labeled the "four modernizations."

6. *Peking Review*, no. 4 (January 24, 1975), p. 23.

7. For information on the career of Teng Hsiao-ping (Deng Xiaoping) in the 1950s and how he developed the strong power base which was crucial to his reemergence after Mao's death, see Donald W. Klein and Anne B. Clark, eds., *Biographic Dictionary of Chinese Communism, 1921–1965* (Harvard University Press, 1971), vol. 2, pp. 819–26; Howard L. Boorman, ed., *Biographical Dictionary of Republican China* (Columbia University Press, 1970), vol. 3, pp. 252–54; and Union Research Service, *Who's Who in Communist China* (Hong Kong: URI, 1970), vol. 2, pp. 610–12.

8. For texts smuggled out of China and published in Taiwan, see "On the General Program of All Work of the (Whole) Party and the (Whole) Country," *Issues and Studies* (Taiwan), vol. 13, no. 8 (August 1977), pp. 77–99; "Some Problems in Speeding Up Industrial Development" (often referred to as the "twenty points," although actually there were eighteen), *Issues and Studies*, vol. 13, no. 7 (July 1977), pp. 90–112; and "Several Questions Concerning the Work of Science and Technology," *Issues and Studies*, vol. 13, no. 9 (September 1977), pp. 63–70. For information on the background of these documents, see John Gittings, "New Material on Teng Hsiao-ping," *China Quarterly*, no. 67 (September 1976), pp. 489–93.

9. This criticism explicitly named Teng as the target after his second purge. (The Central Committee ousted him from all posts on April 7, 1976, the same day Hua Kuo-feng [Hua Guofeng] was appointed first Vice Chairman of the Central Committee and Premier.) Criticism reached a peak between then and Mao's death in September 1976. *Peking Review* carried a series of articles strongly criticizing both Teng personally and the three documents: Chin Chih-po (Jin Zhibo or Qin Zhibo?), "Denial of the Difference between Socialism and Capitalism Is Not Allowed—Repudiating the Theme about 'White Cat, Black Cat,'" no. 16 (April 16, 1976), pp. 18–21; Li Chang (Li Chang), "Teng Hsiao-ping's Total Betrayal of Marxism," no. 23 (June 4, 1976), pp. 13–18; Chung Shih (Zhong Shi or Chong Shi?), "Criticize Teng Hsiao-ping's Revisionist Fallacies on the Industrial and Transport Front," no. 24 (June 11, 1976), pp. 8–12; Mass Criticism Group of Peking and Tsinghua (Qinghua) universities, "A Confession of Attempts at Reversal of Verdicts and Restoration—Criticizing an Article Concocted at Teng Hsiao-ping's Bidding," no. 28 (July 9, 1976), pp. 9–12; *People's Daily* (*Jen-min Jih-pao* or *Renmin Ribao*)

editorial on August 23, 1976, "Grasp the Crucial Point and Deepen the Criticism of Teng Hsiao-ping," no. 35 (August 27, 1976), pp. 5–6; and Kao Lu (Gao Lu) and Chang Ko (Zhang Ke or Chang Ge?), "Comments on Teng Hsiao-ping's Economic Ideas of the Compradore Bourgeoisie," no. 35 (August 27, 1976), pp. 6–9.

10. "On the Ten Major Relationships" (or "On Ten Great Relationships") was first delivered by Mao as a speech to an enlarged Politburo meeting on April 25, 1956, but it was not published at that time. For the new official version (first published in China on December 25, 1976), see *Peking Review*, no. 1 (January 1, 1977), pp. 10–25. See also note 85.

11. Immediately after Mao's death the standard adjectives describing him were "most esteemed and beloved great leader and teacher" (see Hua Kuo-feng, "Speech at the Second National Conference on Learning from Tachai [Dazhai] in Agriculture," *Peking Review*, no. 1 [January 1, 1977], p. 33). However, within a year he generally was referred to simply as "our great leader and teacher" (see "Vice Chairman Yeh Chien-ying's [Ye Jianying's] Speech at the Grand Rally Celebrating the 50th Anniversary of the Founding of the Chinese People's Liberation Army," *Peking Review*, no. 32 [August 5, 1977], p. 32). From the start Chou En-lai (Zhou Enlai) was labeled "our esteemed and beloved Premier" (see the sources cited above). This label stuck, and the praise of Chou became increasingly fulsome over time; see Theoretical Group of the General Office of the State Council, "In Commemoration of the First Anniversary of the Passing of Our Esteemed and Beloved Premier Chou En-lai," *Peking Review*, no. 3 (January 14, 1977), pp. 8–21, reprinted from *Red Flag*, no. 1 (1977).

12. See National Foreign Assessment Center, Central Intelligence Agency, *China: In Pursuit of Economic Modernization*, Research Paper ER 78-10680, December 1978, pp. 1–2; and CIA, *Current Economic Problems and the Prospects for 1985*, March 9, 1978, pp. 1–2.

13. See table 1-1 for GNP estimate. In writing the section that follows I have made extensive use of the general sources listed in note 1, but for statistics I have relied primarily on CIA estimates for the years when no official Chinese data were published, and on available Chinese official figures for the 1950s and for the years since 1977 (see table 1-3). Some of the earlier CIA statistical compendia that I used are CIA, *People's Republic of China: Handbook of Economic Indicators*, Research Aid A ER 75-72, August 1975, and *People's Republic of China: Handbook of Economic Indicators*, Research Aid ER 76-10540, August 1976; NFAC, CIA, *China: Economic Indicators*, Reference Aid ER 77-10508, October 1977, and *China: Economic Indicators*, Reference Aid ER 78-10750, December 1978. Tables 1-1 and 1-2 contain selected figures and estimates from these sources. However, since mid-1979 China's State Statistical Bureau (SSB) and Ministry of Finance again have published communiqués and other reports containing fairly extensive statistics, and I have used them; see tables 1-3 and 1-4. The CIA also has used these figures and has revised or updated its own previous estimates; see NFAC, CIA, *China: A Statistical Compendium*, Reference Aid ER 79-10374, July 1979 (selected figures from this source are given in appendix tables 1 and 2).

14. See table 3-2.

15. During personal trips to China in October–November 1977 and October 1979, every factory that I visited reported slowdowns, disruptions, or closures during the Cultural Revolution; at some, there were still visible physical signs of destructive struggles. For one analysis of the economic effects of that political strife, see Robert Michael Field, Kathleen M. McGlynn, and William B. Abnett, "Political Conflict and Industrial Growth in China: 1965–77," in JEC, *Chinese Economy Post-Mao*, pp. 239–47.

16. See table 1-1.

17. Nicholas R. Lardy ("Current Chinese Economic Policy Problems," in "Briefing Packet," China Council [Asia Society], July 1977, mimeographed, p. 11), argued, "Political disruptions and the earthquake, rather than long-term structural causes, appear to be the most important variables explaining the relatively poor performance of the economy in recent years." In 1978 Lardy maintained that "the major causes of the downturn in economic performance in recent years appear to be transitory and potentially reversible," stressing once again that political disruptions and the 1976 earthquake were the key factors; see Nicholas Lardy, "China: Starting On an Uphill Road," *Asian Wall Street Journal*, June 8, 1978. Some Chinese—possibly many—may have shared this view. However, subsequent evidence supports the view that structural problems were basic, and Peking's recent policies have called for fundamental changes in the economy.

18. In this study, when I say "from x year through y year," the first year is the base year, not included in the period mentioned; therefore, "from 1970 through 1977" is a seven-year period. In contrast, "1971–77" includes the first year and thus is also a seven-year period.

19. My calculations, from tables 1-1 and 1-2.

20. For representative statements (apart from major policy statements by leaders, which will be cited later) that appeared in articles published or republished in *Peking Review* during 1977 and early 1978, see Chi Wei (Ji Wei or Qi Wei?) "How the 'Gang of Four' Opposed Socialist Modernization," *Peking Review*, no. 11 (March 11, 1977), pp. 6–9; Chu Chin-ping (Zhu Qinping or Chu Jinbing?), "The Basic Policy for Socialist Revolution and Construction—Notes on Studying Chairman Mao's 'On the Ten Major Relationships,'" *Peking Review*, no. 12 (March 18, 1977), pp. 10–13; Chung Chin (Zhong Qin or Chong Jin?), "China's Road to Industrialization, Notes on Studying Chairman Mao's 'On the Ten Major Relationships,'" *Peking Review*, no. 14 (April 1, 1977), pp. 12–15; *Renmin Ribao* editorials, "Carry Out in an All-Round Way the Strategic Decision on Grasping the Key Link in Running the Country Well," *Peking Review*, no. 16 (April 15, 1977), pp. 8–10, and "Grasp the Key Link in Running the Country Well and Promote a New Leap Forward in the National Economy," *Peking Review*, no. 18 (April 29, 1977), pp. 21–25; and Chin Yen (Jin Yan or Qin Yan?), "Why Did the 'Gang of Four' Wield the Big Stick of the 'Theory of Productive Forces,'" *Peking Review*, no. 26 (June 24, 1977), pp. 25–29. See also Hsiang Chun (Xiang Jun or Xiang Qun?), "An Attempt to Restore Capitalism under the Signboard of Opposing Restoration—Refuting the 'Gang of Four's' So-Called Criticism of 'On the General

Programme for All Work of the Whole Party and the Whole Country,' "
Peking Review, no. 33 (August 12, 1977), pp. 28–32, and *Peking Review*, no.
34 (August 19, 1977), pp. 29–32, 37; Mass Group, State Planning Commission,
"Why Did the 'Gang of Four' Attack the 'Twenty Points?' " *Peking Review*,
no. 42 (October 14, 1977), pp. 5–13; Su Hsing (Su Xing), "China's Industrialization: How to Achieve It—Notes on Studying Volume 5 of the 'Selected
Works of Mao Tse-tung,' " *Peking Review*, no. 5 (February 3, 1978), pp.
11–15; Su Shao-chih (Su Shaozhi) and Feng Lan-jui (Feng Lanrui), "Refuting
Yao Wen-yuan's [Yao Wenyuan's] Fallacy that the Principle 'To Each According to His Work' Breeds Bourgeoisie," *Peking Review*, no. 6 (February
10, 1978), pp. 11–14; *Renmin Ribao* editorial, "Press on with the Three Great
Revolutionary Movements Simultaneously," *Peking Review*, no. 17 (April 28,
1978), pp. 4–6; and Chi Ti (Ji Ti), "General Task for the New Period, Industrial Modernization," *Peking Review*, no. 26 (June 30, 1978), pp. 7–9.

21. See sources cited in note 9 in the Introduction. Even though many
analysts have been skeptical, and rightly so, of the possibilities of transferring
the Maoist model to other countries, some have argued that all or part of it
deserves emulation. See the books by Gurley and by Wheelwright and Mc-
Farlane cited in the Introduction, note 9. Although these writers believed
that much of the model deserved wide diffusion, even they acknowledged that
ideological and political revolutions probably would be requisites for its effective diffusion. Today, in view of the basic changes occurring in China, there
is considerably less interest in the transferability of the Maoist model, and
many of those who believed that it deserved wide emulation have modified
their views.

22. These and the following figures, unless otherwise indicated, are based
on data from table 1-1, and the rates are my calculations from those data.
(The data in appendix table 1 indicate a 5.7 percent rate in the period from
1952 through 1977 and a 5.4 percent rate in the period from 1957 through
1977. With the use of estimates for gross national product [GNP] through
1978 in that table, the rate is 5.9 percent from 1952 through 1978 and 5.7 percent from 1957 through 1978.) What rate one obtains depends very much on
the years as well as the data used; my estimated rates, like those of others,
should be regarded as only an approximate indication of realities.

23. For an analysis of the pattern of, and reasons for, the fluctuations in
China's growth, see Alexander Eckstein, "Economic Fluctuations in Com-
munist China's Domestic Development," in Ping-ti Ho and Tang Tsou, eds.,
China in Crisis, vol. 1, book 2: *China's Heritage and the Communist Political
System* (University of Chicago Press, 1968), pp. 691–729.

24. For comparative purposes, see the figures on India and Indonesia in
U.S. Arms Control and Disarmament Agency, *World Military Expenditures
and Arms Transfers, 1966–75*, ACDA Publication 90, December 1976 (GPO,
1976), pp. 25, 33. See also Thomas E. Weisskopf, "The Political Economy of
Development in Non-Revolutionary Asia: A Comparative Survey of India,
Pakistan, and Indonesia," paper prepared for the Research Conference on the
Lessons of China's Development Experience for the Developing Countries,

Puerto Rico, January–February 1976, mimeographed; and Kuan-I Chen and J. S. Uppal, eds., *Comparative Development of India and China* (Free Press, 1971). JERC, *A Study on Japan-China Economic Relations*, p. 29, gives relatively low rates for China, but the estimates it includes are still above India's.

25. Dwight H. Perkins, "Growth and Changing Structure of China's Twentieth-Century Economy," in Perkins, ed., *China's Modern Economy in Historical Perspective*, p. 134.

26. Robert Michael Field, "Real Capital Formation in the People's Republic of China: 1952–1973," July 12, 1976, mimeographed, p. 68, estimated that gross domestic fixed capital formation was 24.5 percent of gross domestic product in 1970 (in 1957 prices). Perkins, "Growth and Changing Structure of China's Twentieth-Century Economy," p. 134, estimated that gross domestic capital formation in 1970 was 28 to 29 percent in 1957 prices, or 31 to 32 percent in 1952 prices. On capital formation, see also K. C. Yeh, "Capital Formation," in Eckstein and others, *Economic Trends in Communist China*, pp. 509 ff.; Shigeru Ishikawa, *National Income and Capital Formation in Mainland China* (Tokyo: Institute of Asian Economic Affairs, 1965); Chu-yuan Cheng, *China's Allocation of Fixed Capital Investment, 1952–1957*, Michigan Papers in Chinese Studies 17 (University of Michigan, Center for Chinese Studies, 1974); and the works by Kang Chao, William W. Hollister, and others cited in these studies. In recent years the investment rate has been above 30 percent; for official Chinese statements on recent rates, see part II, p. 209 and note 211.

27. Weisskopf, "The Political Economy of Development in Non-Revolutionary Asia," table 12, estimated that in India during 1968–70 gross capital formation was 15.7 percent of gross domestic product. Other data indicate that in 1962–63, aggregate investment (including net capital inflow from abroad) in India was 12.7 percent of national income, but domestic investment alone was just under 10 percent of national income; see Ruddar Datt and K. P. M. Sundharam, "Various Estimates of Physical Capital Formation for the Indian Economy," in Chen and Uppal, *India and China*, p. 226.

28. The CIA in 1976 estimated that during 1970–75 new fixed investment in the Soviet Union was 24 to 25 percent of GNP; see *Allocation of Resources in the Soviet Union and China, 1976*, Hearings before the Subcommittee on Priorities and Economy in Government of the Joint Economic Committee, 94 Cong. 2 sess. (GPO, 1976), p. 10. However, in 1977 it estimated that "up to 30 percent" of GNP went into capital investment; see *Allocation of Resources in the Soviet Union and China, 1977*, Hearings before the Subcommittee on Priorities and Economy in Government of the Joint Economic Committee, 95 Cong. 1 sess. (GPO, 1977), p. 2.

29. The following figures for the 1950s and 1960s are from table 1-2, and figures for 1975–78 are from appendix table 2. The rates are my calculations. For general background, see Robert Michael Field, "Civilian Industrial Production in the People's Republic of China: 1949–74," in JEC, *China: A Reassessment of the Economy*, pp. 146–74; and the five articles on manufacturing and extractive industries in JEC, *Chinese Economy Post-Mao*, vol. 1, pp. 239 ff.

30. On regional distribution of industry, see Field, "Civilian Industrial Production in the People's Republic of China: 1949–74," pp. 153–57; Field and others, "Political Conflict and Industrial Growth in China: 1965–1977," pp. 244–46; and Robert Michael Field, Nicholas R. Lardy, and John Philip Emerson, *Provincial Industrial Output in the People's Republic of China: 1949–75*, Bureau of Economic Analysis, Foreign Economic Report 12 (Department of Commerce, 1976).

31. See American Rural Small-Scale Industry Delegation (Dwight H. Perkins, chairman), *Rural Small-Scale Industry in the People's Republic of China* (University of California Press, 1977); CIA, *China: Role of Small Plants in Economic Development*, Research Aid A ER 74-60, May 1974; and Jon Sigurdson, "Rural Industrialization in China," in JEC, *China: A Reassessment of the Economy*, pp. 411–435.

32. From table 1-2 and appendix table 2.

33. See table 1-2.

34. See appendix table 2.

35. The 283-million-ton figure is Peking's official estimate; it is 3 million tons below the CIA's previous estimate; see table 1-2 and appendix table 2. For further details, see part III, pp. 315 ff. and table 3-2. The rates of growth and per capita figures below are my calculations; see the detailed discussion in part III.

36. My calculations, from table 1-2.

37. See part III, pp. 277–83.

38. See the discussion in Keesing, "Economic Lessons from China" (and the other sources cited in note 9 in the introduction); Eckstein, *China's Economic Development*, especially chap. 12, pp. 341 ff.; Lardy, "Economic Planning and Income Distribution in China," *Current Scene* (Hong Kong), vol. 14, no. 11 (November 1976), pp. 1–12, and "Centralization and Decentralization in China's Fiscal Management," *China Quarterly*, no. 61 (March 1975), pp. 25–60.

39. Roger D. Hansen and others, *The U.S. and World Development: Agenda for Action, 1976* (Praeger for the Overseas Development Council, 1976), p. 148.

40. Most objective observers visiting China in recent years have noted this; however, the areas observed have been limited. Improved food distribution and rationing have been major factors responsible for the progress made. Ensuring basic food requirements to all has been possible only during the last two decades, however; in the early 1960s China experienced severe food shortages which caused widespread malnutrition, and nutritional deficiencies still cause health problems. See Samuel D. J. Yeh and Bacon T. Chow, "Nutrition," in Joseph R. Quinn, ed., *Medicine and Public Health in the People's Republic of China*, U.S. Department of Health, Education, and Welfare, Public Health Service, publication no. (NIH) 72-67 (HEW, June 1972), pp. 211–31; and R. O. Whyte, *Rural Nutrition in China* (Oxford: Oxford University Press, 1972). Interviews with refugees in Hong Kong also reveal continued hunger

in certain areas; see Miriam London and Ivan D. London, "Hunger in China: The Failure of a System?" *Worldview*, no. 10 (1979), pp. 44–49.

41. For background, see Quinn, *Medicine and Public Health in the People's Republic of China*; China Health Care Study Group, *Health Care in China: An Introduction* (Geneva: Christian Medical Commission, 1974); Joshua S. Horn, *Away with All Pests: An English Surgeon in People's China, 1954–1969* (New York: Monthly Review Press, 1969); David M. Lampton, *The Politics of Medicine in China: The Policy Process, 1949–1977* (Boulder, Colo.: Westview Press, 1977); Victor W. Sidel and Ruth Sidel, *Serve the People: Observations on Medicine in the People's Republic of China* (Josiah Macy, Jr., Foundation, 1973); M. E. Wegman, ed., *Public Health in the People's Republic of China* (Josiah Macy, Jr., Foundation, 1973); and relevant specialized reports published by the Committee on Scholarly Communication with the People's Republic of China, Washington, D.C.

42. Many of the general works cited in note 1 deal to some extent with the wage system and income distribution. For additional background, see Barry M. Richman, *Industrial Society in Communist China* (Random House, 1969); Christopher Howe, *Wage Patterns and Wage Policy in Modern China* (Cambridge University Press, 1973); Charles Hoffman, *The Chinese Worker* (State University of New York Press, 1974); and Carl Riskin, "Workers' Incentives in Chinese Industry," in JEC, *China: A Reassessment of the Economy*, pp. 199–224.

43. For background on the commune system, see Benedict Stavis, *People's Communes and Rural Development in China* (Rural Development Committee, Cornell University, 1974); Frederick W. Crook, "The Commune System in the People's Republic of China, 1963–74," in JEC, *China: A Reassessment of the Economy*, pp. 366–410; Gordon Bennett, *Huadong* [Hua-tung]: *The Story of a Chinese People's Commune* (Westview Press, 1978); Gargi Dutt, *Rural Communes in China* (Delhi: Asian Publishing House, 1967); and the studies by Parris Chang and Byung-joon Ahn cited in note 2. Recent Chinese articles reveal Peking's current views on why the communes, as operated in recent years, have been less than optimally efficient. One striking example is Zhao Ziyang (Chao Tzu-yang), "Study New Conditions and Implement the Principle of Readjustment in an All-Round Way," in Foreign Broadcast Information Service, *Daily Report—People's Republic of China*, Department of Commerce, National Technical Information Service, January 18, 1980, pp. L3–L11. (Hereafter, FBIS, *Daily Report—PRC*.) (Chao was Party head in Szechwan [Sichuan] Province when he was elevated to the Politburo Standing Committee in February 1980.)

44. The "agriculture first" policy was evolved and publicized during the post-Great Leap depression in China between the summer of 1960 and early 1961 and it was clearly enunciated following the January 1961 meeting of the Party Central Committee. See Chang, *Power and Policy in China*, pp. 126–29; and Ahn, *Chinese Politics and the Cultural Revolution*, pp. 48 ff.

45. See part III, pp. 341–42 and notes 265, 266, and 267.

46. Susan B. Rifkin, "Health Care for Rural Areas," in Quinn, *Medicine and Public Health in the People's Republic of China*, pp. 137–47.

47. These and the following percentages are my calculations, from data in CIA, *China: Economic Indicators*, December 1978, pp. 22–25.

48. New China News Agency (NCNA) in 1979 carried an article titled "Consolidate and Vigorously Develop Small Local Coal Mines," which stated that more than 20,000 small local coal mines produced 276 million tons, or close to 45 percent of total national output, in 1978; FBIS, *Daily Report—PRC*, June 7, 1979, p. L12. In 1979 the head of China's State Planning Commission, Yu Chiu-li (Yu Qiuli), said that of the 1979 coal output target of 620 million tons (barely above the 1978 figure), between 354 million and 366 million tons (57 to 59 percent) were to come from mines (mainly larger ones) whose output is "distributed under the unified state plan"; FBIS, *Daily Report—PRC*, July 2, 1979, p. L19. For other data on small plants and mines in other fields, see CIA, *China: Role of Small Plants in Economic Development*.

49. See Schurmann, *Ideology and Organization in Communist China*, pp. 382, 400–03; and Morris B. Ullman, *Cities of Mainland China: 1953 and 1958*, Department of Commerce, Bureau of the Census, Foreign Manpower Research Office, International Population Reports, Series P-95, no. 59 (Department of Commerce, 1961), p. 12.

50. Estimates and official statements vary on how many were involved in the "hsia fang (xiafang)" and "hsia hsiang (xiaxiang)" programs to send youth to the countryside. Thomas P. Bernstein, *Up to the Mountains and Down to the Villages: The Transfer of Youth from Urban to Rural China* (Yale University Press, 1977), p. 2, cited official Chinese figures indicating totals of 1.2 million people transferred between 1956 and 1966 and 12 million between 1968 and 1975. Eckstein, *China's Economic Revolution*, p. 144, estimated that between 1959 and late 1963, urban population was reduced from 130 million to 110 million, largely as a result of sending people to the countryside.

51. Chen-siang Chen, "Population Growth and Urbanization in China," *Geographic Review* (January 1973), pp. 55–72, gave figures, using Chinese sources, showing that China's population in urban municipalities in 1953 was 51 million and that its total urban population grew from 140 million in 1964 to 160 million in 1970. His list of cities with populations of more than a half million people showed that all grew, but some only very slightly, some moderately, and only a very few rapidly, between 1957 and 1970. (His 1953 figures differ, however, from those in Ullman, *Cities of Mainland China: 1953 and 1958*, p. 10, which indicated that China's total urban population in 1953 was more than 77 million—almost 44 million in municipalities of 100,000 or more and just under 34 million in smaller urban areas.) In the early 1970s Shanghai (Shanghai), at least, was one major city whose urban population declined. Chen gave a figure of 7 million for Shanghai's urban population in 1970. Thereafter it dropped to a low of about 5.6 million; see Judith Banister, "Mortality, Fertility, and Contraceptive Use in Shanghai," *China Quarterly*, no. 70 (June 1977), p. 260. An official in Shanghai told me in 1977 that the city's urban population was a "little over 5.6 million" (out of a "municipal" population, he

said, that totaled 10.8 million) (from personal notes on an interview with Lin Teh-ming [Lin Deming], Shanghai, October 31, 1977). Then from 1978 on, youths sent to the countryside began to return to Shanghai; Chinese officials told me in the fall of 1979 that during the year they had found jobs for 350,000 of those who had returned (from personal notes on interviews with Lin Chu-wen [Lin Zhuwen] and municipal economic planning officials, Shanghai, October 26, 1979).

52. "Serve the people"—"wei jen-min fu-wu (wei renmin fuwu)"—was, like "self-reliance," one of the regime's key slogans in the 1960s and early 1970s. As in the case of most key Chinese slogans, its origin is traceable to Mao; a short speech with that title (delivered by Mao on September 8, 1944) is included in *Selected Works of Mao Tse-tung*, vol. 3 (Peking: Foreign Languages Press, 1967), pp. 177–78.

53. On the first major steps toward decentralization in the late 1950s, see Schurmann, *Ideology and Organization in Communist China*, pp. 173–219, which remains one of the most thorough analyses of the problems, dilemmas, and varieties of decentralization in China.

54. Creeping inflation began to be visible in early 1979. Soon thereafter, having raised the state purchase prices for many agricultural goods, the Party Central Committee and State Council issued a circular announcing that on November 1, 1979, there would be sizable price rises (for consumers) of key non-staple foods (pork, beef, mutton, poultry, eggs, vegetables, aquatic products, and milk); in most cases prices were increased by about one-third compared with 1978. Peking also stated that "the prices of more than 10,000 farming rural side-line, handicraft, and other miscellaneous products in China are no longer to be fixed by government but adjusted according to market supply and demand"; see Xinhua She (Hsin-hua She), NCNA, "Prices of Rural and Miscellaneous Products in China to Be Adjusted by Market Supply and Demand," in FBIS, *Daily Report—PRC*, November 2, 1979, pp. L1–L7; and other NCNA articles in FBIS, *Daily Report—PRC*, October 31, 1979, pp. L12–L13, and November 6, 1979, pp. L5–L8; as well as "Non-Staple Food Prices Raised," *Beijing Review*, no. 45 (November 9, 1979), p. 4. See also Jay Mathews, "In China: Prices Rise," *Washington Post*, November 2, 1979; and "Mark-ups in the Marketplace," *Economist* (November 10, 1979), pp. 77–78. To try to counterbalance these moves, the authorities announced that food allowances for non-staples would be given to urban workers and staff, that they would be given another raise (of about 40 percent) in wages, and that the sale prices would not change for staples such as grain, edible oils, cotton cloth, sugar, and coal. All of these actions were part of a broad attempt to move toward a more market-oriented economy, but their effects clearly were inflationary.

55. See part III, pp. 309 ff., and the sources cited in part III, notes 144 and 152.

56. U.S. estimates had indicated that the rate might have been about 1.6 percent in 1975; the Chinese now claim that it dropped to 1.2 percent in 1978. Peking has set targets of 0.5 percent in 1985 and zero in 2000. See part III, pp. 310 and 314.

57. See the detailed discussion in part II, pp. 214–15 and 223–26.

58. My calculations, from tables 1-2 and 3-2.

59. Hu Chiao-mu (Hu Qiaomu), "Act in Accordance with Economic Laws, Step Up the Four Modernizations," *People's Daily*, October 6, 1978, in FBIS, *Daily Report—PRC*, October 11, 1978, pp. E1–E21 (the quotation is from page E17). This extremely important article (which will be cited frequently in this discussion) was approved by Peking's top leadership before it was published and was one of the first comprehensive statements outlining proposals for restructuring the Chinese economy. (It will be referred to in the following discussion simply as Hu, "Act in Accordance with Economic Laws.") During much of his long Party career, Hu has been what one might call a "Party intellectual," engaged in writing key official documents (including one early official Party history), preparing speeches for Mao and reports for the top leadership, and engaging in work relating to propaganda, education, culture, and journalism. Although once close to Mao, for some years he has been very close to Teng. Today, he is one of the Party's top intellectuals, or idea men, in key fields including economic policy. According to some reports, he also has overall supervisory responsibility in the fields of culture and education. Together with Hu Yao-pang (Hu Yaobang), who has emerged as the leading Party organization man under Teng, and Hu Chi-wei (Hu Jiwei), editor of the *People's Daily*, he is referred to as one of the "three Hu's," all of whom are regarded as key advisers to Teng.

60. Jay Mathews, "Chinese Official Reportedly Sees Economic Crisis," *Washington Post*, June 15, 1979. *Ming Pao* (*Ming Bao*) stated that in Li Hsien-nien's (Li Xiannian's) speech (reportedly given at a Party central work conference in April), Li also said that China had 20 million unemployed and faced a budget deficit amounting to more than $6 billion.

61. Hu, "Act in Accordance with Economic Laws," p. E11.

62. "Speech at Opening of National Science Conference," *Peking Review*, no. 12 (March 24, 1978), p. 12.

63. Some Western studies of employment in China have stressed the problem of rural unemployment and the growing problem of absorbing people from the villages into urban areas; see Thomas G. Rawski, *Economic Growth and Employment in China* (Oxford University Press for the World Bank, 1979). Urban underemployment has been highly visible to any visitor (see my observations in *Uncertain Passage*, pp. 152–54), and recently the Chinese themselves have increasingly underlined this as a problem; see, for example, *Renmin Ribao* Commentator, "Implementing the Socialist Principle 'To Each According to His Work,'" *Peking Review*, no. 31 (August 4, 1978), pp. 6–15, and *Peking Review*, no. 33 (August 18, 1978), pp. 11–19; "For Higher Efficiency," *Beijing Review*, no. 17 (April 27, 1979), p. 7; and "Iron Rice Bowl," *Beijing Review*, no. 8 (February 23, 1979), p. 7. Hu, "Act in Accordance with Economic Laws," p. E11, stated that if the growth of labor productivity had continued at the 1950s rate, "the total number of workers [in urban China] could be two-thirds less."

64. This, if correct, implied that about one-fifth of the urban workforce

was unemployed. Wei Min (Wei Min), "1979: More Than 7 Million People Employed" (interview with director of the State Bureau of Labor), *Beijing Review*, no. 6 (February 11, 1980), pp. 13–23, discussed the unemployment problem at length and outlined the measures that Peking is taking to try to create new jobs. This article asserted that although 7 million new jobs were created in 1979, there still was a need to create many more, especially in light industries, commerce, and service trades, particularly in medium and small cities. The Chinese now are also pushing early retirement; see Jay Mathews, "China Retires Aged to Spur Economy," *Washington Post*, July 16, 1979.

65. Based on several personal interviews in China, October 1977. See also Chen, "Economic Modernization in Post-Mao China: Policies, Problems, and Prospects," in JEC, *Chinese Economy Post-Mao*, p. 174. Chen estimated that bonuses formerly amounted to 6 to 8 percent of workers' wages.

66. The question of incentives was one of the most critical issues in the political and ideological debates of 1975–76. A flood of articles in that period attacked "material incentives"; key articles in 1975 were by two top radical leaders: Yao Wen-yuan, "On the Social Basis of the Lin Piao [Lin Biao] Anti-Party Clique," *Peking Review*, no. 10 (March 7, 1975), pp. 5–10; and Chang Chun-chiao (Zhang Chunqiao), "On Exercising All-Round Dictatorship over the Bourgeoisie," *Peking Review*, no. 14 (April 4, 1975), pp. 5–11. Typical of follow-up articles were Li Chang, "Teng Hsiao-ping's Total Betrayal of Marxism," pp. 13–18; and the Mass Criticism Group of Peking and Tsinghua Universities, "A Confession of Attempts at Reversal of Verdicts and Restoration," *Peking Review*, no. 28 (July 29, 1976), pp. 9–12. Virtually every major official speech from 1977 on (including most of those cited elsewhere in part I) stressed the need for greater use of material incentives. These were echoed in numerous press articles, for example, Su and Feng, "Refuting Yao Wen-yuan's Fallacy," pp. 11–14; and *Renmin Ribao* Commentator, "Implementing the Socialist Principle 'To Each According to His Work,'" *Peking Review*, no. 31 (August 4, 1978), pp. 6–15, and no. 33 (August 18, 1978), pp. 11–19. (The latter articles followed one written by a leading economist, Hsueh Mu-chiao [Xue Muqiao], "Some Ideas on the Employment Question in Urban Areas," originally published in July; see "Should the 'Iron Rice Bowl' Be Smashed?" *Beijing Review*, no. 48 [November 30, 1979], p. 4.) The need to improve incentives greatly for both peasants and urban workers continues to be strongly stressed; see, for example, "More Work, More Pay," *Beijing Review*, no. 16 (April 20, 1979); and "Increased Wages" and "Higher Purchase Prices Bring Good Results," *Beijing Review*, no. 45 (November 9, 1979), p. 5. Some articles have suggested, however, that debate on the issue has continued. See, for example, "Iron Rice Bowl," p. 7; and "Stress on Moral Encouragement or Material Reward?" *Beijing Review*, no. 22 (June 1, 1979), p. 7.

67. In the late 1960s this erupted in unrest and demands for improvements in livelihood, which Peking's leaders at that time denounced as "economism"; see Stanley Karnow, *Mao and China: From Revolution to Revolution* (Viking, 1972), pp. 261–75. Any visitor to China since 1979 has been able to observe the upsurge of consumerism.

68. Earlier studies suggested that, overall, China's capital–output ratio in · the 1950s was relatively low; see Cheng, *China's Allocation of Fixed Capital Investment, 1952–1957*, pp. 38–41, which indicated that the net capital–output ratio was 2.8 for the whole economy—which was relatively low. JERC, *A Study on Japan-China Economic Relations*, pp. 28–31, uses 3 or 4 as a co-efficient of marginal capital output nationally in making hypothetical economic projections for the period ahead. However, numerous articles in the Chinese press during 1978–79 made it clear that Peking's own planners recognized that use of capital has been extremely inefficient in some major industries. See, for example, the data cited in note 301 on the automobile industry.

69. See Hans Heymann, Jr., *China's Approach to Technology Acquisition*, pt. 3: *Summary Observations*, Rand Report R-1575—ARPA (Rand Corp., February 1975), pp. 34–35.

70. See Thomas G. Rawski, "Choice of Technology and Technological Innovation in China's Economic Development," November 1975, mimeographed, especially pp. 31–32, 48; and Rawski, "The Growth of Producer Industries, 1900–1971," in Perkins, *China's Modern Economy in Historical Perspective*, pp. 231–32.

71. See, for example, American Rural Small-Scale Industry Delegation, *Rural Small-Scale Industry in the People's Republic of China*, p. 75.

72. For a discussion of the pros and cons and possible consequences of mixing different levels of production technology and methods in Chinese plants, see Richard Baum, "Diabolus Ex Machina: Technological Development and Social Change in Chinese Industry," in Frederick J. Fleron, Jr., ed., *Technology and Communist Culture, The Socio-Cultural Impact of Technology Under Socialism* (Praeger, 1977), especially pp. 319–22. Many visitors have observed inefficiencies everywhere, and recently the Chinese themselves have increasingly discussed these inefficiencies in China's public media.

73. Hua Kuo-feng, "Unite and Strive to Build a Modern Powerful Socialist Country!" a "Report on the Work of the Government," February 26, 1978, in FBIS, *Daily Report—PRC*, March 7, 1978, p. D16. This important report was the first major comprehensive public explication and outline of China's new modernization program. (Hereafter, "Report on the Work of the Government," February 26, 1978.) (Hua made a second "Report on the Work of the Government" in 1979; it will be identified with its date of delivery.) No comparable report on government policies, problems, and plans had been published in China for more than a decade, and none with so much economic data had been released since the 1950s. Although delivered by Hua (who thereby associated himself closely with the policies described), these reports were collective products of China's top leadership, and Teng and his closest supporters doubtless played the principal roles in drafting them.

74. Ibid., p. D4. For discussion of the rates—and problems—of converting yuan to dollars, see part II, notes 154 and 288.

75. See, for example, Field and others, "Political Conflict and Industrial Growth in China," pp. 246–47.

76. See Wu, *The Economy of Communist China*, chap. 3, pp. 47 ff. Hu,

"Act in Accordance with Economic Laws"; and Hsueh Mu-chiao, "A Study in the Planned Management of the Socialist Economy," *Beijing Review*, no. 43 (October 26, 1979), and "On Reforming the Economic Management System," *Beijing Review*, no. 5 (February 4, 1980), pp. 16–22, and *Beijing Review*, no. 12 (March 24, 1980), pp. 21–26, are among the most important Chinese critiques of past pricing policies. Both Hu and Hsueh argue for much greater reliance on "the law of value" and realistic pricing, that is, on market forces. (Hsueh Mu-chiao is one of a small group of leading Chinese economists who were prominent in the 1950s and 196s, disappeared during the Cultural Revolution, and recently have returned to prominence. His views generally parallel Hu Chiao-mu's but probably are not as influential.)

77. This is clear from recent Chinese critiques of past planning. On the planning system in earlier years, see a basic explanation in Wu, *The Economy of Communist China*, chap. 3, and "Planning, Management, and Economic Development in Communist China," in JEC, *An Economic Profile of Mainland China*, vol. 1: *General Economic Setting, The Economic Sectors*, pp. 99–119.

78. On earlier shifts in the prevailing forms of management, see Schurmann, *Ideology and Organization in Communist China*, especially pp. 239–308. For sympathetic accounts of management trends and experiments in the late 1960s and early 1970s, see the Marxist assessment made by Charles Bettelheim, *Cultural Revolution and Industrial Organization in China, Changes in Management and Division of Labor* (Monthly Review Press, 1974); and the analysis of Stephen Andors, *China's Industrial Revolution: Politics, Planning, and Management, 1949 to the Present* (Pantheon, 1977).

79. Hua, "Report on the Work of the Government," February 26, 1978, p. D22.

80. Fang Yi (Fang Yi), "Outline National Plan for the Development of Science and Technology, Relevant Policies and Measures," *Peking Review*, no. 14 (April 7, 1978), pp. 6–7. This is one of the key documents outlining China's current science policy.

81. See estimates for certain fields in Chen, "Economic Modernization in Post-Mao China: Policies, Problems, and Prospects," p. 173, note 40.

82. Genevieve Dean, "Research and Technological Innovation in Industry," in OECD, *Science and Technology in the People's Republic of China*, pp. 157 ff.; and Rensselaer W. Lee III, "Mass Innovation and Communist Culture: The Soviet and Chinese Cases," in Fleron, ed., *Technology and Communist Culture*, pp. 265 ff. Both discuss certain types of innovation that largely, however, consist of adaptation. Hans Heymann, Jr., "Acquisition and Diffusion of Technology in China," in JEC, *China: A Reassessment of the Economy*, pp. 678 ff., argues that China's weaknesses are more in design and management technology than in manufacturing technology, although China still faces serious problems in developing the latter.

83. *Peking Review*, no. 12 (March 24, 1978), p. 12.

84. See the articles cited in note 20.

85. See note 10. The official version published after Mao's death differs in

a number of respects from earlier unofficial versions smuggled out of China; for example, it contains many statements critical of the Soviet Union. For comparison, see the earlier text in Schram, *Chairman Mao Talks to the People*, pp. 61–83.

86. In *Selected Works of Mao Tse-tung*, vol. 5, the first item is dated September 21, 1949, and the last is dated November 18, 1957—shortly before the Great Leap Forward. On October 8, 1976, a month after Mao's death, the Central Committee decided that volume 5 should be published "at the soonest possible date" and that Mao's "Collected Works" now should be compiled, edited, and published under the direct leadership of the Politburo and Hua Kuo-feng; see *Peking Review*, no. 42 (October 15, 1976), pp. 3–4. The compilation and editing of the "Collected Works" will reflect the basic ideological changes now under way in China; producing it will not be easy. Hu Chiao-mu reportedly is playing a key role in the process.

87. See, for example, the contrast between Teng's March 18, 1978, speech to China's National Science Conference in *Peking Review*, no. 12 (March 24, 1978), pp. 9 ff., and Hua's speech to the same conference on March 24, in *Peking Review*, no. 13 (March 31, 1978), pp. 6 ff. Teng stressed the key role of "outstanding scientists and technicians," the "great revolution" under way in modern science and technology, the need for basic research, the critical importance of sophisticated fields such as electronic computers and cybernetics, and the fact that in a socialist society the majority of "brain workers" (that is, intellectuals) are "part of the proletariat." Hua stressed the need to "carry forward the three great revolutionary movements of class struggle, the struggle for production, and scientific experiment," the continuing importance of mass mobilization, and the need to involve ordinary people and "raise the scientific and cultural level of the entire Chinese nation."

88. Over time, as will be noted later, Teng's influence in all fields, including those relating to political and ideological issues, became progressively stronger, and by 1979 his policy positions had achieved clear primacy.

89. See the texts in *Peking Review*, no. 1 (January 1, 1977), pp. 31 ff.; no. 21 (May 20, 1977), pp. 7 ff.; and no. 22 (May 27, 1977), pp. 5 ff.

90. See the Congress "Press Communiqué" and "Political Report" delivered by Hua; texts of both are in *Peking Review*, no. 35 (August 26, 1977), pp. 6 ff.

91. "Press Communiqué."

92. Yu Chiu-li, "Development of China's National Economy"; speech text in *Peking Review*, no. 45 (November 4, 1977), pp. 6–9.

93. Fang Yi, "On the Situation in China's Science and Education"; speech text in *Peking Review*, no. 2 (January 13, 1978), pp. 15–19.

94. Speech text in FBIS, *Daily Report—PRC*, March 7, 1978, pp. D1–D38.

95. Ibid., pp. D2 and D11.

96. See note 80.

97. The text of Teng's speech is in *Peking Review*, no. 18 (May 5, 1978), pp. 6–12.

98. *Peking Review*, no. 30 (July 28, 1978), pp. 3, 6–17.

99. "Draft Decision Concerning Some Problems in Speeding Up the Development of Industry," *Peking Review*, no. 28 (July 14, 1978), p. 3. For the text, see *Issues and Studies* (Taiwan), vol. 14, no. 11 (November 1978), pp. 89–97, and vol. 15, no. 1 (January 1979), pp. 69–98, with commentary on pp. 48–63. (The Central Committee drafted this as a resolution in April 1978; see Hu, "Act in Accordance with Economic Laws," p. E21.) These "thirty points" clearly were based on the earlier "twenty points" (see note 8) originally drafted in 1975 under Teng Hsiao-ping's supervision. However, there are differences in emphasis in them; these differences are discussed in Thierry Pairault, "Industrial Strategy (1975–1979): In Search of New Policies for Industrial Growth," typescript, September 11, 1979.

100. See note 59. Certain Chinese officials have told me in interviews that this was discussed by the State Council and approved by the Council in the summer of 1978; it also received Politburo approval. It did not merely spell out policies already agreed upon; rather it articulated the ideas that were still tentative to guide new experimental policies.

101. See, for example, "Canton [Kuang-chou or Guangzhou] 43—New Flexibility, New Era?" *China Business Review*, vol. 5, no. 3 (May–June 1978), pp. 33–40. See also the discussion in part II.

102. The following discussion is based mainly on Hua, "Report on the Work of the Government," February 26, 1978, pp. D1–D38.

103. Ibid., p. D12.

104. Ibid.

105. My rough calculation, based on the assumptions that agricultural and industrial output will, as now, make up roughly 26 percent and 41 percent, respectively, of GNP, and that services and other elements making up the rest of GNP will grow at approximately the same rate as industry. For background see the discussion in note 288. Of course the proportions and rates will change at least some.

106. See Jen Min (Ren Min), "Reclaiming Wasteland," *Peking Review*, no. 26 (June 30, 1978), p. 10.

107. Hua, "Report on the Work of the Government," February 26, 1978, p. D12.

108. Ibid., concerning the target; the rate required is my calculation, based on table 3-2.

109. Hua, "Report on the Work of the Government," February 26, 1978, p. D14.

110. Ibid., p. D12.

111. Ibid., p. D14.

112. Ibid., pp. D16–D17; see also ibid., p. D12.

113. The specified projects are listed in ibid., p. D17; it is assumed from press reports that many of the unspecified projects will be in the fields mentioned.

114. Ibid., pp. D12, D14.

115. Ibid., p. D21.

116. A subsequent article stated that state profits and revenues from light

and textile industries "from 1950 to 1977" were equivalent to thirteen times the state's investments in capital construction in these industries and accounted for 29 percent of the state's income and 70 percent of the state's total investment in capital construction; see *Renmin Ribao* Commentator, "Adopt Special Measures to Advance Light and Textile Industries," June 3, 1979, in FBIS, *Daily Report—PRC*, June 15, 1979, p. L3.

117. Hua, "Report on the Work of the Government," February 26, 1978, p. D18.

118. Lardy, "The Impact of Technology Transfer on China's Domestic Economy," paper prepared for the Workshop on the Development of Industrial Science and Technology in the PRC, Bermuda, January 1979, mimeographed, p. 22, argues the case that it could have been.

119. Hua Guofeng, "Report on the Work of the Government," June 18, 1979 (his second report with this title), in FBIS, *Daily Report—PRC*, Supplement 015, July 2, 1979, pp. 1–32.

120. See Hua, "Report on the Work of the Government," February 26, 1978, pp. D17–D18. Emphasis on these fields had begun considerably earlier; see Sy Yuan, "China's Chemicals" (and other articles), *U.S.-China Business Review*, vol. 2, no. 6 (November–December 1975), pp. 37–53.

121. Hua, "Report on the Work of the Government," February 26, 1978, D25.

122. See, for example, Tung Yuan (Dong Yuan or Tong Yuan?), "Create a High Speed," *Red Flag*, no. 2, 1978, in FBIS, *Daily Report—PRC*, March 3, 1978, pp. E9–E11; Commentator, "Seriously Grasp the Key Work for the Sake of Great Order and Quick Progress," *Renmin Ribao*, February 28, 1978, in FBIS, *Daily Report—PRC*, March 10, 1978, pp. E9–E10; Li Lieh (Li Lie), "A Great Undertaking," *Renmin Ribao*, March 14, 1978, in FBIS, *Daily Report—PRC*, March 22, 1978, pp. E14–E15; and Chi Ti, "General Task for the New Period," cited in note 20.

123. The following estimates of rates are my calculations. I used the 1977 estimate in table 1-1 as a base figure. These and the following calculations are in constant 1977 prices; obviously they would be larger stated in current prices.

124. My calculation, from table 1-1.

125. See p. 77 and note 244.

126. This was attributed to Li Hsien-nien but first appeared in the *Japan Economic Journal* (October 1978) (see *China Business Review*, vol. 6, no. 2 [March–April 1979], p. 5), and some observers doubt if the original report was correct; in 1980 Teng Hsiao-ping stated that past investment had totaled 600 billion yuan, not dollars (see note 244 and p. 77), and previously Hua Kuo-feng had stated that 1978–85 investment would equal all past investment since 1949 (see note 103). However, a number of Japanese bankers and businessmen subsequently used the figure of $600 billion as an estimate of China's possible investments during 1978–85, and some calculated that China might need to obtain $200 billion to $300 billion of this from abroad; see Henry Scott-Stokes, "Japan Studies Loans for China," *New York Times*, December

27, 1978, and "Teng Criticizes the U.S. for a Lack of Firmness on Japan," *New York Times*, February 8, 1979.

127. Li Hsien-nien told a visiting American delegation (from the United Nations Association of the United States), in an interview in Peking on March 10, 1979, that $600 billion was too high an estimate for probable capital investment during the period 1978–85 and that, in his opinion, the figure probably would be lower (from the notes of a participant, unattributable).

128. Robert F. Dernberger, "China's Economic Future," in Whiting and Dernberger, *China's Future*, pp. 140–49, 152.

129. Arthur G. Ashbrook, Jr., "China: Shift of Economic Gears in Mid-1970s," in JEC, *Chinese Economy Post-Mao*, pp. 206, 225–29.

130. This judgment is based on the analysis of China's agricultural problems and prospects in part III.

131. These are rates that I personally believe to be plausible if Peking's current "readjustment" policies succeed to any reasonable extent.

132. Dernberger, "China's Economic Future," pp. 4–5.

133. Ashbrook, "China: Shift of Economic Gears in Mid-1970s," p. 229.

134. See the discussion in part III, p. 310.

135. China's new economic policies have evolved in a step-by-step fashion since 1977. The following discussion draws upon the extensive reporting about these policies in the Chinese and Western press throughout this period. A few of these press reports will be cited specifically below. However, the discussion is based mainly on official Chinese policy statements that have presented new data and articulated the new policies. The first comprehensive statement on the new policies was Hua's "Report on the Work of the Government," February 26, 1978, presented at the first session of the Fifth National People's Congress (NPC). Not long thereafter the "Communiqué" of the Third Plenum of the Eleventh Central Committee, December 22, 1978 (FBIS, *Daily Report—PRC*, December 26, 1978, pp. E4–E13), called for adjustments, including a slowdown in the pace of development and increased attention to agriculture. It also decided to distribute a draft decision, "Some Questions Concerning the Acceleration of Agricultural Development," and new draft regulations on the communes; the draft decision on agriculture was adopted by the Fourth Plenum on September 28, 1979; see the text in FBIS, *Daily Report—PRC*, Supplement 023, October 25, 1979, and the Plenum's "Communiqué" in *Beijing Review*, no. 40 (October 5, 1979), pp. 32–34. In 1978 the Central Committee also issued the draft "Thirty Points" on industry (cited in note 99). The leadership's decision to "adjust" the regime's original economic plans was elaborated on in many articles in early 1979; a notable example was the *People's Daily* editorial of February 24, 1979, titled "Emancipate the Mind for an Overall Balance in Economic Development," in FBIS, *Daily Report—PRC*, February 26, 1979, pp. E12–E16, which called not only for a slowdown in investment in heavy industry (especially in steel) but also for other policy changes. Then, Hua Kuo-feng's second "Report on the Work of the Government" at the second session of the Fifth NPC, June 18, 1979, discussed in some detail the regime's policies for a three-year period of "readjustment"; text in

FBIS, *Daily Report—PRC*, Supplement 015, July 2, 1979, pp. 1–32. Throughout this period spokesmen for the regime put increasing emphasis on the need to alter the economic *system*. The first comprehensive statement of proposals for systemic change was the article by Hu Chiao-mu, "Act in Accordance with Economic Laws," cited earlier. Among subsequent statements of considerable importance were those by Hsueh Mu-chiao; see Xue Muqiao, "A Study in the Planned Management of the Socialist Economy," *Beijing Review*, no. 43 (October 26, 1979), pp. 14–20, and "On Reforming the Economic Management System," *Beijing Review*, no. 5 (February 4, 1980), pp. 16–22, no. 12 (March 24, 1980), pp. 21–26, and no. 14 (April 7, 1980), pp. 20–27. The provincial leader who played the pacesetting role in experimenting with the new policies and wrote about them was Chao Tzu-yang, the head of Szechwan; see Zhao Ziyang, "Study New Conditions and Implement the Principle of Readjustment in an All-Round Way," *Red Flag*, no. 1 (1980), in FBIS, *Daily Report—PRC*, January 18, 1980, pp. L3–L11. On January 16, 1980, and February 10, 1980, Teng Hsiao-ping and Li Hsien-nien, respectively, gave major reports (Teng's very important speech, which was published later, is discussed below and cited in note 239); both mainly reinforced the new economic policies. (Also see the "Communiqué" of the Fifth Plenum, February 9, 1980, in FBIS, *Daily Report—PRC*, February 29, 1980, pp. L1–L5.) For outsiders' comments on Teng's speech, see *Ming Pao* (Hong Kong), "Deng Xiaoping Makes Important Speech on Targets of Four Modernizations," in FBIS, *Daily Report—PRC*, February 12, 1980, pp. U1–U3; and Jay Mathews, "Deng Pledges China to Match Taiwan's Thriving Economy," *Washington Post*, March 11, 1980. Also see Deng Xiaoping, "Why China Has Opened Its Doors," *Bangkok Post*, February 10, 1980, in FBIS, *Daily Report—PRC*, February 12, 1980, pp. L1–L5. In the mass of journalistic Western writings and articles during 1978–79 that discussed the evolution of China's new policies, a few general summaries were particularly noteworthy. These included "China in the 1980s," *Economist* (London) (December 29, 1979), pp. 17–30; and "China '79, Overview, Astonishing Reversions to Pre-1966 Social Policies," *Far Eastern Economic Review* (Hong Kong) (October 5, 1979), pp. 50–82. Useful overviews and analyses by scholars were provided by Nai-Ruenn Chen, "Economic Modernization in Post-Mao China: Policies, Problems, and Prospects," in JEC, *Chinese Economy Post-Mao*, pp. 165–203; Kenneth Lieberthal, "China Faces the Fundamental Revolution," *Asia* (May-June 1978), pp. 3–9, "A 'Second Revolution' Begins in China," *Fortune* (October 23, 1978), pp. 94 ff., and "China: The Politics behind the New Economics," *Fortune* (December 31, 1979), pp. 44–50; and Joyce K. Kallgren, "China in 1979: On Turning Thirty," *Asian Survey*, vol. 20, no. 1 (January 1980), pp. 1–18. See also major special reports in mass circulation magazines, including "Visionary of a New China," *Time* (January 1, 1979), pp. 11 ff.; "Teng's Great Leap Outward," *Time* (February 5, 1979), pp. 24 ff.; and "The New China, Special Report," *Newsweek* (February 5, 1979), pp. 32 ff.

136. See Hua Kuo-feng, "Political Report to the Eleventh National Con-

gress of the Communist Party of China," *Peking Review*, no. 35 (August 26, 1977), p. 38. A parallel slogan expressing the regime's priority political goal of restoring unity was "great order."

137. From late 1976 on, there was a "nationwide mass movement to expose and criticize Lin Piao and the Gang of Four." The Third Plenum's "Communiqué" on December 12, 1978, declared that this campaign "had in the main been completed victoriously," and that "the stress of the Party's work should shift to socialist modernization as of 1979"; FBIS, *Daily Report—PRC*, December 26, 1978, p. E4. Many subsequent Chinese statements indicated that the present leadership was determined not to repeat the costly, disruptive campaigns characteristic of the period from the 1950s through the early 1970s.

138. Hua, "Report on the Work of the Government," February 26, 1978, stated that the regime would "uphold the principle of 'from each according to his ability, to each according to his work,'" and would "oppose equalitarianism"; see FBIS, *Daily Report—PRC*, March 7, 1978, p. D20. For illustrative articles in which the importance of developing material incentives and opposing egalitarianism was stressed, see Su Shao-chih and Feng Lan-jui, "Refuting Yao Wen-yuan's Fallacy," pp. 11–14; *Renmin Ribao* editorial, April 9, 1978, "Integrating Moral Encouragement with Material Reward," *Peking Review*, no. 16 (April 21, 1978), pp. 6–7; *Renmin Ribao* Commentator, "Implementing the Socialist Principle 'To Each According to His Work'"; and Jin Wen, "Egalitarianism Is a Major Enemy of Distribution According to Work," *Guangming Ribao (Kuang-ming Jih-pao)*, June 16, 1979, in FBIS, *Daily Report—PRC*, June 29, 1979, pp. L13–L17.

139. The most important statements by radical leaders on this issue were Yao Wen-yuan, "On the Social Basis of the Lin Piao Anti-Party Clique," *Red Flag*, no. 3 (1975), in *Peking Review*, no. 10 (March 7, 1975), pp. 5–10; and Chang Chun-chiao, "On Exercising All-Round Dictatorship over the Bourgeoisie," *Red Flag*, no. 4 (1975), in *Peking Review*, no. 14 (April 4, 1975), pp. 5–11. (The official translators of these articles used the term "bourgeois right" in the singular, but "bourgeois rights" seems more appropriate.)

140. The use of bonuses has grown rapidly since they were reinstituted in 1978, but this has continued to be a subject of debate, with some arguing that bonuses should supplement but not replace moral incentives, and others charging that bonuses have been abused and given indiscriminately without regard to performance; see *Renmin Ribao*, "The Situation of Wantonly Giving Away Bonuses Must Be Corrected," January 25, 1979, in FBIS, *Daily Report—PRC*, January 26, 1979, pp. E22–E23; "Discussion of Bonuses," *Beijing Review*, no. 16, April 20, 1979, pp. 5–6; and "Further Report on State Council Circular on Spending, Bonuses," in FBIS, *Daily Report—PRC*, November 6, 1979, pp. L4–L5.

141. *Peking Review*, no. 49 (December 2, 1977), p. 3, reported that the government decided to raise wages starting October 1, 1977, and that these raises affected 46 percent of urban workers and staff. *Beijing Review*, no. 45 (November 9, 1979), p. 4, reported that in 1978 a very small number (2 per-

cent) received wage increases, but that another wage increase, the third since Mao's death, was to be carried out starting in November 1979 and would affect 40 percent of urban workers and staff.

142. Television sets have become a major symbol of growing consumerism. High priority is placed on domestic production of television sets, and output has grown rapidly. See "More TV Sets," *Beijing Review*, no. 33 (August 17, 1979), p. 27; and "More and Better Radios and TV Sets," *Beijing Review*, no. 49 (December 7, 1979), p. 6. China also now imports some Japanese sets (which, as I observed in China in October 1979, are greatly desired and attract huge crowds at department stores when displayed). See also Jay Mathews, "Television: A Symbol of China's Desire for Consumer Goods," *Washington Post*, August 1, 1978.

143. See various quotations in *People's Daily* Commentator, "Implementing the Socialist Principle 'To Each According to His Work,' " *Peking Review*, no. 31 (August 4, 1978), pp. 7, 11; and *Peking Review*, no. 33 (August 18, 1978), pp. 12, 13. These statements appear in Mao's *Selected Works;* see, for example, *Selected Works*, vol. 4 (Peking: Foreign Languages Press, 1961), p. 236.

144. While this may sound like an overstatement, I believe that it is essentially correct. In the 1950s and 1960s many refugees that I interviewed in Hong Kong detailed the way political and social pressures inhibited any tendencies toward consumerism.

145. As indicated in note 54, by late 1979 there were clear signs of inflationary pressures resulting from the rise in the purchase prices for many agricultural goods, wage raises, and increases in the prices of consumer goods in the cities. See also "Further Report on Joint Circular on Food Prices," in FBIS, *Daily Report—PRC*, November 6, 1979, pp. L5–L6; "Higher Purchasing Prices Bring Good Results," *Beijing Review*, no. 45 (November 9, 1979), p. 5; Ernst Kux, "Notes from China," *Swiss Review of World Affairs*, vol. 29, no. 10 (January 1980), pp. 16–21; and Fox Butterfield, "In Peking: Food Ration Cards Sell Briskly," *New York Times*, July 7, 1979.

146. The State Statistical Bureau stated that the "overall level of retail prices" (including state list prices, negotiated prices and prices on the rural market) were 5.8 percent higher in December 1979 than a year earlier; see SSB, "Communiqué on the Fulfilment of China's 1979 National Economic Plan," in FBIS, *Daily Report—PRC*, April 30, 1980, p. L7.

147. See, for example Hu, "Act in Accordance with Economic Laws," pp. E18–E19, and Zhao, "Study New Conditions," pp. L4–L8, for discussions of proposed ways to increase peasant incentives and productivity.

148. Ibid.

149. Chao Tzu-yang, as governor of Szechwan, was by far the most experiment-minded in this respect; see Zhao, "Study New Conditions," especially pp. L7–L8, and "China in the 1980s," *Economist* (December 29, 1979), especially pp. 23–25.

150. Hu, "Act in Accordance with Economic Laws," p. E17. See also part III, pp. 307 and 342.

151. "Communiqué" of Third Plenum, in FBIS, *Daily Report—PRC*, December 26, 1978, p. E8, announced a 20 percent increase in the purchase price of quota grain and an additional 50 percent for above-quota purchases.

152. By November 1979 state purchase prices had been raised 25 percent for fats and oils, 15 percent for quota cotton (and an additional 30 percent for above-quota cotton), 26 percent for pigs, and 20 to 50 percent for fourteen other products; *Beijing Review*, no. 45 (November 9, 1979), p. 5.

153. This is Hu Chiao-mu's phrase, in "Act in Accordance with Economic Laws," p. E13. The following discussion relies heavily on this article plus the writings of Hsueh Mu-chiao and Chao Tzu-yang, cited earlier.

154. *China Business Review*, vol. 6, no. 5 (September–October 1979), p. 9, lists and describes some new top bodies, including the Financial and Economic Commission; *China Business Review*, vol. 6, no. 4 (July–August 1979), pp. 16–17, analyzes the reestablished State Planning Commission.

155. See Jay Mathews, "China Promotes 3 Financial Experts," *Washington Post*, July 2, 1979; Frank Ching, "China's Congress Names 3 Vice Premiers in Session Seen as Turning Point for Nation," *Wall Street Journal*, July 2, 1979; and "Economic Expert Back in Peking Leadership," *New York Times*, July 2, 1979. For a listing of all of the positions held by these men, see *China Business Review*, vol. 6, no. 5 (September–October, 1979), p. 9. The technocratic nature of the new leadership became even clearer in early 1980, when a new Party Secretariat was established; see pp. 79–80 and notes 248 and 249.

156. This commission is headed by Fang Yi, who now is overall coordinator of scientific and technical affairs in China.

157. These regions were first mentioned in Hua, "Report on the Work of the Government," February 28, 1978, p. D12, but relatively little has been said about them subsequently.

158. On Sun Yeh-fang (Sun Yefang), see the interview in *Tanjug* (Yugoslavia), August 18, 1978, in FBIS, *Daily Report—PRC*, August 23, 1978, pp. A26–A28; Sun was then reported to be working on a book, *Political Economy of Socialism*. On the Academy of Social Sciences, headed by Hu Chiao-mu, see Committee on Scholarly Communication with the People's Republic of China (CSCPRC), *China Exchange Newsletter*, vol. 6, nos. 3–4 (June–August 1978), pp. 9–14. As of late 1979 the Academy was giving special priority to developing work in economics, law, and international relations, including foreign area studies. On the social sciences generally, see George Braybrooke, "Recent Developments in Chinese Social Sciences, 1977–79," *China Quarterly*, no. 79 (September 1979), pp. 593–607; Zhang Wen (Chang Wen), "Social Science: A Hundred Schools of Thought Contend," *Beijing Review*, no. 14 (August 6, 1979), pp. 9–14; and Zhou Xun (Chou Hsun), "The Present State and Future Outlook for Social Science Research in Communist China," *The Seventies* (*Chi-shih Nien-tai* or *Qishi Niandai*) (Hong Kong), no. 7 (December 1978), translated by Alexander P. De Angelis, CSCPRC, mimeographed; and Harry Harding, "Social Science in the People's Republic of China," 1979, mimeographed, to appear in a book edited by Leo Orleans, scheduled to be published

in 1980 by Stanford University Press and titled *Science in Contemporary China*.

159. See Saburo Okita, "Japan, China, and the United States: Economic Relations and Prospects," *Foreign Affairs*, vol. 57, no. 5 (Summer 1979), p. 1103.

160. Most of the following quotations are from Hu, "Act in Accordance with Economic Laws," but comparable ones could be cited from many other sources.

161. Ibid., pp. E5–E6.

162. Ibid., pp. E9–E10.

163. Ibid., pp. E2–E9.

164. Ibid., pp. E2, E5, E7–E8.

165. Ibid., pp. E13–E14, E19.

166. Ibid., pp. E12–E13.

167. See p. 37 and note 99.

168. There now is much greater stress on accounting, quality, and cost-cutting, as well as on profits. See Hu, "Act in Accordance with Economic Laws," pp. E8, E10, E13–E14.

169. On profits, see Fox Butterfield, "Chinese Province Tests Profit Incentive in Industry," *New York Times*, January 27, 1980. Experimental factories in Szechwan have been authorized to keep 5 percent of planned profits and 20 percent of above-plan profits; although the amounts may sound modest, they should significantly increase the incentive of enterprises to increase efficiency and profits. See also "China Gives Factories a Freer Hand," *China Business Review*, vol. 6, no. 5 (September–October 1979), p. 53. In early 1980 Hsueh Mu-chiao gave many details on the new experiments stressing profits; see Xue Muqiao, "On Reforming the Economic Management System," *Beijing Review*, no. 12 (1980), pp. 21 ff. An accompanying article stated that in July 1979 the State Council issued five documents to provide guidelines for new experiments in enterprise self-management (including regulations on retaining shares of profits and depreciation funds, taxation of fixed assets, and provision of working capital through loans); see "Self-Management Enlivens Enterprises," *Beijing Review*, no. 12 (March 24, 1980), pp. 25–26.

170. Hu, in "Act in Accordance with Economic Laws," p. E10, stated bluntly, "We must adhere to the principle illustrated in Lenin's instruction to give awards to enterprises that have run themselves well and made money, and punish those that do not run themselves well and lose money. Legal action must be taken against the responsible leaders of enterprises where management is alarmingly chaotic, laws and discipline are defied, and there are heavy financial losses. They should be punished or fined. New leading groups must be organized to replace old ones. Those derelict in their duties must not be left unpunished by law."

171. Ibid., p. E10. With a group of U.S. governors, I visited factories in several Chinese cities in October 1979. My interviews with managers and technical personnel indicated that, as of that date, the amount of profits that they could keep had been increased to some extent. One manager in Tsinan,

for example, reported that the factory could keep 10 percent of above-quota profits (personal interview notes, October 22, 1979). However, none of the factories visited had been designated "experimental" factories, where the percentage is reported to be larger (see note 169). As of late 1979, one report stated that there were about 2,000 designated experimental enterprises in China; their experiments clearly will provide the basis for policy applied generally later; see *Economist* (December 29, 1979), p. 26. However, a later Chinese report, in early 1980, said that there were 2,600 state-owned enterprises of an experimental type in 1979; see "Self-Management Enlivens Enterprises," *Beijing Review*, no. 12 (March 24, 1980), p. 25. Later in 1980, it was reported that this number had risen to over 6,000.

172. During 1979 increasing stress was placed on the need both to promote technicians and specialists into leading posts and to train Party members to be specialists and professionals. See, for example, "Training Managerial Cadres in Rotation," *Beijing Review*, no. 25 (June 22, 1979), p. 7; "Technicians Become Leading Cadres," *Beijing Review*, no. 51 (December 21, 1979), p. 4; and "Leading Cadres Receive Training in Management," *Beijing Review*, no. 8 (February 25, 1980), p. 6. Teng Hsiao-ping, in his January 16, 1980, "Report on the Current Situation and Tasks," stated, "We should gradually attain a situation in which people with specialized knowledge are undertaking leadership work in professional organs at all levels, including the Party committees at all levels"; FBIS, *Daily Report*—PRC, March 11, 1980, Supplement, p. 21.

173. On general policy regarding specialized companies (or trusts), see Hu, "Act in Accordance with Economic Laws," pp. E14–E15. On the early 1960s experience with trusts, see the sources cited in note 3.

174. See NFAC, CIA, *China: In Pursuit of Economic Modernization*, Research Paper ER 78-10680, December 1978, pp. 10–11; "A Guide to China's New Industrial Corporations," *China Business Review*, vol. 5, no. 5 (September–October 1978), pp. 21–26; and "Ten New PRC Industrial Corporations Identified," *China Business Review*, vol. 6, no. 3 (May–June 1979), pp. 21–24.

175. Hu, "Act in Accordance with Economic Laws," p. E14.

176. Ibid., pp. E5–E6.

177. Ibid. On management see Xue Muqiao, "On Reforming the Economic Management System," cited earlier, and "A Study in the Planned Management of the Socialist Economy," *Beijing Review*, no. 43 (October 26, 1979), pp. 14–20; Ren Luosen (Jen Lo-sen), "Changes in China's Economic Management," *Beijing Review*, no. 5 (February 4, 1980), pp. 16–22; Li Chih-sheng (Li Zhisheng), "Take Management as a Way to Win Victory," *Kwangming Daily*, November 4, 1978, in FBIS, *Daily Report*—PRC, November 17, 1978, pp. E12 ff.; *Renmin Ribao* Commentary, "We Must Be Bold in Reforming the Economic Management System," February 6, 1979, in FBIS, *Daily Report*—PRC, February 14, 1979, p. E10; Chiang Hsueh-mo (Jiang Xuemo or Qiang Xuemo), "A Talk on Learning from Enterprise Management of Capitalist Countries," *Kwangming Daily*, September 28, 1978, in FBIS, *Daily Report*—PRC, October 4, 1978, pp. E23–E25; and "Enterprise Management Tentative Practice," *Beijing Review*, no. 32 (August 10, 1979), p. 6.

178. Hu, "Act in Accordance with Economic Laws," pp. E2–E4. Also see Tung Chih-min (Tong Zhimin), member of the Institute of Foreign Economic Management, Chinese People's University, "How Did Lenin View the Introduction of Advanced Technology and the Admission of Foreign Capital?" *Kwangming Daily*, August 18, 1978, in FBIS, *Daily Report—PRC*, August 25, 1978, pp. E4–E7; Jou Shui (Rou Shui), "What Is the Difference between a Name and Reality—Talk Based on Taochuan [Taoquan]," *People's Daily*, August 25, 1978, in FBIS, *Daily Report—PRC*, August 28, 1978, pp. E1–E5; Chiang Hsueh-mo (Jiang Xuemo) (a commentator), "A Talk on Learning from Enterprise Management of Capitalist Countries," *Kwangming Daily*, September 23, 1978, in FBIS, *Daily Report—PRC*, October 4, 1978, pp. E23–E24; and "Industry Vice Minister on Learning from Capitalist Management," FBIS, *Daily Report—PRC*, January 22, 1979, pp. E15–E16. On learning from Japan, Yugoslavia, and Rumania, see "Why China Imports Technology and Equipment," *Peking Review*, no. 41 (October 13, 1978), pp. 11–13. Hungary, whose experience in many respects may be more relevant to China, also has been of great interest to Peking, but for foreign policy reasons the Chinese stressed more strongly their interest in Yugoslavia and Rumania. Chao Tzu-yang, however, has talked of China's interest in the experience in Hungary as well as Yugoslavia and other areas; see Fox Butterfield, "Chinese Province Tests Profit Incentive in Industry," *New York Times*, January 27, 1980.

179. Hu, "Act in Accordance with Economic Laws," p. E15.

180. Ibid., p. E16.

181. See Special Feature, "Prospect and Retrospect, China's Socialist Legal System," *Beijing Review*, no. 2 (January 12, 1979), pp. 25–30; Xing Zhong (Hsing Chung), "Judicial Organs and Judicial Procedure in China," *Beijing Review*, no. 2 (January 12, 1979), pp. 30–34; "The Law of the People's Republic of China on Joint Ventures Using Chinese and Foreign Investment," *Beijing Review*, no. 29 (July 20, 1979), pp. 24–26; "The New Criminal Law and the Law of Criminal Procedure," *Beijing Review*, no. 33 (August 17, 1979), pp. 16–22; and Cheng Zihua (Cheng Tzu-hua), "On China's Electoral Law," *Beijing Review*, no. 37 (September 14, 1979), pp. 15–18. See also "China's New Revolution Introduces Democracy," *China Business Review*, vol. 6, no. 5 (September–October 1979), pp. 45–49. For background on law in the period before Mao's death, see Jerome Alan Cohen, *The Criminal Process in the People's Republic of China, 1949–1963* (Harvard University Press, 1968), and "Chinese Law: At the Crossroads," *China Quarterly*, no. 53 (January–March 1973), pp. 139–43; Victor H. Li, *Law Without Lawyers* (Stanford Alumni Association, 1977), and "The Role of Law in Communist China," *China Quarterly*, no. 44 (October–December 1970), pp. 66–111; Stanley Lubman, "On Understanding Chinese Law and Legal Institutions," *American Bar Association Journal*, vol. 62 (May 1976), pp. 597–99; and Shao-chuan Leng, *Justice in Communist China* (Oceana Publications, 1967). On economic contracts, see Richard M. Pfeffer, "The Institution of Contracts in the Chinese People's Republic," and "Contracts in China Revisited," *China Quarterly*, no. 14 (April–June 1963), pp. 153–77, no. 15 (July–September 1963), pp. 115–39,

and no. 28 (October–December 1966), pp. 106–29; and Gene T. Hsiao, "The Role of Contracts in Communist China," *California Law Review*, vol. 53, no. 4 (October 1965), pp. 1029–60.

182. Hundreds of Chinese articles as well as official statements, including most cited elsewhere in these notes, help to provide a basis for understanding the recent change in ideology in China. For a recent Western analysis, see Brantly Womack, "Politics and Epistemology in China since Mao," *China Quarterly*, no. 80 (December 1979), pp. 768–92; the author is more tentative. than I, however, in judging whether or not the recent changes are a "watershed." A leading Chinese scholar involved in a Peking institute dealing with ideological issues stated in December 1979, when I asked him how he viewed China's present problem of redefining its ideology, "We have to go back to absolute basics and fundamentals, and take a new look at everything."

183. Until recently, many American scholars objected to the use of the term "pragmatism" to describe the outlook of any Chinese leaders, including Teng and others who now dominate decision making in Peking. Personally, I have long believed "pragmatic" to be the correct term for such men. The radicals recognized it and labeled their views pragmatism. They openly attacked Teng for what they called his "new version of the notorious bourgeois philosophy of pragmatism"; see Chin Chih-po, "Denial of the Difference between Socialism and Capitalism," p. 20. All of Teng's recent statements have openly and strongly stressed pragmatic and empirical values and approaches.

184. This shift of emphasis was predictable; see Barnett, *Uncertain Passage*, p. 31, which stated, in 1974, "It would not be surprising, for example, if future leaders, motivated by the desire to use the Thought of Mao to justify relatively pragmatic policies, decide to put increasing emphasis on the elements in Mao's writings that stress pragmatic approaches. . . . they can easily do so by emphasizing the importance of certain of his writings (for example, 'On Practice')." An article in the *Kwangming Daily* on May 11, 1978, titled "Practice Is the Only Standard for Evaluating Truth" (reprinted the next day in *People's Daily*), signaled the start of this ideological shift (it was soon made the centerpiece of a Teng speech on June 2); see Womack, "Politics and Epistemology in China since Mao," p. 768. See also C. L. Chiou, "Maoism in the 'Three Great Debates,'" *Issues and Studies* (Taiwan), vol. 15, no. 10 (October 1979), pp. 34–49. The Third Plenum of the Central Committee discussed the issue and endorsed the principle of "seeking truth from facts" and "linking theory with practice," stating that the Party "highly valued the discussion of whether practice is the sole criterion for testing truth." This appears to have been the subject of some continuing debate, however; see "Discussion of the Criterion of Truth," *Beijing Review*, no. 39 (September 28, 1979), pp. 3–4. Nevertheless, a top leader of the Chinese Academy of Social Sciences told me in 1980 that he considered the May 11, 1978, article on "practice" and Hu Chiao-mu's article on "economic laws" to be the two most important articles laying the foundations for new policies in 1978.

185. This slogan, perhaps even more than ones emphasizing "practice," has become the key popular phrase symbolizing Teng's pragmatic values.

186. One of the most important early statements clarifying the new policy

toward intellectuals was Teng Hsiao-ping's speech at the 1978 National Science Conference; see the text in *Peking Review*, no. 12 (March 24, 1978), pp. 9–18. His statement that "the overwhelming majority of them [intellectuals] are part of the proletariat" was a basic reformulation of the Party's previous ideological position defining intellectuals' status in society. See also *Renmin Ribao* Commentator, "Comprehensively and Accurately Understand the Party's Policy towards Intellectuals," abridged version, *Beijing Review*, no. 5 (February 2, 1979), pp. 10–15. Also see the following earlier articles: Shen Ko-ting (Shen Keting or Shen Geding), "Refuting the Gang of Four's Theory of 'The Notorious Ninth Category,' " *Red Flag*, no. 7 (1977), in FBIS, *Daily Report—PRC*, July 12, 1977, pp. E15–E21; Mass Criticism Group of Shensi (Shaanxi) Normal University, "A Correct Attitude Must Be Taken toward Intellectuals," *Red Flag*, no. 7 (1977), in FBIS, *Daily Report—PRC*, July 14, 1977, pp. E1–E5; NCNA, "Conscientious Efforts Must Be Made to Implement the Party's Policy on Intellectuals and Bring Their Socialist Enthusiasm into Full Play," in FBIS, *Daily Report—PRC*, February 25, 1977, pp. E1–E2.

187. A brief summary of the conference and the text of Teng Hsiao-ping's speech are in *Peking Review*, no. 18 (May 5, 1978), pp. 6–12.

188. Chinese writings on education since then have continued to stress these themes; see, for example, several articles (labeled "Special Feature/Education") in *Beijing Review*, no. 1 (January 7, 1980), pp. 17–27.

189. On education in the 1960s and early 1970s, see P. J. Seybolt, *Chinese Education* (Sharpe, 1968); R. F. Price, *Education in Communist China* (Praeger, 1970); R. D. Barendsen, *The Educational Revolution in China*, Department of Health, Education, and Welfare, Office of Education (GPO, 1973); Donald J. Munro, "Egalitarian Ideal and Educational Fact in Communist China," in Lindbeck, *China: Management of a Revolutionary Society*, pt. 3, pp. 256–304; and T. H. E. Chen, "The Maoist Model of Education: Origins and Ideology," *Asian Affairs* (July–August 1976), pp. 384–400.

190. For Western analyses of recent developments in Chinese education, see Suzanne Pepper, "Education and Revolution: The 'Chinese Model,' Revisited," *Asian Survey*, vol. 18, no. 9 (September 1978), pp. 847–90; Susan L. Shirk, "Educational Reform and Political Backlash: Recent Changes in Chinese Educational Policy," *Comparative Education Review*, vol. 23, no. 2 (June 1979), pp. 183–217, and "The Politics of Education in Post-Mao China," China Council (Asia Society), April 1979, mimeographed; and J. W. Munro, "A Major Turnabout in China," *Chronicle of Higher Education*, vol. 15, no. 10 (November 7, 1977), pp. 1–10. On "key schools," see Theoretical Group of the Ministry of Education, "It Is Imperative to Run a Group of Key Schools Well," *Kwangming Daily*, January 13, 1978, in FBIS, *Daily Report—PRC*, January 20, 1978, pp. E17–E20; and Committee on Scholarly Communication with the People's Republic of China and National Association of Foreign Student Affairs, U.S.-China Education Clearing House, *An Introduction to Education in the People's Republic of China and U.S.-China Educational Exchanges* (CSCPRC and NAFSA, 1980), pp. 49–59. This source lists "key" universities and colleges.

191. SSB, "Communiqué on Fulfilment of China's 1979 National Economic Plan," April 30, 1980, in FBIS, *Daily Report—PRC*, April 30, 1980, p. L8. See also CSCPRC and NAFSA, *An Introduction to Education*, pp. 8–11.

192. FBIS, *Daily Report—PRC*, April 30, 1980, p. L8.

193. CSCPRC and NAFSA, *An Introduction to Education*, pp. 6–7.

194. Estimates vary; none can be accurate because of the difficulty of determining valid standards for defining and testing literacy, and because of incomplete statistics. The literacy among China's youth has unquestionably risen, however, to a fairly high level.

195. CSCPRC and NAFSA, *An Introduction to Education*, pp. 15–23. See also International Communication Agency (ICA), Office of Research and Evaluation, *Student Exchange Programs of the People's Republic of China*, Research Report R-20-78, August 9, 1978, and *International Scientific and Technical Exchanges of the People's Republic of China*, Research Report R-2-79, January 31, 1979; Elizabeth MacCallum, "China, In Crash Program, Will Send 10,000 Students Overseas in Next 2 Years," *Chronicle of Higher Education* (September 5, 1978), pp. 3–5; Frank Ching, "Scholars from China Set to Begin Study in U.S. Next Month," *Asian Wall Street Journal*, September 22, 1978; and Melinda Liu, "Replacing a Lost Generation," *Far Eastern Economic Review* (September 15, 1978).

196. Personal interview, unattributable, February 23, 1979. (To reach this figure, the flow clearly will have to be stepped up during 1980–82.)

197. The State Statistical Bureau Communiqué on 1979 stated that during the year 1,762 "students were sent to study abroad by educational departments"; see FBIS, *Daily Report—PRC*, April 30, 1980, p. L8. However, by early 1980, American officials estimated that by then close to 2,000 persons (students and scholars) from China were studying in the United States alone. (Some had come with private funding.) Thereafter the number rose rapidly and by late 1980 was over 5,000.

198. CSCPRC and NAFSA, *An Introduction to Education*, pp. 15–17. The overwhelming majority (about 96 percent in the United States in 1979) were studying science and technology; ibid.

199. "On the Situation in China's Science and Education," Report to the Standing Committee of the Fourth National Committee of the Chinese People's Consultative Conference, *Peking Review*, no. 2 (January 13, 1978), p. 16. See also Pierre Perrolle, ed., "The 1978 National Science Conference: Speeches and Commentary," *Chinese Science and Society* (Sharpe, 1979).

200. Hua, "Report on the Work of the Government," February 26, 1978, p. D22.

201. *Peking Review*, no. 12 (March 24, 1978), pp. 10–11.

202. Ibid., p. 11.

203. See, for example, Chien San-chiang (Qian Sanqiang) radio commentary, "Chairman Mao Guides Us Continuously to Scale the Peaks of Science and Technology," in FBIS, *Daily Report—PRC*, January 4, 1977, pp. E13–E17; "Eliminate the Four Evils, Make Science Flourish," *People's Daily*, March 9, 1977, in FBIS, *Daily Report—PRC*, March 22, 1977, pp. E2–E4; Commentator, "Get Mobilized and Accelerate the Modernization of Science and Tech-

nology," *Red Flag*, no. 7 (1977), in FBIS, *Daily Report—PRC*, June 5, 1977, pp. E4–E8; Chien Hsueh-sen (Qian Xueshen), "Science and Technology Must Catch Up with and Surpass Advanced World Levels before the End of the Century," *Red Flag*, no. 7 (1977), in FBIS, *Daily Report—PRC*, July 8, 1977, pp. E2–E5.

204. Tse-tsung Chow, *The May Fourth Movement, Intellectual Revolution in Modern China* (Stanford University Press, 1967), especially p. 59; and John King Fairbank, *The United States and China* (Harvard University Press, 1955), p. 181.

205. Genevieve Dean and Thomas Fingar, "Developments in PRC Science and Technology Policy," April–June 1977, *United States-China Relations S and T Summary*, no. 3, Stanford University, United States-China Relations Program, pp. 11–12, and no. 4 (July–September 1977), pp. 1–10, mimeographed; and Fang Yi, "Report to the National Science Conference," March 18, 1978, in FBIS, *Daily Report—PRC*, March 29, 1978, pp. E1–E22.

206. Fang Yi, "Report," p. E8.

207. CSCPRC, *China Exchange Newsletter*, vol. 6, nos. 3–4 (June–August 1978), pp. 9–14.

208. Fang Yi, "Report," pp. E8–E14.

209. Top leaders already had underlined the importance of work in special fields that are on the frontiers of high technology; see, for example, Hua, "Report on the Work of the Government," February 26, 1978, pp. D22–D23.

210. See the 1978–79 issues of CSCPRC, *China Exchange Newsletter;* and CSCPRC and NAFSA, *An Introduction to Education*, pp. 40–47.

211. It is now possible to talk frankly with many Party as well as non-Party cadres in China (especially those involved in affairs at the national level), most of whom are prepared to give accounts of their personal histories; it is clear from such accounts that events from the mid-1960s to the mid-1970s had an even more devastating effect on China's best-qualified professionals than most outside observers realized. During 1978–79 I talked with many such people (who had been recently reappointed to significant positions) about their personal histories; in almost every case, their lives were literally wrecked for many years. Some frankly stated that they had considered suicide (and that they knew many others who had taken this course). The talents of some—especially intellectuals—had been wasted not just during the decade of the Cultural Revolution but for two whole decades, ever since the Anti-Rightist Campaign of 1957.

212. The Central Committee largely resolved this problem in early 1980 (see the later discussion of the results of the Central Committee's Fifth Plenum), but tensions clearly still exist at lower levels in the Party and bureaucracies.

213. Although some analysts have consistently maintained that Teng, if he were able to do so, would probably eventually try to seize the regime's top posts for himself, on repeated occasions during 1978–79 he told Westerners that he did not wish to have these posts. For example, in his interview with Robert Novak in late 1978, he stated that he could have acquired the premier-

ship after Mao's death but chose not to take it; see Rowland Evans and Robert Novak, "An Interview with China's Teng Hsiao-ping," *Washington Post*, November 28, 1978. He and others apparently did, however, require Hua Kuo-feng to make a self-criticism in late 1978; see Kyodo report, in FBIS, *Daily Report—PRC*, February 5, 1979, p. E2.

214. For a detailed account and analysis of internal politics during 1977–79, which generally rings true (and which stresses the antagonism between Hua Kuo-feng and Teng Hsiao-ping) and correctly assesses the gradually increasing predominance of Teng and his views, see Warren Kuo, "Power Struggle and Struggle over the Party's Line among the Chinese Communist Power Holders," in Institute of International Studies, University of South Carolina, *The Enduring Chinese Dimension* (IIS, University of South Carolina, 1979), pp. 349–61. Also see Joyce K. Kallgren, "China 1978: The New Long March," *Asian Survey*, vol. 19, no. 1 (January 1979), especially pp. 11–19.

215. Teng's second rehabilitation in 1977 really began the process. It was speeded up and greatly extended in late 1978; see the reports on the Central Committee meeting and follow-up in FBIS, *Daily Report—PRC*, December 22 and December 26, 1978. It was, in effect, completed by early 1980; see later discussion of Liu Shao-chi's final rehabilitation.

216. See Kuo, "Power Struggle," p. 352. On the significance of the title "Secretary-General," see p. 80 and note 248.

217. Third Plenum Communiqué, in FBIS, *Daily Report—PRC*, December 26, 1978, pp. E4 and E6.

218. Ibid., pp. E4 and E12.

219. Chen Yung-kuei (Chen Yonggui), a former peasant and head of the famous Tachai Brigade, and Ni Chih-fu (Ni Zhifu), a former worker, were elevated to the Politburo during the Cultural Revolution as representatives of the "masses." For a period of time, it appeared that Chen was acquiring significant influence; his absence from the purge list in early 1980 (see p. 79) may have been a sop to Hua. Li Teh-sheng (Li Desheng), who clearly had been influential, seemed to have been successful in making his peace with Teng temporarily. But Chen was ousted soon thereafter.

220. For one analysis by U.S. government specialists, see FBIS, "Chinese Political Debate since the December Third Plenum," *Analysis Report*, FB 79-10017 (August 1, 1979). See also Fox Butterfield, "A High-Level Discussion Has Been Going on in Peking for Weeks, Updating China's Economy Is Not Easy," *New York Times*, May 6, 1979, and "Deng, under Attack, Hits Back in China," *New York Times*, May 25, 1979; and Jay Mathews, "Heated Debates Reported among China's Leaders," *Washington Post*, January 20, 1979, and "China Admits Some Oppose Post-Mao Policies," *Washington Post*, June 6, 1979.

221. This was a major focus of Western correspondents' reports on domestic trends in China in late 1978 and early 1979. See, as examples, Jay Mathews, "Chinese Posters Attack System of Secret Police," *Washington Post*, November 22, 1978, and "Reform-Minded Chinese Becoming More Open about Varying Opinions," *Washington Post*, January 22, 1979; Fox

Butterfield, "Posters in Chinese City Call Rallies to Air Grievances," *New York Times*, December 27, 1978, "Freer Expression Typifies a New Dynamism in China," *New York Times*, January 14, 1979, and "China Backs Poster as Citizens' Forum," *New York Times*, January 1, 1979; John Fraser, "Calls for More Democracy Echo in New Peking March," *Washington Post*, November 29, 1978, and "Poster Attacks China's Rights Record," *Washington Post*, December 9, 1978; and "China's Winds of Change," *Newsweek* (December 11, 1978), pp. 41–43.

222. This slogan was revived soon after the winding down of the Cultural Revolution. In early 1978 Yeh Chien-ying, reporting on China's new state constitution, for the first time stated that it would be inserted into the constitution; see Jay Mathews, *Washington Post*, March 2, 1978.

223. Several handwritten, mimeographed publications were started by small groups and circulated in limited numbers, especially at "Democracy Wall"; the best-known was titled *Exploration*.

224. On criticism of Mao and some other Chinese leaders, see Jay Mathews, "Mao Tse-tung Criticized in Peking Wall Poster," *Washington Post*, November 20, 1978; and Agence France Press (AFP), "Member of Chinese Politburo Attacked in Peking Wallposter," *Washington Post*, November 25, 1978. On posters calling for Western-style democracy, see Fox Butterfield, "New Peking Posters Ask for Democracy and Praise the U.S.," *New York Times*, November 26, 1978. The most publicized of the calls for full democracy was an eloquent article written somewhat later, in March 1979, by Wei Ching-sheng (Wei Jingsheng), published in *Exploration* and titled "Human Rights, Equality, Democracy—On to the Fifth Modernization"; text in *Issues and Studies* (Taiwan), vol. 15, no. 11 (November 1979), pp. 86–95. A group calling itself the Chinese Human Rights Alliance, established on January 1, 1979, adopted on January 17 a "Declaration of Chinese Human Rights," which was put up on a poster and distributed in mimeographed form; see the text in *Issues and Studies*, vol. 15, no. 11, pp. 96–101.

225. From the start it seemed highly unlikely that the leadership would permit unfettered criticism or agitation for Western-style pluralistic democracy; see A. Doak Barnett, "Ferment in China," *New York Times*, November 12, 1978. By the spring of 1979 the regime began to impose limits, and it tried to draw a line on permissible dissent; see Jay Mathews, "China Muffles Pro-Democracy Critic," *Washington Post*, March 24, 1979. "Democracy Wall" was transferred to an out-of-the-way place in Peking (in most other cities comparable walls were closed down), and gradually the nonofficial mimeographed papers were stopped. Ultimately, Wei Ching-sheng was tried and jailed. The official press tried to define the limits of dissent while still advocating democratization; see Wu Jialin (Wu Chia-lin), "Some Questions concerning Socialist Democracy," *Beijing Review*, no. 24 (June 15, 1979), pp. 9–13; and Li Honglin (Li Hung-lin), "What Kind of Dictatorship of the Proletariat Should We Uphold?" *Renmin Ribao*, June 22, 1979, in FBIS, *Daily Report—PRC*, June 26, 1979, pp. L11–L14.

226. NCNA, "CCP Central Committee Decides to Remove 'Labels, Designations,'" January 28, 1979, in FBIS, *Daily Report—PRC*, January 30, 1979,

pp. E1–E3; Editorial, "An Important Party Decision in Suiting [*sic*] the Changed Situation," *Renmin Ribao*, January 29, 1979, in FBIS, *Daily Report—PRC*, January 30, 1979, pp. E3–E6; and *Renmin Ribao* Commentator, "Liberate Our Thinking, Hasten Our Speed," February 3, 1979, in FBIS, *Daily Report—PRC*, February 5, 1979, pp. E6–E10.

227. See note 265.

228. See sources cited in note 181. Another notable major trend was toward increased freedom of religion. In one extraordinary development, it was revealed that in the revived All-China Youth Federation, the YMCA and YWCA would be two of its four legally recognized constituent organizational members, along with the Communist Youth League and the All-China Students' Federation; see *Beijing Review*, no. 20 (May 18, 1979), p. 3.

229. Bennett Lee, "China Adds Spice to Its Cultural Fare," *Asian Wall Street Journal*, July 23, 1979.

230. On my October 1979 trip to China, the trend toward more individualistic hairstyles and clothing was quite visible in major cities. Perhaps the most striking change in social mores was the new public expression of romantic relationships between young men and women. In Shanghai the promenade along the Bund bordering the Whangpoo (Huangpu) River was crowded in the evening with couples, many indulging in what can only be called old-fashioned "necking."

231. An early harbinger of this was a short article in the *People's Daily* in late 1977: Huang Ching-lin (Huang Jinglin or Huang Qingling), "Chin Shih-huang [Qin Shihuang] [the first emperor of a unified China] Did Not Belong to the Communist Party," *Renmin Ribao*, November 5, 1977, in FBIS, *Daily Report—PRC*, November 14, 1977, p. E14. By early 1978, the trend was clear; see Fox Butterfield, "China Is Quietly Moderating Worshipful Treatment of Mao," *New York Times*, April 26, 1978; and Jay Mathews, "Chinese Leadership Disputes Mao's Legacy," *Washington Post*, May 5, 1978. The official press carried articles such as Niu Geng (Niu Keng), "Leaders Are Not Infallible," *Gongren Ribao* (*Kung-jen Jih-pao* or *Workers' Daily*), February 24, 1979, in FBIS, *Daily Report—PRC*, March 8, 1979, pp. E7–E8.

232. Article by Lu Dingyi (Lu Ting-yi), *Renmin Ribao*, March 8, 1979, NCNA summary, March 8, 1979, in FBIS, *Daily Report—PRC*, March 8, 1979, pp. E1–E4.

233. Article by Dong Tai (Tung Tai), *Renmin Ribao*, March 9, 1979, NCNA summary, March 9, 1979, in FBIS, *Daily Report—PRC*, March 9, 1979, pp. E5–E6.

234. See Lu Tingyi's article, in FBIS, *Daily Report—PRC*, March 8, 1979, p. E2. See also Fu Chongli (Fu Chung-li), " 'The Big Tree Reaches the Sky and Protects the Elite,' " *Renmin Ribao*, January 7, 1979, in FBIS, *Daily Report—PRC*, January 8, 1979, pp. E1–E6; and "Peking Throng Pays Homage to Chou," *New York Times*, January 8, 1979.

235. This, obviously, is a subjective judgment (no polls are available), but it is based on observation in China and numerous interviews and conversations with Chinese in both China and the United States.

236. Growing youth problems now are discussed openly in official Chinese

publications; see, for example, Zhou Zheng (Chou Cheng), "Save the Teen-age Delinquents," *Beijing Review*, no. 44 (November 2, 1979), pp. 18–26. For one analysis of relevant youth motivations and behavior during the Cultural Revolution, see David M. Raddock, *Political Behavior of Adolescents in China, The Cultural Revolution in Kwangchow* (University of Arizona Press, 1977).

237. Demonstrations during the winter of 1978–79 included some by dis-satisfied peasants who went to Peking to express their grievances; see, for example, Fox Butterfield, "Freer Expression Typifies a New Dynamism in China," *New York Times*, January 14, 1979.

238. See the discussion on pp. 105–07 and the analyses by Jammes and Pollack, cited in notes 282 and 283.

239. The following quotations are from the text, printed in FBIS, *Daily Report—PRC*, March 11, 1980, Supplement, pp. 1–27.

240. Teng stated that China's per capita national output now is "something over 200 U.S. dollars." This figure is roughly half the estimate made by U.S. government analysts. It highlighted the problem of converting Chinese data and yuan figures into dollar equivalents. Perhaps Teng's dollar estimate was arrived at simply by converting yuan estimates to dollar figures at official exchange rates, which would substantially underestimate what a realistic dol-lar figure should be. On the problems of estimating China's output in dollars, see my later discussion in note 288, below.

241. See the text in *Beijing Review*, no. 40 (October 5, 1979), pp. 7–32. When I visited Peking a few days after this speech was delivered, everyone with whom I talked regarded the speech as a milestone.

242. For an analysis of fear of chaos (*luan*) as a central theme in Chinese politics, see Solomon, *Mao's Revolution and the Chinese Political Culture*.

243. In discussions with Chinese intellectuals in early 1980, I found, some-what to my surprise, considerable support for the banning of "big character posters" from non-Communist intellectuals who argued that during the Cul-tural Revolution such posters had been a primary instrument for irresponsible attacks by the radicals on them, and that because there was no accountability for what was written on such posters they were dangerous.

244. The following quotations are from the text, titled "Why China Has Opened Its Doors," in FBIS, *Daily Report—PRC*, February 12, 1980, pp. L1–L5.

245. Fox Butterfield, "Deng Reported Set to Yield Post," *New York Times*, March 17, 1980. There was no implication that he was relinquishing power, but rather the move implied that his power was sufficient to "rule" without holding that post.

246. The following quotations are from the text, in FBIS, *Daily Report—PRC*, February 29, 1980, pp. L1–L5.

247. UPI, "Deng Says His Protégé Runs China's Government," *New York Times*, April 18, 1980.

248. See Donald W. Klein and Anne B. Clark, *Biographic Dictionary of Chinese Communism, 1921–1965* (Harvard University Press, 1971), vol. 2, pp. 823–24.

249. For current official biographies of these men, see FBIS, *Daily Report—PRC*, March 3, 1980, pp. L8–L15.

250. "Report on Hua Address," in FBIS, *Daily Report—PRC*, May 8, 1980, p. L4.

251. In May 1980 huge memorial services for Liu were held in Peking and throughout the country; see Jay Mathews, "China Erases Official Leader to Honor Ex-Leader," *Washington Post*, May 16, 1980.

252. See "Guiding Principles for Inner-Party Political Life," *Beijing Review*, no. 14 (April 7, 1980), pp. 11–20.

253. See part II, pp. 132 ff.

254. Huan Hsiang (Huan Xiang), vice president of the Chinese Academy of Social Sciences, discussed this at some length during a visit to the Brookings Institution in Washington, D.C., on April 17, 1979.

255. Third Plenum Communiqué, December 22, 1978, in FBIS, *Daily Report—PRC*, December 26, 1978, p. E7.

256. *Renmin Ribao*, February 24, 1979, in FBIS, *Daily Report—PRC*, February 26, 1979, pp. E12–E16.

257. This and the following quotations are from the editorial in ibid.

258. After returning from a trip to Peking to advise China's economic planners, the noted Japanese economist Saburo Okita (who became Japan's Foreign Minister in November 1979) stated that he believed the target probably had been cut to about 45 million tons (personal interview, August 1, 1979).

259. Huan Hsiang, during the visit mentioned in note 254, discussed the changes in agricultural policy, including the slowdown in mechanization. On revised mechanization policy, see also "China's New Agriculture Mechanization Guidelines," *China Business Review*, vol. 6, no. 4 (July–August 1979), p. 66.

260. A large percentage of China's negotiations with large foreign corporations during 1978–79 concerned possible development of basic resources; see part II.

261. Jay Mathews, "Chinese Official Reportedly Sees Economic Crisis," *Washington Post*, June 15, 1979.

262. Publicly, the Chinese did not use any figure of this sort. However, in early 1980 the director of the State Bureau of Labor, after stating that 7 million new jobs had been created in 1979, discussed at length the many types of people in urban areas still waiting to obtain jobs, clearly implying that the number of unemployed was still sizable; see Wei Min, "1979: More Than 7 Million People Employed," *Beijing Review*, no. 6 (February 11, 1980), pp. 13–23.

263. This and the following quotations are from Hua's "Report on the Work of the Government," June 18, 1979.

264. On Liu Shao-chi's position (articulated in the late 1950s) that "class struggle has in the main ended," a position the radicals later strongly attacked, see Dittmer, *Liu Shao-chi and the Chinese Cultural Revolution*, pp. 221–27.

265. From the early 1950s until after Mao's death, large numbers of Chinese were subject to severe discrimination because they had been labeled (and con-

tinued to bear the "caps" of) the "five [bad] elements": landlords, rich peasants, counterrevolutionaries, Rightists, and other "bad elements"; see A. Doak Barnett, *Cadres, Bureaucracy, and Political Power in Communist China* (Columbia University Press, 1967), pp. 231–33, 395, 404–10.

266. See Chou En-lai, *Report on the Question of Intellectuals*, a speech delivered January 14, 1956 (Peking: Foreign Languages Press, 1956), especially pp. 4 ff., where he discusses "the connection between the question of intellectuals and our present task of hastening the building of socialism."

267. Hua, "Report on the Work of the Government," June 18, 1979, p. 23. Hua also urged that "we popularize and improve the system of electing cadres." In early 1980 it was announced that the NPC Standing Committee had decided to hold elections in 1980 for county-level congresses (although it was not clear whether or not these would involve multiple candidacies); see press release no. 80/008, Embassy of the People's Republic of China, Washington, D.C., February 20, 1980, pp. 2–3.

268. This commission was established July 1, 1980, directly under the State Council. Its membership included China's top economic and financial leaders with Chen Yun (Chen Yun) as chairman, Li Hsien-nien as Vice Chairman, and Yao Yi-lin (Yao Yilin) as Secretary-General; the other members included Yu Chiu-li, Wang Chen (Wang Zhen), Fang Yi, Ku Mu (Gu Mu), Po Yi-po (Bo Yibo), Wang Jen-chung (Wang Renzhong), Chen Kuo-tung (Chen Guodong), Kang Shih-en (Kang Shien), Chang Ching-fu (Zhang Jingfu), and Chin Ming (Jin Ming); see *China Business Review*, vol. 6, no. 5 (September–October 1979), p. 9. It was designed "to strengthen unified leadership over financial and economic work." A leading Chinese official stated to me in a private conversation on September 17, 1979, that the Commission had become, in fact, the top body determining broad economic policy in China, despite the fact that Chen Yun, because of age and ill health, was only able to work about half time (unattributable interview).

269. The quotations and data from Yu and Chang that follow are from Yu Qiuli, "Report on the Draft of the 1979 National Economic Plan," text in FBIS, *Daily Report—PRC*, July 2, 1979, pp. L13–L28; and Zhang Jingfu, "Report on the Final State Accounts of 1978 and the Draft State Budget for 1979," text in FBIS, *Daily Report—PRC*, July 3, 1979, pp. L6–L19.

270. This promise will be difficult to fulfill because of likely inflationary pressures; see note 145 on the signs of such pressures.

271. Vice Premier Chen Muhua (Chen Mu-hua), "Controlling Population Growth in a Planned Way," *Beijing Review*, no. 46 (November 16, 1979), p. 18. See also, in the same issue, Zhou Jinghua (Chou Ching-hua), "Interview with a Specialist on Population," pp. 20–22; and Ouyang Huiyun (Ou-yang Hui-yun), "Marked Results in China's Most Populous Province," pp. 22–27.

272. "Communiqué of the State Statistical Bureau of the People's Republic of China on Fulfilment of China's 1978 National Economic Plan," June 27, 1979, text in FBIS, *Daily Report—PRC*, June 27, 1979, pp. L11–L19.

273. The figures used in this discussion are drawn from the NPC reports and SSB Communiqués unless otherwise noted. Figures for 1978 and targets

for 1979 were given by the Chinese in concrete terms; many of those for 1977 are inferred from statements about percentage increases over 1977. The figures are given in Chinese yuan rather than dollar equivalents because of the difficulty of determining valid dollar equivalents. For a discussion of this problem, see note 288. The yuan figures are extremely useful for analyzing trends and relative values within the Chinese economy, even though they do not provide a basis for international comparisons.

274. Chang's figures are slightly confusing. He stated that 1978 revenues were 24.600 billion yuan above the 1977 figures (on the basis of "final state accounts"), implying that 1978 revenues were 87.511 billion yuan. (He also noted that 1978 revenues were 28.2 percent above 1977.) However, he also said that in terms of "comparable items" in 1977, revenues in 1978 were 20.400 billion yuan, or 23.4 percent, above 1977.

275. Again, however, this direct comparison may be misleading to a degree. Finance Minister Chang stated that if "calculated in terms of comparable items," the 1979 budget would have been 128.600 billion yuan, or 14.7 percent above 1978; the reason it would be officially 16.600 billion yuan less than 128.600 billion yuan, he said, was that the 1979 figures would not include funds already "deducted" for raises in the purchase prices of farm and sideline products, reductions or exemptions of rural taxes, wage increases, creation of new employment opportunities, and the implementation of the new "system of enterprises' funds."

276. The SSB said that of total investment in 1978, "fixed assets made available by capital construction departments all over the country" totaled 35.600 billion yuan, which it said was 37 percent above 1977.

277. These percentage figures are difficult to reconcile with his other figures and statements, however. Of his 111.093 billion yuan figure for total central state expenditures in 1978, 40.7 percent would be 45.215 billion yuan, which is close to his figure for *central and local* expenditures on capital construction, whereas 34.8 percent of his 112 billion yuan figure for total central state expenditures in 1979 would be 38.976 billion yuan, which is close to his figure for just *central* budget appropriations for capital construction, without including local government capital construction.

278. See table 1-3.

279. These figures appear plausible. If one applies Yu's percentages on sectoral allocation of investments to the 36 billion yuan figure for 1979 (without including foreign loans), they would indicate a drop in investment in heavy industry of 4.759 billion yuan, or 22 percent, to 16.848 billion yuan (in 1979) and a rise in investment in agriculture of 813 million yuan, or 19 percent, to 5.040 billion yuan. However, they would indicate a *drop* in investment in light industry (which does *not* seem plausible) by 45 million yuan, or 2 percent, to 2.088 billion yuan.

280. For purposes of comparison, the planned allocation of investment in China at the start of its first Five Year Plan was 61.8 percent for industry and 6.2 percent for agriculture; see Eckstein, *China's Economic Development*, p. 264.

281. Hua, "Report on the Work of the Government," June 18, 1979, p. 12.

282. A study in 1979 by a leading CIA analyst of Chinese military affairs indicated that China's budget figures for defense probably include only costs for operations, including personnel, and that most other defense expenditures are under budget categories. He estimated that total defense expenditures in 1979 may have been around 40 billion yuan. (This is difficult to convert realistically to dollars but may be equivalent to something between 5 and 10 percent of GNP; earlier estimates were close to 10 percent.) The study estimated that military expenditures increased at an average of 10 percent a year (a very high rate) between 1961 and 1971 (despite a temporary decline in 1967), dropped almost 15 percent in 1972, then started slowly upward in 1973, increasing at an average rate of only about 1 percent or a little more a year between 1972 and 1977. He attributed the sizable increases in military expenditures that occurred in 1978 and 1979 mainly to the operating costs of the Sino-Vietnamese hostilities and judged that the increase therefore was "temporary"; see Sydney H. Jammes, "Chinese Military Expenditures: Implications for the Future," November 1979, mimeographed. A published CIA study in mid-1980 gave further details on the probable breakdown of Chinese military spending by category, as well as new estimates of China's total military manpower (4.3 million in combat and combat support units and another 3 million to 4 million in administrative and service units). It estimated that China's total defense spending in 1978 was still below the 1971 peak, and that military modernization will continue at a very modest pace; see NFAC, CIA, *Chinese Defense Spending, 1965–79*, Research Paper SR 80-10091, July 1980. For earlier U.S. government estimates, see Arms Control and Disarmament Agency, *World Military Expenditures and Arms Transfers, 1968–1977* (ACDA, 1979), p. 155, and earlier issues of this ACDA serial publication.

283. Military modernization clearly still is fourth in priority; in addition to the sources cited in note 282, see Jonathan D. Pollack, *Defense Modernization in the People's Republic of China*, Rand Note N-1214-1-AF, October 1979 (Rand Corp., 1979); and Ellis Joffe, "The Chinese Army," *Quadrant*, vol. 22, no. 11 (November 1978), pp. 10–11 (Truman Institute Reprints, 1979). Teng, in his January 16, 1980, speech (cited earlier), stressed, "National defense construction cannot be carried out without a certain economic foundation."

284. On China's worldwide window shopping for arms and military equipment, see Paul H. B. Godwin, "China and the Second World: The Search for Defense Technology," *Contemporary China*, vol. 2, no. 3 (Fall 1978), pp. 3–9; and my discussion in part II, p. 138 and note 55.

285. See Pollack, *Defense Modernization in the People's Republic of China*, especially pp. 13–16.

286. The figures that follow on 1977–78, unless otherwise noted, are from the State Statistical Bureau's Communiqué issued June 27, 1979, in FBIS, *Daily Report—PRC*, June 27, 1979, pp. L11–L19. A few figures in the reports by Yu and Chang differ slightly. Additional data are presented in tables 1-3 and 1-4.

287. SSB Communiqué, June 27, 1979, p. L12, gives these percentages. The 1978 yuan figure is my calculation from the 1979 figure and its percentage over 1978, in the SSB Communiqué, April 30, 1980, in FBIS, *Daily Report— PRC*, April 30, 1980, p. L1.

288. Chinese "national income" statistics, following Soviet practices, differ from Western calculations of gross domestic product (GDP) and gross national product (GNP). The State Statistical Bureau, in its communiqué on performance in 1979, which stated that the national income was 337 billion yuan and was 7 percent above 1978, defined it briefly as "net output value of material-producing departments including industry, agriculture, building construction, communications and transport and commerce" (FBIS, *Daily Report—PRC*, April 30, 1980, p. L1). The concept excludes the service sector and other items included in Western GDP and GNP calculations (for further details, see Chen, *Chinese Economic Statistics*, pp. 10–13). Two major steps are required to convert Chinese national income figures into estimates of GDP in dollars. The first is to convert yuan national income figures into yuan GDP estimates, and the second is to convert the yuan estimates into dollars. Recently published Chinese data are helpful in regard to the first step. In 1979, according to SSB figures, output of industry (459.1 billion yuan) accounted for 74.4 percent and agriculture (158.4 billion yuan) for 25.7 percent of gross industrial and agricultural output, and new data suggest that in 1977–78 the *net* value of output was probably 31.1 percent of *gross* value in industry and 67.5 percent in agriculture (Robert Michael Field, typed memorandum, March 21, 1980, citing *Jingji Yenjiu* [*Ching-chi, Yen-chiu*, or *Economic Research*], no. 4 [1979], p. 51, and no. 12 [1979], p. 9). If one assumes that the percentages were the same in 1979, the net value of output in industry in 1979 was 142.78 billion yuan, and in agriculture it was 106.92 yuan; the two combined totaled 249.70 billion yuan. A CIA study has estimated that in 1971 the net value of China's industrial and agricultural output, with depreciation added, was just over 66 percent (industry, 40.5 percent; agriculture, 25.7 percent) of the gross domestic product (calculated from figures in Robert Michael Field, "Real Capital Formation in the People's Republic of China: 1952–1973," July 12, 1976, mimeographed, p. 131). If one assumes that this percentage was the same in 1979, China's GDP in 1979 was about 373 billion yuan. The second step, converting this into a dollar estimate, poses more difficult questions. If one makes conversions at the average exchange rate of $1.00 = 1.56 yuan, the GDP dollar figure would be $239 billion—far below the CIA's estimate of China's GNP even in 1978: $407 billion, in 1977 dollars, or $444 billion, in 1978 dollars (see table 1-1 and appendix table 1). However, this clearly would not reflect real "purchasing power parities." Studies sponsored by the United Nations of purchasing power parities indicate that the real dollar values of GNP (stated in local currencies) in some developing countries are two or more times those obtained by other methods relying mainly on exchange rates (see *World Bank Atlas*, 1977 [Washington, D.C.: World Bank, no date but presumably 1978], pp. 2, 31–32, citing Irving B. Kravis, Alan Heston, and Robert Summers, *International Comparisons of*

Real Product and Purchasing Power [Johns Hopkins University Press, 1978]).
For example, their estimates of certain countries' GDP in 1975, based on new
estimates of purchasing power parities, were 183 percent of the *World Bank
Atlas* GNP estimates (based on average 1974–76 exchange rates and prices plus
a U.S. GNP deflator) in the case of Kenya, 227 percent in the case of Co-
lombia, and 348 percent in the case of India (my calculations, from data in
World Bank Atlas, p. 31). The CIA, in calculating China's GNP in dollars,
used a U.S. GNP deflator to try to reflect real purchasing power parities (see
Ashbrook, "China: Shift of Economic Gears in Mid-1970s," p. 233). In 1979,
after studying recently published Chinese statistics, CIA analysts tentatively
concluded that their previous dollar estimates of China's GNP and its growth
might have been "somewhat" too high (see CIA, *China: A Preliminary Reconciliation of Official and CIA National Product Data*, ER M 79-10690, December 1979, p. 3). However, in my judgment they may not have been very far
off the mark, and it is conceivable that more sophisticated estimates of purchasing power parities made in the future could show that their dollar estimates actually have been too low. The CIA's estimate for China's GNP in
1979 was $468 billion (in 1978 dollars), a 5 percent rise over their estimate of
$444 billion (in 1978 dollars) for 1978; see NFAC, CIA, *China: The Continu-
ing Search for a Modernization Strategy*, Research Paper ER 80-10248, April
1980, p. 1.

289. The following figures are from the SSB Communiqué of June 27,
1979, and the Yu and Chang reports cited in note 269. Additional data are in
table 1-4.

290. The per capita electricity figure for China is calculated from the output figure in table 1-4, and the Chinese population figure from table 3-1. The
figure on U.S. per capita electricity is based on 1976 electricity and population figures in CIA, *Handbook of Economic Statistics, 1977*, Research Aid
ER 77-10537, September 1977, pp. 22, 86. The per kilometer railway figure is
calculated from the figure for operating rail lines in the SSB Communiqué,
June 27, 1979, p. L16, and a CIA figure for China's area (roughly 3.7 million
square miles, or 9.6 million square kilometers) in CIA, *People's Republic of
China Atlas*, November 1971, p. 5. The per capita bicycle figure is calculated
from population and bicycle figures in tables 1-4 and 3-1.

291. See table 3-2 for grain output data for earlier years, from which these
figures are calculated.

292. "Education Industry Thrives despite Fewer Customers," *Washington
Post*, September 3, 1979. The estimated figure of 12 million for 1979–80 covered junior and community colleges and specialized higher education institutions as well as regular colleges and universities, but it excluded 4 million
noncredit students in other kinds of higher education.

293. See Yu Chiu-li, "Report on the Draft of the 1979 National Economic
Plan," June 21, 1979, in FBIS, *Daily Report—PRC*, July 2, 1979, pp. L13–L28.

294. Unless otherwise noted, the following statistics for 1979 are from
SSB, "Communiqué on the Fulfilment of China's 1979 Economic Plan," April

30, 1980, in FBIS, *Daily Report—PRC*, April 30, 1980, pp. L1–L10. For additional data on 1979–80, see *Beijing Review*, no. 2 (January 14, 1978), pp. 3–5, and no. 9 (March 3, 1980), pp. 5–6; and "Yuan Baohua [Yuan Pao-hua] Outlines 1980 Tasks," in FBIS, *Daily Report—PRC*, February 12, 1980, pp. L9–L12.

295. For further discussion of 1979 grain output, see part III, p. 316.

296. *Beijing Review*, no. 6 (February 11, 1980), pp. 13 ff.

297. "China's Economy: 1979 Performance and 1980 Plan," Department of State telegram from American Consulate-General, Hong Kong, April 1980 (R1409302, unclassified). This report stated (citing a Chinese source) that even though these 3,000 enterprises were a tiny fraction of the 380,000 industrial and communication enterprises in China, they accounted for 7 percent of "key state industrial enterprises," more than 30 percent of state industries' output, and more than 45 percent of their profits.

298. NCNA, "Zhao Ziyang Discusses Economic Reform Contradictions," in FBIS, *Daily Report—PRC*, April 21, 1980, pp. L2–L4; and "Second Part of Zhao Ziyang's Speech on Economic Reform," in FBIS, *Daily Report—PRC*, April 22, 1980, pp. L1–L7.

299. NFAC, CIA, *China: The Continuing Search for a Modernization Strategy*, p. 11.

300. "Communiqué of the Fifth Plenary Session of the Eleventh Central Committee of the Communist Party of China," February 29, 1980, in FBIS, *Daily Report—PRC*, February 29, 1980, p. L1.

301. Qin Wen, "Why Has It Not Been Possible to Scale Down Capital Construction?" *Renmin Ribao*, January 31, 1980, in FBIS, *Daily Report—PRC*, March 3, 1980, pp. L18–L22. The author also asserted that "there is no long-term program upon which the readjustment can be based," and the only guidelines were the State Planning Commission's "six don'ts" (prohibiting investment in projects that did not fulfill certain specified criteria). He analyzed the practical difficulties created by the lack of "objective criteria," "departmental egoism," and "the tendency toward excessive decentralization." There are over thirty of the "kind of channels outside the budget" through which some investment flows, and they are difficult to control, he said; local authorities circumvent restrictions by shifting funds from one year to the next. He, like others, also stressed the inefficiency of existing plants. China, he said, has 106 car manufacturing plants, but in 1978 they were operating "57 percent below their designed capacity" and 9 plants accounted for 68.6 percent of national production.

302. NCNA, "Li Renjun [Li Jen-chun] Reports on Economy to NPC Standing Committee," and "Proposed 1980 Plan," April 8, 1980, in FBIS, *Daily Report—PRC*, April 9, 1980, especially p. L4.

303. "Seminar on China's Economy in the 1980s," Department of State telegram from the American Consulate-General, Hong Kong, March 1980 (R170302Z, unclassified).

304. See the estimates cited on p. 45; see also *Chase International Finance* (Chase Manhattan Bank, June 1979), p. 8, which predicted a rate of 5 to 6

percent (2.5 percent in agriculture, and 7 to 10 percent in industry) during 1978–85.

305. Okita, "Japan, China, and the United States," p. 1107.

306. "Why China Has Opened Its Doors," *Bangkok Post*, February 10, 1980, in FBIS, *Daily Report—PRC*, February 12, 1980, p. L2.

Part II

1. Alexander Eckstein, "China's Trade Policy and Sino-American Relations," *Foreign Affairs*, vol. 54, no. 1 (October 1975), especially pp. 135, 139–40, 147. The author dates the change in policy to late 1971 and 1972, following the fall of Lin Piao (Lin Biao). In 1972, trade began to rise rapidly; see table 2-1.

2. For general background on the debate, see Allen S. Whiting, *Chinese Domestic Politics and Foreign Policy in the 1970s*, Michigan Papers in Chinese Studies, 36 (University of Michigan, Center for Chinese Studies, 1979).

3. "Chairman of Chinese Delegation Teng Hsiao-ping's [Deng Xiaoping's] Speech," *Peking Review* (later, *Beijing Review*), no. 16 (April 19, 1974), p. 10.

4. Li Chiang (Li Qiang), "New Developments in China's Foreign Trade," *Foreign Trade* (Peking), no. 1 (July 1974), p. 4. Initiation of this new journal was in itself a significant sign of Peking's increased stress on trade.

5. Article by Chin Feng (Jin Feng or Qin Feng), *Selections from People's Republic of China Magazines*, CMP-SPRCM 74-15, September 20, 1974 (Hong Kong: American Consulate-General, 1974), pp. 1–3. "Chin Feng" was a pseudonym for the Writing Group of the Communist Party's Shanghai Committee, which at that time was a major base for power for radical leaders; see Kuo Chi-tsu (Guo Jizu or Guo Qizu), "Usurping Party and State Power in the Name of Criticising Slavish Compradore Philosophy," in Foreign Broadcast Information Service, *Daily Report—People's Republic of China*, Department of Commerce, National Technical Information Service, May 5, 1978, p. E2. (Hereafter, FBIS, *Daily Report—PRC*.)

6. "Some Problems in Speeding Up Industrial Development," *Issues and Studies* (Taiwan), vol. 13, no. 7 (July 1977), pp. 106–08. This was the precursor of the 1978 Central Committee decision (bearing the same title) discussed in part I, p. 37 and note 99.

7. "Several Questions Concerning the Work of Science and Technology" (also referred to as "Outline of a Briefing on the Work of the Academy of Sciences"), *Issues and Studies*, vol. 13, no. 9 (September 1977), pp. 67–68. This preceded the 1978 "Outline National Plan" on science and technology, presented by Fang Yi (Fang Yi), discussed in part I, p. 32 and note 80.

8. Article by Li Hsin (Li Xin), in *Peking Review*, no. 32 (August 8, 1975), pp. 14, 23.

9. *Red Flag*, no. 8 (August 1, 1975), in *Selections from People's Republic of China Magazines*, CMP-SPRCM 75-25, August 25–September 2, 1975, pp.

17–18. "Liang Hsiao" (Liang Xiao) was a pseudonym used by the Mass Criticism Group of Peking and Tsinghua (Ching-hua or Qinghua) Universities, a group of more than thirty people used as a mouthpiece by Chiang Ching (Jiang Qing) and other top radical leaders; see "Who Is Liang Hsiao?" *Peking Review*, no. 43 (October 21, 1977), pp. 22–23.

10. *Historical Research* (*Li-shih Yen-chiu* or *Lishi Yanjiu*), no. 5 (October 20, 1975), in *Selections from People's Republic of China Magazines*, CMP-SPRCM 75-36, December 16, 1975, pp. 2–3, 5, 8.

11. Article by "Chin Feng," in *Kwangming Daily* (*Kwang-ming Jih-pao* or *Guangming Ribao*), April 21, 1976, in *Survey of People's Republic of China Press*, CMP-SPRCP 76-18, no. 6086, May 3, 1976, pp. 2, 5.

12. Kao Lu (Gao Lu) and Chang Ko (Zhang Ke or Chang Ge), "Comments on Teng Hsiao-ping's Economic Ideas of Compradore Bourgeoisie," *Peking Review*, no. 35 (August 27, 1976), p. 8.

13. *Peking Review*, no. 1 (January 1, 1977), p. 23.

14. New China News Agency (NCNA) Correspondent, "A Grave Step for Usurping Party and State Power—Exposing the Towering Crimes of the 'Gang of Four' in Rampantly Opposing Chairman Mao [Mao] and the Party Central Committee and in Viciously Attacking Premier Chou [Zhou] in Foreign Trade," in FBIS, *Daily Report—PRC*, January 14, 1977, pp. E1–E8, especially pp. E1, E7.

15. Article by Kuo Chi (Guo Ji or Guo Qi), in *Peking Review*, no. 9 (February 25, 1977), pp. 16–18.

16. Article by Lo Yuan-cheng (Luo Yuanzheng or Luo Yuancheng), in *Peking Review*, no. 28 (July 8, 1977), pp. 9–11, especially p. 10.

17. *Peking Review*, no. 42 (October 14, 1977), pp. 5–13, especially p. 11.

18. Radio talk, Peking, October 29, 1977, in FBIS, *Daily Report—PRC*, November 3, 1977, pp. E3–E5.

19. Radio talk, Peking, "We Should Learn All Good Things—Criticizing the Gang of Four's Fallacies against Studying and Introducing Advanced Foreign Technology," November 14, 1977, in FBIS, *Daily Report—PRC*, November 16, 1977, pp. E3–E5, especially p. E4.

20. Hua Kuo-feng (Hua Guofeng), "Unite and Strive to Build a Modern, Powerful Socialist Country!—Report on the Work of the Government," February 26, 1978, in FBIS, *Daily Report—PRC*, March 7, 1978, p. D18.

21. Speech, March 18, 1978, in FBIS, *Daily Report—PRC*, March 21, 1978, p. E8.

22. "Outline National Plan for the Development of Science and Technology, Relevant Policies and Measures," March 18, 1978, *Peking Review*, no. 14 (April 7, 1978), p. 13.

23. Speech of June 20, 1978, *Peking Review*, no. 30 (July 28, 1978), p. 16.

24. Hu Chiao-mu (Hu Qiaomu), "Act in Accordance with Economic Laws, Step Up the Four Modernizations," *Renmin Ribao* (*Jen-min Jih-pao* or *People's Daily*), October 6, 1978, in FBIS, *Daily Report—PRC*, October 11, 1978, p. E4.

25. Article by Tung Chih-min (Tong Zhimin) of the People's University Institute of Foreign Economic Management, *Kwangming Daily*, August 18, 1978, in FBIS, *Daily Report—PRC*, August 25, 1978, pp. E4–E7.

26. *Renmin Ribao*, August 25, 1978, in FBIS, *Daily Report—PRC*, August 28, 1978, pp. E1–E5.

27. Article by Ching Wen (Qing Wen or Jing Wen), *Kwangming Daily*, December 2, 1978, in FBIS, *Daily Report—PRC*, December 8, 1978, pp. E25–E27.

28. Hua Guofeng, "Report on the Work of the Government," June 18, 1979, in FBIS, *Daily Report—PRC*, Supplement 015, July 2, 1979, p. 15.

29. Yu Qiuli (Yu Chiu-li), "Report on the Draft of the 1979 National Economic Plan," June 21, 1979, in FBIS, *Daily Report—PRC*, July 2, 1979, pp. L14, L22–L24; State Statistical Bureau, "Communiqué on Fulfilment of China's 1978 National Economic Plan," June 27, 1979, in FBIS, *Daily Report— PRC*, June 27, 1979, p. L17.

30. See pp. 142 ff. and note 66.

31. See all 1977 issues of *China Business Review*, especially the sections titled "China International Notes." This journal and the *Far Eastern Economic Review* provide the most comprehensive regular reporting on developments relating to China's foreign economic relations.

32. Here and in the discussion that follows I use U.S. dollar figures; see table 2-1. The figures in this table are CIA statistics based on calculations of China's exports f.o.b. (free on board) and imports c.i.f. (cost, insurance, freight; insurance and freight are estimated). For 1978 I also give in table 2-1, in parentheses, the CIA's more recent figures based on calculations of both China's exports and imports f.o.b. Unfortunately, until recently, the two U.S. government agencies issuing the best statistics on China's trade have used different bases for calculations. CIA publications through 1978 used f.o.b. for exports and c.i.f. for imports. The Department of Commerce has used figures that give both exports and imports f.a.s. (free alongside ship); f.a.s. figures are close to f.o.b. figures (the latter simply add loading costs). Starting in 1979, the CIA began using f.o.b. figures for both exports and imports (and issued new figures for 1976, 1977, and 1978 calculated on this basis). This means that until 1979 the figures from the CIA and the Department of Commerce differed, especially on China's imports; since 1979, however, the differences have been minor. In the following discussion I have relied (except where otherwise noted) on the CIA's earlier figures, giving exports f.o.b. and imports c.i.f. Their data have been especially useful because not only have they been relatively comprehensive, but they have included breakdowns by country, region, and commodity. (However, in my discussion of U.S.-China trade in part V, I rely primarily on Department of Commerce figures, which I found to be more useful for this aspect of China's trade.)

33. Based on table 2-1. The CIA's recent statistics for 1978 giving both exports and imports f.o.b. indicate that China's trade rose 38 percent in 1978 to $20.3 billion. See National Foreign Assessment Center, Central Intelligence Agency, *China: International Trade Quarterly Review, First Quarter 1979*,

Reference Aid ER CIT 79-001, September 1979, pp. 3–6. The official Chinese figures for trade in 1978 were total trade, 35.5 billion yuan; imports, 18.74 billion yuan; exports, 16.76 billion yuan (see FBIS, *Daily Report—PRC*, June 27, 1979, p. L17). If these figures are converted to dollars at the average exchange rate for 1978 ($1.00 = 1.682 yuan), they are virtually identical to the CIA's f.o.b./c.i.f. figures. However, Chinese figures on growth in 1978 (total trade, 30.3 percent; imports, 41.1 percent; exports, 20 percent) were different from the CIA's, which reflected the appreciation of the yuan against the dollar during the year.

34. NFAC, CIA, *China: Post-Mao Search for Civilian Industrial Technology*, Research Paper ER 79-10020U, February 1979, pp. 4–6, estimated actual contracts at about $7 billion. Later, the NFAC, CIA, *China: International Trade Quarterly Review, Fourth Quarter 1979*, Research Paper ER CIT 80-003, May 1980, pp. 24–25, estimated the 1978 total to be $6.787 billion. In early 1980 Li Jen-chun (Li Renjun), Vice Minister of the State Planning Commission, stated that in 1978 China signed contracts for imports of "complete sets of equipment and separate units of machinery totaling $7.8 billion" (he himself used the dollar figure); see FBIS, *Daily Report—PRC*, April 9, 1980, p. L2.

35. *China Business Review*, vol. 5, no. 5 (September–October 1978), p. 65; plus detailed listings obtained from James B. Stepanek of the National Council for U.S.-China Trade, January 1979.

36. *China Business Review*, vol. 6, no. 2 (March–April 1979), p. 57, summarizes the National Council's study, "Sales to China, 1978, and Negotiations for Sales," April 1979.

37. For a general summary of these long-term agreements, see *China Business Review*, vol. 6, no. 2 (March–April 1979), p. 70. On the Japan-China agreement, see Japan External Trade Organization (Tokyo), *JETRO China Newsletter* (later JETRO, *China Newsletter*), no. 18 (June 1978), pp. 1–26.

38. *China Business Review*, vol. 6, no. 2 (March–April 1979), p. 70; speech by W. Michael Blumenthal, "U.S. Eyes Enlarged China Trade," *China Mail* (June 1979), p. 9.

39. Sueo Kojima, "Sino-Japanese Economic Relations," paper prepared for the Seminar on PRC's New Business System, American Management Association, April 1980, p. 26.

40. Bing Wong, "China's Outward Reach Reaps Reward in Japan," *Washington Star*, October 19, 1978. (Kojima, in "Sino-Japanese Economic Relations," p. 19, predicted two-way Sino-Japanese trade of $20 billion in 1985.) Nomura Institute (Tokyo) in 1979 estimated that China would import $35 billion of plants in five years, of which Japan would sell $9 billion; *Economist* (September 29, 1979), p. 82. The Japan Economic Research Center in 1979 published a study by a group of economists headed by Faeo Sekiguchi estimating that in the period ahead China would need to import about $6.5 billion of "capital" a year, a large part from Japan; see Leonard Silk, "How Japan Sees the China Market," *New York Times*, May 18, 1979.

41. Text in *China Business Review*, vol. 5, no. 2 (March–April 1978), pp. 50–51.

42. Andreas Freund, "French Get Trade Pact with China," *New York Times*, December 5, 1978; Thomas O'Toole, "China, France Sign Treaty on Trade, A-Plants," *Washington Post*, December 5, 1978; and "Teng Hsiaoping at French Trade Pact Signing Ceremony" and other articles, in FBIS, *Daily Report—PRC*, December 4, 1978, pp. A14–A17.

43. Freund, in "French Get Trade Pact," estimated the two atomic power plants might be worth $2.2 billion; Thomas O'Toole, in "U.S. Says France Could Sell Chinese an A-Power Plant," *Washington Post*, November 26, 1978, estimated the plants might be worth $4.5 billion. By late 1979, however, it appeared that these projects had been postponed and possibly canceled.

44. *China Business Review*, vol. 6, no. 2 (March–April 1979), pp. 69–70. See also "Promises, Promises," *Economist* (March 10, 1979). For other developments in Sino-British economic relations, see "Premier Hua's Visit to Britain, New Impetus for Closer Cooperation," *Beijing Review*, no. 45 (November 9, 1979), pp. 8–11.

45. "FRG Signs DM 8 Billion Mining Equipment Deal with PRC," in FBIS, *Daily Report—PRC*, September 25, 1978, p. A17. On the $150 million of German credits offered in 1979, see JETRO, *China Newsletter*, no. 22 (July 1979), p. 6. See also Roger Boyes, "West Germany Prepared to Increase China Credits," *Financial Times* (London), October 19, 1979.

46. *China Business Review*, vol. 6, no. 2 (March–April 1979), p. 70.

47. On the Paoshan (Baoshan) steel plant agreement, see NCNA, "Agreement Signed with Japan on Building Steel Plant," in FBIS, *Daily Report—PRC*, May 24, 1978, pp. A5–A6; Henry Scott-Stokes, "Japanese to Build Giant Steel Mill for Chinese in $2.03 Billion Deal," *New York Times*, December 6, 1978; and Staff Reporter, "China, Nippon Steel Joint Effort on Mill to Start This Month," *Wall Street Journal*, December 6, 1978. On the discussion of an even larger steel mill in Chitung (Jidung), North China, see Kyodo News Service (Tokyo), "Japanese Steel Firm Chairman on Cooperation with PRC," in FBIS, *Daily Report—PRC*, December 28, 1978, pp. A6–A7; and Kyodo, "PRC Seeks Japanese Aid in Steelworks Construction," in FBIS, *Daily Report—PRC*, September 21, 1978, p. A4. For general listings of major "deals" in 1978, see also "China: The Start of a $350 Billion Long March," *Business Week* (November 6, 1978), pp. 76–78; "China: Over 900 Million Customers," *Economist* (October 14, 1978), pp. 114–15; David Pauly, with Lloyd H. Norman, "The New China Trade," *Newsweek* (December 18, 1978), p. 62; John Srades, "Counting on Each Other," *Far Eastern Economic Review* (December 29, 1975), pp. 41–42; Frank Ching, "U.S. Steel Agrees to Assist China on Iron Ore Job," *Wall Street Journal*, January 8, 1979; and Jay Mathews, "China, U.S. Steel Sign Contract for $1 Billion Plant," *Washington Post*, January 6, 1979.

48. Based on NFAC, CIA, *China: International Trade, 1977–78*, Research Paper ER 78-10721, December 1978, p. 21. This source, which is very conservative and only includes final, confirmed contracts known to the CIA at the time,

lists a total of $887 million for 1978, through September, of which $576 million were with Japanese firms.

49. NFAC, CIA, *China: Post-Mao Search*, p. 2.

50. Special to *New York Times*, "Fluor Studying Chinese Project," *New York Times*, March 13, 1979. For articles summarizing other major U.S.-China projects under discussion in 1978, see Fox Butterfield, "The China Trade: Companies Mob Peking," *New York Times*, International Economic Survey section, February 4, 1979, p. 55; News Roundup, "Contracts Flow to U.S. Firms as China Bids to Catch Up with Industrial West," *Wall Street Journal*, December 12, 1978; and "American Business Activities with China Are Proceeding in Many Areas," *Asian Wall Street Journal*, supplement, June 25, 1979. See also discussion in part V. On oil deals, see part IV.

51. NFAC, CIA, *China: Post-Mao Search*, p. 5, which simply says it will cost "billions." One study, made in 1976, when China's oil output was about 84 million tons, estimated that to reach an output of 335 million tons by 1985, an annual investment of $4.5 billion would be required (which implied a total of perhaps $40 billion to $50 billion); see C. Y. Cheng study cited in Selig H. Harrison, *China, Oil, and Asia: Conflict Ahead?* (Columbia University Press, 1977). An American oil company executive estimated in 1978 that to develop 100 billion barrels of recoverable reserves in offshore areas would require investments of more than $100 billion; see H. I. Goodman, "Energy—A Major Determinant of the Asian Power Balance," paper prepared for the Conference on the Balance of Power in Asia, Ditchley Foundation (England), February 1978, p. 3.

52. On the port, railway, and ship projects cited below, see Special to *Wall Street Journal*, "Dutch Group Gets China Port Job Exceeding $2 Billion," *Wall Street Journal*, October 17, 1978; Richard Witkin, "China Acts to Improve Railroads, Japan Giving Technical Advice," *New York Times*, January 15, 1979; and the *Economist*, *Newsweek*, and *Far Eastern Economic Review* articles cited in note 47. On the communications satellite project, see Peter J. Schuyten, "China Shops for a Satellite System in U.S.," *New York Times*, November 23, 1978; and Bernard Weintraub, "U.S. Approves Satellite Sale to Chinese," *Washington Star*, October 31, 1978. On the Boeing sale, see Richard Witkin, "Boeing Gets 3-Jet Order from China," *New York Times*, December 20, 1978.

53. General Motors (GM) began serious negotiations with the Chinese in 1978 on the possibility of building two huge truck plants in China that, with ancillary facilities, theoretically could involve investments of perhaps several billion dollars (personal interview with a high-ranking GM official, January 5, 1979, unattributable).

54. Frank Ching, "Pan Am Air Unit Agrees to Build Hotels in China," *Wall Street Journal*, November 9, 1978; and S. Karene Witcher, "China's Rethinking of Construction Plans May Endanger U.S. Firms' Hotel Projects," *Wall Street Journal*, April 9, 1979. On the Coca-Cola agreement, see N. R. Kleinfield, "Coca-Cola to Go on Sale in China as U.S. Links with Peking Gain," *New York Times*, December 20, 1978. On the trade center, see Henry

Scott-Stokes, "Trade Mart Is Reported Set in China," *New York Times*, January 9, 1979.

55. Reuters, "Agreement on Sale of Missiles to China Confirmed by France," *Washington Post*, October 21, 1978; Jim Browning, "France Moves Ahead on China Arms Sales," *Christian Science Monitor*, October 24, 1978; "Arms for China, My Enemy's Enemy," *Economist* (November 11, 1978); Flora Lewis, "Britain Will Sell Fighters to China, Callahan Says at Summit Meeting," *New York Times*, January 6, 1979; and Leonard Downie, Jr., "Britain Tells Hua It Is Willing to Sell Harrier Jets," *Washington Post*, November 2, 1979. See also Roger Kelly, "The Rush to Catch Up Slips into High Gear," *Far Eastern Economic Review* (October 6, 1978), pp. 49–50; David Bonavia, "Ridding the Army of Dogma," *Far Eastern Economic Review* (November 4, 1979), p. 24; Paul H. B. Godwin, "China and the Second World: The Search for Defense Technology," *Contemporary China*, vol. 2, no. 3 (Fall 1978), pp. 3–9; and Harry G. Gelber, *Technology, Defense, and External Relations in China, 1975–1978* (Boulder, Colo.: Westview Press, 1979), chap. 2, pp. 49–88, and chap. 4, pp. 141–81.

56. William Chapman, "Chinese Suspend Deals with Japan Worth $2.5 Billion," *Washington Post*, March 1, 1979; *China Business Review*, vol. 6, no. 3 (May–June 1979), p. 59; and Henry Scott-Stokes, "Japan's Shift toward China Takes a Lurch into Reverse," *New York Times*, March 25, 1979. On the general (but temporary) slowdown, see Louis Kraar, "China's Narrow Door to the West," *Fortune* (March 26, 1979), pp. 63–69; Jay Mathews, "China's Expanding Foreign Trade Comes into Question," *Washington Post*, March 17, 1979; Jerome Alan Cohen, "China Trade: After the 'Slowdown,'" *Asian Wall Street Journal*, July 2, 1979; and Donald W. Green and Miriam Karr, "China Lets the Flowers Bloom—But Slowly," *Chase International Finance*, vol. 14, no. 12 (June 11, 1979), pp. 7–8. On the "pick up" of purchases, see William Schwartz, "Japanese Preparing for Renegotiation of 'Frozen' Export Contracts with China," *Asian Wall Street Journal*, May 14, 1979; and Roundup, "China to Reactivate Some Suspended Contracts with Japanese Companies," *Asian Wall Street Journal*, June 11, 1979. On China's continued stress on importing equipment and technology but modifying priorities and methods, see "Trade Policy Revamped, Suitability of Imports Stressed," *China Business Review*, vol. 6, no. 3 (May–June 1979), pp. 49–50; "Minister Li Qiang on Expanding China's Foreign Trade to Speed Up the Four Modernizations," *Beijing Review*, no. 17 (April 27, 1979), pp. 15–16; and "Importing Technology, Plans Readjusted, Policy Unchanged" (interview with Ku Ming [Gu Ming], Vice Minister, State Planning Commission), *Beijing Review*, no. 30 (July 27, 1979), pp. 9–11. Ku discussed the problems of unified planning, the trade balance, the ability to absorb imported technology, and the need to give greater stress to imports that give quick returns on capital and to manufacturing technology as well as plants and equipment. "But," he said, "as a basic policy, the import of technology will not change. We will continue to import technology, and do it better than before." He stated that China imported technology and equipment to equip more than

80 construction projects from 1962 to 1965 and nearly 200 projects between 1973 and 1977 and that then, in 1978, China's imports of technology were "the largest in the history of the People's Republic" and "twice the total for the five years from 1973 through 1977 and involved hundreds of companies from a dozen countries."

57. Hints of change began as early as 1976; see "First U.S. Insurance Agreement with the PRC Established a Good Precedent," *U.S.-China Business Review* (later, *China Business Review*), vol. 3, no. 2 (March–April 1976), pp. 3–5; and "China's Trade Structure, Decentralizing, Specializing, Reorganizing," *U.S.-China Business Review*, vol. 3, no. 5 (September–October 1976), p. 42. Many other signs of flexibility were evident in late 1977; see, for example, the following articles or items in *China Business Review*, vol. 4, no. 6 (November–December 1977): "Packaging Study Group Tours America," p. 14; "Milestone Case in Dispute Settlement in Trade with the PRC," pp. 16–17; Sally Winder, "Exclusives from the PRC," pp. 19–21; and John T. Kamm, "Canton 42, Down to Business Cordially," p. 35.

58. During the first six months of 1978 more than 250 "seminars" were presented by foreign businesses in China; during 1977–78 about 2,000 Chinese technicians and officials visited major non-Communist industrial nations on economic missions, and in 1978 China moved increasingly to decentralize trading decisions and started recognizing foreign patents and trademarks; see NFAC, CIA, *China: Post-Mao Search*, pp. 2–9. For examples of other innovations in 1978–79, see Staff Reporter, "Chinese Will Permit Foreign Companies to Advertise Wares," *Wall Street Journal*, February 28, 1979; Ho Kwon Ping, "Birth of the Second Generation," *Far Eastern Economic Review* (May 18, 1979), pp. 76–78; "Chinese Province Sets Up Firm to Accept Investments," *Asian Wall Street Journal Weekly*, June 4, 1979; John T. Kamm, "End-User Corporations Emerge in China," *Asian Wall Street Journal Weekly*, Supplement; Associated Press, "China to Set Up Business Zones," *New York Times*, December 12, 1979; and Fox Butterfield, "China Trade Plan Has a Capitalist Tinge," *New York Times*, December 27, 1979. See also Li Chiang, "Distinguish between Right and Wrong in Line and Actively Develop Socialist Foreign Trade," *Hungchi* (*Hongqi* or *Red Flag*), no. 10 (October 8, 1977), in FBIS, *Daily Report—PRC*, October 20, 1977, pp. E1–E8.

59. See, for example, "Minister Li Chiang on China's Foreign Trade," *Peking Review*, no. 26 (June 30, 1978), pp. 17–18; and editorial, "There Should Be a Big Growth of Foreign Trade," *Renmin Ribao*, December 4, 1978, in FBIS, *Daily Report—PRC*, December 6, 1978. The developments that began in 1978 were reported in much greater detail in 1979; see, for example, Chinese discussions of new policies in "Some Questions on Developing Economic and Technological Exchanges with Foreign Countries" (interview with Zou Siyu [Tsou Ssu-yu], Ministry of Foreign Trade, Export Bureau), *Beijing Review*, no. 17 (April 27, 1979), pp. 17–20; interviews with Li Qiang and Gu Ming cited in note 56; and Yu Qiuli, "Report on the Draft of the 1979 National Economic Plan," pp. L14, L22–L24.

60. "China Province Cites 300 Contracts with Hong Kong, Macao" (citing NCNA), *Asian Wall Street Journal*, July 2, 1979. See also Barry Kramer, "How a Chinese Factory Leads a Leap Forward into Capitalist Ways," *Wall Street Journal*, July 5, 1979.

61. NCNA, "Peking Factories Produce Goods for Foreign Companies," in FBIS, *Daily Report—PRC*, November 29, 1978, p. K4.

62. NCNA, "Li Chiang Comments on Trade while in Hong Kong, Macao," in FBIS, *Daily Report—PRC*, December 19, 1978, pp. A1–A3; and Staff Reporter, "China Official Spells Out Trade Policies, Says U.S. Gets Equal Footing with Others," *Wall Street Journal*, December 19, 1978.

63. Interview with Swedish reporter, in FBIS, *Daily Report—PRC*, December 8, 1978, pp. E7–E9.

64. Personal interview with a high-ranking official of General Motors Corporation, January 5, 1979, unattributable.

65. "China Is Looking to Joint Ventures for Importing Plants and Technology," *Asian Wall Street Journal*, Supplement, June 25, 1979, p. 2.

66. For the text, see *Beijing Review*, July 20, 1979, pp. 24–27. See also Fox Butterfield, "China Announces Guidelines for Foreign Investment," *New York Times*, July 9, 1979; Geoffrey Owen, "China: Risks and Rewards for Foreign Ventures," *Financial Times*, July 10, 1979; Staff Reporter, "Foreign Partners in Ventures with China Offered Package of Incentives, Protection," *Wall Street Journal*, July 9, 1979; NCNA, "New Law on Joint Ventures Reviewed," July 8, 1979, in FBIS, *Daily Report—PRC*, July 9, 1979, pp. 10–13; and Barry Kramer, "China Spells Out Law Governing Joint Ventures," *Asian Wall Street Journal*, July 16, 1979. Some Chinese articles appeared to be mainly defenses against possible criticism in China; see Li Yongji (Li Yung-chi), "Talk on Current Events," *Jiefangjun Ribao* (*Chieh-fang-chun Jih-pao* or *Liberation Army Daily*), July 21, 1979, in FBIS, *Daily Report—PRC*, July 23, 1979, pp. L17–L21.

67. NCNA, "China International Trust, Investment Corporation, Founded," in FBIS, *Daily Report—PRC*, October 5, 1979, pp. L8–L10; and Staff Reporter, "China Is Establishing Two Key Commissions for Joint Ventures," *Wall Street Journal*, August 1, 1979.

68. Ibid.; and Fox Butterfield, "Peking Promises Profits on Foreign Investments," *New York Times*, October 2, 1979; "Investment in China: An Exclusive Interview with Rong Yiren [Jung Yi-jen]," *China Business Review*, vol. 6, no. 5 (September–October 1979), pp. 4–6; "Investment, Rong Yiren: The Man to See about Joint Ventures," *China Business Review*, vol. 6, no. 5 (September–October 1979), pp. 7–8; and Jerome Alan Cohen and Owen D. Nee, Jr., "A Look at China's Joint Venture Law," *Asian Wall Street Journal Weekly*, July 30, 1979.

69. "Foreign Firms Are Seen Undaunted by Chinese Control of Joint Ventures" (unsigned article quoting James McGregor, director, Hong Kong General Chamber of Commerce), *Asian Wall Street Journal*, June 30, 1979.

70. Butterfield, "Peking Promises Profits on Foreign Investments."

71. See, for example, David E. Birenbaum, "Doing Business with China,"

Wall Street Journal, August 31, 1979. NCNA, "On Foreign Investment," September 28, 1979, in FBIS, *Daily Report—PRC,* September 28, 1979, p. L10, reported that more than thirty possible joint ventures were already under discussion. However, many foreign corporations were holding back until further laws and regulations resolved unanswered questions.

72. For the results of their analysis, see JETRO, "China's Foreign Investment Laws and Problems Involved," *China Newsletter,* no. 23 (October 1979), pp. 18–22.

73. David L. Denny and Frederic M. Surls, "China's Foreign Financial Liabilities," *China Business Review,* vol. 4, no. 2 (March–April 1977), p. 15; "China's Green for Go," *China Business Review,* vol. 4, no. 6 (November–December 1977), p. 41; "British Banks Negotiating Deposit Facility with Bank of China," *Times* (London), August 17, 1978, in FBIS, *Daily Report—PRC,* August 18, 1978, p. A26; and Chen Fang (Chen Fang or Zhen Fang), "Socialist China Attracts Foreign Capital," distributed by the Embassy of the People's Republic of China, Washington, D.C., October 1979, mimeographed.

74. JETRO, "World Extension of Credit to China," *China Newsletter,* no. 22 (July 1979), pp. 5–6, gives a detailed listing of credits offered to the Chinese between December 1978 and mid-1979, totaling $21.143 billion. Cary Reich, "China: The Bankers' Grand Illusion?" *Institutional Investor* (January 1979), pp. 37–46, includes a broad discussion of China's borrowing; the author stated that credits of "at least $25 billion . . . have been discussed" in the "past four months." See also "Peking Jumping into Worldwide Borrowing Market," *Asian Wall Street Journal Weekly,* May 14, 1979, which estimated that in the previous five weeks China had "signed for over $8 billion in borrowings from British, French, Arab, Canadian, and Australian banks." (This was an overestimate.)

75. These and the following data are from JETRO, "World Extension of Credit to China," and other press sources cited. Not all of the data are consistent, as will be noted. The interest rates and periods for the loans are given in these sources.

76. For additional information, especially on the British and French credits, see the following press reports (which in some cases differ, however, from the JETRO data regarding the dates of agreements and even the amounts): Jim Browning, "China Signs Multibillion-Dollar Export Credit Agreement with French Banks," *Asian Wall Street Journal Weekly,* May 14, 1979; Paul Lewis, "Big French Loan Pact with China," *New York Times,* May 10, 1979; Special to the *New York Times,* "Chinese Get Credits in Britain," *New York Times,* December 7, 1978 (prior to the agreement date that JETRO reported); Staff Reporter, "Seven Banks in U.K. Sign Pacts with China," *Wall Street Journal,* December 12, 1978; and "China Takes Out Insurance," *Far Eastern Economic Review* (January 19, 1979). See also "Peking's Jumping into Worldwide Borrowing Market," *Asian Wall Street Journal Weekly,* May 14, 1979.

77. On the Japanese credits, which were negotiated over a period of about eight months, see Kyodo, "PRC Ready to Accept 'Private' Japanese Loans,"

August 24, 1978, in FBIS, *Daily Report—PRC,* August 24, 1978, p. A1; Susumu Awanohara, "Japan Gives an Extra Push to Its Trade with China," *Far Eastern Economic Review* (September 22, 1978), pp. 96–98; and Henry Scott-Stokes, "Japan Studies Loans for China," *New York Times,* December 27, 1978, "China-Japan Import Finance Accord Nears," *New York Times,* February 2, 1979, and "China Sets $10 Billion Japan Loan," *New York Times,* May 16, 1979.

78. Reich, "China: The Bankers' Grand Illusion?" p. 37.

79. Hamburg DPA, "FRG Signs DM 8 Billion Mining Equipment Deal with PRC," in FBIS, *Daily Report—PRC,* September 25, 1978, p. A17; Roger Boyes, "West Germany Prepared to Increase China Credits"; and Colin Lawson, "Red Carpets All the Way for Hua," *Far Eastern Economic Review* (November 9, 1979), p. 66.

80. Reuters, "Canada Grants Credit to China," *New York Times,* August 22, 1979, and "China Gets Line of Credit," *New York Times,* January 30, 1980.

81. JETRO, "World Extension of Credit to China," gives the terms of all major loan offers.

82. "China Asks Japan for Government Loan to Aid Modernization," *Wall Street Journal,* June 25, 1979; Robert Trumbull, "China Asks Japan for $5.5 Billion Loan for 8 Rail, Port, and Power Projects," *New York Times,* September 7, 1979, and "Japan-China Meeting Strengthening Economic Ties," *New York Times,* December 9, 1979. Also see part V, p. 574 and note 162.

83. See part V, pp. 532–33 and notes 133 and 134.

84. The United Nations Development Program (UNDP) grant was for eleven projects, including development of computer technology, weather forecasting, and automatic mail sorting; see Kathleen Teltsch, "Peking, in a Shift, Is Seeking U.N. Aid," *New York Times,* November 16, 1978, and "U.N. Gives China 15 Million to Modernize," *New York Times,* February 14, 1979; and Associated Press, "U.N. Aid to China Approved," *Washington Post,* January 28, 1979.

85. *Washington Post* Foreign Service, "U.N. Gives China $20 Million for Aid to Refugees," *Washington Post,* November 12, 1979; and Bernard D. Nossiter, "U.N. Agency Aids China to Curb Population Growth," *New York Times,* March 6, 1980.

86. *Sino-American Relations: A New Turn,* a Trip Report to the Committee on Foreign Relations, 96 Cong. 1 sess. (GPO, 1979); and Kyodo, "Deng Discusses International Issues in Kyodo Interview," February 26, 1979, in FBIS, *Daily Report—PRC,* February 27, 1979, p. A1.

87. Secretary of Commerce Juanita M. Kreps, "Comments at a State Department Briefing," *Department of State Bulletin,* vol. 79, no. 2023 (February 1979), p. 18.

88. NFAC, CIA, *China: Post-Mao Search,* pp. 14–17.

89. A study by Japan's Nomura Research Institute in 1979 estimated that China might need to borrow $50 billion to pay for plant imports through 1985; see "China's Economy, Big Deals," *Economist* (September 29, 1979),

p. 82. A Japan Economic Research Center (JERC) study in 1979 estimated that to achieve the ambitious targets initially set in 1978 for the year 1985, China might need as much as $200 billion of foreign capital over eight years; see Japan Economic Research Center, *A Study on Japan-China Economic Relations* (Tokyo: JERC, February 1979), p. 42.

90. NFAC, CIA, *China: Post-Mao Search*, pp. 14–17.

91. For background on China's foreign trade in the pre-Communist period, see C. F. Remer, *The Foreign Trade of China* (Shanghai: Commercial Press, 1925). For background on China's foreign trade during the 1950s and 1960s, see Alexander Eckstein, *Communist China's Economic Growth and Foreign Trade* (McGraw-Hill for the Council on Foreign Relations, 1966); Feng-hwa Mah, *The Foreign Trade of Mainland China* (Chicago: Aldine, 1971); and Allen S. Whiting and Robert F. Dernberger, *China's Future, Foreign Policy and Economic Development in the Post-Mao Era* (McGraw-Hill for the Council on Foreign Relations, 1977). Many of the most useful analyses of China's trade, especially since the mid-1960s, are in chapters of volumes published by the U.S. Congress Joint Economic Committee (JEC) and in trade journals; these include Robert L. Price, "International Trade of Communist China, 1950–65," in JEC, *An Economic Profile of Mainland China*, vol. 2, 90 Cong. 1 sess. (GPO, 1967), pp. 583–608; A. H. Usack and R. E. Batsavage, "The International Trade of the People's Republic of China," in JEC, *People's Republic of China: An Economic Assessment*, 92 Cong. 2 sess. (GPO, 1972), pp. 335–70; Nai-Ruenn Chen, "China's Foreign Trade, 1950–74," in JEC, *China: A Reassessment of the Economy*, 94 Cong. 1 sess. (GPO, 1975), pp. 617–52; Richard E. Batsavage and John L. Davie, "China's International Trade and Finance," in JEC, *Chinese Economy Post-Mao*, vol. 1 (GPO, 1978), pp. 707–41; Alexander Eckstein, "China's Economic Growth and Foreign Trade," *U.S.-China Business Review*, vol. 1, no. 4 (July–August 1974), pp. 15–20; and Dwight H. Perkins, "Forecasting China's Trade over the Long Term," *U.S.-China Business Review*, vol. 2, no. 2 (March–April 1975), pp. 41–47. Other useful sources include K. C. Yeh, "Communist China's Foreign Trade: Recent Trends in a Long Term Perspective," *Issues and Studies* (Taiwan), vol. 13, no. 5 (May 1977), pp. 59–86, "Foreign Trade under the Hua Regime: Policy, Performance, and Prospects," *Issues and Studies*, vol. 14, no. 8 (August 1978), pp. 12–43; Alexander Eckstein, "The Role of Foreign Trade in China's Economic Development," in *China's Economic Revolution* (Cambridge University Press, 1977), chap. 7, pp. 233–76; and Japan External Trade Organization, *China: A Business Guide* (Tokyo: JETRO, 1979), chaps. 5–11, pp. 67–176. Journals of particular value for continuing reporting on China's foreign trade are *China Business Review* (formerly *U.S.-China Business Review*), JETRO (Tokyo), *China Newsletter*, and *Far Eastern Economic Review* (Hong Kong). As indicated earlier (see note 32), the statistics on China's foreign trade used throughout this discussion are, unless otherwise noted, CIA statistics giving China's exports f.o.b. and imports c.i.f. These are drawn not only from the writings cited above by Price, Usack, Batsavage, and Davie (all of them CIA analysts) but also from the following specialized CIA publications: CIA,

People's Republic of China: International Trade Handbook (four annual issues), Research Aid A72-38, December 1972, Research Aid A ER 74-63, September 1974, Research Aid A ER 75-73, October 1975, and Research Aid ER 76-10610, October 1976; NFAC, CIA, *China: International Trade, 1976–77,* Research Paper ER 77-10674, November 1977, and *China: International Trade, 1977–78.* For the most recent figures I have used NFAC, CIA, *China: International Trade Quarterly Review* (the title of each issue includes also the quarter and the year), *First Quarter 1979,* Reference Aid ER CIT 79-001, September 1979, *Second Quarter 1979,* ER CIT 80-001, January 1980, *Third Quarter 1979,* ER CIT 80-002, February 1980, and *Fourth Quarter 1979,* ER CIT 80-003, May 1980, which give both exports and imports f.o.b. In this discussion I generally avoid using U.S. Department of Commerce or Chinese statistics because they are not exactly comparable with CIA figures (but I use Department of Commerce figures on U.S.-China trade in part V, as explained in part V, note 38).

92. Eckstein, *China's Economic Revolution,* p. 253.

93. Ibid., pp. 234–35. Eckstein estimated that in the 1950s and 1960s total trade turnover as a percentage of GNP was in the 4 to 8 percent range and possibly around 6 percent.

94. My calculations, from data on 1977 and 1978 in tables 1-1 and 2-1, data on 1979 from the State Statistical Bureau (SSB) Communiqué, in FBIS, *Daily Report—PRC,* April 30, 1980, pp. L1, L7, and data from NFAC, CIA, *China: The Continuing Search for a Modernization Strategy,* Research Paper ER 80-10248, April 1980, p. 1. With just the SSB's yuan figures for national income and foreign trade in 1979, trade was 13.5 percent of national income. This almost certainly exaggerates the real proportion of trade to national income, and a comparison of the two in estimated dollar equivalents is more justifiable; see the discussion in part I, note 288.

95. Eckstein, *China's Economic Revolution,* p. 234.

96. The figure was 15.5 percent, according to my calculation from data in NFAC, CIA, *Handbook of Economic Statistics, 1979,* Research Aid ER 79-10274, August 1979, pp. 1, 78–79.

97. Eckstein, *China's Economic Revolution,* p. 234.

98. This is Eckstein's judgment regarding the 1952–74 period; see ibid., p. 235.

99. My calculations from data in tables 1-1 and 2-1.

100. My calculations from data in NFAC, CIA, *China: Real Trends in Trade with Non-Communist Countries since 1970,* Research Paper ER 77-10477, October 1977, p. 10.

101. My calculation, from data in Eckstein, *China's Economic Revolution,* p. 246.

102. See Arthur N. Young, *China's Nation-Building Effort, 1927–1937: The Financial and Economic Record* (Hoover Institution Press, 1971), pp. 492–93. In current dollars (of that period) China's total trade (including Manchuria's trade) was $1.570 billion in 1928 and $1.489 billion in 1929.

103. In real terms, imports probably surpassed the 1928–29 peak in 1954

and exports did so in 1955 or 1956; see Eckstein, *Communist China's Economic Growth and Foreign Trade*, p. 94.

104. These and the following percentage rates are my calculations, from data in table 2-1.

105. Eckstein, *China's Economic Revolution*, p. 245.

106. NFAC, CIA, *China: International Trade Quarterly Review, Fourth Quarter 1979*, pp. 9–11. Converted to yuan at the average exchange rate for the year, 1.552, the CIA's figures are close to but not identical with the Chinese figures.

107. State Statistical Bureau Communiqué, in FBIS, *Daily Report—PRC*, April 30, 1980, p. L7.

108. My calculations, from data in NFAC, CIA, *China: Real Trends in Trade*, pp. 12–13, 16–17. The figures in this source give both exports and imports f.o.b.

109. See the discussion in Eckstein, *China's Economic Revolution*, pp. 235, 245–49. The figures I use, however, are my own calculations, based on data in tables 1-1 and 2-1; my figures differ slightly from Eckstein's.

110. On the latest Chinese official figures for the period 1977–79, see p. 207.

111. Until recently, the Chinese appear to have viewed foreign trade essentially as the "balancing sector" in their strategy of economic development; see Eckstein, *Communist China's Economic Growth and Foreign Trade*, p. 89; and, for background, C. P. Kindleberger, *Foreign Trade and the National Economy* (Yale University Press, 1962), chap. 12.

112. For a good general discussion of China's basic motivations and strategies regarding trade in the 1950s and 1960s, see Eckstein, *China's Economic Revolution*, pp. 233–76.

113. On the fertilizer plants, see "U.S. Technicians in China: The Pullman Kellogg Story," *U.S.-China Business Review*, vol. 3, no. 5 (September–October 1976), pp. 33–39; and Alva Lewis Erisman, "China: Agriculture in the 1970s," in JEC, *China: A Reassessment of the Economy*, p. 334. On plant purchases since the mid-1970s, see pp. 193–94 and notes 165–69.

114. See Marshall I. Goldman, "The Soviet Economy Is Not Immune," *Foreign Policy*, no. 21 (Winter 1975–76), pp. 76–85.

115. See, for example, Audrey Donnithorne, *China's Economic System* (London: Allen and Unwin, 1967), pp. 318–36; and Gene T. Hsiao, "The Organization of China's Foreign Trade," *U.S.-China Business Review*, vol. 1, no. 3 (May–June 1974), pp. 9–14.

116. Hans Heymann, Jr., "Acquisition and Diffusion of Technology in China," in JEC, *China: A Reassessment of the Economy*, p. 685. See also the discussion on pp. 188 ff.

117. My calculations, from data in Robert Michael Field, "Real Capital Formation in the People's Republic of China, 1952–1973," July 12, 1976, mimeographed, p. 131.

118. See the discussion below, pp. 171 ff. See also Perkins, "Forecasting China's Trade over the Long Term," p. 42. Perkins estimated that of China's

total exports, 87.4 percent in 1959 and 72.2 percent in 1973 were "agriculture related"; he included manufactured textile goods in this category.

119. For figures on deficits, see table 2-1; on Soviet loans, see discussion on pp. 212–14.

120. If China's exports are calculated f.o.b. and its imports c.i.f., as they have been in determining the figures used above, the deficit was only $255 million; but if both imports and exports are calculated f.o.b., it was $1.100 billion. The Chinese themselves said that their 1978 trade deficit was 1.980 billion yuan, which if converted to dollars at the average exchange rate of 1.68 amounted to $1.178 billion; see the sources cited in note 29.

121. See Robert F. Dernberger, "Prospects for Trade between China and the United States," pt. 3, in Alexander Eckstein, ed., *China Trade Prospects and U.S. Policy* (New York: Praeger for the National Committee on United States-China Relations, 1971), especially pp. 230–37.

122. These and the following percentages for the years through 1978 are my calculations, based mainly on table 2-1. For a breakdown of China's trade with various Communist countries, see Chen, "China's Foreign Trade, 1950–74," p. 648; Usack and Batsavage, "The International Trade of the People's Republic of China," p. 347; and table 2-1. (There are some differences in the figures in table 2-1, based on CIA sources giving exports f.o.b. and imports c.i.f., and the above-mentioned chapter by Chen, based on Department of Commerce sources.) See also Eckstein, *Communist China's Economic Growth and Foreign Trade*, especially pp. 94–95, 98, 146, 158, which gives slightly different figures. Figures for 1979 are from NFAC, CIA, *China: International Trade Quarterly Review, Fourth Quarter 1979*, which gives both exports and imports f.o.b.

123. My calculations, from data in NFAC, CIA, *China: International Trade Quarterly Review, Fourth Quarter 1979*, pp. 9–12.

124. On Chinese views on the economic and trade significance of the Third World, see, for example, the following official speeches in the early 1970s: Chiao Kuan-hua (Qiao Guanhua), Speech to UN General Assembly, *Peking Review*, no. 47 (November 19, 1971), especially p. 8; Huang Hua (Huang Hua), Speech to UN General Assembly, *Peking Review*, no. 44 (November 3, 1972), pp. 21–22; Teng Hsiao-ping, Speech to UN General Assembly, *Peking Review*, no. 16 (April 19, 1974), pp. 6–11; Huang Hua, Speech to UN General Assembly, *Peking Review*, no. 19 (May 10, 1974), pp. 9–11; Chiao Kuan-hua, Speech to UN General Assembly, *Peking Review*, no. 41 (October 11, 1974), pp. 9–16; Li Chiang, Speech to UN General Assembly, *Peking Review*, no. 37 (September 12, 1975), pp. 11–16; Chiao Kuan-hua, Speech to UN General Assembly, *Peking Review*, no. 40 (October 3, 1975), pp. 10–17. See also Chin Yi-wu (Qin Yiwu or Jin Yiwu), "China's Economic and Technical Cooperation with Friendly Countries," *Peking Review*, no. 43 (October 25, 1974), pp. 16–18; and NCNA commentary, "Third World Countries' Surging Struggle against Hegemonism in International Economic Spheres," in FBIS, *Daily Report—PRC*, December 7, 1977, pp. A6–A8. For background, see Dick Wilson, "China and the Third World," *Pacific Community* (Tokyo),

vol. 7, no. 2 (January 1976), pp. 216–29; Carol H. Fogarty, "China's Economic Relations with the Third World," in JEC, *China: A Reassessment of the Economy*, pp. 730–37; and Bruce Larkin, "China and the Third World," *Current History* (September 1975), pp. 75–79, 103.

125. Gene T. Hsiao, "Non-Recognition and Trade: A Case Study of the Fourth Sino-Japanese Trade Agreement," in Jerome A. Cohen, ed., *China's Practice of International Law: Some Case Studies* (Harvard University Press, 1972), and "The Role of Trade in China's Diplomacy with Japan," in Jerome A. Cohen, ed., *The Dynamics of China's Foreign Relations*, East Asian Monograph 39 (Harvard University Press, 1970).

126. The following are my calculations, based on breakdowns of China's trade with non-Communist developed countries (DCs) and less developed countries (LDCs) from 1961 through 1977; see table 2-2; Usack and Batsavage, "The International Trade of the People's Republic of China," pp. 347, 350–51; and Price, "International Trade of Communist China, 1950–65," p. 600. The figures for Hong Kong and Macao, excluding entrepôt trade with third countries, are subtracted from the totals of China's trade with developing nations. Where there are slight differences between the Usack and Batsavage figures and the Price figures, I have used the former. The 1979 figures are based on NFAC, CIA, *International Trade Quarterly Review, Fourth Quarter 1979*, pp. 9–12; since this source gives both exports and imports f.o.b., its figures are not exactly comparable with the figures for earlier years.

127. The following percentages are my calculations, based on data in the sources cited in note 126; the 1961 and 1977 data give exports f.o.b. and imports c.i.f., while the 1979 figures give both f.o.b., and therefore they are not exactly comparable; they nevertheless reveal trends accurately. The figures for Hong Kong include its re-exports to third countries, which were $534 million in 1977. See NFAC, CIA, *China: International Trade, 1977–78*, p. 18, for a breakdown of where Hong Kong's re-exports went.

128. These and the following figures on Hong Kong include some trade with the nearby Portuguese colony of Macao, but the latter's trade is not large.

129. See table 2-2.

130. These and the following figures for 1977 on specific countries or areas are from table 2-2. The figures for 1979 are from NFAC, CIA, *China: International Trade Quarterly Review, Fourth Quarter 1979*, pp. 9–12, 17–19.

131. NFAC, CIA, *China: International Trade Quarterly Review, Fourth Quarter 1979*, pp. 16–17; the percentages are my calculations. Japanese statistics are somewhat different. For 1979, for example, Japan External Trade Organization figures show Japanese trade with China rising about 31 percent to $6.7 million, with Japanese exports to China rising 21.3 percent to $3.7 billion and imports from China increasing 45.5 percent to $3.0 billion; see Sueo Kojima, "Sino-Japanese Economic Relations."

132. See part V, pp. 506 ff.

133. For 1977 figures, see table 2-2; for 1978 figures, see NFAC, CIA, *China: International Trade Quarterly Review, Third Quarter 1979*, pp. 3–7. As noted earlier, these are not exactly comparable; the 1977 figures in the *China: Inter-*

national Trade Quarterly Review issue cited are $2.421 billion for two-way trade and $1.067 billion for China's imports (including $293 million from Rumania, $162 million from the Soviet Union, and $115 million from East Germany).

134. These calculations include Manchuria; see Young, *China's Nation-Building Effort*, especially pp. 325–28, 492–93. See also Department of Agriculture, Economic Research Service, *Agricultural Trade of the People's Republic of China, 1935–69*, Foreign Agricultural Economic Report 83 (ERS, August 1972).

135. Young, *China's Nation-Building Effort*, pp. 495–96.

136. Data on the commodity composition of 1959 and 1962 trade, on which the following discussion is based, are in Usack and Batsavage, "The International Trade of the People's Republic of China," p. 348; and Price, "International Trade of Communist China, 1950–65," p. 586. Where there are differences, I use the Usack and Batsavage figures. The percentages are my calculations.

137. Data on the commodity composition of 1965 trade are from Usack and Batsavage, "The International Trade of the People's Republic of China," p. 353. The percentages are my calculations.

138. On totals for the second half of the 1960s, see table 2-1. The earlier CIA estimates, in ibid., contain slight differences in totals for those years.

139. Data on the commodity breakdown for 1977 are in table 2-3 (parts 1 and 2). (NFAC, CIA, *China: International Trade Quarterly Review, Third Quarter 1979*, pp. 14–25, contains commodity breakdowns for the years 1977 and 1978.) The percentages are my calculations.

140. See part III, pp. 351 ff. and note 293. The percentages for 1974–76 are my calculations from data in CIA, *People's Republic of China: International Trade Handbook*, October 1976, p. 17; and NFAC, CIA, *China: International Trade, 1976–77*, November 1977, p. 13. The average (14 percent) for food imports during 1974–76 disguises sizable year-to-year differences and a decline (from 19.9 percent in 1974 to 11.56 percent in 1975 to 9 percent in 1976).

141. These steel figures are from table 2-3 (parts 1 and 2); and NFAC, CIA, *China: International Trade, 1977–78*, December 1978, p. 4. For revised, and more detailed, figures, see NFAC, CIA, *China: The Steel Industry in the 1970s and 1980s*, Research Paper ER 79-10245, May 1979, especially p. 6. For fertilizer figures, see table 2-3; and part III, p. 332 and note 229. For figures on fibers and rubber, see table 2-3; and NFAC, CIA, *China: Economic Indicators*, Reference Aid ER 78-10750, December 1978, p. 43.

142. This discussion comparing 1977 and 1965 is based on table 2-3 (parts 1 and 2); and Usack and Batsavage, "The International Trade of the People's Republic of China," p. 353.

143. See Chen, "China's Foreign Trade, 1950–74," pp. 646–47; CIA, *People's Republic of China: International Trade Handbook*, October 1975, p. 13, and *People's Republic of China: International Trade Handbook*, October 1976, p. 16; NFAC, CIA, *China: International Trade, 1977–78*, p. 14; and the discussion in part IV.

144. *JETRO China Newsletter*, no. 18 (June 1978), p. 1.

145. *China Business Review* contains many articles describing Chinese efforts from 1978 on to expand consumer goods exports.

146. See Perkins, "Forecasting China's Trade over the Long Term," pp. 41–45, for an analysis of changes in China's comparative advantage in exports.

147. My calculations, from data in table 2-3 (parts 1 and 2); and NFAC, CIA, *China: International Trade, 1977–78*, p. 16. All figures for Hong Kong include Macao.

148. For an interesting South Korean analysis, see Ungsuh K. Park, *The Modernization Program of the PRC and Its Impact on Korea*, KIEI Working Paper KWP-79-04, serial no. 709, June 1979 (Seoul: Korean International Economic Institute, 1979).

149. The noted economist, Simon Kuznets, in his classic study *Modern Economic Growth, Rate, Structure, and Spread* (Yale University Press, 1966), stated (pp. 286–87): "modern economic growth . . . could best be viewed as a process based on an epochal innovation—a complex of additions to useful knowledge which raises sharply the stock of technological and social knowledge in the world, and which when exploited is the source of the high rate of aggregate increase and of the high rate of structural shifts that characterize modern economics . . . the increase in the stock of useful knowledge and the extension of its application are of the essence in modern economic growth . . . technological and social innovation . . . are largely the product of the developed countries," but the results become a "transnational stock of useful knowledge" on which all nations depend. For useful background on technology transfers generally, and especially between the Western industrial nations and the Soviet Union and East European Communist nations, see Frederic J. Fleron, Jr., ed., *Technology and Communist Culture: The Socio-Cultural Impact of Technology under Socialism* (Praeger, 1977); JEC, *Issues in East-West Commercial Relations*, 95 Cong. 2 sess. (GPO, 1979); R. J. Carrick, *East-West Technology Transfers in Perspective*, Policy Papers in International Affairs (Institute of International Studies, University of California, Berkeley, 1978); William H. Gruber and Donald G. Marquis, eds., *Factors in the Transfer of Technology* (MIT Press, 1969); Edwin Mansfield, "Determinants of the Speed of Application of New Technology," in B. R. Williams, ed., *Science and Technology in Economic Growth* (Wiley, 1973), pp. 199–216, and "International Technology Transfer: Forms, Resource Requirements, and Policies," *American Economic Review*, vol. 65, no. 2 (May 1975, *Papers and Proceedings, 1974*), pp. 372–76; Philip Hanson, "The Import of Western Technology," in Archie Brown and Michael Kaser, eds., *The Soviet Union since the Fall of Khrushchev* (New York: Free Press, 1976), pp. 16–48; John P. Hardt, "The Role of Western Technology in Soviet Economic Plans," in North Atlantic Treaty Organization, *East-West Technological Change* (NATO, 1976), pp. 315–27; Marshall I. Goldman, "Autarchy or Integration—The U.S.S.R. and the World Economy," in JEC, *Soviet Economy in a New Perspective*, 94 Cong. 2 sess. (JEC, October 14, 1976), pp. 81–96; Edward A. Hewett, "The Economics of East European Technology Imports from the

West," *American Economic Review* (May 1975, *Papers and Proceedings, 1974*), pp. 377–82; Robert Starr, ed., *East-West Business Transactions* (Praeger, 1974); James A. Ramsey, "East-West Business Cooperation: The Twain Meets [*sic*]," *Columbia Journal of World Business* (July–August 1970), pp. 17–20; W. Paul Strassmann, *Technological Change and Economic Development* (Cornell University Press, 1968); and John P. Hardt, George D. Holliday, and Young C. Kim, *Western Investment in Communist Economies*, prepared for the Subcommittee on Multinational Corporations of the Senate Committee on Foreign Relations (GPO, 1974).

150. Eckstein, "China's Economic Growth and Foreign Trade," p. 15.

151. The estimates of China's imports of machinery and equipment used in the following discussion are, unless otherwise noted, from table 2-4. Other sources I have used, which have estimates that differ somewhat, include Chu-yuan Cheng, *The Machine-Building Industry in Communist China* (Chicago: Aldine-Atherton, 1971), especially pp. 62–64; Heymann, "Acquisition and Diffusion of Technology in China," pp. 678–729, especially p. 685; Shannon R. Brown, "Foreign Technology and Economic Growth," *Problems of Communism*, vol. 26, no. 4 (July–August 1977), pp. 30–40, especially p. 32; JETRO, *China: A Business Guide*, especially pp. 94–98; and Eckstein, *Communist China's Economic Growth and Foreign Trade*, especially pp. 106–07. See also data in table 2-3; Usack and Batsavage, "The International Trade of the People's Republic of China," pp. 353, 355; and Price, "International Trade of Communist China, 1950–65," p. 586.

152. Hans Heymann, Jr., *China's Approach to Technology Acquisition, Part III, Summary Observations*, Report R-1575-ARPA (Santa Monica, Calif.: Rand Corp., February 1975), p. 6.

153. NFAC, CIA, *China: Real Trends in Trade*, p. 17 (the figures in this source are for all "capital goods"); and CIA, *Foreign Trade in Machinery and Equipment Since 1952*, Reference Aid A ER 75-60, January 1975, p. 6.

154. My calculation, from figures in Yu Qiuli, "Report on the Draft of the 1979 National Economic Plan," in FBIS, *Daily Report—PRC*, July 2, 1979, p. L23, giving a target figure of 4.730 billion yuan for 1979, which he said was 220 percent over 1978. I have converted yuan figures to dollars at $1.00 = 1.682 yuan for 1978 and $1.00 = 1.552 yuan for 1979.

155. My calculation, from State Statistical Bureau, "Communiqué on the Fulfilment of China's 1979 National Economic Plan," in FBIS, *Daily Report—PRC*, July 2, 1979, p. L7, which says that imports of new technology and complete sets of equipment increased 190 percent over 1978, implying that in 1979 they totaled 4.286 billion yuan, or $2.762 billion.

156. One CIA study calculated that China's imports of "capital goods" from non-Communist countries (in current dollars) rose from $292 million (f.o.b.) in 1970 (a figure different from CIA's figure of $249 million in 1970 for just machinery and equipment imports from non-Communist countries) to $1.707 billion in 1975, and in constant 1970 dollars rose from $292 million to $846 million (in short, in real terms, instead of increasing almost six times, they roughly tripled); see NFAC, CIA, *China: Real Trends in Trade*, pp.

16–17. CIA, *Foreign Trade in Machinery and Equipment*, pp. 1, 6, estimated that in current dollars, China's imports of all machinery and equipment totaled $193 million in 1952 and $797 million in 1973, roughly a four-fold rise, but that in constant 1957 dollars the rise was from $195 million in 1952 to $574 million in 1973, roughly a tripling. In regard to complete plant purchases, Eckstein estimated that, during the 1950s, of 291 Soviet aid projects agreed upon, 130 were completed by 1960 (when aid was cut off), and of 64 East European aid projects agreed upon, 27 were completed; the value of those completed, he estimated, was $1.8 billion in current dollars (or about $3 billion in 1973 dollars). He also estimated that China's contracts for complete plant purchases signed in 1973–74 alone, after appropriate price adjustments, totaled perhaps 50 percent of the dollar value of the Soviet and East European plants completed in the 1950s; but that since the deliveries on the latter were generally over seven to eight years, while most of the new contracts in the 1970s called for deliveries in about three years, the new contracts might result in about $700 million a year of plant deliveries, compared with about $430 million a year in the 1950s; see Eckstein, *China's Economic Revolution*, pp. 260–61.

157. My calculations, from table 2-4.

158. My calculations, from CIA data in sources cited earlier.

159. Despite the diversity, the Chinese have concentrated their largest expenditures on certain key industrial sectors; see Heymann, "Acquisition and Diffusion of Technology in China."

160. Calculated from data in NFAC, CIA, *China: International Trade, 1977–78*, p. 15.

161. Calculated from data in CIA, *Foreign Trade in Machinery and Equipment*, p. 13. The Soviet source cited indicated that from 1952 through 1961, China purchased $2.850 billion of machinery and equipment from the Soviet Union, of which $1.770 billion consisted of complete plants. The overall Soviet figures on exports of machinery and equipment to China, it should be noted, differ from CIA estimates. The ruble figure for such exports during 1952–61 in the Soviet source cited equals only $2.850 billion, converted to dollars at official rates, while the CIA estimated the total for those years to be $4.757 billion.

162. Eckstein, *China's Economic Revolution*, pp. 260–61.

163. Calculated from data in Heymann, "Acquisition and Diffusion of Technology in China," p. 685.

164. Batsavage and Davie, "China's International Trade and Finance," p. 711.

165. Estimates on the number (and value) of contracts for complete plants actually signed since 1972 vary, in part because of confusion between firm contracts and preliminary agreements and letters of intent, many of which have not to date resulted in firm contracts. The following figures are conservative CIA estimates which include only confirmed contracts. See NFAC, CIA, *China: International Trade Quarterly Review, Fourth Quarter 1979*, pp. 21–30.

166. JETRO, *China: A Business Guide*, pp. 98–99, listed, by country, a

total of $9.189 billion in industrial plant contracts signed by China during 1972–78 (of which $4.978 billion were with Japan). If one adds the CIA estimate of $1.706 billion for 1979, the total for 1972–79 would be $10.895 billion, only slightly below the CIA's $11.191 billion total. However, JETRO's figures for particular years were different. They were higher than the CIA's for all years except 1978 and considerably lower for that year. JETRO estimated that plant purchase contracts signed during 1978 totaled $5.771 billion, of which $3.835 billion were with Japan. The National Council for U.S.-China Trade (NCUSCT) estimated (in early 1979) that during 1978 China had contracted for about $10 billion of capital goods and technology (including complete plants and other machinery and equipment) for delivery over the next several years; see "CBR Forecast, China's Trade through 1985," *China Business Review*, vol. 6, no. 3 (May–June 1979), p. 10, and NCUSCT, "Sales to China, 1978," unpublished listing, received from James Stepanek of the NCUSCT staff (which listed a total of $17.482 billion of contracted sales to China during 1978, of which an estimated $11 billion consisted of capital goods; it also listed numerous other projects, totaling an estimated $43.333 billion, which were "under discussion or negotiation" during 1978). These NCUSCT estimates of contract totals were too high. Their detailed listings are nevertheless useful; see *U.S.-China Business Review*, vol. 1, no. 1 (January–February 1974), pp. 36–38; vol. 1, no. 2 (March–April 1974), p. 10; vol. 1, no. 3 (May–June 1974), pp. 36–41; vol. 1, no. 5 (September–October 1974), pp. 8–15; vol. 2, no. 1 (January–February 1975), pp. 36–37; vol. 2, no. 4 (July–August 1975), pp. 21, 40; vol. 2, no. 6 (November–December 1975), pp. 44–45; vol. 3, no. 1 (January–February 1976), p. 44; vol. 3, no. 3 (May–June 1976), p. 38; and vol. 3, no. 4 (July–August 1977), pp. 40–43; *China Business Review*, vol. 4, no. 4 (July–August 1977), pp. 10–11; vol. 6, no. 1 (January–February 1979), pp. 88–89; vol. 6, no. 2 (March–April 1979), pp. 75–80; vol. 6, no. 3 (May–June 1979), pp. 61–63; vol. 6, no. 4 (July–August 1979), pp. 71–76; vol. 6, no. 6 (November–December 1979), pp. 65–69; and vol. 7, no. 1 (January–February 1980), pp. 84–85. *JETRO China Newsletter* also has very useful listings, especially of Japanese plant and machinery sales to China. For a summary of 1973–77, see issue no. 19 (September 1978), pp. 8–10, and for lists of later sales and negotiations see no. 20 (December 1978), pp. 18–21; no. 21 (March 1979), pp. 19–21; no. 23 (October 1979), p. 2; and no. 25 (March 1980), p. 22.

167. NFAC, CIA, *China: International Trade Quarterly Review, Fourth Quarter 1979*, pp. 21–30.

168. Projections from NFAC, CIA, *China: Post-Mao Search*, pp. 14–17, suggest possible lows of $4 billion or more a year and a possible high of over $12 billion a year during 1980–84, but these estimates were made before the readjustment of mid-1979, and today the same analysts probably would make lower estimates.

169. My calculations, based on tables 2-1 and 2-4. The real figures should be adjusted slightly since table 2-1 gives total imports c.i.f. and table 2-4 gives machinery imports f.o.b. The figures for machinery and equipment in the sources cited below, in note 170, which give imports c.i.f., total over $8.6 billion, while those in tables 2-1 and 2-4 total about $8.5 billion.

NOTES TO PART II

170. These figures on machinery and equipment are from table 2-4; those on iron, steel, nonferrous metals, and grain are from CIA, *People's Republic of China: International Trade Handbook*, September 1974, p. 13, October 1975, p. 13, October 1976, p. 13; and NFAC, CIA, *China: International Trade, 1977–78*, p. 15.

171. My calculation, from the machinery index in NFAC, CIA, *China: Economic Indicators*, December 1978, p. 1.

172. Eckstein, *China's Economic Revolution*, p. 235. For details, see Field, "Real Capital Formation"; on p. 60, he gives figures that indicate that the percentages for imports in relation to all machinery and equipment delivered to sites were 39 percent in 1952, 45 percent in 1955, 28 percent in 1957, averaged about 38 percent during 1952–60, and by 1973 had dropped to about 8 percent. See also Robert F. Dernberger, "China's Economic Future," in Whiting and Dernberger, *China's Future*, p. 97. Elsewhere, this analyst has estimated that in the 1950s and 1960s as a whole, machinery and equipment imports accounted for over one-tenth of China's total domestic supply of machinery and equipment, that from 1952 through 1960 it accounted for over one-fourth, and that in 1961–73 it was less than one-tenth; see Robert F. Dernberger, "Economic Development and Modernization in Contemporary China: The Attempt to Limit Dependence on the Transfer of Modern Industrial Technology from Abroad and to Control Its Corruption of the Maoist Social Revolution," revised version of paper prepared for the Conference on Technology and Culture, Bellagio, Italy, August 1975 (December 1976), mimeographed, pp. 23–24.

173. Heymann, "Acquisition and Diffusion of Technology in China," pp. 688–89.

174. Brown, "Foreign Technology and Economic Growth," p. 34.

175. Hanson, "The Import of Western Technology," pp. 28–31.

176. See Robert F. Dernberger, "The Transfer of Technology to China," paper prepared for the Workshop on Science and Technology in China's Development, Sussex, England, January 1972, p. 16; and Eckstein, *Communist China's Economic Growth and Foreign Trade*, p. 124. Eckstein estimated that from 1952 through 1957 the rate of GNP growth actually might have been 3 to 5 percent rather than 6 to 7 percent.

177. Cited by Hardt, "The Role of Western Technology in Soviet Economic Plans," p. 317.

178. For general discussions of the methods of technology transfer and the problems of absorption, see the works cited in note 149. For background on these problems relating specifically to China, see Richard Baum, ed., *China's Four Modernizations: The New Technological Revolution* (Boulder, Colo.: Westview Press, 1980); Organization for Economic Cooperation and Development, *Science and Technology in the People's Republic of China* (Paris: OECD, 1977); and Gelber, *Technology, Defense, and External Relations in China, 1975–1978*. A useful bibliography is *Annotated Bibliography on Science and Technology in China*, prepared for the Subcommittee on Domestic and International Scientific Planning and Analysis of the House Committee on Science and Technology, 94 Cong. 2 sess. (GPO, 1976).

179. See, for example, Joseph Berliner, *The Innovation Decision in Soviet*

Industry (MIT Press, 1976); Fleron, *Technology and Communist Culture;* Mansfield, "International Technology Transfer: Forms, Resource Requirements, and Policies," pp. 374–75; Hanson, "The Import of Western Technology," pp. 24–29, 42–44; and Hardt, "The Role of Western Technology in Soviet Economic Plans," pp. 321–27.

180. *Peking Review,* no. 41 (October 13, 1978), pp. 11–12.

181. Estimate of Derek Price, cited by Susan Cozzens, in "Science and Technology: Diffusion, Adaptation, and Development," papers of the Advanced Training Seminar on Subnational Politics and Development in the PRC, October 1975–May 1976 (Columbia University, East Asian Institute, 1976), mimeographed, pp. 199–200.

182. Mansfield, "Determinants of the Speed of Application of New Technology," p. 202.

183. Ibid., pp. 199–200.

184. See part I, pp. 60 ff.

185. The United Nations Conference on Trade and Development (UNCTAD) has tried to urge the developed countries to adopt new policies to facilitate greater and faster technology transfers to the LDCs on improved terms; see United Nations Conference on Trade and Development, *Guidelines for the Study of the Transfer of Technology to Developing Countries,* A Study by the UNCTAD Secretariat (UN, 1972).

186. For a discussion of the problems, see Franklyn D. Holzman and Robert Legvold, "The Economics and Politics of East-West Relations," in C. Fred Bergsten and Lawrence B. Krause, eds., *World Politics and International Economics* (Brookings, 1975), pp. 275–80.

187. Edward F. Denison, *The Sources of Economic Growth in the U.S.* (New York: Committee for Economic Development, 1962), p. 234, cited in Brown, "Foreign Technology and Economic Growth," p. 30.

188. Hanson, "The Impact of Western Technology," p. 28.

189. These are discussed in detail in the sources cited in notes 149 and 178.

190. See, for example, Fleron, *Technology and Communist Culture,* pp. 30–45; and Heymann, "Acquisition and Diffusion of Technology in China," pp. 699–700.

191. Sources relating to the new policies regarding training and research were cited in part I. For additional background on Chinese science and technology, see Baum, *China's Four Modernizations;* OECD, *Science and Technology in the People's Republic of China;* Richard P. Suttmeier, *Research and Revolution: Science Policy and Societal Change in China* (Lexington, Mass.: Lexington Books, 1974), and "Recent Developments in the Politics of Chinese Science," *Asian Survey,* vol. 17, no. 4 (April 1977), pp. 376–92; Charles P. Ridley, *China's Scientific Policies: Implications for International Cooperation* (American Enterprise Institute–Hoover Institution, 1976); Genevieve Dean, "Science, Technology, and Development: China as a Case Study," *China Quarterly,* no. 51 (July–September 1972), pp. 520–34; and Thomas Fingar and Genevieve Dean, "Recent Policy Trends in Industrial Science and Technology: An Overview," paper prepared for the Workshop on the Development of Industrial Science and Technology in the PRC, Bermuda, January

1979. Also useful are numerous reports on particular scientific fields published by the Committee on Scholarly Communication with the People's Republic of China (Washington, D.C.). Basic studies of the state of the sciences and the supply of scientific manpower in China in the 1950s and early 1960s include Chu-yuan Cheng, *Scientific and Engineering Manpower in Communist China, 1949–1963* (Washington, D.C.: National Science Foundation, 1965); and Sidney H. Gould, ed., *Sciences in Communist China* (Washington, D.C.: American Association for the Advancement of Science, 1961). A new study of science in China, sponsored by the Committee on Scholarly Communication with the People's Republic of China and edited by Leo A. Orleans, is scheduled for publication soon by Stanford University Press. Additional sources are listed in the *Annotated Bibliography on Science and Technology in China*, cited in note 178.

192. See the discussion by Richard Baum, "Diabolus Ex Machina: Technological Development and Social Change in Chinese Industry," in Fleron, *Technology and Communist Culture*, chap. 7, pp. 315–56.

193. Heymann, "Acquisition and Diffusion of Technology in China," pp. 702–03.

194. Ibid., pp. 691–96. See also Jon Sigurdson, "Transfer of Technology to the Rural and Collective Sectors in China," in OECD, *Science and Technology in the People's Republic of China*, chap. 10, pp. 171–84; and Genevieve Dean, "Research and Technological Innovation in Industry," in ibid., chap. 9, pp. 157–70.

195. See part I, note 301.

196. See, for example, Dean, "Research and Technological Innovation in Industry," pp. 164–67.

197. See C. H. Geoffrey Oldham, "The Scientific Revolution and China," Newsletter CHGO-37 (New York: Institute of Current World Affairs, December 2, 1964), processed; and Rensselaer W. Lee III, "The Politics of Technology in Communist China," in Chalmers Johnson, ed., *Ideology and Politics in Contemporary China* (University of Washington Press, 1973), pp. 301–25.

198. Thomas G. Rawski, "Problems of Technology Absorption in Chinese Industry," *American Economic Review*, vol. 65, no. 2 (May 1975, *Papers and Proceedings, 1974*), pp. 383–88.

199. Jeffrey Schultz, "The Fourth Modernization: Chinese Industrial Science and Technology and Its Implications for American China Policy" (New York: Asia Society, China Council, March 1978), mimeographed, p. 10.

200. Hans Heymann, Jr., *China's Approach to Technology Acquisition, Part 1: The Aircraft Industry*, Rand Report R-1573-ARPA (Rand Corp., 1975), especially pp. 20–25.

201. This kind of problem has created difficulties for most Chinese aircraft production; see ibid., pp. 55–57.

202. William Clarke, "China's Electric Power Industry," in JEC, *Chinese Economy Post-Mao*, pp. 409–10.

203. Personal interview, September 27, 1979, with an American oil industry specialist who has made extensive visits to Chinese oil sites; unattributable.

204. See p. 207 and notes 106 and 107.

205. State Statistical Bureau Communiqué, in FBIS, *Daily Report—PRC*, June 27, 1979, p. L17.

206. NFAC, CIA, *China: International Trade Quarterly Review, Fourth Quarter 1979*, pp. 9–14. The percentages are my calculations. In 1977 China had a sizable trade surplus; if this had not been the case, the disparity in import and export growth rates would have produced a much bigger deficit in 1978.

207. State Statistical Bureau Communiqué, in FBIS, *Daily Report—PRC*, April 30, 1980, p. 17. The official percentage figures differ slightly from what the rounded figures indicate.

208. NFAC, CIA, *China: International Trade Quarterly Review, Fourth Quarter 1979*, pp. 9–14.

209. These and the following figures are my calculations, from data from my tables and sources already cited.

210. My calculations.

211. The director made these statements in a meeting in Hong Kong; see "Seminar on China's Economy in the 1980s," Department of State incoming telegram from American Consulate-General, Hong Kong, March 1980 (04108, 01 of 02 180545Z, R 170302Z, unclassified).

212. See Field, "Real Capital Formation," pp. 52, 60. His estimates (in 1952 yuan) indicated that of China's gross domestic fixed capital formation in 1957 (21.748 billion yuan, in 1952 yuan), 5.305 billion yuan, or 24.39 percent, consisted of machinery and equipment delivered to sites, of which 3.116 billion yuan, or 15.02 percent, was domestically produced and 2.130 billion yuan, or 9.79 percent, was imported (imports therefore accounted for about 40 percent of machinery and equipment delivered to sites). See also ibid., p. 60, which gives slightly different figures in 1957 yuan. Field estimated that in 1957 total machinery and equipment delivered to sites was 4.171 billion yuan, or 21 percent of total fixed capital formation, which amounted to 19.522 billion yuan, and that in 1973 the comparable figure for machinery and equipment was 20.302 billion yuan, or almost 30 percent of total fixed capital formation, which amounted to 61.013 billion yuan.

213. Based on the figures in NFAC, CIA, *China: Post-Mao Search*, p. 14.

214. For useful background, see David L. Denny, "China's Foreign Financial Liabilities," *U.S.-China Business Review*, vol. 2, no. 1 (January–February 1975), pp. 34–38, "International Finance in the People's Republic of China," in JEC, *China: A Reassessment of the Economy*, pp. 653–77; and Denny and Surls, "China's Foreign Financial Liabilities," pp. 13–21. For background on earlier years, see Directorate of Intelligence, CIA, *Communist China's Balance of Payments, 1950–65*, Intelligence Report CIA/RR ER 66-17, August 1966.

215. State Statistical Bureau Communiqué, in FBIS, *Daily Report—PRC*, June 27, 1979, p. 17. The yuan figures have been converted to dollars at the average exchange rate for the year, $1 = 1.682 yuan. (This average rate is based on calculations made by the National Council for U.S.-China Trade. The CIA calculated that the 1978 average rate was $1 = 1.6802 yuan.)

216. The average exchange rate in 1979, according to NCUSCT calcula-

tions, was $1 = 1.560 yuan. (On this, too, the CIA calculation was slightly different, $1 = 1.5519 yuan.)

217. See p. 207 and note 208.

218. "CBR Forecast—China's Trade through 1985," p. 12.

219. NFAC, CIA, *China: Post-Mao Search*, p. 15.

220. JETRO, *China: A Business Guide*, pp. 100, 106, 120.

221. CIA, "Communist China's Balance of Payments, 1950–1965," in JEC, *An Economic Profile of Mainland China*, pp. 621–60, especially pp. 638–40. The percentages are my calculations.

222. The trade figures for 1950–64 that follow calculate both imports and exports f.o.b. and consequently differ somewhat from those in table 2-1, which gives imports c.i.f. The combined totals of figures on trade and figures on "nontrade" items in ibid. show that trade accounted for 83.2 percent of "credits" and 81.4 percent of "debits" in the overall balance of payments during 1950–64 and 94.0 percent of credits and 98.0 percent of debits in the merchandise trade balance during that period.

223. These are mainly funds sent to relatives in China by Chinese living abroad, mostly in Southeast Asia, but also in North America and elsewhere.

224. My calculations, based on CIA, "Communist China's Balance of Payments, 1950–1965." In the "total balance," I include capital movements as well as current account items.

225. Mah, *Foreign Trade of Mainland China*, pp. 173 ff.

226. Based on Chen, "China's Foreign Trade, 1950–74," p. 648. China's trade deficits with the Soviet Union steadily grew during the five years 1951–55 and totaled $1.070 billion; the annual figures were: 1951, $140 million; 1952, $135 million; 1953, $215 million; 1954, $170 million; and 1975, $410 million.

227. Based on Price, "International Trade of Communist China, 1950–65," especially p. 593.

228. Mah, *Foreign Trade of Mainland China*, pp. 148–61, especially the summaries on pp. 152, 156.

229. Eckstein, *Communist China's Economic Growth and Foreign Trade*, pp. 154–61, 167.

230. Mah, *Foreign Trade of Mainland China*, p. 155.

231. Ibid., p. 163.

232. CIA, "Communist China's Balance of Payments, 1950–1965," p. 638.

233. Ibid. Mah, *Foreign Trade of Mainland China*, p. 167, estimated that during 1961–64, China drew $909 million in credits ($874 million in short-term grain credits and $35 million other credits) and repaid $701 million ($683 million grain credits and $18 million other credits) and that it paid a total of $39 million in interest on these credits during 1961–64.

234. For general background on China's foreign aid programs, see John Franklin Copper, *China's Foreign Aid: An Instrument of Peking's Foreign Policy* (Lexington Books, 1976); Wolfgang Bartke, *China's Economic Aid* (Holmes and Meier for the Hamburg Institute of Asian Affairs, 1975); Carol H. Fogarty, "Chinese Relations with the Third World," in JEC, *Chinese Economy Post-Mao*, pp. 851–59; Leo Tansky, "Chinese Foreign Aid," in JEC,

People's Republic of China: An Economic Assessment; John Franklin Copper, *China's Foreign Aid in 1978,* Occasional Paper 8-1979 (29) (University of Maryland Law School); and NFAC, CIA, *Communist Aid Activities in Non-Communist Less Developed Countries, 1978,* Research Paper ER 79-10412U, September 1979. Generally, when figures differ I have relied on those used by CIA analysts.

235. CIA, "Communist China's Balance of Payments, 1950–1965," pp. 638–40.

236. Tansky, "Chinese Foreign Aid," pp. 372, 381. For aid to Communist nations, see ibid., p. 378. Milton Korner, "Communist China's Foreign Aid to Less-Developed Countries," in JEC, *An Economic Profile of Mainland China,* p. 612, gave a higher estimate for 1956–65: $845.5 million (of which only $59 million was committed in 1965, so his 1956–64 total was $786.5 million).

237. CIA, "Communist China's Balance of Payments, 1950–1965," p. 629.

238. Ibid. China's monetary gold reserves in 1962 were estimated to be $165 million. However, it owed Communist countries an estimated $205 million in clearing account balances, so that its net international financial resources had dropped to $115 million.

239. Mah, *Foreign Trade of Mainland China,* pp. 248–49.

240. NFAC, CIA, *China: International Trade, 1977–78,* p. 23. For somewhat different Japanese estimates of China's current accounts with the non-Communist countries in 1970, see JETRO, *China: A Business Guide,* p. 119, which estimated China's deficit in invisibles at $78 million.

241. NFAC, CIA, *China: International Trade, 1977–78,* p. 23.

242. JETRO, *China: A Business Guide,* p. 120.

243. State Statistical Bureau Communiqué, in FBIS, *Daily Report—PRC,* June 22, 1979, p. L17.

244. "CBR Forecast—China's Trade through 1985," p. 10. Japanese estimates for 1978 differ somewhat; see JETRO, *China: A Business Guide,* p. 120. JETRO estimated China's net earnings from invisibles in 1978 totaled $679 million. Their breakdown was as follows for revenues: $421 million was from Overseas Chinese remittances, $392 million from "travel" (tourism), $8 million from water revenue (from China's supply to Hong Kong), and $27 million from foreign diplomatic missions. On the expenditure side, $38 million was for shipping, $7 million for travel, $41 million in Chinese foreign aid, and $83 million for Chinese diplomatic missions abroad. These figures may underestimate deliveries on Chinese foreign aid, and for some reason JETRO stated (probably erroneously) that China's "revenue from shipping" was still "assumed to be either non-existent or negligible"; ibid., p. 117.

245. Zhang Jingfu (Chang Ching-fu), "Report on the Final State Accounts of 1978 and the Draft Budget for 1979," in FBIS, *Daily Report—PRC,* July 3, 1979, p. L14.

246. Unless otherwise noted, the data below are from Irwin Millard Heine, "China's Merchant Marine," in *U.S.-China Business Review,* vol. 3, no. 2

(March–April 1976), pp. 7–18. For additional background, see CIA, *Chinese Merchant Marine Production*, Research Aid ER 76-10193, March 1976; JETRO, *China: A Business Guide*, pp. 116–18; George Lauriat, "China's Merchant Marine Sails a New Course," *Far Eastern Economic Review* (November 24, 1978), pp. 42–44; "Red China, the New Maritime Superpower," *Sea Power Magazine* (February 1975), pp. 14–16; Stephen Uhalley, "China in the Pacific," Honolulu, 1978, typescript; and Daniel J. Dzurek, "The People's Republic of China: Maritime Policy," Chicago, June 18, 1976, typescript.

247. JETRO, *China: A Business Guide*, pp. 116–17.

248. *China Business Review*, vol. 6, no. 3 (May–June 1979), p. 13. If correct, this represents a huge jump compared to a few years before; Heine, "China's Merchant Marine," p. 9, estimated that in the mid-1970s China carried slightly more than one-third of its trade in its own vessels.

249. Heine, "China's Merchant Marine," p. 18.

250. Ibid., pp. 10–11. The Chinese are giving high priority to port improvement in their current development programs, and reportedly they are preparing to enter the general world shipping and charter market in a big way; see Staff Reporter, "China Soon to Enter World Shipping Arena by Chartering Its Fleet," *Wall Street Journal*, November 16, 1979.

251. *China Business Review*, vol. 6, no. 3 (May–June 1979), p. 12.

252. For general background, see "Tourism: New Chinese Industry on the Rise," *China Business Review*, vol. 5, no. 2 (March–April 1978), pp. 5–9. Both the Chinese and Western press were full of articles relating to tourism during 1978–80. Major expansion of hotel facilities was begun, and some continued even after the readjustment of mid-1979, although thereafter greatest emphasis was placed on relatively modest projects; some of the most grandiose ones initially discussed were postponed or abandoned.

253. *China Business Review*, vol. 6, no. 3 (May–June 1979), p. 13. The Chinese press reported that "over 100,000 foreign tourists" visited China in 1978; see JETRO, *China: A Business Guide*, p. 109.

254. FBIS, *Daily Report—PRC*, April 30, 1980, p. L8. JETRO had estimated $385.4 million; see *China: A Business Guide*, p. 112. Other Chinese reports indicated that "foreign tourists" (not counting visiting Chinese relatives) totaled 160,000 in 1979, a 60 percent increase over 1968, and that the total number of tourists in 1979, including visitors from Macao, Hong Kong, and varied Overseas Chinese communities, was 960,000. A conference on tourism held in China in September 1979 projected 3.5 million foreign tourists spending $2.5 billion in 1985, but another report indicated a hope for 6 million tourists of all kinds spending $5 billion in 1985. See "China's Tourist Industry," Department of State incoming telegram, from Hong Kong Consulate-General, July 1980 (R 8309352).

255. For these and the following figures, see James P. Sterba (with erroneous headline "F.B.I. Assailed by U.S. Court in Black Panther Case"!), *New York Times*, May 6, 1979. The low figure for Japan and the discrepancies among per capita spending of tourists in different places raise questions about

the reliability of some of these figures, but they nevertheless indicate the importance of earnings from tourism throughout most of Asia and the potential of such earnings for China.

256. *China Business Review*, vol. 6, no. 3 (May–June 1979), p. 13.

257. JETRO, *China: A Business Guide*, p. 112.

258. See, for example, Fox Butterfield, "China, Short of Capital, Looking for Philanthropists," *New York Times*, April 10, 1979; and Melinda Liu, "China's Investments Grow and the Vibes Are Good," *Far Eastern Economic Review* (October 6, 1978), pp. 59–66. For background on Overseas Chinese remittances in the earlier years, see Remer, *The Foreign Trade of China*, pp. 215–21; and Donnithorne, *China's Economic System*, pp. 513–14.

259. *China Business Review*, vol. 6, no. 3 (May–June 1979), p. 13.

260. JETRO, *China: A Business Guide*, p. 110.

261. Liu, "China's Investments Grow and the Vibes Are Good," p. 59.

262. This was the National Council for U.S.-China Trade's estimate, in *China Business Review*, vol. 6, no. 3 (May–June 1979), p. 13. JETRO, *China: A Business Guide*, p. 110, estimated a possible rise to $873 million by 1982.

263. NFAC, CIA, *Communist Aid Activities in Non-Communist Less Developed Countries, 1978*, pp. 7, 11. For specific annual figures in the discussion that follows, I use estimates from Fogarty, "Chinese Relations with the Third World," pp. 851–59, for the years through 1976, even though there are discrepancies between them and the more recent CIA estimates (for example, Fogarty says China's 1976 aid deliveries to LDCs totaled $285 million; the recent CIA figure is $315 million). For 1977–78, I have used the recent CIA estimates.

264. Fogarty, "Chinese Relations with the Third World," p. 854.

265. The actual amount was $2.216 billion ($4.756 billion committed, minus $2.540 billion delivered) according to the figures in NFAC, CIA, *Communist Aid Activities in Non-Communist Less Developed Countries, 1978*, pp. 7, 11.

266. The yuan figure is from official 1979 budget projections, in FBIS, *Daily Report—PRC*, July 3, 1979, p. L14. The average 1978 exchange rate used here is $1 = 1.56 yuan.

267. "CBR Forecast—China's Trade through 1985," p. 12, projects a steady $220 million a year in total Chinese foreign aid deliveries during 1978–85. JETRO, *China: A Business Guide*, pp. 118, 120, projects $41 million each year, during 1980–82, in aid deliveries, but this is probably too low. (JETRO's estimates for actual deliveries in recent years are substantially lower than the CIA's.)

268. Mah, *Foreign Trade of Mainland China*, pp. 165–66.

269. Ibid., pp. 164–65.

270. Indicated in the hypothetical projection in NFAC, CIA, *China: Post-Mao Search*, p. 14.

271. Indicated in the hypothetical projection of the National Council for U.S.-China Trade, in "CBR Forecast—China's Trade through 1985," p. 12. JETRO's projections indicate that in 1982, China's net earnings from invisibles could be $1.48 billion; see JETRO, *China: A Business Guide*, p. 120.

272. NFAC, CIA, *China: Post-Mao Search*, p. 14, projected cumulative net invisible earnings during 1978–85 at $12.3 billion, or 9.7 percent of projected cumulative exports (of $127.3 billion). "CBR Forecast—China's Trade through 1985," p. 12, projected cumulative net invisible earnings during the same period at $11.870 billion, or over 8 percent of projected cumulative exports of $145.800 billion.

273. The following are my calculations, based on the estimated repayment schedule in Mah, *Foreign Trade of Mainland China*, pp. 162–63. For figures on China's trade with the Soviet Union and all other Communist nations, see Chen, "China's Foreign Trade, 1950–74," p. 648, and for figures on China's overall trade, see table 2-1.

274. Calculated from data in table 2-5.

275. Calculated from data in tables 2-1 and 2-6.

276. Batsavage and Davie, "China's International Trade and Finance," p. 720. For CIA estimates for the period 1960–70, see Usack and Batsavage, "The International Trade of the People's Republic of China," p. 342.

277. Li made the statement to Japanese business leaders; see Kyodo, July 13, 1978, in FBIS, *Daily Report—PRC*, July 13, 1978, p. A2.

278. Recent reports and estimates of Chinese total reserves (including gold) vary; they include the following: *Economist* (October 14, 1978), p. 114—more than $3 billion (including $1 billion in gold); *Business Week* (November 6, 1978), p. 76—less than $5 billion; *Far Eastern Economic Review* (October 14, 1978), p. 41—$5 billion; and *Chase International Finance*, vol. 14, no. 12 (June 11, 1979), p. 8—$6.5 billion ($2.5 billion currency reserves and estimated gold holdings of $4 billion). (In early 1980, the National Council for U.S.-China Trade estimated that China's "net deposit position" in the Eurocurrency and Asian dollar markets had dropped between mid-1978 and mid-1979 from $2.314 billion to $670 million, but these figures did not reveal China's total currency reserves; see *China Business Review*, vol. 7, no. 1 [January–February 1980], p. 56.)

279. World Bank, *World Debt Tables*, vol. 1: *External Public Debt of Developing Countries*, Document EC-167/77 (Washington, D.C.: World Bank, 1977).

280. In 1978 the USSR's repayments ($1.459 billion) and interest ($1.769 billion) on Western credits totaled $3.228 billion, or 19 percent of its hard currency imports ($16.886 billion). Its gross debt (from Western credits) outstanding as of the end of 1978 was $17.224 billion; see NFAC, CIA, *Handbook of Economic Statistics, 1979*, pp. 67–69.

281. See Lawrence S. Theriot, "Communist Country Hard Currency Debt in Perspective," project no. D-66-78 (Office of East-West Policy and Planning, Department of Commerce, 1976), mimeographed, p. 10. For additional background, see Richard Portes, "East Europe's Debt to the West: Interdependence Is a Two-Way Street," *Foreign Affairs*, vol. 55, no. 4 (July 1977), pp. 751 ff.

282. Batsavage and Davie, "China's International Trade and Finance," p. 732.

283. NFAC, CIA, *China: Post-Mao Search*, pp. 14–17.

284. My calculation, from estimates in "CBR Forecast—China's Trade through 1985," pp. 12–13.

285. Ibid., p. 16.

286. Obtained by dividing the price index of exports by the price index of imports.

287. NFAC, CIA, *China: Real Trends in Trade*, p. 3.

288. Obtained by multiplying the commodity terms of trade index by the export quantity index (which provides a measure of capacity to import based on exports alone).

289. See NFAC, CIA, *Least Developed Countries: Economic Characteristics and Stake in North-South Issues*, Research Paper ER 78-10253, May 1978, especially pp. 34–35.

290. In September 1979 Vice Premier Ku Mu (Gu Mu) acknowledged "that worldwide economic recession would inevitably affect China's export of industrial goods"; however, he argued that "the commodities China exports are what other countries want," claiming they "have a market abroad whatever the situation." See "Gu Mu Comments on Economic Questions at Press Conference," in FBIS, *Daily Report—PRC*, September 28, 1979, p. L9.

291. For background, see James B. Stepanek, "How Are China's Exchange Rates Set?" *U.S.-China Business Review*, vol. 3, no. 1 (January–February 1976), pp. 11–15; "An Introduction to the Renminbi," *U.S.-China Business Review*, vol. 1, no. 1 (January–February 1974), pp. 50–51, and vol. 1, no. 3 (May–June 1974), pp. 33–35; and Denny, "International Finance in the People's Republic of China," especially pp. 664 ff.

292. Hobart Rowen, "Hong Kong's Partnership with Peking," *Washington Post*, November 2, 1978.

293. On China-Europe textile problems, see Francis Deron, Agence France Press, "EEC-PRC Textile Talks Stalled over PRC Export Quotas," in FBIS, *Daily Report—PRC*, July 16, 1979, p. G1. On U.S.-China textile problems, see part V, pp. 527 ff.

294. For broad background on China's participation in the United Nations and UN-affiliated bodies, see Samuel S. Kim, *China, the United Nations and World Order* (Princeton University Press, 1979); on China's relative passivity until recently, see ibid., especially pp. 365–66.

295. See p. 147.

296. Paul Hofmann, "China Displays Interest in World Nuclear Agency," *New York Times*, April 1, 1979.

297. Bhushan Bahree, "China Stepping Up Its Role at World Commodity Talks," *Asian Wall Street Journal*, October 17, 1978.

298. A high Chinese official told me this in an unattributable interview in Peking in October 1979. He implied that at that time passage of the trade agreement was Peking's first priority objective in U.S.-China economic relations, that Chinese leaders did not wish to jeopardize this, and that they recognized that moving first to join the International Monetary Fund (IMF) and the World Bank might create problems since some influential U.S. congress-

men opposed the ousting of Taiwan from these bodies (a move which Peking insisted upon).

299. Associated Press, "China Admitted to I.M.F.," *New York Times*, April 18, 1980; and Clyde H. Farnsworth, "China Gets World Bank Seat," *New York Times*, May 16, 1980.

300. James B. Stepanek, "China, the IMF, and the World Bank," *China Business Review*, vol. 7, no. 1 (January–February 1980), pp. 55–62.

301. Stepanek, in ibid., p. 58, stated that eventually China will be eligible for at least $1 billion to $3 billion in loans from the World Bank and sizable amounts from the International Development Association (IDA) and the International Finance Corporation (IFC), but he pointed out that these agencies will not have the funds necessary immediately to loan China such large amounts.

302. From private conversations with top World Bank officials, May 27 and June 4, 1980; unattributable.

303. See, for example, Maurice Samuelson, "Peking Interest In Tokyo Round," *Financial Times* (London), October 19, 1979. In private conversations, Chinese officials showed some interest in the General Agreement on Tariffs and Trade (GATT) in early 1980.

304. "Duty Free Treatment for Chinese Goods?" *China Business Review*, vol. 6, no. 4 (July–August 1979), p. 32.

305. Ibid.

306. China's past statements to, and activities in, these and other UN-related institutions have been regularly reported in some detail in the "Quarterly Chronicle and Documentation" section of the *China Quarterly* (London) issues since no. 49 (January–March 1972), following Peking's seating in the United Nations in the fall of 1971. For a general discussion of China's expanding participation, recently, in UN-related and other international organizations, see Natalie G. Lichtenstein, "China's Participation in International Organizations," *China Business Review*, vol. 6, no. 3 (May–June 1979), pp. 28–36.

307. For Chinese statements typical of those made during the early 1970s, see "Discussion on Drafting Charter of Economic Rights and Duties of States," and "Third World Struggle Against Hegemony in the Economic Sphere," both in *Peking Review*, no. 3 (August 17, 1973), pp. 12–14; "7th Special Session of U.N. General Assembly Closes," *Peking Review*, no. 39 (September 26, 1975), pp. 19–25, 29; and the major speeches made by Chinese representatives at the UN General Assembly, cited earlier in note 124.

308. A survey (done for me in 1978 by Neal Hoptman) of the amount of coverage (measured in numbers of articles and pages) on "North-South issues" in articles in *Peking Review*, from the start of 1974 through the fall of 1978, showed a very significant drop from thirty-four articles totaling more than ninety-nine pages in 1974 to ten articles totaling nineteen pages in 1977. (In 1977 there were also eight articles, totaling more than forty-seven pages, on "three world" theory—thirty pages of which, however, were accounted for by a single article by the *People's Daily* editorial department

discussing Mao's concept of "three worlds," and by 1978 the space devoted to this theme began to decline.)

309. For example, Wei Yu-ming (Wei Yuming), in 1977 appointed Vice Minister of the Ministry of Economic Relations with Foreign Countries, stated at a UN Conference on Technical Cooperation among Developing Countries, "Some Second World countries have increased their economic ties and technical exchange with third world countries on the basis of equality and mutual benefit, expressed willingness to revise certain unreasonable stipulations in their technical cooperation with developing countries, provide technical assistance on relatively preferential terms and support technical cooperation among developing countries. We appreciate all this." See "Conference on Technical Cooperation," *Peking Review*, no. 37 (September 15, 1978), p. 31.

310. Bahree, "China Stepping Up Its Role at World Commodity Talks."

311. Ibid. However, China has offered to make a contribution to the so-called common fund, designed to provide a mechanism for management of commodity markets, which has been strongly promoted by many Third World countries.

312. For an example of earlier Chinese attacks on multinationals, see Cheng Wei-min[g] (Zheng Weiming or Cheng Weiming), "U.S. Trans-National Corporations' Plunder and Exploitation of Developing Countries," *Peking Review*, no. 23 (June 7, 1974), pp. 24–25, 28. For an example of their more restrained and pragmatic—but still "pro-Third World"—recent line, see NCNA, "PRC Supports Developing Countries on Transfer of Technology," October 19, 1978, in FBIS, *Daily Report—PRC*, October 20, 1978, p. A1.

313. For background on Chinese views on the laws of the sea, see sources cited in part IV, notes 405–08. On most of China's island claims there is still no sign of significant change from past positions; see, for example, "China's Indisputable Sovereignty over the Xisha [Hsi-sha] and Nansha [Nan-sha] Islands," *Beijing Review*, no. 7 (February 18, 1980), pp. 15–24. Reportedly, in mid-1979, Vice Premiers Li Hsien-nien and Wang Chen (Wang Zhen) expressed interest in joint oil development near the Tiaoyutai (Diaoyutai)/ Senkaku islands, but within the framework of Chinese laws, and the Japanese were unwilling to consider this; see "Chronology of Japan-China Negotiation on Joint Oil Development," JETRO, *China Newsletter*, no. 24 (December 1979), p. 29.

314. China's new cooperation with the United Nations in population matters is discussed in Bernard D. Nossiter, "U.N. Agency Aids China to Curb Population Growth," *New York Times*, March 16, 1980. China also is expanding its cooperation, internationally, in pollution control and has passed its first comprehensive law relating to it; see "China's First Environmental Protection Law," *Beijing Review*, no. 24 (November 9, 1979), p. 24.

315. The concept of "three worlds," though attributed to Mao, was most dramatically articulated by Teng Hsiao-ping in speeches at the United Nations in April 1974; see *Peking Review*, no. 15, Supplement (April 12, 1974),

pp. 1–5, and no. 16 (April 19, 1974), pp. 6–11. It was given renewed emphasis, briefly, in the fall of 1977 in the *People's Daily* editorial, "Chairman Mao's Theory of the Differentiation of the Three Worlds Is a Major Contribution to Marxism-Leninism"; see *Peking Review*, no. 45 (November 4, 1977), pp. 10–41. However, by 1979, though not repudiated, the three worlds idea clearly was deemphasized.

316. Unless otherwise noted, the following data are from Kojima, "Sino-Japanese Economic Relations." (Kojima was a member of the China Team of the Overseas Research Department of the Japan External Trade Organization.) The Japanese statistics he used were close to but not identical with American estimates used in this volume.

317. Kojima's list included credits of $2 billion from a twenty-two bank consortium for four and a half years at an interest rate of LIBOR plus 0.50 percent; $6 billion of six-month tied loans from a thirty-one bank consortium at LIBOR plus 0.25 percent; $1.6 billion to $1.7 billion of untied EX-IM Bank loans for fifteen years at 6.25 percent for oil, coal, and other resource development; and an initial $200 million of concessionary credit, at 3.0 percent for thirty years, from the Overseas Economic Cooperation Fund for infrastructure projects.

318. Import and export percentages are from ibid., p. 7.

319. Ibid., p. 7; Kojima predicted that China would account for "around 10 percent" of both Japan's exports and its imports by 1985. The Japan Economic Research Center, *A Study on Japan-China Economic Relations*, pp. 11, 13, calculating that in 1978 China accounted for less than 2.5 percent of total Japanese trade, predicted that by 1985 it might account for around 5 percent.

320. Several JETRO officials emphasized this in conversations with me during 1979–80. Kojima, "Sino-Japanese Economic Relations," pp. 22–23, stated, "We do not intend to monopolize the [China] market, even if we could. . . . As to cooperation between the U.S. and Japan in China trade, I think there is a good potential, but that potential may be somewhat limited in scope. . . . There is a natural compatibility between China's needs, American high technology, and the strategically situated Japanese manufacturing centers." What he favored most strongly was that "the U.S. provide licensing and key items while Japan builds the actual equipment and ships it to the PRC." Immediately thereafter, however, he recognized that, "of course, I am sure that American companies would be less interested in licensing and tapping [Japanese] trading company know-how than in making down-to-earth sales." The kind of relationships he described as ideal from the Japanese viewpoint seem unlikely to arouse enthusiasm in U.S. government or business circles interested in China trade.

321. My calculations, from data on the trade of all European Community (EC) nations, in Department of State, Bureau of Public Affairs, *Trade Patterns of the West, 1978*, Special Report no. 63 (BPA, December 1979), table 1, p. 3. Of the EC countries' overall trade, totaling $923 billion, only $3.1 billion, or 0.34 percent, was with China; of their total exports amounting to

$461 billion, $1.9 billion, or 0.41 percent, were to China; and of total EC imports amounting to $462 billion, $1.2 billion, or 0.26 percent, came from China. (These statistics gave exports f.o.b. and imports c.i.f. They differed slightly, in some cases, from the CIA figures used throughout most of this study.)

322. Estimate of Endymion Wilkinson, China expert on the EC Commission; see "China and the International Community," *Trialogue* (New York: Trilateral Commission), no. 20 (Summer 1979), p. 21. Wilkinson believed that in 1985 China's total imports might reach $30 billion and that the EC nations might provide about one-third of the total, or $10 billion, and he calculated that this would be 2.3 percent of projected total EC exports, worldwide, in 1985.

323. Total U.S. foreign trade in 1978, according to CIA figures, was $327 billion ($144 billion exports and $183 billion imports); see CIA, *Handbook of Economic Statistics, 1979*, pp. 77, 79. Trade with China in 1978 was 0.36 percent of total U.S. trade, 0.60 percent of U.S. exports, and 0.18 percent of U.S. imports.

324. Juanita Kreps, "China Trade Speech," *Congressional Record*, daily ed. (June 12, 1979), p. S7500.

325. A long, official U.S. report in early 1980 provides extensive details on the newly developing relationships; see "Hong Kong Official Perspectives on the Growing Economic Relationship with China," Department of State airgram from American Consulate-General, Hong Kong, March 27, 1980 (message reference A-29, unclassified). In addition to discussing the possible increase in cross-border supply of fuel and electricity as well as water, it deals with the large two-way flow of people (including increasing immigration to Hong Kong, which supplies the colony with useful labor but also creates new problems); the development of new special economic zones in China adjacent to Hong Kong; the increasing importance to China of Hong Kong's transport, storage, communications, finance, insurance, and other services; the development of new direct transportation links; growing Chinese investments in Hong Kong; and the establishment of joint manufacturing enterprises in China, with foreign investment, involving Hong Kong as well as other entrepreneurs. It also discusses China's strong desire for joint ventures in Kwangtung (Guangdong) to obtain new technology and managerial techniques as well as capital and to help in export marketing; the value to Hong Kong of developing enterprises on Chinese land (because land is such a scarce commodity in Hong Kong) and using Chinese labor (which is cheaper in China than in Hong Kong); and the benefits to both places of growing overall economic cooperation. It cites Chinese leaders' assurances to Hong Kong business leaders and investors, quoting statements made by them about "Hong Kong being a possible bridge between China and Taiwan." For another optimistic view, articulated by one of Hong Kong's prominent business leaders, see Sir Lawrence Kadoorie, "Kadoorie Looks at Hong Kong's Future," *Asian Wall Street Journal*, July 23, 1979. See also a report on Governor Sir Murray MacLehose's "historic trip to China" in Melinda Liu, "China Puts Hong Kong Investors at Ease," *Far Eastern Economic Review* (April

20, 1979), pp. 42–43; and the statement by Foreign Trade Minister Li Chiang that "there are many things we can learn from Hong Kong," in Dende Montilla, *South China Morning Post* (Hong Kong), in FBIS, *Daily Report—PRC*, December 20, 1978, p. A26.

326. Peking has strongly pushed this moderate line since 1978, and particularly since Peking's National People's Congress, on January 1, 1979, issued a special "Message to Compatriots in Taiwan"; see text in *Beijing Review*, no. 1 (January 5, 1979), pp. 16–17. Teng Hsiao-ping spelled out China's new flexible position in several interviews with Americans; see, as examples, his interview with A. T. Steele, *New York Times*, December 13, 1978, and his January 1979 interview with U.S. Senator John Glenn and others from the U.S. Senate Committee on Foreign Relations, summarized in Senate Committee on Foreign Relations, *Sino-American Relations: A New Turn*, pp. 3–4.

327. It is difficult to know exactly how large such indirect trade is now, but American government specialists estimate that it already totals tens of millions of dollars and is still growing fairly rapidly. Peking is actively encouraging its growth and often proclaims its desire to learn from Taiwan as well as from Hong Kong, and Taipei (Taibei) is at least tolerating the trade, and perhaps in some ways encouraging it; see James P. Sterba, "China and Taiwan Urging U.S. to Trade with Both," *New York Times*, April 9, 1980; and Fox Butterfield, "Chinese Region Imitates Taiwan in Search for International Trade," *New York Times*, April 21, 1980. In April 1980 the General Administration of Customs in China announced that to promote trade with Taiwan it would grant permission to Chinese foreign trade corporations to ship goods there; press release no. 80/015, Embassy of the People's Republic of China, Washington, D.C., April 9, 1980, mimeographed.

328. American officials report that it has been extremely difficult, even in secret negotiations, to have fruitful discussions with the Chinese on issues relating to Korea, presumably because of Peking's fears that any sign of policy change could affect its relations with Pyongyang adversely and create problems that Moscow might exploit.

329. For an objective South Korean analysis of possible Chinese economic competition, which concludes that Korea has advantages in certain fields and areas and China in others and urges greater Korean emphasis on sophisticated high-quality products, see Ungsuh K. Park, *The Modernization Program of the PRC and Its Impact on Korea*, especially pp. 40–52. The author urges the development of trade with China, starting with indirect trade.

330. See, for example, "The Search for Cheap Labor, China and South Asia Are at the Forefront of the New Waves of Areas Attracting Investment," *Far Eastern Economic Review*, May 18, 1979, pp. 79–80. Privately, South and Southeast Asian officials have increasingly expressed concern about the possible adverse effects on their countries of increased Chinese competition for capital and markets.

331. NFAC, CIA, *China: International Trade Quarterly Review, Fourth Quarter 1979*, pp. 10, 12.

332. Both publicly and privately, for many years the Russians have stressed the mutual advantage of expanded Sino-Soviet economic relations and have

emphasized the two countries' potential economic complementarity. M. Sladkovsky, director of the Institute of the Far East, stated to me in an interview in Moscow on April 16, 1974: "Our [Soviet and Chinese] economies are complementary. We can buy and sell in a way the United States cannot. What can the United States buy from China? This economic complementarity will be important in the long run" (from personal interview notes). Moscow periodically has proposed steps to expand Sino-Soviet economic relationships. Its desire for restored economic ties also is reflected in many articles in *Far Eastern Affairs* (Moscow: Institute of the Far East); see, for example, O. Rakhmainin, "Twenty Years of Soviet-Chinese Friendship," no. 2 (1978), pp. 61–62.

333. After abrogation of the Sino-Soviet treaty, and after China's Vietnam incursion, wide-ranging Sino-Soviet discussions were proposed "without preconditions"; they started in May 1979. This was seen by many as a potentially significant attempt to reduce the level of tensions in government-to-government relations. But the attempt was aborted, and the talks adjourned, as a result of Moscow's Afghanistan invasion in late 1979.

334. Hua Guofeng, "Report on the Work of the Government," June 18, 1979, in FBIS, *Daily Report—PRC*, Supplement 015, July 2, 1979, p. 12.

335. The Soviet case, while not exactly analogous, is instructive. Moscow, too, has alternately turned outward and inward, and U.S. specialists on Soviet affairs are divided on whether or not increased Soviet interdependence with the global economy is reversible. Marshall I. Goldman, "Autarchy or Integration—The U.S.S.R. and the World Economy," p. 95, first argued that "a return to autarchy is possible" but then stated, "No one move by itself has been all that far-reaching, but the totality of these processes in recent years, and in years to come, may eventually bring about a qualitative change. As of now, the U.S.S.R. may still be able to extract itself without too much trouble, but it is clear that if the present trend continues, the cost of severing ties with the West will mount rapidly." Hanson, "The Import of Western Technology," pp. 42–44, cited differing views on this question and ended somewhat agnostically, stating that while "great and increasing importance has been attributed by Soviet policy makers over the past decade and a half to technology transfer from the West," nevertheless, "I conclude . . . with no firm views about the future development of East-West economic interdependence but with at least some grounds for expecting it to increase, so far as Soviet interests are concerned."

336. International Monetary Fund statistics show world imports of non-Communist nations in 1978 totaling $1.23 trillion; see IMF, *International Financial Statistics*, vol. 32, no. 5 (May 1979), pp. 36–37.

337. Ibid., p. 37. The figures for Africa and the Middle East are for 1977; those for the Western Hemisphere and Asia are for 1978.

338. Ibid.; where 1978 figures are not complete, I have used 1977 figures.

339. See part V for details on the evolution of U.S. official views.

340. Hua Guofeng, "Report on the Work of the Government," June 18, 1979, p. 31.

341. "Report on the Current Situation and Tasks," January 16, 1980, in FBIS, *Daily Report—PRC*, March 11, 1980, p. 2.

342. See John R. Garson, "COCOM, CHINCOM, and a Note on Third Country Trade with China," in Eckstein, ed., *China Trade Prospects and U.S. Policy*, chap. 4.

343. Reuters, "Agreement on Sale of Missiles to China Confirmed by France"; Browning, "France Moves Ahead on China Arms Sales"; and Downie, "Britain Tells Hua It Is Willing to Sell Harrier Jets."

344. See, for example, Dusko Doder, "Brezhnev Warns Britain on Sale of Jets to China," *Washington Post*, November 24, 1978; David K. Willis, "Soviets Tie Arms Deal to Other Gains," *Christian Science Monitor*, October 24, 1978; Don Oberdorfer, "Soviets Warn Not to Sell Peking Arms," *Washington Post*, October 27, 1978; and R. W. Apple, Jr., "Brezhnev Reported to Warn U.S. on Arming China," *New York Times*, January 30, 1980.

345. Gelber, *Technology, Defense, and External Relations in China, 1975–1978*, p. 81.

346. See part V, p. 502 and note 24.

347. See part V, pp. 554–56 and notes 175 and 186.

348. Innumerable Soviet articles reveal this; for examples, see A. Kruchinin "From Anti-Imperialism to Alliance with Imperialism and Reaction," *Far Eastern Affairs* (Moscow: Institute of the Far East), no. 4 (1979), pp. 102–17; and S. Yurkov, "China and Western Europe," in ibid., pp. 87–101. Yurkov's article ended (p. 101): "Those Western European leaders who are willing to make use of China's leaders' adventurism and anti-Sovietism are politically near-sighted, since this will eventually lead them to a sorry pass, like those leaders, who, on the eve of World War II, tried to appease Hitler's Germany at Munich and to push it against the Soviet Union. Peking may jeopardize world peace and plunge their countries into a nuclear holocaust." Kruchinin's article concluded (pp. 116–17): "When it unleashed the second World War, Hitler's Germany was by no means the strongest among the imperialist powers. But this country happened to have the most adventuristic and irresponsible leadership guided by chauvinistic and hegemonistic ambitions of Hitlerism, which naturally resulted in the policy of aggression and war. The last two decades have irrefutably shown that Maoism is a Great Power ideology and policy with chauvinist aspirations at world domination and hence an ideology and policy of aggression and war. . . . The situation is likely to deteriorate as the Peking militarists extend their collaboration with the like-minded imperialist warmongers. Unfortunately, there is increasingly plentiful and alarming evidence of their growing collaboration."

Part III

1. Fred H. Sanderson, "The Great Food Fumble," *Science*, vol. 188, no. 4188 (May 9, 1975), p. 503.

2. These world population estimates are from Central Intelligence Agency,

Potential Implications of Trends in World Population, Food Production, and Climate, OPR-401, August 1974, p. 5.

3. See ibid. for figures on 1930 and 1960; for figures on 1965–75, see Population Reference Bureau, *World Population Growth and Response, 1965–1975, A Decade of Global Action* (PRB, April 1976), and *1977 World Population Data Sheet* (PRB, 1977). These publications provide excellent background information on global population problems and trends. The PRB has estimated that on July 1, 1978, world population totaled 4.219 billion; see Arthur Haumpt and Thomas T. Kane, *Population Handbook* (PRB, December 1978), p. 5. The U.S. Census Bureau has estimated that from the mid-1950s to 1970 the world's population grew at 2.0 percent a year, that since 1970 the rate has dropped to 1.9 percent, and that in mid-1977 world population totaled 4.3 billion; see Susanna McBee, "For First Time, Population Rise Is Less Rapid," *Washington Post,* November 20, 1978.

4. CIA, *Potential Implications of Trends,* annex 1, p. 1.

5. Recent evidence indicates that world fertility continues to decline. The natural global increase rate may now be well below 2.0 percent (although it is too early to say whether this trend will last). Some studies indicate that the worldwide rate has dropped to 1.7 percent; see Reuters, "Worldwide Birth Rate Hits Historical Low Level," *Washington Post,* April 19, 1978; Joanne Omang, "Scientists Find World Population Growth Is Declining," *Washington Post,* February 15, 1978; "Population Growth Declining," *The IDRC Reports* (Canada: International Development Research Centre), vol. 7, no 2 (June 1978), p. 24; and Leon Tabah, "World Population at a Turning Point?" in PRB, *Intercom,* vol. 5, no. 12 (December 1977), pp. 7–9.

6. From United Nations estimates, cited in CIA, *Potential Implications of Trends,* annex 1, p. 1.

7. See McBee, "For First Time, Population Rise Is Less Rapid."

8. Amy Ong Tsui and Donald J. Bogue, "Declining World Fertility: Trends, Causes, and Implications," cited by Associated Press, "Population Crisis Held Resolvable if Trends Continue," *Washington Post,* October 10, 1978.

9. Robert S. McNamara, "World Change and World Security," address to the Massachusetts Institute of Technology, April 28, 1977, p. 52. McNamara also stated, "For every decade of delay in achieving a net reproduction rate of 1.0—replacement level—the world's ultimate steady-state population will be about 15 percent greater." Ibid., p. 10.

10. Lester R. Brown, "The Next Crisis? Food," *Foreign Policy,* no. 13 (Winter 1973–74), p. 4.

11. Ibid.

12. T. T. Poleman, "World Food: A Perspective," *Science,* vol. 188, no. 4188 (May 9, 1975), pp. 510 ff. In 1973 the 3.8 billion people in the world had about one-fifth more food, per capita, than did the 2.7 billion people in 1954; see U.S. Department of Agriculture, *The World Food Situation and Prospects to 1985,* Foreign Agricultural Economic Report 98, December 1974, p. 12. (This book-length study by the USDA, prepared following Secretary of State Henry Kissinger's proposal in 1973 that the United Nations sponsor a World

Food Conference, provides excellent data on general world food problems and trends.)

13. USDA, *World Agricultural Situation*, WAS-17 (USDA, October 1978), p. 34. For CIA estimates, see CIA, *Handbook of Economic Statistics, 1977*, ER 77-10537, September 1977, pp. 125–28. The totals include wheat, coarse grains, and milled rice.

14. All grain tonnage figures are in metric tons; 1 metric ton = 1,000 kilograms or 1.1 tons. USDA converts "paddy" (unhusked) rice to milled rice at 68 percent, which is the conversion rate used throughout this study. USDA's trade figures are usually based on grain marketing years, but its rice production figures are usually based on calendar years. A grain marketing year is indicated by a slash (for example, 1960/61).

15. USDA, *World Agricultural Situation*, WAS-17 (October 1978), p. 34.

16. My calculations. Total output of *food* (not just grain) increased 69 percent (based on trend values), at an annual rate of 2.8 percent, during 1954–73; see USDA, *World Food Situation and Prospects*, p. 12. The CIA's figures were somewhat different: 874 million tons in 1960 and 1.44 billion tons in 1976; see CIA, *Handbook of Economic Statistics, 1977*, p. 125.

17. USDA, *World Agricultural Situation*, WAS-22 (June 1980), p. 39.

18. USDA, *World Food Situation and Prospects*, p. 14. The average rate of increase in grain output, 1960–62 to 1969–71, was 3 percent. The global rate of increase in total food production was 2.8 percent a year, 1954–73; ibid., p. 12.

19. While world output of food (not just grain) increased during 1954–73 at a 2.8 percent rate, world population grew at 2.0 percent, producing a 0.8 percent rate of increase in per capita food supply. (China is not included in these figures.) However, during the 1976/77–1979/80 period, the rate of increase in grain output was probably more than 2 percent above the rate of population growth.

20. James P. Grant, "Food, Energy, and the Changing World Order," Overseas Development Council, May 1975 processed, p. 6, stated that 30 million tons a year were required; subsequently, it has continued to increase.

21. USDA, *World Agricultural Situation*, WAS-22 (June 1980), p. 39.

22. USDA, *World Food Situation and Prospects*, pp. 35–36. These figures were the lower two of the four projections presented; the higher projections (based on different assumptions) were for a 2.8 or 3.0 percent rate of growth in demand for grain, resulting in a total demand of either 1.62 million tons or 1.64 million tons in 1985. This same source gave UN Food and Agriculture Organization (FAO) estimates, which were only marginally different.

23. Henry A. Kissinger, "The Global Community and the Struggle against Famine," speech, November 5, 1974, Department of State, Bureau of Public Affairs, p. 3.

24. See, for example, the discussion in USDA, *World Food Situation and Prospects*, pp. v, 32–39. A key variable will be how much the developing nations increase their use of grain for animal feed.

25. CIA, *Potential Implications of Trends*, p. 19. USDA, *World Food Situation and Prospects*, p. 36, made four projections based on four rates—2.2, 2.4, 2.7, and 2.8 percent—between 1969–71 and 1985.

26. USDA, *World Food Situation and Prospects*, p. 35.

27. All estimates of this sort are theoretical, of course; they are based on technical possibilities, but the key factors influencing output often are prices and government policies.

28. CIA, *Potential Implications of Trends*, p. 6; this source estimated that in 1970, 70 percent of the world's population was in developing nations (21 percent in China and 49 percent in other countries).

29. Grant, "Food, Energy, and the Changing World Order," p. 5; and USDA, *World Food Situation and Prospects*, p. 80.

30. PRB, *World Population Growth and Response*, p. 265.

31. USDA, *World Food Situation and Prospects*, pp. 12, 14. See also CIA, *Potential Implications of Trends*, p. 6.

32. USDA, *World Food Situation and Prospects*, p. 14.

33. See the sources cited in note 5; more recently it has been estimated that the average birth rate in the developing countries as a group (excluding China) was thirty-six per thousand (3.6 percent) in 1977, compared with forty-two per thousand (4.2 percent) in 1970.

34. See, for example, the discussion in Philip M. Hauser, "Population Policies Affecting Fertility: A Sociological Perspective on Family Planning Programs," in *International Population Conference, International Union for the Scientific Study of Population* (Liege, Belgium: IUSSP/UIESP, 1973), vol. 3, pp. 303–18; "The World Population Outlook," *Revista Interamericana Review*, vol. 4, no. 1 (Spring, 1974), pp. 1 ff.; and C. T. Chang and P. M. Hauser, "The Impact on Fertility of Singapore's Family Planning Program," in C. Chandrasekaran and Albert L. Hermalin, *Measuring the Effect of Family Planning Programs on Fertility* (Liege, Belgium: IUSSP, Ordina Editions, 1975), pp. 381–425.

35. Poleman, "World Food," p. 515.

36. Ibid.

37. CIA, *Potential Implications of Trends*, annex 1, p. 1.

38. Ibid. These UN estimates indicated a 1.3 percent average annual rate in China during 1970–2000, producing a total Chinese population of 1.127 billion in the year 2000. For other estimates, see table 3-1 and my discussion of China's population on pp. 309 ff.

39. USDA, *World Food Situation and Prospects*, p. 12.

40. Henry Giniger, "In Ottawa, UN's Food Talks Open to Gloomy Report," *New York Times*, September 5, 1979.

41. See USDA, *World Food Situation and Prospects*, p. 12, for these figures and those on developing nations that follow.

42. My calculation, from data on China's population and grain output in tables 3-1 and 3-2.

43. USDA, *World Food Situation and Prospects*, pp. 12, 14.

44. Department of State, Office of Media Services, "World Food Situation," publication 8769 (Department of State, July 1974), p. 3.

45. My calculations from data in USDA, *World Agricultural Situation*, WAS-19 (July 1979), p. 40.

46. FAO estimates were in USDA, *World Food Situation and Prospects*, p. 35; the figure given here for China's grain deficit (an average for 1969–71) was 3.0 million tons. China's average annual gross import of grain during those years was 4.0 million tons; but its *net* imports averaged 3 million tons; see table 3-6. Fred H. Sanderson, "Export Opportunities for Agricultural Products: Implications for U.S. Agricultural and Trade Policies," *Columbia Journal of World Business*, vol. 10, no. 3 (Fall 1975), p. 17, used an FAO figure of 16 million tons for the average net grain imports of the developing countries during 1969–71 (but this appeared not to include the Asian Communist nations).

47. My calculations from data in USDA, *World Agricultural Situation*, WAS-22 (June 1980), p. 39.

48. USDA, *World Food Situation and Prospects*, p. 35. The lowest estimate of the grain deficit was 22.5 million tons, the medium estimates were 52.4 million and 58.8 million tons, and the highest estimate was 77.5 million tons a year. The estimates for the Asian Communist nations' deficit ranged from a low of 4.1 million to a high of 6.7 million tons a year; China's deficits are likely to be considerably higher, as will be discussed. The FAO has estimated that the grain import needs of all developing nations will rise to 85 million tons in 1985; see Sanderson, "Export Opportunities," p. 17. The International Food Policy Research Institute has estimated that the growth of developing countries' grain deficits would be about 100 million tons if the trends of the 1960s and early 1970s were to persist, and up to 200 million tons if the trends of just the early 1970s were to persist; see Sterling Wortman, "Food and Agriculture," *Scientific American*, vol. 235, no. 3 (September 1976), p. 32.

49. Cited in W. Howard Wriggins and Gunnar Adler-Karlsson, *Reducing Global Inequities* (McGraw-Hill, 1978), p. 128. In 1979 the head of the UN World Food Council stated that the number probably already was larger; see the article by Giniger cited in note 40.

50. FAO, *The Fourth World Food Survey* (Rome: FAO, 1977), app. C, pp. 77–80.

51. *FAO Food Balances, 1964–66*, cited in USDA, *World Food Situation and Prospects*, p. 49. For the United States the average was 3,156 calories, of which 649 came directly from grain. The UN Department of Economic and Social Affairs Statistical Office estimated that in 1970 the per capita caloric intake averaged 2,659 calories globally, 3,079 in the developed countries, and 2,239 in the developing countries; see *Statistical Yearbook, 1972*, UN publication no. E/F.75 XVII.I, table 162, pp. 524–30, cited in Overseas Development Council, Roger Hansen, and others, *The U.S. and World Development: Agenda for Action*, 1976 (Praeger, 1976), p. 142. (An annual publication; hereafter ODC, *Agenda for Action*, with the year.)

52. Organization for Economic Cooperation and Development, *Development Cooperation, 1974 Review*, Report by the Chairman of the Development Assistance Committee (Paris: OECD, 1974), p. 98, cited in ODC, *Agenda for Action*, 1975, p. 209. (OECD's estimate for China was 420 pounds in 1964–66 and 430 pounds in 1972–74.) For estimates of per capita consumption of other

foods, see ODC, *Agenda for Action, 1975*, p. 208. Some estimates of average per capita grain consumption in the developing nations have been lower, showing only a 2 percent rise between 1969–71 and 1973–74.

53. See ODC, *Agenda for Action, 1975*, p. 209, for these and the figures on the Soviet Union that follow.

54. OECD, *Meat Balances in OECD Member Countries* (Paris: OECD, February 1976), pp. 14–17. See also CIA, *Potential Implications of Trends*, p. 11; and USDA, *Agricultural Statistics 1977* (Government Printing Office, 1977), p. 357.

55. Lyle P. Schertz, "World Food: Prices and the Poor," in William P. Bundy, ed., *The World Economic Crisis* (Norton, 1975), p. 181. See also Brown, "The Next Crisis?" pp. 5–7.

56. My calculations from data in USDA, "Grain Supply Utilization Tables," 1977, computer tape, processed, pages unnumbered. John A. Schnittker, "Grain Reserves—Now," *Foreign Policy*, no. 20 (Fall 1975), p. 226, asserted that by then nearly half of the world's grain was used to feed livestock, but this estimate probably was too high.

57. Figures on Japan are from USDA, "Grain Supply Utilization Tables." Figures on the Soviet Union are from USDA, *Livestock Feed Balance for the USSR*, Economic Research Service (ERS) Foreign, no. 355 (undated, probably 1974), p. 9. In the 1976/77 grain year, "grain availabilities" (production plus stocks) were: United States, 292.0 million tons; Western Europe, 142.8 million; Japan, 17.6 million; and the Soviet Union, 221.2 million. The amounts of grain used as feed were: United States, 115.1 million tons; Western Europe, 96.4 million; Japan, 13.3 million; and the Soviet Union, 101.5 million. See USDA, *World Agricultural Situation*, WAS-14 (October 1977), p. 36.

58. Lester R. Brown and Erik P. Eckholm, "Next Steps toward Global Food Security," in ODC, *Agenda for Action, 1975*, pp. 79–80.

59. USDA, *World Food Situation and Prospects*, pp. 58–59. Herman Kahn and others, *The Next 200 Years* (Hudson Institute, 1976), pp. 145–46, asserted that "potential farm acreage is over four times that now being harvested"; on agricultural prospects in general, this study made forecasts that were notably optimistic.

60. USDA, *World Food Situation and Prospects*, p. 64.

61. Ibid.

62. Cited in ibid.

63. USDA, *Foreign Agricultural Circular*, November 11, 1977, p. 32.

64. Lester R. Brown, "Crop Yields and Food Policies," *Washington Post*, November 16, 1978.

65. These and the following figures are from USDA, *World Food Situation and Prospects*, pp. 18, 64.

66. The following figures are from ibid., p. 18.

67. Ibid.

68. Ibid., pp. 60–64. For other statistics, see ODC, *Agenda for Action, 1975*, pp. 238, 251, and *Agenda for Action, 1976*, p. 157.

69. See USDA, *World Food Situation and Prospects*, p. 61, and *World Agricultural Situation*, WAS-19 (July 1979), p. 38.

70. The FAO/UNIDO/World Bank Working Group on Fertilizers, cited in USDA, *World Agricultural Situation*, WAS-14 (October 1977), p. 27. This group's estimate of likely world supply in 1981/82 was 137 million tons; see ibid., p. 28.

71. Cited in USDA, *World Agricultural Situation*, WAS-19 (July 1979), p. 38.

72. The figures that follow are from USDA, *World Food Situation and Prospects*, p. 61. For CIA figures on fertilizer consumption in particular countries, see CIA, *Handbook of Economic Statistics, 1977*, p. 138.

73. Cited in USDA, *World Food Situation and Prospects*, p. 63.

74. See their March 1979 study, cited in USDA, *World Agricultural Situation*, WAS-19 (July 1979), p. 38.

75. Unless otherwise stated, the following figures for world grain trade are from USDA, *Foreign Agricultural Circular*, November 11, 1977, pp. 13, 15, 18, 30–32, and *World Agricultural Situation*, WAS-14 (October 1977), pp. 32–35. The USDA estimated that between 1966/67 and 1976/77 total world exports of all grains rose from 108.5 million tons to 158 million tons (1976/77 was not a high export year). Thereafter world exports rose to 169.6 million tons in 1975/76 and reached 168.6 million tons in 1977/78; USDA, *Foreign Agricultural Circular*, November 11, 1977, p. 32.

76. Preliminary estimates, in USDA, *Foreign Agricultural Circular*, March 12, 1980, pp. 4, 5, 8. The figure for rice is for the calendar year 1979.

77. The statistics that follow on particular years are based on Sanderson, "Export Opportunities"; and Philip H. Trezise, *Rebuilding Grain Reserves: Toward an International System* (Brookings, 1976) (in addition to the sources cited in note 75).

78. Sanderson, "Export Opportunities," p. 21.

79. USDA, *World Agricultural Situation*, WAS-22 (June 1980), p. 39.

80. Ibid. For earlier years, including 1960/61–1962/63, see Sanderson, "Export Opportunities," pp. 15–22; and Trezise, *Rebuilding Grain Reserves*, pp. 5–20. See also ODC, *Agenda for Action, 1976*, p. 153; and USDA, *World Agricultural Situation*, WAS-14 (October 1977), pp. 32–35, for regional breakdowns for earlier years.

81. In 1979 USDA officials estimated that the Soviet Union might import 30.5 million tons in the 1979/80 grain year; Dan Balz, "New Soviet Grain Deal," *Washington Post*, August 2, 1979.

82. See table 3-6 and the discussion on pp. 351 ff.

83. See note 48.

84. For data on prices, on which this discussion is based, see USDA, *Foreign Agricultural Circular*, November 11, 1977, p. 25, and *World Food Situation and Prospects*, pp. 3, 24–31; Sanderson, "Export Opportunities," p. 15; and ODC, *Agenda for Action, 1975*, pp. 228–29, and *Agenda for Action, 1976*, pp. 170–71.

85. FAO, Economic and Social Policy Department, Statistics Division,

Trade Yearbook, 1974, vol. 28 (Rome: FAO, 1975), cited in ODC, *Agenda for Action, 1976,* p. 156.

86. FAO, *Ceres: FAO Review on Development* (FAO, March–April 1975), p. 7, cited in ODC, *Agenda for Action, 1976,* p. 157.

87. USDA, *World Agricultural Situation,* WAS-19 (July 1979), pp. 3, 7 ff.

88. During the past decade the terms of trade have moved against developing nations that produce mainly primary commodities other than petroleum (although in the early 1970s they had moved briefly in their favor); see United Nations Conference on Trade and Development (UNCTAD), *Commodity Trade: Indexation,* publication no. TD/B/563, July 7, 1975, pp. 1–6, cited in ODC, *Agenda for Action, 1976,* p. 178. See also USDA, *World Food Situation and Prospects,* pp. 6–8.

89. Interview with Fred H. Sanderson, January 1978.

90. Reserves are analyzed in detail in Trezise, *Rebuilding Grain Reserves,* and also are discussed in USDA, *World Food Situation and Prospects,* pp. 40–47. Other estimates can be found in ODC, *Agenda for Action, 1975,* p. 244, and *Agenda for Action, 1976,* p. 152.

91. ODC, *The United States and World Development, Agenda, 1979* (Praeger, 1979), p. 189. For estimates based only on exporting nations, see Lester R. Brown, *The Politics and Responsibility of the North American Breadbasket,* Worldwatch Paper 2 (Worldwatch Institute, October 1975), p. 8.

92. Trezise, *Rebuilding Grain Reserves,* pp. 8–9.

93. USDA, *World Agricultural Situation,* WAS-14 (October 1977), p. 31.

94. See USDA, *World Agricultural Situation,* WAS-19 (July 1979), p. 11, and "World Grain Situation Outlook for 1979/80," *Foreign Agricultural Circular,* January 26, 1979, p. 3, and March 12, 1980, p. 3. The breakdown by type of grain in 1977/78 was wheat, 82.3 million tons; coarse grains, 84.1 million tons; and rice, 20.3 million tons; see USDA, *Foreign Agricultural Circular,* January 26, 1979, pp. 4, 5, 6.

95. USDA, *World Agricultural Situation,* WAS-19 (July 1979), p. 11.

96. Ibid., pp. 11 ff.; see also Dan Balz, "New Soviet Grain Deal," *Washington Post,* August 2, 1978; and Seth S. King, "Is the Year's Grain Harvest a Possible Crop of Trouble?" *New York Times,* July 1, 1979.

97. See USDA, *Agricultural Situation, Review of 1979 and Outlook for 1980, U.S.S.R.,* supplement 1 to *World Agricultural Situation,* WAS-21 (April 1980), especially pp. 1–2, 22–23, and "World Grain Situation Outlook for 1979/80," *Foreign Agricultural Circular,* March 12, 1980, pp. 1–3.

98. USDA, "World Grain Situation Outlook for 1979/80," p. 3.

99. USDA, *World Food Situation and Prospects,* p. 42.

100. Ibid.

101. Trezise, *Rebuilding Grain Reserves,* p. 17.

102. Lance Taylor, Alexander H. Sarris, and Philip C. Abbott, "Grain Reserves, Emergency Relief, and Food Aid," in William R. Cline, ed., *Policy Alternatives for a New International Economic Order: An Economic Analysis* (Praeger, 1979).

103. Fred H. Sanderson, "Next Step on Grain Reserves," *Food Policy*

(November 1977), pp. 269–70. See also Lester R. Brown and Erik P. Eckholm, "Next Steps toward Global Food Security," in ODC, *Agenda for Action, 1975,* p. 81; and Martin M. McLaughlin, "The World Food Situation and the U.S. Role," in ODC, *Agenda for Action, 1976,* p. 75. The 1974 U.S. proposal was made by Henry Kissinger in "The Global Community and the Struggle against Famine," p. 8.

104. Sanderson, "Next Step on Grain Reserves," p. 273.

105. See the general discussion on weather in USDA, *World Food Situation and Prospects,* pp. 71–74. See also Sanderson, "The Great Food Fumble," pp. 503–04; and Brown, "The Next Crisis?" p. 22.

106. Except where noted, these and following figures on shortfalls are from USDA, *World Food Situation and Prospects,* pp. 41–42.

107. USDA, *Agricultural Situation, Review of 1979 and Outlook for 1980, U.S.S.R.,* supplement 1 to *World Agricultural Situation,* WAS-21 (April 1980), p. 2.

108. CIA, *Potential Implications of Trends,* pp. 26–42; and a report by the U.S. Interdepartmental Committee for Atmospheric Sciences, 1974, cited in USDA, *World Food Situation and Prospects,* p. 73.

109. Ibid.

110. *Newsweek* (January 23, 1978), pp. 74–76.

111. The literature on agricultural development is now vast. Good collections of articles written by recognized experts for nonspecialized audiences are in *Scientific American,* vol. 235, no. 3 (September 1976); and *Science,* vol. 188, no. 4188 (May 9, 1975). Important scholarly studies include Theodore W. Schultz, *Transforming Traditional Agriculture* (Yale University Press, 1964); and Ester Boserup, *The Conditions of Agricultural Growth: The Economics of Agrarian Change under Population Pressure* (Chicago: Aldine, 1965).

112. USDA figures indicated that China's grain output was 15.38 percent of the world's total in 1978/79; see *World Agricultural Situation,* WAS-22 (June 1980), p. 39. Based on 1977 global population data and grain statistics from sources cited earlier and data on China in tables 1-1 and 1-2, the figure was also about 15 percent in 1977. (To compare China's grain output with the world's total, one must subtract soybeans and potatoes from the total Chinese "grain" figures and convert unmilled rice figures to milled rice figures.) CIA, *Potential Implications of Trends,* p. 7 and annex 1, pp. 1–2, estimated that China in 1970 accounted for 21 percent of world population, and in 1969/70–1971/72 for a little over 14 percent of world grain output. Using the estimate for China's population in 1975 in table 3-1 and the world estimate for that year in PRB, *World Population Growth and Response,* p. 265, China accounted for 23 percent of the world's population.

113. My calculations from data in USDA, *World Agricultural Situation,* WAS-22 (June 1980), pp. 39–41.

114. Based on CIA, *Handbook of Economic Statistics, 1977,* pp. 108–11.

115. USDA, *Agricultural Trade of the People's Republic of China, 1935–69,* Foreign Agricultural Economic Report no. 83, August 1972, pp. vi, 11, 21.

116. USDA, *Foreign Agricultural Circular,* March 12, 1980, pp. 4, 8.

117. Gerald F. Winfield, "The Impact of Urbanization on Agricultural Processes," in American Academy of Political and Social Science, *Annals*, vol. 405 (January 1973), p. 73.

118. Dwight H. Perkins, "Constraints Influencing China's Agricultural Performance," in Joint Economic Committee (JEC), *China: A Reassessment of the Economy*, 94 Cong. 1 sess. (GPO, 1975), p. 350.

119. Ibid.

120. See Kung-chuan Hsiao, *Rural China, Imperial Control in the Nineteenth Century* (University of Washington Press, 1960), chaps. 4, 5.

121. For general background on Chinese agriculture, see Dwight H. Perkins, *Agricultural Development in China, 1368–1968* (Aldine, 1969), the best volume to date on the subject; it deals with both traditional and modern China, including the post-1949 years. See also Robert F. Dernberger, "China's Economic Future," in Allen S. Whiting and Robert F. Dernberger, *China's Future, Foreign Policy and Economic Development in the Post-Mao Era* (McGraw-Hill, 1977). Important sources on pre-1949 agriculture include John L. Buck, *Land Utilization in China* (University of Nanking, 1937), and *China's Farm Economy* (University of Chicago, 1930); R. H. Tawney, *Land and Labor in China* (London: Allen and Unwin, 1932); T. H. Shen, *Agricultural Resources of China* (Cornell University Press, 1951); Ramon Myers, *The Chinese Peasant Economy: Agricultural Development in Hopei and Shantung, 1890–1949* (Harvard University Press, 1970); F. H. King, *Farmers of Forty Centuries* (London: Jonathan Cope, 1949); and Gerald F. Winfield, *China: The Land and the People* (William Sloane, 1950). Agriculture is dealt with in a broad economic context in numerous basic studies of the Chinese economy, including Alexander Eckstein, *China's Economic Development: The Interplay of Scarcity and Ideology* (University of Michigan Press, 1975), and *China's Economic Revolution* (Cambridge University Press, 1977); Ta-chung Liu and Kung-chia Yeh, *The Economy of the Chinese Mainland: National Income and Economic Development, 1933–1959* (Princeton University Press, 1965); Nai-Ruenn Chen and Walter Galenson, *The Chinese Economy under Communism* (Aldine, 1969); Alexander Eckstein, Walter Galenson, and Ta-chung Liu, eds., *Economic Trends in Communist China* (Aldine, 1968); Yuan-li Wu and others, *The Economic Potential of Communist China*, 3 vols. (Stanford Research Institute, 1963); Chu-yuan Cheng, *Communist China's Economy, 1949–1962* (Seton Hall University Press, 1963); and Choh-ming Li, *Economic Development of Communist China* (University of California Press, 1959). A useful statistical source is Nai-Ruenn Chen, ed., *Chinese Economic Statistics: A Handbook for Mainland China* (Aldine, 1967). On the Chinese Communists' land reform, see Kuo-chun Chao, *Agrarian Policy of the Chinese Communist Party, 1921–1959* (Bombay: Asia Publishing House, 1960). For other sources, see Patricia Blair, ed., with an essay by A. Doak Barnett, *Development in the People's Republic of China: A Selected Bibliography* (ODC, 1976).

122. Eckstein, *China's Economic Development*, p. 264.

123. These and the figures that follow are based on population statistics and grain figures in tables 3-1 and 3-2.

124. On collectivization and the communes, see Chao, *Agrarian Policy;* Gargi Dutt, *Rural Communes of China* (New York: Asia Publishing House, 1967); Frederick W. Crook, "The Commune System in the People's Republic of China, 1963–74," in JEC, *China: A Reassessment of the Economy*, pp. 336–410; and Benedict Stavis, *People's Communes and Rural Development in China* (Cornell University, Rural Development Committee, 1974).

125. On the Great Leap Forward, its background, its aftermath, and the policy issues involved, see Franz Schurmann, *Ideology and Organization in Communist China* (University of California Press, 1966), chap. 7, pp. 464 ff.; Parris H. Chang, *Power and Policy in China* (Pennsylvania State University Press, 1975); and Byung-joon Ahn, *Chinese Politics and the Cultural Revolution, Dynamics of Policy Processes* (University of Washington Press, 1976).

126. On the Great Leap crisis, see Jacques Guillermaz, *The Chinese Communist Party in Power, 1949–1976* (Boulder, Colo.: Westview Press, 1976), pp. 226 ff.

127. On the post-Leap policies in the early 1960s, see Franz Schurmann, "China's 'New Economic Policy'—Transition or Beginning," *China Quarterly*, no. 17 (January–March 1964), pp. 65 ff.; and Chang, *Power and Policy in China*, pp. 122 ff.

128. See Edwin F. Jones, "The Impact of the Food Crisis on Peiping's Policies," *Asian Survey*, vol. 2, no. 10 (December 1962), pp. 1–11; and Alva Lewis Erisman, "China: Agriculture in the 1970s," in JEC, *China: A Reassessment of the Economy*, pp. 330 ff.

129. These efforts sometimes have involved more than 100 million peasants a year; see USDA, *Agricultural Situation, Review of 1979 and Outlook for 1980, People's Republic of China*, supplement 6 to *World Agricultural Situation*, WAS-6 (June 1980), pp. 36–37.

130. Benedict Stavis, *Making Green Revolution: The Policies of Agricultural Development in China* (Cornell University, Rural Development Committee, 1974), pp. 1 ff.

131. Erisman, "China: Agriculture in the 1970s," p. 330.

132. Ibid., p. 334.

133. See American Rural Small-Scale Industry Delegation (Dwight H. Perkins, Chairman), *Rural Small-Scale Industry in the People's Republic of China* (University of California Press, 1977), pp. 117 ff.

134. Robert Michael Field and James A. Kilpatrick, "Chinese Grain Production: An Interpretation of the Data," *China Quarterly*, no. 74 (June 1978), p. 739.

135. For varying views on "the Chinese model" including its Maoist elements stressing agriculture and the rural population, see Michel Oksenberg, ed., *China's Development Experience* (Columbia University, Academy of Political Science, 1973); Donald B. Keesing, "Economic Lessons from China," *Journal of Development Economics*, no. 2 (1975); "China's Road to Development," papers prepared for a symposium, in *World Development*, vol. 3, nos. 7 and 8 (1975); John C. Gurley, *China's Economy and the Maoist Strategy* (Monthly Review Press, 1976); and A. Doak Barnett, *Uncertain Passage: China's Transition to the Post-Mao Era* (Brookings, 1974), especially

chap. 3, "Strategies for Economic Development," pp. 117 ff. Robert F. Dernberger, "The Relevance of China's Experience for Other Developing Countries," in Social Science Research Council, *Items*, vol. 31, no. 3 (September 1977), summarized a 1976 SSRC conference on the "Lessons of China's Development Experience for the Developing Countries."

136. For background, see Crook, "The Commune System in the People's Republic of China."

137. This and the following statement on per capita incomes were in "Decisions of the CCP [Chinese Communist Party] Central Committee on Some Problems in Accelerating Agricultural Development (draft)" (hereafter "Decisions"), in Foreign Broadcast Information Service, *Daily Report—People's Republic of China*, Department of Commerce, National Technical Information Service, August 31, 1979, p. L22. (Hereafter FBIS, *Daily Report—PRC*.) The text of the document finally adopted by the Central Committee's Fourth Plenum on September 28, 1979, is in FBIS, *Daily Report—PRC*, October 25, 1979, supplement 032, pp. 1–18. Its title was "Decision of the CCP Central Committee on Some Questions Concerning the Acceleration of Agricultural Development."

138. Ibid.; see also the source cited in part I, note 60.

139. The following goals were elaborated upon in Hua Kuo-feng's (Hua Guofeng's) report, in FBIS, *Daily Report—PRC*, March 7, 1978.

140. See Communiqué of the Third Plenum, in FBIS, *Daily Report—PRC*, December 26, 1978, pp. E4–E13.

141. Ibid., p. E8.

142. See part I, p. 104.

143. The following discussion is based on "Decisions," in FBIS, *Daily Report—PRC*, August 31, 1979, pp. L22–L37; and "The Agricultural Development Programme," *Beijing Review* (formerly *Peking Review*), no. 12 (March 24, 1980), pp. 14–20, which summarized the finally adopted "Decisions."

144. For estimates of China's population, see John S. Aird, "Population Growth in the People's Republic of China," U.S. Department of Commerce, Demographic Analysis Division, April 1978, processed, p. 22 (also see table 3-1), and "Population Growth in the People's Republic of China," in JEC, *Chinese Economy Post-Mao*, 95 Cong. 2 sess. (GPO, 1978), pp. 439–75. For other estimates and general background, see National Foreign Assessment Center, CIA, *China: Economic Indicators*, Research Aid ER 77-10508, October 1977, p. 8; John Aird, *Estimates and Projections of the Population of Mainland China, 1953–1986*, U.S. Department of Commerce, Bureau of the Census, International Population Reports, Series P-91, no. 17 (Department of Commerce 1968), "Population Policy and Demographic Prospects in the People's Republic of China," in JEC, *People's Republic of China: An Economic Assessment*, 92 Cong. 2 sess. (GPO, 1972), and "Population Growth," in Eckstein and others, *Economic Trends in Communist China;* Pi-chao Chen, "The Prospects of Demographic Transition in a Mobilization System: China," in Richard L. Clinton and R. Kenneth Godwin, eds., *Research in the Politics of Population* (Lexington Books, 1972); K. C. Yeh and Carolyn Lee,

"Communist China's Population Problem in the 1980's," paper prepared for a Sino-American Conference on Mainland China (no date); Thomas T. Kane, "Demography's Big Question Mark," in PRB, *Intercom*, vol. 5, no. 4 (April 1977), pp. 8–9; and Leo A. Orleans, "China's Population: Can the Contradictions Be Resolved?" in JEC, *China: A Reassessment of the Economy*, pp. 69–80, *China's Birth Rate, Death Rate, and Population Growth: Another Perspective*, prepared for the House International Relations Committee, 95 Cong. 1 sess. (GPO, 1977), and "China's Population Statistics: An Illusion?" *China Quarterly*, no. 21 (January–March 1965).

145. In 1964 there was a population survey, which the Chinese sometimes have referred to as a census, but apparently it was less thorough than the 1953 census. In 1979 it was reported that Peking was planning a new census for 1980; subsequent reports indicated that it probably will be in 1981 or 1982.

146. Perkins, "Constraints," p. 352.

147. See *Economist* (November 5, 1977), p. 103; and Aird, "Population Growth in the People's Republic of China," p. 22.

148. Aird, "Population Growth in the People's Republic of China," p. 21.

149. The official figure published by Peking's State Statistical Bureau (SSB) for all of China, including Taiwan, in 1978 was 975.23 million (see FBIS, *Daily Report—PRC*, June 27, 1979, p. L20); subtracting 17 million (for Taiwan) gives a figure of 958 million. The 1977 figure is inferred based on the SSB's statement that population grew 1.2 percent in 1978.

150. SSB Communiqué, April 30, 1980, in FBIS, *Daily Report—PRC*, April 30, 1980, p. L10. It is interesting that this time the official figure did not include Taiwan.

151. I have used Aird's "low model" estimates (instead of "intermediate model" estimates, which Aird himself thought might be the "best guess" model). The low model estimates are nearer to the official Chinese figures, and in my judgment the indicated rates of natural increase are plausible.

152. On Chinese birth control methods, see, in addition to sources cited in note 144 above, Leo A. Orleans, "China's Experience with Motivation for Family Planning," in Agency for International Development, *Development Digest*, vol. 14, no. 4 (October 1976), pp. 25 ff., and *China's Experience in Population Control: The Elusive Model*, House Committee on Foreign Affairs, 93 Cong. 2 sess. (GPO, 1974); Pi-chao Chen, "Lessons from the Chinese Experience: China's Planned Birth Program and Its Transferability," in Population Council, *Studies in Family Planning*, vol. 6, no. 10 (October 1975), pp. 354 ff., and "China's Population Program at the Grassroots Level," in Harrison Brown and Alan Sweezy, eds., *Population: Perspective, 1972* (Freeman, Cooper, 1973); and Victor Bostrom Fund and the Population Crisis Committee, *Population and Family Planning in the People's Republic of China* (Victor Bostrom Fund and the Population Crisis Committee, Spring 1971).

153. See National Academy of Sciences, *Oral Contraceptives and Steroid Chemistry in the People's Republic of China*, Committee on Scholarly Communication with the People's Republic of China, report no. 5 (NAS, 1977), pp. 1 ff.

154. The following details are on Kwangtung (Guangdong) Province; they were summarized in Chi-hsien Tuan, "Chinese Population Perspectives," paper prepared for a Symposium Commemorating the Twentieth Anniversary of the Founding of the East-West Center, Washington, D.C., May 14, 1980, mimeographed, pp. 75 ff. On October 25, 1979, I obtained similar information from interviews with persons at the Shanghai Petrochemical Company, in a satellite town near Shanghai; at that time I was told, however, that the monthly subsidy for one-child families was 3 yuan, not 5 yuan.

155. Chen Muhua (Chen Mu-hua), "Controlling Population Growth in a Planned Way," Beijing Review, no. 46 (November 16, 1979), p. 19.

156. Targets for 1979 and 1985 were in Hua Kuo-feng's 1979 National People's Congress (NPC) report; see FBIS, Daily Report—PRC, July 2, 1979, Supplement, p. 19. The target for the year 2000 was revealed soon thereafter; see James B. Sterba, "China Will Try to Halt Growth of Population by End of Century," New York Times, August 13, 1979. See also the article by Chen Mu-hua, cited in note 155.

157. William L. Parish, Jr., and Martin K. Whyte, "Social Change in Rural Mainland China: Family, Lineage, and Market since 1949," paper prepared for the Fourth Annual Sino-American Conference on Mainland China, December 1974 (processed), argued (on the basis of extensive interviewing in Hong Kong of refugees from South China) that many of the traditional incentives for having several children, especially males, persisted in rural China.

158. CIA, Potential Implications of Trends, p. 6, estimated that China had 21 percent of the world's population at the time of publication and would have 18 percent in 2000.

159. Field and Kilpatrick, "Chinese Grain Production," p. 382.

160. NFAC, CIA, China: Economic Indicators, October 1977, p. 3.

161. Ibid.

162. USDA, World Food Situation and Prospects, p. 12.

163. Chinese grain statistics for the 1950s were published official figures. Figures for the 1960s and 1970s (until 1977) are estimates. In the early 1970s, a consensus appeared to emerge among Western scholars on a statistical series on grain output in China for the post-1960 period; although there were some differences in estimates, generally they were not large. CIA figures used through 1966 reflected that consensus; see CIA, People's Republic of China: Handbook of Economic Indicators, Research Aid ER 76-10540, August 1976, p. 11. However, in 1977 CIA analysts concluded that their previously used series was faulty because in some years the figures included soybeans and in others they did not, and in some years they included tubers (potatoes) at a rate of four to one (4 tons of tubers = 1 ton of grain) and in others at a rate of five to one. Using the best new information available, these analysts adjusted the entire series to make the figures consistent. The result was the series of figures in Field and Kilpatrick, "Chinese Grain Production," p. 380; and in Henry J. Groen and James A. Kilpatrick, "China's Agricultural Production," in JEC, Chinese Economy Post-Mao, p. 649. The adjusted figures all included soybeans, and for all years tubers were converted to grain at a 5 to 1 ratio. This new series has provided the best available data to analyze trends in China

during the 1952–77 period. These figures have been used throughout this study, together with official Chinese figures for 1977 through 1979. (To compare the Chinese figures with grain output in other countries, soybeans and tubers must be subtracted; this has been done in making the comparisons in this study.) For useful background data on Chinese national agricultural statistics, see Thomas B. Wiens, "Agricultural Statistics in the People's Republic of China: Another Look," paper prepared for the Conference on Quantitative Measures of China's Economic Output, sponsored by the Joint Committee on Contemporary China, Washington, D.C., January 1975, processed.

164. The original CIA estimate for 1977 was 285 million tons. The 283 million ton figure is China's official one, made public in mid-1979; see FBIS, *Daily Report—PRC*, June 27, 1979, p. L14.

165. A similar figure, in Field and Kilpatrick, "Chinese Grain Production," p. 377, was arrived at through calculating trends by regressing the logarithms of the actual values against time for the period 1952–76.

166. NFAC, CIA, *China: A Statistical Compendium*, Reference Aid ER 79-10374, July 1979, p. 7.

167. SSB Communiqué, in FBIS, *Daily Report—PRC*, June 27, 1979, p. L14.

168. SSB Communiqué, in FBIS, *Daily Report—PRC*, April 30, 1980, p. L3.

169. "Li Renjun [Li Jen-chun] Reports on Economy to NPC Standing Committee," in FBIS, *Daily Report—PRC*, p. L1.

170. Ibid., p. L6.

171. For figures on output of rice, wheat, and coarse grains and potatoes, the main components of total "grain" output in China, see CIA estimates in Field and Kilpatrick, "Chinese Grain Production," p. 380. For USDA estimates, see "People's Republic of China," *Agricultural Situation*, Supplement 6 to WAS-18 (June 1979), p. 30, and Supplement 6 to WAS-21 (June 1980), p. 36. The latter source estimated the output of different grains in 1979 to be rice, 140.5 million tons; coarse grains, 77.5 million tons; and wheat, 60.5 million tons. (It also gave estimates for 1977 and 1978.)

172. It has been estimated that from the late fourteenth century to the late eighteenth century, the growth of grain output in China averaged about 0.5 percent a year, and that in the first part of the twentieth century it was about 1 percent a year—in both cases roughly equal to the rate of population growth; see Perkins, *Agricultural Development*, chap. 2.

173. My calculations. Field and Kilpatrick, "Chinese Grain Production," p. 380, gave estimates of 279 kilograms in 1952 and 287 kilograms in 1977. However, they used population estimates that I believe were too high.

174. FBIS, *Daily Report—PRC*, August 31, 1979, p. L22, and October 25, 1979, supplement 032, p. 1.

175. The USDA's conversion rate of 68 percent for rice (paddy rice to milled rice) is used here. The figures used for various grains are from Field and Kilpatrick, "Chinese Grain Production," p. 380. Estimated output in 1952 was: rice, 68 million tons; wheat, 18 million tons; coarse grains, 48.75 million tons. Output in 1976 was: rice, 126 million tons; wheat, 41 million tons; and coarse grains, 73 million tons. (The coarse grain figures here subtract potatoes from the table's figures for "coarse grains and potatoes" combined.)

176. Vaclav Smil, "Food Energy in the PRC," *Current Scene* (Hong Kong), vol. 15, nos. 6 and 7 (June–July 1977), p. 3. See also Smil, "Food Availability in Communist China: 1957 and 1974," *Issues and Studies* (Taiwan), vol. 13, no. 5 (May 1977), pp. 39 ff.

177. ODC, *Agenda for Action, 1975*, p. 209.

178. Chu Chin-chih (Zhu Jinzhi or Chu Qinzhi?), *China's Grain Policy and the Supply of Grain to Cities and Towns* (in Chinese), pp. 11–13, cited in Audrey Donnithorne, *China's Grain: Output, Procurement, Transfers and Trade* (Chinese University of Hong Kong, 1970), p. 15.

179. Whiting and Dernberger, *China's Future*, pp. 105–06. The surveys showed that national average per capita consumption of cotton cloth was 6 to 8 meters; pork, 10 kilograms; and vegetables, 125 kilograms. Grain, together with these commodities, accounted for over 50 percent of consumers' budgets. Since the 1950s, supplies of vegetables and· some manufactured consumer goods have gradually improved in some areas, but per capita grain supplies have remained approximately the same.

180. *FAO Food Balances, 1964–66*, cited in USDA, *World Food Situation and Prospects*, pp. 48–49. In USDA, *Agriculture in the United States and the People's Republic of China, 1967–1971*, Foreign Agricultural Economic Report 94 (February 1974), p. 34, the estimate of China's average caloric intake was 2,050 (compared with 3,140 in the United States).

181. Smil, "Food Energy in the PRC," p. 4. He also gave other estimates, using lower population estimates.

182. See USDA, *World Food Situation and Prospects*, p. 49; and Smil, "Food Energy in the PRC," p. 9. See also Kenneth R. Walker, "Grain Self-Sufficiency in North China, 1953–57," *China Quarterly*, no. 71 (September 1977), p. 583.

183. NFAC, CIA, *China: Demand for Foreign Grain*, ER 79-10073, January 1979, p. 2; rations have varied depending on the physical needs of persons in different occupations (and other factors) as estimated by Peking's planners.

184. Smil, "Food Energy in the PRC," p. 5. The USDA estimate broke down the components of the average of 2,045 daily calories as follows: grain, 1,383; starch crops, 224; sugar, 35; pulses and nuts, 134; vegetables, 33; fruit, 6; meat, 134; eggs, 12; fish, 14; milk, 5; and fats and oils, 65. See USDA, *World Food Situation and Prospects*, p. 49.

185. CIA, *China: Demand for Foreign Grain*, p. 2.

186. "Decisions," in FBIS, *Daily Report—PRC*, August 31, 1979, p. L22.

187. SSB Communiqué, in FBIS, *Daily Report—PRC*, April 30, 1980, p. L4.

188. Perkins, *Agricultural Development in China*, pp. 15–17. See also Whiting and Dernberger, *China's Future*, p. 126.

189. Perkins, "Constraints," p. 353.

190. The 107 million hectare estimate was in USDA, *Agriculture in the United States and the People's Republic of China*, p. 10. In 1979 a Chinese article stated that the country had 47 million hectares under irrigation and that this was half of all farmland in China, implying that total cultivated land was 94 million hectares; see Tian Sang (Tien Sang), "China: Winning Its

Battle with the Land," mimeographed, p. 3, distributed by the People's Republic of China Embassy, October 1979. This author may have been using "half" as an approximation, however; some recent reports have indicated that China's cultivated land now may be just under 100 million hectares.

191. Perkins, "Constraints," p. 353.

192. Figures on India and Japan are from ibid., p. 354. The China figure is my calculation. Perkins, using a different population estimate, gave a figure of 0.134 hectare per capita in China. USDA's figure for China, in *Agriculture in the United States and the People's Republic of China*, was 0.162 hectare per capita.

193. Perkins, "Constraints," p. 354. The figures for the United States, India, and Japan are based on the year 1965.

194. "Decisions," in FBIS, *Daily Report—PRC*, August 31, 1979, p. L27.

195. Erisman, "China: Agriculture in the 1970s," p. 342. Some synthetic cloth now is unrationed. A recent estimate of the average ration of vegetable oil was 0.5 catty (0.25 kilogram) a month; see CIA, *China: Demand for Foreign Grain*, p. 2.

196. For data on cotton and textiles (production and trade), see USDA, "People's Republic of China," *Agricultural Situation*, Supplement 6 to WAS-18 (June 1979), p. 34; National Council for U.S.-China Trade, *China's Agriculture* (NCUSCT, 1976), p. 90; NFAC, CIA, *China: Economic Indicators*, October 1977, pp. 11, 24, 41; CIA, *Handbook of Economic Statistics, 1977*, p. 137; NFAC, CIA, *China: A Statistical Compendium*, ER 79-10374, July 1979, p. 8; and SSB Communiqué, in FBIS, *Daily Report—PRC*, April 30, 1980, p. L3.

197. NFAC, CIA, *China: International Trade Quarterly Review, Fourth Quarter 1979*, Research Paper EC CIT 80-003, May 1980, p. 32.

198. The following data are from USDA, "People's Republic of China," *Agricultural Situation*, Supplement 6 to WAS-18 (June 1979), p. 38.

199. CIA, *China: International Trade Quarterly Review, Fourth Quarter 1979*, p. 32.

200. See Erisman, "China: Agriculture in the 1970s," p. 344; and USDA, *Agricultural Trade of the People's Republic of China*, p. 20.

201. Hsu Ti-hsin (Xu Dixin), director of Peking's Economic Research Institute; reported in American Consulate-General, Hong Kong, "Seminar on China's Economy in the 1980's," telegram to the Secretary of State, R 17032Z, March 1980, unclassified.

202. See USDA, "People's Republic of China," in *Agricultural Situation*, Supplement 6 to WAS-18 (June 1979), p. 30.

203. See USDA, *Foreign Agricultural Circular*, November 11, 1977, pp. 28–32, and *World Food Situation and Prospects*, pp. 14–15, 64–66.

204. USDA, *Agriculture in the United States and the People's Republic of China*, p. 21, compared Chinese and U.S. yields in 1967–71. My comparison is between recent Chinese yields and U.S. yields in 1967–71.

205. National Academy of Sciences, *Plant Studies in the People's Republic of China* (NAS, 1975), p. 22.

206. Fred H. Sanderson, *Japan's Food Prospects and Policies* (Brookings, 1978), p. 8.

207. These and following data are from Perkins, "Constraints," p. 360. See also Field and Kilpatrick, "Chinese Grain Production," pp. 378–79; and Erisman, "China: Agriculture in the 1970s," pp. 335–37. T. H. Shen, *Agricultural Resources of China* (Cornell University Press, 1951), p. 80 (reporting the results of a survey by J. L. Buck), presented extensive data on the 1930s.

208. Perkins, "Constraints," p. 360. Some other estimates were lower, however; for example, the USDA estimated that in the early 1970s 33.5 million hectares, or about one-third of all cultivated land, were irrigated; see USDA, *Agriculture in the United States and the People's Republic of China*, p. 18.

209. See Tian Sang, "China: Winning Its Battle with the Land"; and Groen and Kilpatrick, "China's Agricultural Production," p. 630.

210. Erisman, "China: Agriculture in the 1970s," p. 336.

211. NFAC, CIA, *China: Economic Indicators*, October 1977, pp. 13, 18.

212. FBIS, *Daily Report—PRC*, April 30, 1980, p. L4.

213. USDA, *Agriculture in the United States and the People's Republic of China*, p. 10; 150 hectares of sown area and 107 hectares of cultivated area gives a cropping index of 140.

214. Erisman, "China: Agriculture in the 1970s," p. 337.

215. Hua Kuo-feng in early 1978 said, "The State must . . . build projects to direct water from the Yangtze to areas north of the Yellow River"; see "Report on the Work of the Government," in FBIS, *Daily Report—PRC*, March 7, 1978, p. D15. Shortly thereafter, Fang Yi (Fang Yi), head of the State Scientific and Technological Commission, said, "We will study projects for diverting water from the south to the north"; see *Peking Review*, no. 14 (April 7, 1978), p. 8. Subsequent discussions between Chinese and American officials indicated that the Chinese give high priority to power and irrigation projects on the Yangtze, as well as elsewhere.

216. Perkins, "Constraints," pp. 359–61.

217. "Decisions," in FBIS, *Daily Report—PRC*, August 31, 1979, p. L34.

218. Whiting and Dernberger, *China's Future*, pp. 135–39.

219. Frank Ching, "China's Legendary Farming Commune Falsified Output, People's Daily Says," *Wall Street Journal*, July 8, 1980.

220. See part I, p. 29 and note 62.

221. See NFAC, CIA, *China: Economic Indicators*, October 1977, p. 13; and Groen and Kilpatrick, "China's Agricultural Production," p. 102.

222. USDA, *Agriculture in the United States and the People's Republic of China*, p. 18.

223. SSB Communiqué, in FBIS, *Daily Report—PRC*, April 30, 1980, p. L4.

224. Sometimes the phrase was "in the main" mechanized by 1980; see speeches by Hua Kuo-feng and Politburo member Chen Yung-kuei (Chen Yonggui) at the Second National Conference on Learning from Tachai (Dazhai) in Agriculture, in *Peking Review*, no. 1 (January 1, 1977), pp. 31 ff., and no. 2 (January 7, 1977), pp. 5 ff. For background on mechanization, see Scott H. Hallford, "Mechanization in the PRC," *Current Scene*, vol. 14, no. 5 (May 1976), pp. 1 ff.; Chou Chin (Zhou Jin or Zhou Qin?), "Mechanization:

Fundamental Way Out for Agriculture," *Peking Review*, no. 9 (February 25, 1977), pp. 11 ff.; Amir V. Khan, "Agricultural Mechanization and Machinery Production in the People's Republic of China," *U.S.-China Business Review*, vol. 3, no. 6 (November–December 1976), pp. 17 ff.; and American Rural Small-Scale Industry Delegation, *Rural Small-Scale Industry*, pp. 117 ff.

225. Conversation with Huan Hsiang (Huan Xiang), vice president, Chinese Academy of Social Sciences, in Washington, D.C., April 17, 1979. This theme recurred in many subsequent press articles.

226. Perkins, "Constraints," p. 355.

227. For statistics on fertilizer output, supply, consumption, and trade used in the following discussion, see NFAC, CIA, *China: Economic Indicators*, October 1977, pp. 12, 22, 41; Groen and Kilpatrick, "China's Agricultural Production," p. 650; CIA, *Handbook of Economic Statistics, 1977*, pp. 110–11, 138–41; National Council for U.S.-China Trade, *China's Agriculture*, pp. 212–13; NFAC, CIA, *China: International Trade, 1976–1977*, ER 77-10676, November 1977, p. 13; NFAC, CIA, *China: Real Trends in Trade with Non-Communist Countries Since 1970*, Research Paper ER 77-10477, October 1977, pp. 16–17; and Erisman, "China: Agriculture in the 1970s," pp. 333–35. For background, see Jung-chao Liu, *China's Fertilizer Economy* (Aldine, 1970); and Kang Chao, "The Production and Application of Chemical Fertilizers in China," *China Quarterly*, no. 64 (December 1975), pp. 712 ff. The production figures I use for 1977 and 1978 are from the SSB Communiqué in 1979; see FBIS, *Daily Report—PRC*, June 27, 1979, p. L12.

228. SSB Communiqué, in FBIS, *Daily Report—PRC*, April 30, 1980, p. L2.

229. Groen and Kilpatrick, "China's Agricultural Production," p. 650; and NFAC, CIA, *China: International Trade, 1977–78*, Research Paper ER 78-10721, December 1978, p. 18.

230. CIA, *China: International Trade Quarterly Review, Fourth Quarter 1979*, p. 8.

231. USDA, *World Food Situation and Prospects*, p. 61.

232. Perkins, "Constraints," p. 357, stated that 8 to 1 is a "modest yield result."

233. Figures for 1971–72 are from CIA, *People's Republic of China: International Trade Handbook*, A ER 74-63 (September 1974); 1973–74 figures are from the October 1975 issue of the same serial, A ER 75-73; and 1975–76 figures are from CIA, *China: International Trade, 1976–77*.

234. Erisman, "China: Agriculture in the 1970s," p. 334.

235. The members of the American Rural Small-Scale Industry Delegation in their report (cited in note 133) concluded that small fertilizer plants clearly serve an important function in China at its present stage of development but their output is obviously inferior to that of large modern plants.

236. The sources cited in note 227 give data on phosphates and potassium as well as nitrogen.

237. Erisman, "China: Agriculture in the 1970s," p. 333.

238. See CIA, *Handbook of Economic Statistics, 1977*, p. 138; and SSB Communiqué, in FBIS, *Daily Report—PRC*, June 27, 1979, p. L15.

239. Perkins, "Constraints," p. 357.

240. Perkins, "Constraints," pp. 355–57, estimated 55 kilograms; subsequently he concluded that the figure was considerably higher. Other estimates of organic fertilizers have varied. Dernberger, "China's Economic Future," p. 128, estimated that there might be 75 kilograms of nutrient per hectare. Stavis, *Making Green Revolution*, p. 42, estimated that the total national availability in the early 1970s was between 6.07 million and 14.8 million tons. Winfield, "The Impact of Urbanization," p. 73, estimated that the national total was 4.62 million tons.

241. See CIA, *Handbook of Economic Statistics, 1977*, p. 138; and Erisman, "China: Agriculture in the 1970s," p. 335.

242. CIA, *Handbook of Economic Statistics, 1977*, p. 138.

243. Erisman, "China: Agriculture in the 1970s," p. 335.

244. "Decisions," in FBIS, *Daily Report—PRC*, August 31, 1979, p. L28.

245. Whiting and Dernberger, *China's Future*, pp. 129–30. For additional data and estimates, see also Liu, *China's Fertilizer Economy;* and Kuan-I Chen and Robert T. Tsuchigane, "An Assessment of China's Foodgrain Supplies in 1980," *Asian Survey*, vol. 16, no. 10 (October 1976), especially pp. 936 ff. These sources had various estimates of yield ratios in China.

246. The figures in table 3-4 relate total chemical fertilizer use to total grain output. Actually, some fertilizer is used on other crops (there are no data on exactly how much). The real response ratio therefore probably is somewhat higher than indicated; nevertheless, these figures give a picture of trends.

247. Erisman, "China: Agriculture in the 1970s," p. 334.

248. My calculations are from data in CIA, *Handbook of Economic Statistics, 1977*, pp. 139–41. The ratio for 1973/74, calculated from data in CIA, *Handbook of Economic Statistics, 1976*, pp. 137–39, was 100/46/5.7.

249. Erisman, "China: Agriculture in the 1970s," p. 335.

250. John W. Mellor, "The Agriculture of India," *Scientific American*, vol. 235, no. 3 (September 1976), p. 157.

251. Ibid., p. 155.

252. Stavis, *Making Green Revolution*, p. 33. See also NAS, *Plant Studies*, pp. 25–26.

253. FBIS, *Daily Report—PRC*, September 29, 1977, p. E2, December 19, 1977, pp. E13–E14, and July 26, 1978, p. E11. See also Thomas B. Wiens, "The Evolution of Policy and Capabilities in China's Agricultural Technology," in JEC, *Chinese Economy Post-Mao*, pp. 671–703 (which discusses recent changes in agricultural technology in China). The 1978 figure is from the SSB Communiqué, in FBIS, *Daily Report—PRC*, June 27, 1979, p. L15.

254. NAS, *Plant Studies*, p. 25.

255. The optimistic statement quoted above was by Haldore Hanson, who went to China with Norman Borlaug; see "Statement of Haldore Hanson, director-general of CIMMYT [International Maize and Wheat Improvement Center], to International Centers Week, September 13, 1972" (processed), p. 6. The less optimistic judgment was made by Erisman, "China: Agriculture in the 1970s," p. 337.

256. Stavis, *Making Green Revolution*, pp. 76 ff., and Siu-kai Lau, "The People's Commune and the Diffusion of Agri-Technology in China," paper prepared for conference, East-West Communications Institute, Hawaii, November 1977, processed.

257. Perkins, "Constraints," p. 350.

258. NAS, *Plant Studies*, pp. 118–20. See also Leo A. Orleans, *The Role of Science and Technology in China's Population/Food Balance*, House Committee on Science and Technology, 95 Cong. 1 sess. (GPO, 1977). The author pointed out that a considerable amount of applied research continued, but that basic research had been neglected.

259. On the new policy, see speech by Vice Premier Fang Yi, *Peking Review*, no. 14 (April 7, 1978), pp. 7–8.

260. On private plots, see Kenneth R. Walker, *Planning in Chinese Agriculture* (Aldine, 1965).

261. Article 7; for the text, see *Peking Review*, no. 4 (January 24, 1975), p. 14.

262. Chang, *Power and Policy in China*, pp. 138–40.

263. Nicholas Lardy, "China: Starting on an Uphill Road," *Asian Wall Street Journal*, June 8, 1978.

264. Perkins, "Constraints," p. 363.

265. Ibid., p. 362.

266. FBIS, *Daily Report—PRC*, July 26, 1978, pp. E10, E11.

267. FBIS, *Daily Report—PRC*, October 11, 1978, p. E17.

268. "Li Renjun Reports on Economy to NPC Standing Committee," in FBIS, *Daily Report—PRC*, April 9, 1980, p. L1.

269. Ibid., p. L3.

270. USDA, *World Food Situation and Prospects*, p. 18.

271. Professor Anthony M. Tang of Vanderbilt University pointed this out to me in correspondence in 1978. In "Food and Agriculture in China," a study for the International Food Policy Research Institute (May 1979, processed), p. 7, he asserted that this would be a plausible figure for the likely real income elasticity for demand for all food in China if there were no rationing or other limiting controls.

272. For these and the following data on some Chinese proposals regarding reserves, see Donnithorne, *China's Grain*, pp. 16–17.

273. Ibid., p. 17.

274. Edgar Snow, "Talks with Chou En-lai: The Open Door," *New Republic* (March 27, 1971), p. 20.

275. Hao Chung-shih (Hao Zhongshi), speech; see text in *Peking Review*, no. 46 (November 15, 1974), pp. 9 ff. The granaries in counties and communes store state grain, while those in brigades and teams store collective grain. The granaries' capacities generally range from 10 to 250 tons. See "Storing Grain," *Peking Review*, no. 4 (January 27, 1978), pp. 30–31.

276. Tang, "Food and Agriculture in China," p. 53.

277. Ibid., pp. 43, 47.

278. Ibid., p. 8.

279. Shigeru Ishikawa, cited in ibid., p. 9.

280. Hsu Ti-hsin, statement; see note 201.

281. Tang, "Food and Agriculture in China," pp. 60–61, 67–68.

282. USDA, *Agricultural Trade of the People's Republic of China*, pp. 6 ff., 21, 41–42.

283. Ibid., pp. 7, 41–42.

284. Ibid., p. vi.

285. In current dollars, based on data in CIA, *China: Real Trends in Trade*, p. 12. (This source also indicated what the figure should be in constant 1970 dollars; see p. 13.)

286. Based on USDA, *Agricultural Trade of the People's Republic of China*, p. 12.

287. CIA, *China: Real Trends in Trade*, p. 16.

288. CIA, *China: International Trade, 1976–77*, pp. 12–13.

289. CIA, *China: International Trade, 1977–78*, pp. 14–15. Foodstuffs made up 25 percent of exports and 16 percent of imports in 1977.

290. USDA, *Agricultural Trade of the People's Republic of China*, p. 14.

291. Ibid., pp. 26, 33.

292. CIA, *China: International Trade Quarterly Review, Fourth Quarter 1979*, p. 32. For data on 1978, see CIA, *China: Demand for Foreign Grain*, p. 1; and Frederic M. Surls, "China's Grain Trade," in JEC, *Chinese Economy Post-Mao*, p. 655. The latter sources have similar but not identical figures. On 1979, see USDA, "World Grain Situation, Outlook for 1979/80," *Foreign Agricultural Circular*, March 12, 1980, p. 2 (its figures for July/June grain years for China are 11.1 million tons for 1978/79 and 10.5 million tons for 1979/80).

293. CIA, *Handbook of Economic Statistics, 1977*, p. 62, and *China: International Trade 1977–78*, p. 18.

294. CIA, *China: International Trade Quarterly Review, Fourth Quarter 1979*, pp. 31, 10–11.

295. Based on data in CIA, *China: International Trade, 1977–78*, p. 18.

296. Ibid. I have relied on this source for dollar figures. Certain of its tonnage figures (especially the one for 1967) differ from those that I use in my later discussion of China's grain trade.

297. CIA, *China: International Trade Quarterly Review, Fourth Quarter 1979*, p. 8.

298. Data on rice exports are from Erisman, "China: Agriculture in the 1970s," p. 344; Groen and Kilpatrick, "China's Agricultural Production," p. 81; USDA, *Agricultural Trade of the People's Republic of China*, p. 33, *Foreign Agricultural Circular*, November 11, 1977, p. 13; Surls, "China's Grain Trade," p. 655; and CIA, *China: International Trade Quarterly Review, Fourth Quarter 1979*, p. 32. All figures are given in milled rice rather than paddy rice. I have used USDA figures for the years through 1960, Erisman and Groen and Kilpatrick figures for 1961–70, and CIA, *China: International Trade Quarterly* figures for 1971–79.

299. See table 3-6.

300. The Chinese imported $268.5 million worth of corn from the United States in 1979; see CIA, *China: International Trade Quarterly Review, Fourth Quarter 1979*, p. 19.

301. Dollar figures for 1961–77 were obtained or calculated from USDA, *Agricultural Trade of the People's Republic of China*, pp. 26–27, 32–33; and CIA, *China: International Trade, 1976–77*, pp. 12–13, and *Handbook of Economic Statistics, 1977*, pp. 61–62.

302. For example, see Chen and Tsuchigane, "An Assessment of China's Foodgrain Supplies in 1980," pp. 946–47; these authors estimated, wrongly, that China would be a net grain exporter in 1980.

303. CIA, *China: Demand for Foreign Grain*, p. 1. See also USDA, "People's Republic of China," *Agricultural Situation*, Supplement 6 to WAS-18 (June 1979), p. 10; and James Risser, "China-U.S. Farm Trade Appears Set for Big Leap," *Washington Post*, November 16, 1978.

304. USDA, "People's Republic of China," *Agricultural Situation*, Supplement 6 to WAS-18 (June 1979), pp. 10–11.

305. Associated Press, "Grain Imports by China Soar," *Washington Post*, March 1, 1979.

306. The figure is closer to 3 percent than 2 percent if one subtracts tubers and soybeans from the Chinese "grain" figures. During 1966–73 Chinese rice exports averaged about 1.7 percent of China's total rice production. (This calculation is based on figures on paddy rice output converted to milled rice figures; a 104 million ton average of paddy rice output during 1966–73 was equivalent to an average of 71 million tons of milled rice. Rice exports, milled, averaged 1.2 million tons during 1966–73.)

307. Eckstein and others, *Economic Trends in Communist China*, p. 79.

308. Ibid.

309. Donnithorne, *China's Grain*, p. 8. See also Perkins, "Constraints," p. 364, and *Agricultural Development in China*, pp. 157–58.

310. "Li Renjun Reports on Economy," p. L1.

311. My calculation, based on figures in USDA, "People's Republic of China," *Agricultural Situation*, Supplement 6 to WAS-21 (June 1980), pp. 25, 36–37.

312. Perkins, "Constraints," p. 364, argued that grain imports are essentially "an investment in agricultural production incentives," since they substitute for grain that would have to be extracted from the peasantry. He estimated that if grain collected by the state was about 60 million tons, perhaps 30 million should be considered "involuntary" (that is, he estimated that the peasants might sell 30 million voluntarily); if so, net grain imports amounted to 17 or 18 percent of the involuntary portion.

313. Chu Chin-chih, cited in Donnithorne, *China's Grain*, p. 15.

314. Perkins, *Agricultural Development in China*, p. 159.

315. Donnithorne, *China's Grain*, p. 36.

316. Perkins, *Agricultural Development in China*, p. 160, pointed out that even before the recent increase, the level of grain imports had been large enough to feed two-thirds of the population of large cities (over 100,000) in

Northeast China and Hopeh (Ho-pei or Hebei), plus Shanghai and Canton (Kuang-chou or Guangzhou). He stated that imported grain may, in effect, have provided supplies sufficient to feed the entire post-1938 increase in population in these cities, thereby reducing the burden that these cities otherwise would have placed on China's rural areas.

317. My calculations, based on data in USDA, *Foreign Agricultural Circular*, November 11, 1977, p. 13. (The figure for 1978 was an estimate.)

318. USDA, "World Grain Situation, Outlook for 1979/80," *Foreign Agricultural Circular*, March 12, 1980, p. 8.

319. Ibid., pp. 4, 10.

320. These and the following figures are calculated from USDA, *Foreign Agricultural Circular*, November 11, 1977, pp. 15–18. The wheat figures included flour. The 1977/78 figures in this source were preliminary estimates. The figures for grain marketing years are different from the grain figures I use elsewhere in this study.

321. My calculations, from data in USDA, "People's Republic of China," *Agricultural Situation*, Supplement 6 to WAS-21 (June 1980), p. 25. The figures are for calendar years. They differ slightly from CIA figures that I use elsewhere.

322. *Peking Review*, no. 46 (November 15, 1974), pp. 10 ff.

323. Listed in National Council for U.S.-China Trade, *China's Agriculture*, p. 222.

324. USDA, "People's Republic of China," *Agricultural Situation*, Supplement 6 to WAS-18 (June 1979), pp. 10–11.

325. USDA, "People's Republic of China," *Agricultural Situation*, Supplement 6 to WAS-21 (June 1980), p. 12.

326. Interview with a member of Japanese Foreign Ministry, Tokyo, October 17, 1977.

327. *China Exchange Newsletter*, vol. 6, no. 2 (April 1978), pp. 1–2.

328. Details on these delegations are reported in *China Exchange Newsletter* (published by the Committee on Scholarly Communication with the People's Republic of China). Many of the reports of these delegations remain the best sources available to date relating to Chinese agriculture. Published by the National Academy of Sciences, the reports include *Plant Studies in the People's Republic of China* (1975); *Insect Control in the People's Republic of China* (1977); *Wheat Studies in the People's Republic of China* (1977); and others. Another useful delegation report was James E. Nickum, U.S. Water Resources Delegation, *Hydraulic Engineering and Water Resources in the People's Republic of China*, U.S.-China Relations Report no. 2 (Stanford University, 1977).

329. *China Exchange Newsletter*, vol. 6, no. 2 (April 1978), pp. 1–2.

330. USDA, "People's Republic of China," *Agricultural Situation*, Supplement 6 to WAS-21 (June 1980), pp. 48–49.

331. Haldore Hanson in "Statement," cited above, reports on an exchange program between the International Maize and Wheat Improvement Center (CIMMYT) in Mexico and the Chinese Academy of Agricultural and For-

estry Sciences under the Ministry of Agriculture. As early as 1977, four groups, two from each organization, were exchanged to study grain, mainly wheat and maize; these visits led to significant exchanges of germ plasm. The wheat group visiting China was impressed with many aspects of China's agriculture, and Hanson's report was one of the most optimistic made by any foreign specialist on Chinese research on seeds; however, he also reported various problems, including the disruption of research by the Cultural Revolution, and he stressed the need—and the possibility—of increasing China's yields. Hanson reported that China also had begun an exchange program with the International Rice Research Institute (in the Philippines) in 1976. (Reportedly, the Chinese are now on the board of IRRI.)

332. Samuel S. Kim, *China, the United Nations, and World Order* (Princeton University Press, 1979), pp. 365 ff. The discussion below on China's role in FAO is based mainly on this source.

333. Ibid., pp. 373–74.

334. Martin M. McLaughlin, "The World Food Situation and the U.S. Role," in ODC, *Agenda for Action, 1976*, pp. 67 ff., briefly described international organizations related to agriculture.

335. In 1977 China had agricultural technical assistance programs in at least five Third World countries: Sri Lanka, Nepal, Guinea, Ethiopia, and Sierra Leone; see *China Exchange Newsletter*, vol. 6, no. 2 (April 1978), pp. 1–2.

336. Giniger, "In Ottawa, UN's Food Talks Open to Gloomy Report."

337. Trezise, *Rebuilding Grain Reserves*, p. 36, argued that a workable system would be possible even if the Soviet Union did not join, if members were prepared to discriminate against nonmembers in times of shortages.

338. Under the 1975 U.S.-Soviet agreement, the Soviet Union agreed to buy at least 6 million tons of American grain a year, and could buy up to 8 million tons if they chose, but they would have to obtain U.S. government permission to buy more than 8 million tons. By the fall of 1979, the Russians had bought, with permission, about 15 million tons from the United States. That fall the U.S. government agreed that the Soviet Union could buy another 2 million tons in the current grain year and an additional 8 million in the next year. The prospect of such large Soviet purchases—plus those of China—exerted strong upward pressure on prices. (See Dan Balz, "New Soviet Grain Deal," *Washington Post*, August 2, 1979.) Then in early 1980, following the Soviet decision to send troops into Afghanistan, the U.S. government severely restricted grain sales to the Soviet Union.

Part IV

1. In the vast literature on world energy, there are numerous sources for statistical data; among those that I have used extensively are Joel Darmstadter and others, *Energy in the World Economy: A Statistical Review of Trends in Output, Trade, and Consumption since 1925* (Johns Hopkins Press, 1971) (hereafter Darmstadter, *Energy*); United Nations, Economic

and Social Affairs Department, *World Energy Supplies, 1950–1974*, Statistical Papers, Series J, no. 19 (UN, 1976) (hereafter UN, *WES 1950–74*), *World Energy Supplies, 1971–1975*, Statistical Papers, Series J, no. 20 (UN, 1977) (hereafter UN, *WES 1971–75*); and United Nations, International Economic and Social Affairs Department, *World Energy Supplies, 1973–1978*, Statistical Papers, Series J, no. 22 (UN, 1979) (hereafter UN, *WES 1973–78*). I have used UN figures for global totals and for data on countries other than China. For statistics on Chinese energy production and trade, I have used Central Intelligence Agency (CIA) data. On very recent statistics on world oil, I also have used data from the CIA's *International Energy Biweekly Statistical Review*, *International Energy Statistical Review* (published by the CIA's National Foreign Assessment Center [NFAC]), and *International Oil Developments Statistical Survey* (issued by its Office of Economic Research [OER]). In addition, I have made use of the *Oil and Gas Journal*, a leading oil industry publication. Several general CIA studies have been particularly useful: CIA, *The International Energy Situation: Outlook to 1985*, ER 77-10240U, April 1977; NFAC, CIA, *The World Oil Market in the Years Ahead*, ER 79-10327U, August 1979; and CIA, *Handbook of Economic Statistics, 1977*, ER 77-10537, September 1977; as well as detailed country oil studies on China, the Soviet Union, and Saudi Arabia, cited below. Several other analytical studies that attempt to project future trends also have been particularly useful, including Congressional Research Service, *Project Interdependence: U.S. and World Energy Outlook through 1990*, report printed for the Subcommittee on Energy and Power of the House Committee on Interstate and Foreign Commerce, and for the Senate Committee on Energy and Natural Resources, 95 Cong. 1 sess. (Government Printing Office, 1977) (hereafter, CRS, *Project Interdependence*); Carroll L. Wilson and others, *Energy: Global Prospects, 1985–2000*, Report of the Workshop on Alternative Energy Strategies (McGraw-Hill, 1977) (hereafter, Wilson, *Energy: Global Prospects*); and Joseph A. Yager and Eleanor B. Steinberg, *Energy and U.S. Foreign Policy*, Report to the Energy Policy Project, Ford Foundation (Ballinger, 1975). (The Wilson book is summarized in Andrew R. Flower, "World Oil Production," *Scientific American*, vol. 238, no. 3 [March 1978], pp. 42–49, which will be cited for some of the workshop's conclusions.) Useful analyses of the significance of the 1973 oil crisis are in articles from *Foreign Affairs*, republished in William P. Bundy, ed., *The World Economic Crisis* (Norton, 1975), and valuable data on trends affecting the Third World are in annual volumes published by the Overseas Development Council (ODC): *The U.S. and the Developing World: Agenda for Action*, and *The United States and World Development: Agenda* (Praeger for ODC, each volume dated by year, 1974 through 1979) (hereafter *Agenda for Action* or *Agenda*, with the year covered identified).

2. UN, *WES 1971–75*, p. 3. In 1975 liquid fuels accounted for 3.526 billion tons of "coal equivalent" (CE) and solid fuels for 2.623 billion tons

CE; total world consumption of "primary commercial energy" was 8.003 billion tons CE. The United Nations converts all forms of energy into CE. Conversion rates are discussed briefly in note 21 below and in greater detail in UN, *WES 1950–74*, pp. x–xxvii. "Primary energy" (or "primary commercial energy") includes solid fuels (coal, lignite, and peat), liquid fuels (crude petroleum and natural gas liquids), natural gas, hydroelectricity, and nuclear electric power. (The UN statistics generally do not include uranium in the figures on solid fuels.)

3. The term "oil" will be used in this discussion (as in most nontechnical writing) interchangeably with "crude petroleum," except where otherwise qualified. UN statistics include detailed figures not only on crude petroleum but also on petroleum products.

4. UN, *WES 1971–75*, p. 2. In 1975 world imports and exports of primary commercial energy totaled, respectively, 2.958 billion and 2.939 billion tons CE, out of the world production of 8.555 billion tons CE. (These figures do not include nuclear fuels; import and export figures do not match exactly because they may fall into different reporting periods.) In 1975 imports and exports of crude petroleum totaled 1.431 billion and 1.409 billion tons, equivalent to 2.147 billion and 2.114 billion tons CE; see ibid., p. 62. World imports and exports of "energy petroleum products" in 1975 totaled 303 million and 310 million tons, equivalent to 455 million and 465 million tons CE; see ibid., p. 92.

5. See discussions on pp. 403 ff.

6. According to UN estimates, for example, in 1950 China produced only 43 million tons of primary energy; 42.920 million tons CE of this was coal, which was less than 2 percent of world production that year (which amounted to 2.664 billion tons CE; see UN, *WES 1950–74*, pp. 2, 92).

7. See note 130 below. Figures on the United States, the Soviet Union, and Saudi Arabia (for 1975) are from UN, *WES 1971–75*, pp. 18, 19, 26, 36, 37. Figures on consumption that year were United States, 2.350 billion tons CE; Soviet Union, 1.411 billion tons. Figures on production were United States, 2.037 billion tons CE; Soviet Union, 1.650 billion tons; and Saudi Arabia, 530 million tons. The UN figures for 1975 showed China's energy consumption as 570 million tons CE and its production as 597 million tons CE; see ibid., pp. 30–31. This indicated that China's production was already above that of Saudi Arabia; however, these UN figures probably were too high. The estimate for China that I use, obtained from CIA sources, placed China's total energy supply in 1975 (477 million tons) below that of Saudi Arabia. CIA, *Handbook of Economic Statistics, 1977*, pp. 75–76, gave figures on energy production and consumption of major nations, in oil equivalent, for 1960–76, which differ somewhat from UN figures (and its estimates for China were higher than the later estimates that I use).

8. Based on CIA figures for China's coal and oil, in NFAC, CIA, *China: A Statistical Compendium*, Research Aid ER 79-10374, July 1979, p. 9; figures on China's natural gas in NFAC, CIA, *Electric Power for China's Moderniza-*

tion: The Hydroelectric Option, Research Paper ER 80-10089U, May 1980, p. 23; and statistics on coal, oil, and gas in other countries in UN, *WES 1971–75,* pp. 2–39; and CIA, *Handbook of Economic Statistics, 1977,* pp. 80, 83–84. The CIA estimates for China's natural gas in *Handbook of Economic Statistics, 1977* were far too high (they indicated that China's output was sixth in the world). In 1980 the CIA revised its estimates downward on the basis of official Chinese data; the new figures are in NFAC, CIA, *Electric Power for China's Modernization.* The cubic meter figures in this source, converted to cubic feet (1 cubic meter equals 35.315 cubic feet), indicate that in 1975 China ranked eleventh worldwide. The major energy producers and their output in 1975 (in CE), according to UN sources, were: for solid fuels (mostly coal), United States, 574 million tons CE; Soviet Union, 507 million tons CE; China, 318 million tons CE; for natural gas, United States, 707 million tons CE; Soviet Union, 405 million tons CE; Netherlands, 109 million tons CE; Canada, 99 million tons CE; United Kingdom, 49 million tons CE; and China, 46 million tons CE (however, the estimate for China was too high; see table 4-10 and pp. 422 ff.); and for oil, see table 4-6 (the figures in the table can be converted to CE by multiplying by 1.5).

9. In 1978 China's crude oil output (104 million tons) was far behind that of the Soviet Union (561 million tons), the United States (435 million tons), Saudi Arabia (403 million tons), and Iran (262 million tons), but it was very close to that of Iraq (128 million tons) and Venezuela (108 million tons) and just above that of Libya (99 million tons), Kuwait (95 million tons), and Mexico (63 million tons); see NFAC, CIA, *International Energy Statistical Review,* ER IESR 80–008, April 23, 1980, p. 1. (This source gives production in barrels a day, which I have converted to tons per year.)

10. Oil statistics are presented in three forms: millions or billions of barrels; thousands or millions of barrels a day; and tons. In this study, most figures will be given in tons. When the original sources have used other measures, I have converted them to standard equivalents: 1 million barrels a day (b/d) equal 50 million tons a year; 7.33 barrels equal 1 ton. (See note 21 for further discussion of conversion rates.)

11. China's exports of crude oil and petroleum products in 1978, totaling slightly over 14 million tons, were just over 1 percent of total exports by the world's major exporters; see the figures on China in table 4-14 and figures on other countries in NFAC, CIA, *Handbook of Economic Statistics, 1979,* Research Aid ER 79-10274, August 1979, p. 137.

12. See table 4-7. NFAC, CIA, *Handbook of Economic Statistics, 1979,* reported that in 1978 Saudi Arabia exported 8.135 million b/d (about 406.75 million tons) and Iran 4.685 million b/d (about 234.25 million tons) of oil, including refined products (but excluding bunkers). NFAC, CIA, *The World Oil Market in the Years Ahead,* predicted that Saudi Arabian production, after rising in 1979, would drop and stabilize at about 8.5 million b/d (about 425 million tons) and that Iran's output, after dropping in 1979, would rise and might stabilize at about 4.0 million b/d (about 200 million tons). Both countries export most of their output.

13. In 1975 the exports of Saudi Arabia (328 million tons), Iran (234 million tons), and Iraq (103 million tons) accounted for 665 million tons, or close to half, of total world exports of 1.409 billion in 1975. These, plus the exports of six other countries—the Soviet Union (93 million tons), Kuwait (91 million tons), Nigeria (85 million tons), United Arab Emirates (80 million tons), Venezuela (77 million tons), and Libya (69 million tons)—totaled 1.160 billion tons, or 82 percent of the world total; see table 4-6. In 1978, not much had changed; the three largest exporters together exported 762 million tons, and the other six, 639 million tons, for a total of 1.401 billion tons (the big increases coming from Saudi Arabia and the Soviet Union); see table 4-7.

14. In addition to those listed in note 13, in 1975 the countries were Indonesia (49 million tons), Algeria (41 million tons), Qatar (21 million tons), Oman (17 million tons), Gabon (10 million tons), Mexico (6 million tons), and China. (The UN statistics gave a figure of 8.7 million tons for China's exports in 1975; I use CIA figures: 10.5 million tons, including petroleum products.) Both Canada and Trinidad also exported more than 5 million tons, but imported more than they exported.

15. See UN, *WES 1973–78*, pp. 126–35. (In my ranking I have excluded Canada, which exported more than 5 million tons but imported more.) There are substantial differences between the UN figures and the CIA figures. For China, the UN figure for crude oil exports in 1978 was 9 million tons, but the CIA figure was 11.9 million tons. (For the CIA figures, see table 4-15.)

16. See the discussions of the energy/GNP (gross national product) elasticity coefficient in Darmstadter, *Energy*, pp. 32–39; and OER, CIA, "China: Energy Balance Projections, 1980 and 1985," in CRS, *Project Interdependence*, pp. 864–65 (hereafter OER, CIA, "Energy Balance Projections"). See also Joel Darmstadter, "Economic Growth and Energy Conservation, Historical and International Lessons," paper prepared for the annual meeting of the American Association for the Advancement of Science, Washington, D.C., February 1978 (Washington, D.C.: Resources for the Future, Reprint 154).

17. Many types of high-grade steel are essential for oil pipelines, drilling bits, and so on; see p. 446 and note 305.

18. CIA analysts have attempted to calculate what impact, under various conditions, large Chinese oil exports might have on domestic GNP growth; in some studies they may have overestimated the adverse impact; see OER, CIA, "Energy Balance Projections," pp. 868–69, and note 337.

19. "Primary commercial energy" excludes traditional fuels such as straw, shale, and fuelwood.

20. For a useful discussion of traditional energy sources, see Arjun Makhijani, *Energy and Agriculture in the Third World* (Ballinger, 1975).

21. See Darmstadter, *Energy*, p. 10; and UN, *WES 1971–75*, p. 3. Three measures are commonly used to aggregate statistics on different types of energy: CE, oil equivalent (OE), and British thermal units (Btu). I have generally used CE, as most UN sources and many CIA sources do. A "standard" ton of "coal equivalent" is one containing 7,000 kilocalories per kilogram (calories/gramme). The UN conversion coefficients are given in UN, *WES 1950–74*, pp.

xx–xxiv. Some of the most important are 1 ton of crude petroleum equals 1.47 tons of standard coal equivalent, 1,000 cubic meters of natural gas equal 1.332 tons CE, and 1,000 kilowatt-hours of electricity equal 0.123 ton CE. Since the quality of coal varies, it too must be converted to standard CE; generally, the UN converts anthracite and bituminous coal at a ratio of 1.00 to 1.00 but lignite, brown coal, and peat at lower rates. Darmstadter in his study used the following conversion factors: hard coal, 1 ton equals 1 ton CE; crude petroleum, 1 ton equals 1.5 tons CE; natural gas, 1,000 cubic meters equal 1.332 tons CE; and 1,000 kilowatt-hours equal 0.125 ton CE; see Darmstadter, *Energy*, pp. 827–31. In recent studies, the CIA has used the following conversion factors for China: raw coal from large mines—1 ton equals 0.8 ton CE; raw coal from small mines—1 ton equals 0.6 ton CE (nationally, the average raw coal/coal equivalent rate has varied, depending on the relative size of the output of large and small mines; it was 0.79 in 1957, 0.77 in 1965, and 0.744 in 1974–76); crude oil—1 ton equals 1.5 tons CE; natural gas and hydroelectricity—1,000 cubic meters equal 1.332 tons CE and 1,000 kilowatt-hours equal 0.125 ton CE; see OER, CIA, "Energy Balance Projections," p. 872. World oil statistics are given, in different sources, in three forms: tons, barrels, or barrels a day. In making conversions among these, I have used the widely accepted rough conversion rate of 1 million b/d equals 50 million tons of oil a year (which implies that 1 ton equals, on a worldwide average, 7.33 barrels, although different types of oil have different weights). When I have used statistics directly from other sources, I have accepted their conversion factors. When I have converted oil to CE I have used the 1.5 rate. All tonnage figures cited in this study are in metric tons. (One metric ton equals 2,204.6 pounds.) In converting barrels of oil to CE I have used 7.33 or a rounded 7.3 figure.

22. Makhijani, *Energy and Agriculture*, p. 1, estimates that the total "probably" is around 30 million b/d of oil (1.5 billion tons of oil or 2.25 billion tons CE), which is close to the amount of oil that now enters world trade.

23. My calculations from data in Darmstadter, *Energy*, p. 10; and UN, *WES 1950–74*, p. 3. (The exact 1950 figure is 2.49 billion tons CE.)

24. My calculations from data in ibid.; and UN, *Wes 1971–75*, p. 3.

25. My calculations from data in sources cited in notes 23 and 24.

26. These and the following figures are from Darmstadter, *Energy*, p. 10.

27. My calculations from data in UN, *WES 1971–75*, pp. 17, 19, 27, 31, 35, 37.

28. My calculations from data in ibid., pp. 3, 35.

29. Based on Darmstadter, *Energy*, p. 10; UN, *WES 1950–74*, pp. 3, 93, and *WES 1971–75*, pp. 3, 31. I have had to adjust some of Darmstadter's categories for 1925 to make them comparable to the other sources.

30. These and the per capita figures below are from UN, *WES 1971–75*, pp. 3, 19, 29, 35.

31. Ibid., pp. 5, 7, 27, gives the following regional figures for per capita energy in 1975: Africa, 395 kilograms; Caribbean America, 1,174 kilograms; the rest of Latin America, 813 kilograms; Middle East, 1,055 kilograms; and the Far East (non-Communist developing countries of Asia), 242 kilograms.

32. These and the following rates are my calculations, based on Darm-

stadter, *Energy*, p. 10; UN, *WES 1950–74*, p. 3, and *WES 1971–75*, p. 3. As indicated earlier, in part I, when I state "from x year through y year," x year is a base year, not included in the period for which rates of change are calculated; but when I state "x year–y year," x year is included in the period and the base year for calculated rates of change is the year preceding x year.

33. My calculations from data in UN, *WES 1950–74*, pp. 3, 93, 107, and *WES 1971–75*, pp. 3, 31, 35. The UN figures for Asian Communist nations are given here, but elsewhere I use CIA estimates and official Chinese figures which are, I believe, closer to reality; see notes 127 and 130.

34. The rates are my calculations from data in UN, *WES 1950–74*, pp. 43, 79, and *WES 1971–75*, pp. 19, 27.

35. My calculations from data in UN, *WES 1950–74*, pp. 5, 7, and *WES 1971–75*, pp. 5, 7.

36. My calculations from statistics in Arms Control and Disarmament Agency, *World Military Expenditures and Arms Transfers, 1966–1975*, ACDA Publication 90 (GPO, 1976), p. 14.

37. My calculations from statistics in CIA, *Handbook of Economic Statistics, 1977*, p. 31. The statistics here indicate a 7 percent GNP growth rate for China during 1965–75; the long-term rate in China since the 1950s has been closer to 5.5 (see part I, p. 17).

38. Darmstadter, *Energy*, p. 32, discussed the correlations between GNP and energy consumption.

39. The correlation between economic growth and energy consumption can vary significantly and depends on stages of development, the structures of economies, prices, the efficiency with which energy is used, and so on; see Sam H. Schurr, "Energy, Economic Growth, and Human Welfare," *EPRI Journal* (Washington. D.C., Electric Power Research Institute, May 1978), pp. 14–18; and Darmstadter, "Economic Growth and Energy Conservation, Historical and International Lessons," in Charles J. Hitch, ed., *Energy Conservation and Economic Growth* (Boulder, Colo.: Westview Press, 1978), pp. 113–24.

40. Darmstadter, *Energy*, p. 37. The figures for 1950–65 for various countries range from lows of 0.62 in the United Kingdom, 0.76 in West Germany, and 0.81 in the United States to highs of 2.16 in Italy and 2.14 in Bulgaria. About half of the national figures given, however, are between 1.00 and 1.50. Since the oil crisis of 1973, conservation and the effects of increased prices have led to a significant decline in the coefficient in a number of countries. In the United States, according to some estimates, it may have dropped to perhaps 0.60 to 0.65 by 1977; see John H. Lichtblau, "American Oil Imports and World Needs," *Washington Post*, April 2, 1978; and Steven Rattner, "Energy: Where Did the Crisis Go?" *New York Times*, April 16, 1978.

41. In 1925, solid fuels (mainly coal, but also lignite) accounted for 1.230 billion tons CE (of total energy consumption of 1.485 billion); by comparison, liquid fuels accounted for only 197 million tons CE, natural gas for 48 million, and hydroelectricity for 10 million; see Darmstadter, *Energy*, p. 13.

42. My calculations from data in ibid.; and UN, *WES 1950–74*, p. 3.

43. In 1950 solid fuels accounted for 1.534 billion tons CE (of total world

energy consumption of 2.493 billion); liquid fuels accounted for 672 million tons CE, natural gas for 244 million tons CE, and hydroelectricity for 42 million tons CE; see UN, *WES 1950–74*, p. 3.

44. My calculations from data in UN, *WES 1971–75*, p. 3.

45. My calculations from data in ibid. In 1975 the consumption figures were solid fuels, 2.623 billion tons CE; liquid fuels, 3.526 billion tons CE; natural gas, 1.633 billion tons CE; and hydroelectricity and nuclear electricity, 221 million tons CE.

46. The rates of growth in consumption of different types of primary commercial energy during 1951–75 were solid fuels, 2.2 percent; liquid fuel, 6.9 percent; natural gas, 7.9 percent; and hydroelectricity and nuclear electricity, 6.9 percent; my calculations from data in ibid.

47. In 1925 energy consumption and production figures for major developed areas were North America, 779 million tons CE (produced) and 749 million tons CE (consumed); Western Europe, 532 million and 517 million tons CE; and Japan, 33 million and 31 million tons CE. Their ratios of energy production to energy consumption were North America, 1.04; Western Europe, 1.03; and Japan, 1.06; based on Darmstadter, *Energy*, p. 22.

48. In 1950 North America produced 1.196 billion tons CE and consumed 1.187 billion; Western Europe produced 507 million tons CE and consumed 574 million; and Japan produced 44 million tons CE and consumed 46 million. Their respective production-consumption ratios in 1950, therefore, were North America, 1.01; Western Europe, 0.88; and Japan, 0.96; my calculations from data in UN, *WES 1950–74*, pp. 4–7, 78–79.

49. In 1975 North America produced 2.305 billion tons CE and consumed 2.576 billion (for the United States the figures were 2.037 billion and 2.350 billion tons CE); Western Europe produced 653 million tons CE and consumed 1.408 billion; and Japan produced 37 million tons CE and consumed 402 million. Their respective production-consumption ratios in 1975, therefore, were North America, 0.89 (United States, 0.87); Western Europe, 0.44; and Japan, 0.09. My calculations from data in UN, *WES 1971–75*, pp. 4–7, 18–19, 26–27.

50. Darmstadter, *Energy*, p. 25. The breakdown by types was solid fuel, 146 million tons CE; liquid fuel, 68 million tons CE; natural gas, 5,000 tons CE; and electricity, 200,000 tons CE.

51. UN, *WES 1950–74*, p. 2.

52. See Darmstadter, *Energy*, p. 25; and UN, *WES 1971–75*, pp. 2, 62.

53. In 1975 the non-Communist developed nations consumed 4.635 billion tons CE but produced only 3.185 billion tons; see UN, *WES 1971–75*, pp. 2, 3.

54. In 1975 the non-Communist developed countries produced 1.091 billion tons CE of solid fuels (mainly coal) and consumed 1.106 billion tons; they produced 1.032 billion tons CE of natural gas and consumed 1.080 billion tons; see ibid.

55. In 1975 liquid fuel (mainly oil) consumption in the non-Communist developed countries was 2.322 billion tons CE; see ibid., p. 3.

56. In 1975 the Communist nations produced 2.774 billion tons CE of pri-

mary energy, consumed 2.590 billion tons, and exported 328 million tons (the equivalent of 219 million tons of oil); see ibid., pp. 2, 3.

57. In 1975 in the European Communist nations, solid fuel accounted for 849 million tons CE of their total consumption of primary energy, which amounted to 1.965 billion tons CE; natural gas accounted for 467 million tons CE; and hydropower and nuclear power, 20 million tons CE; see ibid., p. 35. For data on China, see later discussion.

58. In 1975 the developing non-Communist nations produced 2.593 billion tons CE and consumed 778 million tons CE; see ibid., pp. 2, 3.

59. As of mid-1979, the members of the Organization of Petroleum Exporting Countries (OPEC) were Algeria, Ecuador, Gabon, Indonesia, Iran, Iraq, Kuwait, Libya, Neutral Zone, Nigeria, Qatar, Saudi Arabia, United Arab Emirates (Abu Dhabi, Dubai, Sharjah), and Venezuela (Egypt was suspended in April 1979). Of these, eleven had installed production capacities of more than 50 million tons (1 million b/d). See NFAC, CIA, *International Energy Statistical Review*, ER IESR 79-012, September 5, 1979, p. 3.

60. In 1975 in the developing non-Communist nations, liquid fuels accounted for 475 million tons CE of their total primary energy consumption of 778 million tons; solid fuels accounted for only 154 million tons; natural gas for 119 million tons; and hydroelectric power for 30 million tons; see UN, *WES 1971-75*, p. 3.

61. The figures on liquid fuel consumption and total energy consumption were as follows for particular regions in 1975: Africa, 70 million tons and 158 million tons CE; Caribbean America, 112 million tons and 145 million tons CE; other Latin America, 113 million tons and 166 million tons CE; Middle East, 78 million tons and 127 million tons CE; non-Communist developing Asia, 124 million tons and 272 million tons CE; see ibid., pp. 5-6, 27.

62. Rumania in 1857; the United States in 1859; see M. King Hubbert, "World Oil and Natural Gas Reserves and Resources," in CRS, *Project Interdependence*, p. 636.

63. UN, *WES 1950-74*, p. 193.

64. UN, *WES 1971-75*, p. 62. In 1976 it was 2.822 billion tons, or about 56 million b/d. CIA statistics on world oil production indicated that total output was 53 million b/d in 1975 and more than 59 million b/d (about 3 billion tons) in 1977; see NFAC, CIA, *International Energy Statistical Review*, May 17, 1978, p. 1.

65. My calculations from data in UN, *WES 1950-74*, pp. 193, 280, and *WES 1971-75*, pp. 62, 92. Crude oil production was 520 million tons in 1950 and 2.647 billion tons in 1975. Consumption of energy petroleum products was 433 million tons in 1950 and 2.284 billion tons in 1975. (In CE, all of these figures should be roughly 50 percent higher.)

66. The United States consumed 279 million tons, the world consumed 433 million tons; see UN, *WES 1950-74*, pp. 280, 296.

67. The figures on consumption of energy petroleum products in 1950 and 1975 for different areas were North America, 294 million and 737 million tons; Western Europe, 45 million and 526 million tons; and Japan, 1.28

million and 193 million tons; see ibid., pp. 295, 314, 322, and UN, *WES 1971–75*, pp. 95, 99–100.

68. In 1950 the European Communist countries consumed 36 million tons of energy petroleum products; in 1975, 410 million tons; see UN, *WES 1950–74*, p. 328, and *WES 1971–75*, p. 102.

69. In 1950 the non-Communist developing countries consumed 50 million tons of energy petroleum products; in 1975, 308 million tons; see UN, *WES 1950–74*, p. 280, and *WES 1971–75*, p. 92.

70. For these and the following figures, see UN, *WES 1971–75*, pp. 92, 99–100. Total world consumption of energy petroleum products was 2.284 billion tons in 1975. (The figures given here are lower than those for total consumption of all liquid fuels, which were world, 3.526 billion tons; North America, 1.153 billion tons; Western Europe, 803 million tons; Japan, 295 million tons; see ibid., pp. 3, 5, 7, 27, 31.)

71. Ibid., p. 102. The European Communist nations' consumption of all liquid fuels in 1975 was 630 million tons, and their supply of crude petroleum was 493 million tons; see ibid., pp. 35, 70.

72. In 1975, 308 million tons were consumed in the non-Communist developing countries and 65 million tons in the Asian Communist nations, for a total of 373 million tons; see ibid., pp. 92, 100. In 1975 the consumption of all liquid fuels in these countries totaled 574 million tons (475 million and 99 million tons, respectively, in the non-Communist and Communist developing nations), and their supply of crude petroleum was 581 million tons (516 million and 65 million tons, respectively); see ibid., pp. 3, 7, 62, 68.

73. Ibid., pp. 92, 100. In 1975, the world average per capita consumption of energy petroleum products was 579 kilograms; in the developed nations it was 1,974 kilograms; in the non-Communist developing nations it was 159 kilograms; and in the Communist developing nations, according to the UN figures, it was 73 kilograms.

74. My calculations from data in UN, *WES 1950–74*, p. 193, and *WES 1971–75*, p. 62. World production of crude oil was 520 million tons in 1950 and 2.647 billion tons in 1975. In the non-Communist developed nations, it was 275 million tons in 1950 and 537 million tons in 1975. In the non-Communist developing nations, it was 201 million tons in 1950 and 1.519 billion tons in 1975. According to these UN figures, world production was 2.779 billion tons in 1973, before the oil crisis (587 million tons in the non-Communist developed countries, 1.693 billion tons in the non-Communist developing countries, and 489 million tons in the Communist countries). By 1976 it was only slightly higher: 2.822 billion tons (530 million tons in the non-Communist developed countries, 1.660 billion tons in the non-Communist developing countries, and 631 million tons in the Communist countries). CIA figures indicated that world crude oil production that year was 2.975 billion tons (59.490 million b/d)—2.329 billion tons in the non-Communist countries (46.580 million b/d) and 646 million tons in the Communist countries (12.910 million b/d); see NFAC, CIA, *International Energy Statistical Review*, ER IESR 78-008, May 17, 1978, p. 1.

75. UN, *WES 1971–75*, p. 62.

76. For figures on oil production of particular countries, see table 4-6, based on ibid., pp. 62–71.

77. Ibid., pp. 64, 70. In 1975 the United States imported 203 million tons (4.06 million b/d), and the Soviet Union exported 93 million tons (1.86 million b/d). Between 1973 and 1977 U.S. oil imports rose by 38 percent. In 1977 about 46 percent of U.S. supply was imported, and U.S. oil imports accounted for about one-quarter of all world oil trade (roughly four-fifths of these U.S. imports came from OPEC nations, and they amounted, in 1977, to about 22 percent of OPEC's exports); see John H. Lichtblau, "American Oil Imports and World Needs," *Washington Post*, April 2, 1978.

78. By 1977 Saudi production had risen to 460 million tons (9.2 million b/d); see NFAC, CIA, *International Energy Statistical Review*, May 17, 1978, p. 1. In 1978 Saudi output was about 403 million tons (8.1 million b/d), while Iranian output was 262 million tons (5.2 million b/d); see note 9.

79. UN, *WES 1971–75*, p. 62.

80. See table 4-6.

81. Calculated from the data in table 4-6. In 1975 the exports of these eleven countries, totaling 1.196 billion tons, made up 85 percent of total world exports of 1.409 billion tons. Since then, there have been some changes in OPEC's membership; see note 59.

82. UN, *WES 1971–75*, pp. 64, 67–68. The *net* figure for North America was 213 million tons, and for Western Europe it was 573 million tons.

83. The problems, as seen by a number of leading experts after the oil crisis of 1973, were reviewed in the following articles from *Foreign Affairs*, published in Bundy, *The World Economic Crisis:* James E. Akins, "The Oil Crisis: This Time the Wolf Is Here"; Carroll L. Wilson, "A Plan for Energy Independence"; Jahangir Amuzegar, "The Oil Story: Facts, Fiction and Fair Play"; Gerald A. Pollack, "The Economic Consequences of the Energy Crisis"; and Walter J. Levy, "World Oil Cooperation or International Chaos."

84. Useful background information is in Yager and Steinberg, *Energy and U.S. Foreign Policy*.

85. Ibid., p. 10. Many other writings focus on the seven largest—the so-called seven sisters.

86. Ibid., pp. 12–17.

87. Akins, "The Oil Crisis," p. 28.

88. Levy, "World Oil Cooperation," p. 206, emphasized that the producing countries had gained "complete control of the oil industry" in their countries.

89. Ali A. Mazrui, "The New Interdependence, from Hierarchy to Symmetry," in ODC, *Agenda 1975*, pp. 118–34, reflected the Third World perspective.

90. On the Third World's desire for cartels similar to OPEC, see C. Fred Bergsten, "The Threat from the Third World," *Foreign Policy*, no. 11 (Summer 1973), pp. 102–24; and Zuhayr Mikdashi, "Collusion Could Work," *Foreign Policy*, no. 14 (Spring 1974), pp. 57–68. On the obstacles to copying OPEC, see Stephen D. Krasner, "Oil Is the Exception," *Foreign Policy*, no. 14

(Spring 1974), pp. 68–83; and Bension Varon and Kenji Takeuchi, "Developing Countries and Non-Fuel Minerals," in Bundy, *The World Economic Crisis*, pp. 165–78.

91. See Edward R. Fried and Charles L. Schultze, eds., *Higher Oil Prices and the World Economy* (Brookings, 1975).

92. In 1976 the demand for oil in the non-OPEC developing countries was 6.7 million b/d (335 million tons); since this same group of countries exported 3.7 million b/d (185 million tons), their net imports were 3.0 million b/d (150 million tons); see CIA, *The International Energy Situation: Outlook to 1985*, p. 15. (If one crudely calculates the average cost of the net imports at that time at $13 a barrel, or $95 a ton, the import bill was $14 billion to $15 billion.)

93. James P. Grant, "Energy Shock and the Development Prospect," in James W. Howe and others, ODC, *Agenda for Action 1974*, pp. 33 ff.

94. The external debt of the oil-importing developing nations jumped in the years between 1973 and 1976 from $80 billion to $140 billion; see Bruce K. MacLaury, "OPEC's Billions," *Brookings Bulletin*, vol. 15, no. 2 (Fall 1978), p. 3. For other details, see Ann Crittenden, "Managing OPEC's Money," *New York Times*, June 24, 1979. She reported the current account deficit of the developing nations to be $238 billion as of 1979.

95. See John H. Lichtblau, "World Oil Supply and Demand: 1950–76 and Forecast to 1990," in CRS, *Project Interdependence*, p. 677; and Amurzegar, "The Oil Story," p. 74.

96. Many observers, even at that time, pointed out that this could not last long. Daniel Yergin, "The Real Meaning of the Energy Crunch," *New York Times Magazine*, June 4, 1978, p. 32, quoted Sheik Ahmed Zaki Yamani of Saudi Arabia as saying, "Once the [present] surplus is eliminated, neither the United States nor any other superpower will be able to bring about a freeze in oil prices." Yamani predicted that oil prices would almost certainly double within a decade. Joseph A. Yager, "Trends in the International Oil Market," 1978, processed, p. 3, stated, "Early in the 1980s, Saudi Arabia will probably be able to determine the price of internationally traded oil simply by varying its own production."

97. See, for example, Anthony J. Parisi, "Experts Dispute Administration, Doubt World Oil Shortage in '80s," *New York Times*, January 18, 1978; Steven Rattner, "Energy: Where Did the Crisis Go?" *New York Times*, April 16, 1978; and "The Glut Goes On," *Newsweek* (June 5, 1978), pp. 77–78.

98. Based on UN, *Yearbook of International Trade Statistics, 1976*, vol. II (UN, 1977), p. 88; and International Monetary Fund, *International Financial Statistics*, vol. 29, no. 6 (June 1976), pp. 38–41. The figures showed that the value of crude oil imports increased 4.37 times between 1972 and 1975, while the value of total trade increased only 2.1 times.

99. MacLaury, "OPEC's Billions," p. 3.

100. See John Williamson, "The International Financial System," in Fried and Schultze, *Higher Oil Prices*, pp. 197–225; and Guy F. Erb, "Petrodollars and Multilateral Development Financing," in ODC, *Agenda for Action, 1975*,

pp. 105–17. Pollack, "The Economic Consequence of the Energy Crisis," p. 121, estimated that OPEC surpluses could accumulate to more than $600 billion by 1985.

101. The discussion of recent trends that follow is, except where otherwise noted, based on NFAC, CIA, *The World Oil Market in the Years Ahead*, especially pp. 1–15. This gave energy statistics in OE, which I have converted to CE (at the ratio of 1 ton OE to 1.5 tons CE).

102. Where figures are in tons and barrels, the tonnage figures generally are my calculations and the figures in barrels are those in the sources cited. For tonnage in oil equivalent, the figures are generally those in the original sources; coal equivalent tonnage figures are usually my calculations.

103. Based on statistics in NFAC, CIA, *International Energy Biweekly Statistical Review*, ER IEBSR 78-002, January 25, 1978, pp. 6–7, and *International Energy Statistical Review*, September 5, 1979, pp. 5–6.

104. See David B. Ottaway, "Nigeria Warns West on Recognition of Rhodesia," *Washington Post*, May 31, 1979; and "Qaddafi Threat Seen Hardened by Translation," *Washington Post*, July 1, 1979.

105. NFAC, CIA, *The World Oil Market in the Years Ahead*, pp. 37–42; also see note 338 below.

106. Ibid., p. 5.

107. Strictly speaking, of course, supply and demand curves will always meet, at some price; if demand grows more rapidly than supply, the price will rise. In this discussion, statements about "demand" or "need" exceeding supply mean the demand/supply situation results in prices that create constraints on oil use that (without adequate substitutes) tend to reduce economic growth.

108. These and the data below are from Hubbert, "World Oil," p. 635. His figures are in barrels; I have converted them at 7.3 barrels to the ton.

109. CIA, *Handbook of Economic Statistics, 1977*, p. 8, gives figures in barrels, which I have converted at 7.3 barrels to the ton.

110. Wilson, *Energy: Global Prospects*, p. 118.

111. See NFAC, CIA, *International Energy Statistical Review*, May 17, 1978, p. 4, which estimated world petroleum reserves to be 657 billion barrels (90 billion tons, converted at a 7.3 ratio)—592 billion barrels in the free world and 65 billion barrels in the Communist countries. The *Oil and Gas Journal* made an estimate for 1977 of 646 billion barrels; see Anthony J. Parisi and Steven Rattner, "Experts Dispute Administration, Doubt World Oil Shortage in '80s," *New York Times*, January 18, 1978.

112. Hubbert, "World Oil," p. 638. Wilson, *Energy: Global Prospects*, p. 115, listed other estimates.

113. Bernardo F. Grossling, "A Critical Survey of World Petroleum Opportunities," in CRS, *Project Interdependence*, pp. 645–58. Some "highly speculative" estimates have gone as high as 5 trillion barrels; see *Newsweek* (June 5, 1978), p. 77.

114. William Greider, "Bank Spurs Oil Search in Third-World Nations," *Washington Post*, May 24, 1978.

115. NFAC, CIA, *The World Oil Market in the Years Ahead*, p. iii.

116. Hubbert, "World Oil," pp. 636–37.

117. My calculations, based on data in UN, *WES 1950–74*, p. 3. Total world consumption of liquid fuels from 1950 through 1959 was 9.55 billion tons CE; from 1960 through 1964 it was 7.85 billion tons CE.

118. The following figures are from CIA, *The International Energy Situation: Outlook to 1985*. The original figures were in million b/d; I have converted them to millions of tons (at a ratio of 1 million b/d to 50 million tons).

119. See John P. Hardt, Ronda A. Bresnick, and David Levine, "Soviet Oil and Gas in the Global Perspective," in CRS, *Project Interdependence*, pp. 787–857; George Lardner, Jr., "CIA Chided on Soviet Oil Predictions," *Washington Post*, May 22, 1978; and Richard Harwood and J. P. Smith, "CIA Oil Figures Raise Eyebrows among Experts," *Washington Post*, April 23, 1978.

120. NFAC, CIA, *The World Oil Market in the Years Ahead*, pp. 3, 37–41.

121. Ibid., pp. 8–11.

122. Hubbert, "World Oil," pp. 627, 644. The author's figures were in billions of barrels; I have converted them to tons.

123. Lichtblau, "World Oil Supply and Demand," pp. 675 ff., especially pp. 687–88.

124. Horst Mendershausen, "Worldwide Energy Demand and Supply: Medium-Term Forecast," in CRS, *Project Interdependence*, pp. 659–74, especially pp. 661 ff., which summarized the January 1977 estimates of the Organization for Economic Cooperation and Development, published in OECD, *World Energy Outlook*, which followed a 1974 OECD publication, *Energy Prospects to 1985*.

125. The full study (Wilson, *Energy: Global Prospects*) was cited earlier. A succinct summary, in Flower, "World Oil Production," gave the essential data, cited in the following discussion.

126. Hubbert, "World Oil," p. 638, estimated that in 1975 the ratio world-wide was 29.13 (10.71 in the United States, 18.09 in Latin America, 28.73 in Africa, 46.22 in the Middle East, 16.59 in the Soviet Union), and (on the basis of UN statistics) 30.16 in China. Lichtblau, "World Oil Supply and Demand," p. 686, estimated that it was 30.4 worldwide in 1976 but predicted that it will drop to 20 by 1990.

127. China published no comprehensive statistics on energy from 1960 until recently. Statistical series on China's energy from 1960 through 1976 are estimates, therefore. Because I believe the estimates of the CIA are, in general, the best, I have used them as the main statistical base for the following discussion for the years through 1976. For 1977–79 I rely on recently published official Chinese figures on output of oil, coal, natural gas, and electricity; see especially the State Statistical Bureau (SSB) Communiqués, in Foreign Broadcast Information Service, *Daily Report—People's Republic of China*, Department of Commerce, National Technical Information Service, June 27, 1979, p. L12, and April 30, 1980, p. L2. (Hereafter FBIS, *Daily Report—PRC*.) There also is a growing secondary literature—government reports and schol-

arly studies—on Chinese energy. Although many are already outdated, they provide useful background information. Among the best broad studies are the following: OER, CIA, "Energy Balance Projections," chap. 30, pp. 858–77; CIA, *China, Oil Production Prospects*, ER 77-10030U, June 1977 (hereafter CIA, *China, Oil*); Vaclav Smil, *China's Energy: Achievements, Problems, and Prospects* (Praeger, 1976); and Selig S. Harrison, *China, Oil, and Asia: Conflict Ahead?* (Columbia University Press, 1977). Two particularly valuable recent studies are NFAC, CIA, *Electric Power for China's Modernization;* and Kevin Fountain, "The Development of China's Offshore Oil," *China Business Review*, vol. 7, no. 1 (January–February 1980), pp. 23–36. Other useful books, papers, and articles include Chu-yuan Cheng, *China's Petroleum Industry, Output Growth and Export Potential* (Praeger, 1976); H. C. Ling, *The Petroleum Industry of the People's Republic of China* (Hoover Institution, 1975); Yuan-li Wu, with the assistance of H. C. Ling, *Economic Development and the Use of Energy Resources in Communist China* (Praeger, 1963); Vaclav Smil and Kim Woodard, "Perspectives on Energy in the People's Republic of China," in Jack M. Hollander, ed., *Annual Review of Energy* (Annual Review, Inc., 1977), pp. 307–42; Kim Woodard, "The International Energy Policies of the People's Republic of China" (Ph.D. dissertation, Stanford University, 1976); Vaclav Smil, "Energy in China: Achievements and Prospects," *China Quarterly*, no. 65 (March 1976), pp. 54–82, and "China's Energetics: A System Analysis," in Joint Economic Committee, *Chinese Economy Post-Mao*, 95 Cong. 2 sess. (GPO, 1978), pp. 323–69; A. A. Meyerhoff and Jan-Olaf Willums, "Petroleum Geology and Industry of the People's Republic of China," 1977, processed; Peter W. Colm, Rosemary Hayes, and Edwin Jones, *Implications of Prospective Chinese Petroleum Developments to 1980*, IDA Paper P-1229 (Institute for Defense Analyses, July 1976); H. I. Goodman, "Energy—A Major Determinant of the Asian Power Balance," paper prepared for a Ditchley Foundation Conference, February 1978, processed; Thomas Fingar, *China's Energy Policies and Resource Development*, United States-China Relations Report no. 1 (United States-China Relations Program, Stanford University, June 1976); K. P. Wang, *The People's Republic of China: A New Industrial Power with a Strong Mineral Base* (U.S. Department of the Interior, Bureau of Mines, 1975); K. C. Yeh, *Communist China's Petroleum Situation*, Rand Memorandum RM 3160-PR (Santa Monica, Calif.: Rand Corp., May 1962); K. C. Yeh and Y. L. Wu, "Oil and Strategy," in Institute of International Relations, *Proceedings of the Fifth Sino-American Conference on Mainland China* (Taipei: IIR, 1976), pp. 358–68; Thomas G. Rawski, "The Role of China in the World Energy Situation," May 7, 1973, processed; Yager and Steinberg, "China," in *Energy and U.S. Foreign Policy*, chap. 12, pp. 209–28 (based on Rawski's paper); CIA, *China: Energy Balance Projections*, A ER 75-75, November 1975; Tatsu Kambara, "The Petroleum Industry in China," *China Quarterly*, no. 60 (October–December 1974), pp. 699–719; Bobby A. Williams (a CIA analyst), "The Chinese Petroleum Industry: Growth and Prospects," in JEC, *China: A Reassessment of the Economy*, 94 Cong. 1 sess.

(GPO, 1975), pp. 225–63; Jerome Alan Cohen and Choon-ho Park, "China's Oil Policy," in Shao-chuan Leng, ed., *Post-Mao China and US-China Trade* (University Press of Virginia, 1977), chap. 6, pp. 108–40; Choon-ho Park and Jerome Alan Cohen, "The Politics of China's Oil Weapon," *Foreign Policy*, no. 20 (Fall 1975), pp. 28–49; Choon-ho Park, "Oil under Troubled Waters: The Northeast Asia Sea-Bed Controversy," *Harvard International Law Journal*, vol. 14, no. 2 (Spring 1973), pp. 212–60; Selig S. Harrison, "Time Bomb in East Asia," *Foreign Policy*, no. 20 (Fall 1975), pp. 3–27; Arthur Jay Klinghoffer, "Sino-Soviet Relations and the Politics of Oil," *Asian Survey*, vol. 16, no. 6 (June 1976), pp. 540–52; Jan-Olaf Willums, "China's Offshore Petroleum," *China Business Review*, vol. 4, no. 4 (July–August 1977), pp. 6–14; Nicholas Ludlow, "China's Oil," *U.S.-China Business Review*, vol. 1, no. 1 (January–February 1974), pp. 21–27; Peter Weintraub, "China's Oil Production and Consumption," *U.S.-China Business Review*, vol. 1, no. 1 (January–February 1974), pp. 29–31; CIA, *China: The Coal Industry*, ER 76-10691, November 1976; Genevieve C. Dean, "Energy in the People's Republic of China," *Energy Policy* (March 1974), pp. 33–54; Werner Klatt, "Learning from Taching [Daqing]," *Pacific Affairs*, vol. 50, no. 3 (Fall 1977), pp. 445–59; and King C. Chen, "China's Oil Policy," *Yale Review*, vol. 66, no. 1 (Autumn 1976), pp. 1–13.

128. My estimate, which is based on CIA data, is that China's total energy consumption increased from 42 million tons CE in 1952 to 626 million tons CE in 1979. But there are wide variations in earlier estimates. Smil, *China's Energy*, p. 140, estimated 22.85 million tons CE in 1949 and 377.21 million tons CE in 1974. In "China's Energetics," table 7, the same author estimated 30.4 million tons CE in 1950 and 445.0 million tons CE in 1976. The estimates in Smil and Woodard, "Perspectives on Energy," p. 313, were 42.3 million tons CE in 1952 and 379.7 million tons CE in 1974. Rawski, "Role of China," p. 11, estimated 1,964 trillion Btu in 1952 and 14,521 trillion Btu in 1971. And the estimates in Yager and Steinberg, *Energy and U.S. Foreign Policy*, p. 210, were 1,964 trillion Btu in 1952 and 11,893 trillion Btu in 1971. The UN estimates have been the highest of all; in UN, *WES 1950–74*, p. 92, and *WES 1971–75*, p. 31, they were 43.025 million tons CE in 1950 and 570.467 million tons CE in 1975; for the UN estimate for 1978, see note 129.

129. According to UN estimates, energy consumption in 1950 was 1.114 billion tons CE in the United States, 287 million tons in the Soviet Union, 221 million tons in the United Kingdom, 124 million tons in West Germany, 80 million tons in France, 73 million tons in Canada, 51 million tons in Poland, 49 million tons in East Germany, and 46 million tons in Japan, compared with just over 40 million tons in China; see UN, *WES 1950–74*, pp. 43, 79, 93, 97, 99, 109, 111. In 1978, according to UN statistics, energy consumption in the United States was 2.502 billion tons CE, in the Soviet Union 2.046 billion tons, and in Japan 439 million tons; see UN, *WES 1973–78*, pp. 23, 31, 39. This same source (p. 35) estimated China's total energy consumption in 1978 at 766 million tons CE, but almost certainly this was too high; a better estimate, based on CIA data, is in table 4-9. In my judgment, the UN's esti-

mates for China in 1978, compared with estimates based on CIA data, are much too high for coal because they simply use the official Chinese figure for total coal output, as is done in table 4-10, and do not convert raw coal to CE realistically.

130. UN figures showed the following ranking in energy production in 1950: United States, 1.165 billion tons CE; Soviet Union, 285 million tons; United Kingdom, 220 million tons; West Germany, 153 million tons; Venezuela, 116 million tons; Poland, 80 million tons; France, 54 million tons; Iran, 48 million tons; Japan, 44 million tons; East Germany, 44 million tons; and China, 43 million tons; see UN, *WES 1950–74*, pp. 42, 68, 70, 78, 92, 96, 98, 108, 110. UN figures on energy production show the following ranking in 1978: United States, 2.021 billion tons CE; Soviet Union, 1.854 billion tons; Saudi Arabia, 617 million tons; and China, 786 million tons; see UN, *WES 1973–78*, pp. 22, 30, 34, 38. My 624 million ton CE figure for China's total energy supply (mostly China's own output in 1978; see table 4-11) places China almost exactly on a par with Saudi Arabia. The certainty that China's total energy will rise and the probability that Saudi Arabian output will stabilize virtually ensure that China will be the third largest energy producer in the 1980s.

131. See Edwin O. Reischauer and John K. Fairbank, *East Asia: The Great Tradition* (Houghton Mifflin, 1960), p. 178. Kenneth Scott Latourette, *The Chinese: Their History and Culture* (Macmillan, 1946), pp. 584–85, said coal use probably started in the fifth century and was used for smelting as early as the Tang dynasty.

132. Reischauer and Fairbank, *East Asia*, p. 284.

133. G. C. Allen and Audrey G. Donnithorne, *Western Enterprise in Far Eastern Economic Development* (London: Allen and Unwin, 1954), pp. 149–60.

134. John K. Chang, *Industrial Development in Pre-Communist China* (Aldine, 1969), pp. 100, 122–23.

135. Ibid., p. 76.

136. See table 4-11.

137. These and the figures immediately below are from CIA, *China: Economic Indicators*, ER 77-10508, October 1977, p. 20; and (revised figures) NFAC, CIA, *China: A Statistical Compendium*, p. 9. The figure for 1949 is well above the level indicated in Chang, *Industrial Development*, p. 123 (12 million in 1948); the Chang figure, based on a UN source, probably was too low.

138. The 1977, 1978, and 1979 figures are official Chinese figures from the SSB Communiqués in FBIS, *Daily Report—PRC*, June 27, 1979, p. L12, and April 30, 1980, p. L2.

139. The following figures for large and small mines are from CIA, *China: Economic Indicators*, October 1977, p. 20. In 1977, when the CIA estimated that China's total coal output was 448 million tons, it estimated that 300 million tons were from large mines and 148 million tons from small ones. Smil, "China's Energetics," p. 367, estimated that in 1977, of China's total coal out-

put of 494 million tons, 331 million tons were from large mines, and 163 million tons were from small ones.

140. FBIS, *Daily Report—PRC*, June 7, 1979, p. L12.

141. CIA, *China: The Coal Industry*, p. 10.

142. Because transporting coal long distances is costly, savings on transportation costs may well have been the most important contribution of small mines.

143. See tables 4-10 and 4-11.

144. This was the U.S. government's estimate, as of 1976, in OER, CIA, "Energy Balance Projections," p. 863.

145. NFAC, CIA, *Electric Power for China's Modernization*, pp. 2–3.

146. CIA, *China: The Coal Industry*, p. 14. Smil, *China's Energy*, p. 146, had somewhat different estimates for 1974: industry, 56 percent; household and commercial use, 34 percent; transportation, 9 percent; and agriculture, 1 percent. (Smil broke down industrial use as follows: industry, 45 percent; electric generation, 11 percent.)

147. Theodore Shabad, *China's Changing Map* (Praeger, 1950), p. 56.

148. See Smil, *China's Energy*, p. 11; and Shabad, *China's Changing Map*, pp. 52–56. Compared with the most advanced world standards of coal technology, China is still far behind; probably only about 10 percent of China's coal is mined by large-scale surface recovery methods that are relatively efficient (in the United States the figure is about 50 percent); see Smil and Woodard, "Perspectives on Energy," pp. 314–15.

149. See the discussion in CIA, *China: The Coal Industry*, pp. 11–13. The huge Tangshan (Tangshan) earthquake in 1976 also was a serious blow to the industry.

150. These and the figures below are my calculations, from estimates in ibid., p. 1, for earlier years, and the revised estimates in NFAC, CIA, *China: A Statistical Compendium*, p. 9, for 1970 and 1976. See also table 4-10. Smil, *China's Energy*, p. 23, estimated that the rate from 1913 through 1974, excluding periods of severe military or political disruption, was about 5.4 percent.

151. Hsiao Han (Xiao Han), "Developing Coal Industry at High Speed," *Peking Review*, no. 8 (February 24, 1978), pp. 5–7. Hsiao also stated, "The key to speedy development of the coal industry lies in mechanization."

152. Ibid., p. 6.

153. Chinese Ministry of Information, *China Handbook, 1937–1943* (Macmillan, 1943), p. 480, gave the estimate of the National Geological Survey of China, which was 241 billion tons. Cressey, *Asia's Lands and People* (McGraw-Hill, 1952), p. 79, cited a Geological Survey of China estimate of 284 billion.

154. These were Chinese Ministry of Coal Industry estimates, cited in Smil, *China's Energy*, pp. 7–8.

155. From A. Parker, "World Energy Resources, A Survey," March 3, 1975, cited in Smil, *China's Energy*, p. 172.

156. CIA, *China: The Coal Industry*, pp. 2–3.

157. Vice Premier Chao Tzu-yang (Zhao Ziyang) to Senator Robert C. Byrd; see "Report of Trip to the People's Republic of China," *Congressional Record* (July 23, 1980), p. S9579.

158. Smil, *China's Energy*, pp. 172 ff. Most of China's coal is high quality. It has been estimated that about 77 percent is bituminous and about 19 percent anthracite; see CIA, *China: The Coal Industry*, p. 3. See also Smil, *China's Energy*, p. 11.

159. This is my calculation. CIA analysts, in *China: The Coal Industry*, p. 2, asserted that at current rates of consumption, and with a 50 percent rate of recovery, probable reserves (1.5 trillion tons) would be equal to 1,700 years of supply.

160. Ibid., pp. 1–2, 5–7, 11–13. See also Dean, "Energy in the PRC," p. 53; and Smil and Woodard, "Perspectives on Energy," pp. 317–18.

161. CIA analysts in many studies have converted raw coal from small mines to standard CE at a rate of 0.6, compared with a rate of 0.8 for coal from large mines; see OER, CIA, "Energy Balance Projections," p. 872. Smil has used even lower rates: 0.5 for coal from small mines and 0.7 for coal from large mines.

162. Smil, *China's Energy*, p. 21.

163. Ibid., p. 9. CIA, *China: The Coal Industry*, pp. 2–3, cited a Chinese study that indicated that nearly three-fourths of the country's reserves are in four North China provinces, and a British study that calculated that 91 percent of the country's reserves are in North, Northeast, and Northwest China and only 9 percent in East, Central-South, and Southwest China. At present, nearly five-sixths of China's output comes from the North and West; see ibid., p. 7.

164. See Wang, *People's Republic of China*, pp. 18–19; CIA, *China: The Coal Industry*, p. 7; and Hsiao Han, "Developing Coal," p. 6.

165. Wang, *People's Republic of China*, pp. 21–26.

166. Cited by Smil, *China's Energy*, p. 9.

167. OER, CIA, "Energy Balance Projections," p. 875.

168. See, for example, Smil, *China's Energy*, pp. 23–25. The author stated that he believed it would be difficult for China even to sustain what he estimated to be the 1913–74 growth rate in coal output—5.4 percent.

169. CIA analysts until recently assumed a continuing "substitution of oil for coal" in China; see OER, CIA, "Energy Balance Projections," p. 866.

170. See CIA, *China: The Coal Industry*, pp. 10–11, 16. Even during 1973–74, China imported $116 million of coal mining equipment, mainly from the United Kingdom, West Germany, Poland, and the United States; since 1977 the amounts have risen, and the Chinese have negotiated for some huge purchases. Although China now produces the bulk of its coal mining equipment, it still cannot make all of the sophisticated equipment that it needs, particularly equipment requiring high-grade steel. Imports of coal mining equipment possibly will be large during the next few years.

171. Taching is China's largest oil field, located in the Northeast.

172. Hua Kuo-feng (Hua Guofeng), government work report, February 26, 1978, in FBIS, *Daily Report—PRC*, March 7, 1978, p. D17.

173. This was a statement by a Chinese government minister to a visiting American congressman in early 1978; unattributable. The Chinese press in 1977–78 had many articles stressing the importance of coal, of which the one

by Hsiao Han, cited earlier, was representative. In early 1978, China reported a significant increase in the rate of coal output; see, for example, FBIS, *Daily Report—PRC*, March 31, 1978, p. E17. The Chinese also stressed the need to conserve coal and to make better use of poor-quality coal with low caloric content (including coal tailings, coal pebbles, stone coal, lignite, and peat); see, for example, FBIS, *Daily Report—PRC*, January 25, 1977, p. E6, December 15, 1977, p. E13, and February 23, 1978, p. E13. According to one Chinese estimate, the country could, simply by using more efficient methods in consumption, save 60 million tons of raw coal, 6 million tons of coking coal, and more than 6 million tons of other fuels; see articles in *People's Daily* (*Renmin Ribao*), August 9, 1977, and September 25, 1977, cited in Nai-Ruenn Chen, "Economic Modernization in Post-Mao China: Policies, Problems, and Prospects," in JEC, *Chinese Economy Post-Mao*, p. 180.

174. *Peking Review* (later *Beijing Review*), no. 14 (April 7, 1978), pp. 8–9. These developments also will require a large and expensive expansion of China's power transmission grid. At present, there are some regional grids but no national grid in China; see Dean, "Energy in the PRC," p. 44; Smil and Woodard, "Perspectives on Energy," p. 311; and William W. Clarke, "China's Electric Power Industry," *China Business Review*, vol. 4, no. 5 (September–October 1977), p. 33.

175. See p. 416 and note 151, above.

176. FBIS, *Daily Report—PRC*, November 1, 1978, p. E22.

177. FBIS, *Daily Report—PRC*, June 7, 1979, p. L12.

178. See part I, p. 95.

179. FBIS, *Daily Report—PRC*, June 4, 1979, p. L7.

180. Ibid., p. L8.

181. SSB Communiqué, in FBIS, *Daily Report—PRC*, April 30, 1980, p. L5.

182. Ibid.

183. OER, CIA, "Energy Balance Projections," p. 862, estimated 1976 output at 38 billion cubic meters, or 10 percent of China's energy. But on the basis of official Chinese data on 1979, released in 1980, the CIA reduced its estimate for 1976 to 10.2 billion cubic meters, or 3 percent of China's energy; see tables 4-10 and 4-11.

184. CIA, *Handbook of Economic Statistics, 1977*, p. 78, estimated 24.72 trillion cubic feet, or 700 billion cubic meters. Smil, *China's Energy*, p. 29, cited estimates of 500 billion by Ling and 598 billion by Meyerhoff. Wang, *People's Republic of China*, p. 45, cited one estimate of 850 billion cubic meters. In 1980 the CIA estimated that China's "ultimately recoverable" oil and natural gas together may total the equivalent of 100 billion barrels of "oil and oil equivalents"; see NFAC, CIA, *Electric Power for China's Modernization*, p. 1. Of this, a sizable proportion is natural gas.

185. Conversion rate: 1,000 cubic meters of natural gas equal 1.332 tons of coal equivalent; see OER, CIA, "Energy Balance Projections," p. 872. One ton of CE is roughly equal to 0.666 ton of oil.

186. CIA, *Handbook of Economic Statistics, 1977*, p. 78, listed twelve countries with reserves larger than China (many much larger); its figures for the

United States and the Soviet Union, for example, were 219 trillion and 812 trillion cubic feet, respectively. It is possible that, with further exploration, the estimates for China could rise substantially.

187. Based on table 4-10.

188. The SSB Communiqué on 1979 reported that output was 14.51 billion cubic meters; see FBIS, *Daily Report—PRC*, April 30, 1980, p. L2.

189. OER, CIA, "Energy Balance Projections," p. 872, estimated 80 percent; Smil, *China's Energy*, p. 44, estimated 95 percent; Fingar, *China's Energy Policies*, p. 21, estimated 90 percent.

190. Smil, *China's Energy*, p. 44.

191. When I visited Chengtu (Chengdu), capital city of Szechwan (Sichuan), in October 1977, most of the city's buses were fueled by natural gas, which was carried in huge plastic bags on their roofs.

192. OER, CIA, "Energy Balance Projections," p. 873.

193. Ibid., p. 877. Smil, *China's Energy*, p. 149, estimated that in the mid-1970s, 56 percent was used in industry, 40 percent in residential and commercial use, and 4 percent in electric power generation.

194. See table 4-11.

195. Among known natural gas deposits outside of Szechwan that could be further developed are those at Takang (Dagang) and Shengli (Shengli) oil fields, some in areas south of Shanghai (Shanghai), and others in the Tsaidam basin; see Wang, *Peoples' Republic of China*, pp. 47–48; and Fingar, *China's Energy Policies*, p. 21.

196. On the growth of China's petrochemical industries in the first half of the 1970s, see Sy Yuan, "China's Chemicals," *U.S.-China Business Review*, vol. 2, no. 6 (November–December 1975), pp. 37–53. For later developments, see numerous reports in *China Business Review*.

197. By 1976, perhaps, according to some estimates, 3 billion to 3.5 billion cubic meters were used in fertilizer plants and 1.5 billion to 2 billion cubic meters in other petrochemical plants; see Fingar, *China's Energy Policies*, p. 23.

198. Ibid., p. 21.

199. The Chinese have discussed this with officials of Bridgestone Liquefaction Gas of Tokyo; see Wang, *People's Republic of China*, p. 47.

200. See OER, CIA, "Energy Balance Projections," p. 875. The figures in the original source are in coal equivalent; I have converted them at the rate of 1 ton CE equals 750.75 cubic meters of gas.

201. Based on UN, *WES 1971–75*, pp. 2–39, 166–219.

202. Based on ibid., pp. 18, 36, 193, 200. U.S. electricity production was 2 trillion kilowatt-hours; hydroelectricity production was 306 billion kilowatt-hours (equal to 38.25 million tons CE, at the conversion rate of 1,000 kilowatt-hours equal 0.125 ton CE); total U.S. output of primary energy was 2.037 billion tons CE. Soviet electricity production was 1.039 trillion kilowatt-hours; hydroelectricity output was 126 billion kilowatt-hours (or 15.75 million tons CE); total primary energy output was 1.650 billion tons CE.

203. Smil, *China's Energy*, pp. 67 ff.

204. See ibid., p. 69; and Smil and Woodard, "Perspectives on Energy," p. 308. Also, Chou En-lai (Zhou Enlai) in 1957 stated that China has a potential of 540 million kilowatts (that is, 540 gigawatts); see FBIS, *Daily Report—PRC*, October 17, 1977, p. E16. Smil and Woodard estimated that 300 gigawatts of China's 540 gigawatt potential are suitable for industrial development, but much of it is in remote areas. The potential of the Yangtze (Yangzi) Valley is estimated at 230 million kilowatts, and many power stations have already been built on its tributaries; see FBIS, *Daily Report—PRC*, October 12, 1977, p. E16. In the discussion that follows, capacity is measured in kilowatts, megawatts (thousands of kilowatts), and gigawatts (millions of kilowatts).

205. Vice Premier Chao Tzu-yang gave this 600 gigawatt estimate to Senator Robert C. Byrd on July 8, 1980; see "Report of Trip to the People's Republic of China," *Congressional Record* (July 23, 1980), p. S9579.

206. NFAC, CIA, *Electric Power for China's Modernization*, pp. 1, 8.

207. Calculated from ibid., pp. 1–2; and table 4-10. The figures on hydroelectric power output in my table, obtained orally from the CIA in July 1980, are slightly lower than CIA estimates in *Electric Power for China's Modernization*, which was published in May 1980.

208. In 1976, the Chinese stated that in the previous ten years, some 56,000 medium and small hydropower stations had been built in rural areas in China; see FBIS, *Daily Report—PRC*, June 15, 1976, p. E11. See also Denis Hayes, *Energy for Development: Third World Options*, Worldwatch Paper no. 15, December 1977, p. 28; Fingar, *China's Energy Policies*, p. 16; and Smil and Woodard, "Perspectives on Energy," p. 316. The latter states that 80 percent of these small hydro stations are in eight southern provinces (areas of high rainfall). In early 1973, I visited hydro stations of this sort serving rural communes in Kwangtung (Guangdong); they were primitive but nevertheless functional.

209. Hayes, *Energy for Development*, p. 28, cited an estimate of one-third, but NFAC, CIA, *Electric Power for China's Modernization*, p. 9, estimated that in early 1979, 88,000 small hydropower plants (with an average capacity of 61 kilowatts) had a total capacity of 5.380 gigawatts, which was 42 percent of the CIA's estimate of total hydropower capacity in China in 1979 (which was 12.800 gigawatts).

210. Converted at the following rates: 1,000 kilowatt-hours equal 0.125 ton CE and 0.083 ton OE.

211. The following discussion is based mainly on NFAC, CIA, *Electric Power for China's Modernization*. Although outdated in some respects, Clarke, "China's Electric Power Industry," pp. 43–38, provided useful background.

212. Many articles discussed the completion of China's largest hydropower station, Liuchiahsia (Liujiaxia), on the Yellow River, serving Shensi (Shaanxi), Kansu (Gansu), and Tsinghai (Qinghai) with 220- and 330-kilovolt transforming stations. One stated that by 1975 this station had a capacity of 1.225 gigawatts and generated 5.7 billion kilowatt-hours a year; see "China's Biggest Hydro-Power Station," *Peking Review*, no. 7 (February 14, 1975), pp. 11 ff. Another stated that Liuchiahsia already, by 1977, had three large generating

plants with an installed capacity able to generate 1.68 million kilowatts per hour; FBIS, *Daily Report—PRC*, October 17, 1977, p. E16.

213. See note 174.

214. James P. Sterba, "Mondale Says Talks in Peking Put Ties on New Basis," *New York Times*, August 29, 1979, and "American Aid for the Lamps of China," *New York Times*, September 2, 1979.

215. NFAC, CIA, *Electric Power for China's Modernization*, pp. 9–14. On one major hydro project already under way on the Yangtze River, and debate over others, see *China Business Review*, vol. 7, no. 3 (May–June 1980), pp. 11–23.

216. OER, CIA, "Energy Balance Projections," p. 875, estimated 6 to 10 percent, but this was before the increased stress placed on hydroelectricity starting in 1978.

217. For background, see Kim Woodard, "China's Nuclear Development Program: Problems and Prospects," paper prepared for the International Studies Association Annual Convention, March 1979, processed, and "Evaluating Peking's Nuclear Potential," *Asian Wall Street Journal*, June 4, 1979. Woodard's projections were overoptimistic.

218. Fingar, *China's Energy Policies*, p. 16.

219. Hua Kuo-feng simply stated, "We must . . . set up nuclear power stations"; see FBIS, *Daily Report—PRC*, March 7, 1978, p. D23. Fang Yi (Fang Yi) stated, "We should accelerate our research in atomic power generation and speed up the building of atomic power plants"; see "Outline National Plan," *Peking Review*, no. 14 (April 7, 1978), p. 9. These were the most important public statements on the subject. However, a year earlier, in 1977, Vice Premier Li Hsien-nien (Li Xiannian) had personally told British visitors that China intended to build nuclear power stations (see FBIS, *Daily Report— PRC*, January 5, 1977, p. E-18), and in early 1978 a leading Chinese scientist, Chien San-chiang (Qian Sanqiang) had told a Yugoslav news reporter that China was planning and designing such plants; see FBIS, *Daily Report—PRC*, January 27, 1978, p. E11. In 1978 the Chinese press also published a number of articles that favored developing nuclear power; see, for example, "Utilization of Nuclear Energy and the Struggle against Hegemonism," *Peking Review*, no. 15 (April 14, 1978), pp. 10–12.

220. See, for example, *Current Scene* (Hong Kong, March 1973), p. 7. (China has uranium resources; see Yuan-li Wu, ed., *China: A Handbook* [Praeger, 1973], p. 77.)

221. See part II, p. 135.

222. Kevin Fountain, "On the Back Burner: Nuclear Power in China," *China Business Review*, vol. 6, no. 6 (November–December 1979), p. 38.

223. Ibid., p. 40.

224. Reuters, "China Reportedly Planning Commercial Nuclear Plant," *Washington Post*, April 6, 1980. The report said the plant would have two 900 megawatt reactors.

225. Calculated from data in Warren H. Donnelly, "Nuclear Power through 1990," in CRS, *Project Interdependence*, p. 269.

226. For a general discussion of biogas, see Smil, *China's Energy*, pp. 102 ff.; and Rustan Lalkaka, "Small and Medium Scale Industries in China," UNIDO/ 10 D.172, March 29, 1978, processed.

227. Ibid. Gas from biogas pits that I saw in Szechwan Province in 1977 was used mainly for cooking.

228. In May 1978 the Chinese press stated that in the entire country there were 5,760,010 pits—20 percent more than 1976; of these, more than 4.3 million were in Szechwan, but more than 1,000 of China's counties had at least a few; see FBIS, *Daily Report—PRC*, May 22, 1978, p. E16. In June 1979, the Chinese press reported that 7.1 million peasant families used methane gas (5 million of them in Szechwan); see FBIS, *Daily Report—PRC*, June 8, 1979, p. L16. By early 1980, it was reported that 8 million pits provided cooking and lighting gas for 30 million people; see Kevin Fountain, "New Energy Sources in China," *China Business Review*, vol. 6, no. 5 (September–October 1979), p. 30.

229. Smil, *China's Energy*, p. 105.

230. The following discussion is based on Fountain, "New Energy Sources in China," pp. 28–33; Smil, *China's Energy*, pp. 110–11; Smil and Woodard, "Perspectives on Energy," p. 317; and Fingar, *China's Energy Policies*, p. 15.

231. A 1978 press report discussed solar furnaces and water heaters, solar cells, and the use of solar energy in electric power generation; see FBIS, *Daily Report—PRC*, May 28, 1978, p. E6.

232. Colm and others, *Implications*, pp. 56–57.

233. Rawski, "Role of China," pp. 11–12. See also Yeh, *Communist China's Petroleum Situation*.

234. Colm and others, *Implications*, pp. 56–57.

235. Smil, *China's Energy*, pp. 98–102, 108–09.

236. Colm and others, *Implications*, p. 57. Also see the general discussion of the substitution of commercial for traditional fuels in Darmstadter, *Energy*, pp. 36–38.

237. See Kambara, "Petroleum Industry," p. 699; Smil, *China's Energy*, p. 26; and Park and Cohen, "Politics of China's Oil Weapon," p. 29. The latter source says oil was used in the first century B.C. and the first well was developed in the early sixteenth century, more than 300 years before the first wells in the United States and Europe. When I visited the Tzuliuching (Ziliujing) salt well in 1948, no use was being made of the oil and gas there.

238. Smil, *China's Energy*, p. 26.

239. Cressey, *Asia's Lands and People*, p. 80.

240. These tonnage figures are my calculations; the figures in barrels are those in the sources cited.

241. Chinese Ministry of Information, *China Handbook, 1937–1943*, p. 483.

242. Ibid.

243. Smil, *China's Energy*, p. 31. The three operating wells inherited by the Communists in 1949—Yumen (Yumen) and Tushantzu (Dushanzi) in Sinkiang (Xinjiang) and Yenchang (Yanchang) in Shensi—produced about

100,000 tons a year (less than 2,000 b/d) and the two oil shale plants built by the Japanese at Fushun (Fushun) in Manchuria produced about 50,000 tons (1,000 b/d); see CIA, *China, Oil*, p. 9.

244. CIA, *China, Oil*, p. 9. See also the chart in Smil, *China's Energy*, p. 32. On Sino-Soviet cooperation, see Dean, "Energy in the PRC," pp. 40–42; and Kambara, "Petroleum Industry," pp. 700–02.

245. CIA, *China, Oil*, pp. 11–21, has details on each of China's major oil fields, with production estimates, technical data, and information on the oil's characteristics; the following discussion relies heavily on this source.

246. The Chinese essentially adapted and further developed the technology received from the Russians, although this fact is underplayed now.

247. All output estimates on particular fields, except where otherwise noted, are from CIA, *China, Oil*, p. 9.

248. My calculation from data in ibid.

249. Shengli has received less priority in allocations of money, manpower, and skills than Taching; it is much poorer in equipment. See Stephanie Green, "Shengli Journal," *China Business Review*, vol. 5, no. 1 (January–February 1978), pp. 31–35.

250. Takang is close to Shengli and may be part of the same general formation; the structures in shallow offshore areas in the Pohai (Bohai) Gulf may also be connected geologically. Early exploration in the Pohai appeared to be managed by the authorities at Takang; see CIA, *China, Oil*, p. 13.

251. Ibid., p. 9.

252. CIA estimates of China's oil production appear to have been remarkably close to reality. In 1978 its analysts estimated that China's crude oil output in 1977 was 90.3 million tons; see CIA, *China: Economic Indicators*, December 1978, p. 22. The official Chinese figure for 1977 output (published in 1979) was 93.64 million tons; its subsequently published official figures for 1978 and 1979 were 104.05 million tons and 106.15 million tons; see FBIS, *Daily Report—PRC*, June 27, 1979, p. L12, and April 30, 1980, p. L2. In 1979 the CIA slightly adjusted some of its estimates for earlier years, raising them as follows: for 1965, from 10.961 million to 11.374 million; for 1970, from 28.211 million to 30.129 million; and for 1976, from 83.608 million to 86.760 million; see NFAC, CIA, *China: A Statistical Compendium*, July 1979, p. 9. These revised figures are used in table 4-10; the CIA's earlier estimates are in table 4-12, with the revised estimates in brackets.

253. In 1975 three major shale oil sites—two at Fushun and one at Maoming (Maoming)—produced 1.4 million tons of oil, and Fushun produced 300,000 tons of liquefied coal; see CIA, *China, Oil*, p. 10.

254. See note 252 and table 4-10.

255. Calculated from the 1950 figure in CIA, *China, Oil*, p. 9; and the 1976 figure in table 4-10.

256. The oil rates are my calculations from tables 4-10 and 4-12. The rate of increase in coal output from 1960 through 1976 was 3.5 percent (my calculation from the revised CIA figures in table 4-10; and CIA, *China: The Coal Industry*, p. iii). Also see note 150.

257. These and the following rates are calculated from the latest CIA estimates; see note 252.

258. My calculations from data in UN, *WES 1950–74*, pp. 212, 226, and *WES 1971–75*, pp. 67, 70.

259. FBIS, *Daily Report—PRC*, July 2, 1979, p. L19.

260. Ibid.

261. Minister of Petroleum and Chemical Industries, Kang Shih-en (Kang Shien), in FBIS, *Daily Report—PRC*, February 22, 1978, p. E20. This article also claimed that new discoveries had recently been made in widely separated areas from Sinkiang to Pohai Bay and Heilungkiang (Heilongjiang) to the South China Sea and heralded the start of a "great leap period of development" which would "not only be a powerful force for modernizing China but will also work noticeable changes in China's economic relations with foreign countries."

262. CIA, *China, Oil*, pp. 5, 8.

263. Maurice J. Terman of the U.S. Geological Survey, cited in ibid., p. 5. Some Chinese dispute this, however.

264. China's shale oil deposits have been estimated by the Chinese themselves at 360 billion tons of shale, which could contain (at 6 percent oil per ton of shale) about 20 billion tons of oil; see Park and Cohen, "The Politics of China's Oil Weapon," p. 32. In the 1950s Soviet geologists estimated that China's shale oil reserves totaled about 21 billion tons (153.3 billion barrels); see CIA, *China, Oil*, p. 7. However, CIA analysts believe that "China's large shale oil deposits will be irrelevant in the next ten to twenty years. The exploitation of shale would be prohibitively expensive and irrational as long as liquid oil is available"; see ibid., p. 8.

265. Ibid., p. 5. Meyerhoff and Willums, "Petroleum Geology and Industry," p. 1, used the figure 5.398 billion tons (39.51 billion barrels) for "produced, proved, probable, and potential onshore oil recovery" (this was not counting shale oil). Smil, "China's Energetics," table 5, lists many different estimates.

266. CIA, *China, Oil*, p. 5.

267. Ibid., pp. 5–6.

268. Kambara, "Petroleum Industry," p. 711.

269. *Petroleum Times*, July 11, 1975, p. 25, cited in CIA, *China, Oil*, p. 5. See also Harrison, "Time Bomb in East Asia," p. 6.

270. Goodman, "Energy—A Major Determinant," p. 3.

271. Harrison, *China, Oil, and Asia*, p. 46.

272. CIA, *China, Oil*, p. 6.

273. Ibid. Meyerhoff and Willums, "Petroleum Geology and Industry," p. 1, estimated "proved, probable, and potential" offshore reserves at 4.11 billion tons (30 billion barrels).

274. Goodman, "Energy—A Major Determinant," pp. 3–4. His original figures were in barrels (I have converted them at 7.3 barrels to the ton).

275. Fountain, "The Development of China's Offshore Oil," p. 23.

276. CIA, *China, Oil,* p. 7. In some estimates, the CIA is fairly conservative in totaling China's "proved and probable" reserves; see CIA, *Handbook of Economic Statistics, 1977,* p. 78, which lists such reserves as 2.74 billion tons.

277. Meyerhoff and Willums, "Petroleum Geology and Industry," p. 1.

278. Hubbert, "World Oil," p. 638. CIA figures in *China, Oil,* p. 7, on "proved plus probable" reserves in these areas are slightly higher. Estimates on world energy vary, in part because of definitional problems. See, in addition to the sources cited above, *Oil and Gas Journal,* no. 72 (December 30, 1974), pp. 108–09, which gives a world total of 98 billion tons (which compares with Hubbert's figure of 78 billion). Goodman, "Energy—A Major Determinant," app. exhibit 4, gave a figure of 75 billion tons (550 billion barrels).

279. Hubbert, "World Oil," p. 639.

280. In July 1979, Vice Minister Chen Lieh-min (Chen Liemin) of the Ministry of Petroleum Industry said that China would concentrate on prospecting for more oil deposits for the next three years; see *Asian Wall Street Journal,* July 2, 1979.

281. This was the goal set by Hua Kuo-feng at a "National Conference on Learning from Taching in Industry," in 1977; see *Peking Review,* no. 21 (May 20, 1977), p. 15.

282. See, for example, "Jenchiu [Renqiu]—A New High-Yielding Oil-field," in *Peking Review,* no. 41 (October 13, 1978); "PRC Oil Discovery in Sinkiang," in FBIS, *Daily Report—PRC,* October 13, 1978, p. A8; and "Several New Oil Fields Discovered Outside Taching," *Ta Kung Pao* (Dagong Bao), July 18, 1978, in FBIS, *Daily Report—PRC,* July 18, 1978, p. N3. See also note 292.

283. *Renmin Ribao* (*People's Daily*), July 6, 1978; the editorial said that in the next twenty years China should drill five times as many oil wells as it had in the previous twenty-eight years; FBIS, *Daily Report—PRC,* July 12, 1978, p. E17.

284. My calculation from data in CIA, *China, Oil,* p. 9.

285. Ibid., p. 7; these figures were from the private study cited. See also Smil, "China's Energetics," table 6.

286. The estimate of Taching's ultimate recoverable oil is from Colm and others, *Implications,* p. 9; the figures on Taching's output are from CIA, *China, Oil,* p. 9.

287. CIA, *China, Oil,* p. 22.

288. "China Reports Oil Reserves Up," *New York Times,* September 19, 1979.

289. CIA, *China, Oil,* p. 22.

290. These and the following figures are from ibid., p. 7.

291. Kambara, "Petroleum Industry," p. 717, gave estimates of how much China must discover in new reserves each year to maintain a 30/1 reserve/production (R/P) rate; by the early 1980s, his estimates indicate, the figures will be very large.

292. See "Petroleum Minister Confirms New Discoveries," in FBIS, *Daily*

Report—PRC, February 27, 1978, pp. E20, E21. There are also reports of rich new deposit discoveries in South China; see FBIS, *Daily Report—PRC*, May 11, 1978, p. N5. See also note 282.

293. At Taching it took nine years for production to reach 10 millions tons a year; at Shengli it took more than twelve years. At Takang, production was still under 5 million tons a year after nine years; CIA, *China, Oil*, p. 9.

294. Yu Chiu-li (Yu Qiuli), Vice Premier and head of the State Planning Commission; see "Mobilize the Whole Party and the Nation's Working Class and Strive to Build Taching-Type Enterprises throughout the Country," *Peking Review*, no. 22 (May 27, 1977), p. 17.

295. Vice Minister Sun Ching-wen (Sun Jingwen), on a visit to Japan in February 1978; see *Ta Kung Pao*, February 3, 1978, cited in Nai-Ruenn Chen, "Economic Modernization," p. 197.

296. Hubbert, "World Oil," p. 638.

297. My calculation, based on China's 1976 production of almost 87 million tons and its presumed "proved reserves" of 2.16 billion.

298. My calculation, based on the assumptions that oil production in the North and Northeast was about 68 million tons in 1976 and that likely remaining "proved reserves" may have been about 550 million. The Chinese have stated, however, that Taching has been "maintaining an annual recovery rate of 2 to 3 percent of the subsurface oil reserves, although over 25 percent was recovered in the oldest area over the past 17 years" (this implied an R/P rate of 33/1 to 50/1); see "Taching Oilfield Surpasses World's Advanced Level," in FBIS, *Daily Report—PRC*, April 14, 1977, p. E21.

299. Fingar, *China's Energy Policies*, pp. 33–40. Recently, the Chinese claimed that "per well output consistently remains stable"; see FBIS, *Daily Report—PRC*, March 29, 1978, p. E26, and the FBIS source cited in note 309. However, this seems questionable now.

300. Colm and others, *Implications*, p. 23, gave an estimate for investment in Taching in the 1960s and early 1970s which was below $1 billion, but it probably was too low, perhaps *much* too low.

301. Cheng, *China's Petroleum Industry*, pp. 188–89. Cheng's estimate may have been too high. Goodman, "Energy—A Major Determinant," p. 2, estimated that the costs of developing new oil fields recently has ranged from a low of $500 (in 1977 dollars) for each new daily barrel of production in some Middle Eastern countries to $7,000 in some fields in the North Sea. He estimated (p. 3) that development costs may average $4,000 per new daily barrel in the Western Pacific, or about $4 billion for each million barrels a day (50 million tons a year) of new production. Klatt, "Learning from Taching," p. 456, said that costs range, per field, from a few thousand dollars to as much as $1.5 million. (It is not wholly clear what he meant by "field.")

302. Colm and others, *Implications*, p. 23.

303. A claim made by the chief geological engineer at Taching; FBIS, *Daily Report—PRC*, March 29, 1978, p. E27.

304. This, reportedly, was a U.S. government estimate in 1978; see "The

Scramble to Exploit China's Oil Reserves," *Business Week* (October 30, 1978), p. 155.

305. CIA, *China, Oil*, p. 25. See also Smil, *China's Energy*, pp. 37–39.

306. CIA, *China, Oil*, p. 25.

307. Fingar, *China's Energy Policies*, pp. 35–37. The Chinese could use other ways, besides heating, to move waxy oil; the alternatives include emulsifying the oil in water (a method used in Indonesia) and dispersing the oil in methanol (a method developed for Alaska).

308. CIA, *China, Oil*, p. 26. See also FBIS, *Daily Report—PRC*, August 31, 1976, p. E5.

309. See Smil, *China's Energy*, p. 39; and FBIS, *Daily Report—PRC*, August 31, 1976, p. E5.

310. CIA, *China, Oil*, p. 26.

311. Ibid., p. 5.

312. For data on characteristics of Chinese oil from particular fields, see Smil, "China's Energetics," table F-1; and CIA, *China, Oil*, pp. 8–10, 11 ff.

313. In 1977 the Chinese announced the opening of their first underground water-sealed rock cave oil depot; see FBIS, *Daily Report—PRC*, April 14, 1977, p. E19. They say they will build more depots of that kind because they are cheaper than steel tanks.

314. For data on and discussion of China's energy consumption, see OER, CIA, "Energy Balance Projections," pp. 862–64, 867–71; and NFAC, CIA, *China: A Statistical Compendium*, July 1979, p. 10. Also see Smil, *China's Energy*, p. 138; Smil and Woodard, "Perspectives on Energy," pp. 312 ff.; Colm and others, *Implications*, pp. 51 ff.; Rawski, "The Role of China," pp. 5 ff.; and Yager and Steinberg, *Energy and U.S. Foreign Policy*, pp. 210 ff., 215–20; as well as the CIA's earlier estimates in *China: Energy Balance Projections*, November 1975. UN estimates are in *WES 1950–74*, p. 93, and *WES 1971–75*, p. 31.

315. See table 4-9.

316. My calculations, based on ibid.

317. My calculations from data in Darmstadter, *Energy*, p. 10; UN, *WES 1950–74*, p. 111, and *WES 1971–75*, p. 37.

318. My calculations from data in Darmstadter, *Energy*, p. 10; *WES 1950–74*, p. 79, and *WES 1971–75*, p. 27. Until recently, Japan's total energy consumption surpassed China's, but by 1975 China's was larger. UN statistics indicate Japan's energy consumption in 1975 totaled 402 million tons CE; CIA statistics indicate that China's consumption in 1975 totaled 471 million tons CE (see table 4-9).

319. My calculations from data in UN, *WES 1950–74*, pp. 85, 91, and *WES 1971–75*, pp. 29, 31.

320. My calculation from data in UN, *WES 1950–74*, p. 83, and *WES 1971–75*, p. 29.

321. These and the following figures are from OER, CIA, "Energy Balance Projections," pp. 864–65. For somewhat different estimates, see Smil, *China's Energy*, p. 144.

322. NFAC, CIA, *Electric Power for China's Modernization*, p. 2.

323. Smil, *China's Energy*, pp. 139–41.

324. Colm and others, *Implications*, pp. 58–60, citing CIA figures for 1957. This study stated that CIA figures for 1974 showed a drop in the share of these four industries in energy consumption to 54 percent, but the authors question the validity of these later figures.

325. Although limited personal observation provides no basis for generalizing about such matters, I was impressed, during trips to China in 1972–73, 1977, and 1979, by widespread evidence of wasteful and inefficient use of energy in some small rural plants; other observers also have noted this.

326. These and the figures below are based on NFAC, CIA, *China: A Statistical Compendium*, p. 10; see table 4-9.

327. Ibid., and table 4-11.

328. On energy, see "Li Renjun [Li Jen-chun] Reports on Economy to NPC Standing Committee," in FBIS, *Daily Report—PRC*, April 9, 1980, p. L2; as well as tables 4-9, 4-10, and 4-11. On national income, see part I, p. 113 and table 1-3. For CIA's 1979 GNP estimate, see CIA, *China: The Continuing Search for a Modernization Strategy*, Research Paper ER 80-10248, April 1980, p. 1.

329. This is not to imply that China is on the verge of a consumer economy in any way comparable to that in the major non-Communist industrial nations; it will continue to restrict personal energy consumption. Nevertheless, increases in living standards, which the leaders have promised, are likely to result in some increases in per capita household and personal energy consumption, at least in urban areas.

330. The world figures here and below are from UN, *WES 1950–74*, p. 3, and *WES 1971–75*, p. 3. The Chinese figures are my calculations, based on population figures from table 3-1, and the energy consumption figures in table 4-9.

331. In 1975, per capita energy consumption in these countries was as follows: India, 221 kilograms CE; Indonesia, 178; Egypt, 405; Nigeria, 90; Zaire, 78; Chile, 765; Brazil, 670; Lebanon, 928; Turkey, 630; South Korea, 1,038; and peninsular Malaysia, 552; see UN, *WES 1971–75*, pp. 11, 13, 15, 19, 27, 29. If China in 1975 had had the same per capita energy consumption as Japan (3,622 kilograms CE; see ibid., p. 27), it would have consumed 3.31 billion tons CE (about seven times the 471 million that it actually consumed). (This is my calculation on the basis of figures in the sources cited in note 330.)

332. The following discussion relies heavily on OER, CIA, "Energy Balance Projections," pp. 865–71, 874–77.

333. The study gives "high," "medium," and "low" estimates. It was apparent, however, that CIA analysts were inclined to believe that the "medium" estimates were most plausible; these were based on a projected GNP growth rate of about 6 percent. More recently, some CIA analysts have been inclined to believe that in the period from 1980 on, a GNP growth rate closer to 5 percent is more plausible.

334. Smil and Woodard, "Perspectives on Energy," pp. 334–38, estimated

that China's energy consumption may be between 660 million and 715 million tons CE in 1985 and will peak at between 1.1 billion and 1.2 billion in 2000. The difference between their estimates and CIA projections illustrate how large the possible margin of error in future projections is.

335. (CE converted to OE at rate of 0.666.) The estimates by Smil and Woodard, "Perspectives on Energy," p. 336, differed substantially from these CIA projections. Smil and Woodard calculated that China could have exportable surpluses (of oil or other energy expressed in terms of "oil equivalent") amounting to 25 million to 55 million tons in 1980, 45 million to 170 million tons in 1985, and 65 million to 295 million tons in 1990; their estimates for 1980 and 1985 were too high; however, as will be indicated below, it is possible that China's exports during the second half of the 1980s could be more than 50 million tons a year.

336. Their summary judgment was, "China clearly can benefit from exporting oil to help finance capital imports, but it is unlikely that it will become important in the world petroleum market. High domestic demand for energy and low foreign demand for the types of crude China sells have constrained exports"; see OER, CIA, "Energy Balance Projections," p. 858. This was a more pessimistic judgment than an earlier CIA estimate in *China: Energy Balance Projections*, p. 1, in which it was projected that by 1980 China's oil exports could be between 27 million and 33 million tons, and would grow thereafter, but probably would not exceed 65 million tons by 1985.

337. In 1977, in OER, CIA, "Energy Balance Projections," pp. 868–69, CIA analysts estimated that exports of 50 million tons of oil (75 million tons CE) in 1980 might well cause a drop of around 3 percent in China's annual GNP growth rate. In my opinion, even though China's 1980 exports are not close to that level, the CIA estimate of the possible effects were very debatable, if one thinks in longer-range terms. The adverse effect of reduced domestic energy supply must be balanced by the positive effects of increased imports of capital and technology. Moreover, many variables (such as the degree of efficiency in energy use) will affect the situation.

338. Hardt and others, "Soviet Oil and Gas in the Global Perspective," pp. 787 ff., especially pp. 812–17. In 1975 the USSR earned more than $3 billion from oil exports, $52 million from gas exports, and $385 million from coal exports. In 1977 the authors estimated that the Soviet Union hoped to sell 45 million tons of oil to the West by 1980 (35 million tons of it to hard currency countries) and to export 59 billion cubic meters of natural gas (33 billion to Eastern Europe and 26 billion to Western Europe), and might earn $5.4 billion from oil exports and $1.4 billion from gas exports. However, as noted earlier, the CIA now believes that the Soviet Union's capacity to export energy is likely to decline in the period ahead. In CIA, *Prospects for Soviet Oil Production*, ER 77-10270, April 1977, p. 8, the agency's analysts predicted that Soviet oil output will peak soon and that, actually, in the 1980s the Soviet Union could become a significant oil importer. Hardt and his coauthors doubted this and argued that the Russians would try hard to achieve (and perhaps come close to) their stated goals because of the enormous importance of oil in their

foreign as well as domestic economic relations. (Soviet oil exports recently have supplied three-fourths of Eastern Europe's needs and constitute the Soviet Union's largest single source of hard currency.) However, in 1979, another CIA analysis predicted that Soviet oil exports would decline, perhaps to near zero by 1985, while East European net oil imports will continue to rise; see NFAC, CIA, *The World Oil Market in the Years Ahead*, pp. 40–41.

339. Chinese Ministry of Information, *China Handbook, 1937–1943*, p. 541.

340. World exports of solid fuels (mainly coal) fluctuated; they were 120 million tons in 1933, 150 million tons in 1937, and 130 million tons in 1938; in 1950 they were 120 million tons; see Darmstadter, *Energy*, pp. 303–04. The largest exporters in the late 1930s were Germany and the United Kingdom (each of which exported close to 40 million tons); Poland (which exported 10 million tons) and the United States (which exported 12 million tons) were next; all others exported much smaller amounts (Belgium-Luxembourg, the Netherlands, Denmark, and Japan each exported 5 million or 6 million tons). No developing nation other than China exported any significant amount.

341. Chinese Ministry of Information, *China Handbook, 1937–1943*, p. 540.

342. The following figures on China's imports of oil and oil products are from Smil, *China's Energy*, pp. 119–21 (they are based on Soviet sources); also see table 4-13. Kambara, "Petroleum Industry," p. 703, gave figures, also from Soviet sources, that were slightly different.

343. UN, *WES 1950–74*, pp. 215, 316.

344. China's domestic crude oil output exceeded imports of oil and oil products for the first time in 1960; in that year, domestic output reached 5.1 million tons, and imports were 3.875 million tons (2.963 million tons of crude and 0.913 million of oil products); see Smil, *China's Energy*, p. 121; and CIA, *China, Oil*, p. 9.

345. Even since achieving self-sufficiency in oil, China has needed to import some specialized oil products, but in very small amounts.

346. See CIA, *China, Oil*, p. 9; and Smil, *China's Energy*, p. 121.

347. This was the first time China exported oil to non-Communist nations. It had begun exporting some oil to North Korea and North Vietnam in the mid-1960s; see Yager and Steinberg, *Energy and U.S. Foreign Policy*, p. 220.

348. Early in their negotiations with the Japanese, the Chinese asked if Japan wished to buy 50 million tons of oil and 5 million tons of coal a year within five years (as, reportedly, some Japanese earlier had proposed); see *JETRO* [Japan External Trade Organization] *China Newsletter* (later JETRO, *China Newsletter*) no. 14 (October 1977), p. 17. This was soon reflected in many Japanese estimates of future possibilities, even those made by certain government bodies; see "Outlook on China's Foreign Trade and Oil Exports," *JETRO China Newsletter*, no. 7 (April 1975), pp. 11 ff.; JETRO projected several possibilities, ranging from 30 million to 50 million tons by 1980, which were far too high.

349. Ping-ti Ho, "China's Oil Reserves Far Exceed Western Estimates," in the *Nineteen-Seventies (Chi-shih Nien-tai)* (Hong Kong, February 1975), pp. 6–14; cited in *JETRO China Newsletter*, no. 7 (April 1975), p. 11.

350. Ryutaro Hasegawa, chairman of Japan-China Oil Import Council, predicted that by 1980 China would produce 400 million tons a year (8 million b/d) and export as much as 100 million(!); see Ralph N. Clough, "Chinese Oil, Japanese Markets, and U.S. Technology," January 20, 1975, processed, p. 1; and Clyde H. Farnsworth, "Big Rise in China Oil Output Foreseen," *New York Times*, May 12, 1975. See also Yeh and Wu, "Oil and Strategy," pp. 1–3.

351. See Klatt, "Learning from Taching," p. 454; and JETRO estimate of 30 million to 50 million tons (see note 348). Williams, "Chinese Petroleum Industry," p. 247, predicted Chinese oil exports of 50 million to 65 million tons, and Smil, *China's Energy*, pp. 131–32, exports of perhaps 20 million tons in 1980 but possibly more than 30 million tons in the early 1980s (up to a maximum of about 50 million tons in the mid-1980s and 80 million tons in 1990). Cohen and Park, "The Politics of China's Oil Weapon," p. 40, predicted China might possibly export 50 million tons by 1980. CIA analysts, in *China: Energy Balance Projections*, p. 1, predicted it could export 27 million to 33 million tons (0.54 million to 0.66 million b/d) by 1980.

352. In table 4-14, the original figures are in barrels a day; the tonnage figures are my calculations using a standard conversion ratio of 1 million b/d equal 50 million tons. Some other estimates differ, in part because of different information on delivery dates; see, for example, *JETRO China Newsletter*, no. 16 (January 1978), p. 9, no. 17 (April 1978), pp. 4–5, and no. 20 (December 1978), p. 7.

353. See also Fountain, "The Development of China's Offshore Oil," p. 36. For earlier years, Fountain gives the following figures on Chinese exports of crude oil alone: 1975, 9.0 million tons; 1976, 8.0 million tons; and 1977, 8.8 million tons. He breaks down these figures by country.

354. Harrison, *China, Oil, and Asia*, pp. 146 ff., especially pp. 157–65, analyzes the Sino-Japanese negotiations and the reasons for the limited enthusiasm for Chinese oil among some Japanese. A detailed account of the negotiations during 1977 is in Tadao Iguchi, "The Japan-China Long-Term Trade Agreement," *JETRO China Newsletter*, no. 16 (January 1978), pp. 1–18. He implied that at that time the Chinese clearly wished to sell more than the Japanese were willing to commit themselves to buy (a fact confirmed to me by a Japanese diplomat). See also Williams, "Chinese Petroleum Industry," pp. 239–40.

355. On the problem of price, see Iguchi, "Japan-China," pp. 13–14; Williams, "Chinese Petroleum Industry," p. 240; Cohen and Park, "China's Oil Policy," pp. 125–26; and Klatt, "Learning from Taching," pp. 453, 456. The Japanese reportedly tried to get the Chinese to reduce their price slightly (by between $0.50 and $1.00 a barrel), which they felt was necessary to put it on a par with Arabian oil (according to a Japanese diplomat's account, to me), and some Japanese said that removal of wax from Chinese oil would add $2 to $3 to the cost of a barrel—which may have been an exaggeration—and that this should be taken into account by the Chinese in the pricing (see Cohen and Park, "China's Oil Policy," p. 125). In general, the Chinese have used, as a yardstick for their prices, the prices of Indonesian Minas oil, which is generally

pegged to Arabian oil prices—but with adjustments made for different transport costs. There is considerable room for difference about how much adjustment is necessary to take account of quality differences, and so on.

356. Smil and Woodard, "Perspectives on Energy," p. 323.

357. See Kuo Chi (Guo Ji or Guo Qi?), "Foreign Trade: Why the 'Gang of Four' Created Confusion," *Peking Review*, no. 9 (February 25, 1977), pp. 16–18; and Fang Hai (Fang Hai), "Criticize the Slavish Compradore Philosophy," *Selections from People's Republic of China Magazines* (SPRCM), nos. 867–68 (Hong Kong: American Consulate-General, April 1976), pp. 22–23.

358. The trend of policy from late 1976 on was foreshadowed by policy changes pushed by Chou En-lai and Teng Hsiao-ping (Deng Xiaoping) in 1975. A key party document on industry, prepared in 1975 under the direction of Teng, stated, "In order to usher in more advanced technology from foreign countries, it is necessary to increase exports and to raise as soon as possible the proportion of industrial and mining products in commodity exports. . . . In order to speed up the development of our country's coal and petroleum, it is permissible to sign contracts, under deferred and installment payments which are common practices in international trade, with foreign countries and to fix several production points to which they will supply modern and complete sets of equipment suitable to our needs and we will pay back with the coal and petroleum produced"; see "Some Problems in Speeding up Industrial Development," *Issues and Studies* (Taiwan), vol. 13, no. 7 (July 1977), pp. 107–08. The need to increase exports of mineral products, including oil, was stated with increasing frequency in public statements starting in early 1977; see, for example, Hua Kuo-feng's 1978 National People's Congress (NPC) report, in FBIS, *Daily Report—PRC*, March 7, 1978, p. D18.

359. Teng stated this in an interview with myself and others in Peking, October 23, 1977; the quotes are from my interview notes.

360. For the text of the agreement, see *China Business Review*, vol. 5, no. 2 (March–April 1978), pp. 46–47; see also "The Long-Term Trade Agreement and the Future of Japan-China Trade," *JETRO China Newsletter*, no. 18 (June 1978), pp. 1 ff.

361. My calculations based on table 4-14.

362. In 1979 Chinese oil exports to the United States totaled $96.5 million; see NFAC, CIA, *China: International Trade Quarterly Review, Fourth Quarter 1979*, Research Paper ER CIT 80-003, May 1980, p. 18.

363. See Department of Commerce, *China's Economy and Foreign Trade, 1978–79* (GPO, June 30, 1979), p. 10; JETRO, *China Newsletter*, no. 22 (July 1979), pp. 3–4; and Fountain, "The Development of China's Offshore Oil," p. 36.

364. See CIA, *International Trade Handbook*, Research Aid ER 76-10610, October 1976, p. 16; and NFAC, CIA, *China: International Trade, 1977–78*, Research Paper ER 78-10721, December 1978, p. 14.

365. JETRO, *China Newsletter*, no. 25 (March 1980), p. 27, and no. 26 (June 1980), p. 27.

366. The following data are from JETRO, *China Newsletter*, no. 26 (June 1980), pp. 26–28.

367. JETRO, *China Newsletter*, no. 27 (August 1980), pp. 16–27.

368. Ibid., p. 16.

369. OER, CIA, "Energy Balance Projections," p. 869.

370. Smil, *China's Energy*, p. 132.

371. Melvin Conant and Fern Gold, "U.S. Foreign Policy Implications of the Energy Situation," in CRS, *Project Interdependence*, p. 712.

372. Harrison, *China, Oil, and Asia*, pp. 20–22.

373. Woodard, "China's Nuclear Development Program: Problems and Prospects," pp. 7–8.

374. Fountain, "The Development of China's Offshore Oil," p. 36.

375. Strobe Talbott, "Schlesinger Tours China's Oil Heartland," *Washington Star*, October 29, 1978.

376. Kuo, "Foreign Trade: Why the 'Gang of Four' Created Confusion," pp. 16–68.

377. Hua Kuo-feng, government work report, in FBIS, *Daily Report—PRC*, March 7, 1978, pp. D11–D12, D16–D18.

378. Fang Yi, "Outline National Plan for the Development of Science and Technology, Relevant Policies and Measures," *Peking Review*, no. 14 (April 7, 1978), pp. 8–9.

379. See, especially, the 1979 reports of Hua Kuo-feng and Yu Chiu-li, cited in part I, notes 135 and 269.

380. These and the following figures (except for 1979) are from CIA, *International Trade Handbook*, Research Aid A ER 75-73, October 1975, p. 13, and *International Trade Handbook*, October 1976, p. 16; NFAC, CIA, *China: International Trade, 1976–77*, Research Paper ER 77-10674, November 1977, p. 12, *China: International Trade, 1977–78*, p. 14, and *China: International Trade Quarterly Review, Second Quarter 1979*, Research Paper ER CIT 80-001, January 1980, p. 14.

381. This and the following figures for 1979 are preliminary CIA estimates, obtained orally from the CIA on August 1980. The large rise was partly from increased volume, partly from sizable price increases.

382. My calculations.

383. See NFAC, CIA, *China: International Trade, 1976–77*, p. 12, and *China: International Trade, 1977–78*, p. 14.

384. See part II, pp. 179 and 182.

385. This preliminary estimate was obtained orally from the CIA on August 22, 1980.

386. On early Chinese purchases of oil equipment, see *China Business Review*, vol. 4, no. 1 (January–February 1977), p. 37, vol. 4, no. 4 (July–August 1977), pp. 10–11, vol. 4, no. 5 (September–October 1977), pp. 38–39, vol. 5, no. 1 (January–February 1978), p. 9, and vol. 5, no. 2 (March–April 1978), p. 49; Cheng, *China's Petroleum Industry*, pp. 127 ff.; Melvin W. Searls, Jr., "Sales of Petroleum-Related Equipment to the PRC," speech, pp. 1–13, June 23, 1976, processed; Martha Avery and William Clarke, "The Sino-American Commercial Relationship," in JEC, *Chinese Economy Post-Mao*, p. 754; and numerous articles in the *Washington Post*, including ones on August 28, 1977, November 27, 1977, December 10, 1977, and April 27, 1978.

387. Searls, "Sales of Petroleum-Related Equipment," p. 2.

388. Harrison, *China, Oil, and Asia*, pp. 28–30.

389. See Harrison, *China, Oil, and Asia*, pp. 64 ff., 82, and "Oil Claims and the 'One China' Policy," *Asian Wall Street Journal*, December 20, 1977; *China Business Review*, vol. 4, no. 5 (September–October 1977), p. 38; and "The Scramble to Exploit China's Oil Reserves," p. 156.

390. "China: A New Frontier for the Oil Industry," *World Business Weekly* (*Financial Times*, London, September 3, 1979), p. 20.

391. Harrison, *China, Oil, and Asia*, pp. 21–30.

392. Ibid., p. 86.

393. Willums, "China's Offshore Petroleum," p. 9.

394. At the start, five major American firms were invited; Hobart Rowen, "China's Oil, Peking Turns to West for Its Technology," *Washington Post*, August 11, 1978. Thereafter, the number multiplied rapidly.

395. See "The Scramble to Exploit China's Oil Reserves," p. 155.

396. For details, see "China's Offshore Oil Surveys," in *China Business Review*, vol. 6, no. 4 (July–August 1979), p. 62; "China: A New Frontier for the Oil Industry," pp. 20–21. For additional background on early developments, see Edward K. Wu, "China, Foreign Oil Firms Discuss Co-operation," *Baltimore Sun*, October 18, 1978; Don Oberdorfer, "U.S. Oil Giants May Explore China Sea," *Washington Post*, June 1, 1979; Clyde H. Farnsworth, "China Expects to Sign Oil Agreements," *New York Times*, June 4, 1979; "Two U.S. Oil Firms to Conduct Surveys in Chinese Waters," *Asian Wall Street Journal*, June 11, 1979; and Devin Done, "China Signs Oil Exploration Pacts," *Financial Times*, June 14, 1979.

397. *China Business Review*, vol. 6, no. 4 (July–August 1979), p. 62, contained preliminary maps of these various areas which indicated their sizes.

398. For details, see Fountain, "The Development of China's Offshore Oil," pp. 23–36, including maps on pp. 26 and 33. Except where otherwise noted, the following data on agreements reached during 1979 are from this source.

399. Ibid., p. 30.

400. Ibid., pp. 28–29.

401. See ibid., p. 31; and Fox Butterfield, "70 Are Reported Killed in Collapse of Chinese Oil Rig," *New York Times*, July 7, 1980.

402. Fountain, "The Development of China's Offshore Oil," pp. 31–32. In conversations with me in the summer and fall of 1979, several U.S. oil company representatives made similar estimates. A top executive of Pennzoil stated, in a published interview in late 1978, that following agreement with the Chinese, it would probably "take two to three years to complete exploration and five to eight years to get into substantial production"; although this estimate was more pessimistic than some on the time required to get into production, it highlights the fact that considerable time will be required, at best, to get Chinese offshore oil into production; see Hobart Rowen, "China's Oil, Peking Turns to West for Its Technology."

403. Fountain, "The Development of China's Offshore Oil," p. 31.

404. Ibid., p. 32.

405. Excellent background information is in Park, "Oil under Troubled Waters," pp. 212 ff.; Harrison, *China, Oil, and Asia,* chaps. 5–9; Hungdah Chiu, "China and the Law of the Sea Conference," paper prepared for the Washington and Southeast Regional Seminar on China, University of Maryland, February 10, 1978, processed; and many other articles.

406. See *Peking Review,* no. 6 (February 8, 1974), p. 3, and no. 25 (June 17, 1977), pp. 16–17.

407. UN General Assembly, "Working Paper on Sea Area within the Limits of National Jurisdiction," A/AC.138/SC.II/L.34, July 16, 1973, submitted by the Chinese delegation, July 16, 1973, processed, p. 3.

408. *Peking Review,* no. 25 (June 17, 1977), p. 17.

409. This is because of the deterioration of Sino-Vietnamese relations and increasing Soviet naval involvement in the area; see Fountain, "The Development of China's Offshore Oil," pp. 25–27. When China issued invitations to fifty-seven foreign oil companies to participate in surveying different parts of the South China Sea, and later announced specific agreements covering the areas south and west of Hainan, Hanoi strongly protested. Vietnam itself has signed cooperation agreements with five Communist nations (the Soviet Union, Bulgaria, Czechoslovakia, Hungary, and Poland) and several Western companies, including Bow Valley (Canada), AGIP (Italy), and Deminex (West Germany) for surveying blocks in the Gulf of Tonkin. In July 1979 a Vietnamese gunboat attacked two oil rig supply ships west of Hainan, and surveys were postponed in that area. In October 1979 Peking declared that four areas east of Hainan were "danger zones."

Part V

1. On the dominance of strategic factors and military-security factors in the shaping of Chinese foreign policy, see A. Doak Barnett, *China and the Major Powers in East Asia* (Brookings, 1977).

2. See part II, pp. 254 ff.

3. For background on recent developments in U.S.-China relations, see A. Doak Barnett, *China Policy: Old Problems and New Challenges* (Brookings, 1977); William J. Barnds, ed., *China and America: The Search for a New Relationship* (New York University Press for the Council on Foreign Relations, 1977); Michel Oksenberg and Robert B. Oxnam, *Dragon and Eagle: United States-China Relations, Past and Future* (Basic Books for the China Council of the Asia Society, 1978); and Robert G. Sutter, *China Watch: Toward Sino-American Reconciliation* (Johns Hopkins University Press, 1978). Numerous congressional hearings also provide useful background information; recent ones of particular value include *Normalization of Relations with the People's Republic of China: Practical Implications,* Hearings before the Subcommittee on Asian and Pacific Affairs of the House Committee on International Relations, 95 Cong. 1 sess. (Government Printing Office, 1977); and *Taiwan,* Hearings before the Senate Committee on Foreign Relations, 96

Cong. 1 sess. (GPO, 1979). A good overall survey of American China policy from 1949 until the reopening of U.S.-China contacts is in Foster Rhea Dulles, *American Policy toward Communist China: The Historical Record, 1949–1969* (Crowell, 1972).

4. Press conference with Secretary of State William Rogers, April 7, 1969, *Department of State Bulletin*, vol. 60, no. 1557 (April 28, 1969), p. 361.

5. Henry Kissinger, *White House Years* (Little, Brown, 1979), pp. 693–94, 700, 763–65, 1053.

6. Under Secretary of State Elliot L. Richardson, "The Foreign Policy of the Nixon Administration: Its Aims and Strategy," address, September 5, 1969, *Department of State Bulletin*, vol. 61, no. 1578 (September 22, 1969), p. 260.

7. John Newhouse, *Cold Dawn: The Story of SALT* (Holt, Rinehart, and Winston, 1973), p. 189.

8. Kissinger, *White House Years*, pp. 691, 716–17, 735, 763–70.

9. Department of State, Bureau of Public Affairs, Office of Public Communication, *U.S. Policy toward China, July 15, 1971–January 15, 1979*, Selected Documents, no. 9, p. 7. (For the full text of the February 27, 1972, communiqué, see pp. 6–8.)

10. Secretary of State Henry Kissinger, excerpt from an address, June 23, 1975, in ibid., p. 21.

11. Secretary of State Henry Kissinger, excerpt from an address, September 22, 1975, in ibid., p. 22.

12. Secretary of State Henry Kissinger, excerpts from toasts, Peking, October 19 and 22, 1975, in ibid., p. 22.

13. President Gerald R. Ford, excerpt from a toast, Peking, December 1, 1975, in ibid., p. 23.

14. President Jimmy Carter, excerpt from an address, May 22, 1977, in ibid., p. 32.

15. Secretary of State Cyrus R. Vance, excerpt from an address, June 29, 1977, in ibid., p. 32.

16. Secretary of State Cyrus R. Vance, excerpt from a news conference, November 2, 1977, in ibid., p. 36.

17. Assistant Secretary of State Richard C. Holbrooke, excerpts from a statement before the Subcommittee on Asian and Pacific Affairs, House Committee on International Relations, March 9, 1978, in ibid., p. 36.

18. National Security Adviser Zbigniew Brzezinski, excerpts from toasts, Peking, May 20 and 22, 1978, in ibid., p. 38.

19. Ibid.

20. Ibid., pp. 38–39.

21. President Jimmy Carter, excerpt from a news conference, June 26, 1978, in ibid., p. 41.

22. Secretary of State Cyrus R. Vance, excerpt from a news conference, July 10, 1978, in ibid., p. 42.

23. President Jimmy Carter, excerpt from question and answer sessions

with Western European and Japanese reporters and with a reporter from *Der Spiegel*, July 11, 1978, in ibid., p. 42.

24. Secretary of State Cyrus R. Vance, excerpts from a news conference, November 3, 1978, in ibid., p. 44.

25. See, for example, Bernard Gwertzman, "Vance and Brzezinski Differ Again on Peking Tie and Effect on Soviet," *New York Times*, January 16, 1979. For a summary of differing views, see Robert G. Sutter and Michael Baron, *Playing the China Card: Implications for United States-Soviet-Chinese Relations*, prepared for the Subcommittee on Asian and Pacific Affairs of the House Foreign Affairs Committee by the Congressional Research Service, Library of Congress (GPO, 1979).

26. For background on the normalization negotiations provided in briefings by U.S. officials, see Department of State, Daily Briefing DPC 236, December 18, 1978, typescript; White House Press Office of Media Liaison, "Background Report," January 4, 1979; "Remarks of Dr. Zbigniew Brzezinski . . . to Members of the National Council for U.S.-China Trade and the U.S.-R.O.C. Economic Council," press release, Office of the White House Press Secretary, January 15, 1979, typescript; Cyrus R. Vance, "Stability in East Asia: The U.S. Role," address, in press release no. 13, Department of State, January 15, 1979, typescript; Department of State, Bureau of Public Affairs, Office of Public Communication, "Diplomatic Relations with the People's Republic of China and Future Relations with Taiwan," news release, December 1978; and Department of State, Bureau of Public Affairs, Office of Public Communication, "China: Special Briefing on Normalization with the People's Republic of China," *Current Policy*, no. 52 (January 1979). For particularly useful press accounts, see Don Oberdorfer and Edward Walsh, "Evolution of Normalization: Six Months of Secret Talks," *Washington Post*, December 16, 1978; and Martin Tolchin, "How China and the U.S. Toppled Barriers to Normalized Relations," *New York Times*, December 18, 1978.

27. Terrence Smith, "U.S. and China Opening Full Relations; Teng [Deng] Will Visit Washington on Jan. 29," *New York Times*, December 16, 1978. The date set for normalization of relations was January 1, 1979. For discussion of the compromises made, see the sources cited in note 26. In the U.S.-China joint communiqué of December 15, 1978, announcing the decision, the U.S. government stated that it "acknowledges the Chinese position that there is but one China and Taiwan is part of China"; see President Jimmy Carter, Address to the Nation, December 15, 1978, in Department of State, *U.S. Policy toward China, July 15, 1975–January 15, 1979*, pp. 45–46. The Chinese text used the term "cheng jen" (chengren), which is sometimes translated "recognizes" rather than "acknowledges"; this wording went further than the Shanghai Communiqué (however, for the United States, the English text is the operative one).

28. From the text of the joint communiqué, in *Department of State Bulletin*, vol. 79, no. 2022 (January 1979), p. 25.

29. Ibid.

30. For general coverage of Mondale's 1979 trip, see *New York Times*, August 27, 28, and 29, and September 2; *Washington Post*, August 24, 27, 28, and 30; and *Wall Street Journal*, August 28 and September 3.

31. From speech text, in *Department of State Bulletin*, vol. 79, no. 2031 (October 1979), p. 11.

32. The following Mondale quotations are all from ibid., pp. 11–12.

33. Mondale made this statement at a Peking news conference; see James P. Sterba, "Mondale Says Talks in Peking [Beijing] Put Ties on a Concrete Basis," *New York Times*, August 29, 1979.

34. Frank Ching and Pam Lambert, "Mondale's China Trip Wins Plaudits in U.S.," *Asian Wall Street Journal*, September 3, 1979.

35. Ibid.

36. James P. Sterba, "Mondale and Deng Urge Bolstering of U.S.-China Ties to Aid Stability," *New York Times*, August 27, 1979.

37. For background, see Alexander Eckstein, *China Trade Prospects and U.S. Policy* (Praeger for the National Committee on United States-China Relations, 1971), especially part 3, by Robert F. Dernberger, "Prospects for Trade between China and the United States." For data on trade trends in the early 1970s, see Stanley B. L. Lubman, "Trade between the United States and the People's Republic of China: Practice, Policy, and Law," *Law and Policy in International Business*, vol. 8, no. 1 (1976), pp. 1–79; Shao-chuan Leng, ed., *Post-Mao China and U.S.-China Trade* (University Press of Virginia, 1977); and W. W. Whitson, ed., *Doing Business with China: American Trade Opportunities in the '70s* (Praeger, 1974).

38. See table 5-1. In this discussion of U.S.-China trade, unless otherwise noted, I have used Department of Commerce statistics (which the Department obtains from the Bureau of the Census, Foreign Trade Division). The figures on both exports and imports are f.a.s. (free alongside ship), which are very close to f.o.b. (free on board, which adds the cost of loading). As noted earlier, the Central Intelligence Agency's (CIA's) figures on China's trade until recently (that is, through the year 1978) gave China's exports f.o.b. and its imports c.i.f. (cost, insurance, and freight, based on estimates of the insurance and freight costs). Consequently, the CIA's figures prior to 1979 for China's imports from the United States differed substantially from the Commerce Department's (although figures for China's exports to the United States were similar). The CIA's earlier figures on U.S.-China trade are in various issues of National Foreign Assessment Center (NFAC), CIA, *China: International Trade*, and CIA, *People's Republic of China: International Trade Handbook*. Because the CIA began calculating China's exports and imports on an f.o.b. basis (at the port of origin), its figures are close to those of the Commerce Department for the years from 1978 on. I have relied to a considerable extent on Commerce Department figures on U.S.-China trade for the same reason that I have relied mainly on CIA figures for China's overall trade— because in some respects they are more detailed and have useful breakdowns. I nevertheless use CIA figures as well, and the reader should remember that for many years they were based on different types of calculations.

39. My calculations, from figures in CIA, *People's Republic of China: International Trade Handbook*, Research Aid A ER 74-63, September 1974, p. 14 (based on c.i.f. figures on China's imports).

40. My calculations, based on figures from William Clarke and Martha Avery, "The Sino-American Commercial Relationship," July 10, 1975, in Joint Economic Committee (JEC), *China: A Reassessment of the Economy*, 94 Cong. 1 sess. (GPO, 1975), pp. 512–13. (These are Commerce Department figures, based on f.a.s. calculations.)

41. Ibid.

42. My calculations, based on figures from CIA, *People's Republic of China: International Trade Handbook*, Research Aid A ER 75-73, October 1975, p. 10 (based on c.i.f. figures). Department of Commerce analysts calculate that over 29 percent of China's total imports in 1974 came from Japan, 13 percent from the United States, 7.5 percent from Canada, and 6.3 percent from West Germany; see Clarke and Avery, "The Sino-American Commercial Relationship," July 10, 1975, p. 513.

43. See table 5-1.

44. My calculations, based on figures from CIA, *People's Republic of China: International Trade Handbook*, October 1975, p. 10.

45. Ibid., pp. 10–11.

46. My calculations, based on figures from NFAC, CIA, *China: International Trade, 1976–1977*, Research Paper ER 77-10674, p. 10.

47. See part II, p. 160 and table 2-1.

48. This point was stressed by numerous Chinese officials (including members of the first delegation sent to the United States by the China Council for the Promotion of International Trade) in several conversations with me during this period.

49. China's total imports of manufactured goods amounted to $3.805 billion in 1974 and $4.560 billion in 1975; its imports from the United States totaled only $134 million in 1974 and $217 million in 1975; see CIA, *People's Republic of China: International Trade Handbook*, October 1975, pp. 13, 15; and CIA, *People's Republic of China: International Trade Handbook*, Research Aid ER 76-10610, October 1976, pp. 17, 19. In 1974 China imported $1.180 billion of grain, of which $412 million came from the United States; see CIA, *People's Republic of China: International Trade Handbook*, October 1976, p. 17, and *People's Republic of China: International Trade Handbook*, October 1975, p. 15.

50. The CIA figures (giving exports f.o.b., imports c.i.f.) in table 2-1, indicated a rise in China's total trade in 1977 of 13.4 percent. Revised CIA figures (giving exports and imports f.o.b.) indicated a rise of 13.9 percent; my calculations are based on data in NFAC, CIA, *China: International Trade Quarterly Review, First Quarter 1979*, Reference Aid ER CIT 79-001, September 1979, pp. 3, 5. The figures on U.S.-China trade in the latter source indicate a rise in 1977 of 11 percent, as do the Commerce Department figures in table 5-1.

51. See Martha Avery and William Clarke, "The Sino-American Com-

mercial Relationship," November 9, 1978, in JEC, *Chinese Economy Post-Mao*, 95 Cong. 2 sess. (GPO, 1978), p. 753.

52. Ibid.

53. My calculations, based on data from ibid.

54. My calculations, based on data from CIA, *China: International Trade Quarterly Review, First Quarter 1979*, pp. 3, 5.

55. One-tenth of 1 percent of U.S. exports and two-tenths of 1 percent of U.S. imports; see Avery and Clarke, "The Sino-American Commercial Relationship," November 9, 1978, p. 751.

56. See part II, p. 207 and note 206.

57. Table 5-1. The ranking in 1978 is calculated from NFAC, CIA, *China: International Trade Quarterly Review, Fourth Quarter 1979*, Research Paper ER CIT 80-003 (May 1980), pp. 9–12.

58. My calculations, from data in ibid., p. 19; and Department of Commerce, Industry and Trade Administration, *China's Economy and Foreign Trade, 1978–79* (GPO, 1979), p. 17. See also note 61.

59. Department of Commerce, *China's Economy and Foreign Trade, 1978–79*, p. 17.

60. Ibid.

61. The lower figure for total U.S. sales to China is from Commerce Department data in ibid.; the higher figure, and the figures for other countries' exports to China, are from NFAC, CIA, *China: International Trade Quarterly Review, Fourth Quarter 1979*, p. 11. The difference of $46.3 million between the Commerce Department figures and the CIA figures for Chinese imports from the United States is due almost entirely to U.S. grain exports to China that go via Canada (through the St. Lawrence Seaway), which CIA includes but the Commerce Department does not. The Commerce Department and CIA figures for China's exports to the United States in 1978 were almost identical (Commerce Department, $324.0 million; CIA, $323.6 million); the figures here on Chinese exports to other areas are CIA statistics.

62. These and the percentages below are my calculations, based on data in NFAC, CIA, *China: International Trade Quarterly Review, Fourth Quarter 1979*, pp. 9–14. These data indicate that China had trade deficits of $1.077 billion with Western Europe, $676.5 billion with West Germany, $1.126 billion with Japan, $359.3 million with Canada, and $342.3 million with Australia. For the United States, I have (as in table 5-1) calculated the deficit on the basis of U.S. Customs Bureau figures (see ibid., pp. 18–19), which excludes U.S. grain exports to China via Canada. If those are included, China's deficit in U.S.-China trade amounted to $541 million in 1978 (ibid., p. 13).

63. Ibid., p. 13.

64. The 1979 figures are from ibid., pp. 9–12, 18–19.

65. Ibid., p. 18. See also *Asian Wall Street Journal*, August 20, 1979; and Jay Mathews, "Petroleum Becomes Peking's Top Export to the U.S.," *Washington Post*, August 27, 1979. (Actually, petroleum remained well behind all textiles as a group.)

66. See National Council for U.S.-China Trade, "China Trade Predic-

tions," news release, in *China Trade News*, January 16, 1980, pp. 1–2. Preliminary studies made by the CIA of China's trade in 1979 indicated a slowdown in imports during the second half of the year, but the pace picked up again in 1980 (based on an interview with CIA staff members, February 13, 1980).

67. See part II, pp. 208 and 247.

68. *U.S. News and World Report* (April 30, 1979), p. 29; and NCUSCT, "China Trade Predictions," p. 3. (The NCUSCT figures are in current dollars and take into account price rises, which are not, however, specified.) In February Secretary of Commerce Kreps had made lower estimates, predicting that two-way U.S.-China trade perhaps would reach $3.5 billion in 1985 (and that total U.S.-China trade might total $18 billion to $19 billion during 1978–85); see *China Business Review*, vol. 6, no. 1 (January–February 1979), p. 31. Although it was not specified, Kreps' estimates were probably in current, not constant prices. They were also probably too conservative.

69. U.S. Department of Commerce figures indicated that U.S.-China trade in 1980 totaled $4.2 billion through November ($3.3 billion Chinese imports and $900 million Chinese exports), and the department's China specialists estimated that by year-end total two-way trade would reach close to $4.5 billion; from interview with department staff, February 3, 1981. Actually, a year-end surge raised two-way trade to over $4.5 billion.

70. See the discussion on pp. 519 ff. and the source cited in note 85.

71. See *The National Council for U.S.-China Trade* (brochure by NCUSCT, Washington, D.C., undated).

72. See *U.S.-China Business Review*, vol. 1, no. 1 (January–February 1974), pp. 1–6, and vol. 2, no. 5 (September–October 1975), pp. 18–23. (This journal, retitled *China Business Review* in 1979, has been one of the best sources of month-to-month developments in U.S.-China trade since it began publication in 1974.) A good brief summary of the early developments in this trade is in Avery and Clarke, "The Sino-American Commercial Relationship," November 9, 1978, especially pp. 742–50.

73. As of late 1978 it was estimated that about twenty Chinese delegations a month were visiting the United States (*U.S. News and World Report* [December 11, 1978], p. 36); however, according to a high U.S. official attending a meeting in Peking of the U.S.-China Joint Commission on Scientific and Technological Cooperation, which I attended also, by January 1980 the flow had risen to about sixty a month. By mid-1980 State Department and Chinese Embassy personnel stated that it had risen to between seventy and eighty delegations a month, but it dropped in late 1980.

74. NCUSCT, "China Trade Predictions," p. 3.

75. Department of Commerce, *China's Economy and Foreign Trade, 1978–79*, p. 19.

76. NCUSCT, "China Trade Predictions," p. 1.

77. See *China Business Review*, vol. 5, no. 4 (July–August 1978), pp. 20–21; and Robert Reinhold, "U.S.-China Exchange in Science Is Sought," *New York Times*, July 15, 1978.

78. *China Business Review*, vol. 5, no. 6 (November–December 1978),

pp. 45–47. See also United Press International, "U.S. Offers to Aid China in Energy Development," *New York Times*, November 7, 1978.

79. Committee on Scholarly Communication with the People's Republic of China (Washington, D.C.), *Notes on Student Exchanges with China*, issue 1 (November 1978), pp. 1–2. (I was fortunate to be able to attend the Chou-Atkinson meetings in Washington as an adviser to the U.S. delegation.)

80. *China Business Review*, vol. 5, no. 6 (November–December 1978), pp. 43–45. See also Fox Butterfield, "China Seen as Bigger Buyer of U.S. Grain," *New York Times*, November 15, 1978; and James Risser, "China-U.S. Farm Trade Appears Set for Big Leap," *Washington Post*, November 26, 1978.

81. See Peter J. Schuyten, "China Shops for a Satellite System in U.S.," *New York Times*, November 23, 1978; and Robert Toth, "U.S. Reportedly Discusses Sale, Launch of Satellite for China," *Washington Post*, October 4, 1978. Both report discussions regarding the purchase of a communications satellite. For text of the "understanding" on selling both communications and Landsat satellite equipment, see *China Business Review*, vol. 6, no. 1 (January–February 1979), p. 28; for additional discussion of cooperation in this field, see that issue, pp. 69–70. (A memorandum of understanding on the Landsat station was signed in January 1980 during the meeting of the U.S.-China Joint Commission on Scientific and Technological Cooperation, which I attended.) See also "Press Discusses U.S., PRC Communications Satellite," in Foreign Broadcast Information Service, *Daily Report—People's Republic of China*, Department of Commerce, National Technical Information Service, January 28, 1980, p. B1. (Hereafter FBIS, *Daily Report—PRC*.)

82. Agis Salpukas, "Teng's American Business Trip," *New York Times*, February 1, 1979.

83. For the texts of the agreements and understandings, signed or endorsed officially at that time, relating to science and technology, agricultural exchanges, cooperation in space technology, cooperation in high-energy physics, exchanges of students and scholars, consular relations, and cultural exchanges, see *Department of State Bulletin*, vol. 79, no. 2024 (March 1979), pp. 6–11.

84. From a private interview with a U.S. official, June 24, 1979; unattributable.

85. For background, see John R. Garson, "The American Trade Embargo against China," pt. 1, in Alexander Eckstein, ed., *China Trade Prospects and U.S. Policy* (Praeger for the National Committee on United States-China Relations, 1971).

86. Earlier, different estimates were used ($196.5 million for U.S. claims and $76.5 million for the frozen assets); see "Claims/Assets Settlement," *China Business Review*, vol. 6, no. 1 (January–February 1979), pp. 50–51. (A listing of the major U.S. claimants is in ibid., pp. 52–53.)

87. See ibid., p. 50; and Hobart Rowan, "Blumenthal, in China, Foresees Closer Trade Ties," *Washington Post*, February 25, 1979, and "Blumenthal Talks in Peking Seen Going Smoothly," *Washington Post*, February 27, 1979;

and Associated Press, "China to Pay $80 Million on Claims," *Washington Post*, March 2, 1979.

88. See "Claims/Assets Settlement, Still Unsettled," *China Business Review*, vol. 6, no. 5 (September–October 1979), p. 22.

89. See Jay Mathews, "Peking, U.S. Sign Agreement on Assets," *Washington Post*, May 11, 1979; Leonard Silk, "Payment Pact Set, U.S. and China near a Trade Agreement," *New York Times*, May 12, 1979; "Cutting a Deal with China," *Newsweek* (March 12, 1979), pp. 72, 75; and "China Claims Finally Settled," *New York Times*, March 4, 1979.

90. See "The Way Ahead: MFN Status for China This Year?" *China Business Review*, vol. 6, no. 2 (March–April 1979), pp. 6–7; "The Sino-U.S. Trade Agreement," text in *China Business Review*, vol. 6, no. 4 (July–August 1979), pp. 24–26; and "The Way Ahead, U.S.-China Trade Agreement, Eleventh-Hour Switch," *China Business Review*, vol. 6, no. 5 (September–October 1979), p. 17. Also see Jay Mathews, "China and U.S. Initial Accord Aiding Trade," *Washington Post*, May 15, 1979; Leonard Silk, "U.S.-Chinese Accord on Trade Reported Set for Initialing," *New York Times*, May 13, 1979; and Kenneth H. Bacon, "U.S.-China Initial Accord to Widen Trade But Benefits Aren't Expected for a While," *Wall Street Journal*, May 15, 1979.

91. See Jay F. Henderson, Nicholas H. Ludlow, and Eugene A. Theroux, "China and the Trade Act of 1974," *U.S.-China Business Review*, vol. 2, no. 1 (January–February 1975), pp. 3–10.

92. Leonard Silk, "Strain Evident but Mrs. Kreps Achieves Goal," *New York Times*, May 15, 1979.

93. See Fox Butterfield, "China Signs Treaty on Trade with U.S., Looks to Tariff Cuts," *New York Times*, July 8, 1979; and Hobart Rowan, "U.S. Signs Pact to Grant China Favored Status," *Washington Post*, July 8, 1979.

94. "Preparing for Economic Normalization: The Impact of MFN on Our Future Trade with China," *China Business Review*, vol. 6, no. 4 (July–August 1979), pp. 20–23. See also David Buchan, "U.S. Hopes Pact Will Bring Rapid Rise in China Trade," *Financial Times* (London), July 9, 1979; and Hobart Rowan, "China: Unfinished Business," *Washington Post*, August 30, 1979.

95. See Helen Raffel, Robert E. Teal, and Cheryl McQueen, "The Impact of U.S. Most-Favored-Nation Tariff Treatment on PRC Exports," in JEC, *Chinese Economy Post-Mao*, pp. 840–50, especially p. 841.

96. "Preparing for Economic Normalization," pp. 20–23, especially p. 23.

97. Philip T. Lincoln, Jr., and James A. Kilpatrick, "The Impact of Most-Favored-Nation Tariff Treatment on U.S. Imports from the People's Republic of China," in JEC, *Chinese Economy Post-Mao*, pp. 812–27, especially pp. 825–27.

98. The following citations are from the text of the agreement, in *China Business Review*, vol. 6, no. 4 (July–August 1979), pp. 24–26.

99. "The Way Ahead: MFN Status for China This Year?" p. 6.

100. Robert Parry, "China Pact Hits Snag on Emigration," *Washington Post*, November 2, 1979.

101. Teng is reported to have told Senator Jackson that, if the United States wished, it "would have one million Chinese in Seattle Monday morning"; see Leonard Silk, "Doing Business with Peking," *New York Times*, May 30, 1979.

102. See Don Oberdorfer, "U.S. Moves to Grant Soviets Trade and Tariff Benefits," *Washington Post*, May 17, 1979; and Bernard Gwertzman, "U.S. Seeking Pledge Soviet Union Won't Curb Rate of Emigration," *New York Times*, May 18, 1979.

103. Robert G. Kaiser, "Trade Benefits for Russia, China Eyed," *Washington Post*, January 5, 1979. See also Keith Richburg, "Trade Benefits for Soviet Focus of New Hill Battle," *Washington Post*, June 13, 1979.

104. Robert G. Kaiser, "Senate Trade Proposal Seeks to Treat Soviets, China Alike," *Washington Post*, February 3, 1979.

105. See Leonard Silk, "Strain Evident but Mrs. Kreps Achieves Goal," *New York Times*, May 15, 1979, and "U.S. and China Reach 6 Cooperative Accords on Eve of Trade Pact," *New York Times*, May 14, 1979. UPI, "China Talks on Textiles Bog Down," *New York Times*, May 31, 1979, reported that, in May, Kreps had said the trade agreement "could not be signed and sent to Congress" until a textile agreement had been signed.

106. On the delay, see Special to the *New York Times*, "U.S. Delays Action on Tariff Concessions to China," *New York Times*, August 7, 1979.

107. When I visited China in October 1979 with a group of seven U.S. governors, the desirability of rapid implementation of the trade agreement and MFN treatment was emphasized by virtually every Chinese official we met, including Teng Hsiao-ping (Deng Xiaoping). The Chinese press also consistently emphasized this.

108. See Silk, "U.S. and China Reach 6 Cooperative Accords"; and *Beijing Review*, no. 21 (May 25, 1979), p. 6.

109. See A. O. Sulzberger, "NASA Awaits China Decision on Space Flights in '82," *New York Times*, May 18, 1979; and U.S. Postal Service, "U.S. and China to Discuss Direct Mail Exchange," *News*, General Release no. 34, May 21, 1979.

110. Committee on Scholarly Communication with the People's Republic of China, *China Exchange Newsletter*, vol. 7, no. 3 (June 1979), pp. 4–6.

111. On the visit of Kang Shih-en (Kang Shien), see *China Business Review*, vol. 6, no. 4 (July–August 1979), p. 19. On Chang's (Zhang's) visit, see *China Business Review*, vol. 6, no. 5 (September–October 1979), p. 21. In a speech at a luncheon given by David Rockefeller on July 13, Chang spoke of the "great potentials" for U.S.-China trade and called U.S. goods "highly competitive" (from the text, mimeographed, p. 1).

112. See Clyde H. Farnsworth, "U.S. Imposes Quotas on Chinese Textiles," *New York Times*, June 1, 1979; UPI, "China Talks on Textiles Bog Down"; and Silk, "Doing Business with Peking."

113. See Bhushan Bahree, "Textile Accord Passes Review; Renewal Likely," *Asian Wall Street Journal*, November 11, 1976; and Pamela G. Hollie,

"Tensions in Textiles: A Challenge from Asia," *New York Times* (International Economic Survey), February 5, 1978.

114. Farnsworth, "U.S. Imposes Quotas on Chinese Textiles."

115. Helen Dewar, "Strauss, Textiles Reach Agreement," *Washington Post*, January 19, 1979. See also Clyde H. Farnsworth, "Curb Asked on Cotton from China," *New York Times*, December 7, 1978.

116. Staff Reporter, "U.S. to Seek Limits on Textile Exports from China in Talks," *Wall Street Journal*, January 3, 1979.

117. *China Business Review*, vol. 6, no. 2 (March–April 1979), p. 7.

118. See "Deadline Set by Strauss on Chinese Textile Pact," *New York Times*, May 5, 1979; and Farnsworth, "U.S. Imposes Quotas on Chinese Textiles."

119. See Farnsworth, "U.S. Imposes Quotas on Chinese Textiles"; and "U.S. Curbs Imports of Chinese Apparel after Talks Fail" (no author listed), *Asian Wall Street Journal*, June 4, 1979.

120. Farnsworth, "U.S. Imposes Quotas on Chinese Textiles."

121. See ibid.; and Clyde H. Farnsworth, "U.S. Options on Chinese Textiles," *New York Times*, May 30, 1979.

122. Ibid.

123. Jay Mathews, "China and U.S. Initial Accord Aiding Trade."

124. See Avery and Clarke, "The Sino-American Commercial Relationship," November 9, 1978, p. 753; Department of Commerce, *China's Economy and Foreign Trade, 1978–79* (Department of Commerce, September 1979), p. 17; and NFAC, CIA, *China: International Trade Quarterly Review, Fourth Quarter 1979*, pp. 18–19. In 1979, China exported $202 million of textiles to the United States and imported $357 million of cotton from the United States.

125. Special to the *New York Times*, "U.S. to Maintain Quotas on Apparel from China," *New York Times*, May 21, 1980.

126. New China News Agency, "China Opposed to U.S. Quotas, Says Textile Chief," Press release no. 80/023, Embassy of the People's Republic of China, Washington, D.C., May 28, 1980.

127. *Department of State Bulletin*, vol. 79, no. 2031 (October 1979), pp. 10–11.

128. Ibid.

129. AP, "China Gets Favored Trade Status," *New York Times*, January 25, 1980.

130. "U.S. Aid to China, How to Obtain It," *China Business Review*, vol. 6, no. 5 (September–October 1979), pp. 18–19.

131. The departments of Agriculture, Commerce, Defense, Health and Human Services (formerly HEW), Labor, Transportation, and Treasury, as well as the Environmental Protection Agency, Federal Aviation Administration, Federal Highway Administration, U.S. Geological Survey, General Services Administration, Internal Revenue Service, Bureau of Mines, Coast Guard, Customs Service, Bureau of Reclamation, and Army Corp of Engineers, all can participate in such programs; see ibid., p. 19.

132. See ibid.; and Sterba, "Mondale Says Talks in Peking Put Ties on a Concrete Basis."

133. *Department of State Bulletin,* vol. 79, no. 2031 (October 1979), p. 11.

134. Except where otherwise noted, the following discussion of the Ex-Im Bank is based mainly on "Now, Exim for China?" *China Business Review,* vol. 6, no. 5 (September–October 1979), p. 21.

135. The total without interest was more than $26 million but would be higher if interest were to be included. See ibid., p. 21; and David Buchan, "No U.S. Credit Seen till 1980," *Financial Times* (London), August 30, 1979.

136. Teng Hsiao-ping and Bank of China officials indicated such a desire in meetings with representatives of the House Banking, Finance, and Urban Affairs Committee; see Fox Butterfield, "Teng Invites Senator Goldwater to Peking for a Talk," *New York Times,* January 3, 1979.

137. See part II, pp. 144 ff.

138. "Now, Exim for China?" p. 21.

139. This and the data below are from ibid.; and Judith Miller, "Ex-Im Bank Facing Mounting Pressure," *New York Times,* June 23, 1980.

140. "Now, Exim for China?" p. 21.

141. Ibid.

142. Ibid.

143. Ibid. However, the U.S. Ex-Im Bank charged a very low rate, 3.75 percent, for part of a $100 million loan to Tunisia in 1979.

144. Jim Browning, "China Cancels Preliminary Agreement with Chase Bank for $30 million Credit," *Wall Street Journal,* May 30, 1979.

145. See Special to the *New York Times,* "China Loan Set by Bank in Chicago," *New York Times,* June 7, 1979; and Jim Browning, "First Chicago Wooing of China Yields a Result—But Not the One Expected," *Asian Wall Street Journal,* June 11, 1979.

146. *China Business Review,* vol. 6, no. 3 (May–June 1979), p. 56.

147. The following discussion is based on "OPIC: Three Steps Remain," *China Business Review,* vol. 6, no. 5 (September–October 1979), p. 20.

148. By late March 1979, a U.S. government interagency working committee was "finalizing details of a shipping agreement" with China; see *China Business Review,* vol. 6, no. 2 (March–April 1979), p. 46. However, little real progress was made during the rest of 1979.

149. See ibid., pp. 46–48; and *China Business Review,* vol. 6, no. 4 (July–August 1979), p. 29.

150. See *China Business Review,* vol. 6, no. 2 (March–April 1979), p. 48.

151. Ibid.

152. See Richard Witkin, "Pan Am Asking U.S. Permission to Offer First Flights to Peking," *New York Times,* December 19, 1978; A. O. Sulzberger, Jr., "Pact Signed for Flights by China," *New York Times,* August 16, 1979; and Carole Shifrin, "CAB Rejects Deadline Request from China," *Washington Post,* August 24, 1979.

153. Special to the *New York Times,* "China May Increase U.S. Grain Purchases," *New York Times,* January 20, 1980.

154. "Duty-Free Treatment for Chinese Goods?" *China Business Review,* vol. 6, no. 14 (July–August 1979), pp. 31–32.

155. Ibid.

156. "Text of Press Communiqué [dated December 9, 1979] on Prime Minister Ohira's Visit to China," clause 11, in Press release no. 79/013, Embassy of the People's Republic of China, Washington, D.C., December 12, 1979.

157. In late 1979, Canada also agreed to grant China general preferential tariff treatment, starting January 1, 1980; see "Canada Lowers Duty on Chinese Imports," *Asian Wall Street Journal,* October 29, 1979.

158. "Duty-Free Treatment for Chinese Goods?" p. 32.

159. See ibid., p. 31; and Jay F. Henderson, Nicholas H. Ludlow, and Eugene A. Theroux, "China and the Trade Act of 1974," *U.S.-China Business Review,* vol. 2, no. 1 (January–February 1975), p. 9.

160. Henderson, Ludlow, and Theroux, "China and the Trade Act of 1974," p. 9.

161. Based on an off-the-record interview with an official of a leading Japanese bank involved in these loans, in Washington, D.C., January 9, 1980; unattributable.

162. Jay Mathews, "Japan and China Agree on Loan, Oil Exploration," *Washington Post,* December 8, 1979. See also the press communiqué cited in note 156.

163. Robert Trumbull, "Japan-China Meeting Strengthening Economic Ties," *New York Times,* December 9, 1979.

164. For background on the policy issues for the United States, see JEC, *Issues in East-West Commercial Relations,* 95 Cong. 2 sess. (GPO, 1979).

165. Hedija Kravalis, Allen J. Lenz, Helen Raffel, and John Young, "Quantification of Western Exports of High Technology Products to Communist Countries," in JEC, *Issues in East-West Commercial Relations,* pp. 34–45, especially pp. 38, 42.

166. For background, see George Holiday and John P. Hardt, "Export Controls," *Issue Brief,* no. IB 75003, Congressional Research Service, Library of Congress, December 11, 1978, mimeographed. In 1978, Presidential Review Memorandum (PRM) 31 dealt with the issues (see Thomas O'Toole, "White House to Monitor Exports to Communists," *Washington Post,* October 27, 1978). However, debate has continued; see Richard Burt, "Technology Sales Rules under Fire," *New York Times,* June 18, 1979. Debate within Coordinating Committee (COCOM) countries also has continued; see Jack Aboaf, "NATO Group Mulls Revising Sales Curbs on Strategic Technology to Communists," *Wall Street Journal,* November 15, 1978. On China, specifically, see Bernard Weintraub, "U.S. Aides Split on Defense Technology for China," *New York Times,* January 4, 1978; and "Export Controls, Faster Process Ahead for China Sales?" *China Business Review,* vol. 6, no. 4 (July–August 1979), pp. 54–56.

167. Department of Defense, Office of the Director of Defense Research and Engineering, *An Analysis of Export Control of U.S. Technology—A*

DOD Perspective (the "Bucy Report") (DOD, February 4, 1976). See also Richard Burt, "U.S. Seeks to Guard Technological Edge," *New York Times,* December 11, 1977.

168. Richard Halloran, "U.S. Bars Exports to Soviet of Sophisticated Technology and Machinery," *New York Times,* January 10, 1980.

169. Richard Burt, "U.S. Looks to China for Aid to Pakistan," *New York Times,* January 3, 1980.

170. Ibid.

171. For this and the following quotation, see Jay Mathews, "Brown Seeks China's Cooperation," *Washington Post,* January 7, 1980. See also Fox Butterfield, "Brown, In Peking, Urges Cooperation to Counter Moscow," *New York Times,* January 7, 1980.

172. Fox Butterfield, "Defense Secretary Arrives in China for 8-Day Visit," *New York Times,* January 6, 1980.

173. See Fox Butterfield, "Brown Sees Accord on China's Defense," *New York Times,* January 10, 1979; and Jay Mathews, "Brown, Chinese Reportedly Find 'Convergence of Views,' " *Washington Post,* January 8, 1980.

174. Jay Mathews, "U.S., China to Strengthen Afghan Area, Brown Says," *Washington Post,* January 10, 1980.

175. See Mathews, "U.S., China to Strengthen Afghan Area, Brown Says"; and Butterfield, "Brown Sees Accord on China's Defense."

176. Mathews, "Brown Seeks China's Cooperation."

177. Jay Mathews, "Brown in China for Talks on Security, Afghanistan," *Washington Post,* January 6, 1980.

178. Mathews, "U.S., China to Strengthen Afghan Area, Brown Says."

179. Butterfield, "Defense Secretary Arrives in China for 8-Day Visit."

180. Ibid.

181. Jay Mathews, "Brown Says China Fears Buying Arms Restricts Independence," *Washington Post,* January 11, 1980.

182. See Butterfield, "Brown Sees Accord on China's Defense"; and Jay Mathews, "Sino-U.S. Accord Seen on Reaction to Soviets," *Washington Post,* January 9, 1980.

183. Jay Mathews, "Brown's Trip Strong on Symbolism but Not Treaties," *Washington Post,* January 12, 1980.

184. The contrast in the terms used by the Americans and those used by the Chinese in each country's publicity on Brown's trip was notable; see "Deng Xiaoping Urges Unity against Soviet Expansionism" and "Secretary Brown's Visit Important for Contacts between Chinese and U.S. Defense Establishments," Press release no. 80/003, Embassy of the People's Republic of China, Washington, D.C., January 16, 1980, pp. 1–3.

185. Mathews, "Sino-U.S. Accord Seen on Reaction to Soviets." The final memorandum of understanding concerning details of the Landsat arrangement (which was signed on January 24, 1980, at the end of the first meeting of the U.S.-China Joint Commission on Scientific and Technological Cooperation) was essentially similar to other agreements the United States has signed with non-Communist countries to which it has sold Landsat stations.

186. See Bernard Gwertzman, "U.S., In New Rebuff to Soviet, Announces It Will Sell China Military Support Equipment," *New York Times*, January 25, 1980; and Michael Getler, "Pentagon Willing to Sell China Some Military Equipment," *Washington Post*, January 25, 1980.

187. Department of State, *Munitions Control Newsletter*, no. 81 (March 1980). See also Michael Getler, "U.S. Willing to Sell China Copters, Transport Planes," *Washington Post*, March 19, 1980.

188. See George C. Wilson, "New Military Relationship with China Is Developing," *Washington Post*, May 29, 1980; UPI, "U.S. Will Sell Aircraft and Defense Radar to China," *New York Times*, May 30, 1980; and Reuters, "U.S. Clears Way to Sell Military Gear to China," *Washington Post*, May 30, 1980.

189. Assistant Secretary of State Richard Holbrooke, "China and the U.S.: Into the 1980s," speech to NCUSCT, Washington, D.C., June 4, 1980, in *Current Policy*, no. 187 (June 4, 1980).

190. Drew Middleton, "Pentagon Studies Prospect of Military Links with China," *New York Times*, January 4, 1980.

191. *China Business Review*, vol. 6, no. 4 (July–August 1979), p. 55.

192. Based on an interview on December 10, 1979, in Washington, D.C.; unattributable.

193. Cong Linzhong (Tsung Lin-chung), "Courtesy and Dignity," *People's Daily*, November 27, 1979, in FBIS, *Daily Report—PRC*, December 12, 1979, pp. L1–L3.

194. Jay Mathews, "Scathing Critique of American Life Surfaces in Peking," *Washington Post*, March 31, 1980.

195. NFAC, CIA, *The U.S. Position in World Markets*, Research Paper ER 79-10466, August 1979, p. 3.

Index

Afghanistan, Soviet invasion of, 370, 498, 553–54

Agricultural production: as GNP determinant, 158; increase in, 109, 110, 113, 114, 299, 315; lag in, 28, 183, 300, 301, 304; need for accelerated, 93; and population growth, 22–23, 315; ten year plan target, 38–39

Agriculture: capital construction investment in, 104–05; collectivization, 24, 300–01; crisis in, *1959–61,* 271; decisions on development of, 306–09, 318; as determinant of trade, 158; extension services, 303, 304, 338; foreign machinery contracts, 133; "green revolution," 337; growth rate, 22–23; high-yield seed varieties, 337–38; international contacts on, 364–66; investment, 271–72, 347; labor intensity, 302, 328–29, 367; land reform, 299–300; mechanization, 85, 93, 329–31, 348; mobilization of labor, 300, 302, 328; modernization, 6, 271, 296, 302, 347; priority, 84, 85, 93, 271, 305–06; specialization, 39, 54, 55, 348; state efforts to raise prices, 24, 49, 97, 214, 307, 341–42, 348–49; trade, 171–72, 183, 308, 350–51, 507–08, 511, 513. *See also* Communes; Rural areas

Agriculture, U.S. Department of (USDA), 284, 343; exchange program with China, 365; per capita calorie consumption estimates, 282; predictions of world grain demand and production, 278–79, 281; world grain reserve estimate, 292–93

Aircraft: problems in producing, 205; technology transfer for support equipment, 550, 556

Aird, John S., population estimates, 310, 315

Air service agreement, U.S.-China, 538, 539n

Algeria, oil production and exports, 392–93

Argentina: grain exports, 287–88; grain exports to China, 359, 363–64; oil production, 392

Asian Development Bank, 219

Assets-claims issue, 514, 519–21, 526, 529

Australia: grain exports, 287–88; grain exports to China, 359, 363–64; oil production, 392; trade with China, 170, 508

Automobiles and automotive equipment, 137, 205

Bailer, Benjamin F., 527

Balance of payments, 210; aid assistance to LDCs and, 220–21; changes in, 215–17; deficits in, 159–60, 207, 210–11; foreign currency expropriations and, 214; loans and credits and, 211, 212–14; oil exports and, 476; Overseas Chinese remittances and, 212, 216, 217; projected, 219–22; short-term commercial credits and, 215; tourism and, 218–19

Balance of trade: deficits in, 159–60, 207, 210–11, 509, 512, 513; surplus with LDCs, 164, 165

Banking system, 55

Bergland, Robert, 517

Bethlehem Steel, 136

Bicycle production, 110, 115, 116

Biogas, 430–31

Biomass energy, 431–32

Birth control, 280, 305, 314. *See also* Population planning program

Birth rate, 98, 276, 280

Blumenthal, W. Michael, 519, 520, 522

741